SO-BCT-488

Spark: The Definitive Guide
Big Data Processing Made Simple

Bill Chambers and Matei Zaharia

Beijing · Boston · Farnham · Sebastopol · Tokyo

Spark: The Definitive Guide

by Bill Chambers and Matei Zaharia

Copyright © 2018 Databricks. All rights reserved.

Published by O'Reilly Media, Inc., 1005 Gravenstein Highway North, Sebastopol, CA 95472.

O'Reilly books may be purchased for educational, business, or sales promotional use. Online editions are also available for most titles (*http://oreilly.com/safari*). For more information, contact our corporate/institutional sales department: 800-998-9938 or *corporate@oreilly.com*.

Editor: Nicole Tache
Production Editor: Justin Billing
Copyeditor: Octal Publishing, Inc., Chris Edwards, and Amanda Kersey
Proofreader: Jasmine Kwityn

Indexer: Judith McConville
Interior Designer: David Futato
Cover Designer: Karen Montgomery
Illustrator: Rebecca Demarest

February 2018:   First Edition

Revision History for the First Edition
2018-02-08:   First Release
2018-03-16:   Second Release

See *http://oreilly.com/catalog/errata.csp?isbn=9781491912218* for release details.

978-1-491-91221-8

[LSI]

Table of Contents

Part VI. Advanced Analytics and Machine Learning

Preface

Welcome to this first edition of *Spark: The Definitive Guide*! We are excited to bring you the most complete resource on Apache Spark today, focusing especially on the new generation of Spark APIs introduced in Spark 2.0.

Apache Spark is currently one of the most popular systems for large-scale data processing, with APIs in multiple programming languages and a wealth of built-in and third-party libraries. Although the project has existed for multiple years—first as a research project started at UC Berkeley in 2009, then at the Apache Software Foundation since 2013—the open source community is continuing to build more powerful APIs and high-level libraries over Spark, so there is still a lot to write about the project. We decided to write this book for two reasons. First, we wanted to present the most comprehensive book on Apache Spark, covering all of the fundamental use cases with easy-to-run examples. Second, we especially wanted to explore the higher-level "structured" APIs that were finalized in Apache Spark 2.0—namely DataFrames, Datasets, Spark SQL, and Structured Streaming—which older books on Spark don't always include. We hope this book gives you a solid foundation to write modern Apache Spark applications using all the available tools in the project.

In this preface, we'll tell you a little bit about our background, and explain who this book is for and how we have organized the material. We also want to thank the numerous people who helped edit and review this book, without whom it would not have been possible.

About the Authors

Both of the book's authors have been involved in Apache Spark for a long time, so we are very excited to be able to bring you this book.

Bill Chambers started using Spark in 2014 on several research projects. Currently, Bill is a Product Manager at Databricks where he focuses on enabling users to write various types of Apache Spark applications. Bill also regularly blogs about Spark and presents at conferences and meetups on the topic. Bill holds a Master's in Information Management and Systems from the UC Berkeley School of Information.

Matei Zaharia started the Spark project in 2009, during his time as a PhD student at UC Berkeley. Matei worked with other Berkeley researchers and external collaborators to design the core Spark APIs and grow the Spark community, and has continued to be involved in new initiatives such as the structured APIs and Structured Streaming. In 2013, Matei and other members of the Berkeley Spark team co-founded Databricks to further grow the open source project and provide commercial offerings around it. Today, Matei continues to work as Chief Technologist at Databricks, and also holds a position as an Assistant Professor of Computer Science at Stanford University, where he does research on large-scale systems and AI. Matei received his PhD in Computer Science from UC Berkeley in 2013.

Who This Book Is For

We designed this book mainly for data scientists and data engineers looking to use Apache Spark. The two roles have slightly different needs, but in reality, most application development covers a bit of both, so we think the material will be useful in both cases. Specifically, in our minds, the data scientist workload focuses more on interactively querying data to answer questions and build statistical models, while the data engineer job focuses on writing maintainable, repeatable production applications— either to use the data scientist's models in practice, or just to prepare data for further analysis (e.g., building a data ingest pipeline). However, we often see with Spark that these roles blur. For instance, data scientists are able to package production applications without too much hassle and data engineers use interactive analysis to understand and inspect their data to build and maintain pipelines.

While we tried to provide everything data scientists and engineers need to get started, there are some things we didn't have space to focus on in this book. First, this book does not include in-depth introductions to some of the analytics techniques you can use in Apache Spark, such as machine learning. Instead, we show you how to invoke these techniques using libraries in Spark, assuming you already have a basic background in machine learning. Many full, standalone books exist to cover these techniques in formal detail, so we recommend starting with those if you want to learn about these areas. Second, this book focuses more on application development than on operations and administration (e.g., how to manage an Apache Spark cluster with dozens of users). Nonetheless, we have tried to include comprehensive material on monitoring, debugging, and configuration in Parts V and VI of the book to help engineers get their application running efficiently and tackle day-to-day maintenance. Finally, this book places less emphasis on the older, lower-level APIs in Spark— specifically RDDs and DStreams—to introduce most of the concepts using the newer, higher-level structured APIs. Thus, the book may not be the best fit if you need to maintain an old RDD or DStream application, but should be a great introduction to writing new applications.

Conventions Used in This Book

The following typographical conventions are used in this book:

Italic
    Indicates new terms, URLs, email addresses, filenames, and file extensions.

`Constant width`
    Used for program listings, as well as within paragraphs to refer to program elements such as variable or function names, databases, data types, environment variables, statements, and keywords.

`Constant width bold`
    Shows commands or other text that should be typed literally by the user.

`Constant width italic`
    Shows text that should be replaced with user-supplied values or by values determined by context.

This element signifies a tip or suggestion.

This element signifies a general note.

This element indicates a warning or caution.

Using Code Examples

We're very excited to have designed this book so that all of the code content is runnable on real data. We wrote the whole book using Databricks notebooks and have posted the data and related material on GitHub (*https://github.com/databricks/Spark-*

The-Definitive-Guide). This means that you can run and edit all the code as you follow along, or copy it into working code in your own applications.

We tried to use real data wherever possible to illustrate the challenges you'll run into while building large-scale data applications. Finally, we also include several larger standalone applications in the book's GitHub repository for examples that it does not make sense to show inline in the text.

The GitHub repository will remain a living document as we update based on Spark's progress. Be sure to follow updates there.

This book is here to help you get your job done. In general, if example code is offered with this book, you may use it in your programs and documentation. You do not need to contact us for permission unless you're reproducing a significant portion of the code. For example, writing a program that uses several chunks of code from this book does not require permission. Selling or distributing a CD-ROM of examples from O'Reilly books does require permission. Answering a question by citing this book and quoting example code does not require permission. Incorporating a significant amount of example code from this book into your product's documentation does require permission.

We appreciate, but do not require, attribution. An attribution usually includes the title, author, publisher, and ISBN. For example: "*Spark: The Definitive Guide* by Bill Chambers and Matei Zaharia (O'Reilly). Copyright 2018 Databricks, Inc., 978-1-491-91221-8."

If you feel your use of code examples falls outside fair use or the permission given above, feel free to contact us at *permissions@oreilly.com*.

O'Reilly Safari

 *Safari* (formerly Safari Books Online) is a membership-based training and reference platform for enterprise, government, educators, and individuals.

Members have access to thousands of books, training videos, Learning Paths, interactive tutorials, and curated playlists from over 250 publishers, including O'Reilly Media, Harvard Business Review, Prentice Hall Professional, Addison-Wesley Professional, Microsoft Press, Sams, Que, Peachpit Press, Adobe, Focal Press, Cisco Press, John Wiley & Sons, Syngress, Morgan Kaufmann, IBM Redbooks, Packt, Adobe Press, FT Press, Apress, Manning, New Riders, McGraw-Hill, Jones & Bartlett, and Course Technology, among others.

For more information, please visit *http://oreilly.com/safari*.

How to Contact Us

Please address comments and questions concerning this book to the publisher:

O'Reilly Media, Inc.
1005 Gravenstein Highway North
Sebastopol, CA 95472
800-998-9938 (in the United States or Canada)
707-829-0515 (international or local)
707-829-0104 (fax)

To comment or ask technical questions about this book, send email to *bookquestions@oreilly.com*.

For more information about our books, courses, conferences, and news, see our website at *http://www.oreilly.com*.

Find us on Facebook: *http://facebook.com/oreilly*

Follow us on Twitter: *http://twitter.com/oreillymedia*

Watch us on YouTube: *http://www.youtube.com/oreillymedia*

Acknowledgments

There were a huge number of people that made this book possible.

First, we would like to thank our employer, Databricks, for allocating time for us to work on this book. Without the support of the company, this book would not have been possible. In particular, we would like to thank Ali Ghodsi, Ion Stoica, and Patrick Wendell for their support.

Additionally, there are numerous people that read drafts of the book and individual chapters. Our reviewers were best-in-class, and provided invaluable feedback.

These reviewers, in alphabetical order by last name, are:

- Lynn Armstrong
- Mikio Braun
- Jules Damji
- Denny Lee
- Alex Thomas

In addition to the formal book reviewers, there were numerous other Spark users, contributors, and committers who read over specific chapters or helped formulate how topics should be discussed. In alphabetical order by last name, the people who helped are:

- Sameer Agarwal
- Bagrat Amirbekian
- Michael Armbrust
- Joseph Bradley
- Tathagata Das
- Hossein Falaki
- Wenchen Fan
- Sue Ann Hong
- Yin Huai
- Tim Hunter
- Xiao Li
- Cheng Lian
- Xiangrui Meng
- Kris Mok
- Josh Rosen
- Srinath Shankar
- Takuya Ueshin
- Herman van Hövell
- Reynold Xin
- Philip Yang
- Burak Yavuz
- Shixiong Zhu

Lastly, we would like to thank friends, family, and loved ones. Without their support, patience, and encouragement, we would not have been able to write the definitive guide to Spark.

## PART I

Gentle Overview of Big Data and Spark

## CHAPTER 1

What Is Apache Spark?

Apache Spark is a unified computing engine and a set of libraries for parallel data processing on computer clusters. As of this writing, Spark is the most actively developed open source engine for this task, making it a standard tool for any developer or data scientist interested in big data. Spark supports multiple widely used programming languages (Python, Java, Scala, and R), includes libraries for diverse tasks ranging from SQL to streaming and machine learning, and runs anywhere from a laptop to a cluster of thousands of servers. This makes it an easy system to start with and scale-up to big data processing or incredibly large scale.

Figure 1-1 illustrates all the components and libraries Spark offers to end-users.

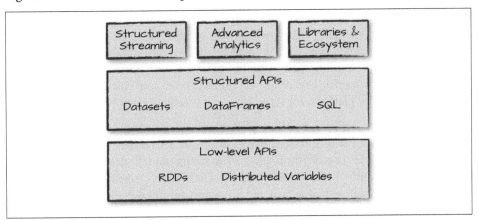

Figure 1-1. Spark's toolkit

You'll notice the categories roughly correspond to the different parts of this book. That should really come as no surprise; our goal here is to educate you on all aspects of Spark, and Spark is composed of a number of different components.

Given that you're reading this book, you might already know a little bit about Apache Spark and what it can do. Nonetheless, in this chapter, we want to briefly cover the overriding philosophy behind Spark as well as the context it was developed in (why is everyone suddenly excited about parallel data processing?) and its history. We will also outline the first few steps to running Spark.

Apache Spark's Philosophy

Let's break down our description of Apache Spark—a unified computing engine and set of libraries for big data—into its key components:

Unified

Spark's key driving goal is to offer a unified platform for writing big data applications. What do we mean by unified? Spark is designed to support a wide range of data analytics tasks, ranging from simple data loading and SQL queries to machine learning and streaming computation, over the same computing engine and with a consistent set of APIs. The main insight behind this goal is that real-world data analytics tasks—whether they are interactive analytics in a tool such as a Jupyter notebook, or traditional software development for production applications—tend to combine many different processing types and libraries.

Spark's unified nature makes these tasks both easier and more efficient to write. First, Spark provides consistent, composable APIs that you can use to build an application out of smaller pieces or out of existing libraries. It also makes it easy for you to write your own analytics libraries on top. However, composable APIs are not enough: Spark's APIs are also designed to enable high performance by optimizing across the different libraries and functions composed together in a user program. For example, if you load data using a SQL query and then evaluate a machine learning model over it using Spark's ML library, the engine can combine these steps into one scan over the data. The combination of general APIs and high-performance execution, no matter how you combine them, makes Spark a powerful platform for interactive and production applications.

Spark's focus on defining a unified platform is the same idea behind unified platforms in other areas of software. For example, data scientists benefit from a unified set of libraries (e.g., Python or R) when doing modeling, and web developers benefit from unified frameworks such as Node.js or Django. Before Spark, no open source systems tried to provide this type of unified engine for parallel data processing, meaning that users had to stitch together an application out of multiple APIs and systems. Thus, Spark quickly became the standard for this type of development. Over time, Spark has continued to expand its built-in APIs to cover more workloads. At the same time, the project's developers have continued to refine its theme of a unified engine. In particular, one major focus of this book will be the "structured APIs" (DataFrames, Datasets, and SQL) that were finalized in Spark 2.0 to enable more powerful optimization under user applications.

Computing engine

At the same time that Spark strives for unification, it carefully limits its scope to a computing engine. By this, we mean that Spark handles loading data from storage systems and performing computation on it, not permanent storage as the end itself. You can use Spark with a wide variety of persistent storage systems, including cloud storage systems such as Azure Storage and Amazon S3, distributed file systems such as Apache Hadoop, key-value stores such as Apache Cassandra, and message buses such as Apache Kafka. However, Spark neither stores data long term itself, nor favors one over another. The key motivation here is that most data already resides in a mix of storage systems. Data is expensive to move so Spark focuses on performing computations over the data, no matter where it resides. In user-facing APIs, Spark works hard to make these storage systems look largely similar so that applications do not need to worry about where their data is.

Spark's focus on computation makes it different from earlier big data software platforms such as Apache Hadoop. Hadoop included both a storage system (the Hadoop file system, designed for low-cost storage over clusters of commodity servers) and a computing system (MapReduce), which were closely integrated together. However, this choice makes it difficult to run one of the systems without the other. More important, this choice also makes it a challenge to write applications that access data stored anywhere else. Although Spark runs well on Hadoop storage, today it is also used broadly in environments for which the Hadoop architecture does not make sense, such as the public cloud (where storage can be purchased separately from computing) or streaming applications.

Libraries

Spark's final component is its libraries, which build on its design as a unified engine to provide a unified API for common data analysis tasks. Spark supports both standard libraries that ship with the engine as well as a wide array of external libraries published as third-party packages by the open source communities. Today, Spark's standard libraries are actually the bulk of the open source project: the Spark core engine itself has changed little since it was first released, but the libraries have grown to provide more and more types of functionality. Spark includes libraries for SQL and structured data (Spark SQL), machine learning (MLlib), stream processing (Spark Streaming and the newer Structured Streaming), and graph analytics (GraphX). Beyond these libraries, there are hundreds of open source external libraries ranging from connectors for various storage systems to machine learning algorithms. One index of external libraries is available at spark-packages.org (*https://spark-packages.org/*).

Context: The Big Data Problem

Why do we need a new engine and programming model for data analytics in the first place? As with many trends in computing, this is due to changes in the economic factors that underlie computer applications and hardware.

For most of their history, computers became faster every year through processor speed increases: the new processors each year could run more instructions per second than the previous year's. As a result, applications also automatically became faster every year, without any changes needed to their code. This trend led to a large and established ecosystem of applications building up over time, most of which were designed to run only on a single processor. These applications rode the trend of improved processor speeds to scale up to larger computations and larger volumes of data over time.

Unfortunately, this trend in hardware stopped around 2005: due to hard limits in heat dissipation, hardware developers stopped making individual processors faster, and switched toward adding more parallel CPU cores all running at the same speed. This change meant that suddenly applications needed to be modified to add parallelism in order to run faster, which set the stage for new programming models such as Apache Spark.

On top of that, the technologies for storing and collecting data did not slow down appreciably in 2005, when processor speeds did. The cost to store 1 TB of data continues to drop by roughly two times every 14 months, meaning that it is very inexpensive for organizations of all sizes to store large amounts of data. Moreover, many of the technologies for collecting data (sensors, cameras, public datasets, etc.) continue to drop in cost and improve in resolution. For example, camera technology continues to improve in resolution and drop in cost per pixel every year, to the point where a 12-megapixel webcam costs only $3 to $4; this has made it inexpensive to collect a wide range of visual data, whether from people filming video or automated sensors in an industrial setting. Moreover, cameras are themselves the key sensors in other data collection devices, such as telescopes and even gene-sequencing machines, driving the cost of these technologies down as well.

The end result is a world in which collecting data is extremely inexpensive—many organizations today even consider it negligent *not* to log data of possible relevance to the business—but processing it requires large, parallel computations, often on clusters of machines. Moreover, in this new world, the software developed in the past 50 years cannot automatically scale up, and neither can the traditional programming models for data processing applications, creating the need for new programming models. It is this world that Apache Spark was built for.

History of Spark

Apache Spark began at UC Berkeley in 2009 as the Spark research project, which was first published the following year in a paper entitled "Spark: Cluster Computing with Working Sets" (*https://www.usenix.org/legacy/event/hotcloud10/tech/full_papers/Zaha ria.pdf*) by Matei Zaharia, Mosharaf Chowdhury, Michael Franklin, Scott Shenker, and Ion Stoica of the UC Berkeley AMPlab. At the time, Hadoop MapReduce was the dominant parallel programming engine for clusters, being the first open source system to tackle data-parallel processing on clusters of thousands of nodes. The AMPlab had worked with multiple early MapReduce users to understand the benefits and drawbacks of this new programming model, and was therefore able to synthesize a list of problems across several use cases and begin designing more general computing platforms. In addition, Zaharia had also worked with Hadoop users at UC Berkeley to understand their needs for the platform—specifically, teams that were doing large-scale machine learning using iterative algorithms that need to make multiple passes over the data.

Across these conversations, two things were clear. First, cluster computing held tremendous potential: at every organization that used MapReduce, brand new applications could be built using the existing data, and many new groups began using the system after its initial use cases. Second, however, the MapReduce engine made it both challenging and inefficient to build large applications. For example, the typical machine learning algorithm might need to make 10 or 20 passes over the data, and in MapReduce, each pass had to be written as a separate MapReduce job, which had to be launched separately on the cluster and load the data from scratch.

To address this problem, the Spark team first designed an API based on functional programming that could succinctly express multistep applications. The team then implemented this API over a new engine that could perform efficient, in-memory data sharing across computation steps. The team also began testing this system with both Berkeley and external users.

The first version of Spark supported only batch applications, but soon enough another compelling use case became clear: interactive data science and ad hoc queries. By simply plugging the Scala interpreter into Spark, the project could provide a highly usable interactive system for running queries on hundreds of machines. The AMPlab also quickly built on this idea to develop Shark, an engine that could run SQL queries over Spark and enable interactive use by analysts as well as data scientists. Shark was first released in 2011.

After these initial releases, it quickly became clear that the most powerful additions to Spark would be new libraries, and so the project began to follow the "standard library" approach it has today. In particular, different AMPlab groups started MLlib, Spark Streaming, and GraphX. They also ensured that these APIs would be highly interoperable, enabling writing end-to-end big data applications in the same engine for the first time.

In 2013, the project had grown to widespread use, with more than 100 contributors from more than 30 organizations outside UC Berkeley. The AMPlab contributed Spark to the Apache Software Foundation as a long-term, vendor-independent home for the project. The early AMPlab team also launched a company, Databricks, to harden the project, joining the community of other companies and organizations contributing to Spark. Since that time, the Apache Spark community released Spark 1.0 in 2014 and Spark 2.0 in 2016, and continues to make regular releases, bringing new features into the project.

Finally, Spark's core idea of composable APIs has also been refined over time. Early versions of Spark (before 1.0) largely defined this API in terms of *functional operations*—parallel operations such as maps and reduces over collections of Java objects. Beginning with 1.0, the project added Spark SQL, a new API for working with *structured data*—tables with a fixed data format that is not tied to Java's in-memory representation. Spark SQL enabled powerful new optimizations across libraries and APIs by understanding both the data format and the user code that runs on it in more detail. Over time, the project added a plethora of new APIs that build on this more powerful structured foundation, including DataFrames, machine learning pipelines, and Structured Streaming, a high-level, automatically optimized streaming API. In this book, we will spend a signficant amount of time explaining these next-generation APIs, most of which are marked as production-ready.

The Present and Future of Spark

Spark has been around for a number of years but continues to gain in popularity and use cases. Many new projects within the Spark ecosystem continue to push the boundaries of what's possible with the system. For example, a new high-level streaming engine, Structured Streaming, was introduced in 2016. This technology is a huge part of companies solving massive-scale data challenges, from technology companies like Uber and Netflix using Spark's streaming and machine learning tools, to institutions like NASA, CERN, and the Broad Institute of MIT and Harvard applying Spark to scientific data analysis.

Spark will continue to be a cornerstone of companies doing big data analysis for the foreseeable future, especially given that the project is still developing quickly. Any data scientist or engineer who needs to solve big data problems probably needs a copy of Spark on their machine—and hopefully, a copy of this book on their bookshelf!

Running Spark

This book contains an abundance of Spark-related code, and it's essential that you're prepared to run it as you learn. For the most part, you'll want to run the code interactively so that you can experiment with it. Let's go over some of your options before we begin working with the coding parts of the book.

You can use Spark from Python, Java, Scala, R, or SQL. Spark itself is written in Scala, and runs on the Java Virtual Machine (JVM), so therefore to run Spark either on your laptop or a cluster, all you need is an installation of Java. If you want to use the Python API, you will also need a Python interpreter (version 2.7 or later). If you want to use R, you will need a version of R on your machine.

There are two options we recommend for getting started with Spark: downloading and installing Apache Spark on your laptop, or running a web-based version in Databricks Community Edition, a free cloud environment for learning Spark that includes the code in this book. We explain both of those options next.

Downloading Spark Locally

If you want to download and run Spark locally, the first step is to make sure that you have Java installed on your machine (available as `java`), as well as a Python version if you would like to use Python. Next, visit the project's official download page (*http://spark.apache.org/downloads.html*), select the package type of "Pre-built for Hadoop 2.7 and later," and click "Direct Download." This downloads a compressed TAR file, or tarball, that you will then need to extract. The majority of this book was written using Spark 2.2, so downloading version 2.2 or later should be a good starting point.

Downloading Spark for a Hadoop cluster

Spark can run locally without any distributed storage system, such as Apache Hadoop. However, if you would like to connect the Spark version on your laptop to a Hadoop cluster, make sure you download the right Spark version for that Hadoop version, which can be chosen at *http://spark.apache.org/downloads.html* by selecting a different package type. We discuss how Spark runs on clusters and the Hadoop file system in later chapters, but at this point we recommend just running Spark on your laptop to start out.

> In Spark 2.2, the developers also added the ability to install Spark for Python via `pip install pyspark`. This functionality came out as this book was being written, so we weren't able to include all of the relevant instructions.

Building Spark from source

We won't cover this in the book, but you can also build and configure Spark from source. You can select a source package on the Apache download page to get just the source and follow the instructions in the README file for building.

After you've downloaded Spark, you'll want to open a command-line prompt and extract the package. In our case, we're installing Spark 2.2. The following is a code snippet that you can run on any Unix-style command line to unzip the file you downloaded from Spark and move into the directory:

```
cd ~/Downloads
tar -xf spark-2.2.0-bin-hadoop2.7.tgz
cd spark-2.2.0-bin-hadoop2.7.tgz
```

Note that Spark has a large number of directories and files within the project. Don't be intimidated! Most of these directories are relevant only if you're reading source code. The next section will cover the most important directories—the ones that let us launch Spark's different consoles for interactive use.

Launching Spark's Interactive Consoles

You can start an interactive shell in Spark for several different programming languages. The majority of this book is written with Python, Scala, and SQL in mind; thus, those are our recommended starting points.

Launching the Python console

You'll need Python 2 or 3 installed in order to launch the Python console. From Spark's home directory, run the following code:

```
./bin/pyspark
```

After you've done that, type "spark" and press Enter. You'll see the SparkSession object printed, which we cover in Chapter 2.

Launching the Scala console

To launch the Scala console, you will need to run the following command:

```
./bin/spark-shell
```

After you've done that, type "spark" and press Enter. As in Python, you'll see the SparkSession object, which we cover in Chapter 2.

Launching the SQL console

Parts of this book will cover a large amount of Spark SQL. For those, you might want to start the SQL console. We'll revisit some of the more relevant details after we actually cover these topics in the book.

```
./bin/spark-sql
```

Running Spark in the Cloud

If you would like to have a simple, interactive notebook experience for learning Spark, you might prefer using Databricks Community Edition. Databricks, as we mentioned earlier, is a company founded by the Berkeley team that started Spark, and offers a free community edition of its cloud service as a learning environment. The Databricks Community Edition includes a copy of all the data and code examples for this book, making it easy to quickly run any of them. To use the Databricks Community Edition, follow the instructions at *https://github.com/databricks/Spark-The-Definitive-Guide*. You will be able to use Scala, Python, SQL, or R from a web browser–based interface to run and visualize results.

Data Used in This Book

We'll use a number of data sources in this book for our examples. If you want to run the code locally, you can download them from the official code repository in this book as desribed at *https://github.com/databricks/Spark-The-Definitive-Guide*. In short, you will download the data, put it in a folder, and then run the code snippets in this book!

## CHAPTER 2

A Gentle Introduction to Spark

Now that our history lesson on Apache Spark is completed, it's time to begin using and applying it! This chapter presents a gentle introduction to Spark, in which we will walk through the core architecture of a cluster, Spark Application, and Spark's structured APIs using DataFrames and SQL. Along the way we will touch on Spark's core terminology and concepts so that you can begin using Spark right away. Let's get started with some basic background information.

Spark's Basic Architecture

Typically, when you think of a "computer," you think about one machine sitting on your desk at home or at work. This machine works perfectly well for watching movies or working with spreadsheet software. However, as many users likely experience at some point, there are some things that your computer is not powerful enough to perform. One particularly challenging area is data processing. Single machines do not have enough power and resources to perform computations on huge amounts of information (or the user probably does not have the time to wait for the computation to finish). A *cluster*, or group, of computers, pools the resources of many machines together, giving us the ability to use all the cumulative resources as if they were a single computer. Now, a group of machines alone is not powerful, you need a framework to coordinate work across them. Spark does just that, managing and coordinating the execution of tasks on data across a cluster of computers.

The cluster of machines that Spark will use to execute tasks is managed by a cluster manager like Spark's standalone cluster manager, YARN, or Mesos. We then submit Spark Applications to these cluster managers, which will grant resources to our application so that we can complete our work.

Spark Applications

Spark Applications consist of a *driver* process and a set of *executor* processes. The driver process runs your main() function, sits on a node in the cluster, and is responsible for three things: maintaining information about the Spark Application; responding to a user's program or input; and analyzing, distributing, and scheduling work across the executors (discussed momentarily). The driver process is absolutely essential—it's the heart of a Spark Application and maintains all relevant information during the lifetime of the application.

The *executors* are responsible for actually carrying out the work that the driver assigns them. This means that each executor is responsible for only two things: executing code assigned to it by the driver, and reporting the state of the computation on that executor back to the driver node.

Figure 2-1 demonstrates how the cluster manager controls physical machines and allocates resources to Spark Applications. This can be one of three core cluster managers: Spark's standalone cluster manager, YARN, or Mesos. This means that there can be multiple Spark Applications running on a cluster at the same time. We will discuss cluster managers more in Part IV.

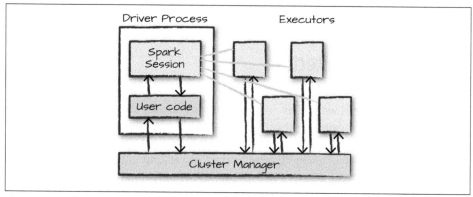

Figure 2-1. The architecture of a Spark Application

In Figure 2-1, we can see the driver on the left and four executors on the right. In this diagram, we removed the concept of cluster nodes. The user can specify how many executors should fall on each node through configurations.

> Spark, in addition to its cluster mode, also has a *local mode*. The driver and executors are simply processes, which means that they can live on the same machine or different machines. In local mode, the driver and executurs run (as threads) on your individual computer instead of a cluster. We wrote this book with local mode in mind, so you should be able to run everything on a single machine.

Here are the key points to understand about Spark Applications at this point:

- Spark employs a cluster manager that keeps track of the resources available.
- The driver process is responsible for executing the driver program's commands across the executors to complete a given task.

The executors, for the most part, will always be running Spark code. However, the driver can be "driven" from a number of different languages through Spark's language APIs. Let's take a look at those in the next section.

Spark's Language APIs

Spark's language APIs make it possible for you to run Spark code using various programming languages. For the most part, Spark presents some core "concepts" in every language; these concepts are then translated into Spark code that runs on the cluster of machines. If you use just the Structured APIs, you can expect all languages to have similar performance characteristics. Here's a brief rundown:

Scala
  Spark is primarily written in Scala, making it Spark's "default" language. This book will include Scala code examples wherever relevant.

Java
  Even though Spark is written in Scala, Spark's authors have been careful to ensure that you can write Spark code in Java. This book will focus primarily on Scala but will provide Java examples where relevant.

Python
  Python supports nearly all constructs that Scala supports. This book will include Python code examples whenever we include Scala code examples and a Python API exists.

SQL
  Spark supports a subset of the ANSI SQL 2003 standard. This makes it easy for analysts and non-programmers to take advantage of the big data powers of Spark. This book includes SQL code examples wherever relevant.

R
  Spark has two commonly used R libraries: one as a part of Spark core (SparkR) and another as an R community-driven package (sparklyr). We cover both of these integrations in Chapter 32.

Figure 2-2 presents a simple illustration of this relationship.

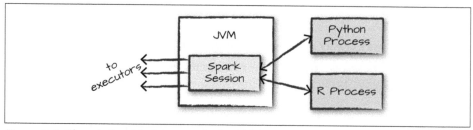

Figure 2-2. The relationship between the SparkSession and Spark's Language API

Each language API maintains the same core concepts that we described earlier. There is a SparkSession object available to the user, which is the entrance point to running Spark code. When using Spark from Python or R, you don't write explicit JVM instructions; instead, you write Python and R code that Spark translates into code that it then can run on the executor JVMs.

Spark's APIs

Although you can drive Spark from a variety of languages, what it makes available in those languages is worth mentioning. Spark has two fundamental sets of APIs: the low-level "unstructured" APIs, and the higher-level structured APIs. We discuss both in this book, but these introductory chapters will focus primarily on the higher-level structured APIs.

Starting Spark

Thus far, we covered the basic concepts of Spark Applications. This has all been conceptual in nature. When we actually go about writing our Spark Application, we are going to need a way to send user commands and data to it. We do that by first creating a SparkSession.

To do this, we will start Spark's local mode, just like we did in Chapter 1. This means running `./bin/spark-shell` to access the Scala console to start an interactive session. You can also start the Python console by using `./bin/pyspark`. This starts an interactive Spark Application. There is also a process for submitting standalone applications to Spark called `spark-submit`, whereby you can submit a precompiled application to Spark. We'll show you how to do that in Chapter 3.

When you start Spark in this interactive mode, you implicitly create a SparkSession that manages the Spark Application. When you start it through a standalone application, you must create the SparkSession object yourself in your application code.

The SparkSession

As discussed in the beginning of this chapter, you control your Spark Application through a driver process called the SparkSession. The SparkSession instance is the way Spark executes user-defined manipulations across the cluster. There is a one-to-one correspondence between a SparkSession and a Spark Application. In Scala and Python, the variable is available as `spark` when you start the console. Let's go ahead and look at the `SparkSession` in both Scala and/or Python:

```
spark
```

In Scala, you should see something like the following:

```
res0: org.apache.spark.sql.SparkSession = org.apache.spark.sql.SparkSession@...
```

In Python you'll see something like this:

```
<pyspark.sql.session.SparkSession at 0x7efda4c1ccd0>
```

Let's now perform the simple task of creating a range of numbers. This range of numbers is just like a named column in a spreadsheet:

```
// in Scala
val myRange = spark.range(1000).toDF("number")

# in Python
myRange = spark.range(1000).toDF("number")
```

You just ran your first Spark code! We created a *DataFrame* with one column containing 1,000 rows with values from 0 to 999. This range of numbers represents a *distributed collection*. When run on a cluster, each part of this range of numbers exists on a different executor. This is a Spark DataFrame.

DataFrames

A DataFrame is the most common Structured API and simply represents a table of data with rows and columns. The list that defines the columns and the types within those columns is called the *schema*. You can think of a DataFrame as a spreadsheet with named columns. Figure 2-3 illustrates the fundamental difference: a spreadsheet sits on one computer in one specific location, whereas a Spark DataFrame can span thousands of computers. The reason for putting the data on more than one computer should be intuitive: either the data is too large to fit on one machine or it would simply take too long to perform that computation on one machine.

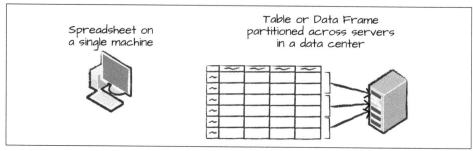

Figure 2-3. Distributed versus single-machine analysis

The DataFrame concept is not unique to Spark. R and Python both have similar concepts. However, Python/R DataFrames (with some exceptions) exist on one machine rather than multiple machines. This limits what you can do with a given DataFrame to the resources that exist on that specific machine. However, because Spark has language interfaces for both Python and R, it's quite easy to convert Pandas (Python) DataFrames to Spark DataFrames, and R DataFrames to Spark DataFrames.

 Spark has several core abstractions: Datasets, DataFrames, SQL Tables, and Resilient Distributed Datasets (RDDs). These different abstractions all represent distributed collections of data. The easiest and most efficient are DataFrames, which are available in all languages. We cover Datasets at the end of Part II, and RDDs in Part III.

Partitions

To allow every executor to perform work in parallel, Spark breaks up the data into chunks called *partitions*. A partition is a collection of rows that sit on one physical machine in your cluster. A DataFrame's partitions represent how the data is physically distributed across the cluster of machines during execution. If you have one partition, Spark will have a parallelism of only one, even if you have thousands of executors. If you have many partitions but only one executor, Spark will still have a parallelism of only one because there is only one computation resource.

An important thing to note is that with DataFrames you do not (for the most part) manipulate partitions manually or individually. You simply specify high-level transformations of data in the physical partitions, and Spark determines how this work will actually execute on the cluster. Lower-level APIs do exist (via the RDD interface), and we cover those in Part III.

Transformations

In Spark, the core data structures are *immutable*, meaning they cannot be changed after they're created. This might seem like a strange concept at first: if you cannot change it, how are you supposed to use it? To "change" a DataFrame, you need to instruct Spark how you would like to modify it to do what you want. These instructions are called *transformations*. Let's perform a simple transformation to find all even numbers in our current DataFrame:

```
// in Scala
val divisBy2 = myRange.where("number % 2 = 0")

# in Python
divisBy2 = myRange.where("number % 2 = 0")
```

Notice that these return no output. This is because we specified only an abstract transformation, and Spark will not act on transformations until we call an action (we discuss this shortly). Transformations are the core of how you express your business logic using Spark. There are two types of transformations: those that specify *narrow dependencies*, and those that specify *wide dependencies*.

Transformations consisting of narrow dependencies (we'll call them narrow transformations) are those for which each input partition will contribute to only one output partition. In the preceding code snippet, the `where` statement specifies a narrow dependency, where only one partition contributes to at most one output partition, as you can see in Figure 2-4.

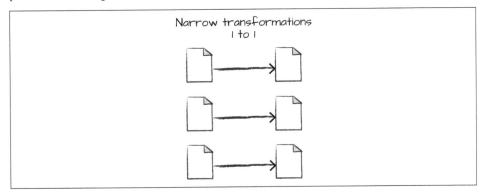

Figure 2-4. A narrow dependency

A wide dependency (or wide transformation) style transformation will have input partitions contributing to many output partitions. You will often hear this referred to as a *shuffle* whereby Spark will exchange partitions across the cluster. With narrow transformations, Spark will automatically perform an operation called *pipelining*, meaning that if we specify multiple filters on DataFrames, they'll all be performed in-memory. The same cannot be said for shuffles. When we perform a shuffle, Spark writes the results to disk. Wide transformations are illustrated in Figure 2-5.

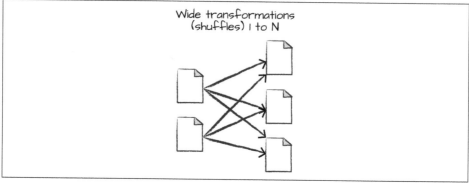

Wide transformations
(shuffles) 1 to N

Figure 2-5. A wide dependency

You'll see a lot of discussion about shuffle optimization across the web because it's an important topic, but for now, all you need to understand is that there are two kinds of transformations. You now can see how transformations are simply ways of specifying different series of data manipulation. This leads us to a topic called *lazy evaluation*.

Lazy Evaluation

Lazy evaulation means that Spark will wait until the very last moment to execute the graph of computation instructions. In Spark, instead of modifying the data immediately when you express some operation, you build up a *plan* of transformations that you would like to apply to your source data. By waiting until the last minute to execute the code, Spark compiles this plan from your raw DataFrame transformations to a streamlined physical plan that will run as efficiently as possible across the cluster. This provides immense benefits because Spark can optimize the entire data flow from end to end. An example of this is something called *predicate pushdown* on Data-Frames. If we build a large Spark job but specify a filter at the end that only requires us to fetch one row from our source data, the most efficient way to execute this is to access the single record that we need. Spark will actually optimize this for us by pushing the filter down automatically.

Actions

Transformations allow us to build up our logical transformation plan. To trigger the computation, we run an *action*. An action instructs Spark to compute a result from a series of transformations. The simplest action is count, which gives us the total number of records in the DataFrame:

```
divisBy2.count()
```

The output of the preceding code should be 500. Of course, count is not the only action. There are three kinds of actions:

- Actions to view data in the console
- Actions to collect data to native objects in the respective language
- Actions to write to output data sources

In specifying this action, we started a Spark job that runs our filter transformation (a narrow transformation), then an aggregation (a wide transformation) that performs the counts on a per partition basis, and then a collect, which brings our result to a native object in the respective language. You can see all of this by inspecting the Spark UI, a tool included in Spark with which you can monitor the Spark jobs running on a cluster.

Spark UI

You can monitor the progress of a job through the Spark web UI. The Spark UI is available on port 4040 of the driver node. If you are running in local mode, this will be *http://localhost:4040*. The Spark UI displays information on the state of your Spark jobs, its environment, and cluster state. It's very useful, especially for tuning and debugging. Figure 2-6 shows an example UI for a Spark job where two stages containing nine tasks were executed.

Figure 2-6. The Spark UI

This chapter will not go into detail about Spark job execution and the Spark UI. We will cover that in Chapter 18. At this point, all you need to understand is that a Spark *job* represents a set of transformations triggered by an individual action, and you can monitor that job from the Spark UI.

An End-to-End Example

In the previous example, we created a DataFrame of a range of numbers; not exactly groundbreaking big data. In this section, we will reinforce everything we learned previously in this chapter with a more realistic example, and explain step by step what is happening under the hood. We'll use Spark to analyze some flight data (*https://github.com/databricks/Spark-The-Definitive-Guide/tree/master/data/flight-data*) from the United States Bureau of Transportation statistics.

Inside of the CSV folder, you'll see that we have a number of files. There's also a number of other folders with different file formats, which we discuss in Chapter 9. For now, let's focus on the CSV files.

Each file has a number of rows within it. These files are CSV files, meaning that they're a semi-structured data format, with each row in the file representing a row in our future DataFrame:

```
$ head /data/flight-data/csv/2015-summary.csv

DEST_COUNTRY_NAME,ORIGIN_COUNTRY_NAME,count
United States,Romania,15
United States,Croatia,1
United States,Ireland,344
```

Spark includes the ability to read and write from a large number of data sources. To read this data, we will use a DataFrameReader that is associated with our SparkSession. In doing so, we will specify the file format as well as any options we want to specify. In our case, we want to do something called *schema inference*, which means that we want Spark to take a best guess at what the schema of our DataFrame should be. We also want to specify that the first row is the header in the file, so we'll specify that as an option, too.

To get the schema information, Spark reads in a little bit of the data and then attempts to parse the types in those rows according to the types available in Spark. You also have the option of strictly specifying a schema when you read in data (which we recommend in production scenarios):

```scala
// in Scala
val flightData2015 = spark
  .read
  .option("inferSchema", "true")
  .option("header", "true")
  .csv("/data/flight-data/csv/2015-summary.csv")
```

```python
# in Python
flightData2015 = spark\
  .read\
  .option("inferSchema", "true")\
```

```
.option("header", "true")\
.csv("/data/flight-data/csv/2015-summary.csv")
```

Each of these DataFrames (in Scala and Python) have a set of columns with an unspecified number of rows. The reason the number of rows is unspecified is because reading data is a transformation, and is therefore a lazy operation. Spark peeked at only a couple of rows of data to try to guess what types each column should be. Figure 2-7 provides an illustration of the CSV file being read into a DataFrame and then being converted into a local array or list of rows.

Figure 2-7. Reading a CSV file into a DataFrame and converting it to a local array or list of rows

If we perform the `take` action on the DataFrame, we will be able to see the same results that we saw before when we used the command line:

```
flightData2015.take(3)

Array([United States,Romania,15], [United States,Croatia...
```

Let's specify some more transformations! Now, let's sort our data according to the count column, which is an integer type. Figure 2-8 illustrates this process.

Remember, `sort` does not modify the DataFrame. We use `sort` as a transformation that returns a new DataFrame by transforming the previous DataFrame. Let's illustrate what's happening when we call take on that resulting DataFrame (Figure 2-8).

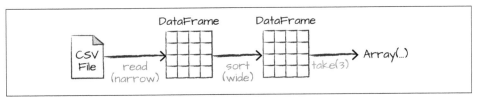

Figure 2-8. Reading, sorting, and collecting a DataFrame

Nothing happens to the data when we call sort because it's just a transformation. However, we can see that Spark is building up a plan for how it will execute this across the cluster by looking at the `explain` plan. We can call `explain` on any DataFrame object to see the DataFrame's lineage (or how Spark will execute this query):

```
flightData2015.sort("count").explain()
```

```
== Physical Plan ==
*Sort [count#195 ASC NULLS FIRST], true, 0
+- Exchange rangepartitioning(count#195 ASC NULLS FIRST, 200)
   +- *FileScan csv [DEST_COUNTRY_NAME#193,ORIGIN_COUNTRY_NAME#194,count#195] ...
```

Congratulations, you've just read your first explain plan! Explain plans are a bit arcane, but with a bit of practice it becomes second nature. You can read explain plans from top to bottom, the top being the end result, and the bottom being the source(s) of data. In this case, take a look at the first keywords. You will see sort, exchange, and FileScan. That's because the sort of our data is actually a wide transformation because rows will need to be compared with one another. Don't worry too much about understanding everything about explain plans at this point, they can just be helpful tools for debugging and improving your knowledge as you progress with Spark.

Now, just like we did before, we can specify an action to kick off this plan. However, before doing that, we're going to set a configuration. By default, when we perform a shuffle, Spark outputs 200 shuffle partitions. Let's set this value to 5 to reduce the number of the output partitions from the shuffle:

```
spark.conf.set("spark.sql.shuffle.partitions", "5")

flightData2015.sort("count").take(2)

... Array([United States,Singapore,1], [Moldova,United States,1])
```

Figure 2-9 illustrates this operation. Notice that in addition to the logical transformations, we include the physical partition count, as well.

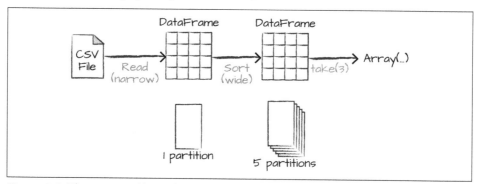

Figure 2-9. The process of logical and physical DataFrame manipulation

The logical plan of transformations that we build up defines a lineage for the DataFrame so that at any given point in time, Spark knows how to recompute any partition by performing all of the operations it had before on the same input data. This sits at the heart of Spark's programming model—functional programming where the same inputs always result in the same outputs when the transformations on that data stay constant.

We do not manipulate the physical data; instead, we configure physical execution characteristics through things like the shuffle partitions parameter that we set a few moments ago. We ended up with five output partitions because that's the value we specified in the shuffle partition. You can change this to help control the physical execution characteristics of your Spark jobs. Go ahead and experiment with different values and see the number of partitions yourself. In experimenting with different values, you should see drastically different runtimes. Remember that you can monitor the job progress by navigating to the Spark UI on port 4040 to see the physical and logical execution characteristics of your jobs.

DataFrames and SQL

We worked through a simple transformation in the previous example, let's now work through a more complex one and follow along in both DataFrames and SQL. Spark can run the same transformations, regardless of the language, in the exact same way. You can express your business logic in SQL or DataFrames (either in R, Python, Scala, or Java) and Spark will compile that logic down to an underlying plan (that you can see in the explain plan) before actually executing your code. With Spark SQL, you can register any DataFrame as a table or view (a temporary table) and query it using pure SQL. There is no performance difference between writing SQL queries or writing DataFrame code, they both "compile" to the same underlying plan that we specify in DataFrame code.

You can make any DataFrame into a table or view with one simple method call:

```
flightData2015.createOrReplaceTempView("flight_data_2015")
```

Now we can query our data in SQL. To do so, we'll use the `spark.sql` function (remember, `spark` is our SparkSession variable) that conveniently returns a new DataFrame. Although this might seem a bit circular in logic—that a SQL query against a DataFrame returns another DataFrame—it's actually quite powerful. This makes it possible for you to specify transformations in the manner most convenient to you at any given point in time and not sacrifice any efficiency to do so! To understand that this is happening, let's take a look at two explain plans:

```scala
// in Scala
val sqlWay = spark.sql("""
SELECT DEST_COUNTRY_NAME, count(1)
FROM flight_data_2015
GROUP BY DEST_COUNTRY_NAME
""")

val dataFrameWay = flightData2015
  .groupBy('DEST_COUNTRY_NAME)
  .count()
```

```
sqlWay.explain
dataFrameWay.explain

# in Python
sqlWay = spark.sql("""
SELECT DEST_COUNTRY_NAME, count(1)
FROM flight_data_2015
GROUP BY DEST_COUNTRY_NAME
""")

dataFrameWay = flightData2015\
  .groupBy("DEST_COUNTRY_NAME")\
  .count()

sqlWay.explain()
dataFrameWay.explain()

== Physical Plan ==
*HashAggregate(keys=[DEST_COUNTRY_NAME#182], functions=[count(1)])
+- Exchange hashpartitioning(DEST_COUNTRY_NAME#182, 5)
   +- *HashAggregate(keys=[DEST_COUNTRY_NAME#182], functions=[partial_count(1)])
      +- *FileScan csv [DEST_COUNTRY_NAME#182] ...
== Physical Plan ==
*HashAggregate(keys=[DEST_COUNTRY_NAME#182], functions=[count(1)])
+- Exchange hashpartitioning(DEST_COUNTRY_NAME#182, 5)
   +- *HashAggregate(keys=[DEST_COUNTRY_NAME#182], functions=[partial_count(1)])
      +- *FileScan csv [DEST_COUNTRY_NAME#182] ...
```

Notice that these plans compile to the exact same underlying plan!

Let's pull out some interesting statistics from our data. One thing to understand is that DataFrames (and SQL) in Spark already have a huge number of manipulations available. There are hundreds of functions that you can use and import to help you resolve your big data problems faster. We will use the max function, to establish the maximum number of flights to and from any given location. This just scans each value in the relevant column in the DataFrame and checks whether it's greater than the previous values that have been seen. This is a transformation, because we are effectively filtering down to one row. Let's see what that looks like:

```
spark.sql("SELECT max(count) from flight_data_2015").take(1)

// in Scala
import org.apache.spark.sql.functions.max

flightData2015.select(max("count")).take(1)

# in Python
from pyspark.sql.functions import max

flightData2015.select(max("count")).take(1)
```

Great, that's a simple example that gives a result of 370,002. Let's perform something a bit more complicated and find the top five destination countries in the data. This is our first multi-transformation query, so we'll take it step by step. Let's begin with a fairly straightforward SQL aggregation:

```scala
// in Scala
val maxSql = spark.sql("""
SELECT DEST_COUNTRY_NAME, sum(count) as destination_total
FROM flight_data_2015
GROUP BY DEST_COUNTRY_NAME
ORDER BY sum(count) DESC
LIMIT 5
""")

maxSql.show()
```

```python
# in Python
maxSql = spark.sql("""
SELECT DEST_COUNTRY_NAME, sum(count) as destination_total
FROM flight_data_2015
GROUP BY DEST_COUNTRY_NAME
ORDER BY sum(count) DESC
LIMIT 5
""")

maxSql.show()
```

```
+-----------------+-----------------+
|DEST_COUNTRY_NAME|destination_total|
+-----------------+-----------------+
|    United States|           411352|
|           Canada|             8399|
|           Mexico|             7140|
|   United Kingdom|             2025|
|            Japan|             1548|
+-----------------+-----------------+
```

Now, let's move to the DataFrame syntax that is semantically similar but slightly different in implementation and ordering. But, as we mentioned, the underlying plans for both of them are the same. Let's run the queries and see their results as a sanity check:

```scala
// in Scala
import org.apache.spark.sql.functions.desc

flightData2015
  .groupBy("DEST_COUNTRY_NAME")
  .sum("count")
  .withColumnRenamed("sum(count)", "destination_total")
  .sort(desc("destination_total"))
  .limit(5)
  .show()
```

```python
# in Python
from pyspark.sql.functions import desc
```

```
flightData2015\
  .groupBy("DEST_COUNTRY_NAME")\
  .sum("count")\
  .withColumnRenamed("sum(count)", "destination_total")\
  .sort(desc("destination_total"))\
  .limit(5)\
  .show()

+-----------------+-----------------+
|DEST_COUNTRY_NAME|destination_total|
+-----------------+-----------------+
|    United States|           411352|
|           Canada|             8399|
|           Mexico|             7140|
|   United Kingdom|             2025|
|            Japan|             1548|
+-----------------+-----------------+
```

Now there are seven steps that take us all the way back to the source data. You can see this in the explain plan on those DataFrames. Figure 2-10 shows the set of steps that we perform in "code." The true execution plan (the one visible in `explain`) will differ from that shown in Figure 2-10 because of optimizations in the physical execution; however, the llustration is as good of a starting point as any. This execution plan is a *directed acyclic graph* (DAG) of transformations, each resulting in a new immutable DataFrame, on which we call an action to generate a result.

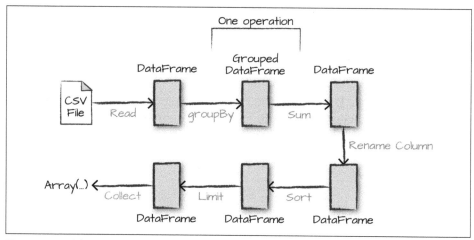

Figure 2-10. The entire DataFrame transformation flow

The first step is to read in the data. We defined the DataFrame previously but, as a reminder, Spark does not actually read it in until an action is called on that Data-Frame or one derived from the original DataFrame.

The second step is our grouping; technically when we call groupBy, we end up with a RelationalGroupedDataset, which is a fancy name for a DataFrame that has a grouping specified but needs the user to specify an aggregation before it can be queried further. We basically specified that we're going to be grouping by a key (or set of keys) and that now we're going to perform an aggregation over each one of those keys.

Therefore, the third step is to specify the aggregation. Let's use the sum aggregation method. This takes as input a column expression or, simply, a column name. The result of the sum method call is a new DataFrame. You'll see that it has a new schema but that it does know the type of each column. It's important to reinforce (again!) that no computation has been performed. This is simply another transformation that we've expressed, and Spark is simply able to trace our type information through it.

The fourth step is a simple renaming. We use the withColumnRenamed method that takes two arguments, the original column name and the new column name. Of course, this doesn't perform computation: this is just another transformation!

The fifth step sorts the data such that if we were to take results off of the top of the DataFrame, they would have the largest values in the destination_total column.

You likely noticed that we had to import a function to do this, the desc function. You might also have noticed that desc does not return a string but a Column. In general, many DataFrame methods will accept strings (as column names) or Column types or expressions. Columns and expressions are actually the exact same thing.

Penultimately, we'll specify a limit. This just specifies that we only want to return the first five values in our final DataFrame instead of all the data.

The last step is our action! Now we actually begin the process of collecting the results of our DataFrame, and Spark will give us back a list or array in the language that we're executing. To reinforce all of this, let's look at the explain plan for the previous query:

```scala
// in Scala
flightData2015
  .groupBy("DEST_COUNTRY_NAME")
  .sum("count")
  .withColumnRenamed("sum(count)", "destination_total")
  .sort(desc("destination_total"))
  .limit(5)
  .explain()
```

```python
# in Python
flightData2015\
  .groupBy("DEST_COUNTRY_NAME")\
  .sum("count")\
  .withColumnRenamed("sum(count)", "destination_total")\
  .sort(desc("destination_total"))\
```

```
  .limit(5)\
  .explain()

== Physical Plan ==
TakeOrderedAndProject(limit=5, orderBy=[destination_total#16194L DESC], outpu...
+- *HashAggregate(keys=[DEST_COUNTRY_NAME#7323], functions=[sum(count#7325L)])
   +- Exchange hashpartitioning(DEST_COUNTRY_NAME#7323, 5)
      +- *HashAggregate(keys=[DEST_COUNTRY_NAME#7323], functions=[partial_sum...
         +- InMemoryTableScan [DEST_COUNTRY_NAME#7323, count#7325L]
            +- InMemoryRelation [DEST_COUNTRY_NAME#7323, ORIGIN_COUNTRY_NA...
               +- *Scan csv [DEST_COUNTRY_NAME#7578,ORIGIN_COUNTRY_NAME...
```

Although this explain plan doesn't match our exact "conceptual plan," all of the pieces are there. You can see the limit statement as well as the orderBy (in the first line). You can also see how our aggregation happens in two phases, in the partial_sum calls. This is because summing a list of numbers is commutative, and Spark can perform the sum, partition by partition. Of course we can see how we read in the DataFrame, as well.

Naturally, we don't always need to collect the data. We can also write it out to any data source that Spark supports. For instance, suppose we want to store the information in a database like PostgreSQL or write them out to another file.

Conclusion

This chapter introduced the basics of Apache Spark. We talked about transformations and actions, and how Spark lazily executes a DAG of transformations in order to optimize the execution plan on DataFrames. We also discussed how data is organized into partitions and set the stage for working with more complex transformations. In Chapter 3 we take you on a tour of the vast Spark ecosystem and look at some more advanced concepts and tools that are available in Spark, from streaming to machine learning.

A Tour of Spark's Toolset

In Chapter 2, we introduced Spark's core concepts, like transformations and actions, in the context of Spark's Structured APIs. These simple conceptual building blocks are the foundation of Apache Spark's vast ecosystem of tools and libraries (Figure 3-1). Spark is composed of these primitives—the lower-level APIs and the Structured APIs—and then a series of standard libraries for additional functionality.

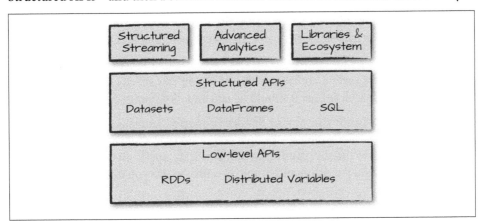

Figure 3-1. Spark's toolset

Spark's libraries support a variety of different tasks, from graph analysis and machine learning to streaming and integrations with a host of computing and storage systems. This chapter presents a whirlwind tour of much of what Spark has to offer, including some of the APIs we have not yet covered and a few of the main libraries. For each section, you will find more detailed information in other parts of this book; our purpose here is provide you with an overview of what's possible.

This chapter covers the following:

- Running production applications with `spark-submit`
- Datasets: type-safe APIs for structured data
- Structured Streaming
- Machine learning and advanced analytics
- Resilient Distributed Datasets (RDD): Spark's low level APIs
- SparkR
- The third-party package ecosystem

After you've taken the tour, you'll be able to jump to the corresponding parts of the book to find answers to your questions about particular topics.

Running Production Applications

Spark makes it easy to develop and create big data programs. Spark also makes it easy to turn your interactive exploration into production applications with `spark-submit`, a built-in command-line tool. `spark-submit` does one thing: it lets you send your application code to a cluster and launch it to execute there. Upon submission, the application will run until it exits (completes the task) or encounters an error. You can do this with all of Spark's support cluster managers including Standalone, Mesos, and YARN.

`spark-submit` offers several controls with which you can specify the resources your application needs as well as how it should be run and its command-line arguments.

You can write applications in any of Spark's supported languages and then submit them for execution. The simplest example is running an application on your local machine. We'll show this by running a sample Scala application that comes with Spark, using the following command in the directory where you downloaded Spark:

```
./bin/spark-submit \
  --class org.apache.spark.examples.SparkPi \
  --master local \
  ./examples/jars/spark-examples_2.11-2.2.0.jar 10
```

This sample application calculates the digits of pi to a certain level of estimation. Here, we've told `spark-submit` that we want to run on our local machine, which class and which JAR we would like to run, and some command-line arguments for that class.

We can also run a Python version of the application using the following command:

```
./bin/spark-submit \
  --master local \
  ./examples/src/main/python/pi.py 10
```

By changing the `master` argument of `spark-submit`, we can also submit the same application to a cluster running Spark's standalone cluster manager, Mesos or YARN.

`spark-submit` will come in handy to run many of the examples we've packaged with this book. In the rest of this chapter, we'll go through examples of some APIs that we haven't yet seen in our introduction to Spark.

Datasets: Type-Safe Structured APIs

The first API we'll describe is a type-safe version of Spark's structured API called *Datasets*, for writing statically typed code in Java and Scala. The Dataset API is not available in Python and R, because those languages are dynamically typed.

Recall that DataFrames, which we saw in the previous chapter, are a distributed collection of objects of type `Row` that can hold various types of tabular data. The Dataset API gives users the ability to assign a Java/Scala class to the records within a Data-Frame and manipulate it as a collection of typed objects, similar to a Java `ArrayList` or Scala `Seq`. The APIs available on Datasets are *type-safe*, meaning that you cannot accidentally view the objects in a Dataset as being of another class than the class you put in initially. This makes Datasets especially attractive for writing large applications, with which multiple software engineers must interact through well-defined interfaces.

The `Dataset` class is parameterized with the type of object contained inside: `Dataset<T>` in Java and `Dataset[T]` in Scala. For example, a `Dataset[Person]` will be guaranteed to contain objects of class `Person`. As of Spark 2.0, the supported types are classes following the JavaBean pattern in Java and case classes in Scala. These types are restricted because Spark needs to be able to automatically analyze the type T and create an appropriate schema for the tabular data within your Dataset.

One great thing about Datasets is that you can use them only when you need or want to. For instance, in the following example, we'll define our own data type and manipulate it via arbitrary map and filter functions. After we've performed our manipulations, Spark can automatically turn it back into a DataFrame, and we can manipulate it further by using the hundreds of functions that Spark includes. This makes it easy to drop down to lower level, perform type-safe coding when necessary, and move higher up to SQL for more rapid analysis. Here is a small example showing how you can use both type-safe functions and DataFrame-like SQL expressions to quickly write business logic:

```scala
// in Scala
case class Flight(DEST_COUNTRY_NAME: String,
                  ORIGIN_COUNTRY_NAME: String,
```

```
              count: BigInt)
  val flightsDF = spark.read
    .parquet("/data/flight-data/parquet/2010-summary.parquet/")
  val flights = flightsDF.as[Flight]
```

One final advantage is that when you call `collect` or `take` on a Dataset, it will collect objects of the proper type in your Dataset, not DataFrame Rows. This makes it easy to get type safety and securely perform manipulation in a distributed and a local manner without code changes:

```
// in Scala
flights
  .filter(flight_row => flight_row.ORIGIN_COUNTRY_NAME != "Canada")
  .map(flight_row => flight_row)
  .take(5)

flights
  .take(5)
  .filter(flight_row => flight_row.ORIGIN_COUNTRY_NAME != "Canada")
  .map(fr => Flight(fr.DEST_COUNTRY_NAME, fr.ORIGIN_COUNTRY_NAME, fr.count + 5))
```

We cover Datasets in depth in Chapter 11.

Structured Streaming

Structured Streaming is a high-level API for stream processing that became production-ready in Spark 2.2. With Structured Streaming, you can take the same operations that you perform in batch mode using Spark's structured APIs and run them in a streaming fashion. This can reduce latency and allow for incremental processing. The best thing about Structured Streaming is that it allows you to rapidly and quickly extract value out of streaming systems with virtually no code changes. It also makes it easy to conceptualize because you can write your batch job as a way to prototype it and then you can convert it to a streaming job. The way all of this works is by incrementally processing that data.

Let's walk through a simple example of how easy it is to get started with Structured Streaming. For this, we will use a retail dataset (*https://github.com/databricks/Spark-The-Definitive-Guide/tree/master/data/retail-data*), one that has specific dates and times for us to be able to use. We will use the "by-day" set of files, in which one file represents one day of data.

We put it in this format to simulate data being produced in a consistent and regular manner by a different process. This is retail data so imagine that these are being produced by retail stores and sent to a location where they will be read by our Structured Streaming job.

It's also worth sharing a sample of the data so you can reference what the data looks like:

```
InvoiceNo,StockCode,Description,Quantity,InvoiceDate,UnitPrice,CustomerID,Country
536365,85123A,WHITE HANGING HEART T-LIGHT HOLDER,6,2010-12-01 08:26:00,2.55,17...
536365,71053,WHITE METAL LANTERN,6,2010-12-01 08:26:00,3.39,17850.0,United Kin...
536365,84406B,CREAM CUPID HEARTS COAT HANGER,8,2010-12-01 08:26:00,2.75,17850...
```

To ground this, let's first analyze the data as a static dataset and create a DataFrame to do so. We'll also create a schema from this static dataset (there are ways of using schema inference with streaming that we will touch on in Part V):

```scala
// in Scala
val staticDataFrame = spark.read.format("csv")
  .option("header", "true")
  .option("inferSchema", "true")
  .load("/data/retail-data/by-day/*.csv")

staticDataFrame.createOrReplaceTempView("retail_data")
val staticSchema = staticDataFrame.schema
```

```python
# in Python
staticDataFrame = spark.read.format("csv")\
  .option("header", "true")\
  .option("inferSchema", "true")\
  .load("/data/retail-data/by-day/*.csv")

staticDataFrame.createOrReplaceTempView("retail_data")
staticSchema = staticDataFrame.schema
```

Because we're working with time–series data, it's worth mentioning how we might go along grouping and aggregating our data. In this example we'll take a look at the sale hours during which a given customer (identified by `CustomerId`) makes a large purchase. For example, let's add a total cost column and see on what days a customer spent the most.

The window function will include all data from each day in the aggregation. It's simply a window over the time–series column in our data. This is a helpful tool for manipulating date and timestamps because we can specify our requirements in a more human form (via intervals), and Spark will group all of them together for us:

```scala
// in Scala
import org.apache.spark.sql.functions.{window, column, desc, col}
staticDataFrame
  .selectExpr(
    "CustomerId",
    "(UnitPrice * Quantity) as total_cost",
    "InvoiceDate")
  .groupBy(
    col("CustomerId"), window(col("InvoiceDate"), "1 day"))
  .sum("total_cost")
  .show(5)
```

```python
# in Python
from pyspark.sql.functions import window, column, desc, col
```

```
staticDataFrame\
  .selectExpr(
    "CustomerId",
    "(UnitPrice * Quantity) as total_cost",
    "InvoiceDate")\
  .groupBy(
    col("CustomerId"), window(col("InvoiceDate"), "1 day"))\
  .sum("total_cost")\
  .show(5)
```

It's worth mentioning that you can also run this as SQL code, just as we saw in the previous chapter.

Here's a sample of the output that you'll see:

```
+----------+--------------------+------------------+
|CustomerId|              window|  sum(total_cost)|
+----------+--------------------+------------------+
|   17450.0|[2011-09-20 00:00...|          71601.44|
...
|      null|[2011-12-08 00:00...|31975.590000000007|
+----------+--------------------+------------------+
```

The null values represent the fact that we don't have a `customerId` for some transactions.

That's the static DataFrame version; there shouldn't be any big surprises in there if you're familiar with the syntax.

Because you're likely running this in local mode, it's a good practice to set the number of shuffle partitions to something that's going to be a better fit for local mode. This configuration specifies the number of partitions that should be created after a shuffle. By default, the value is 200, but because there aren't many executors on this machine, it's worth reducing this to 5. We did this same operation in Chapter 2, so if you don't remember why this is important, feel free to flip back to review.

```
spark.conf.set("spark.sql.shuffle.partitions", "5")
```

Now that we've seen how that works, let's take a look at the streaming code! You'll notice that very little actually changes about the code. The biggest change is that we used readStream instead of read, additionally you'll notice the maxFilesPerTrigger option, which simply specifies the number of files we should read in at once. This is to make our demonstration more "streaming," and in a production scenario this would probably be omitted.

```
val streamingDataFrame = spark.readStream
    .schema(staticSchema)
    .option("maxFilesPerTrigger", 1)
    .format("csv")
    .option("header", "true")
    .load("/data/retail-data/by-day/*.csv")
```

```python
# in Python
streamingDataFrame = spark.readStream\
    .schema(staticSchema)\
    .option("maxFilesPerTrigger", 1)\
    .format("csv")\
    .option("header", "true")\
    .load("/data/retail-data/by-day/*.csv")
```

Now we can see whether our DataFrame is streaming:

```
streamingDataFrame.isStreaming // returns true
```

Let's set up the same business logic as the previous DataFrame manipulation. We'll perform a summation in the process:

```scala
// in Scala
val purchaseByCustomerPerHour = streamingDataFrame
    .selectExpr(
      "CustomerId",
      "(UnitPrice * Quantity) as total_cost",
      "InvoiceDate")
    .groupBy(
      $"CustomerId", window($"InvoiceDate", "1 day"))
    .sum("total_cost")
```

```python
# in Python
purchaseByCustomerPerHour = streamingDataFrame\
    .selectExpr(
      "CustomerId",
      "(UnitPrice * Quantity) as total_cost",
      "InvoiceDate")\
    .groupBy(
      col("CustomerId"), window(col("InvoiceDate"), "1 day"))\
    .sum("total_cost")
```

This is still a lazy operation, so we will need to call a streaming action to start the execution of this data flow.

Streaming actions are a bit different from our conventional static action because we're going to be populating data somewhere instead of just calling something like count (which doesn't make any sense on a stream anyways). The action we will use will output to an in-memory table that we will update after each *trigger*. In this case, each trigger is based on an individual file (the read option that we set). Spark will mutate the data in the in-memory table such that we will always have the highest value as specified in our previous aggregation:

```scala
// in Scala
purchaseByCustomerPerHour.writeStream
    .format("memory") // memory = store in-memory table
    .queryName("customer_purchases") // the name of the in-memory table
    .outputMode("complete") // complete = all the counts should be in the table
    .start()
```

```python
# in Python
purchaseByCustomerPerHour.writeStream\
    .format("memory")\
    .queryName("customer_purchases")\
    .outputMode("complete")\
    .start()
```

When we start the stream, we can run queries against it to debug what our result will look like if we were to write this out to a production sink:

```scala
// in Scala
spark.sql("""
  SELECT *
  FROM customer_purchases
  ORDER BY `sum(total_cost)` DESC
  """)
  .show(5)
```

```python
# in Python
spark.sql("""
  SELECT *
  FROM customer_purchases
  ORDER BY `sum(total_cost)` DESC
  """)\
  .show(5)
```

You'll notice that the composition of our table changes as we read in more data! With each file, the results might or might not be changing based on the data. Naturally, because we're grouping customers, we hope to see an increase in the top customer purchase amounts over time (and do for a period of time!). Another option you can use is to write the results out to the console:

```
purchaseByCustomerPerHour.writeStream
    .format("console")
    .queryName("customer_purchases_2")
    .outputMode("complete")
    .start()
```

You shouldn't use either of these streaming methods in production, but they do make for convenient demonstration of Structured Streaming's power. Notice how this window is built on event time, as well, not the time at which Spark processes the data. This was one of the shortcomings of Spark Streaming that Structured Streaming has resolved. We cover Structured Streaming in depth in Part V.

Machine Learning and Advanced Analytics

Another popular aspect of Spark is its ability to perform large-scale machine learning with a built-in library of machine learning algorithms called MLlib. MLlib allows for preprocessing, munging, training of models, and making predictions at scale on data. You can even use models trained in MLlib to make predictions in Strucutred Streaming. Spark provides a sophisticated machine learning API for performing a variety of machine learning tasks, from classification to regression, and clustering to deep learning. To demonstrate this functionality, we will perform some basic clustering on our data using a standard algorithm called k-means.

What Is k-Means?

k-means is a clustering algorithm in which "k" centers are randomly assigned within the data. The points closest to that point are then "assigned" to a class and the center of the assigned points is computed. This center point is called the *centroid*. We then label the points closest to that centroid, to the centroid's class, and shift the centroid to the new center of that cluster of points. We repeat this process for a finite set of iterations or until convergence (our center points stop changing).

Spark includes a number of preprocessing methods out of the box. To demonstrate these methods, we will begin with some raw data, build up transformations before getting the data into the right format, at which point we can actually train our model and then serve predictions:

```
staticDataFrame.printSchema()

root
 |-- InvoiceNo: string (nullable = true)
 |-- StockCode: string (nullable = true)
 |-- Description: string (nullable = true)
 |-- Quantity: integer (nullable = true)
 |-- InvoiceDate: timestamp (nullable = true)
 |-- UnitPrice: double (nullable = true)
 |-- CustomerID: double (nullable = true)
 |-- Country: string (nullable = true)
```

Machine learning algorithms in MLlib require that data is represented as numerical values. Our current data is represented by a variety of different types, including timestamps, integers, and strings. Therefore we need to transform this data into some numerical representation. In this instance, we'll use several DataFrame transformations to manipulate our date data:

```scala
// in Scala
import org.apache.spark.sql.functions.date_format
val preppedDataFrame = staticDataFrame
  .na.fill(0)
  .withColumn("day_of_week", date_format($"InvoiceDate", "EEEE"))
  .coalesce(5)
```

```python
# in Python
from pyspark.sql.functions import date_format, col
preppedDataFrame = staticDataFrame\
  .na.fill(0)\
```

```
.withColumn("day_of_week", date_format(col("InvoiceDate"), "EEEE"))\
.coalesce(5)
```

We are also going to need to split the data into training and test sets. In this instance, we are going to do this manually by the date on which a certain purchase occurred; however, we could also use MLlib's transformation APIs to create a training and test set via train validation splits or cross validation (these topics are covered at length in Part VI):

```
// in Scala
val trainDataFrame = preppedDataFrame
  .where("InvoiceDate < '2011-07-01'")
val testDataFrame = preppedDataFrame
  .where("InvoiceDate >= '2011-07-01'")

# in Python
trainDataFrame = preppedDataFrame\
  .where("InvoiceDate < '2011-07-01'")
testDataFrame = preppedDataFrame\
  .where("InvoiceDate >= '2011-07-01'")
```

Now that we've prepared the data, let's split it into a training and test set. Because this is a time–series set of data, we will split by an arbitrary date in the dataset. Although this might not be the optimal split for our training and test, for the intents and purposes of this example it will work just fine. We'll see that this splits our dataset roughly in half:

```
trainDataFrame.count()
testDataFrame.count()
```

Note that these transformations are DataFrame transformations, which we cover extensively in Part II. Spark's MLlib also provides a number of transformations with which we can automate some of our general transformations. One such transformer is a StringIndexer:

```
// in Scala
import org.apache.spark.ml.feature.StringIndexer
val indexer = new StringIndexer()
  .setInputCol("day_of_week")
  .setOutputCol("day_of_week_index")

# in Python
from pyspark.ml.feature import StringIndexer
indexer = StringIndexer()\
  .setInputCol("day_of_week")\
  .setOutputCol("day_of_week_index")
```

This will turn our days of weeks into corresponding numerical values. For example, Spark might represent Saturday as 6, and Monday as 1. However, with this numbering scheme, we are implicitly stating that Saturday is greater than Monday (by pure numerical values). This is obviously incorrect. To fix this, we therefore need to use a

OneHotEncoder to encode each of these values as their own column. These Boolean flags state whether that day of week is the relevant day of the week:

```scala
// in Scala
import org.apache.spark.ml.feature.OneHotEncoder
val encoder = new OneHotEncoder()
  .setInputCol("day_of_week_index")
  .setOutputCol("day_of_week_encoded")
```

```python
# in Python
from pyspark.ml.feature import OneHotEncoder
encoder = OneHotEncoder()\
  .setInputCol("day_of_week_index")\
  .setOutputCol("day_of_week_encoded")
```

Each of these will result in a set of columns that we will "assemble" into a vector. All machine learning algorithms in Spark take as input a Vector type, which must be a set of numerical values:

```scala
// in Scala
import org.apache.spark.ml.feature.VectorAssembler

val vectorAssembler = new VectorAssembler()
  .setInputCols(Array("UnitPrice", "Quantity", "day_of_week_encoded"))
  .setOutputCol("features")
```

```python
# in Python
from pyspark.ml.feature import VectorAssembler

vectorAssembler = VectorAssembler()\
  .setInputCols(["UnitPrice", "Quantity", "day_of_week_encoded"])\
  .setOutputCol("features")
```

Here, we have three key features: the price, the quantity, and the day of week. Next, we'll set this up into a pipeline so that any future data we need to transform can go through the exact same process:

```scala
// in Scala
import org.apache.spark.ml.Pipeline

val transformationPipeline = new Pipeline()
  .setStages(Array(indexer, encoder, vectorAssembler))
```

```python
# in Python
from pyspark.ml import Pipeline

transformationPipeline = Pipeline()\
  .setStages([indexer, encoder, vectorAssembler])
```

Preparing for training is a two-step process. We first need to fit our transformers to this dataset. We cover this in depth in Part VI, but basically our StringIndexer needs to know how many unique values there are to be indexed. After those exist, encoding is easy but Spark must look at all the distinct values in the column to be indexed in order to store those values later on:

```scala
// in Scala
val fittedPipeline = transformationPipeline.fit(trainDataFrame)
```

```python
# in Python
fittedPipeline = transformationPipeline.fit(trainDataFrame)
```

After we fit the training data, we are ready to take that fitted pipeline and use it to transform all of our data in a consistent and repeatable way:

```scala
// in Scala
val transformedTraining = fittedPipeline.transform(trainDataFrame)
```

```python
# in Python
transformedTraining = fittedPipeline.transform(trainDataFrame)
```

At this point, it's worth mentioning that we could have included our model training in our pipeline. We chose not to in order to demonstrate a use case for caching the data. Instead, we're going to perform some hyperparameter tuning on the model because we do not want to repeat the exact same transformations over and over again; specifically, we'll use caching, an optimization that we discuss in more detail in Part IV. This will put a copy of the intermediately transformed dataset into memory, allowing us to repeatedly access it at much lower cost than running the entire pipeline again. If you're curious to see how much of a difference this makes, skip this line and run the training without caching the data. Then try it after caching; you'll see the results are significant:

```
transformedTraining.cache()
```

We now have a training set; it's time to train the model. First we'll import the relevant model that we'd like to use and instantiate it:

```scala
// in Scala
import org.apache.spark.ml.clustering.KMeans
val kmeans = new KMeans()
  .setK(20)
  .setSeed(1L)
```

```python
# in Python
from pyspark.ml.clustering import KMeans
kmeans = KMeans()\
  .setK(20)\
  .setSeed(1L)
```

In Spark, training machine learning models is a two-phase process. First, we initialize an untrained model, and then we train it. There are always two types for every algorithm in MLlib's DataFrame API. They follow the naming pattern of Algorithm, for the untrained version, and AlgorithmModel for the trained version. In our example, this is KMeans and then KMeansModel.

Estimators in MLlib's DataFrame API share roughly the same interface that we saw earlier with our preprocessing transformers like the `StringIndexer`. This should come as no surprise because it makes training an entire pipeline (which includes the model) simple. For our purposes here, we want to do things a bit more step by step, so we chose to not do this in this example:

```scala
// in Scala
val kmModel = kmeans.fit(transformedTraining)
```

```python
# in Python
kmModel = kmeans.fit(transformedTraining)
```

After we train this model, we can compute the cost according to some success merits on our training set. The resulting cost on this dataset is actually quite high, which is likely due to the fact that we did not properly preprocess and scale our input data, which we cover in depth in Chapter 25:

```
kmModel.computeCost(transformedTraining)
```

```scala
// in Scala
val transformedTest = fittedPipeline.transform(testDataFrame)
```

```python
# in Python
transformedTest = fittedPipeline.transform(testDataFrame)
```

```
kmModel.computeCost(transformedTest)
```

Naturally, we could continue to improve this model, layering more preprocessing as well as performing hyperparameter tuning to ensure that we're getting a good model. We leave that discussion for Part VI.

Lower-Level APIs

Spark includes a number of lower-level primitives to allow for arbitrary Java and Python object manipulation via Resilient Distributed Datasets (RDDs). Virtually everything in Spark is built on top of RDDs. As we will discuss in Chapter 4, DataFrame operations are built on top of RDDs and compile down to these lower-level tools for convenient and extremely efficient distributed execution. There are some things that you might use RDDs for, especially when you're reading or manipulating raw data, but for the most part you should stick to the Structured APIs. RDDs are lower level than DataFrames because they reveal physical execution characteristics (like partitions) to end users.

One thing that you might use RDDs for is to parallelize raw data that you have stored in memory on the driver machine. For instance, let's parallelize some simple numbers and create a DataFrame after we do so. We then can convert that to a DataFrame to use it with other DataFrames:

```scala
// in Scala
spark.sparkContext.parallelize(Seq(1, 2, 3)).toDF()
```

```python
# in Python
from pyspark.sql import Row

spark.sparkContext.parallelize([Row(1), Row(2), Row(3)]).toDF()
```

RDDs are available in Scala as well as Python. However, they're not equivalent. This differs from the DataFrame API (where the execution characteristics are the same) due to some underlying implementation details. We cover lower-level APIs, including RDDs in Part IV. As end users, you shouldn't need to use RDDs much in order to perform many tasks unless you're maintaining older Spark code. There are basically no instances in modern Spark, for which you should be using RDDs instead of the structured APIs beyond manipulating some very raw unprocessed and unstructured data.

SparkR

SparkR is a tool for running R on Spark. It follows the same principles as all of Spark's other language bindings. To use SparkR, you simply import it into your environment and run your code. It's all very similar to the Python API except that it follows R's syntax instead of Python. For the most part, almost everything available in Python is available in SparkR:

```r
# in R
library(SparkR)
sparkDF <- read.df("/data/flight-data/csv/2015-summary.csv",
        source = "csv", header="true", inferSchema = "true")
take(sparkDF, 5)

# in R
collect(orderBy(sparkDF, "count"), 20)
```

R users can also use other R libraries like the pipe operator in magrittr to make Spark transformations a bit more R-like. This can make it easy to use with other libraries like ggplot for more sophisticated plotting:

```r
# in R
library(magrittr)
sparkDF %>%
  orderBy(desc(sparkDF$count)) %>%
  groupBy("ORIGIN_COUNTRY_NAME") %>%
  count() %>%
  limit(10) %>%
  collect()
```

We will not include R code samples as we do in Python, because almost every concept throughout this book that applies to Python also applies to SparkR. The only difference will by syntax. We cover SparkR and sparklyr in Part VII.

Spark's Ecosystem and Packages

One of the best parts about Spark is the ecosystem of packages and tools that the community has created. Some of these tools even move into the core Spark project as they mature and become widely used. As of this writing, the list of packages is rather long, numbering over 300—and more are added frequently. You can find the largest index of Spark Packages at spark-packages.org (*https://spark-packages.org/*), where any user can publish to this package repository. There are also various other projects and packages that you can find on the web; for example, on GitHub.

Conclusion

We hope this chapter showed you the sheer variety of ways in which you can apply Spark to your own business and technical challenges. Spark's simple, robust programming model makes it easy to apply to a large number of problems, and the vast array of packages that have crept up around it, created by hundreds of different people, are a true testament to Spark's ability to robustly tackle a number of business problems and challenges. As the ecosystem and community grows, it's likely that more and more packages will continue to crop up. We look forward to seeing what the community has in store!

The rest of this book will provide deeper dives into the product areas in Figure 3-1.

You may read the rest of the book any way that you prefer, we find that most people hop from area to area as they hear terminology or want to apply Spark to certain problems they're facing.

## PART II

Structured APIs—DataFrames, SQL, and Datasets

## CHAPTER 4

Structured API Overview

This part of the book will be a deep dive into Spark's Structured APIs. The Structured APIs are a tool for manipulating all sorts of data, from unstructured log files to semi-structured CSV files and highly structured Parquet files. These APIs refer to three core types of distributed collection APIs:

- Datasets
- DataFrames
- SQL tables and views

Although they are distinct parts of the book, the majority of the Structured APIs apply to both *batch* and *streaming* computation. This means that when you work with the Structured APIs, it should be simple to migrate from batch to streaming (or vice versa) with little to no effort. We'll cover streaming in detail in Part V.

The Structured APIs are the fundamental abstraction that you will use to write the majority of your data flows. Thus far in this book, we have taken a tutorial-based approach, meandering our way through much of what Spark has to offer. This part offers a more in-depth exploration. In this chapter, we'll introduce the fundamental concepts that you should understand: the typed and untyped APIs (and their differences); what the core terminology is; and, finally, how Spark actually takes your Structured API data flows and executes it on the cluster. We will then provide more specific task-based information for working with certain types of data or data sources.

Before proceeding, let's review the fundamental concepts and definitions that we covered in Part I. Spark is a distributed programming model in which the user specifies *transformations*. Multiple transformations build up a directed acyclic graph of instructions. An action begins the process of executing that graph of instructions, as a single job, by breaking it down into stages and tasks to execute across the cluster. The logical structures that we manipulate with transformations and actions are DataFrames and Datasets. To create a new DataFrame or Dataset, you call a transformation. To start computation or convert to native language types, you call an action.

DataFrames and Datasets

Part I discussed DataFrames. Spark has two notions of structured collections: DataFrames and Datasets. We will touch on the (nuanced) differences shortly, but let's define what they both represent first.

DataFrames and Datasets are (distributed) table-like collections with well-defined rows and columns. Each column must have the same number of rows as all the other columns (although you can use null to specify the absence of a value) and each column has type information that must be consistent for every row in the collection. To Spark, DataFrames and Datasets represent immutable, lazily evaluated plans that specify what operations to apply to data residing at a location to generate some output. When we perform an action on a DataFrame, we instruct Spark to perform the actual transformations and return the result. These represent plans of how to manipulate rows and columns to compute the user's desired result.

Tables and views are basically the same thing as DataFrames. We just execute SQL against them instead of DataFrame code. We cover all of this in Chapter 10, which focuses specifically on Spark SQL.

To add a bit more specificity to these definitions, we need to talk about schemas, which are the way you define the types of data you're storing in this distributed collection.

Schemas

A schema defines the column names and types of a DataFrame. You can define schemas manually or read a schema from a data source (often called *schema on read*). Schemas consist of types, meaning that you need a way of specifying what lies where.

Overview of Structured Spark Types

Spark is effectively a programming language of its own. Internally, Spark uses an engine called *Catalyst* that maintains its own type information through the planning and processing of work. In doing so, this opens up a wide variety of execution optimizations that make significant differences. Spark types map directly to the different language APIs that Spark maintains and there exists a lookup table for each of these in Scala, Java, Python, SQL, and R. Even if we use Spark's Structured APIs from Python or R, the majority of our manipulations will operate strictly on *Spark types*, not Python types. For example, the following code does not perform addition in Scala or Python; it actually performs addition *purely in Spark*:

```scala
// in Scala
val df = spark.range(500).toDF("number")
df.select(df.col("number") + 10)
```

```python
# in Python
df = spark.range(500).toDF("number")
df.select(df["number"] + 10)
```

This addition operation happens because Spark will convert an expression written in an input language to Spark's internal Catalyst representation of that same type information. It then will operate on that internal representation. We touch on why this is the case momentarily, but before we can, we need to discuss Datasets.

DataFrames Versus Datasets

In essence, within the Structured APIs, there are two more APIs, the "untyped" DataFrames and the "typed" Datasets. To say that DataFrames are untyped is aslightly inaccurate; they have types, but Spark maintains them completely and only checks whether those types line up to those specified in the schema at *runtime*. Datasets, on the other hand, check whether types conform to the specification at *compile time*. Datasets are only available to Java Virtual Machine (JVM)–based languages (Scala and Java) and we specify types with case classes or Java beans.

For the most part, you're likely to work with DataFrames. To Spark (in Scala), DataFrames are simply Datasets of Type Row. The "Row" type is Spark's internal representation of its optimized in-memory format for computation. This format makes for highly specialized and efficient computation because rather than using JVM types, which can cause high garbage-collection and object instantiation costs, Spark can operate on its own internal format without incurring any of those costs. To Spark (in Python or R), there is no such thing as a Dataset: everything is a DataFrame and therefore we always operate on that optimized format.

The internal Catalyst format is well covered in numerous Spark presentations. Given that this book is intended for a more general audience, we'll refrain from going into the implementation. If you're curious, there are some excellent talks by Josh Rosen (*https://youtu.be/5ajs8EIPWGI*) and Herman van Hovell (*https://youtu.be/GDeePbbCz2g*), both of Databricks, about their work in the development of Spark's Catalyst engine.

Understanding DataFrames, Spark Types, and Schemas takes some time to digest. What you need to know is that when you're using DataFrames, you're taking advantage of Spark's optimized internal format. This format applies the same efficiency gains to all of Spark's language APIs. If you need strict compile-time checking, read Chapter 11 to learn more about it.

Let's move onto some friendlier and more approachable concepts: columns and rows.

Columns

Columns represent a *simple type* like an integer or string, a *complex type* like an array or map, or a *null value*. Spark tracks all of this type information for you and offers a variety of ways, with which you can transform columns. Columns are discussed extensively in Chapter 5, but for the most part you can think about Spark `Column` types as columns in a table.

Rows

A row is nothing more than a record of data. Each record in a DataFrame must be of type `Row`, as we can see when we collect the following DataFrames. We can create these rows manually from SQL, from Resilient Distributed Datasets (RDDs), from data sources, or manually from scratch. Here, we create one by using a range:

```scala
// in Scala
spark.range(2).toDF().collect()
```

```python
# in Python
spark.range(2).collect()
```

These both result in an array of `Row` objects.

Spark Types

We mentioned earlier that Spark has a large number of internal type representations. We include a handy reference table on the next several pages so that you can most easily reference what type, in your specific language, lines up with the type in Spark.

Before getting to those tables, let's talk about how we instantiate, or declare, a column to be of a certain type.

To work with the correct Scala types, use the following:

```
import org.apache.spark.sql.types._
val b = ByteType
```

To work with the correct Java types, you should use the factory methods in the following package:

```
import org.apache.spark.sql.types.DataTypes;
ByteType x = DataTypes.ByteType;
```

Python types at times have certain requirements, which you can see listed in Table 4-1, as do Scala and Java, which you can see listed in Tables 4-2 and 4-3, respectively. To work with the correct Python types, use the following:

```
from pyspark.sql.types import *
b = ByteType()
```

The following tables provide the detailed type information for each of Spark's language bindings.

Table 4-1. Python type reference

Data type	Value type in Python	API to access or create a data type
ByteType	int or long. Note: Numbers will be converted to 1-byte signed integer numbers at runtime. Ensure that numbers are within the range of −128 to 127.	ByteType()
ShortType	int or long. Note: Numbers will be converted to 2-byte signed integer numbers at runtime. Ensure that numbers are within the range of −32768 to 32767.	ShortType()
IntegerType	int or long. Note: Python has a lenient definition of "integer." Numbers that are too large will be rejected by Spark SQL if you use the IntegerType(). It's best practice to use LongType.	IntegerType()
LongType	long. Note: Numbers will be converted to 8-byte signed integer numbers at runtime. Ensure that numbers are within the range of −9223372036854775808 to 9223372036854775807. Otherwise, convert data to decimal.Decimal and use DecimalType.	LongType()
FloatType	float. Note: Numbers will be converted to 4-byte single-precision floating-point numbers at runtime.	FloatType()
DoubleType	float	DoubleType()
DecimalType	decimal.Decimal	DecimalType()
StringType	string	StringType()
BinaryType	bytearray	BinaryType()
BooleanType	bool	BooleanType()
TimestampType	datetime.datetime	TimestampType()
DateType	datetime.date	DateType()

Data type	Value type in Python	API to access or create a data type
ArrayType	list, tuple, or array	ArrayType(elementType, [containsNull]). Note: The default value of containsNull is True.
MapType	dict	MapType(keyType, valueType, [valueContainsNull]). Note: The default value of valueContainsNull is True.
StructType	list or tuple	StructType(fields). Note: `fields` is a list of StructFields. Also, fields with the same name are not allowed.
StructField	The value type in Python of the data type of this field (for example, Int for a StructField with the data type IntegerType)	StructField(name, dataType, [nullable]) Note: The default value of nullable is True.

Table 4-2. Scala type reference

Data type	Value type in Scala	API to access or create a data type
ByteType	Byte	ByteType
ShortType	Short	ShortType
IntegerType	Int	IntegerType
LongType	Long	LongType
FloatType	Float	FloatType
DoubleType	Double	DoubleType
DecimalType	java.math.BigDecimal	DecimalType
StringType	String	StringType
BinaryType	Array[Byte]	BinaryType
BooleanType	Boolean	BooleanType
TimestampType	java.sql.Timestamp	TimestampType
DateType	java.sql.Date	DateType
ArrayType	scala.collection.Seq	ArrayType(elementType, [containsNull]). Note: The default value of containsNull is true.
MapType	scala.collection.Map	MapType(keyType, valueType, [valueContainsNull]). Note: The default value of valueContainsNull is true.
StructType	org.apache.spark.sql.Row	StructType(fields). Note: fields is an Array of StructFields. Also, fields with the same name are not allowed.
StructField	The value type in Scala of the data type of this field (for example, Int for a StructField with the data type IntegerType)	StructField(name, dataType, [nullable]). Note: The default value of nullable is true.

Table 4-3. Java type reference

Data type	Value type in Java	API to access or create a data type
ByteType	byte or Byte	DataTypes.ByteType
ShortType	short or Short	DataTypes.ShortType
IntegerType	int or Integer	DataTypes.IntegerType
LongType	long or Long	DataTypes.LongType
FloatType	float or Float	DataTypes.FloatType
DoubleType	double or Double	DataTypes.DoubleType
DecimalType	java.math.BigDecimal	DataTypes.createDecimalType() DataTypes.createDecimalType(precision, scale).
StringType	String	DataTypes.StringType
BinaryType	byte[]	DataTypes.BinaryType
BooleanType	boolean or Boolean	DataTypes.BooleanType
TimestampType	java.sql.Timestamp	DataTypes.TimestampType
DateType	java.sql.Date	DataTypes.DateType
ArrayType	java.util.List	DataTypes.createArrayType(elementType). Note: The value of containsNull will be true DataTypes.createArrayType(elementType, containsNull).
MapType	java.util.Map	DataTypes.createMapType(keyType, valueType). Note: The value of valueContainsNull will be true. DataTypes.createMapType(keyType, valueType, valueContainsNull)
StructType	org.apache.spark.sql.Row	DataTypes.createStructType(fields). Note: fields is a List or an array of StructFields. Also, two fields with the same name are not allowed.
StructField	The value type in Java of the data type of this field (for example, int for a StructField with the data type IntegerType)	DataTypes.createStructField(name, dataType, nullable)

It's worth keeping in mind that the types might change over time as Spark SQL continues to grow so you may want to reference Spark's documentation (*http://bit.ly/2EdflXW*) for future updates. Of course, all of these types are great, but you almost never work with purely static DataFrames. You will always manipulate and transform them. Therefore it's important that we give you an overview of the execution process in the Structured APIs.

Overview of Structured API Execution

This section will demonstrate how this code is actually executed across a cluster. This will help you understand (and potentially debug) the process of writing and executing code on clusters, so let's walk through the execution of a single structured API query from user code to executed code. Here's an overview of the steps:

1. Write DataFrame/Dataset/SQL Code.

2. If valid code, Spark converts this to a *Logical Plan*.

3. Spark transforms this *Logical Plan* to a *Physical Plan*, checking for optimizations along the way.

4. Spark then executes this *Physical Plan* (RDD manipulations) on the cluster.

To execute code, we must write code. This code is then submitted to Spark either through the console or via a submitted job. This code then passes through the Catalyst Optimizer, which decides how the code should be executed and lays out a plan for doing so before, finally, the code is run and the result is returned to the user. Figure 4-1 shows the process.

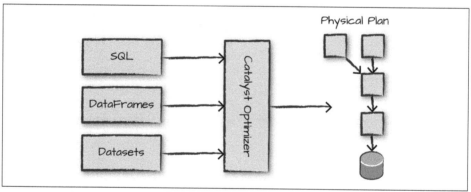

Figure 4-1. The Catalyst Optimizer

Logical Planning

The first phase of execution is meant to take user code and convert it into a logical plan. Figure 4-2 illustrates this process.

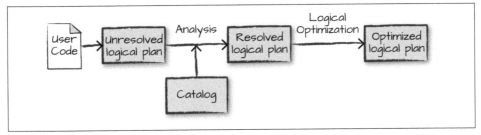

Figure 4-2. The structured API logical planning process

This logical plan only represents a set of abstract transformations that do not refer to executors or drivers, it's purely to convert the user's set of expressions into the most optimized version. It does this by converting user code into an *unresolved logical plan*. This plan is unresolved because although your code might be valid, the tables or columns that it refers to might or might not exist. Spark uses the *catalog*, a repository of all table and DataFrame information, to *resolve* columns and tables in the *analyzer*. The analyzer might reject the unresolved logical plan if the required table or column name does not exist in the catalog. If the analyzer can resolve it, the result is passed through the Catalyst Optimizer, a collection of rules that attempt to optimize the logical plan by pushing down predicates or selections. Packages can extend the Catalyst to include their own rules for domain-specific optimizations.

Physical Planning

After successfully creating an optimized logical plan, Spark then begins the physical planning process. The *physical plan*, often called a Spark plan, specifies how the logical plan will execute on the cluster by generating different physical execution strategies and comparing them through a cost model, as depicted in Figure 4-3. An example of the cost comparison might be choosing how to perform a given join by looking at the physical attributes of a given table (how big the table is or how big its partitions are).

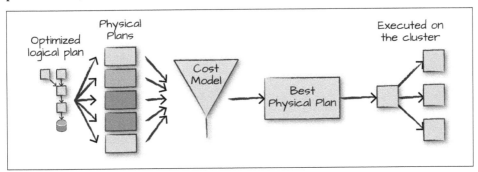

Figure 4-3. The physical planning process

Physical planning results in a series of RDDs and transformations. This result is why you might have heard Spark referred to as a compiler—it takes queries in DataFrames, Datasets, and SQL and compiles them into RDD transformations for you.

Execution

Upon selecting a physical plan, Spark runs all of this code over RDDs, the lower-level programming interface of Spark (which we cover in Part III). Spark performs further optimizations at runtime, generating native Java bytecode that can remove entire tasks or stages during execution. Finally the result is returned to the user.

Conclusion

In this chapter, we covered Spark Structured APIs and how Spark transforms your code into what will physically execute on the cluster. In the chapters that follow, we cover core concepts and how to use the key functionality of the Structured APIs.

## CHAPTER 5

Basic Structured Operations

In Chapter 4, we introduced the core abstractions of the Structured API. This chapter moves away from the architectural concepts and toward the tactical tools you will use to manipulate DataFrames and the data within them. This chapter focuses exclusively on fundamental DataFrame operations and avoids aggregations, window functions, and joins. These are discussed in subsequent chapters.

Definitionally, a DataFrame consists of a series of *records* (like rows in a table), that are of type Row, and a number of *columns* (like columns in a spreadsheet) that represent a computation expression that can be performed on each individual record in the Dataset. *Schemas* define the name as well as the type of data in each column. *Partitioning* of the DataFrame defines the layout of the DataFrame or Dataset's physical distribution across the cluster. The *partitioning scheme* defines how that is allocated. You can set this to be based on values in a certain column or nondeterministically.

Let's create a DataFrame with which we can work:

```scala
// in Scala
val df = spark.read.format("json")
  .load("/data/flight-data/json/2015-summary.json")
```

```python
# in Python
df = spark.read.format("json").load("/data/flight-data/json/2015-summary.json")
```

We discussed that a DataFame will have columns, and we use a schema to define them. Let's take a look at the schema on our current DataFrame:

```
df.printSchema()
```

Schemas tie everything together, so they're worth belaboring.

Schemas

A schema defines the column names and types of a DataFrame. We can either let a data source define the schema (called *schema-on-read*) or we can define it explicitly ourselves.

> Deciding whether you need to define a schema prior to reading in your data depends on your use case. For ad hoc analysis, schema-on-read usually works just fine (although at times it can be a bit slow with plain-text file formats like CSV or JSON). However, this can also lead to precision issues like a long type incorrectly set as an integer when reading in a file. When using Spark for production Extract, Transform, and Load (ETL), it is often a good idea to define your schemas manually, especially when working with untyped data sources like CSV and JSON because schema inference can vary depending on the type of data that you read in.

Let's begin with a simple file, which we saw in Chapter 4, and let the semi-structured nature of line-delimited JSON define the structure. This is flight data from the United States Bureau of Transportation statistics (*https://github.com/databricks/Spark-The-Definitive-Guide/tree/master/data/flight-data*):

```scala
// in Scala
spark.read.format("json").load("/data/flight-data/json/2015-summary.json").schema
```

Scala returns the following:

```
org.apache.spark.sql.types.StructType = ...
StructType(StructField(DEST_COUNTRY_NAME,StringType,true),
StructField(ORIGIN_COUNTRY_NAME,StringType,true),
StructField(count,LongType,true))
```

```python
# in Python
spark.read.format("json").load("/data/flight-data/json/2015-summary.json").schema
```

Python returns the following:

```
StructType(List(StructField(DEST_COUNTRY_NAME,StringType,true),
StructField(ORIGIN_COUNTRY_NAME,StringType,true),
StructField(count,LongType,true)))
```

A schema is a `StructType` made up of a number of fields, `StructFields`, that have a name, type, a Boolean flag which specifies whether that column can contain missing or `null` values, and, finally, users can optionally specify associated metadata with that column. The metadata is a way of storing information about this column (Spark uses this in its machine learning library).

Schemas can contain other `StructTypes` (Spark's complex types). We will see this in Chapter 6 when we discuss working with complex types. If the types in the data (at runtime) do not match the schema, Spark will throw an error. The example that follows shows how to create and enforce a specific schema on a DataFrame.

```scala
// in Scala
import org.apache.spark.sql.types.{StructField, StructType, StringType, LongType}
import org.apache.spark.sql.types.Metadata

val myManualSchema = StructType(Array(
  StructField("DEST_COUNTRY_NAME", StringType, true),
  StructField("ORIGIN_COUNTRY_NAME", StringType, true),
  StructField("count", LongType, false,
    Metadata.fromJson("{\"hello\":\"world\"}"))
))

val df = spark.read.format("json").schema(myManualSchema)
  .load("/data/flight-data/json/2015-summary.json")
```

Here's how to do the same in Python:

```python
# in Python
from pyspark.sql.types import StructField, StructType, StringType, LongType

myManualSchema = StructType([
  StructField("DEST_COUNTRY_NAME", StringType(), True),
  StructField("ORIGIN_COUNTRY_NAME", StringType(), True),
  StructField("count", LongType(), False, metadata={"hello":"world"})
])
df = spark.read.format("json").schema(myManualSchema)\
  .load("/data/flight-data/json/2015-summary.json")
```

As discussed in Chapter 4, we cannot simply set types via the per-language types because Spark maintains its own type information. Let's now discuss what schemas define: columns.

Columns and Expressions

Columns in Spark are similar to columns in a spreadsheet, R dataframe, or pandas DataFrame. You can select, manipulate, and remove columns from DataFrames and these operations are represented as *expressions*.

To Spark, columns are logical constructions that simply represent a value computed on a per-record basis by means of an expression. This means that to have a real value for a column, we need to have a row; and to have a row, we need to have a DataFrame. You cannot manipulate an individual column outside the context of a DataFrame; you must use Spark transformations within a DataFrame to modify the contents of a column.

Columns

There are a lot of different ways to construct and refer to columns but the two simplest ways are by using the `col` or `column` functions. To use either of these functions, you pass in a column name:

```scala
// in Scala
import org.apache.spark.sql.functions.{col, column}
col("someColumnName")
column("someColumnName")
```

```python
# in Python
from pyspark.sql.functions import col, column
col("someColumnName")
column("someColumnName")
```

We will stick to using `col` throughout this book. As mentioned, this column might or might not exist in our DataFrames. Columns are not *resolved* until we compare the column names with those we are maintaining in the *catalog*. Column and table resolution happens in the *analyzer* phase, as discussed in Chapter 4.

We just mentioned two different ways of referring to columns. Scala has some unique language features that allow for more shorthand ways of referring to columns. The following bits of syntactic sugar perform the exact same thing, namely creating a column, but provide no performance improvement:

```scala
// in Scala
$"myColumn"
'myColumn
```

The $ allows us to designate a string as a special string that should refer to an expression. The tick mark (') is a special thing called a *symbol*; this is a Scala-specific construct of referring to some identifier. They both perform the same thing and are shorthand ways of referring to columns by name. You'll likely see all of the aforementioned references when you read different people's Spark code. We leave it to you to use whatever is most comfortable and maintainable for you and those with whom you work.

Explicit column references

If you need to refer to a specific DataFrame's column, you can use the `col` method on the specific DataFrame. This can be useful when you are performing a join and need to refer to a specific column in one DataFrame that might share a name with another column in the joined DataFrame. We will see this in Chapter 8. As an added benefit, Spark does not need to resolve this column itself (during the *analyzer* phase) because we did that for Spark:

```
df.col("count")
```

Expressions

We mentioned earlier that columns are expressions, but what is an expression? An *expression* is a set of transformations on one or more values in a record in a DataFrame. Think of it like a function that takes as input one or more column names, resolves them, and then potentially applies more expressions to create a single value for each record in the dataset. Importantly, this "single value" can actually be a complex type like a `Map` or `Array`. We'll see more of the complex types in Chapter 6.

In the simplest case, an expression, created via the `expr` function, is just a DataFrame column reference. In the simplest case, `expr("someCol")` is equivalent to `col("someCol")`.

Columns as expressions

Columns provide a subset of expression functionality. If you use `col()` and want to perform transformations on that column, you must perform those on that column reference. When using an expression, the `expr` function can actually parse transformations and column references from a string and can subsequently be passed into further transformations. Let's look at some examples.

`expr("someCol - 5")` is the same transformation as performing `col("someCol") - 5`, or even `expr("someCol") - 5`. That's because Spark compiles these to a logical tree specifying the order of operations. This might be a bit confusing at first, but remember a couple of key points:

- Columns are just expressions.
- Columns and transformations of those columns compile to the same logical plan as parsed expressions.

Let's ground this with an example:

```
(((col("someCol") + 5) * 200) - 6) < col("otherCol")
```

Figure 5-1 shows an overview of that logical tree.

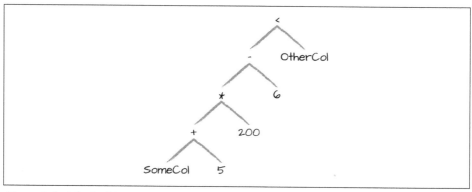

Figure 5-1. A logical tree

This might look familiar because it's a directed acyclic graph. This graph is represented equivalently by the following code:

```scala
// in Scala
import org.apache.spark.sql.functions.expr
expr("(((someCol + 5) * 200) - 6) < otherCol")
```

```python
# in Python
from pyspark.sql.functions import expr
expr("(((someCol + 5) * 200) - 6) < otherCol")
```

This is an extremely important point to reinforce. Notice how the previous expression is actually valid SQL code, as well, just like you might put in a SELECT statement? That's because this SQL expression and the previous DataFrame code compile to the same underlying logical tree prior to execution. This means that you can write your expressions as DataFrame code or as SQL expressions and get the exact same performance characteristics. This is discussed in Chapter 4.

Accessing a DataFrame's columns

Sometimes, you'll need to see a DataFrame's columns, which you can do by using something like printSchema; however, if you want to programmatically access columns, you can use the columns property to see all columns on a DataFrame:

```
spark.read.format("json").load("/data/flight-data/json/2015-summary.json")
  .columns
```

Records and Rows

In Spark, each row in a DataFrame is a single record. Spark represents this record as an object of type Row. Spark manipulates Row objects using column expressions in order to produce usable values. Row objects internally represent arrays of bytes. The byte array interface is never shown to users because we only use column expressions to manipulate them.

You'll notice commands that return individual rows to the driver will always return one or more Row types when we are working with DataFrames.

 We use lowercase "row" and "record" interchangeably in this chapter, with a focus on the latter. A capitalized Row refers to the Row object.

Let's see a row by calling `first` on our DataFrame:

```
df.first()
```

Creating Rows

You can create rows by manually instantiating a Row object with the values that belong in each column. It's important to note that only DataFrames have schemas. Rows themselves do not have schemas. This means that if you create a Row manually, you must specify the values in the same order as the schema of the DataFrame to which they might be appended (we will see this when we discuss creating DataFrames):

```scala
// in Scala
import org.apache.spark.sql.Row
val myRow = Row("Hello", null, 1, false)
```

```python
# in Python
from pyspark.sql import Row
myRow = Row("Hello", None, 1, False)
```

Accessing data in rows is equally as easy: you just specify the position that you would like. In Scala or Java, you must either use the helper methods or explicitly coerce the values. However, in Python or R, the value will automatically be coerced into the correct type:

```scala
// in Scala
myRow(0) // type Any
myRow(0).asInstanceOf[String] // String
myRow.getString(0) // String
myRow.getInt(2) // Int
```

```python
# in Python
myRow[0]
myRow[2]
```

You can also explicitly return a set of Data in the corresponding Java Virtual Machine (JVM) objects by using the Dataset APIs. This is covered in Chapter 11.

DataFrame Transformations

Now that we briefly defined the core parts of a DataFrame, we will move onto manipulating DataFrames. When working with individual DataFrames there are some fundamental objectives. These break down into several core operations, as depicted in Figure 5-2:

- We can add rows or columns
- We can remove rows or columns
- We can transform a row into a column (or vice versa)
- We can change the order of rows based on the values in columns

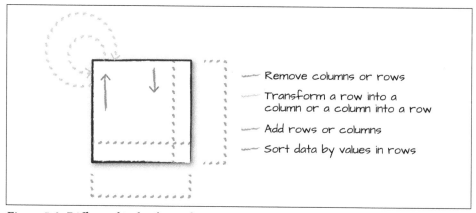

Figure 5-2. Different kinds of transformations

Luckily, we can translate all of these into simple transformations, the most common being those that take one column, change it row by row, and then return our results.

Creating DataFrames

As we saw previously, we can create DataFrames from raw data sources. This is covered extensively in Chapter 9; however, we will use them now to create an example DataFrame (for illustration purposes later in this chapter, we will also register this as a temporary view so that we can query it with SQL and show off basic transformations in SQL, as well):

```scala
// in Scala
val df = spark.read.format("json")
  .load("/data/flight-data/json/2015-summary.json")
df.createOrReplaceTempView("dfTable")
```

```python
# in Python
df = spark.read.format("json").load("/data/flight-data/json/2015-summary.json")
df.createOrReplaceTempView("dfTable")
```

We can also create DataFrames on the fly by taking a set of rows and converting them to a DataFrame.

```scala
// in Scala
import org.apache.spark.sql.Row
import org.apache.spark.sql.types.{StructField, StructType, StringType, LongType}

val myManualSchema = new StructType(Array(
  new StructField("some", StringType, true),
  new StructField("col", StringType, true),
  new StructField("names", LongType, false)))
val myRows = Seq(Row("Hello", null, 1L))
val myRDD = spark.sparkContext.parallelize(myRows)
val myDf = spark.createDataFrame(myRDD, myManualSchema)
myDf.show()
```

In Scala, we can also take advantage of Spark's implicits in the console (and if you import them in your JAR code) by running toDF on a Seq type. This does not play well with null types, so it's not necessarily recommended for production use cases.

```scala
// in Scala
val myDF = Seq(("Hello", 2, 1L)).toDF("col1", "col2", "col3")
```

```python
# in Python
from pyspark.sql import Row
from pyspark.sql.types import StructField, StructType, StringType, LongType
myManualSchema = StructType([
  StructField("some", StringType(), True),
  StructField("col", StringType(), True),
  StructField("names", LongType(), False)
])
myRow = Row("Hello", None, 1)
myDf = spark.createDataFrame([myRow], myManualSchema)
myDf.show()
```

Giving an output of:

```
+-----+----+-----+
| some| col|names|
+-----+----+-----+
|Hello|null|    1|
+-----+----+-----+
```

Now that you know how to create DataFrames, let's take a look at their most useful methods that you're going to be using: the select method when you're working with columns or expressions, and the selectExpr method when you're working with expressions in strings. Naturally some transformations are not specified as methods on columns; therefore, there exists a group of functions found in the `org.apache.spark.sql.functions` package.

With these three tools, you should be able to solve the vast majority of transformation challenges that you might encounter in DataFrames.

select and selectExpr

`select` and `selectExpr` allow you to do the DataFrame equivalent of SQL queries on a table of data:

```
-- in SQL
SELECT * FROM dataFrameTable
SELECT columnName FROM dataFrameTable
SELECT columnName * 10, otherColumn, someOtherCol as c FROM dataFrameTable
```

In the simplest possible terms, you can use them to manipulate columns in your DataFrames. Let's walk through some examples on DataFrames to talk about some of the different ways of approaching this problem. The easiest way is just to use the `select` method and pass in the column names as strings with which you would like to work:

```
// in Scala
df.select("DEST_COUNTRY_NAME").show(2)

# in Python
df.select("DEST_COUNTRY_NAME").show(2)

-- in SQL
SELECT DEST_COUNTRY_NAME FROM dfTable LIMIT 2
```

Giving an output of:

```
+-----------------+
|DEST_COUNTRY_NAME|
+-----------------+
|    United States|
|    United States|
+-----------------+
```

You can select multiple columns by using the same style of query, just add more column name strings to your `select` method call:

```
// in Scala
df.select("DEST_COUNTRY_NAME", "ORIGIN_COUNTRY_NAME").show(2)

# in Python
df.select("DEST_COUNTRY_NAME", "ORIGIN_COUNTRY_NAME").show(2)

-- in SQL
SELECT DEST_COUNTRY_NAME, ORIGIN_COUNTRY_NAME FROM dfTable LIMIT 2
```

Giving an output of:

```
+-----------------+-------------------+
|DEST_COUNTRY_NAME|ORIGIN_COUNTRY_NAME|
+-----------------+-------------------+
|    United States|            Romania|
|    United States|            Croatia|
+-----------------+-------------------+
```

As discussed in "Columns and Expressions" on page 61, you can refer to columns in a number of different ways; all you need to keep in mind is that you can use them interchangeably:

```
// in Scala
import org.apache.spark.sql.functions.{expr, col, column}
df.select(
    df.col("DEST_COUNTRY_NAME"),
    col("DEST_COUNTRY_NAME"),
    column("DEST_COUNTRY_NAME"),
    'DEST_COUNTRY_NAME,
    $"DEST_COUNTRY_NAME",
    expr("DEST_COUNTRY_NAME"))
  .show(2)
```

```
# in Python
from pyspark.sql.functions import expr, col, column
df.select(
    expr("DEST_COUNTRY_NAME"),
    col("DEST_COUNTRY_NAME"),
    column("DEST_COUNTRY_NAME"))\
  .show(2)
```

One common error is attempting to mix Column objects and strings. For example, the following code will result in a compiler error:

```
df.select(col("DEST_COUNTRY_NAME"), "DEST_COUNTRY_NAME")
```

As we've seen thus far, expr is the most flexible reference that we can use. It can refer to a plain column or a string manipulation of a column. To illustrate, let's change the column name, and then change it back by using the AS keyword and then the alias method on the column:

```
// in Scala
df.select(expr("DEST_COUNTRY_NAME AS destination")).show(2)
```

```
# in Python
df.select(expr("DEST_COUNTRY_NAME AS destination")).show(2)
```

```
-- in SQL
SELECT DEST_COUNTRY_NAME as destination FROM dfTable LIMIT 2
```

This changes the column name to "destination." You can further manipulate the result of your expression as another expression:

```scala
// in Scala
df.select(expr("DEST_COUNTRY_NAME as destination").alias("DEST_COUNTRY_NAME"))
  .show(2)
```

```python
# in Python
df.select(expr("DEST_COUNTRY_NAME as destination").alias("DEST_COUNTRY_NAME"))\
  .show(2)
```

The preceding operation changes the column name back to its original name.

Because `select` followed by a series of `expr` is such a common pattern, Spark has a shorthand for doing this efficiently: `selectExpr`. This is probably the most convenient interface for everyday use:

```scala
// in Scala
df.selectExpr("DEST_COUNTRY_NAME as newColumnName", "DEST_COUNTRY_NAME").show(2)
```

```python
# in Python
df.selectExpr("DEST_COUNTRY_NAME as newColumnName", "DEST_COUNTRY_NAME").show(2)
```

This opens up the true power of Spark. We can treat `selectExpr` as a simple way to build up complex expressions that create new DataFrames. In fact, we can add any valid non-aggregating SQL statement, and as long as the columns resolve, it will be valid! Here's a simple example that adds a new column `withinCountry` to our DataFrame that specifies whether the destination and origin are the same:

```scala
// in Scala
df.selectExpr(
  "*", // include all original columns
  "(DEST_COUNTRY_NAME = ORIGIN_COUNTRY_NAME) as withinCountry")
  .show(2)
```

```python
# in Python
df.selectExpr(
  "*", # all original columns
  "(DEST_COUNTRY_NAME = ORIGIN_COUNTRY_NAME) as withinCountry")\
  .show(2)
```

```sql
-- in SQL
SELECT *, (DEST_COUNTRY_NAME = ORIGIN_COUNTRY_NAME) as withinCountry
FROM dfTable
LIMIT 2
```

Giving an output of:

```
+-----------------+-------------------+-----+-------------+
|DEST_COUNTRY_NAME|ORIGIN_COUNTRY_NAME|count|withinCountry|
+-----------------+-------------------+-----+-------------+
|    United States|            Romania|   15|        false|
|    United States|            Croatia|    1|        false|
+-----------------+-------------------+-----+-------------+
```

With select expression, we can also specify aggregations over the entire DataFrame by taking advantage of the functions that we have. These look just like what we have been showing so far:

```scala
// in Scala
df.selectExpr("avg(count)", "count(distinct(DEST_COUNTRY_NAME))").show(2)
```

```python
# in Python
df.selectExpr("avg(count)", "count(distinct(DEST_COUNTRY_NAME))").show(2)
```

```sql
-- in SQL
SELECT avg(count), count(distinct(DEST_COUNTRY_NAME)) FROM dfTable LIMIT 2
```

Giving an output of:

```
+-----------+---------------------------------+
| avg(count)|count(DISTINCT DEST_COUNTRY_NAME)|
+-----------+---------------------------------+
|1770.765625|                              132|
+-----------+---------------------------------+
```

Converting to Spark Types (Literals)

Sometimes, we need to pass explicit values into Spark that are just a value (rather than a new column). This might be a constant value or something we'll need to compare to later on. The way we do this is through *literals*. This is basically a translation from a given programming language's literal value to one that Spark understands. Literals are expressions and you can use them in the same way:

```scala
// in Scala
import org.apache.spark.sql.functions.lit
df.select(expr("*"), lit(1).as("One")).show(2)
```

```python
# in Python
from pyspark.sql.functions import lit
df.select(expr("*"), lit(1).alias("One")).show(2)
```

In SQL, literals are just the specific value:

```sql
-- in SQL
SELECT *, 1 as One FROM dfTable LIMIT 2
```

Giving an output of:

```
+-----------------+-------------------+-----+---+
|DEST_COUNTRY_NAME|ORIGIN_COUNTRY_NAME|count|One|
+-----------------+-------------------+-----+---+
|    United States|            Romania|   15|  1|
|    United States|            Croatia|    1|  1|
+-----------------+-------------------+-----+---+
```

This will come up when you might need to check whether a value is greater than some constant or other programmatically created variable.

Adding Columns

There's also a more formal way of adding a new column to a DataFrame, and that's by using the withColumn method on our DataFrame. For example, let's add a column that just adds the number one as a column:

```
// in Scala
df.withColumn("numberOne", lit(1)).show(2)
```

```
# in Python
df.withColumn("numberOne", lit(1)).show(2)
```

```
-- in SQL
SELECT *, 1 as numberOne FROM dfTable LIMIT 2
```

Giving an output of:

```
+-----------------+-------------------+-----+---------+
|DEST_COUNTRY_NAME|ORIGIN_COUNTRY_NAME|count|numberOne|
+-----------------+-------------------+-----+---------+
|    United States|            Romania|   15|        1|
|    United States|            Croatia|    1|        1|
+-----------------+-------------------+-----+---------+
```

Let's do something a bit more interesting and make it an actual expression. In the next example, we'll set a Boolean flag for when the origin country is the same as the destination country:

```
// in Scala
df.withColumn("withinCountry", expr("ORIGIN_COUNTRY_NAME == DEST_COUNTRY_NAME"))
  .show(2)
```

```
# in Python
df.withColumn("withinCountry", expr("ORIGIN_COUNTRY_NAME == DEST_COUNTRY_NAME"))\
  .show(2)
```

Notice that the withColumn function takes two arguments: the column name and the expression that will create the value for that given row in the DataFrame. Interestingly, we can also rename a column this way. The SQL syntax is the same as we had previously, so we can omit it in this example:

```
df.withColumn("Destination", expr("DEST_COUNTRY_NAME")).columns
```

Resulting in:

```
... DEST_COUNTRY_NAME, ORIGIN_COUNTRY_NAME, count, Destination
```

Renaming Columns

Although we can rename a column in the manner that we just described, another alternative is to use the withColumnRenamed method. This will rename the column with the name of the string in the first argument to the string in the second argument:

```scala
// in Scala
df.withColumnRenamed("DEST_COUNTRY_NAME", "dest").columns
```

```python
# in Python
df.withColumnRenamed("DEST_COUNTRY_NAME", "dest").columns
```

```
... dest, ORIGIN_COUNTRY_NAME, count
```

Reserved Characters and Keywords

One thing that you might come across is reserved characters like spaces or dashes in column names. Handling these means escaping column names appropriately. In Spark, we do this by using backtick (`) characters. Let's use `withColumn`, which you just learned about to create a column with reserved characters. We'll show two examples—in the one shown here, we don't need escape characters, but in the next one, we do:

```scala
// in Scala
import org.apache.spark.sql.functions.expr

val dfWithLongColName = df.withColumn(
  "This Long Column-Name",
  expr("ORIGIN_COUNTRY_NAME"))
```

```python
# in Python
dfWithLongColName = df.withColumn(
    "This Long Column-Name",
    expr("ORIGIN_COUNTRY_NAME"))
```

We don't need escape characters here because the first argument to `withColumn` is just a string for the new column name. In this example, however, we need to use backticks because we're referencing a column in an expression:

```scala
// in Scala
dfWithLongColName.selectExpr(
    "`This Long Column-Name`",
    "`This Long Column-Name` as `new col`")
  .show(2)
```

```python
# in Python
dfWithLongColName.selectExpr(
    "`This Long Column-Name`",
    "`This Long Column-Name` as `new col`")\
  .show(2)
```

```
dfWithLongColName.createOrReplaceTempView("dfTableLong")
```

```sql
-- in SQL
SELECT `This Long Column-Name`, `This Long Column-Name` as `new col`
FROM dfTableLong LIMIT 2
```

We can refer to columns with reserved characters (and not escape them) if we're doing an explicit string-to-column reference, which is interpreted as a literal instead of an expression. We only need to escape expressions that use reserved characters or keywords. The following two examples both result in the same DataFrame:

```scala
// in Scala
dfWithLongColName.select(col("This Long Column-Name")).columns
```

```python
# in Python
dfWithLongColName.select(expr("`This Long Column-Name`")).columns
```

Case Sensitivity

By default Spark is case insensitive; however, you can make Spark case sensitive by setting the configuration:

```sql
-- in SQL
set spark.sql.caseSensitive true
```

Removing Columns

Now that we've created this column, let's take a look at how we can remove columns from DataFrames. You likely already noticed that we can do this by using `select`. However, there is also a dedicated method called `drop`:

```
df.drop("ORIGIN_COUNTRY_NAME").columns
```

We can drop multiple columns by passing in multiple columns as arguments:

```
dfWithLongColName.drop("ORIGIN_COUNTRY_NAME", "DEST_COUNTRY_NAME")
```

Changing a Column's Type (cast)

Sometimes, we might need to convert from one type to another; for example, if we have a set of `StringType` that should be integers. We can convert columns from one type to another by casting the column from one type to another. For instance, let's convert our `count` column from an integer to a type Long:

```
df.withColumn("count2", col("count").cast("long"))
```

```sql
-- in SQL
SELECT *, cast(count as long) AS count2 FROM dfTable
```

Filtering Rows

To filter rows, we create an expression that evaluates to true or false. You then filter out the rows with an expression that is equal to false. The most common way to do this with DataFrames is to create either an expression as a String or build an expression by using a set of column manipulations. There are two methods to perform this operation: you can use `where` or `filter` and they both will perform the same operation and accept the same argument types when used with DataFrames. We will stick to `where` because of its familiarity to SQL; however, `filter` is valid as well.

When using the Dataset API from either Scala or Java, `filter` also accepts an arbitrary function that Spark will apply to each record in the Dataset. See Chapter 11 for more information.

The following filters are equivalent, and the results are the same in Scala and Python:

```
df.filter(col("count") < 2).show(2)
df.where("count < 2").show(2)

-- in SQL
SELECT * FROM dfTable WHERE count < 2 LIMIT 2
```

Giving an output of:

```
+-----------------+-------------------+-----+
|DEST_COUNTRY_NAME|ORIGIN_COUNTRY_NAME|count|
+-----------------+-------------------+-----+
|    United States|            Croatia|    1|
|    United States|          Singapore|    1|
+-----------------+-------------------+-----+
```

Instinctually, you might want to put multiple filters into the same expression. Although this is possible, it is not always useful, because Spark automatically performs all filtering operations at the same time regardless of the filter ordering. This means that if you want to specify multiple AND filters, just chain them sequentially and let Spark handle the rest:

```
// in Scala
df.where(col("count") < 2).where(col("ORIGIN_COUNTRY_NAME") =!= "Croatia")
  .show(2)

# in Python
df.where(col("count") < 2).where(col("ORIGIN_COUNTRY_NAME") != "Croatia")\
  .show(2)

-- in SQL
SELECT * FROM dfTable WHERE count < 2 AND ORIGIN_COUNTRY_NAME != "Croatia"
LIMIT 2
```

Giving an output of:

```
+-----------------+-------------------+-----+
|DEST_COUNTRY_NAME|ORIGIN_COUNTRY_NAME|count|
+-----------------+-------------------+-----+
|    United States|          Singapore|    1|
|          Moldova|      United States|    1|
+-----------------+-------------------+-----+
```

Getting Unique Rows

A very common use case is to extract the unique or distinct values in a DataFrame. These values can be in one or more columns. The way we do this is by using the distinct method on a DataFrame, which allows us to deduplicate any rows that are in that DataFrame. For instance, let's get the unique origins in our dataset. This, of course, is a transformation that will return a new DataFrame with only unique rows:

```scala
// in Scala
df.select("ORIGIN_COUNTRY_NAME", "DEST_COUNTRY_NAME").distinct().count()
```

```python
# in Python
df.select("ORIGIN_COUNTRY_NAME", "DEST_COUNTRY_NAME").distinct().count()
```

```sql
-- in SQL
SELECT COUNT(DISTINCT(ORIGIN_COUNTRY_NAME, DEST_COUNTRY_NAME)) FROM dfTable
```

Results in 256.

```scala
// in Scala
df.select("ORIGIN_COUNTRY_NAME").distinct().count()
```

```python
# in Python
df.select("ORIGIN_COUNTRY_NAME").distinct().count()
```

```sql
-- in SQL
SELECT COUNT(DISTINCT ORIGIN_COUNTRY_NAME) FROM dfTable
```

Results in 125.

Random Samples

Sometimes, you might just want to sample some random records from your DataFrame. You can do this by using the sample method on a DataFrame, which makes it possible for you to specify a fraction of rows to extract from a DataFrame and whether you'd like to sample with or without replacement:

```scala
val seed = 5
val withReplacement = false
val fraction = 0.5
df.sample(withReplacement, fraction, seed).count()
```

```python
# in Python
seed = 5
withReplacement = False
fraction = 0.5
df.sample(withReplacement, fraction, seed).count()
```

Giving an output of 126.

Random Splits

Random splits can be helpful when you need to break up your DataFrame into a random "splits" of the original DataFrame. This is often used with machine learning algorithms to create training, validation, and test sets. In this next example, we'll split our DataFrame into two different DataFrames by setting the weights by which we will split the DataFrame (these are the arguments to the function). Because this method is designed to be randomized, we will also specify a seed (just replace seed with a number of your choosing in the code block). It's important to note that if you don't specify a proportion for each DataFrame that adds up to one, they will be normalized so that they do:

```Scala
// in Scala
val dataFrames = df.randomSplit(Array(0.25, 0.75), seed)
dataFrames(0).count() > dataFrames(1).count() // False
```

```Python
# in Python
dataFrames = df.randomSplit([0.25, 0.75], seed)
dataFrames[0].count() > dataFrames[1].count() # False
```

Concatenating and Appending Rows (Union)

As you learned in the previous section, DataFrames are immutable. This means users cannot append to DataFrames because that would be changing it. To append to a DataFrame, you must *union* the original DataFrame along with the new DataFrame. This just concatenates the two DataFramess. To union two DataFrames, you must be sure that they have the same schema and number of columns; otherwise, the union will fail.

Unions are currently performed based on location, not on the schema. This means that columns will not automatically line up the way you think they might.

```Scala
// in Scala
import org.apache.spark.sql.Row
val schema = df.schema
val newRows = Seq(
  Row("New Country", "Other Country", 5L),
  Row("New Country 2", "Other Country 3", 1L)
)
val parallelizedRows = spark.sparkContext.parallelize(newRows)
val newDF = spark.createDataFrame(parallelizedRows, schema)
df.union(newDF)
  .where("count = 1")
  .where($"ORIGIN_COUNTRY_NAME" =!= "United States")
  .show() // get all of them and we'll see our new rows at the end
```

In Scala, you must use the =!= operator so that you don't just compare the unevaluated column expression to a string but instead to the evaluated one:

```python
# in Python
from pyspark.sql import Row
schema = df.schema
newRows = [
  Row("New Country", "Other Country", 5L),
  Row("New Country 2", "Other Country 3", 1L)
]
parallelizedRows = spark.sparkContext.parallelize(newRows)
newDF = spark.createDataFrame(parallelizedRows, schema)

# in Python
df.union(newDF)\
  .where("count = 1")\
  .where(col("ORIGIN_COUNTRY_NAME") != "United States")\
  .show()
```

Giving the output of:

```
+-----------------+-------------------+-----+
|DEST_COUNTRY_NAME|ORIGIN_COUNTRY_NAME|count|
+-----------------+-------------------+-----+
|    United States|            Croatia|    1|
...
|    United States|            Namibia|    1|
|    New Country 2|    Other Country 3|    1|
+-----------------+-------------------+-----+
```

As expected, you'll need to use this new DataFrame reference in order to refer to the DataFrame with the newly appended rows. A common way to do this is to make the DataFrame into a view or register it as a table so that you can reference it more dynamically in your code.

Sorting Rows

When we sort the values in a DataFrame, we always want to sort with either the largest or smallest values at the top of a DataFrame. There are two equivalent operations to do this sort and orderBy that work the exact same way. They accept both column expressions and strings as well as multiple columns. The default is to sort in ascending order:

```scala
// in Scala
df.sort("count").show(5)
df.orderBy("count", "DEST_COUNTRY_NAME").show(5)
df.orderBy(col("count"), col("DEST_COUNTRY_NAME")).show(5)
```

```python
# in Python
df.sort("count").show(5)
df.orderBy("count", "DEST_COUNTRY_NAME").show(5)
df.orderBy(col("count"), col("DEST_COUNTRY_NAME")).show(5)
```

To more explicitly specify sort direction, you need to use the `asc` and `desc` functions if operating on a column. These allow you to specify the order in which a given column should be sorted:

```scala
// in Scala
import org.apache.spark.sql.functions.{desc, asc}
df.orderBy(expr("count desc")).show(2)
df.orderBy(desc("count"), asc("DEST_COUNTRY_NAME")).show(2)
```

```python
# in Python
from pyspark.sql.functions import desc, asc
df.orderBy(expr("count desc")).show(2)
df.orderBy(col("count").desc(), col("DEST_COUNTRY_NAME").asc()).show(2)
```

```sql
-- in SQL
SELECT * FROM dfTable ORDER BY count DESC, DEST_COUNTRY_NAME ASC LIMIT 2
```

An advanced tip is to use `asc_nulls_first`, `desc_nulls_first`, `asc_nulls_last`, or `desc_nulls_last` to specify where you would like your null values to appear in an ordered DataFrame.

For optimization purposes, it's sometimes advisable to sort within each partition before another set of transformations. You can use the `sortWithinPartitions` method to do this:

```scala
// in Scala
spark.read.format("json").load("/data/flight-data/json/*-summary.json")
  .sortWithinPartitions("count")
```

```python
# in Python
spark.read.format("json").load("/data/flight-data/json/*-summary.json")\
  .sortWithinPartitions("count")
```

We will discuss this more when we look at tuning and optimization in Part III.

Limit

Oftentimes, you might want to restrict what you extract from a DataFrame; for example, you might want just the top ten of some DataFrame. You can do this by using the `limit` method:

```scala
// in Scala
df.limit(5).show()
```

```python
# in Python
df.limit(5).show()
```

```sql
-- in SQL
SELECT * FROM dfTable LIMIT 6
```

```scala
// in Scala
df.orderBy(expr("count desc")).limit(6).show()
```

```python
# in Python
df.orderBy(expr("count desc")).limit(6).show()

-- in SQL
SELECT * FROM dfTable ORDER BY count desc LIMIT 6
```

Repartition and Coalesce

Another important optimization opportunity is to partition the data according to some frequently filtered columns, which control the physical layout of data across the cluster including the partitioning scheme and the number of partitions.

Repartition will incur a full shuffle of the data, regardless of whether one is necessary. This means that you should typically only repartition when the future number of partitions is greater than your current number of partitions or when you are looking to partition by a set of columns:

```scala
// in Scala
df.rdd.getNumPartitions // 1
```

```python
# in Python
df.rdd.getNumPartitions() # 1
```

```scala
// in Scala
df.repartition(5)
```

```python
# in Python
df.repartition(5)
```

If you know that you're going to be filtering by a certain column often, it can be worth repartitioning based on that column:

```scala
// in Scala
df.repartition(col("DEST_COUNTRY_NAME"))
```

```python
# in Python
df.repartition(col("DEST_COUNTRY_NAME"))
```

You can optionally specify the number of partitions you would like, too:

```scala
// in Scala
df.repartition(5, col("DEST_COUNTRY_NAME"))
```

```python
# in Python
df.repartition(5, col("DEST_COUNTRY_NAME"))
```

Coalesce, on the other hand, will not incur a full shuffle and will try to combine partitions. This operation will shuffle your data into five partitions based on the destination country name, and then coalesce them (without a full shuffle):

```scala
// in Scala
df.repartition(5, col("DEST_COUNTRY_NAME")).coalesce(2)
```

```python
# in Python
df.repartition(5, col("DEST_COUNTRY_NAME")).coalesce(2)
```

Collecting Rows to the Driver

As discussed in previous chapters, Spark maintains the state of the cluster in the driver. There are times when you'll want to collect some of your data to the driver in order to manipulate it on your local machine.

Thus far, we did not explicitly define this operation. However, we used several different methods for doing so that are effectively all the same. `collect` gets all data from the entire DataFrame, `take` selects the first N rows, and `show` prints out a number of rows nicely.

```scala
// in Scala
val collectDF = df.limit(10)
collectDF.take(5) // take works with an Integer count
collectDF.show() // this prints it out nicely
collectDF.show(5, false)
collectDF.collect()
```

```python
# in Python
collectDF = df.limit(10)
collectDF.take(5) # take works with an Integer count
collectDF.show() # this prints it out nicely
collectDF.show(5, False)
collectDF.collect()
```

There's an additional way of collecting rows to the driver in order to iterate over the entire dataset. The method `toLocalIterator` collects partitions to the driver as an iterator. This method allows you to iterate over the entire dataset partition-by-partition in a serial manner:

```
collectDF.toLocalIterator()
```

> Any collection of data to the driver can be a very expensive operation! If you have a large dataset and call `collect`, you can crash the driver. If you use `toLocalIterator` and have very large partitions, you can easily crash the driver node and lose the state of your application. This is also expensive because we can operate on a one-by-one basis, instead of running computation in parallel.

Conclusion

This chapter covered basic operations on DataFrames. You learned the simple concepts and tools that you will need to be successful with Spark DataFrames. Chapter 6 covers in much greater detail all of the different ways in which you can manipulate the data in those DataFrames.

Working with Different Types of Data

Chapter 5 presented basic DataFrame concepts and abstractions. This chapter covers building expressions, which are the bread and butter of Spark's structured operations. We also review working with a variety of different kinds of data, including the following:

- Booleans
- Numbers
- Strings
- Dates and timestamps
- Handling null
- Complex types
- User-defined functions

Where to Look for APIs

Before we begin, it's worth explaining where you as a user should look for transformations. Spark is a growing project, and any book (including this one) is a snapshot in time. One of our priorities in this book is to teach where, as of this writing, you should look to find functions to transform your data. Following are the key places to look:

DataFrame (Dataset) *Methods*

This is actually a bit of a trick because a DataFrame is just a Dataset of Row types, so you'll actually end up looking at the Dataset methods, which are available at this link. (*http://bit.ly/2rKkALY*)

Dataset submodules like `DataFrameStatFunctions` (*http://bit.ly/2DPYhJC*) and `Data FrameNaFunctions` (*http://bit.ly/2DPAqd3*) have more methods that solve specific sets of problems. `DataFrameStatFunctions`, for example, holds a variety of statistically related functions, whereas `DataFrameNaFunctions` refers to functions that are relevant when working with null data.

`Column` *Methods*

These were introduced for the most part in Chapter 5. They hold a variety of general column-related methods like `alias` or `contains`. You can find the API Reference for Column methods here (*http://bit.ly/2FloFbr*).

`org.apache.spark.sql.functions` contains a variety of functions for a range of different data types. Often, you'll see the entire package imported because they are used so frequently. You can find SQL and DataFrame functions here. (*http://bit.ly/2DPAycx*)

Now this may feel a bit overwhelming but have no fear, the majority of these functions are ones that you will find in SQL and analytics systems. All of these tools exist to achieve one purpose, to transform rows of data in one format or structure to another. This might create more rows or reduce the number of rows available. To begin, let's read in the `DataFrame` that we'll be using for this analysis:

```scala
// in Scala
val df = spark.read.format("csv")
  .option("header", "true")
  .option("inferSchema", "true")
  .load("/data/retail-data/by-day/2010-12-01.csv")
df.printSchema()
df.createOrReplaceTempView("dfTable")
```

```python
# in Python
df = spark.read.format("csv")\
  .option("header", "true")\
  .option("inferSchema", "true")\
  .load("/data/retail-data/by-day/2010-12-01.csv")
df.printSchema()
df.createOrReplaceTempView("dfTable")
```

Here's the result of the schema and a small sample of the data:

```
root
 |-- InvoiceNo: string (nullable = true)
 |-- StockCode: string (nullable = true)
 |-- Description: string (nullable = true)
 |-- Quantity: integer (nullable = true)
 |-- InvoiceDate: timestamp (nullable = true)
 |-- UnitPrice: double (nullable = true)
 |-- CustomerID: double (nullable = true)
 |-- Country: string (nullable = true)
```

```
+---------+---------+--------------------+--------+-------------------+----...
|InvoiceNo|StockCode|         Description|Quantity|        InvoiceDate|Unit...
+---------+---------+--------------------+--------+-------------------+----...
|   536365|   85123A|WHITE HANGING HEA...|       6|2010-12-01 08:26:00|   ...
|   536365|    71053| WHITE METAL LANTERN|       6|2010-12-01 08:26:00|   ...
...
|   536367|    21755|LOVE BUILDING BLO...|       3|2010-12-01 08:34:00|   ...
|   536367|    21777|RECIPE BOX WITH M...|       4|2010-12-01 08:34:00|   ...
+---------+---------+--------------------+--------+-------------------+----...
```

Converting to Spark Types

One thing you'll see us do throughout this chapter is convert native types to Spark types. We do this by using the first function that we introduce here, the lit function. This function converts a type in another language to its correspnding Spark representation. Here's how we can convert a couple of different kinds of Scala and Python values to their respective Spark types:

```scala
// in Scala
import org.apache.spark.sql.functions.lit
df.select(lit(5), lit("five"), lit(5.0))
```

```python
# in Python
from pyspark.sql.functions import lit
df.select(lit(5), lit("five"), lit(5.0))
```

There's no equivalent function necessary in SQL, so we can use the values directly:

```sql
-- in SQL
SELECT 5, "five", 5.0
```

Working with Booleans

Booleans are essential when it comes to data analysis because they are the foundation for all filtering. Boolean statements consist of four elements: *and, or, true,* and *false.* We use these simple structures to build logical statements that evaluate to either *true* or *false.* These statements are often used as conditional requirements for when a row of data must either pass the test (evaluate to true) or else it will be filtered out.

Let's use our retail dataset to explore working with Booleans. We can specify equality as well as less-than or greater-than:

```scala
// in Scala
import org.apache.spark.sql.functions.col
df.where(col("InvoiceNo").equalTo(536365))
  .select("InvoiceNo", "Description")
  .show(5, false)
```

Scala has some particular semantics regarding the use of == and ===. In Spark, if you want to filter by equality you should use === (equal) or =!= (not equal). You can also use the not function and the equalTo method.

```scala
// in Scala
import org.apache.spark.sql.functions.col
df.where(col("InvoiceNo") === 536365)
  .select("InvoiceNo", "Description")
  .show(5, false)
```

Python keeps a more conventional notation:

```python
# in Python
from pyspark.sql.functions import col
df.where(col("InvoiceNo") != 536365)\
  .select("InvoiceNo", "Description")\
  .show(5, False)
```

```
+---------+----------------------------+
|InvoiceNo|Description                 |
+---------+----------------------------+
|536366   |HAND WARMER UNION JACK      |
...
|536367   |POPPY'S PLAYHOUSE KITCHEN   |
+---------+----------------------------+
```

Another option—and probably the cleanest—is to specify the predicate as an expression in a string. This is valid for Python or Scala. Note that this also gives you access to another way of expressing "does not equal":

```
df.where("InvoiceNo = 536365")
  .show(5, false)

df.where("InvoiceNo <> 536365")
  .show(5, false)
```

We mentioned that you can specify Boolean expressions with multiple parts when you use and or or. In Spark, you should always chain together and filters as a sequential filter.

The reason for this is that even if Boolean statements are expressed serially (one after the other), Spark will flatten all of these filters into one statement and perform the filter at the same time, creating the and statement for us. Although you can specify your statements explicitly by using and if you like, they're often easier to understand and to read if you specify them serially. or statements need to be specified in the same statement:

```scala
// in Scala
val priceFilter = col("UnitPrice") > 600
val descripFilter = col("Description").contains("POSTAGE")
```

```
df.where(col("StockCode").isin("DOT")).where(priceFilter.or(descripFilter))
  .show()

# in Python
from pyspark.sql.functions import instr
priceFilter = col("UnitPrice") > 600
descripFilter = instr(df.Description, "POSTAGE") >= 1
df.where(df.StockCode.isin("DOT")).where(priceFilter | descripFilter).show()

-- in SQL
SELECT * FROM dfTable WHERE StockCode in ("DOT") AND(UnitPrice > 600 OR
    instr(Description, "POSTAGE") >= 1)

+---------+---------+--------------+--------+-------------------+---------+...
|InvoiceNo|StockCode|   Description|Quantity|        InvoiceDate|UnitPrice|...
+---------+---------+--------------+--------+-------------------+---------+...
|   536544|      DOT|DOTCOM POSTAGE|       1|2010-12-01 14:32:00|   569.77|...
|   536592|      DOT|DOTCOM POSTAGE|       1|2010-12-01 17:06:00|   607.49|...
+---------+---------+--------------+--------+-------------------+---------+...
```

Boolean expressions are not just reserved to filters. To filter a DataFrame, you can also just specify a Boolean column:

```
// in Scala
val DOTCodeFilter = col("StockCode") === "DOT"
val priceFilter = col("UnitPrice") > 600
val descripFilter = col("Description").contains("POSTAGE")
df.withColumn("isExpensive", DOTCodeFilter.and(priceFilter.or(descripFilter)))
  .where("isExpensive")
  .select("unitPrice", "isExpensive").show(5)

# in Python
from pyspark.sql.functions import instr
DOTCodeFilter = col("StockCode") == "DOT"
priceFilter = col("UnitPrice") > 600
descripFilter = instr(col("Description"), "POSTAGE") >= 1
df.withColumn("isExpensive", DOTCodeFilter & (priceFilter | descripFilter))\
  .where("isExpensive")\
  .select("unitPrice", "isExpensive").show(5)

-- in SQL
SELECT UnitPrice, (StockCode = 'DOT' AND
  (UnitPrice > 600 OR instr(Description, "POSTAGE") >= 1)) as isExpensive
FROM dfTable
WHERE (StockCode = 'DOT' AND
       (UnitPrice > 600 OR instr(Description, "POSTAGE") >= 1))
```

Notice how we did not need to specify our filter as an expression and how we could use a column name without any extra work.

If you're coming from a SQL background, all of these statements should seem quite familiar. Indeed, all of them can be expressed as a where clause. In fact, it's often easier to just express filters as SQL statements than using the programmatic DataFrame interface and Spark SQL allows us to do this without paying any performance penalty. For example, the following two statements are equivalent:

```scala
// in Scala
import org.apache.spark.sql.functions.{expr, not, col}
df.withColumn("isExpensive", not(col("UnitPrice").leq(250)))
  .filter("isExpensive")
  .select("Description", "UnitPrice").show(5)
df.withColumn("isExpensive", expr("NOT UnitPrice <= 250"))
  .filter("isExpensive")
  .select("Description", "UnitPrice").show(5)
```

Here's our state definition:

```python
# in Python
from pyspark.sql.functions import expr
df.withColumn("isExpensive", expr("NOT UnitPrice <= 250"))\
  .where("isExpensive")\
  .select("Description", "UnitPrice").show(5)
```

One "gotcha" that can come up is if you're working with null data when creating Boolean expressions. If there is a null in your data, you'll need to treat things a bit differently. Here's how you can ensure that you perform a null-safe equivalence test:

```
df.where(col("Description").eqNullSafe("hello")).show()
```

Although not currently available (Spark 2.2), IS [NOT] DISTINCT FROM will be coming in Spark 2.3 to do the same thing in SQL.

Working with Numbers

When working with big data, the second most common task you will do after filtering things is counting things. For the most part, we simply need to express our computation, and that should be valid assuming that we're working with numerical data types.

To fabricate a contrived example, let's imagine that we found out that we misrecorded the quantity in our retail dataset and the true quantity is equal to (the current quantity * the unit price)^2 + 5. This will introduce our first numerical function as well as the pow function that raises a column to the expressed power:

```scala
// in Scala
import org.apache.spark.sql.functions.{expr, pow}
val fabricatedQuantity = pow(col("Quantity") * col("UnitPrice"), 2) + 5
df.select(expr("CustomerId"), fabricatedQuantity.alias("realQuantity")).show(2)
```

```python
# in Python
from pyspark.sql.functions import expr, pow
```

```
fabricatedQuantity = pow(col("Quantity") * col("UnitPrice"), 2) + 5
df.select(expr("CustomerId"), fabricatedQuantity.alias("realQuantity")).show(2)
```

```
+----------+------------------+
|CustomerId|      realQuantity|
+----------+------------------+
|   17850.0|239.08999999999997|
|   17850.0|          418.7156|
+----------+------------------+
```

Notice that we were able to multiply our columns together because they were both numerical. Naturally we can add and subtract as necessary, as well. In fact, we can do all of this as a SQL expression, as well:

```
// in Scala
df.selectExpr(
  "CustomerId",
  "(POWER((Quantity * UnitPrice), 2.0) + 5) as realQuantity").show(2)
```

```
# in Python
df.selectExpr(
  "CustomerId",
  "(POWER((Quantity * UnitPrice), 2.0) + 5) as realQuantity").show(2)
```

```
-- in SQL
SELECT customerId, (POWER((Quantity * UnitPrice), 2.0) + 5) as realQuantity
FROM dfTable
```

Another common numerical task is rounding. If you'd like to just round to a whole number, oftentimes you can cast the value to an integer and that will work just fine. However, Spark also has more detailed functions for performing this explicitly and to a certain level of precision. In the following example, we round to one decimal place:

```
// in Scala
import org.apache.spark.sql.functions.{round, bround}
df.select(round(col("UnitPrice"), 1).alias("rounded"), col("UnitPrice")).show(5)
```

By default, the round function rounds up if you're exactly in between two numbers. You can round down by using the bround:

```
// in Scala
import org.apache.spark.sql.functions.lit
df.select(round(lit("2.5")), bround(lit("2.5"))).show(2)
```

```
# in Python
from pyspark.sql.functions import lit, round, bround

df.select(round(lit("2.5")), bround(lit("2.5"))).show(2)
```

```
-- in SQL
SELECT round(2.5), bround(2.5)
```

```
+-------------+--------------+
|round(2.5, 0)|bround(2.5, 0)|
+-------------+--------------+
```

```
|            3.0|            2.0|
|            3.0|            2.0|
+--------------+--------------+
```

Another numerical task is to compute the correlation of two columns. For example, we can see the Pearson correlation coefficient for two columns to see if cheaper things are typically bought in greater quantities. We can do this through a function as well as through the DataFrame statistic methods:

```scala
// in Scala
import org.apache.spark.sql.functions.{corr}
df.stat.corr("Quantity", "UnitPrice")
df.select(corr("Quantity", "UnitPrice")).show()
```

```python
# in Python
from pyspark.sql.functions import corr
df.stat.corr("Quantity", "UnitPrice")
df.select(corr("Quantity", "UnitPrice")).show()
```

```sql
-- in SQL
SELECT corr(Quantity, UnitPrice) FROM dfTable
```

```
+-----------------------+
|corr(Quantity, UnitPrice)|
+-----------------------+
|   -0.04112314436835551|
+-----------------------+
```

Another common task is to compute summary statistics for a column or set of columns. We can use the `describe` method to achieve exactly this. This will take all numeric columns and calculate the count, mean, standard deviation, min, and max. You should use this primarily for viewing in the console because the schema might change in the future:

```scala
// in Scala
df.describe().show()
```

```python
# in Python
df.describe().show()
```

```
+-------+------------------+------------------+-----------------+
|summary|          Quantity|         UnitPrice|       CustomerID|
+-------+------------------+------------------+-----------------+
|  count|              3108|              3108|             1968|
|   mean| 8.627413127413128| 4.151946589446603|15661.388719512195|
| stddev|26.371821677029203|15.638659854603892|1854.4496996893627|
|    min|               -24|               0.0|          12431.0|
|    max|               600|            607.49|          18229.0|
+-------+------------------+------------------+-----------------+
```

If you need these exact numbers, you can also perform this as an aggregation yourself by importing the functions and applying them to the columns that you need:

```scala
// in Scala
import org.apache.spark.sql.functions.{count, mean, stddev_pop, min, max}
```

```python
# in Python
from pyspark.sql.functions import count, mean, stddev_pop, min, max
```

There are a number of statistical functions available in the StatFunctions Package (accessible using `stat` as we see in the code block below). These are DataFrame methods that you can use to calculate a variety of different things. For instance, you can calculate either exact or approximate quantiles of your data using the `approxQuan tile` method:

```scala
// in Scala
val colName = "UnitPrice"
val quantileProbs = Array(0.5)
val relError = 0.05
df.stat.approxQuantile("UnitPrice", quantileProbs, relError) // 2.51
```

```python
# in Python
colName = "UnitPrice"
quantileProbs = [0.5]
relError = 0.05
df.stat.approxQuantile("UnitPrice", quantileProbs, relError) # 2.51
```

You also can use this to see a cross-tabulation or frequent item pairs (be careful, this output will be large and is omitted for this reason):

```scala
// in Scala
df.stat.crosstab("StockCode", "Quantity").show()
```

```python
# in Python
df.stat.crosstab("StockCode", "Quantity").show()
```

```scala
// in Scala
df.stat.freqItems(Seq("StockCode", "Quantity")).show()
```

```python
# in Python
df.stat.freqItems(["StockCode", "Quantity"]).show()
```

As a last note, we can also add a unique ID to each row by using the function `monoton ically_increasing_id`. This function generates a unique value for each row, starting with 0:

```scala
// in Scala
import org.apache.spark.sql.functions.monotonically_increasing_id
df.select(monotonically_increasing_id()).show(2)
```

```python
# in Python
from pyspark.sql.functions import monotonically_increasing_id
df.select(monotonically_increasing_id()).show(2)
```

There are functions added with every release, so check the documentation for more methods. For instance, there are some random data generation tools (e.g., `rand()`, `randn()`) with which you can randomly generate data; however, there are potential determinism issues when doing so. (You can find discussions about these challenges on the Spark mailing list.) There are also a number of more advanced tasks like bloom filtering and sketching algorithms available in the stat package that we mentioned (and linked to) at the beginning of this chapter. Be sure to search the API documentation for more information and functions.

Working with Strings

String manipulation shows up in nearly every data flow, and it's worth explaining what you can do with strings. You might be manipulating log files performing regular expression extraction or substitution, or checking for simple string existence, or making all strings uppercase or lowercase.

Let's begin with the last task because it's the most straightforward. The `initcap` function will capitalize every word in a given string when that word is separated from another by a space.

```scala
// in Scala
import org.apache.spark.sql.functions.{initcap}
df.select(initcap(col("Description"))).show(2, false)
```

```python
# in Python
from pyspark.sql.functions import initcap
df.select(initcap(col("Description"))).show()
```

```sql
-- in SQL
SELECT initcap(Description) FROM dfTable
```

```
+--------------------------------+
|initcap(Description)            |
+--------------------------------+
|White Hanging Heart T-light Holder|
|White Metal Lantern             |
+--------------------------------+
```

As just mentioned, you can cast strings in uppercase and lowercase, as well:

```scala
// in Scala
import org.apache.spark.sql.functions.{lower, upper}
df.select(col("Description"),
  lower(col("Description")),
  upper(lower(col("Description")))).show(2)
```

```python
# in Python
from pyspark.sql.functions import lower, upper
df.select(col("Description"),
    lower(col("Description")),
    upper(lower(col("Description")))).show(2)
```

```sql
-- in SQL
SELECT Description, lower(Description), Upper(lower(Description)) FROM dfTable
```

```
+--------------------+--------------------+------------------------+
|         Description| lower(Description)|upper(lower(Description))|
+--------------------+--------------------+------------------------+
|WHITE HANGING HEA...|white hanging hea...|    WHITE HANGING HEA...|
| WHITE METAL LANTERN| white metal lantern|    WHITE METAL LANTERN|
+--------------------+--------------------+------------------------+
```

Another trivial task is adding or removing spaces around a string. You can do this by using lpad, ltrim, rpad and rtrim, trim:

```scala
// in Scala
import org.apache.spark.sql.functions.{lit, ltrim, rtrim, rpad, lpad, trim}
df.select(
    ltrim(lit("    HELLO    ")).as("ltrim"),
    rtrim(lit("    HELLO    ")).as("rtrim"),
    trim(lit("    HELLO    ")).as("trim"),
    lpad(lit("HELLO"), 3, " ").as("lp"),
    rpad(lit("HELLO"), 10, " ").as("rp")).show(2)
```

```python
# in Python
from pyspark.sql.functions import lit, ltrim, rtrim, rpad, lpad, trim
df.select(
    ltrim(lit("    HELLO    ")).alias("ltrim"),
    rtrim(lit("    HELLO    ")).alias("rtrim"),
    trim(lit("    HELLO    ")).alias("trim"),
    lpad(lit("HELLO"), 3, " ").alias("lp"),
    rpad(lit("HELLO"), 10, " ").alias("rp")).show(2)
```

```sql
-- in SQL
SELECT
  ltrim('    HELLLOOOO  '),
  rtrim('    HELLLOOOO  '),
  trim('    HELLLOOOO  '),
  lpad('HELLOOOO  ', 3, ' '),
  rpad('HELLOOOO  ', 10, ' ')
FROM dfTable
```

```
+---------+---------+-----+---+----------+
|    ltrim|    rtrim| trim| lp|        rp|
+---------+---------+-----+---+----------+
|HELLO    |    HELLO|HELLO| HE|HELLO     |
|HELLO    |    HELLO|HELLO| HE|HELLO     |
+---------+---------+-----+---+----------+
```

Note that if lpad or rpad takes a number less than the length of the string, it will always remove values from the right side of the string.

Regular Expressions

Probably one of the most frequently performed tasks is searching for the existence of one string in another or replacing all mentions of a string with another value. This is often done with a tool called *regular expressions* that exists in many programming languages. Regular expressions give the user an ability to specify a set of rules to use to either extract values from a string or replace them with some other values.

Spark takes advantage of the complete power of Java regular expressions. The Java regular expression syntax departs slightly from other programming languages, so it is worth reviewing before putting anything into production. There are two key functions in Spark that you'll need in order to perform regular expression tasks: regexp_extract and regexp_replace. These functions extract values and replace values, respectively.

Let's explore how to use the regexp_replace function to replace substitute color names in our description column:

```scala
// in Scala
import org.apache.spark.sql.functions.regexp_replace
val simpleColors = Seq("black", "white", "red", "green", "blue")
val regexString = simpleColors.map(_.toUpperCase).mkString("|")
// the | signifies `OR` in regular expression syntax
df.select(
  regexp_replace(col("Description"), regexString, "COLOR").alias("color_clean"),
  col("Description")).show(2)
```

```python
# in Python
from pyspark.sql.functions import regexp_replace
regex_string = "BLACK|WHITE|RED|GREEN|BLUE"
df.select(
  regexp_replace(col("Description"), regex_string, "COLOR").alias("color_clean"),
  col("Description")).show(2)
```

```sql
-- in SQL
SELECT
  regexp_replace(Description, 'BLACK|WHITE|RED|GREEN|BLUE', 'COLOR') as
  color_clean, Description
FROM dfTable
```

```
+--------------------+--------------------+
|         color_clean|         Description|
+--------------------+--------------------+
|COLOR HANGING HEA...|WHITE HANGING HEA...|
| COLOR METAL LANTERN| WHITE METAL LANTERN|
+--------------------+--------------------+
```

Another task might be to replace given characters with other characters. Building this as a regular expression could be tedious, so Spark also provides the translate function to replace these values. This is done at the character level and will replace all instances of a character with the indexed character in the replacement string:

```scala
// in Scala
import org.apache.spark.sql.functions.translate
df.select(translate(col("Description"), "LEET", "1337"), col("Description"))
  .show(2)
```

```python
# in Python
from pyspark.sql.functions import translate
df.select(translate(col("Description"), "LEET", "1337"),col("Description"))\
  .show(2)
```

```sql
-- in SQL
SELECT translate(Description, 'LEET', '1337'), Description FROM dfTable
```

```
+-----------------------------------+--------------------+
|translate(Description, LEET, 1337)|         Description|
+-----------------------------------+--------------------+
|               WHI73 HANGING H3A...|WHITE HANGING HEA...|
|               WHI73 M37A1 1AN73RN| WHITE METAL LANTERN|
+-----------------------------------+--------------------+
```

We can also perform something similar, like pulling out the first mentioned color:

```scala
// in Scala
import org.apache.spark.sql.functions.regexp_extract
val regexString = simpleColors.map(_.toUpperCase).mkString("(", "|", ")")
// the | signifies OR in regular expression syntax
df.select(
     regexp_extract(col("Description"), regexString, 1).alias("color_clean"),
     col("Description")).show(2)
```

```python
# in Python
from pyspark.sql.functions import regexp_extract
extract_str = "(BLACK|WHITE|RED|GREEN|BLUE)"
df.select(
     regexp_extract(col("Description"), extract_str, 1).alias("color_clean"),
     col("Description")).show(2)
```

```sql
-- in SQL
SELECT regexp_extract(Description, '(BLACK|WHITE|RED|GREEN|BLUE)', 1),
  Description
FROM dfTable
```

```
+------------+--------------------+
| color_clean|         Description|
+------------+--------------------+
|       WHITE|WHITE HANGING HEA...|
|       WHITE| WHITE METAL LANTERN|
+------------+--------------------+
```

Sometimes, rather than extracting values, we simply want to check for their existence. We can do this with the contains method on each column. This will return a Boolean declaring whether the value you specify is in the column's string:

```scala
// in Scala
val containsBlack = col("Description").contains("BLACK")
val containsWhite = col("DESCRIPTION").contains("WHITE")
df.withColumn("hasSimpleColor", containsBlack.or(containsWhite))
  .where("hasSimpleColor")
  .select("Description").show(3, false)
```

In Python and SQL, we can use the `instr` function:

```python
# in Python
from pyspark.sql.functions import instr
containsBlack = instr(col("Description"), "BLACK") >= 1
containsWhite = instr(col("Description"), "WHITE") >= 1
df.withColumn("hasSimpleColor", containsBlack | containsWhite)\
  .where("hasSimpleColor")\
  .select("Description").show(3, False)
```

```sql
-- in SQL
SELECT Description FROM dfTable
WHERE instr(Description, 'BLACK') >= 1 OR instr(Description, 'WHITE') >= 1
```

```
+---------------------------------+
|Description                      |
+---------------------------------+
|WHITE HANGING HEART T-LIGHT HOLDER|
|WHITE METAL LANTERN              |
|RED WOOLLY HOTTIE WHITE HEART.   |
+---------------------------------+
```

This is trivial with just two values, but it becomes more complicated when there are values.

Let's work through this in a more rigorous way and take advantage of Spark's ability to accept a dynamic number of arguments. When we convert a list of values into a set of arguments and pass them into a function, we use a language feature called `var args`. Using this feature, we can effectively unravel an array of arbitrary length and pass it as arguments to a function. This, coupled with `select` makes it possible for us to create arbitrary numbers of columns dynamically:

```scala
// in Scala
val simpleColors = Seq("black", "white", "red", "green", "blue")
val selectedColumns = simpleColors.map(color => {
   col("Description").contains(color.toUpperCase).alias(s"is_$color")
}):+expr("*") // could also append this value
df.select(selectedColumns:_*).where(col("is_white").or(col("is_red")))
  .select("Description").show(3, false)
```

```
+---------------------------------+
|Description                      |
+---------------------------------+
|WHITE HANGING HEART T-LIGHT HOLDER|
|WHITE METAL LANTERN              |
|RED WOOLLY HOTTIE WHITE HEART.   |
+---------------------------------+
```

We can also do this quite easily in Python. In this case, we're going to use a different function, `locate`, that returns the integer location (1 based location). We then convert that to a Boolean before using it as the same basic feature:

```python
# in Python
from pyspark.sql.functions import expr, locate
simpleColors = ["black", "white", "red", "green", "blue"]
def color_locator(column, color_string):
  return locate(color_string.upper(), column)\
          .cast("boolean")\
          .alias("is_" + c)
selectedColumns = [color_locator(df.Description, c) for c in simpleColors]
selectedColumns.append(expr("*")) # has to a be Column type

df.select(*selectedColumns).where(expr("is_white OR is_red"))\
  .select("Description").show(3, False)
```

This simple feature can often help you programmatically generate columns or Boolean filters in a way that is simple to understand and extend. We could extend this to calculating the smallest common denominator for a given input value, or whether a number is a prime.

Working with Dates and Timestamps

Dates and times are a constant challenge in programming languages and databases. It's always necessary to keep track of timezones and ensure that formats are correct and valid. Spark does its best to keep things simple by focusing explicitly on two kinds of time-related information. There are dates, which focus exclusively on calendar dates, and timestamps, which include both date and time information. Spark, as we saw with our current dataset, will make a best effort to correctly identify column types, including dates and timestamps when we enable inferSchema. We can see that this worked quite well with our current dataset because it was able to identify and read our date format without us having to provide some specification for it.

As we hinted earlier, working with dates and timestamps closely relates to working with strings because we often store our timestamps or dates as strings and convert them into date types at runtime. This is less common when working with databases and structured data but much more common when we are working with text and CSV files. We will experiment with that shortly.

There are a lot of caveats, unfortunately, when working with dates and timestamps, especially when it comes to timezone handling. In version 2.1 and before, Spark parsed according to the machine's timezone if timezones are not explicitly specified in the value that you are parsing. You can set a session local timezone if necessary by setting spark.conf.sessionLocalTimeZone in the SQL configurations. This should be set according to the Java TimeZone format (https://docs.oracle.com/javase/7/docs/api/java/util/TimeZone.html).

```
df.printSchema()

root
 |-- InvoiceNo: string (nullable = true)
 |-- StockCode: string (nullable = true)
 |-- Description: string (nullable = true)
 |-- Quantity: integer (nullable = true)
 |-- InvoiceDate: timestamp (nullable = true)
 |-- UnitPrice: double (nullable = true)
 |-- CustomerID: double (nullable = true)
 |-- Country: string (nullable = true)
```

Although Spark will do read dates or times on a best-effort basis. However, sometimes there will be no getting around working with strangely formatted dates and times. The key to understanding the transformations that you are going to need to apply is to ensure that you know exactly what type and format you have at each given step of the way. Another common "gotcha" is that Spark's TimestampType class supports only second-level precision, which means that if you're going to be working with milliseconds or microseconds, you'll need to work around this problem by potentially operating on them as longs. Any more precision when coercing to a Time stampType will be removed.

Spark can be a bit particular about what format you have at any given point in time. It's important to be explicit when parsing or converting to ensure that there are no issues in doing so. At the end of the day, Spark is working with Java dates and timestamps and therefore conforms to those standards. Let's begin with the basics and get the current date and the current timestamps:

```scala
// in Scala
import org.apache.spark.sql.functions.{current_date, current_timestamp}
val dateDF = spark.range(10)
  .withColumn("today", current_date())
  .withColumn("now", current_timestamp())
dateDF.createOrReplaceTempView("dateTable")
```

```python
# in Python
from pyspark.sql.functions import current_date, current_timestamp
dateDF = spark.range(10)\
  .withColumn("today", current_date())\
  .withColumn("now", current_timestamp())
dateDF.createOrReplaceTempView("dateTable")
```

```
dateDF.printSchema()

root
 |-- id: long (nullable = false)
 |-- today: date (nullable = false)
 |-- now: timestamp (nullable = false)
```

Now that we have a simple DataFrame to work with, let's add and subtract five days from today. These functions take a column and then the number of days to either add or subtract as the arguments:

```scala
// in Scala
import org.apache.spark.sql.functions.{date_add, date_sub}
dateDF.select(date_sub(col("today"), 5), date_add(col("today"), 5)).show(1)
```

```python
# in Python
from pyspark.sql.functions import date_add, date_sub
dateDF.select(date_sub(col("today"), 5), date_add(col("today"), 5)).show(1)
```

```sql
-- in SQL
SELECT date_sub(today, 5), date_add(today, 5) FROM dateTable
```

```
+------------------+------------------+
|date_sub(today, 5)|date_add(today, 5)|
+------------------+------------------+
|        2017-06-12|        2017-06-22|
+------------------+------------------+
```

Another common task is to take a look at the difference between two dates. We can do this with the `datediff` function that will return the number of days in between two dates. Most often we just care about the days, and because the number of days varies from month to month, there also exists a function, `months_between`, that gives you the number of months between two dates:

```scala
// in Scala
import org.apache.spark.sql.functions.{datediff, months_between, to_date}
dateDF.withColumn("week_ago", date_sub(col("today"), 7))
  .select(datediff(col("week_ago"), col("today"))).show(1)
dateDF.select(
    to_date(lit("2016-01-01")).alias("start"),
    to_date(lit("2017-05-22")).alias("end"))
  .select(months_between(col("start"), col("end"))).show(1)
```

```python
# in Python
from pyspark.sql.functions import datediff, months_between, to_date
dateDF.withColumn("week_ago", date_sub(col("today"), 7))\
  .select(datediff(col("week_ago"), col("today"))).show(1)

dateDF.select(
    to_date(lit("2016-01-01")).alias("start"),
    to_date(lit("2017-05-22")).alias("end"))\
  .select(months_between(col("start"), col("end"))).show(1)
```

```sql
-- in SQL
SELECT to_date('2016-01-01'), months_between('2016-01-01', '2017-01-01'),
datediff('2016-01-01', '2017-01-01')
FROM dateTable
```

```
+----------------------+
|datediff(week_ago, today)|
+----------------------+
|                   -7|
+----------------------+


+----------------------+
|months_between(start, end)|
+----------------------+
|          -16.67741935|
+----------------------+
```

Notice that we introduced a new function: the to_date function. The to_date function allows you to convert a string to a date, optionally with a specified format. We specify our format in the Java SimpleDateFormat (*http://docs.oracle.com/javase/tuto rial/i18n/format/simpleDateFormat.html*) which will be important to reference if you use this function:

```scala
// in Scala
import org.apache.spark.sql.functions.{to_date, lit}
spark.range(5).withColumn("date", lit("2017-01-01"))
  .select(to_date(col("date"))).show(1)
```

```python
# in Python
from pyspark.sql.functions import to_date, lit
spark.range(5).withColumn("date", lit("2017-01-01"))\
  .select(to_date(col("date"))).show(1)
```

Spark will not throw an error if it cannot parse the date; rather, it will just return null. This can be a bit tricky in larger pipelines because you might be expecting your data in one format and getting it in another. To illustrate, let's take a look at the date format that has switched from year-month-day to year-day-month. Spark will fail to parse this date and silently return null instead:

```
dateDF.select(to_date(lit("2016-20-12")),to_date(lit("2017-12-11"))).show(1)
```

```
+------------------+------------------+
|to_date(2016-20-12)|to_date(2017-12-11)|
+------------------+------------------+
|              null|        2017-12-11|
+------------------+------------------+
```

We find this to be an especially tricky situation for bugs because some dates might match the correct format, whereas others do not. In the previous example, notice how the second date appears as Decembers 11th instead of the correct day, November 12th. Spark doesn't throw an error because it cannot know whether the days are mixed up or that specific row is incorrect.

Let's fix this pipeline, step by step, and come up with a robust way to avoid these issues entirely. The first step is to remember that we need to specify our date format according to the Java SimpleDateFormat standard (*https://docs.oracle.com/javase/8/docs/api/java/text/SimpleDateFormat.html*).

We will use two functions to fix this: to_date and to_timestamp. The former optionally expects a format, whereas the latter requires one:

```scala
// in Scala
import org.apache.spark.sql.functions.to_date
val dateFormat = "yyyy-dd-MM"
val cleanDateDF = spark.range(1).select(
    to_date(lit("2017-12-11"), dateFormat).alias("date"),
    to_date(lit("2017-20-12"), dateFormat).alias("date2"))
cleanDateDF.createOrReplaceTempView("dateTable2")
```

```python
# in Python
from pyspark.sql.functions import to_date
dateFormat = "yyyy-dd-MM"
cleanDateDF = spark.range(1).select(
    to_date(lit("2017-12-11"), dateFormat).alias("date"),
    to_date(lit("2017-20-12"), dateFormat).alias("date2"))
cleanDateDF.createOrReplaceTempView("dateTable2")
```

```sql
-- in SQL
SELECT to_date(date, 'yyyy-dd-MM'), to_date(date2, 'yyyy-dd-MM'), to_date(date)
FROM dateTable2
```

```
+----------+----------+
|      date|     date2|
+----------+----------+
|2017-11-12|2017-12-20|
+----------+----------+
```

Now let's use an example of to_timestamp, which always requires a format to be specified:

```scala
// in Scala
import org.apache.spark.sql.functions.to_timestamp
cleanDateDF.select(to_timestamp(col("date"), dateFormat)).show()
```

```python
# in Python
from pyspark.sql.functions import to_timestamp
cleanDateDF.select(to_timestamp(col("date"), dateFormat)).show()
```

```sql
-- in SQL
SELECT to_timestamp(date, 'yyyy-dd-MM'), to_timestamp(date2, 'yyyy-dd-MM')
FROM dateTable2
```

```
+----------------------------------+
|to_timestamp(`date`, 'yyyy-dd-MM')|
+----------------------------------+
|               2017-11-12 00:00:00|
+----------------------------------+
```

Casting between dates and timestamps is simple in all languages—in SQL, we would do it in the following way:

```
-- in SQL
SELECT cast(to_date("2017-01-01", "yyyy-dd-MM") as timestamp)
```

After we have our date or timestamp in the correct format and type, comparing between them is actually quite easy. We just need to be sure to either use a date/timestamp type or specify our string according to the right format of yyyy-MM-dd if we're comparing a date:

```
cleanDateDF.filter(col("date2") > lit("2017-12-12")).show()
```

One minor point is that we can also set this as a string, which Spark parses to a literal:

```
cleanDateDF.filter(col("date2") > "'2017-12-12'").show()
```

Implicit type casting is an easy way to shoot yourself in the foot, especially when dealing with null values or dates in different time-zones or formats. We recommend that you parse them explicitly instead of relying on implicit conversions.

Working with Nulls in Data

As a best practice, you should always use nulls to represent missing or empty data in your DataFrames. Spark can optimize working with null values more than it can if you use empty strings or other values. The primary way of interacting with null values, at DataFrame scale, is to use the .na subpackage on a DataFrame. There are also several functions for performing operations and explicitly specifying how Spark should handle null values. For more information, see Chapter 5 (where we discuss ordering), and also refer back to "Working with Booleans" on page 85.

Nulls are a challenging part of all programming, and Spark is no exception. In our opinion, being explicit is always better than being implicit when handling null values. For instance, in this part of the book, we saw how we can define columns as having null types. However, this comes with a catch. When we declare a column as not having a null time, that is not actually *enforced*. To reiterate, when you define a schema in which all columns are declared to *not* have null values, Spark will not enforce that and will happily let null values into that column. The nullable signal is simply to help Spark SQL optimize for handling that column. If you have null values in columns that should not have null values, you can get an incorrect result or see strange exceptions that can be difficult to debug.

There are two things you can do with null values: you can explicitly drop nulls or you can fill them with a value (globally or on a per-column basis). Let's experiment with each of these now.

Coalesce

Spark includes a function to allow you to select the first non-null value from a set of columns by using the `coalesce` function. In this case, there are no null values, so it simply returns the first column:

```scala
// in Scala
import org.apache.spark.sql.functions.coalesce
df.select(coalesce(col("Description"), col("CustomerId"))).show()
```

```python
# in Python
from pyspark.sql.functions import coalesce
df.select(coalesce(col("Description"), col("CustomerId"))).show()
```

ifnull, nullIf, nvl, and nvl2

There are several other SQL functions that you can use to achieve similar things. `ifnull` allows you to select the second value if the first is null, and defaults to the first. Alternatively, you could use `nullif`, which returns null if the two values are equal or else returns the second if they are not. `nvl` returns the second value if the first is null, but defaults to the first. Finally, `nvl2` returns the second value if the first is not null; otherwise, it will return the last specified value (`else_value` in the following example):

```sql
-- in SQL
SELECT
  ifnull(null, 'return_value'),
  nullif('value', 'value'),
  nvl(null, 'return_value'),
  nvl2('not_null', 'return_value', "else_value")
FROM dfTable LIMIT 1
```

```
+------------+----+------------+------------+
|           a|  b|           c|           d|
+------------+----+------------+------------+
|return_value|null|return_value|return_value|
+------------+----+------------+------------+
```

Naturally, we can use these in select expressions on DataFrames, as well.

drop

The simplest function is `drop`, which removes rows that contain nulls. The default is to drop any row in which any value is null:

```
df.na.drop()
df.na.drop("any")
```

In SQL, we have to do this column by column:

```
-- in SQL
SELECT * FROM dfTable WHERE Description IS NOT NULL
```

Specifying "any" as an argument drops a row if any of the values are null. Using "all" drops the row only if all values are null or NaN for that row:

```
df.na.drop("all")
```

We can also apply this to certain sets of columns by passing in an array of columns:

```
// in Scala
df.na.drop("all", Seq("StockCode", "InvoiceNo"))

# in Python
df.na.drop("all", subset=["StockCode", "InvoiceNo"])
```

fill

Using the fill function, you can fill one or more columns with a set of values. This can be done by specifying a map—that is a particular value and a set of columns.

For example, to fill all null values in columns of type String, you might specify the following:

```
df.na.fill("All Null values become this string")
```

We could do the same for columns of type Integer by using df.na.fill(5:Integer), or for Doubles df.na.fill(5:Double). To specify columns, we just pass in an array of column names like we did in the previous example:

```
// in Scala
df.na.fill(5, Seq("StockCode", "InvoiceNo"))

# in Python
df.na.fill("all", subset=["StockCode", "InvoiceNo"])
```

We can also do this with with a Scala Map, where the key is the column name and the value is the value we would like to use to fill null values:

```
// in Scala
val fillColValues = Map("StockCode" -> 5, "Description" -> "No Value")
df.na.fill(fillColValues)

# in Python
fill_cols_vals = {"StockCode": 5, "Description" : "No Value"}
df.na.fill(fill_cols_vals)
```

replace

In addition to replacing null values like we did with `drop` and `fill`, there are more flexible options that you can use with more than just null values. Probably the most common use case is to replace all values in a certain column according to their current value. The only requirement is that this value be the same type as the original value:

```
// in Scala
df.na.replace("Description", Map("" -> "UNKNOWN"))

# in Python
df.na.replace([""], ["UNKNOWN"], "Description")
```

Ordering

As we discussed in Chapter 5, you can use `asc_nulls_first`, `desc_nulls_first`, `asc_nulls_last`, or `desc_nulls_last` to specify where you would like your null values to appear in an ordered DataFrame.

Working with Complex Types

Complex types can help you organize and structure your data in ways that make more sense for the problem that you are hoping to solve. There are three kinds of complex types: structs, arrays, and maps.

Structs

You can think of structs as DataFrames within DataFrames. A worked example will illustrate this more clearly. We can create a struct by wrapping a set of columns in parenthesis in a query:

```
df.selectExpr("(Description, InvoiceNo) as complex", "*")

df.selectExpr("struct(Description, InvoiceNo) as complex", "*")

// in Scala
import org.apache.spark.sql.functions.struct
val complexDF = df.select(struct("Description", "InvoiceNo").alias("complex"))
complexDF.createOrReplaceTempView("complexDF")

# in Python
from pyspark.sql.functions import struct
complexDF = df.select(struct("Description", "InvoiceNo").alias("complex"))
complexDF.createOrReplaceTempView("complexDF")
```

We now have a DataFrame with a column `complex`. We can query it just as we might another DataFrame, the only difference is that we use a dot syntax to do so, or the column method `getField`:

```
complexDF.select("complex.Description")
complexDF.select(col("complex").getField("Description"))
```

We can also query all values in the struct by using *. This brings up all the columns to the top-level DataFrame:

```
complexDF.select("complex.*")

-- in SQL
SELECT complex.* FROM complexDF
```

Arrays

To define arrays, let's work through a use case. With our current data, our objective is to take every single word in our Description column and convert that into a row in our DataFrame.

The first task is to turn our Description column into a complex type, an array.

split

We do this by using the split function and specify the delimiter:

```
// in Scala
import org.apache.spark.sql.functions.split
df.select(split(col("Description"), " ")).show(2)

# in Python
from pyspark.sql.functions import split
df.select(split(col("Description"), " ")).show(2)

-- in SQL
SELECT split(Description, ' ') FROM dfTable

+--------------------+
|split(Description,  )|
+--------------------+
| [WHITE, HANGING, ...|
| [WHITE, METAL, LA...|
+--------------------+
```

This is quite powerful because Spark allows us to manipulate this complex type as another column. We can also query the values of the array using Python-like syntax:

```
// in Scala
df.select(split(col("Description"), " ").alias("array_col"))
  .selectExpr("array_col[0]").show(2)

# in Python
df.select(split(col("Description"), " ").alias("array_col"))\
  .selectExpr("array_col[0]").show(2)

-- in SQL
SELECT split(Description, ' ')[0] FROM dfTable
```

This gives us the following result:

```
+------------+
|array_col[0]|
+------------+
|       WHITE|
|       WHITE|
+------------+
```

Array Length

We can determine the array's length by querying for its size:

```scala
// in Scala
import org.apache.spark.sql.functions.size
df.select(size(split(col("Description"), " "))).show(2) // shows 5 and 3
```

```python
# in Python
from pyspark.sql.functions import size
df.select(size(split(col("Description"), " "))).show(2) # shows 5 and 3
```

array_contains

We can also see whether this array contains a value:

```scala
// in Scala
import org.apache.spark.sql.functions.array_contains
df.select(array_contains(split(col("Description"), " "), "WHITE")).show(2)
```

```python
# in Python
from pyspark.sql.functions import array_contains
df.select(array_contains(split(col("Description"), " "), "WHITE")).show(2)
```

```sql
-- in SQL
SELECT array_contains(split(Description, ' '), 'WHITE') FROM dfTable
```

This gives us the following result:

```
+------------------------------------------+
|array_contains(split(Description,  ), WHITE)|
+------------------------------------------+
|                                      true|
|                                      true|
+------------------------------------------+
```

However, this does not solve our current problem. To convert a complex type into a set of rows (one per value in our array), we need to use the explode function.

explode

The explode function takes a column that consists of arrays and creates one row (with the rest of the values duplicated) per value in the array. Figure 6-1 illustrates the process.

Figure 6-1. Exploding a column of text

```scala
// in Scala
import org.apache.spark.sql.functions.{split, explode}

df.withColumn("splitted", split(col("Description"), " "))
  .withColumn("exploded", explode(col("splitted")))
  .select("Description", "InvoiceNo", "exploded").show(2)
```

```python
# in Python
from pyspark.sql.functions import split, explode

df.withColumn("splitted", split(col("Description"), " "))\
  .withColumn("exploded", explode(col("splitted")))\
  .select("Description", "InvoiceNo", "exploded").show(2)
```

```sql
-- in SQL
SELECT Description, InvoiceNo, exploded
FROM (SELECT *, split(Description, " ") as splitted FROM dfTable)
LATERAL VIEW explode(splitted) as exploded
```

This gives us the following result:

```
+--------------------+---------+--------+
|         Description|InvoiceNo|exploded|
+--------------------+---------+--------+
|WHITE HANGING HEA...|   536365|   WHITE|
|WHITE HANGING HEA...|   536365| HANGING|
+--------------------+---------+--------+
```

Maps

Maps are created by using the map function and key-value pairs of columns. You then can select them just like you might select from an array:

```scala
// in Scala
import org.apache.spark.sql.functions.map
df.select(map(col("Description"), col("InvoiceNo")).alias("complex_map")).show(2)
```

```python
# in Python
from pyspark.sql.functions import create_map
df.select(create_map(col("Description"), col("InvoiceNo")).alias("complex_map"))\
  .show(2)
```

```sql
-- in SQL
SELECT map(Description, InvoiceNo) as complex_map FROM dfTable
WHERE Description IS NOT NULL
```

This produces the following result:

```
+--------------------+
|         complex_map|
+--------------------+
|Map(WHITE HANGING...|
|Map(WHITE METAL L...|
+--------------------+
```

You can query them by using the proper key. A missing key returns `null`:

```
// in Scala
df.select(map(col("Description"), col("InvoiceNo")).alias("complex_map"))
  .selectExpr("complex_map['WHITE METAL LANTERN']").show(2)
```

```
# in Python
df.select(map(col("Description"), col("InvoiceNo")).alias("complex_map"))\
  .selectExpr("complex_map['WHITE METAL LANTERN']").show(2)
```

This gives us the following result:

```
+--------------------------------+
|complex_map[WHITE METAL LANTERN]|
+--------------------------------+
|                            null|
|                          536365|
+--------------------------------+
```

You can also explode `map` types, which will turn them into columns:

```
// in Scala
df.select(map(col("Description"), col("InvoiceNo")).alias("complex_map"))
  .selectExpr("explode(complex_map)").show(2)
```

```
# in Python
df.select(map(col("Description"), col("InvoiceNo")).alias("complex_map"))\
  .selectExpr("explode(complex_map)").show(2)
```

This gives us the following result:

```
+--------------------+------+
|                 key| value|
+--------------------+------+
|WHITE HANGING HEA...|536365|
| WHITE METAL LANTERN|536365|
+--------------------+------+
```

Working with JSON

Spark has some unique support for working with JSON data. You can operate directly on strings of JSON in Spark and parse from JSON or extract JSON objects. Let's begin by creating a JSON column:

```scala
// in Scala
val jsonDF = spark.range(1).selectExpr("""
  '{"myJSONKey" : {"myJSONValue" : [1, 2, 3]}}' as jsonString""")
```

```python
# in Python
jsonDF = spark.range(1).selectExpr("""
  '{"myJSONKey" : {"myJSONValue" : [1, 2, 3]}}' as jsonString""")
```

You can use the `get_json_object` to inline query a JSON object, be it a dictionary or array. You can use `json_tuple` if this object has only one level of nesting:

```scala
// in Scala
import org.apache.spark.sql.functions.{get_json_object, json_tuple}
jsonDF.select(
    get_json_object(col("jsonString"), "$.myJSONKey.myJSONValue[1]") as "column",
    json_tuple(col("jsonString"), "myJSONKey")).show(2)
```

```python
# in Python
from pyspark.sql.functions import get_json_object, json_tuple

jsonDF.select(
    get_json_object(col("jsonString"), "$.myJSONKey.myJSONValue[1]") as "column",
    json_tuple(col("jsonString"), "myJSONKey")).show(2)
```

Here's the equivalent in SQL:

```
jsonDF.selectExpr(
  "json_tuple(jsonString, '$.myJSONKey.myJSONValue[1]') as column").show(2)
```

This results in the following table:

```
+------+--------------------+
|column|                  c0|
+------+--------------------+
|     2|{"myJSONValue":[1...|
+------+--------------------+
```

You can also turn a StructType into a JSON string by using the `to_json` function:

```scala
// in Scala
import org.apache.spark.sql.functions.to_json
df.selectExpr("(InvoiceNo, Description) as myStruct")
  .select(to_json(col("myStruct")))
```

```python
# in Python
from pyspark.sql.functions import to_json
df.selectExpr("(InvoiceNo, Description) as myStruct")\
  .select(to_json(col("myStruct")))
```

This function also accepts a dictionary (map) of parameters that are the same as the JSON data source. You can use the `from_json` function to parse this (or other JSON data) back in. This naturally requires you to specify a schema, and optionally you can specify a map of options, as well:

```scala
// in Scala
import org.apache.spark.sql.functions.from_json
import org.apache.spark.sql.types._
val parseSchema = new StructType(Array(
  new StructField("InvoiceNo",StringType,true),
  new StructField("Description",StringType,true)))
df.selectExpr("(InvoiceNo, Description) as myStruct")
  .select(to_json(col("myStruct")).alias("newJSON"))
  .select(from_json(col("newJSON"), parseSchema), col("newJSON")).show(2)
```

```python
# in Python
from pyspark.sql.functions import from_json
from pyspark.sql.types import *
parseSchema = StructType((
  StructField("InvoiceNo",StringType(),True),
  StructField("Description",StringType(),True)))
df.selectExpr("(InvoiceNo, Description) as myStruct")\
  .select(to_json(col("myStruct")).alias("newJSON"))\
  .select(from_json(col("newJSON"), parseSchema), col("newJSON")).show(2)
```

This gives us the following result:

```
+--------------------+--------------------+
|jsontostructs(newJSON)|            newJSON|
+--------------------+--------------------+
|   [536365,WHITE HAN...|{"InvoiceNo":"536...|
|   [536365,WHITE MET...|{"InvoiceNo":"536...|
+--------------------+--------------------+
```

User-Defined Functions

One of the most powerful things that you can do in Spark is define your own functions. These user-defined functions (UDFs) make it possible for you to write your own custom transformations using Python or Scala and even use external libraries. UDFs can take and return one or more columns as input. Spark UDFs are incredibly powerful because you can write them in several different programming languages; you do not need to create them in an esoteric format or domain-specific language. They're just functions that operate on the data, record by record. By default, these functions are registered as temporary functions to be used in that specific SparkSession or Context.

Although you can write UDFs in Scala, Python, or Java, there are performance considerations that you should be aware of. To illustrate this, we're going to walk through exactly what happens when you create UDF, pass that into Spark, and then execute code using that UDF.

The first step is the actual function. We'll create a simple one for this example. Let's write a power3 function that takes a number and raises it to a power of three:

```scala
// in Scala
val udfExampleDF = spark.range(5).toDF("num")
def power3(number:Double):Double = number * number * number
power3(2.0)
```

```python
# in Python
udfExampleDF = spark.range(5).toDF("num")
def power3(double_value):
  return double_value ** 3
power3(2.0)
```

In this trivial example, we can see that our functions work as expected. We are able to provide an individual input and produce the expected result (with this simple test case). Thus far, our expectations for the input are high: it must be a specific type and cannot be a null value (see "Working with Nulls in Data" on page 102).

Now that we've created these functions and tested them, we need to register them with Spark so that we can use them on all of our worker machines. Spark will serialize the function on the driver and transfer it over the network to all executor processes. This happens regardless of language.

When you use the function, there are essentially two different things that occur. If the function is written in Scala or Java, you can use it within the Java Virtual Machine (JVM). This means that there will be little performance penalty aside from the fact that you can't take advantage of code generation capabilities that Spark has for built-in functions. There can be performance issues if you create or use a lot of objects; we cover that in the section on optimization in Chapter 19.

If the function is written in Python, something quite different happens. Spark starts a Python process on the worker, serializes all of the data to a format that Python can understand (remember, it was in the JVM earlier), executes the function row by row on that data in the Python process, and then finally returns the results of the row operations to the JVM and Spark. Figure 6-2 provides an overview of the process.

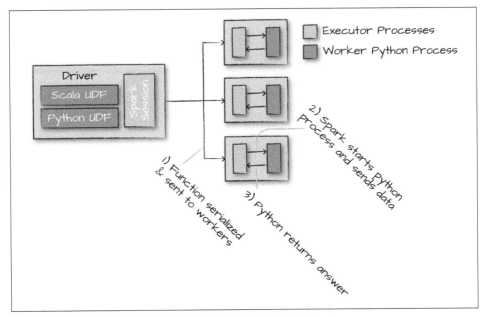

Figure 6-2. Figure caption

Starting this Python process is expensive, but the real cost is in serializing the data to Python. This is costly for two reasons: it is an expensive computation, but also, after the data enters Python, Spark cannot manage the memory of the worker. This means that you could potentially cause a worker to fail if it becomes resource constrained (because both the JVM and Python are competing for memory on the same machine). We recommend that you write your UDFs in Scala or Java—the small amount of time it should take you to write the function in Scala will always yield significant speed ups, and on top of that, you can still use the function from Python!

Now that you have an understanding of the process, let's work through an example. First, we need to register the function to make it available as a DataFrame function:

```scala
// in Scala
import org.apache.spark.sql.functions.udf
val power3udf = udf(power3(_:Double):Double)
```

We can use that just like any other DataFrame function:

```scala
// in Scala
udfExampleDF.select(power3udf(col("num"))).show()
```

The same applies to Python—first, we register it:

```python
# in Python
from pyspark.sql.functions import udf
power3udf = udf(power3)
```

Then, we can use it in our DataFrame code:

```python
# in Python
from pyspark.sql.functions import col
udfExampleDF.select(power3udf(col("num"))).show(2)
```

```
+-----------+
|power3(num)|
+-----------+
|          0|
|          1|
+-----------+
```

At this juncture, we can use this only as a DataFrame function. That is to say, we can't use it within a string expression, only on an expression. However, we can also register this UDF as a Spark SQL function. This is valuable because it makes it simple to use this function within SQL as well as across languages.

Let's register the function in Scala:

```scala
// in Scala
spark.udf.register("power3", power3(_:Double):Double)
udfExampleDF.selectExpr("power3(num)").show(2)
```

Because this function is registered with Spark SQL—and we've learned that any Spark SQL function or expression is valid to use as an expression when working with Data-Frames—we can turn around and use the UDF that we wrote in Scala, in Python. However, rather than using it as a DataFrame function, we use it as a SQL expression:

```python
# in Python
udfExampleDF.selectExpr("power3(num)").show(2)
# registered in Scala
```

We can also register our Python function to be available as a SQL function and use that in any language, as well.

One thing we can also do to ensure that our functions are working correctly is specify a return type. As we saw in the beginning of this section, Spark manages its own type information, which does not align exactly with Python's types. Therefore, it's a best practice to define the return type for your function when you define it. It is important to note that specifying the return type is not necessary, but it is a best practice.

If you specify the type that doesn't align with the actual type returned by the function, Spark will not throw an error but will just return null to designate a failure. You can see this if you were to switch the return type in the following function to be a Double Type:

```python
# in Python
from pyspark.sql.types import IntegerType, DoubleType
spark.udf.register("power3py", power3, DoubleType())
```

```python
# in Python
udfExampleDF.selectExpr("power3py(num)").show(2)
# registered via Python
```

This is because the range creates integers. When integers are operated on in Python, Python won't convert them into floats (the corresponding type to Spark's double type), therefore we see null. We can remedy this by ensuring that our Python function returns a float instead of an integer and the function will behave correctly.

Naturally, we can use either of these from SQL, too, after we register them:

```sql
-- in SQL
SELECT power3(12), power3py(12) -- doesn't work because of return type
```

When you want to optionally return a value from a UDF, you should return None in Python and an Option type in Scala:

```
## Hive UDFs
```

As a last note, you can also use UDF/UDAF creation via a Hive syntax. To allow for this, first you must enable Hive support when they create their SparkSession (via `SparkSession.builder().enableHiveSupport()`). Then you can register UDFs in SQL. This is only supported with precompiled Scala and Java packages, so you'll need to specify them as a dependency:

```sql
-- in SQL
CREATE TEMPORARY FUNCTION myFunc AS 'com.organization.hive.udf.FunctionName'
```

Additionally, you can register this as a permanent function in the Hive Metastore by removing TEMPORARY.

Conclusion

This chapter demonstrated how easy it is to extend Spark SQL to your own purposes and do so in a way that is not some esoteric, domain-specific language but rather simple functions that are easy to test and maintain without even using Spark! This is an amazingly powerful tool that you can use to specify sophisticated business logic that can run on five rows on your local machines or on terabytes of data on a 100-node cluster!

## CHAPTER 7

Aggregations

Aggregating is the act of collecting something together and is a cornerstone of big data analytics. In an aggregation, you will specify a *key* or *grouping* and an *aggregation function* that specifies how you should transform one or more columns. This function must produce one result for each group, given multiple input values. Spark's aggregation capabilities are sophisticated and mature, with a variety of different use cases and possibilities. In general, you use aggregations to summarize numerical data usually by means of some grouping. This might be a summation, a product, or simple counting. Also, with Spark you can aggregate any kind of value into an array, list, or map, as we will see in "Aggregating to Complex Types" on page 125.

In addition to working with any type of values, Spark also allows us to create the following groupings types:

- The simplest grouping is to just summarize a complete DataFrame by performing an aggregation in a select statement.

- A "group by" allows you to specify one or more keys as well as one or more aggregation functions to transform the value columns.

- A "window" gives you the ability to specify one or more keys as well as one or more aggregation functions to transform the value columns. However, the rows input to the function are somehow related to the current row.

- A "grouping set," which you can use to aggregate at multiple different levels. Grouping sets are available as a primitive in SQL and via rollups and cubes in DataFrames.

- A "rollup" makes it possible for you to specify one or more keys as well as one or more aggregation functions to transform the value columns, which will be summarized hierarchically.

- A "cube" allows you to specify one or more keys as well as one or more aggregation functions to transform the value columns, which will be summarized across all combinations of columns.

Each grouping returns a `RelationalGroupedDataset` on which we specify our aggregations.

 An important thing to consider is how exact you need an answer to be. When performing calculations over big data, it can be quite expensive to get an *exact* answer to a question, and it's often much cheaper to simply request an approximate to a reasonable degree of accuracy. You'll note that we mention some approximation functions throughout the book and oftentimes this is a good opportunity to improve the speed and execution of your Spark jobs, especially for interactive and ad hoc analysis.

Let's begin by reading in our data on purchases, repartitioning the data to have far fewer partitions (because we know it's a small volume of data stored in a lot of small files), and caching the results for rapid access:

```scala
// in Scala
val df = spark.read.format("csv")
  .option("header", "true")
  .option("inferSchema", "true")
  .load("/data/retail-data/all/*.csv")
  .coalesce(5)
df.cache()
df.createOrReplaceTempView("dfTable")
```

```python
# in Python
df = spark.read.format("csv")\
  .option("header", "true")\
  .option("inferSchema", "true")\
  .load("/data/retail-data/all/*.csv")\
  .coalesce(5)
df.cache()
df.createOrReplaceTempView("dfTable")
```

Here's a sample of the data so that you can reference the output of some of the functions:

```
+---------+---------+--------------------+--------+--------------+---------+-----
|InvoiceNo|StockCode|         Description|Quantity|   InvoiceDate|UnitPrice|Cu...
+---------+---------+--------------------+--------+--------------+---------+-----
|   536365|   85123A|WHITE HANGING...    |       6|12/1/2010 8:26|     2.55| ...
|   536365|    71053|WHITE METAL...      |       6|12/1/2010 8:26|     3.39| ...
...
|   536367|    21755|LOVE BUILDING BLO...|       3|12/1/2010 8:34|     5.95| ...
|   536367|    21777|RECIPE BOX WITH M...|       4|12/1/2010 8:34|     7.95| ...
+---------+---------+--------------------+--------+--------------+---------+-----
```

As mentioned, basic aggregations apply to an entire DataFrame. The simplest example is the count method:

```
df.count() == 541909
```

If you've been reading this book chapter by chapter, you know that count is actually an action as opposed to a transformation, and so it returns immediately. You can use count to get an idea of the total size of your dataset but another common pattern is to use it to cache an entire DataFrame in memory, just like we did in this example.

Now, this method is a bit of an outlier because it exists as a method (in this case) as opposed to a function and is eagerly evaluated instead of a lazy transformation. In the next section, we will see count used as a lazy function, as well.

Aggregation Functions

All aggregations are available as functions, in addition to the special cases that can appear on DataFrames or via .stat, like we saw in Chapter 6. You can find most aggregation functions in the org.apache.spark.sql.functions package (*http://spark.apache.org/docs/latest/api/scala/index.html#org.apache.spark.sql.functions$*).

> There are some gaps between the available SQL functions and the functions that we can import in Scala and Python. This changes every release, so it's impossible to include a definitive list. This section covers the most common functions.

count

The first function worth going over is count, except in this example it will perform as a transformation instead of an action. In this case, we can do one of two things: specify a specific column to count, or all the columns by using count(*) or count(1) to represent that we want to count every row as the literal one, as shown in this example:

```scala
// in Scala
import org.apache.spark.sql.functions.count
df.select(count("StockCode")).show() // 541909
```

```python
# in Python
from pyspark.sql.functions import count
df.select(count("StockCode")).show() # 541909
```

```sql
-- in SQL
SELECT COUNT(*) FROM dfTable
```

There are a number of gotchas when it comes to null values and counting. For instance, when performing a count(*), Spark will count null values (including rows containing all nulls). However, when counting an individual column, Spark will not count the null values.

countDistinct

Sometimes, the total number is not relevant; rather, it's the number of unique groups that you want. To get this number, you can use the countDistinct function. This is a bit more relevant for individual columns:

```scala
// in Scala
import org.apache.spark.sql.functions.countDistinct
df.select(countDistinct("StockCode")).show() // 4070
```

```python
# in Python
from pyspark.sql.functions import countDistinct
df.select(countDistinct("StockCode")).show() # 4070
```

```sql
-- in SQL
SELECT COUNT(DISTINCT *) FROM DFTABLE
```

approx_count_distinct

Often, we find ourselves working with large datasets and the exact distinct count is irrelevant. There are times when an approximation to a certain degree of accuracy will work just fine, and for that, you can use the approx_count_distinct function:

```scala
// in Scala
import org.apache.spark.sql.functions.approx_count_distinct
df.select(approx_count_distinct("StockCode", 0.1)).show() // 3364
```

```python
# in Python
from pyspark.sql.functions import approx_count_distinct
df.select(approx_count_distinct("StockCode", 0.1)).show() # 3364
```

```sql
-- in SQL
SELECT approx_count_distinct(StockCode, 0.1) FROM DFTABLE
```

You will notice that approx_count_distinct took another parameter with which you can specify the maximum estimation error allowed. In this case, we specified a rather large error and thus receive an answer that is quite far off but does complete more quickly than countDistinct. You will see much greater performance gains with larger datasets.

first and last

You can get the first and last values from a DataFrame by using these two obviously named functions. This will be based on the rows in the DataFrame, not on the values in the DataFrame:

```scala
// in Scala
import org.apache.spark.sql.functions.{first, last}
df.select(first("StockCode"), last("StockCode")).show()
```

```python
# in Python
from pyspark.sql.functions import first, last
df.select(first("StockCode"), last("StockCode")).show()
```

```sql
-- in SQL
SELECT first(StockCode), last(StockCode) FROM dfTable
```

```
+---------------------+--------------------+
|first(StockCode, false)|last(StockCode, false)|
+---------------------+--------------------+
|               85123A|               22138|
+---------------------+--------------------+
```

min and max

To extract the minimum and maximum values from a DataFrame, use the min and max functions:

```scala
// in Scala
import org.apache.spark.sql.functions.{min, max}
df.select(min("Quantity"), max("Quantity")).show()
```

```python
# in Python
from pyspark.sql.functions import min, max
df.select(min("Quantity"), max("Quantity")).show()
```

```sql
-- in SQL
SELECT min(Quantity), max(Quantity) FROM dfTable
```

```
+-------------+-------------+
|min(Quantity)|max(Quantity)|
+-------------+-------------+
|       -80995|        80995|
+-------------+-------------+
```

sum

Another simple task is to add all the values in a row using the sum function:

```scala
// in Scala
import org.apache.spark.sql.functions.sum
df.select(sum("Quantity")).show() // 5176450
```

```python
# in Python
from pyspark.sql.functions import sum
df.select(sum("Quantity")).show() # 5176450
```

```sql
-- in SQL
SELECT sum(Quantity) FROM dfTable
```

sumDistinct

In addition to summing a total, you also can sum a distinct set of values by using the sumDistinct function:

```scala
// in Scala
import org.apache.spark.sql.functions.sumDistinct
df.select(sumDistinct("Quantity")).show() // 29310
```

```python
# in Python
from pyspark.sql.functions import sumDistinct
df.select(sumDistinct("Quantity")).show() # 29310
```

```sql
-- in SQL
SELECT SUM(Quantity) FROM dfTable -- 29310
```

avg

Although you can calculate average by dividing sum by count, Spark provides an easier way to get that value via the avg or mean functions. In this example, we use alias in order to more easily reuse these columns later:

```scala
// in Scala
import org.apache.spark.sql.functions.{sum, count, avg, expr}

df.select(
    count("Quantity").alias("total_transactions"),
    sum("Quantity").alias("total_purchases"),
    avg("Quantity").alias("avg_purchases"),
    expr("mean(Quantity)").alias("mean_purchases"))
  .selectExpr(
    "total_purchases/total_transactions",
    "avg_purchases",
    "mean_purchases").show()
```

```python
# in Python
from pyspark.sql.functions import sum, count, avg, expr

df.select(
    count("Quantity").alias("total_transactions"),
    sum("Quantity").alias("total_purchases"),
    avg("Quantity").alias("avg_purchases"),
    expr("mean(Quantity)").alias("mean_purchases"))\
  .selectExpr(
    "total_purchases/total_transactions",
```

```
    "avg_purchases",
    "mean_purchases").show()
```

```
+---------------------------------+----------------+----------------+
|(total_purchases / total_transactions)|  avg_purchases| mean_purchases|
+---------------------------------+----------------+----------------+
|                 9.55224954743324|9.55224954743324|9.55224954743324|
+---------------------------------+----------------+----------------+
```

You can also average all the distinct values by specifying distinct. In fact, most aggregate functions support doing so only on distinct values.

Variance and Standard Deviation

Calculating the mean naturally brings up questions about the variance and standard deviation. These are both measures of the spread of the data around the mean. The variance is the average of the squared differences from the mean, and the standard deviation is the square root of the variance. You can calculate these in Spark by using their respective functions. However, something to note is that Spark has both the formula for the sample standard deviation as well as the formula for the population standard deviation. These are fundamentally different statistical formulae, and we need to differentiate between them. By default, Spark performs the formula for the sample standard deviation or variance if you use the `variance` or `stddev` functions.

You can also specify these explicitly or refer to the population standard deviation or variance:

```scala
// in Scala
import org.apache.spark.sql.functions.{var_pop, stddev_pop}
import org.apache.spark.sql.functions.{var_samp, stddev_samp}
df.select(var_pop("Quantity"), var_samp("Quantity"),
  stddev_pop("Quantity"), stddev_samp("Quantity")).show()
```

```python
# in Python
from pyspark.sql.functions import var_pop, stddev_pop
from pyspark.sql.functions import var_samp, stddev_samp
df.select(var_pop("Quantity"), var_samp("Quantity"),
  stddev_pop("Quantity"), stddev_samp("Quantity")).show()
```

```sql
-- in SQL
SELECT var_pop(Quantity), var_samp(Quantity),
  stddev_pop(Quantity), stddev_samp(Quantity)
FROM dfTable
```

```
+------------------+------------------+-------------------+-------------------+
| var_pop(Quantity)|var_samp(Quantity)|stddev_pop(Quantity)|stddev_samp(Quan...|
+------------------+------------------+-------------------+-------------------+
|47559.303646609056|47559.391409298754|  218.08095663447796|   218.081157850...|
+------------------+------------------+-------------------+-------------------+
```

skewness and kurtosis

Skewness and kurtosis are both measurements of extreme points in your data. Skewness measures the asymmetry of the values in your data around the mean, whereas kurtosis is a measure of the tail of data. These are both relevant specifically when modeling your data as a probability distribution of a random variable. Although here we won't go into the math behind these specifically, you can look up definitions quite easily on the internet. You can calculate these by using the functions:

```
import org.apache.spark.sql.functions.{skewness, kurtosis}
df.select(skewness("Quantity"), kurtosis("Quantity")).show()

# in Python
from pyspark.sql.functions import skewness, kurtosis
df.select(skewness("Quantity"), kurtosis("Quantity")).show()

-- in SQL
SELECT skewness(Quantity), kurtosis(Quantity) FROM dfTable
```

```
+-------------------+------------------+
| skewness(Quantity)|kurtosis(Quantity)|
+-------------------+------------------+
|-0.2640755761052562|119768.05495536952|
+-------------------+------------------+
```

Covariance and Correlation

We discussed single column aggregations, but some functions compare the interactions of the values in two difference columns together. Two of these functions are cov and corr, for covariance and correlation, respectively. Correlation measures the Pearson correlation coefficient, which is scaled between –1 and +1. The covariance is scaled according to the inputs in the data.

Like the var function, covariance can be calculated either as the sample covariance or the population covariance. Therefore it can be important to specify which formula you want to use. Correlation has no notion of this and therefore does not have calculations for population or sample. Here's how they work:

```
// in Scala
import org.apache.spark.sql.functions.{corr, covar_pop, covar_samp}
df.select(corr("InvoiceNo", "Quantity"), covar_samp("InvoiceNo", "Quantity"),
    covar_pop("InvoiceNo", "Quantity")).show()

# in Python
from pyspark.sql.functions import corr, covar_pop, covar_samp
```

```
df.select(corr("InvoiceNo", "Quantity"), covar_samp("InvoiceNo", "Quantity"),
    covar_pop("InvoiceNo", "Quantity")).show()

-- in SQL
SELECT corr(InvoiceNo, Quantity), covar_samp(InvoiceNo, Quantity),
  covar_pop(InvoiceNo, Quantity)
FROM dfTable

+-----------------------+---------------------------------+--------------------+
|corr(InvoiceNo, Quantity)|covar_samp(InvoiceNo, Quantity)|covar_pop(InvoiceN...|
+-----------------------+---------------------------------+--------------------+
|     4.912186085635685E-4|             1052.7280543902734|         1052.7...|
+-----------------------+---------------------------------+--------------------+
```

Aggregating to Complex Types

In Spark, you can perform aggregations not just of numerical values using formulas, you can also perform them on complex types. For example, we can collect a list of values present in a given column or only the unique values by collecting to a set.

You can use this to carry out some more programmatic access later on in the pipeline or pass the entire collection in a user-defined function (UDF):

```
// in Scala
import org.apache.spark.sql.functions.{collect_set, collect_list}
df.agg(collect_set("Country"), collect_list("Country")).show()

# in Python
from pyspark.sql.functions import collect_set, collect_list
df.agg(collect_set("Country"), collect_list("Country")).show()

-- in SQL
SELECT collect_set(Country), collect_set(Country) FROM dfTable

+--------------------+---------------------+
|collect_set(Country)|collect_list(Country)|
+--------------------+---------------------+
|[Portugal, Italy,...| [United Kingdom, ...|
+--------------------+---------------------+
```

Grouping

Thus far, we have performed only DataFrame-level aggregations. A more common task is to perform calculations based on *groups* in the data. This is typically done on categorical data for which we group our data on one column and perform some calculations on the other columns that end up in that group.

The best way to explain this is to begin performing some groupings. The first will be a count, just as we did before. We will group by each unique invoice number and get the count of items on that invoice. Note that this returns another DataFrame and is lazily performed.

We do this grouping in two phases. First we specify the column(s) on which we would like to group, and then we specify the aggregation(s). The first step returns a `RelationalGroupedDataset`, and the second step returns a `DataFrame`.

As mentioned, we can specify any number of columns on which we want to group:

```
df.groupBy("InvoiceNo", "CustomerId").count().show()

-- in SQL
SELECT count(*) FROM dfTable GROUP BY InvoiceNo, CustomerId
```

```
+---------+----------+-----+
|InvoiceNo|CustomerId|count|
+---------+----------+-----+
|   536846|     14573|   76|
...
|  C544318|     12989|    1|
+---------+----------+-----+
```

Grouping with Expressions

As we saw earlier, counting is a bit of a special case because it exists as a method. For this, usually we prefer to use the `count` function. Rather than passing that function as an expression into a `select` statement, we specify it as within `agg`. This makes it possible for you to pass-in arbitrary expressions that just need to have some aggregation specified. You can even do things like `alias` a column after transforming it for later use in your data flow:

```
// in Scala
import org.apache.spark.sql.functions.count

df.groupBy("InvoiceNo").agg(
  count("Quantity").alias("quan"),
  expr("count(Quantity)")).show()
```

```
# in Python
from pyspark.sql.functions import count

df.groupBy("InvoiceNo").agg(
    count("Quantity").alias("quan"),
    expr("count(Quantity)")).show()
```

```
+---------+----+---------------+
|InvoiceNo|quan|count(Quantity)|
+---------+----+---------------+
|   536596|   6|              6|
...
|  C542604|   8|              8|
+---------+----+---------------+
```

Grouping with Maps

Sometimes, it can be easier to specify your transformations as a series of Maps for which the key is the column, and the value is the aggregation function (as a string) that you would like to perform. You can reuse multiple column names if you specify them inline, as well:

```scala
// in Scala
df.groupBy("InvoiceNo").agg("Quantity"->"avg", "Quantity"->"stddev_pop").show()
```

```python
# in Python
df.groupBy("InvoiceNo").agg(expr("avg(Quantity)"),expr("stddev_pop(Quantity)"))\
  .show()
```

```sql
-- in SQL
SELECT avg(Quantity), stddev_pop(Quantity), InvoiceNo FROM dfTable
GROUP BY InvoiceNo
```

```
+---------+-----------------+-------------------+
|InvoiceNo|    avg(Quantity)|stddev_pop(Quantity)|
+---------+-----------------+-------------------+
|   536596|              1.5|   1.1180339887498947|
...
|  C542604|             -8.0|   15.173990905493518|
+---------+-----------------+-------------------+
```

Window Functions

You can also use *window functions* to carry out some unique aggregations by either computing some aggregation on a specific "window" of data, which you define by using a reference to the current data. This window specification determines which rows will be passed in to this function. Now this is a bit abstract and probably similar to a standard group-by, so let's differentiate them a bit more.

A *group-by* takes data, and every row can go only into one grouping. A window function calculates a return value for every input row of a table based on a group of rows, called a frame. Each row can fall into one or more frames. A common use case is to take a look at a rolling average of some value for which each row represents one day. If you were to do this, each row would end up in seven different frames. We cover defining frames a little later, but for your reference, Spark supports three kinds of window functions: ranking functions, analytic functions, and aggregate functions.

Figure 7-1 illustrates how a given row can fall into multiple frames.

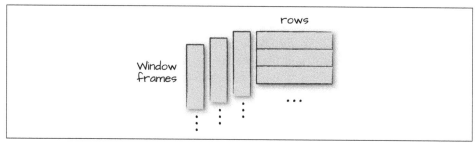

Figure 7-1. Visualizing window functions

To demonstrate, we will add a date column that will convert our invoice date into a column that contains only date information (not time information, too):

```scala
// in Scala
import org.apache.spark.sql.functions.{col, to_date}
val dfWithDate = df.withColumn("date", to_date(col("InvoiceDate"),
  "MM/d/yyyy H:mm"))
dfWithDate.createOrReplaceTempView("dfWithDate")
```

```python
# in Python
from pyspark.sql.functions import col, to_date
dfWithDate = df.withColumn("date", to_date(col("InvoiceDate"), "MM/d/yyyy H:mm"))
dfWithDate.createOrReplaceTempView("dfWithDate")
```

The first step to a window function is to create a window specification. Note that the `partition` by is unrelated to the partitioning scheme concept that we have covered thus far. It's just a similar concept that describes how we will be breaking up our group. The ordering determines the ordering within a given partition, and, finally, the frame specification (the `rowsBetween` statement) states which rows will be included in the frame based on its reference to the current input row. In the following example, we look at all previous rows up to the current row:

```scala
// in Scala
import org.apache.spark.sql.expressions.Window
import org.apache.spark.sql.functions.col
val windowSpec = Window
  .partitionBy("CustomerId", "date")
  .orderBy(col("Quantity").desc)
  .rowsBetween(Window.unboundedPreceding, Window.currentRow)
```

```python
# in Python
from pyspark.sql.window import Window
from pyspark.sql.functions import desc
windowSpec = Window\
  .partitionBy("CustomerId", "date")\
  .orderBy(desc("Quantity"))\
  .rowsBetween(Window.unboundedPreceding, Window.currentRow)
```

Now we want to use an aggregation function to learn more about each specific customer. An example might be establishing the maximum purchase quantity over all time. To answer this, we use the same aggregation functions that we saw earlier by passing a column name or expression. In addition, we indicate the window specification that defines to which frames of data this function will apply:

```
import org.apache.spark.sql.functions.max
val maxPurchaseQuantity = max(col("Quantity")).over(windowSpec)

# in Python
from pyspark.sql.functions import max
maxPurchaseQuantity = max(col("Quantity")).over(windowSpec)
```

You will notice that this returns a column (or expressions). We can now use this in a DataFrame select statement. Before doing so, though, we will create the purchase quantity rank. To do that we use the dense_rank function to determine which date had the maximum purchase quantity for every customer. We use dense_rank as opposed to rank to avoid gaps in the ranking sequence when there are tied values (or in our case, duplicate rows):

```
// in Scala
import org.apache.spark.sql.functions.{dense_rank, rank}
val purchaseDenseRank = dense_rank().over(windowSpec)
val purchaseRank = rank().over(windowSpec)

# in Python
from pyspark.sql.functions import dense_rank, rank
purchaseDenseRank = dense_rank().over(windowSpec)
purchaseRank = rank().over(windowSpec)
```

This also returns a column that we can use in select statements. Now we can perform a select to view the calculated window values:

```
// in Scala
import org.apache.spark.sql.functions.col

dfWithDate.where("CustomerId IS NOT NULL").orderBy("CustomerId")
  .select(
    col("CustomerId"),
    col("date"),
    col("Quantity"),
    purchaseRank.alias("quantityRank"),
    purchaseDenseRank.alias("quantityDenseRank"),
    maxPurchaseQuantity.alias("maxPurchaseQuantity")).show()

# in Python
from pyspark.sql.functions import col

dfWithDate.where("CustomerId IS NOT NULL").orderBy("CustomerId")\
  .select(
    col("CustomerId"),
    col("date"),
    col("Quantity"),
    purchaseRank.alias("quantityRank"),
```

```
    purchaseDenseRank.alias("quantityDenseRank"),
    maxPurchaseQuantity.alias("maxPurchaseQuantity")).show()

-- in SQL
SELECT CustomerId, date, Quantity,
  rank(Quantity) OVER (PARTITION BY CustomerId, date
                        ORDER BY Quantity DESC NULLS LAST
                        ROWS BETWEEN
                          UNBOUNDED PRECEDING AND
                          CURRENT ROW) as rank,

  dense_rank(Quantity) OVER (PARTITION BY CustomerId, date
                              ORDER BY Quantity DESC NULLS LAST
                              ROWS BETWEEN
                                UNBOUNDED PRECEDING AND
                                CURRENT ROW) as dRank,

  max(Quantity) OVER (PARTITION BY CustomerId, date
                        ORDER BY Quantity DESC NULLS LAST
                        ROWS BETWEEN
                          UNBOUNDED PRECEDING AND
                          CURRENT ROW) as maxPurchase
FROM dfWithDate WHERE CustomerId IS NOT NULL ORDER BY CustomerId

+----------+----------+--------+------------+-----------------+--------------+
|CustomerId|      date|Quantity|quantityRank|quantityDenseRank|maxP...Quantity|
+----------+----------+--------+------------+-----------------+--------------+
|     12346|2011-01-18|   74215|           1|                1|         74215|
|     12346|2011-01-18|  -74215|           2|                2|         74215|
|     12347|2010-12-07|      36|           1|                1|            36|
|     12347|2010-12-07|      30|           2|                2|            36|
...
|     12347|2010-12-07|      12|           4|                4|            36|
|     12347|2010-12-07|       6|          17|                5|            36|
|     12347|2010-12-07|       6|          17|                5|            36|
+----------+----------+--------+------------+-----------------+--------------+
```

Grouping Sets

Thus far in this chapter, we've seen simple group-by expressions that we can use to aggregate on a set of columns with the values in those columns. However, sometimes we want something a bit more complete—an aggregation across multiple groups. We achieve this by using *grouping sets*. Grouping sets are a low-level tool for combining sets of aggregations together. They give you the ability to create arbitrary aggregation in their group-by statements.

Let's work through an example to gain a better understanding. Here, we would like to get the total quantity of all stock codes and customers. To do so, we'll use the following SQL expression:

```scala
// in Scala
val dfNoNull = dfWithDate.drop()
dfNoNull.createOrReplaceTempView("dfNoNull")
```

```python
# in Python
dfNoNull = dfWithDate.drop()
dfNoNull.createOrReplaceTempView("dfNoNull")
```

```sql
-- in SQL
SELECT CustomerId, stockCode, sum(Quantity) FROM dfNoNull
GROUP BY customerId, stockCode
ORDER BY CustomerId DESC, stockCode DESC
```

```
+----------+---------+-------------+
|CustomerId|stockCode|sum(Quantity)|
+----------+---------+-------------+
|     18287|    85173|           48|
|     18287|   85040A|           48|
|     18287|   85039B|          120|
...
|     18287|    23269|           36|
+----------+---------+-------------+
```

You can do the exact same thing by using a grouping set:

```sql
-- in SQL
SELECT CustomerId, stockCode, sum(Quantity) FROM dfNoNull
GROUP BY customerId, stockCode GROUPING SETS((customerId, stockCode))
ORDER BY CustomerId DESC, stockCode DESC
```

```
+----------+---------+-------------+
|CustomerId|stockCode|sum(Quantity)|
+----------+---------+-------------+
|     18287|    85173|           48|
|     18287|   85040A|           48|
|     18287|   85039B|          120|
...
|     18287|    23269|           36|
+----------+---------+-------------+
```

Grouping sets depend on null values for aggregation levels. If you do not filter-out null values, you will get incorrect results. This applies to cubes, rollups, and grouping sets.

Simple enough, but what if you *also* want to include the total number of items, regardless of customer or stock code? With a conventional group-by statement, this would be impossible. But, it's simple with grouping sets: we simply specify that we would like to aggregate at that level, as well, in our grouping set. This is, effectively, the union of several different groupings together:

```sql
-- in SQL
SELECT CustomerId, stockCode, sum(Quantity) FROM dfNoNull
GROUP BY customerId, stockCode GROUPING SETS((customerId, stockCode),())
ORDER BY CustomerId DESC, stockCode DESC
```

```
+----------+---------+-------------+
|customerId|stockCode|sum(Quantity)|
+----------+---------+-------------+
|     18287|    85173|           48|
|     18287|   85040A|           48|
|     18287|   85039B|          120|
...
|     18287|    23269|           36|
+----------+---------+-------------+
```

The GROUPING SETS operator is only available in SQL. To perform the same in Data-Frames, you use the rollup and cube operators—which allow us to get the same results. Let's go through those.

Rollups

Thus far, we've been looking at explicit groupings. When we set our grouping keys of multiple columns, Spark looks at those as well as the actual combinations that are visible in the dataset. A rollup is a multidimensional aggregation that performs a variety of group-by style calculations for us.

Let's create a rollup that looks across time (with our new Date column) and space (with the Country column) and creates a new DataFrame that includes the grand total over all dates, the grand total for each date in the DataFrame, and the subtotal for each country on each date in the DataFrame:

```scala
val rolledUpDF = dfNoNull.rollup("Date", "Country").agg(sum("Quantity"))
  .selectExpr("Date", "Country", "`sum(Quantity)` as total_quantity")
  .orderBy("Date")
rolledUpDF.show()
```

```python
# in Python
rolledUpDF = dfNoNull.rollup("Date", "Country").agg(sum("Quantity"))\
  .selectExpr("Date", "Country", "`sum(Quantity)` as total_quantity")\
  .orderBy("Date")
rolledUpDF.show()
```

```
+----------+--------------+--------------+
|      Date|       Country|total_quantity|
+----------+--------------+--------------+
|      null|          null|       5176450|
|2010-12-01|United Kingdom|         23949|
|2010-12-01|       Germany|           117|
|2010-12-01|        France|           449|
...
|2010-12-03|        France|           239|
|2010-12-03|         Italy|           164|
```

```
|2010-12-03|       Belgium|          528|
+----------+--------------+-------------+
```

Now where you see the `null` values is where you'll find the grand totals. A `null` in both rollup columns specifies the grand total across both of those columns:

```
rolledUpDF.where("Country IS NULL").show()

rolledUpDF.where("Date IS NULL").show()

+----+-------+--------------+
|Date|Country|total_quantity|
+----+-------+--------------+
|null|   null|       5176450|
+----+-------+--------------+
```

Cube

A cube takes the rollup to a level deeper. Rather than treating elements hierarchically, a cube does the same thing across all dimensions. This means that it won't just go by date over the entire time period, but also the country. To pose this as a question again, can you make a table that includes the following?

- The total across all dates and countries
- The total for each date across all countries
- The total for each country on each date
- The total for each country across all dates

The method call is quite similar, but instead of calling `rollup`, we call `cube`:

```
// in Scala
dfNoNull.cube("Date", "Country").agg(sum(col("Quantity")))
  .select("Date", "Country", "sum(Quantity)").orderBy("Date").show()

# in Python
from pyspark.sql.functions import sum

dfNoNull.cube("Date", "Country").agg(sum(col("Quantity")))\
  .select("Date", "Country", "sum(Quantity)").orderBy("Date").show()

+----+--------------------+-------------+
|Date|             Country|sum(Quantity)|
+----+--------------------+-------------+
|null|               Japan|        25218|
|null|            Portugal|        16180|
|null|         Unspecified|         3300|
|null|                null|      5176450|
|null|           Australia|        83653|
...
|null|              Norway|        19247|
|null|           Hong Kong|         4769|
```

```
|null|            Spain|      26824|
|null|   Czech Republic|        592|
+----+-----------------+-----------+
```

This is a quick and easily accessible summary of nearly all of the information in our table, and it's a great way to create a quick summary table that others can use later on.

Grouping Metadata

Sometimes when using cubes and rollups, you want to be able to query the aggregation levels so that you can easily filter them down accordingly. We can do this by using the grouping_id, which gives us a column specifying the level of aggregation that we have in our result set. The query in the example that follows returns four distinct grouping IDs:

Table 7-1. Purpose of grouping IDs

Grouping ID	Description
3	This will appear for the highest-level aggregation, which will gives us the total quantity regardless of customerId and stockCode.
2	This will appear for all aggregations of individual stock codes. This gives us the total quantity per stock code, regardless of customer.
1	This will give us the total quantity on a per-customer basis, regardless of item purchased.
0	This will give us the total quantity for individual customerId and stockCode combinations.

This is a bit abstract, so it's well worth trying out to understand the behavior yourself:

```scala
// in Scala
import org.apache.spark.sql.functions.{grouping_id, sum, expr}

dfNoNull.cube("customerId", "stockCode").agg(grouping_id(), sum("Quantity"))
.orderBy(expr("grouping_id()").desc)
.show()
```

```
+----------+---------+-------------+-------------+
|customerId|stockCode|grouping_id()|sum(Quantity)|
+----------+---------+-------------+-------------+
|      null|     null|            3|      5176450|
|      null|    23217|            2|         1309|
|      null|   90059E|            2|           19|
...
+----------+---------+-------------+-------------+
```

Pivot

Pivots make it possible for you to convert a row into a column. For example, in our current data we have a Country column. With a pivot, we can aggregate according to some function for each of those given countries and display them in an easy-to-query way:

```scala
// in Scala
val pivoted = dfWithDate.groupBy("date").pivot("Country").sum()
```

```python
# in Python
pivoted = dfWithDate.groupBy("date").pivot("Country").sum()
```

This DataFrame will now have a column for every combination of country, numeric variable, and a column specifying the date. For example, for USA we have the following columns: `USA_sum(Quantity)`, `USA_sum(UnitPrice)`, `USA_sum(CustomerID)`. This represents one for each numeric column in our dataset (because we just performed an aggregation over all of them).

Here's an example query and result from this data:

```
pivoted.where("date > '2011-12-05'").select("date" ,"`USA_sum(Quantity)`").show()

+----------+-----------------+
|      date|USA_sum(Quantity)|
+----------+-----------------+
|2011-12-06|             null|
|2011-12-09|             null|
|2011-12-08|             -196|
|2011-12-07|             null|
+----------+-----------------+
```

Now all of the columns can be calculated with single groupings, but the value of a pivot comes down to how you would like to explore the data. It can be useful, if you have low enough cardinality in a certain column to transform it into columns so that users can see the schema and immediately know what to query for.

User-Defined Aggregation Functions

User-defined aggregation functions (UDAFs) are a way for users to define their own aggregation functions based on custom formulae or business rules. You can use UDAFs to compute custom calculations over groups of input data (as opposed to single rows). Spark maintains a single `AggregationBuffer` to store intermediate results for every group of input data.

To create a UDAF, you must inherit from the `UserDefinedAggregateFunction` base class and implement the following methods:

- `inputSchema` represents input arguments as a `StructType`
- `bufferSchema` represents intermediate UDAF results as a `StructType`
- `dataType` represents the return `DataType`

- `deterministic` is a Boolean value that specifies whether this UDAF will return the same result for a given input

- `initialize` allows you to initialize values of an aggregation buffer

- `update` describes how you should update the internal buffer based on a given row

- `merge` describes how two aggregation buffers should be merged

- `evaluate` will generate the final result of the aggregation

The following example implements a `BoolAnd`, which will inform us whether all the rows (for a given column) are true; if they're not, it will return false:

```scala
// in Scala
import org.apache.spark.sql.expressions.MutableAggregationBuffer
import org.apache.spark.sql.expressions.UserDefinedAggregateFunction
import org.apache.spark.sql.Row
import org.apache.spark.sql.types._
class BoolAnd extends UserDefinedAggregateFunction {
  def inputSchema: org.apache.spark.sql.types.StructType =
    StructType(StructField("value", BooleanType) :: Nil)
  def bufferSchema: StructType = StructType(
    StructField("result", BooleanType) :: Nil
  )
  def dataType: DataType = BooleanType
  def deterministic: Boolean = true
  def initialize(buffer: MutableAggregationBuffer): Unit = {
    buffer(0) = true
  }
  def update(buffer: MutableAggregationBuffer, input: Row): Unit = {
    buffer(0) = buffer.getAs[Boolean](0) && input.getAs[Boolean](0)
  }
  def merge(buffer1: MutableAggregationBuffer, buffer2: Row): Unit = {
    buffer1(0) = buffer1.getAs[Boolean](0) && buffer2.getAs[Boolean](0)
  }
  def evaluate(buffer: Row): Any = {
    buffer(0)
  }
}
```

Now, we simply instantiate our class and/or register it as a function:

```scala
// in Scala
val ba = new BoolAnd
spark.udf.register("booland", ba)
import org.apache.spark.sql.functions._
spark.range(1)
  .selectExpr("explode(array(TRUE, TRUE, TRUE)) as t")
  .selectExpr("explode(array(TRUE, FALSE, TRUE)) as f", "t")
  .select(ba(col("t")), expr("booland(f)"))
  .show()
```

```
+----------+----------+
|booland(t)|booland(f)|
+----------+----------+
|      true|     false|
+----------+----------+
```

UDAFs are currently available only in Scala or Java. However, in Spark 2.3, you will also be able to call Scala or Java UDFs and UDAFs by registering the function just as we showed in the UDF section in Chapter 6. For more information, go to SPARK-19439 (*https://issues.apache.org/jira/browse/SPARK-19439*).

Conclusion

This chapter walked through the different types and kinds of aggregations that you can perform in Spark. You learned about simple grouping-to window functions as well as rollups and cubes. Chapter 8 discusses how to perform joins to combine different data sources together.

CHAPTER 8
Joins

Chapter 7 covered aggregating single datasets, which is helpful, but more often than not, your Spark applications are going to bring together a large number of different datasets. For this reason, joins are an essential part of nearly all Spark workloads. Spark's ability to talk to different data means that you gain the ability to tap into a variety of data sources across your company. This chapter covers not just what joins exist in Spark and how to use them, but some of the basic internals so that you can think about how Spark actually goes about executing the join on the cluster. This basic knowledge can help you avoid running out of memory and tackle problems that you could not solve before.

Join Expressions

A *join* brings together two sets of data, the *left* and the *right*, by comparing the value of one or more *keys* of the left and right and evaluating the result of a *join expression* that determines whether Spark should bring together the left set of data with the right set of data. The most common join expression, an `equi-join`, compares whether the specified keys in your left and right datasets are equal. If they are equal, Spark will combine the left and right datasets. The opposite is true for keys that do not match; Spark discards the rows that do not have matching keys. Spark also allows for much more sophsticated join policies in addition to equi-joins. We can even use complex types and perform something like checking whether a key exists within an array when you perform a join.

Join Types

Whereas the join expression determines whether two rows *should* join, the join type determines *what* should be in the result set. There are a variety of different join types available in Spark for you to use:

- Inner joins (keep rows with keys that exist in the left and right datasets)
- Outer joins (keep rows with keys in either the left or right datasets)
- Left outer joins (keep rows with keys in the left dataset)
- Right outer joins (keep rows with keys in the right dataset)
- Left semi joins (keep the rows in the left, and only the left, dataset where the key appears in the right dataset)
- Left anti joins (keep the rows in the left, and only the left, dataset where they do not appear in the right dataset)
- Natural joins (perform a join by implicitly matching the columns between the two datasets with the same names)
- Cross (or Cartesian) joins (match every row in the left dataset with every row in the right dataset)

If you have ever interacted with a relational database system, or even an Excel spreadsheet, the concept of joining different datasets together should not be too abstract. Let's move on to showing examples of each join type. This will make it easy to understand exactly how you can apply these to your own problems. To do this, let's create some simple datasets that we can use in our examples:

```scala
// in Scala
val person = Seq(
    (0, "Bill Chambers", 0, Seq(100)),
    (1, "Matei Zaharia", 1, Seq(500, 250, 100)),
    (2, "Michael Armbrust", 1, Seq(250, 100)))
  .toDF("id", "name", "graduate_program", "spark_status")
val graduateProgram = Seq(
    (0, "Masters", "School of Information", "UC Berkeley"),
    (2, "Masters", "EECS", "UC Berkeley"),
    (1, "Ph.D.", "EECS", "UC Berkeley"))
  .toDF("id", "degree", "department", "school")
val sparkStatus = Seq(
    (500, "Vice President"),
    (250, "PMC Member"),
    (100, "Contributor"))
  .toDF("id", "status")
```

```python
# in Python
person = spark.createDataFrame([
    (0, "Bill Chambers", 0, [100]),
```

```
    (1, "Matei Zaharia", 1, [500, 250, 100]),
    (2, "Michael Armbrust", 1, [250, 100])])\
  .toDF("id", "name", "graduate_program", "spark_status")
graduateProgram = spark.createDataFrame([
    (0, "Masters", "School of Information", "UC Berkeley"),
    (2, "Masters", "EECS", "UC Berkeley"),
    (1, "Ph.D.", "EECS", "UC Berkeley")])\
  .toDF("id", "degree", "department", "school")
sparkStatus = spark.createDataFrame([
    (500, "Vice President"),
    (250, "PMC Member"),
    (100, "Contributor")])\
  .toDF("id", "status")
```

Next, let's register these as tables so that we use them throughout the chapter:

```
person.createOrReplaceTempView("person")
graduateProgram.createOrReplaceTempView("graduateProgram")
sparkStatus.createOrReplaceTempView("sparkStatus")
```

Inner Joins

Inner joins evaluate the keys in both of the DataFrames or tables and include (and join together) only the rows that evaluate to true. In the following example, we join the `graduateProgram` DataFrame with the `person` DataFrame to create a new Data-Frame:

```
// in Scala
val joinExpression = person.col("graduate_program") === graduateProgram.col("id")
```

```
# in Python
joinExpression = person["graduate_program"] == graduateProgram['id']
```

Keys that do not exist in both DataFrames will not show in the resulting DataFrame. For example, the following expression would result in zero values in the resulting DataFrame:

```
// in Scala
val wrongJoinExpression = person.col("name") === graduateProgram.col("school")
```

```
# in Python
wrongJoinExpression = person["name"] == graduateProgram["school"]
```

Inner joins are the default join, so we just need to specify our left DataFrame and join the right in the JOIN expression:

```
person.join(graduateProgram, joinExpression).show()
```

```
-- in SQL
SELECT * FROM person JOIN graduateProgram
  ON person.graduate_program = graduateProgram.id
```

```
+---+----------------+----------------+----------------+---+-------+----------+---
| id|            name|graduate_program|    spark_status| id| degree|department|...
+---+----------------+----------------+----------------+---+-------+----------+---
|  0|   Bill Chambers|               0|           [100]|  0|Masters| School...|...
|  1|   Matei Zaharia|               1|[500, 250, 100]|  1|  Ph.D.|      EECS|...
|  2|Michael Armbrust|               1|     [250, 100]|  1|  Ph.D.|      EECS|...
+---+----------------+----------------+----------------+---+-------+----------+---
```

We can also specify this explicitly by passing in a third parameter, the `joinType`:

```
// in Scala
var joinType = "inner"
```

```
# in Python
joinType = "inner"
```

```
person.join(graduateProgram, joinExpression, joinType).show()
```

```
-- in SQL
SELECT * FROM person INNER JOIN graduateProgram
  ON person.graduate_program = graduateProgram.id
```

```
+---+----------------+----------------+----------------+---+-------+-----------+---
| id|            name|graduate_program|    spark_status| id| degree| department...
+---+----------------+----------------+----------------+---+-------+-----------+---
|  0|   Bill Chambers|               0|           [100]|  0|Masters|     School...
|  1|   Matei Zaharia|               1|[500, 250, 100]|  1|  Ph.D.|       EECS...
|  2|Michael Armbrust|               1|     [250, 100]|  1|  Ph.D.|       EECS...
+---+----------------+----------------+----------------+---+-------+-----------+---
```

Outer Joins

Outer joins evaluate the keys in both of the DataFrames or tables and includes (and joins together) the rows that evaluate to true or false. If there is no equivalent row in either the left or right DataFrame, Spark will insert `null`:

```
joinType = "outer"
```

```
person.join(graduateProgram, joinExpression, joinType).show()
```

```
-- in SQL
SELECT * FROM person FULL OUTER JOIN graduateProgram
  ON graduate_program = graduateProgram.id
```

```
+----+----------------+----------------+----------------+---+-------+------------+---
|  id|            name|graduate_program|    spark_status| id| degree| departmen...
+----+----------------+----------------+----------------+---+-------+------------+---
|   1|   Matei Zaharia|               1|[500, 250, 100]|  1|  Ph.D.|        EEC...
|   2|Michael Armbrust|               1|     [250, 100]|  1|  Ph.D.|        EEC...
|null|            null|            null|            null|  2|Masters|        EEC...
|   0|   Bill Chambers|               0|           [100]|  0|Masters|     School...
+----+----------------+----------------+----------------+---+-------+------------+---
```

Left Outer Joins

Left outer joins evaluate the keys in both of the DataFrames or tables and includes all rows from the left DataFrame as well as any rows in the right DataFrame that have a match in the left DataFrame. If there is no equivalent row in the right DataFrame, Spark will insert null:

```
joinType = "left_outer"

graduateProgram.join(person, joinExpression, joinType).show()

-- in SQL
SELECT * FROM graduateProgram LEFT OUTER JOIN person
  ON person.graduate_program = graduateProgram.id
```

```
+---+-------+----------+------------+----+----------------+----------------+---
| id| degree|department|      school| id|            name|graduate_program|...
+---+-------+----------+------------+----+----------------+----------------+---
|  0|Masters| School...|UC Berkeley|   0|   Bill Chambers|               0|...
|  2|Masters|      EECS|UC Berkeley|null|            null|            null|...
|  1|  Ph.D.|      EECS|UC Berkeley|   2|Michael Armbrust|               1|...
|  1|  Ph.D.|      EECS|UC Berkeley|   1|   Matei Zaharia|               1|...
+---+-------+----------+------------+----+----------------+----------------+---
```

Right Outer Joins

Right outer joins evaluate the keys in both of the DataFrames or tables and includes all rows from the right DataFrame as well as any rows in the left DataFrame that have a match in the right DataFrame. If there is no equivalent row in the left DataFrame, Spark will insert null:

```
joinType = "right_outer"

person.join(graduateProgram, joinExpression, joinType).show()

-- in SQL
SELECT * FROM person RIGHT OUTER JOIN graduateProgram
  ON person.graduate_program = graduateProgram.id
```

```
+----+----------------+----------------+----------------+---+-------+-----------+
|  id|            name|graduate_program|    spark_status| id| degree| department|
+----+----------------+----------------+----------------+---+-------+-----------+
|   0|   Bill Chambers|               0|           [100]|  0|Masters|School of...|
|null|            null|            null|            null|  2|Masters|       EECS|
|   2|Michael Armbrust|               1|      [250, 100]|  1|  Ph.D.|       EECS|
|   1|   Matei Zaharia|               1|[500, 250, 100]|  1|  Ph.D.|       EECS|
+----+----------------+----------------+----------------+---+-------+-----------+
```

Left Semi Joins

Semi joins are a bit of a departure from the other joins. They do not actually include any values from the right DataFrame. They only compare values to see if the value exists in the second DataFrame. If the value does exist, those rows will be kept in the result, even if there are duplicate keys in the left DataFrame. Think of left semi joins as filters on a DataFrame, as opposed to the function of a conventional join:

```
joinType = "left_semi"

graduateProgram.join(person, joinExpression, joinType).show()

+---+-------+--------------------+----------+
| id| degree|          department|    school|
+---+-------+--------------------+----------+
|  0|Masters|School of Informa...|UC Berkeley|
|  1|  Ph.D.|                EECS|UC Berkeley|
+---+-------+--------------------+----------+

// in Scala
val gradProgram2 = graduateProgram.union(Seq(
    (0, "Masters", "Duplicated Row", "Duplicated School")).toDF())

gradProgram2.createOrReplaceTempView("gradProgram2")

# in Python
gradProgram2 = graduateProgram.union(spark.createDataFrame([
    (0, "Masters", "Duplicated Row", "Duplicated School")]))

gradProgram2.createOrReplaceTempView("gradProgram2")

gradProgram2.join(person, joinExpression, joinType).show()

-- in SQL
SELECT * FROM gradProgram2 LEFT SEMI JOIN person
  ON gradProgram2.id = person.graduate_program

+---+-------+--------------------+----------------+
| id| degree|          department|          school|
+---+-------+--------------------+----------------+
|  0|Masters|School of Informa...|     UC Berkeley|
|  1|  Ph.D.|                EECS|     UC Berkeley|
|  0|Masters|      Duplicated Row|Duplicated School|
+---+-------+--------------------+----------------+
```

Left Anti Joins

Left anti joins are the opposite of left semi joins. Like left semi joins, they do not actually include any values from the right DataFrame. They only compare values to see if the value exists in the second DataFrame. However, rather than keeping the values that exist in the second DataFrame, they keep only the values that *do not* have a corresponding key in the second DataFrame. Think of anti joins as a NOT IN SQL-style filter:

```
joinType = "left_anti"
graduateProgram.join(person, joinExpression, joinType).show()

-- in SQL
SELECT * FROM graduateProgram LEFT ANTI JOIN person
  ON graduateProgram.id = person.graduate_program

+---+-------+----------+-----------+
| id| degree|department|     school|
+---+-------+----------+-----------+
|  2|Masters|      EECS|UC Berkeley|
+---+-------+----------+-----------+
```

Natural Joins

Natural joins make implicit guesses at the columns on which you would like to join. It finds matching columns and returns the results. Left, right, and outer natural joins are all supported.

Implicit is always dangerous! The following query will give us incorrect results because the two DataFrames/tables share a column name (id), but it means different things in the datasets. You should always use this join with caution.

```
-- in SQL
SELECT * FROM graduateProgram NATURAL JOIN person
```

Cross (Cartesian) Joins

The last of our joins are cross-joins or *cartesian products*. Cross-joins in simplest terms are inner joins that do not specify a predicate. Cross joins will join every single row in the left DataFrame to ever single row in the right DataFrame. This will cause an absolute explosion in the number of rows contained in the resulting DataFrame. If you have 1,000 rows in each DataFrame, the cross-join of these will result in 1,000,000 (1,000 x 1,000) rows. For this reason, you must very explicitly state that you want a cross-join by using the cross join keyword:

```
joinType = "cross"
graduateProgram.join(person, joinExpression, joinType).show()

-- in SQL
SELECT * FROM graduateProgram CROSS JOIN person
  ON graduateProgram.id = person.graduate_program
```

```
+---+-------+----------+-----------+---+------------------+---------------+------
| id| degree|department|     school| id|              name|graduate_program|spar...
+---+-------+----------+-----------+---+------------------+---------------+------
|  0|Masters| School...|UC Berkeley|  0|     Bill Chambers|              0|   ...
|  1|  Ph.D.|      EECS|UC Berkeley|  2|Michael Armbrust|              1| [2...
|  1|  Ph.D.|      EECS|UC Berkeley|  1|    Matei Zaharia|              1|[500...
+---+-------+----------+-----------+---+------------------+---------------+------
```

If you truly intend to have a cross-join, you can call that out explicitly:

```
person.crossJoin(graduateProgram).show()
```

```
-- in SQL
SELECT * FROM graduateProgram CROSS JOIN person
```

```
+---+-----------------+---------------+-----------------+---+-------+-----------+
| id|             name|graduate_program|     spark_status| id| degree|  departm...|
+---+-----------------+---------------+-----------------+---+-------+-----------+
|  0|    Bill Chambers|              0|            [100]|  0|Masters|    School...|
...
|  1|    Matei Zaharia|              1|[500, 250, 100]|  0|Masters|    School...|
...
|  2|Michael Armbrust|              1|      [250, 100]|  0|Masters|    School...|
...
+---+-----------------+---------------+-----------------+---+-------+-----------+
```

You should use cross-joins only if you are absolutely, 100 percent sure that this is the join you need. There is a reason why you need to be explicit when defining a cross-join in Spark. They're dangerous! Advanced users can set the session-level configuration `spark.sql.crossJoin.enable` to true in order to allow cross-joins without warnings or without Spark trying to perform another join for you.

Challenges When Using Joins

When performing joins, there are some specific challenges and some common questions that arise. The rest of the chapter will provide answers to these common questions and then explain how, at a high level, Spark performs joins. This will hint at some of the optimizations that we are going to cover in later parts of this book.

Joins on Complex Types

Even though this might seem like a challenge, it's actually not. Any expression is a valid join expression, assuming that it returns a Boolean:

```
import org.apache.spark.sql.functions.expr

person.withColumnRenamed("id", "personId")
  .join(sparkStatus, expr("array_contains(spark_status, id)")).show()
```

```python
# in Python
from pyspark.sql.functions import expr

person.withColumnRenamed("id", "personId")\
  .join(sparkStatus, expr("array_contains(spark_status, id)")).show()
```

```sql
-- in SQL
SELECT * FROM
  (select id as personId, name, graduate_program, spark_status FROM person)
  INNER JOIN sparkStatus ON array_contains(spark_status, id)
```

```
+--------+---------------+----------------+---------------+---+--------------+
|personId|           name|graduate_program|   spark_status| id|        status|
+--------+---------------+----------------+---------------+---+--------------+
|       0|  Bill Chambers|               0|             [100]|100|   Contributor|
|       1|  Matei Zaharia|               1|[500, 250, 100]|500|Vice President|
|       1|  Matei Zaharia|               1|[500, 250, 100]|250|    PMC Member|
|       1|  Matei Zaharia|               1|[500, 250, 100]|100|   Contributor|
|       2|Michael Armbrust|              1|     [250, 100]|250|    PMC Member|
|       2|Michael Armbrust|              1|     [250, 100]|100|   Contributor|
+--------+---------------+----------------+---------------+---+--------------+
```

Handling Duplicate Column Names

One of the tricky things that come up in joins is dealing with duplicate column names in your results DataFrame. In a DataFrame, each column has a unique ID within Spark's SQL Engine, Catalyst. This unique ID is purely internal and not something that you can directly reference. This makes it quite difficult to refer to a specific column when you have a DataFrame with duplicate column names.

This can occur in two distinct situations:

- The join expression that you specify does not remove one key from one of the input DataFrames and the keys have the same column name
- Two columns on which you are not performing the join have the same name

Let's create a problem dataset that we can use to illustrate these problems:

```
val gradProgramDupe = graduateProgram.withColumnRenamed("id", "graduate_program")
val joinExpr = gradProgramDupe.col("graduate_program") === person.col(
  "graduate_program")
```

Note that there are now two graduate_program columns, even though we joined on that key:

```
person.join(gradProgramDupe, joinExpr).show()
```

The challenge arises when we refer to one of these columns:

```
person.join(gradProgramDupe, joinExpr).select("graduate_program").show()
```

Given the previous code snippet, we will receive an error. In this particular example, Spark generates this message:

```
org.apache.spark.sql.AnalysisException: Reference 'graduate_program' is
ambiguous, could be: graduate_program#40, graduate_program#1079.;
```

Approach 1: Different join expression

When you have two keys that have the same name, probably the easiest fix is to change the join expression from a Boolean expression to a string or sequence. This automatically removes one of the columns for you during the join:

```
person.join(gradProgramDupe,"graduate_program").select("graduate_program").show()
```

Approach 2: Dropping the column after the join

Another approach is to drop the offending column after the join. When doing this, we need to refer to the column via the original source DataFrame. We can do this if the join uses the same key names or if the source DataFrames have columns that simply have the same name:

```
person.join(gradProgramDupe, joinExpr).drop(person.col("graduate_program"))
  .select("graduate_program").show()

val joinExpr = person.col("graduate_program") === graduateProgram.col("id")
person.join(graduateProgram, joinExpr).drop(graduateProgram.col("id")).show()
```

This is an artifact of Spark's SQL analysis process in which an explicitly referenced column will pass analysis because Spark has no need to resolve the column. Notice how the column uses the `.col` method instead of a `column` function. That allows us to implicitly specify that column by its specific ID.

Approach 3: Renaming a column before the join

We can avoid this issue altogether if we rename one of our columns before the join:

```
val gradProgram3 = graduateProgram.withColumnRenamed("id", "grad_id")
val joinExpr = person.col("graduate_program") === gradProgram3.col("grad_id")
person.join(gradProgram3, joinExpr).show()
```

How Spark Performs Joins

To understand how Spark performs joins, you need to understand the two core resources at play: the *node-to-node communication strategy* and *per node computation strategy*. These internals are likely irrelevant to your business problem. However, comprehending how Spark performs joins can mean the difference between a job that completes quickly and one that never completes at all.

Communication Strategies

Spark approaches cluster communication in two different ways during joins. It either incurs a *shuffle join*, which results in an all-to-all communication or a *broadcast join*. Keep in mind that there is a lot more detail than we're letting on at this point, and that's intentional. Some of these internal optimizations are likely to change over time with new improvements to the cost-based optimizer and improved communication strategies. For this reason, we're going to focus on the high-level examples to help you understand exactly what's going on in some of the more common scenarios, and let you take advantage of some of the low-hanging fruit that you can use right away to try to speed up some of your workloads.

The core foundation of our simplified view of joins is that in Spark you will have either a big table or a small table. Although this is obviously a spectrum (and things do happen differently if you have a "medium-sized table"), it can help to be binary about the distinction for the sake of this explanation.

Big table–to–big table

When you join a big table to another big table, you end up with a shuffle join, such as that illustrates in Figure 8-1.

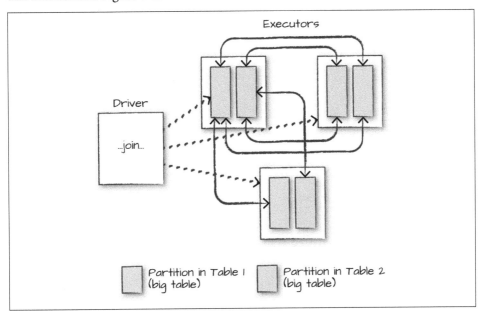

Figure 8-1. Joining two big tables

In a shuffle join, every node talks to every other node and they share data according to which node has a certain key or set of keys (on which you are joining). These joins are expensive because the network can become congested with traffic, especially if your data is not partitioned well.

This join describes taking a big table of data and joining it to another big table of data. An example of this might be a company that receives billions of messages every day from the Internet of Things, and needs to identify the day-over-day changes that have occurred. The way to do this is by joining on `deviceId`, `messageType`, and `date` in one column, and `date - 1 day` in the other column.

In Figure 8-1, DataFrame 1 and DataFrame 2 are both large DataFrames. This means that all worker nodes (and potentially every partition) will need to communicate with one another during the *entire* join process (with no intelligent partitioning of data).

Big table–to–small table

When the table is small enough to fit into the memory of a single worker node, with some breathing room of course, we can optimize our join. Although we can use a big table–to–big table communication strategy, it can often be more efficient to use a broadcast join. What this means is that we will replicate our small DataFrame onto every worker node in the cluster (be it located on one machine or many). Now this sounds expensive. However, what this does is prevent us from performing the all-to-all communication during the *entire* join process. Instead, we perform it only once at the beginning and then let each individual worker node perform the work without having to wait or communicate with any other worker node, as is depicted in Figure 8-2.

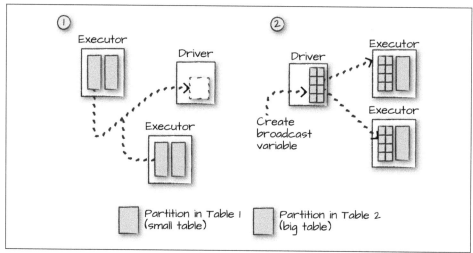

Figure 8-2. A broadcast join

At the beginning of this join will be a large communication, just like in the previous type of join. However, immediately after that first, there will be no further communication between nodes. This means that joins will be performed on every single node individually, making CPU the biggest bottleneck. For our current set of data, we can see that Spark has automatically set this up as a broadcast join by looking at the explain plan:

```
val joinExpr = person.col("graduate_program") === graduateProgram.col("id")

person.join(graduateProgram, joinExpr).explain()

== Physical Plan ==
*BroadcastHashJoin [graduate_program#40], [id#5....
:- LocalTableScan [id#38, name#39, graduate_progr...
+- BroadcastExchange HashedRelationBroadcastMode(....
   +- LocalTableScan [id#56, degree#57, departmen....
```

With the DataFrame API, we can also explicitly give the optimizer a hint that we would like to use a broadcast join by using the correct function around the small DataFrame in question. In this example, these result in the same plan we just saw; however, this is not always the case:

```
import org.apache.spark.sql.functions.broadcast
val joinExpr = person.col("graduate_program") === graduateProgram.col("id")
person.join(broadcast(graduateProgram), joinExpr).explain()
```

The SQL interface also includes the ability to provide *hints* to perform joins. These are not *enforced*, however, so the optimizer might choose to ignore them. You can set one of these hints by using a special comment syntax. MAPJOIN, BROADCAST, and BROAD CASTJOIN all do the same thing and are all supported:

```
-- in SQL
SELECT /*+ MAPJOIN(graduateProgram) */ * FROM person JOIN graduateProgram
  ON person.graduate_program = graduateProgram.id
```

This doesn't come for free either: if you try to broadcast something too large, you can crash your driver node (because that collect is expensive). This is likely an area for optimization in the future.

Little table–to–little table

When performing joins with small tables, it's usually best to let Spark decide how to join them. You can always force a broadcast join if you're noticing strange behavior.

Conclusion

In this chapter, we discussed joins, probably one of the most common use cases. One thing we did not mention but is important to consider is if you partition your data correctly *prior to a join*, you can end up with much more efficient execution because even if a shuffle is planned, if data from two different DataFrames is already located on the same machine, Spark can avoid the shuffle. Experiment with some of your data and try partitioning beforehand to see if you can notice the increase in speed when performing those joins. In Chapter 9, we will discuss Spark's data source APIs. There are additional implications when you decide what order joins should occur in. Because some joins act as filters, this can be a low-hanging improvement in your workloads, as you are guaranteed to reduce data exchanged over the network.

The next chapter will depart from user manipulation, as we've seen in the last several chapters, and touch on reading and writing data using the Structured APIs.

## CHAPTER 9

Data Sources

This chapter formally introduces the variety of other data sources that you can use with Spark out of the box as well as the countless other sources built by the greater community. Spark has six "core" data sources and hundreds of external data sources written by the community. The ability to read and write from all different kinds of data sources and for the community to create its own contributions is arguably one of Spark's greatest strengths. Following are Spark's core data sources:

- CSV
- JSON
- Parquet
- ORC
- JDBC/ODBC connections
- Plain-text files

As mentioned, Spark has numerous community-created data sources. Here's just a small sample:

- Cassandra (*http://bit.ly/2DSafT8*)
- HBase (*http://bit.ly/2FkKN5A*)
- MongoDB (*http://bit.ly/2BwA7yq*)
- AWS Redshift (*http://bit.ly/2GlMsJE*)
- XML (*http://bit.ly/2GitGCK*)
- And many, many others

The goal of this chapter is to give you the ability to read and write from Spark's core data sources and know enough to understand what you should look for when integrating with third-party data sources. To achieve this, we will focus on the core concepts that you need to be able to recognize and understand.

The Structure of the Data Sources API

Before proceeding with how to read and write from certain formats, let's visit the overall organizational structure of the data source APIs.

Read API Structure

The core structure for reading data is as follows:

```
DataFrameReader.format(...).option("key", "value").schema(...).load()
```

We will use this format to read from all of our data sources. `format` is optional because by default Spark will use the Parquet format. `option` allows you to set key-value configurations to parameterize how you will read data. Lastly, `schema` is optional if the data source provides a schema or if you intend to use schema inference. Naturally, there are some required options for each format, which we will discuss when we look at each format.

There is a lot of shorthand notation in the Spark community, and the data source read API is no exception. We try to be consistent throughout the book while still revealing some of the shorthand notation along the way.

Basics of Reading Data

The foundation for reading data in Spark is the `DataFrameReader`. We access this through the `SparkSession` via the `read` attribute:

```
spark.read
```

After we have a DataFrame reader, we specify several values:

- The *format*
- The *schema*
- The *read mode*
- A series of *options*

The format, options, and schema each return a `DataFrameReader` that can undergo further transformations and are all optional, except for one option. Each data source has a specific set of options that determine how the data is read into Spark (we cover these options shortly). At a minimum, you must supply the `DataFrameReader` a path to from which to read.

Here's an example of the overall layout:

```
spark.read.format("csv")
  .option("mode", "FAILFAST")
  .option("inferSchema", "true")
  .option("path", "path/to/file(s)")
  .schema(someSchema)
  .load()
```

There are a variety of ways in which you can set options; for example, you can build a map and pass in your configurations. For now, we'll stick to the simple and explicit way that you just saw.

Read modes

Reading data from an external source naturally entails encountering malformed data, especially when working with only semi-structured data sources. Read modes specify what will happen when Spark does come across malformed records. Table 9-1 lists the read modes.

Table 9-1. Spark's read modes

Read mode	Description
permissive	Sets all fields to `null` when it encounters a corrupted record and places all corrupted records in a string column called `_corrupt_record`
dropMalformed	Drops the row that contains malformed records
failFast	Fails immediately upon encountering malformed records

The default is `permissive`.

Write API Structure

The core structure for writing data is as follows:

```
DataFrameWriter.format(...).option(...).partitionBy(...).bucketBy(...).sortBy(
  ...).save()
```

We will use this format to write to all of our data sources. `format` is optional because by default, Spark will use the arquet format. `option`, again, allows us to configure how to write out our given data. `PartitionBy`, `bucketBy`, and `sortBy` work only for file-based data sources; you can use them to control the specific layout of files at the destination.

Basics of Writing Data

The foundation for writing data is quite similar to that of reading data. Instead of the `DataFrameReader`, we have the `DataFrameWriter`. Because we always need to write out some given data source, we access the `DataFrameWriter` on a per-`DataFrame` basis via the `write` attribute:

```scala
// in Scala
dataFrame.write
```

After we have a `DataFrameWriter`, we specify three values: the `format`, a series of `options`, and the `save` mode. At a minimum, you must supply a path. We will cover the potential for options, which vary from data source to data source, shortly.

```scala
// in Scala
dataframe.write.format("csv")
  .option("mode", "OVERWRITE")
  .option("dateFormat", "yyyy-MM-dd")
  .option("path", "path/to/file(s)")
  .save()
```

Save modes

Save modes specify what will happen if Spark finds data at the specified location (assuming all else equal). Table 9-2 lists the save modes.

Table 9-2. Spark's save modes

Save mode	Description
append	Appends the output files to the list of files that already exist at that location
overwrite	Will completely overwrite any data that already exists there
errorIfExists	Throws an error and fails the write if data or files already exist at the specified location
ignore	If data or files exist at the location, do nothing with the current DataFrame

The default is `errorIfExists`. This means that if Spark finds data at the location to which you're writing, it will fail the write immediately.

We've largely covered the core concepts that you're going to need when using data sources, so now let's dive into each of Spark's native data sources.

CSV Files

CSV stands for commma-separated values. This is a common text file format in which each line represents a single record, and commas separate each field within a record. CSV files, while seeming well structured, are actually one of the trickiest file formats you will encounter because not many assumptions can be made in production scenarios about what they contain or how they are structured. For this reason, the CSV reader has a large number of options. These options give you the ability to work around issues like certain characters needing to be escaped—for example, commas inside of columns when the file is also comma-delimited or `null` values labeled in an unconventional way.

CSV Options

Table 9-3 presents the options available in the CSV reader.

Table 9-3. CSV data source options

Read/write	Key	Potential values	Default	Description
Both	sep	Any single string character	,	The single character that is used as separator for each field and value.
Both	header	true, false	false	A Boolean flag that declares whether the first line in the file(s) are the names of the columns.
Read	escape	Any string character	\	The character Spark should use to escape other characters in the file.
Read	inferSchema	true, false	false	Specifies whether Spark should infer column types when reading the file.
Read	ignoreLeadingWhiteSpace	true, false	false	Declares whether leading spaces from values being read should be skipped.
Read	ignoreTrailingWhiteSpace	true, false	false	Declares whether trailing spaces from values being read should be skipped.
Both	nullValue	Any string character	""	Declares what character represents a `null` value in the file.
Both	nanValue	Any string character	NaN	Declares what character represents a NaN or missing character in the CSV file.
Both	positiveInf	Any string or character	Inf	Declares what character(s) represent a positive infinite value.
Both	negativeInf	Any string or character	-Inf	Declares what character(s) represent a negative infinite value.

Read/write	Key	Potential values	Default	Description
Both	compression or codec	None, uncom pressed, bzip2, deflate, gzip, lz4, or snappy	none	Declares what compression codec Spark should use to read or write the file.
Both	dateFormat	Any string or character that conforms to java's SimpleDataFor mat.	yyyy-MM-dd	Declares the date format for any columns that are date type.
Both	timestampFormat	Any string or character that conforms to java's SimpleDataFor mat.	yyyy-MM-dd'T'HH:mm :ss.SSSZZ	Declares the timestamp format for any columns that are timestamp type.
Read	maxColumns	Any integer	20480	Declares the maximum number of columns in the file.
Read	maxCharsPerColumn	Any integer	1000000	Declares the maximum number of characters in a column.
Read	escapeQuotes	true, false	true	Declares whether Spark should escape quotes that are found in lines.
Read	maxMalformedLogPerPartition	Any integer	10	Sets the maximum number of malformed rows Spark will log for each partition. Malformed records beyond this number will be ignored.
Write	quoteAll	true, false	false	Specifies whether all values should be enclosed in quotes, as opposed to just escaping values that have a quote character.
Read	multiLine	true, false	false	This option allows you to read multiline CSV files where each logical row in the CSV file might span multiple rows in the file itself.

Reading CSV Files

To read a CSV file, like any other format, we must first create a DataFrameReader for that specific format. Here, we specify the format to be CSV:

```
spark.read.format("csv")
```

After this, we have the option of specifying a schema as well as modes as options. Let's set a couple of options, some that we saw from the beginning of the book and others that we haven't seen yet. We'll set the header to true for our CSV file, the mode to be FAILFAST, and inferSchema to true:

```scala
// in Scala
spark.read.format("csv")
  .option("header", "true")
  .option("mode", "FAILFAST")
  .option("inferSchema", "true")
  .load("some/path/to/file.csv")
```

As mentioned, we can use the mode to specify how much tolerance we have for malformed data. For example, we can use these modes and the schema that we created in Chapter 5 to ensure that our file(s) conform to the data that we expected:

```scala
// in Scala
import org.apache.spark.sql.types.{StructField, StructType, StringType, LongType}
val myManualSchema = new StructType(Array(
  new StructField("DEST_COUNTRY_NAME", StringType, true),
  new StructField("ORIGIN_COUNTRY_NAME", StringType, true),
  new StructField("count", LongType, false)
))
spark.read.format("csv")
  .option("header", "true")
  .option("mode", "FAILFAST")
  .schema(myManualSchema)
  .load("/data/flight-data/csv/2010-summary.csv")
  .show(5)
```

Things get tricky when we don't expect our data to be in a certain format, but it comes in that way, anyhow. For example, let's take our current schema and change all column types to LongType. This does not match the *actual* schema, but Spark has no problem with us doing this. The problem will only manifest itself when Spark actually reads the data. As soon as we start our Spark job, it will immediately fail (after we execute a job) due to the data not conforming to the specified schema:

```scala
// in Scala
val myManualSchema = new StructType(Array(
                     new StructField("DEST_COUNTRY_NAME", LongType, true),
                     new StructField("ORIGIN_COUNTRY_NAME", LongType, true),
                     new StructField("count", LongType, false) ))

spark.read.format("csv")
  .option("header", "true")
  .option("mode", "FAILFAST")
  .schema(myManualSchema)
  .load("/data/flight-data/csv/2010-summary.csv")
  .take(5)
```

In general, Spark will fail only at job execution time rather than DataFrame definition time—even if, for example, we point to a file that does not exist. This is due to *lazy evaluation*, a concept we learned about in Chapter 2.

Writing CSV Files

Just as with reading data, there are a variety of options (listed in Table 9-3) for writing data when we write CSV files. This is a subset of the reading options because many do not apply when writing data (like maxColumns and inferSchema). Here's an example:

```scala
// in Scala
val csvFile = spark.read.format("csv")
  .option("header", "true").option("mode", "FAILFAST").schema(myManualSchema)
  .load("/data/flight-data/csv/2010-summary.csv")
```

```python
# in Python
csvFile = spark.read.format("csv")\
  .option("header", "true")\
  .option("mode", "FAILFAST")\
  .option("inferSchema", "true")\
  .load("/data/flight-data/csv/2010-summary.csv")
```

For instance, we can take our CSV file and write it out as a TSV file quite easily:

```scala
// in Scala
csvFile.write.format("csv").mode("overwrite").option("sep", "\t")
  .save("/tmp/my-tsv-file.tsv")
```

```python
# in Python
csvFile.write.format("csv").mode("overwrite").option("sep", "\t")\
  .save("/tmp/my-tsv-file.tsv")
```

When you list the destination directory, you can see that *my-tsv-file* is actually a folder with numerous files within it:

```
$ ls /tmp/my-tsv-file.tsv/

/tmp/my-tsv-file.tsv/part-00000-35cf9453-1943-4a8c-9c82-9f6ea9742b29.csv
```

This actually reflects the number of partitions in our DataFrame at the time we write it out. If we were to repartition our data before then, we would end up with a different number of files. We discuss this trade-off at the end of this chapter.

JSON Files

Those coming from the world of JavaScript are likely familiar with JavaScript Object Notation, or JSON, as it's commonly called. There are some catches when working with this kind of data that are worth considering before we jump in. In Spark, when we refer to JSON files, we refer to *line-delimited* JSON files. This contrasts with files that have a large JSON object or array per file.

The line-delimited versus multiline trade-off is controlled by a single option: multiLine. When you set this option to true, you can read an entire file as one json object and Spark will go through the work of parsing that into a DataFrame. Line-delimited JSON is actually a much more stable format because it allows you to append to a file with a new record (rather than having to read in an entire file and then write it out), which is what we recommend that you use. Another key reason for the popularity of line-delimited JSON is because JSON objects have structure, and JavaScript (on which JSON is based) has at least basic types. This makes it easier to work with because Spark can make more assumptions on our behalf about the data. You'll notice that there are significantly less options than we saw for CSV because of the objects.

JSON Options

Table 9-4 lists the options available for the JSON object, along with their descriptions.

Table 9-4. JSON data source options

Read/write	Key	Potential values	Default	Description
Both	compression or codec	None, uncompressed, bzip2, deflate, gzip, lz4, or snappy	none	Declares what compression codec Spark should use to read or write the file.
Both	dateFormat	Any string or character that conforms to Java's SimpleDataFormat.	yyyy-MM-dd	Declares the date format for any columns that are date type.
Both	timestampFormat	Any string or character that conforms to Java's SimpleDataFormat.	yyyy-MM-dd'T'HH:mm:ss.SSSZZ	Declares the timestamp format for any columns that are timestamp type.
Read	primitiveAsString	true, false	false	Infers all primitive values as string type.
Read	allowComments	true, false	false	Ignores Java/C++ style comment in JSON records.
Read	allowUnquotedFieldNames	true, false	false	Allows unquoted JSON field names.
Read	allowSingleQuotes	true, false	true	Allows single quotes in addition to double quotes.
Read	allowNumericLeadingZeros	true, false	false	Allows leading zeroes in numbers (e.g., 00012).
Read	allowBackslashEscapingAnyCharacter	true, false	false	Allows accepting quoting of all characters using backslash quoting mechanism.

Read/write	Key	Potential values	Default	Description
Read	columnNameOfCorruptRecord	Any string	Value of spark.sql.col umn&NameOfCor ruptRecord	Allows renaming the new field having a malformed string created by permissive mode. This will override the configuration value.
Read	multiLine	true, false	false	Allows for reading in non-line-delimited JSON files.

Now, reading a line-delimited JSON file varies only in the format and the options that we specify:

```
spark.read.format("json")
```

Reading JSON Files

Let's look at an example of reading a JSON file and compare the options that we're seeing:

```
// in Scala
spark.read.format("json").option("mode", "FAILFAST").schema(myManualSchema)
  .load("/data/flight-data/json/2010-summary.json").show(5)

# in Python
spark.read.format("json").option("mode", "FAILFAST")\
  .option("inferSchema", "true")\
  .load("/data/flight-data/json/2010-summary.json").show(5)
```

Writing JSON Files

Writing JSON files is just as simple as reading them, and, as you might expect, the data source does not matter. Therefore, we can reuse the CSV DataFrame that we created earlier to be the source for our JSON file. This, too, follows the rules that we specified before: one file per partition will be written out, and the entire DataFrame will be written out as a folder. It will also have one JSON object per line:

```
// in Scala
csvFile.write.format("json").mode("overwrite").save("/tmp/my-json-file.json")

# in Python
csvFile.write.format("json").mode("overwrite").save("/tmp/my-json-file.json")

$ ls /tmp/my-json-file.json/

/tmp/my-json-file.json/part-00000-tid-543....json
```

Parquet Files

Parquet is an open source column-oriented data store that provides a variety of storage optimizations, especially for analytics workloads. It provides columnar compression, which saves storage space and allows for reading individual columns instead of entire files. It is a file format that works exceptionally well with Apache Spark and is in fact the default file format. We recommend writing data out to Parquet for long-term storage because reading from a Parquet file will always be more efficient than JSON or CSV. Another advantage of Parquet is that it supports complex types. This means that if your column is an array (which would fail with a CSV file, for example), map, or struct, you'll still be able to read and write that file without issue. Here's how to specify Parquet as the read format:

```
spark.read.format("parquet")
```

Reading Parquet Files

Parquet has very few options because it enforces its own schema when storing data. Thus, all you need to set is the format and you are good to go. We can set the schema if we have strict requirements for what our DataFrame should look like. Oftentimes this is not necessary because we can use schema on read, which is similar to the infer Schema with CSV files. However, with Parquet files, this method is more powerful because the schema is built into the file itself (so no inference needed).

Here are some simple examples reading from parquet:

```
spark.read.format("parquet")
// in Scala
spark.read.format("parquet")
  .load("/data/flight-data/parquet/2010-summary.parquet").show(5)

# in Python
spark.read.format("parquet")\
  .load("/data/flight-data/parquet/2010-summary.parquet").show(5)
```

Parquet options

As we just mentioned, there are very few Parquet options—precisely two, in fact—because it has a well-defined specification that aligns closely with the concepts in Spark. Table 9-5 presents the options.

Even though there are only two options, you can still encounter problems if you're working with incompatible Parquet files. Be careful when you write out Parquet files with different versions of Spark (especially older ones) because this can cause significant headache.

Table 9-5. Parquet data source options

Read/Write	Key	Potential Values	Default	Description
Write	compression or codec	None, uncompressed, bzip2, deflate, gzip, lz4, or snappy	None	Declares what compression codec Spark should use to read or write the file.
Read	mergeSchema	true, false	Value of the configuration spark.sql.parquet.mergeSchema	You can incrementally add columns to newly written Parquet files in the same table/folder. Use this option to enable or disable this feature.

Writing Parquet Files

Writing Parquet is as easy as reading it. We simply specify the location for the file. The same partitioning rules apply:

```scala
// in Scala
csvFile.write.format("parquet").mode("overwrite")
  .save("/tmp/my-parquet-file.parquet")
```

```python
# in Python
csvFile.write.format("parquet").mode("overwrite")\
  .save("/tmp/my-parquet-file.parquet")
```

ORC Files

ORC is a self-describing, type-aware columnar file format designed for Hadoop workloads. It is optimized for large streaming reads, but with integrated support for finding required rows quickly. ORC actually has no options for reading in data because Spark understands the file format quite well. An often-asked question is: What is the difference between ORC and Parquet? For the most part, they're quite similar; the fundamental difference is that Parquet is further optimized for use with Spark, whereas ORC is further optimized for Hive.

Reading Orc Files

Here's how to read an ORC file into Spark:

```scala
// in Scala
spark.read.format("orc").load("/data/flight-data/orc/2010-summary.orc").show(5)
```

```python
# in Python
spark.read.format("orc").load("/data/flight-data/orc/2010-summary.orc").show(5)
```

Writing Orc Files

At this point in the chapter, you should feel pretty comfortable taking a guess at how to write ORC files. It really follows the exact same pattern that we have seen so far, in which we specify the format and then save the file:

```scala
// in Scala
csvFile.write.format("orc").mode("overwrite").save("/tmp/my-json-file.orc")
```

```python
# in Python
csvFile.write.format("orc").mode("overwrite").save("/tmp/my-json-file.orc")
```

SQL Databases

SQL datasources are one of the more powerful connectors because there are a variety of systems to which you can connect (as long as that system speaks SQL). For instance you can connect to a MySQL database, a PostgreSQL database, or an Oracle database. You also can connect to SQLite, which is what we'll do in this example. Of course, databases aren't just a set of raw files, so there are more options to consider regarding *how* you connect to the database. Namely you're going to need to begin considering things like authentication and connectivity (you'll need to determine whether the network of your Spark cluster is connected to the network of your database system).

To avoid the distraction of setting up a database for the purposes of this book, we provide a reference sample that runs on SQLite. We can skip a lot of these details by using SQLite, because it can work with minimal setup on your local machine with the limitation of not being able to work in a distributed setting. If you want to work through these examples in a distributed setting, you'll want to connect to another kind of database.

A Primer on SQLite

SQLite is the most used database engine in the entire world (*https://sqlite.org/*), and for good reason. It's powerful, fast, and easy to understand. This is because a SQLite database is just a file. That's going to make it very easy for you to get up and running because we include the source file in the official repository for this book (*https://github.com/databricks/Spark-The-Definitive-Guide/tree/master/data/flight-data/jdbc*). Simply download that file to your local machine, and you will be able to read from it and write to it. We're using SQLite, but all of the code here works with more traditional relational databases, as well, like MySQL. The primary difference is in the properties that you include when you connect to the database. When we're working with SQLite, there's no notion of user or password.

Although SQLite makes for a good reference example, it's probablu not what you want to use in production. Also, SQLite will not necessarily work well in a distributed setting because of its requirement to lock the entire database on write. The example we present here will work in a similar way using MySQL or PostgreSQL, as well.

To read and write from these databases, you need to do two things: include the Java Database Connectivity (JDBC) driver for you particular database on the spark classpath, and provide the proper JAR for the driver itself. For example, to be able to read and write from PostgreSQL, you might run something like this:

```
./bin/spark-shell \
--driver-class-path postgresql-9.4.1207.jar \
--jars postgresql-9.4.1207.jar
```

Just as with our other sources, there are a number of options that are available when reading from and writing to SQL databases. Only some of these are relevant for our current example, but Table 9-6 lists all of the options that you can set when working with JDBC databases.

Table 9-6. JDBC data source options

Property Name	Meaning
url	The JDBC URL to which to connect. The source-specific connection properties can be specified in the URL; for example, *jdbc:postgresql://localhost/test?user=fred&password=secret*.
dbtable	The JDBC table to read. Note that anything that is valid in a FROM clause of a SQL query can be used. For example, instead of a full table you could also use a subquery in parentheses.
driver	The class name of the JDBC driver to use to connect to this URL.
partitionColumn, lowerBound, upperBound	If any one of these options is specified, then all others must be set as well. In addition, numPartitions must be specified. These properties describe how to partition the table when reading in parallel from multiple workers. partitionColumn must be a numeric column from the table in question. Notice that lowerBound and upperBound are used only to decide the partition stride, not for filtering the rows in the table. Thus, all rows in the table will be partitioned and returned. This option applies only to reading.
numPartitions	The maximum number of partitions that can be used for parallelism in table reading and writing. This also determines the maximum number of concurrent JDBC connections. If the number of partitions to write exceeds this limit, we decrease it to this limit by calling coalesce(numPartitions) before writing.
fetchsize	The JDBC fetch size, which determines how many rows to fetch per round trip. This can help performance on JDBC drivers, which default to low fetch size (e.g., Oracle with 10 rows). This option applies only to reading.
batchsize	The JDBC batch size, which determines how many rows to insert per round trip. This can help performance on JDBC drivers. This option applies only to writing. The default is 1000.

Property Name	Meaning
isolationLevel	The transaction isolation level, which applies to current connection. It can be one of NONE, READ_COMMITTED, READ_UNCOMMITTED, REPEATABLE_READ, or SERIALIZABLE, corresponding to standard transaction isolation levels defined by JDBC's Connection object. The default is READ_UNCOMMITTED. This option applies only to writing. For more information, refer to the documentation in java.sql.Connection.
truncate	This is a JDBC writer-related option. When SaveMode.Overwrite is enabled, Spark truncates an existing table instead of dropping and re-creating it. This can be more efficient, and it prevents the table metadata (e.g., indices) from being removed. However, it will not work in some cases, such as when the new data has a different schema. The default is false. This option applies only to writing.
createTableOptions	This is a JDBC writer-related option. If specified, this option allows setting of database-specific table and partition options when creating a table (e.g., CREATE TABLE t (*name string*) ENGINE=InnoDB). This option applies only to writing.
createTableColumn Types	The database column data types to use instead of the defaults, when creating the table. Data type information should be specified in the same format as CREATE TABLE columns syntax (e.g., "name CHAR(64), comments VARCHAR(1024)"). The specified types should be valid Spark SQL data types. This option applies only to writing.

Reading from SQL Databases

When it comes to reading a file, SQL databases are no different from the other data sources that we looked at earlier. As with those sources, we specify the format and options, and then load in the data:

```scala
// in Scala
val driver = "org.sqlite.JDBC"
val path = "/data/flight-data/jdbc/my-sqlite.db"
val url = s"jdbc:sqlite:/${path}"
val tablename = "flight_info"
```

```python
# in Python
driver = "org.sqlite.JDBC"
path = "/data/flight-data/jdbc/my-sqlite.db"
url = "jdbc:sqlite:" + path
tablename = "flight_info"
```

After you have defined the connection properties, you can test your connection to the database itself to ensure that it is functional. This is an excellent troubleshooting technique to confirm that your database is available to (at the very least) the Spark driver. This is much less relevant for SQLite because that is a file on your machine but if you were using something like MySQL, you could test the connection with the following:

```scala
import java.sql.DriverManager
val connection = DriverManager.getConnection(url)
connection.isClosed()
connection.close()
```

If this connection succeeds, you're good to go. Let's go ahead and read the DataFrame from the SQL table:

```scala
// in Scala
val dbDataFrame = spark.read.format("jdbc").option("url", url)
  .option("dbtable", tablename).option("driver",  driver).load()
```

```python
# in Python
dbDataFrame = spark.read.format("jdbc").option("url", url)\
  .option("dbtable", tablename).option("driver",  driver).load()
```

SQLite has rather simple configurations (no users, for example). Other databases, like PostgreSQL, require more configuration parameters. Let's perform the same read that we just performed, except using PostgreSQL this time:

```scala
// in Scala
val pgDF = spark.read
  .format("jdbc")
  .option("driver", "org.postgresql.Driver")
  .option("url", "jdbc:postgresql://database_server")
  .option("dbtable", "schema.tablename")
  .option("user", "username").option("password","my-secret-password").load()
```

```python
# in Python
pgDF = spark.read.format("jdbc")\
  .option("driver", "org.postgresql.Driver")\
  .option("url", "jdbc:postgresql://database_server")\
  .option("dbtable", "schema.tablename")\
  .option("user", "username").option("password", "my-secret-password").load()
```

As we create this DataFrame, it is no different from any other: you can query it, transform it, and join it without issue. You'll also notice that there is already a schema, as well. That's because Spark gathers this information from the table itself and maps the types to Spark data types. Let's get only the distinct locations to verify that we can query it as expected:

```
dbDataFrame.select("DEST_COUNTRY_NAME").distinct().show(5)

+-----------------+
|DEST_COUNTRY_NAME|
+-----------------+
|         Anguilla|
|           Russia|
|         Paraguay|
|          Senegal|
|           Sweden|
+-----------------+
```

Awesome, we can query the database! Before we proceed, there are a couple of nuanced details that are worth understanding.

Query Pushdown

First, Spark makes a best-effort attempt to filter data in the database itself before creating the DataFrame. For example, in the previous sample query, we can see from the query plan that it selects only the relevant column name from the table:

```
dbDataFrame.select("DEST_COUNTRY_NAME").distinct().explain

== Physical Plan ==
*HashAggregate(keys=[DEST_COUNTRY_NAME#8108], functions=[])
+- Exchange hashpartitioning(DEST_COUNTRY_NAME#8108, 200)
   +- *HashAggregate(keys=[DEST_COUNTRY_NAME#8108], functions=[])
      +- *Scan JDBCRelation(flight_info) [numPartitions=1] ...
```

Spark can actually do better than this on certain queries. For example, if we specify a filter on our DataFrame, Spark will push that filter down into the database. We can see this in the explain plan under `PushedFilters`.

```
// in Scala
dbDataFrame.filter("DEST_COUNTRY_NAME in ('Anguilla', 'Sweden')").explain

# in Python
dbDataFrame.filter("DEST_COUNTRY_NAME in ('Anguilla', 'Sweden')").explain()

== Physical Plan ==
*Scan JDBCRel... PushedFilters: [*In(DEST_COUNTRY_NAME, [Anguilla,Sweden])],
...
```

Spark can't translate all of its own functions into the functions available in the SQL database in which you're working. Therefore, sometimes you're going to want to pass an entire query into your SQL that will return the results as a DataFrame. Now, this might seem like it's a bit complicated, but it's actually quite straightforward. Rather than specifying a table name, you just specify a SQL query. Of course, you do need to specify this in a special way; you must wrap the query in parenthesis and rename it to something—in this case, I just gave it the same table name:

```
// in Scala
val pushdownQuery = """(SELECT DISTINCT(DEST_COUNTRY_NAME) FROM flight_info)
  AS flight_info"""
val dbDataFrame = spark.read.format("jdbc")
  .option("url", url).option("dbtable", pushdownQuery).option("driver", driver)
  .load()

# in Python
pushdownQuery = """(SELECT DISTINCT(DEST_COUNTRY_NAME) FROM flight_info)
  AS flight_info"""
dbDataFrame = spark.read.format("jdbc")\
  .option("url", url).option("dbtable", pushdownQuery).option("driver", driver)\
  .load()
```

Now when you query this table, you'll actually be querying the results of that query. We can see this in the explain plan. Spark doesn't even know about the actual schema of the table, just the one that results from our previous query:

```
dbDataFrame.explain()

== Physical Plan ==
*Scan JDBCRelation(
(SELECT DISTINCT(DEST_COUNTRY_NAME)
  FROM flight_info) as flight_info
) [numPartitions=1] [DEST_COUNTRY_NAME#788] ReadSchema: ...
```

Reading from databases in parallel

All throughout this book, we have talked about partitioning and its importance in data processing. Spark has an underlying algorithm that can read multiple files into one partition, or conversely, read multiple partitions out of one file, depending on the file size and the "splitability" of the file type and compression. The same flexibility that exists with files, also exists with SQL databases except that you must configure it a bit more manually. What you can configure, as seen in the previous options, is the ability to specify a maximum number of partitions to allow you to limit how much you are reading and writing in parallel:

```scala
// in Scala
val dbDataFrame = spark.read.format("jdbc")
  .option("url", url).option("dbtable", tablename).option("driver", driver)
  .option("numPartitions", 10).load()
```

```python
# in Python
dbDataFrame = spark.read.format("jdbc")\
  .option("url", url).option("dbtable", tablename).option("driver", driver)\
  .option("numPartitions", 10).load()
```

In this case, this will still remain as one partition because there is not too much data. However, this configuration can help you ensure that you do not overwhelm the database when reading and writing data:

```
dbDataFrame.select("DEST_COUNTRY_NAME").distinct().show()
```

There are several other optimizations that unfortunately only seem to be under another API set. You can explicitly push predicates down into SQL databases through the connection itself. This optimization allows you to control the physical location of certain data in certain partitions by specifying predicates. That's a mouthful, so let's look at a simple example. We only need data from two countries in our data: Anguilla and Sweden. We could filter these down and have them pushed into the database, but we can also go further by having them arrive in their own partitions in Spark. We do that by specifying a list of predicates when we create the data source:

```scala
// in Scala
val props = new java.util.Properties
props.setProperty("driver", "org.sqlite.JDBC")
val predicates = Array(
  "DEST_COUNTRY_NAME = 'Sweden' OR ORIGIN_COUNTRY_NAME = 'Sweden'",
  "DEST_COUNTRY_NAME = 'Anguilla' OR ORIGIN_COUNTRY_NAME = 'Anguilla'")
```

```
spark.read.jdbc(url, tablename, predicates, props).show()
spark.read.jdbc(url, tablename, predicates, props).rdd.getNumPartitions // 2

# in Python
props = {"driver":"org.sqlite.JDBC"}
predicates = [
  "DEST_COUNTRY_NAME = 'Sweden' OR ORIGIN_COUNTRY_NAME = 'Sweden'",
  "DEST_COUNTRY_NAME = 'Anguilla' OR ORIGIN_COUNTRY_NAME = 'Anguilla'"]
spark.read.jdbc(url, tablename, predicates=predicates, properties=props).show()
spark.read.jdbc(url,tablename,predicates=predicates,properties=props)\
  .rdd.getNumPartitions() # 2

+-----------------+-------------------+-----+
|DEST_COUNTRY_NAME|ORIGIN_COUNTRY_NAME|count|
+-----------------+-------------------+-----+
|           Sweden|      United States|   65|
|    United States|             Sweden|   73|
|         Anguilla|      United States|   21|
|    United States|           Anguilla|   20|
+-----------------+-------------------+-----+
```

If you specify predicates that are not disjoint, you can end up with lots of duplicate rows. Here's an example set of predicates that will result in duplicate rows:

```
// in Scala
val props = new java.util.Properties
props.setProperty("driver", "org.sqlite.JDBC")
val predicates = Array(
  "DEST_COUNTRY_NAME != 'Sweden' OR ORIGIN_COUNTRY_NAME != 'Sweden'",
  "DEST_COUNTRY_NAME != 'Anguilla' OR ORIGIN_COUNTRY_NAME != 'Anguilla'")
spark.read.jdbc(url, tablename, predicates, props).count() // 510

# in Python
props = {"driver":"org.sqlite.JDBC"}
predicates = [
  "DEST_COUNTRY_NAME != 'Sweden' OR ORIGIN_COUNTRY_NAME != 'Sweden'",
  "DEST_COUNTRY_NAME != 'Anguilla' OR ORIGIN_COUNTRY_NAME != 'Anguilla'"]
spark.read.jdbc(url, tablename, predicates=predicates, properties=props).count()
```

Partitioning based on a sliding window

Let's take a look to see how we can partition based on predicates. In this example, we'll partition based on our numerical count column. Here, we specify a minimum and a maximum for both the first partition and last partition. Anything outside of these bounds will be in the first partition or final partition. Then, we set the number of partitions we would like total (this is the level of parallelism). Spark then queries our database in parallel and returns numPartitions partitions. We simply modify the upper and lower bounds in order to place certain values in certain partitions. No filtering is taking place like we saw in the previous example:

```
// in Scala
val colName = "count"
```

```
val lowerBound = 0L
val upperBound = 348113L // this is the max count in our database
val numPartitions = 10

# in Python
colName = "count"
lowerBound = 0L
upperBound = 348113L # this is the max count in our database
numPartitions = 10
```

This will distribute the intervals equally from low to high:

```
// in Scala
spark.read.jdbc(url,tablename,colName,lowerBound,upperBound,numPartitions,props)
  .count() // 255

# in Python
spark.read.jdbc(url, tablename, column=colName, properties=props,
                lowerBound=lowerBound, upperBound=upperBound,
                numPartitions=numPartitions).count() # 255
```

Writing to SQL Databases

Writing out to SQL databases is just as easy as before. You simply specify the URI and write out the data according to the specified write mode that you want. In the following example, we specify overwrite, which overwrites the entire table. We'll use the CSV DataFrame that we defined earlier in order to do this:

```
// in Scala
val newPath = "jdbc:sqlite://tmp/my-sqlite.db"
csvFile.write.mode("overwrite").jdbc(newPath, tablename, props)

# in Python
newPath = "jdbc:sqlite://tmp/my-sqlite.db"
csvFile.write.jdbc(newPath, tablename, mode="overwrite", properties=props)
```

Let's look at the results:

```
// in Scala
spark.read.jdbc(newPath, tablename, props).count() // 255

# in Python
spark.read.jdbc(newPath, tablename, properties=props).count() # 255
```

Of course, we can append to the table this new table just as easily:

```
// in Scala
csvFile.write.mode("append").jdbc(newPath, tablename, props)

# in Python
csvFile.write.jdbc(newPath, tablename, mode="append", properties=props)
```

Notice that count increases:

```
// in Scala
spark.read.jdbc(newPath, tablename, props).count() // 765
```

```python
# in Python
spark.read.jdbc(newPath, tablename, properties=props).count() # 765
```

Text Files

Spark also allows you to read in plain-text files. Each line in the file becomes a record in the DataFrame. It is then up to you to transform it accordingly. As an example of how you would do this, suppose that you need to parse some Apache log files to some more structured format, or perhaps you want to parse some plain text for natural-language processing. Text files make a great argument for the Dataset API due to its ability to take advantage of the flexibility of native types.

Reading Text Files

Reading text files is straightforward: you simply specify the type to be `textFile`. With `textFile`, partitioned directory names are ignored. To read and write text files according to partitions, you should use `text`, which respects partitioning on reading and writing:

```
spark.read.textFile("/data/flight-data/csv/2010-summary.csv")
  .selectExpr("split(value, ',') as rows").show()
```

```
+--------------------+
|                rows|
+--------------------+
|[DEST_COUNTRY_NAM...|
|[United States, R...|
...
|[United States, A...|
|[Saint Vincent an...|
|[Italy, United St...|
+--------------------+
```

Writing Text Files

When you write a text file, you need to be sure to have only one string column; otherwise, the write will fail:

```
csvFile.select("DEST_COUNTRY_NAME").write.text("/tmp/simple-text-file.txt")
```

If you perform some partitioning when performing your write (we'll discuss partitioning in the next couple of pages), you can write more columns. However, those columns will manifest as directories in the folder to which you're writing out to, instead of columns on every single file:

```scala
// in Scala
csvFile.limit(10).select("DEST_COUNTRY_NAME", "count")
  .write.partitionBy("count").text("/tmp/five-csv-files2.csv")
```

```python
# in Python
csvFile.limit(10).select("DEST_COUNTRY_NAME", "count")\
  .write.partitionBy("count").text("/tmp/five-csv-files2py.csv")
```

Advanced I/O Concepts

We saw previously that we can control the parallelism of files that we write by controlling the partitions prior to writing. We can also control specific data layout by controlling two things: *bucketing* and *partitioning* (discussed momentarily).

Splittable File Types and Compression

Certain file formats are fundamentally "splittable." This can improve speed because it makes it possible for Spark to avoid reading an entire file, and access only the parts of the file necessary to satisfy your query. Additionally if you're using something like Hadoop Distributed File System (HDFS), splitting a file can provide further optimization if that file spans multiple blocks. In conjunction with this is a need to manage compression. Not all compression schemes are splittable. How you store your data is of immense consequence when it comes to making your Spark jobs run smoothly. We recommend Parquet with gzip compression.

Reading Data in Parallel

Multiple executors cannot read from the same file at the same time necessarily, but they can read different files at the same time. In general, this means that when you read from a folder with multiple files in it, each one of those files will become a partition in your DataFrame and be read in by available executors in parallel (with the remaining queueing up behind the others).

Writing Data in Parallel

The number of files or data written is dependent on the number of partitions the DataFrame has at the time you write out the data. By default, one file is written per partition of the data. This means that although we specify a "file," it's actually a number of files within a folder, with the name of the specified file, with one file per each partition that is written.

For example, the following code

```
csvFile.repartition(5).write.format("csv").save("/tmp/multiple.csv")
```

will end up with five files inside of that folder. As you can see from the list call:

```
ls /tmp/multiple.csv

/tmp/multiple.csv/part-00000-767df509-ec97-4740-8e15-4e173d365a8b.csv
/tmp/multiple.csv/part-00001-767df509-ec97-4740-8e15-4e173d365a8b.csv
```

```
/tmp/multiple.csv/part-00002-767df509-ec97-4740-8e15-4e173d365a8b.csv
/tmp/multiple.csv/part-00003-767df509-ec97-4740-8e15-4e173d365a8b.csv
/tmp/multiple.csv/part-00004-767df509-ec97-4740-8e15-4e173d365a8b.csv
```

Partitioning

Partitioning is a tool that allows you to control what data is stored (and where) as you write it. When you write a file to a partitioned directory (or table), you basically encode a column as a folder. What this allows you to do is skip lots of data when you go to read it in later, allowing you to read in only the data relevant to your problem instead of having to scan the complete dataset. These are supported for all file-based data sources:

```scala
// in Scala
csvFile.limit(10).write.mode("overwrite").partitionBy("DEST_COUNTRY_NAME")
  .save("/tmp/partitioned-files.parquet")
```

```python
# in Python
csvFile.limit(10).write.mode("overwrite").partitionBy("DEST_COUNTRY_NAME")\
  .save("/tmp/partitioned-files.parquet")
```

Upon writing, you get a list of folders in your Parquet "file":

```
$ ls /tmp/partitioned-files.parquet

...
DEST_COUNTRY_NAME=Costa Rica/
DEST_COUNTRY_NAME=Egypt/
DEST_COUNTRY_NAME=Equatorial Guinea/
DEST_COUNTRY_NAME=Senegal/
DEST_COUNTRY_NAME=United States/
```

Each of these will contain Parquet files that contain that data where the previous predicate was true:

```
$ ls /tmp/partitioned-files.parquet/DEST_COUNTRY_NAME=Senegal/

part-00000-tid.....parquet
```

This is probably the lowest-hanging optimization that you can use when you have a table that readers frequently filter by before manipulating. For instance, date is particularly common for a partition because, downstream, often we want to look at only the previous week's data (instead of scanning the entire list of records). This can provide massive speedups for readers.

Bucketing

Bucketing is another file organization approach with which you can control the data that is specifically written to each file. This can help avoid shuffles later when you go to read the data because data with the same bucket ID will all be grouped together into one physical partition. This means that the data is prepartitioned according to how you expect to use that data later on, meaning you can avoid expensive shuffles when joining or aggregating.

Rather than partitioning on a specific column (which might write out a ton of directories), it's probably worthwhile to explore bucketing the data instead. This will create a certain number of files and organize our data into those "buckets":

```
val numberBuckets = 10
val columnToBucketBy = "count"

csvFile.write.format("parquet").mode("overwrite")
  .bucketBy(numberBuckets, columnToBucketBy).saveAsTable("bucketedFiles")

$ ls /user/hive/warehouse/bucketedfiles/

part-00000-tid-1020575097626332666-8....parquet
part-00000-tid-1020575097626332666-8....parquet
part-00000-tid-1020575097626332666-8....parquet
...
```

Bucketing is supported only for Spark-managed tables. For more information on bucketing and partitioning, watch this talk (*https://spark-summit.org/2017/events/ why-you-should-care-about-data-layout-in-the-filesystem/*) from Spark Summit 2017.

Writing Complex Types

As we covered in Chapter 6, Spark has a variety of different internal types. Although Spark can work with all of these types, not every single type works well with every data file format. For instance, CSV files do not support complex types, whereas Parquet and ORC do.

Managing File Size

Managing file sizes is an important factor not so much for writing data but reading it later on. When you're writing lots of small files, there's a significant metadata overhead that you incur managing all of those files. Spark especially does not do well with small files, although many file systems (like HDFS) don't handle lots of small files well, either. You might hear this referred to as the "small file problem." The opposite is also true: you don't want files that are too large either, because it becomes inefficient to have to read entire blocks of data when you need only a few rows.

Spark 2.2 introduced a new method for controlling file sizes in a more automatic way. We saw previously that the number of output files is a derivative of the number of partitions we had at write time (and the partitioning columns we selected). Now, you can take advantage of another tool in order to limit output file sizes so that you can target an optimum file size. You can use the maxRecordsPerFile option and specify a number of your choosing. This allows you to better control file sizes by controlling the number of records that are written to each file. For example, if you set an option for a writer as `df.write.option("maxRecordsPerFile", 5000)`, Spark will ensure that files will contain at most 5,000 records.

Conclusion

In this chapter we discussed the variety of options available to you for reading and writing data in Spark. This covers nearly everything you'll need to know as an everyday user of Spark. For the curious, there are ways of implementing your own data source; however, we omitted instructions for how to do this because the API is currently evolving to better support Structured Streaming. If you're interested in seeing how to implement your own custom data sources, the Cassandra Connector (*https://github.com/datastax/spark-cassandra-connector*) is well organized and maintained and could provide a reference for the adventurous.

In Chapter 10, we discuss Spark SQL and how it interoperates with everything else we've seen so far in the Structured APIs.

Spark SQL

Spark SQL is arguably one of the most important and powerful features in Spark. This chapter introduces the core concepts in Spark SQL that you need to understand. This chapter will not rewrite the ANSI-SQL specification or enumerate every single kind of SQL expression. If you read any other parts of this book, you will notice that we try to include SQL code wherever we include DataFrame code to make it easy to cross-reference with code samples. Other examples are available in the appendix and reference sections.

In a nutshell, with Spark SQL you can run SQL queries against views or tables organized into databases. You also can use system functions or define user functions and analyze query plans in order to optimize their workloads. This integrates directly into the DataFrame and Dataset API, and as we saw in previous chapters, you can choose to express some of your data manipulations in SQL and others in DataFrames and they will compile to the same underlying code.

What Is SQL?

SQL or *Structured Query Language* is a domain-specific language for expressing relational operations over data. It is used in all relational databases, and many "NoSQL" databases create their SQL dialect in order to make working with their databases easier. SQL is everywhere, and even though tech pundits prophesized its death, it is an extremely resilient data tool that many businesses depend on. Spark implements a subset of ANSI SQL:2003 (*https://en.wikipedia.org/wiki/SQL:2003*). This SQL standard is one that is available in the majority of SQL databases and this support means that Spark successfully runs the popular benchmark TPC-DS (*http://www.tpc.org/default.asp*).

Big Data and SQL: Apache Hive

Before Spark's rise, Hive was the de facto big data SQL access layer. Originally developed at Facebook, Hive became an incredibly popular tool across industry for performing SQL operations on big data. In many ways it helped propel Hadoop into different industries because analysts could run SQL queries. Although Spark began as a general processing engine with Resilient Distributed Datasets (RDDs), a large cohort of users now use Spark SQL.

Big Data and SQL: Spark SQL

With the release of Spark 2.0, its authors created a superset of Hive's support, writing a native SQL parser that supports both ANSI-SQL as well as HiveQL queries. This, along with its unique interoperability with DataFrames, makes it a powerful tool for all sorts of companies. For example, in late 2016, Facebook announced that it had begun running Spark workloads (*https://code.facebook.com/posts/1671373793181703/apache-spark-scale-a-60-tb-production-use-case/*) and seeing large benefits in doing so. In the words of the blog post's authors:

> We challenged Spark to replace a pipeline that decomposed to hundreds of Hive jobs into a single Spark job. Through a series of performance and reliability improvements, we were able to scale Spark to handle one of our entity ranking data processing use cases in production.... The Spark-based pipeline produced significant performance improvements (4.5–6x CPU, 3–4x resource reservation, and ~5x latency) compared with the old Hive-based pipeline, and it has been running in production for several months.

The power of Spark SQL derives from several key facts: SQL analysts can now take advantage of Spark's computation abilities by plugging into the Thrift Server or Spark's SQL interface, whereas data engineers and scientists can use Spark SQL where appropriate in any data flow. This unifying API allows for data to be extracted with SQL, manipulated as a DataFrame, passed into one of Spark MLlibs' large-scale machine learning algorithms, written out to another data source, and everything in between.

Spark SQL is intended to operate as an online analytic processing (OLAP) database, not an online transaction processing (OLTP) database. This means that it is not intended to perform extremely low-latency queries. Even though support for in-place modifications is sure to be something that comes up in the future, it's not something that is currently available.

Spark's Relationship to Hive

Spark SQL has a great relationship with Hive because it can connect to Hive metastores. The Hive metastore is the way in which Hive maintains table information for use across sessions. With Spark SQL, you can connect to your Hive metastore (if you already have one) and access table metadata to reduce file listing when accessing information. This is popular for users who are migrating from a legacy Hadoop environment and beginning to run all their workloads using Spark.

The Hive metastore

To connect to the Hive metastore, there are several properties that you'll need. First, you need to set the Metastore version (`spark.sql.hive.metastore.version`) to correspond to the proper Hive metastore that you're accessing. By default, this value is 1.2.1. You also need to set `spark.sql.hive.metastore.jars` if you're going to change the way that the `HiveMetastoreClient` is initialized. Spark uses the default versions, but you can also specify Maven repositories or a classpath in the standard format for the Java Virtual Machine (JVM). In addition, you might need to supply proper class prefixes in order to communicate with different databases that store the Hive metastore. You'll set these as shared prefixes that both Spark and Hive will share (`spark.sql.hive.metastore.sharedPrefixes`).

If you're connecting to your own metastore, it's worth checking the documentation (*http://bit.ly/2DFlcrL*) for further updates and more information.

How to Run Spark SQL Queries

Spark provides several interfaces to execute SQL queries.

Spark SQL CLI

The Spark SQL CLI is a convenient tool with which you can make basic Spark SQL queries in local mode from the command line. Note that the Spark SQL CLI cannot communicate with the Thrift JDBC server. To start the Spark SQL CLI, run the following in the Spark directory:

```
./bin/spark-sql
```

You configure Hive by placing your *hive-site.xml*, *core-site.xml*, and *hdfs-site.xml* files in *conf/*. For a complete list of all available options, you can run `./bin/spark-sql --help`.

Spark's Programmatic SQL Interface

In addition to setting up a server, you can also execute SQL in an ad hoc manner via any of Spark's language APIs. You can do this via the method `sql` on the `SparkSes` sion object. This returns a DataFrame, as we will see later in this chapter. For example, in Python or Scala, we can run the following:

```
spark.sql("SELECT 1 + 1").show()
```

The command `spark.sql("SELECT 1 + 1")` returns a DataFrame that we can then evaluate programmatically. Just like other transformations, this will not be executed eagerly but lazily. This is an immensely powerful interface because there are some transformations that are much simpler to express in SQL code than in DataFrames.

You can express multiline queries quite simply by passing a multiline string into the function. For example, you could execute something like the following code in Python or Scala:

```
spark.sql("""SELECT user_id, department, first_name FROM professors
    WHERE department IN
        (SELECT name FROM department WHERE created_date >= '2016-01-01')""")
```

Even more powerful, you can completely interoperate between SQL and DataFrames, as you see fit. For instance, you can create a DataFrame, manipulate it with SQL, and then manipulate it again as a DataFrame. It's a powerful abstraction that you will likely find yourself using quite a bit:

```
// in Scala
spark.read.json("/data/flight-data/json/2015-summary.json")
    .createOrReplaceTempView("some_sql_view") // DF => SQL

spark.sql("""
SELECT DEST_COUNTRY_NAME, sum(count)
FROM some_sql_view GROUP BY DEST_COUNTRY_NAME
""")
    .where("DEST_COUNTRY_NAME like 'S%'").where("`sum(count)` > 10")
    .count() // SQL => DF

# in Python
spark.read.json("/data/flight-data/json/2015-summary.json")\
    .createOrReplaceTempView("some_sql_view") # DF => SQL

spark.sql("""
SELECT DEST_COUNTRY_NAME, sum(count)
FROM some_sql_view GROUP BY DEST_COUNTRY_NAME
""")\
    .where("DEST_COUNTRY_NAME like 'S%'").where("`sum(count)` > 10")\
    .count() # SQL => DF
```

SparkSQL Thrift JDBC/ODBC Server

Spark provides a Java Database Connectivity (JDBC) interface by which either you or a remote program connects to the Spark driver in order to execute Spark SQL queries. A common use case might be a for a business analyst to connect business intelligence software like Tableau to Spark. The Thrift JDBC/Open Database Connectivity

(ODBC) server implemented here corresponds to the HiveServer2 in Hive 1.2.1. You can test the JDBC server with the beeline script that comes with either Spark or Hive 1.2.1.

To start the JDBC/ODBC server, run the following in the Spark directory:

```
./sbin/start-thriftserver.sh
```

This script accepts all `bin/spark-submit` command-line options. To see all available options for configuring this Thrift Server, run `./sbin/start-thriftserver.sh --help`. By default, the server listens on localhost:10000. You can override this through environmental variables or system properties.

For environment configuration, use this:

```
export HIVE_SERVER2_THRIFT_PORT=<listening-port>
export HIVE_SERVER2_THRIFT_BIND_HOST=<listening-host>
./sbin/start-thriftserver.sh \
  --master <master-uri> \
  ...
```

For system properties:

```
./sbin/start-thriftserver.sh \
  --hiveconf hive.server2.thrift.port=<listening-port> \
  --hiveconf hive.server2.thrift.bind.host=<listening-host> \
  --master <master-uri>
  ...
```

You can then test this connection by running the following commands:

```
./bin/beeline
```

```
beeline> !connect jdbc:hive2://localhost:10000
```

Beeline will ask you for a username and password. In nonsecure mode, simply type the username on your machine and a blank password. For secure mode, follow the instructions given in the beeline documentation (*https://cwiki.apache.org/confluence/display/Hive/HiveServer2+Clients*).

Catalog

The highest level abstraction in Spark SQL is the Catalog. The Catalog is an abstraction for the storage of metadata about the data stored in your tables as well as other helpful things like databases, tables, functions, and views. The catalog is available in the `org.apache.spark.sql.catalog.Catalog` package and contains a number of helpful functions for doing things like listing tables, databases, and functions. We will talk about all of these things shortly. It's very self-explanatory to users, so we will omit the code samples here but it's really just another programmatic interface to Spark SQL. This chapter shows only the SQL being executed; thus, if you're using the programmatic interface, keep in mind that you need to wrap everything in a `spark.sql` function call to execute the relevant code.

Tables

To do anything useful with Spark SQL, you first need to define tables. Tables are logically equivalent to a DataFrame in that they are a structure of data against which you run commands. We can join tables, filter them, aggregate them, and perform different manipulations that we saw in previous chapters. The core difference between tables and DataFrames is this: you define DataFrames in the scope of a programming language, whereas you define tables within a database. This means that when you create a table (assuming you never changed the database), it will belong to the *default* database. We discuss databases more fully later on in the chapter.

An important thing to note is that in Spark 2.X, tables *always contain data*. There is no notion of a temporary table, only a view, which does not contain data. This is important because if you go to drop a table, you can risk losing the data when doing so.

Spark-Managed Tables

One important note is the concept of *managed* versus *unmanaged* tables. Tables store two important pieces of information. The data within the tables as well as the data about the tables; that is, the *metadata*. You can have Spark manage the metadata for a set of files as well as for the data. When you define a table from files on disk, you are defining an unmanaged table. When you use `saveAsTable` on a DataFrame, you are creating a managed table for which Spark will track of all of the relevant information.

This will read your table and write it out to a new location in Spark format. You can see this reflected in the new explain plan. In the explain plan, you will also notice that this writes to the default Hive warehouse location. You can set this by setting the `spark.sql.warehouse.dir` configuration to the directory of your choosing when you create your SparkSession. By default Spark sets this to `/user/hive/warehouse`:

Note in the results that a database is listed. Spark also has databases which we will discuss later in this chapter, but for now you should keep in mind that you can also see tables in a specific database by using the query `show tables IN databaseName`, where *databaseName* represents the name of the database that you want to query.

If you are running on a new cluster or local mode, this should return zero results.

Creating Tables

You can create tables from a variety of sources. Something fairly unique to Spark is the capability of reusing the entire Data Source API within SQL. This means that you do not need to define a table and then load data into it; Spark lets you create one on the fly. You can even specify all sorts of sophisticated options when you read in a file. For example, here's a simple way to read in the flight data we worked with in previous chapters:

```
CREATE TABLE flights (
  DEST_COUNTRY_NAME STRING, ORIGIN_COUNTRY_NAME STRING, count LONG)
USING JSON OPTIONS (path '/data/flight-data/json/2015-summary.json')
```

USING and STORED AS

The specification of the USING syntax in the previous example is of significant importance. If you do not specify the format, Spark will default to a Hive SerDe configuration. This has performance implications for future readers and writers because Hive SerDes are much slower than Spark's native serialization. Hive users can also use the STORED AS syntax to specify that this should be a Hive table.

You can also add comments to certain columns in a table, which can help other developers understand the data in the tables:

```
CREATE TABLE flights_csv (
  DEST_COUNTRY_NAME STRING,
  ORIGIN_COUNTRY_NAME STRING COMMENT "remember, the US will be most prevalent",
  count LONG)
USING csv OPTIONS (header true, path '/data/flight-data/csv/2015-summary.csv')
```

It is possible to create a table from a query as well:

```
CREATE TABLE flights_from_select USING parquet AS SELECT * FROM flights
```

In addition, you can specify to create a table only if it does not currently exist:

In this example, we are creating a Hive-compatible table because we did not explicitly specify the format via USING. We can also do the following:

```
CREATE TABLE IF NOT EXISTS flights_from_select
  AS SELECT * FROM flights
```

Finally, you can control the layout of the data by writing out a partitioned dataset, as we saw in Chapter 9:

```
CREATE TABLE partitioned_flights USING parquet PARTITIONED BY (DEST_COUNTRY_NAME)
AS SELECT DEST_COUNTRY_NAME, ORIGIN_COUNTRY_NAME, count FROM flights LIMIT 5
```

These tables will be available in Spark even through sessions; temporary tables do not currently exist in Spark. You must create a temporary view, which we demonstrate later in this chapter.

Creating External Tables

As we mentioned in the beginning of this chapter, Hive was one of the first big data SQL systems, and Spark SQL is completely compatible with Hive SQL (HiveQL) statements. One of the use cases that you might encounter is to port your legacy Hive statements to Spark SQL. Luckily, you can, for the most part, just copy and paste your Hive statements directly into Spark SQL. For example, in the example that follows, we create an *unmanaged table*. Spark will manage the table's metadata; however, the files are not managed by Spark at all. You create this table by using the CREATE EXTERNAL TABLE statement.

You can view any files that have already been defined by running the following command:

```
CREATE EXTERNAL TABLE hive_flights (
  DEST_COUNTRY_NAME STRING, ORIGIN_COUNTRY_NAME STRING, count LONG)
ROW FORMAT DELIMITED FIELDS TERMINATED BY ',' LOCATION '/data/flight-data-hive/'
```

You can also create an external table from a select clause:

```
CREATE EXTERNAL TABLE hive_flights_2
ROW FORMAT DELIMITED FIELDS TERMINATED BY ','
LOCATION '/data/flight-data-hive/' AS SELECT * FROM flights
```

Inserting into Tables

Insertions follow the standard SQL syntax:

```
INSERT INTO flights_from_select
  SELECT DEST_COUNTRY_NAME, ORIGIN_COUNTRY_NAME, count FROM flights LIMIT 20
```

You can optionally provide a partition specification if you want to write only into a certain partition. Note that a write will respect a partitioning scheme, as well (which may cause the above query to run quite slowly); however, it will add additional files only into the end partitions:

```
INSERT INTO partitioned_flights
  PARTITION (DEST_COUNTRY_NAME="UNITED STATES")
  SELECT count, ORIGIN_COUNTRY_NAME FROM flights
  WHERE DEST_COUNTRY_NAME='UNITED STATES' LIMIT 12
```

Describing Table Metadata

We saw earlier that you can add a comment when creating a table. You can view this by describing the table metadata, which will show us the relevant comment:

```
DESCRIBE TABLE flights_csv
```

You can also see the partitioning scheme for the data by using the following (note, however, that this works only on partitioned tables):

```
SHOW PARTITIONS partitioned_flights
```

Refreshing Table Metadata

Maintaining table metadata is an important task to ensure that you're reading from the most recent set of data. There are two commands to refresh table metadata. REFRESH TABLE refreshes all cached entries (essentially, files) associated with the table. If the table were previously cached, it would be cached lazily the next time it is scanned:

```
REFRESH table partitioned_flights
```

Another related command is REPAIR TABLE, which refreshes the partitions maintained in the catalog for that given table. This command's focus is on collecting new partition information—an example might be writing out a new partition manually and the need to repair the table accordingly:

```
MSCK REPAIR TABLE partitioned_flights
```

Dropping Tables

You cannot delete tables: you can only "drop" them. You can drop a table by using the DROP keyword. If you drop a managed table (e.g., flights_csv), both the data and the table definition will be removed:

```
DROP TABLE flights_csv;
```

Dropping a table deletes the data in the table, so you need to be very careful when doing this.

If you try to drop a table that does not exist, you will receive an error. To only delete a table if it already exists, use DROP TABLE IF EXISTS.

```
DROP TABLE IF EXISTS flights_csv;
```

This deletes the data in the table, so exercise caution when doing this.

Dropping unmanaged tables

If you are dropping an unmanaged table (e.g., hive_flights), no data will be removed but you will no longer be able to refer to this data by the table name.

Caching Tables

Just like DataFrames, you can cache and uncache tables. You simply specify which table you would like using the following syntax:

```
CACHE TABLE flights
```

Here's how you uncache them:

```
UNCACHE TABLE FLIGHTS
```

Views

Now that you created a table, another thing that you can define is a view. A view specifies a set of transformations on top of an existing table—basically just saved query plans, which can be convenient for organizing or reusing your query logic. Spark has several different notions of views. Views can be global, set to a database, or per session.

Creating Views

To an end user, views are displayed as tables, except rather than rewriting all of the data to a new location, they simply perform a transformation on the source data at query time. This might be a filter, select, or potentially an even larger GROUP BY or ROLLUP. For instance, in the following example, we create a view in which the destination is United States in order to see only those flights:

```
CREATE VIEW just_usa_view AS
  SELECT * FROM flights WHERE dest_country_name = 'United States'
```

Like tables, you can create temporary views that are available only during the current session and are not registered to a database:

```
CREATE TEMP VIEW just_usa_view_temp AS
  SELECT * FROM flights WHERE dest_country_name = 'United States'
```

Or, it can be a global temp view. Global temp views are resolved regardless of database and are viewable across the entire Spark application, but they are removed at the end of the session:

```
CREATE GLOBAL TEMP VIEW just_usa_global_view_temp AS
  SELECT * FROM flights WHERE dest_country_name = 'United States'

SHOW TABLES
```

You can also specify that you would like to overwite a view if one already exists by using the keywords shown in the sample that follows. We can overwrite both temp views and regular views:

```
CREATE OR REPLACE TEMP VIEW just_usa_view_temp AS
  SELECT * FROM flights WHERE dest_country_name = 'United States'
```

Now you can query this view just as if it were another table:

```
SELECT * FROM just_usa_view_temp
```

A view is effectively a transformation and Spark will perform it only at query time. This means that it will only apply that filter after you actually go to query the table (and not earlier). Effectively, views are equivalent to creating a new DataFrame from an existing DataFrame.

In fact, you can see this by comparing the query plans generated by Spark Data-Frames and Spark SQL. In DataFrames, we would write the following:

```
val flights = spark.read.format("json")
  .load("/data/flight-data/json/2015-summary.json")
val just_usa_df = flights.where("dest_country_name = 'United States'")
just_usa_df.selectExpr("*").explain
```

In SQL, we would write (querying from our view) this:

```
EXPLAIN SELECT * FROM just_usa_view
```

Or, equivalently:

```
EXPLAIN SELECT * FROM flights WHERE dest_country_name = 'United States'
```

Due to this fact, you should feel comfortable in writing your logic either on Data-Frames or SQL—whichever is most comfortable and maintainable for you.

Dropping Views

You can drop views in the same way that you drop tables; you simply specify that what you intend to drop is a *view* instead of a table. The main difference between dropping a view and dropping a table is that with a view, no underlying data is removed, only the view definition itself:

```
DROP VIEW IF EXISTS just_usa_view;
```

Databases

Databases are a tool for organizing tables. As mentioned earlier, if you do not define one, Spark will use the default database. Any SQL statements that you run from within Spark (including DataFrame commands) execute within the context of a data-base. This means that if you change the database, any user-defined tables will remain in the previous database and will need to be queried differently.

This can be a source of confusion, especially if you're sharing the same context or session for your coworkers, so be sure to set your databases appropriately.

You can see all databases by using the following command:

```
SHOW DATABASES
```

Creating Databases

Creating databases follows the same patterns you've seen previously in this chapter; however, here you use the CREATE DATABASE keywords:

```
CREATE DATABASE some_db
```

Setting the Database

You might want to set a database to perform a certain query. To do this, use the USE keyword followed by the database name:

```
USE some_db
```

After you set this database, all queries will try to resolve table names to this database. Queries that were working just fine might now fail or yield different results because you are in a different database:

```
SHOW tables

SELECT * FROM flights -- fails with table/view not found
```

However, you can query different databases by using the correct prefix:

```
SELECT * FROM default.flights
```

You can see what database you're currently using by running the following command:

```
SELECT current_database()
```

You can, of course, switch back to the default database:

```
USE default;
```

Dropping Databases

Dropping or removing databases is equally as easy: you simply use the DROP DATABASE keyword:

```
DROP DATABASE IF EXISTS some_db;
```

Select Statements

Queries in Spark support the following ANSI SQL requirements (here we list the layout of the SELECT expression):

```
SELECT [ALL|DISTINCT] named_expression[, named_expression, ...]
    FROM relation[, relation, ...]
    [lateral_view[, lateral_view, ...]]
```

```
    [WHERE boolean_expression]
    [aggregation [HAVING boolean_expression]]
    [ORDER BY sort_expressions]
    [CLUSTER BY expressions]
    [DISTRIBUTE BY expressions]
    [SORT BY sort_expressions]
    [WINDOW named_window[, WINDOW named_window, ...]]
    [LIMIT num_rows]

named_expression:
    : expression [AS alias]

relation:
    | join_relation
    | (table_name|query|relation) [sample] [AS alias]
    : VALUES (expressions)[, (expressions), ...]
        [AS (column_name[, column_name, ...])]

expressions:
    : expression[, expression, ...]

sort_expressions:
    : expression [ASC|DESC][, expression [ASC|DESC], ...]
```

case...when...then Statements

Oftentimes, you might need to conditionally replace values in your SQL queries. You can do this by using a case...when...then...end style statement. This is essentially the equivalent of programmatic if statements:

```
SELECT
    CASE WHEN DEST_COUNTRY_NAME = 'UNITED STATES' THEN 1
        WHEN DEST_COUNTRY_NAME = 'Egypt' THEN 0
        ELSE -1 END
FROM partitioned_flights
```

Advanced Topics

Now that we defined where data lives and how to organize it, let's move on to querying it. A SQL query is a SQL statement requesting that some set of commands be run. SQL statements can define manipulations, definitions, or controls. The most common case are the manipulations, which is the focus of this book.

Complex Types

Complex types are a departure from standard SQL and are an incredibly powerful feature that does not exist in standard SQL. Understanding how to manipulate them appropriately in SQL is essential. There are three core complex types in Spark SQL: structs, lists, and maps.

Structs

Structs are more akin to maps. They provide a way of creating or querying nested data in Spark. To create one, you simply need to wrap a set of columns (or expressions) in parentheses:

```
CREATE VIEW IF NOT EXISTS nested_data AS
    SELECT (DEST_COUNTRY_NAME, ORIGIN_COUNTRY_NAME) as country, count FROM flights
```

Now, you can query this data to see what it looks like:

```
SELECT * FROM nested_data
```

You can even query individual columns within a struct—all you need to do is use dot syntax:

```
SELECT country.DEST_COUNTRY_NAME, count FROM nested_data
```

If you like, you can also select all the subvalues from a struct by using the struct's name and select all of the subcolumns. Although these aren't truly subcolumns, it does provide a simpler way to think about them because we can do everything that we like with them as if they were a column:

```
SELECT country.*, count FROM nested_data
```

Lists

If you're familiar with lists in programming languages, Spark SQL lists will feel familiar. There are several ways to create an array or list of values. You can use the `collect_list` function, which creates a list of values. You can also use the function `collect_set`, which creates an array without duplicate values. These are both aggregation functions and therefore can be specified only in aggregations:

```
SELECT DEST_COUNTRY_NAME as new_name, collect_list(count) as flight_counts,
    collect_set(ORIGIN_COUNTRY_NAME) as origin_set
FROM flights GROUP BY DEST_COUNTRY_NAME
```

You can, however, also create an array manually within a column, as shown here:

```
SELECT DEST_COUNTRY_NAME, ARRAY(1, 2, 3) FROM flights
```

You can also query lists by position by using a Python-like array query syntax:

```
SELECT DEST_COUNTRY_NAME as new_name, collect_list(count)[0]
FROM flights GROUP BY DEST_COUNTRY_NAME
```

You can also do things like convert an array back into rows. You do this by using the `explode` function. To demonstrate, let's create a new view as our aggregation:

```
CREATE OR REPLACE TEMP VIEW flights_agg AS
    SELECT DEST_COUNTRY_NAME, collect_list(count) as collected_counts
    FROM flights GROUP BY DEST_COUNTRY_NAME
```

Now let's explode the complex type to one row in our result for every value in the array. The `DEST_COUNTRY_NAME` will duplicate for every value in the array, performing the exact opposite of the original `collect` and returning us to the original Data-Frame:

```
SELECT explode(collected_counts), DEST_COUNTRY_NAME FROM flights_agg
```

Functions

In addition to complex types, Spark SQL provides a variety of sophisticated functions. You can find most of these functions in the DataFrames function reference; however, it is worth understanding how to find these functions in SQL, as well. To see a list of functions in Spark SQL, you use the `SHOW FUNCTIONS` statement:

```
SHOW FUNCTIONS
```

You can also more specifically indicate whether you would like to see the system functions (i.e., those built into Spark) as well as user functions:

```
SHOW SYSTEM FUNCTIONS
```

User functions are those defined by you or someone else sharing your Spark environment. These are the same user-defined functions that we talked about in earlier chapters (we will discuss how to create them later on in this chapter):

```
SHOW USER FUNCTIONS
```

You can filter all `SHOW` commands by passing a string with wildcard (*) characters. Here, we can see all functions that begin with "s":

```
SHOW FUNCTIONS "s*";
```

Optionally, you can include the `LIKE` keyword, although this is not necessary:

```
SHOW FUNCTIONS LIKE "collect*";
```

Even though listing functions is certainly useful, often you might want to know more about specific functions themselves. To do this, use the `DESCRIBE` keyword, which returns the documentation for a specific function.

User-defined functions

As we saw in Chapters 3 and 4, Spark gives you the ability to define your own functions and use them in a distributed manner. You can define functions, just as you did before, writing the function in the language of your choice and then registering it appropriately:

```
def power3(number:Double):Double = number * number * number
spark.udf.register("power3", power3(_:Double):Double)

SELECT count, power3(count) FROM flights
```

You can also register functions through the Hive `CREATE TEMPORARY FUNCTION` syntax.

Subqueries

With subqueries, you can specify queries within other queries. This makes it possible for you to specify some sophisticated logic within your SQL. In Spark, there are two fundamental subqueries. *Correlated subqueries* use some information from the outer scope of the query in order to supplement information in the subquery. *Uncorrelated subqueries* include no information from the outer scope. Each of these queries can return one (scalar subquery) or more values. Spark also includes support for *predicate subqueries*, which allow for filtering based on values.

Uncorrelated predicate subqueries

For example, let's take a look at a predicate subquery. In this example, this is composed of two *uncorrelated* queries. The first query is just to get the top five country destinations based on the data we have:

```
SELECT dest_country_name FROM flights
GROUP BY dest_country_name ORDER BY sum(count) DESC LIMIT 5
```

This gives us the following result:

```
+------------------+
|dest_country_name|
+------------------+
|     United States|
|            Canada|
|            Mexico|
|    United Kingdom|
|             Japan|
+------------------+
```

Now we place this subquery inside of the filter and check to see if our origin country exists in that list:

```
SELECT * FROM flights
WHERE origin_country_name IN (SELECT dest_country_name FROM flights
    GROUP BY dest_country_name ORDER BY sum(count) DESC LIMIT 5)
```

This query is uncorrelated because it does not include any information from the outer scope of the query. It's a query that you can run on its own.

Correlated predicate subqueries

Correlated predicate subqueries allow you to use information from the outer scope in your inner query. For example, if you want to see whether you have a flight that will take you back from your destination country, you could do so by checking whether there is a flight that has the destination country as an origin and a flight that had the origin country as a destination:

```
SELECT * FROM flights f1
WHERE EXISTS (SELECT 1 FROM flights f2
            WHERE f1.dest_country_name = f2.origin_country_name)
AND EXISTS (SELECT 1 FROM flights f2
            WHERE f2.dest_country_name = f1.origin_country_name)
```

EXISTS just checks for some existence in the subquery and returns true if there is a value. You can flip this by placing the NOT operator in front of it. This would be equivalent to finding a flight to a destination from which you won't be able to return!

Uncorrelated scalar queries

Using uncorrelated scalar queries, you can bring in some supplemental information that you might not have previously. For example, if you wanted to include the maximum value as its own column from the entire counts dataset, you could do this:

```
SELECT *, (SELECT max(count) FROM flights) AS maximum FROM flights
```

Miscellaneous Features

There are some features in Spark SQL that don't quite fit in previous sections of this chapter, so we're going to include them here in no particular order. These can be relevant when performing optimizations or debugging your SQL code.

Configurations

There are several Spark SQL application configurations, which we list in Table 10-1. You can set these either at application initialization or over the course of application execution (like we have seen with shuffle partitions throughout this book).

Table 10-1. Spark SQL configurations

Property Name	Default	Meaning
spark.sql.inMemoryColumnar Storage.compressed	true	When set to true, Spark SQL automatically selects a compression codec for each column based on statistics of the data.
spark.sql.inMemoryColumnar Storage.batchSize	10000	Controls the size of batches for columnar caching. Larger batch sizes can improve memory utilization and compression, but risk OutOfMemoryErrors (OOMs) when caching data.
spark.sql.files.maxPartition Bytes	134217728 (128 MB)	The maximum number of bytes to pack into a single partition when reading files.

Property Name	Default	Meaning
`spark.sql.files.openCostIn Bytes`	4194304 (4 MB)	The estimated cost to open a file, measured by the number of bytes that could be scanned in the same time. This is used when putting multiple files into a partition. It is better to overestimate; that way the partitions with small files will be faster than partitions with bigger files (which is scheduled first).
`spark.sql.broadcastTimeout`	300	Timeout in seconds for the broadcast wait time in broadcast joins.
`spark.sql.autoBroadcastJoin Threshold`	10485760 (10 MB)	Configures the maximum size in bytes for a table that will be broadcast to all worker nodes when performing a join. You can disable broadcasting by setting this value to -1. Note that currently statistics are supported only for Hive Metastore tables for which the command `ANALYZE TABLE COMPUTE STA TISTICS noscan` has been run.
`spark.sql.shuffle.partitions`	200	Configures the number of partitions to use when shuffling data for joins or aggregations.

Setting Configuration Values in SQL

We talk about configurations in Chapter 15, but as a preview, it's worth mentioning how to set configurations from SQL. Naturally, you can only set Spark SQL configurations that way, but here's how you can set shuffle partitions:

```
SET spark.sql.shuffle.partitions=20
```

Conclusion

It should be clear from this chapter that Spark SQL and DataFrames are very closely related and that you should be able to use nearly all of the examples throughout this book with only small syntactical tweaks. This chapter illustrated more of the Spark SQL–related specifics. Chapter 11 focuses on a new concept: Datasets that allow for type-safe structured transformations.

Datasets

Datasets are the foundational type of the Structured APIs. We already worked with DataFrames, which are Datasets of type `Row`, and are available across Spark's different languages. Datasets are a strictly Java Virtual Machine (JVM) language feature that work only with Scala and Java. Using Datasets, you can define the object that each row in your Dataset will consist of. In Scala, this will be a case class object that essentially defines a schema that you can use, and in Java, you will define a Java Bean. Experienced users often refer to Datasets as the "typed set of APIs" in Spark. For more information, see Chapter 4.

In Chapter 4, we discussed that Spark has types like `StringType`, `BigIntType`, `Struct Type`, and so on. Those Spark-specific types map to types available in each of Spark's languages like `String`, `Integer`, and `Double`. When you use the DataFrame API, you do not create strings or integers, but Spark manipulates the data for you by manipulating the `Row` object. In fact, if you use Scala or Java, all "DataFrames" are actually Datasets of type `Row`. To efficiently support domain-specific objects, a special concept called an "Encoder" is required. The encoder maps the domain-specific type T to Spark's internal type system.

For example, given a class `Person` with two fields, `name` (string) and `age` (int), an encoder directs Spark to generate code at runtime to serialize the `Person` object into a binary structure. When using DataFrames or the "standard" Structured APIs, this binary structure will be a `Row`. When we want to create our own domain-specific objects, we specify a `case class` in Scala or a `JavaBean` in Java. Spark will allow us to manipulate this object (in place of a `Row`) in a distributed manner.

When you use the Dataset API, for every row it touches, this domain specifies type, Spark converts the Spark Row format to the object you specified (a case class or Java class). This conversion slows down your operations but can provide more flexibility.

You will notice a hit in performance but this is a far different order of magnitude from what you might see from something like a user-defined function (UDF) in Python, because the performance costs are not as extreme as switching programming languages, but it is an important thing to keep in mind.

When to Use Datasets

You might ponder, if I am going to pay a performance penalty when I use Datasets, why should I use them at all? If we had to condense this down into a canonical list, here are a couple of reasons:

- When the operation(s) you would like to perform cannot be expressed using DataFrame manipulations

- When you want or need type-safety, and you're willing to accept the cost of performance to achieve it

Let's explore these in more detail. There are some operations that cannot be expressed using the Structured APIs we have seen in the previous chapters. Although these are not particularly common, you might have a large set of business logic that you'd like to encode in one specific function instead of in SQL or DataFrames. This is an appropriate use for Datasets. Additionally, the Dataset API is type-safe. Operations that are not valid for their types, say subtracting two string types, will fail at compilation time not at runtime. If correctness and bulletproof code is your highest priority, at the cost of some performance, this can be a great choice for you. This does not protect you from malformed data but can allow you to more elegantly handle and organize it.

Another potential time for which you might want to use Datasets is when you would like to reuse a variety of transformations of entire rows between single-node workloads and Spark workloads. If you have some experience with Scala, you might notice that Spark's APIs reflect those of Scala Sequence Types, but they operate in a distributed fashion. In fact, Martin Odersky, the inventor of Scala, said just that in 2015 at Spark Summit Europe (*https://spark-summit.org/eu-2015/events/spark-the-ultimate-scala-collections/*). Due to this, one advantage of using Datasets is that if you define all of your data and transformations as accepting case classes it is trivial to reuse them for both distributed and local workloads. Additionally, when you collect your DataFrames to local disk, they will be of the correct class and type, sometimes making further manipulation easier.

Probably the most popular use case is to use DataFrames and Datasets in tandem, manually trading off between performance and type safety when it is most relevant for your workload. This might be at the end of a large, DataFrame-based extract, transform, and load (ETL) transformation when you'd like to collect data to the driver and manipulate it by using single-node libraries, or it might be at the beginning of a transformation when you need to perform per-row parsing before performing filtering and further manipulation in Spark SQL.

Creating Datasets

Creating Datasets is somewhat of a manual operation, requiring you to know and define the schemas ahead of time.

In Java: Encoders

Java Encoders are fairly simple, you simply specify your class and then you'll encode it when you come upon your DataFrame (which is of type `Dataset<Row>`):

```
import org.apache.spark.sql.Encoders;

public class Flight implements Serializable{
  String DEST_COUNTRY_NAME;
  String ORIGIN_COUNTRY_NAME;
  Long DEST_COUNTRY_NAME;
}

Dataset<Flight> flights = spark.read
  .parquet("/data/flight-data/parquet/2010-summary.parquet/")
  .as(Encoders.bean(Flight.class));
```

In Scala: Case Classes

To create Datasets in Scala, you define a Scala `case class`. A `case class` is a regular class that has the following characteristics:

- Immutable
- Decomposable through pattern matching
- Allows for comparison based on structure instead of reference
- Easy to use and manipulate

These traits make it rather valuable for data analysis because it is quite easy to reason about a case class. Probably the most important feature is that case classes are immutable and allow for comparison by structure instead of value.

Here's how the Scala documentation (*http://docs.scala-lang.org/tutorials/tour/case-classes.html*) describes it:

- Immutability frees you from needing to keep track of where and when things are mutated

- Comparison-by-value allows you to compare instances as if they were primitive values—no more uncertainty regarding whether instances of a class are compared by value or reference

- Pattern matching simplifies branching logic, which leads to less bugs and more readable code.

These advantages carry over to their usage within Spark, as well.

To begin creating a Dataset, let's define a `case class` for one of our datasets:

```
case class Flight(DEST_COUNTRY_NAME: String,
                  ORIGIN_COUNTRY_NAME: String, count: BigInt)
```

Now that we defined a `case class`, this will represent a single record in our dataset. More succinctly, we now have a Dataset of Flights. This doesn't define any methods for us, simply the schema. When we read in our data, we'll get a DataFrame. However, we simply use the `as` method to cast it to our specified row type:

```
val flightsDF = spark.read
  .parquet("/data/flight-data/parquet/2010-summary.parquet/")
val flights = flightsDF.as[Flight]
```

Actions

Even though we can see the power of Datasets, what's important to understand is that actions like `collect`, `take`, and `count` apply to whether we are using Datasets or DataFrames:

```
flights.show(2)

+-----------------+-------------------+-----+
|DEST_COUNTRY_NAME|ORIGIN_COUNTRY_NAME|count|
+-----------------+-------------------+-----+
|    United States|            Romania|    1|
|    United States|            Ireland|  264|
+-----------------+-------------------+-----+
```

You'll also notice that when we actually go to access one of the `case classes`, we don't need to do any type coercion, we simply specify the named attribute of the `case class` and get back, not just the expected value but the expected type, as well:

```
flights.first.DEST_COUNTRY_NAME // United States
```

Transformations

Transformations on Datasets are the same as those that we saw on DataFrames. Any transformation that you read about in this section is valid on a Dataset, and we encourage you to look through the specific sections on relevant aggregations or joins.

In addition to those transformations, Datasets allow us to specify more complex and strongly typed transformations than we could perform on DataFrames alone because we manipulate raw Java Virtual Machine (JVM) types. To illustrate this raw object manipulation, let's filter the Dataset that you just created.

Filtering

Let's look at a simple example by creating a simple function that accepts a Flight and returns a Boolean value that describes whether the origin and destination are the same. This is not a UDF (at least, in the way that Spark SQL defines UDF) but a generic function.

You'll notice in the following example that we're going to create a *function* to define this filter. This is an important difference from what we have done thus far in the book. By specifying a function, we are *forcing* Spark to evaluate this function on every row in our Dataset. This can be very resource intensive. For simple filters it is always preferred to write SQL expressions. This will greatly reduce the cost of filtering out the data while still allowing you to manipulate it as a Dataset later on:

```
def originIsDestination(flight_row: Flight): Boolean = {
  return flight_row.ORIGIN_COUNTRY_NAME == flight_row.DEST_COUNTRY_NAME
}
```

We can now pass this function into the filter method specifying that for each row it should verify that this function returns true and in the process will filter our Dataset down accordingly:

```
flights.filter(flight_row => originIsDestination(flight_row)).first()
```

The result is:

```
Flight = Flight(United States,United States,348113)
```

As we saw earlier, this function does not need to execute in Spark code at all. Similar to our UDFs, we can use it and test it on data on our local machines before using it within Spark.

For example, this dataset is small enough for us to collect to the driver (as an Array of Flights) on which we can operate and perform the exact same filtering operation:

```
flights.collect().filter(flight_row => originIsDestination(flight_row))
```

The result is:

```
Array[Flight] = Array(Flight(United States,United States,348113))
```

We can see that we get the exact same answer as before.

Mapping

Filtering is a simple transformation, but sometimes you need to map one value to another value. We did this with our function in the previous example: it accepts a flight and returns a Boolean, but other times we might actually need to perform something more sophisticated like extract a value, compare a set of values, or something similar.

The simplest example is manipulating our Dataset such that we extract one value from each row. This is effectively performing a DataFrame like select on our Dataset. Let's extract the destination:

```
val destinations = flights.map(f => f.DEST_COUNTRY_NAME)
```

Notice that we end up with a Dataset of type String. That is because Spark already knows the JVM type that this result should return and allows us to benefit from compile-time checking if, for some reason, it is invalid.

We can collect this and get back an array of strings on the driver:

```
val localDestinations = destinations.take(5)
```

This might feel trivial and unnecessary; we can do the majority of this right on DataFrames. We in fact recommend that you do this because you gain so many benefits from doing so. You will gain advantages like code generation that are simply not possible with arbitrary user-defined functions. However, this can come in handy with much more sophisticated row-by-row manipulation.

Joins

Joins, as we covered earlier, apply just the same as they did for DataFrames. However Datasets also provide a more sophisticated method, the joinWith method. joinWith is roughly equal to a co-group (in RDD terminology) and you basically end up with two nested Datasets inside of one. Each column represents one Dataset and these can be manipulated accordingly. This can be useful when you need to maintain more information in the join or perform some more sophisticated manipulation on the entire result, like an advanced map or filter.

Let's create a fake flight metadata dataset to demonstrate joinWith:

```
case class FlightMetadata(count: BigInt, randomData: BigInt)

val flightsMeta = spark.range(500).map(x => (x, scala.util.Random.nextLong))
  .withColumnRenamed("_1", "count").withColumnRenamed("_2", "randomData")
  .as[FlightMetadata]

val flights2 = flights
  .joinWith(flightsMeta, flights.col("count") === flightsMeta.col("count"))
```

Notice that we end up with a Dataset of a sort of key-value pair, in which each row represents a Flight and the Flight Metadata. We can, of course, query these as a Dataset or a DataFrame with complex types:

```
flights2.selectExpr("_1.DEST_COUNTRY_NAME")
```

We can collect them just as we did before:

```
flights2.take(2)

Array[(Flight, FlightMetadata)] = Array((Flight(United States,Romania,1),...
```

Of course, a "regular" join would work quite well, too, although you'll notice in this case that we end up with a DataFrame (and thus lose our JVM type information).

```
val flights2 = flights.join(flightsMeta, Seq("count"))
```

We can always define another Dataset to gain this back. It's also important to note that there are no problems joining a DataFrame and a Dataset—we end up with the same result:

```
val flights2 = flights.join(flightsMeta.toDF(), Seq("count"))
```

Grouping and Aggregations

Grouping and aggregations follow the same fundamental standards that we saw in the previous aggregation chapter, so groupBy rollup and cube still apply, but these return DataFrames instead of Datasets (you lose type information):

```
flights.groupBy("DEST_COUNTRY_NAME").count()
```

This often is not too big of a deal, but if you want to keep type information around there are other groupings and aggregations that you can perform. An excellent example is the groupByKey method. This allows you to group by a specific key in the Dataset and get a typed Dataset in return. This function, however, doesn't accept a specific column name but rather a function. This makes it possible for you to specify more sophisticated grouping functions that are much more akin to something like this:

```
flights.groupByKey(x => x.DEST_COUNTRY_NAME).count()
```

Although this provides flexibility, it's a trade-off because now we are introducing JVM types as well as functions that cannot be optimized by Spark. This means that you will see a performance difference and we can see this when we inspect the explain plan. In the following, you can see that we are effectivelly appending a new column to the DataFrame (the result of our function) and then performing the grouping on that:

```
flights.groupByKey(x => x.DEST_COUNTRY_NAME).count().explain

== Physical Plan ==
*HashAggregate(keys=[value#1396], functions=[count(1)])
+- Exchange hashpartitioning(value#1396, 200)
   +- *HashAggregate(keys=[value#1396], functions=[partial_count(1)])
```

```
      +- *Project [value#1396]
         +- AppendColumns <function1>, newInstance(class ...
         [staticinvoke(class org.apache.spark.unsafe.types.UTF8String, ...
            +- *FileScan parquet [D...
```

After we perform a grouping with a key on a Dataset, we can operate on the Key Value Dataset with functions that will manipulate the groupings as raw objects:

```
def grpSum(countryName:String, values: Iterator[Flight]) = {
  values.dropWhile(_.count < 5).map(x => (countryName, x))
}
flights.groupByKey(x => x.DEST_COUNTRY_NAME).flatMapGroups(grpSum).show(5)
```

```
+--------+--------------------+
|      _1|                  _2|
+--------+--------------------+
|Anguilla|[Anguilla,United ...|
|Paraguay|[Paraguay,United ...|
|  Russia|[Russia,United St...|
| Senegal|[Senegal,United S...|
|  Sweden|[Sweden,United St...|
+--------+--------------------+
```

```
def grpSum2(f:Flight):Integer = {
  1
}
flights.groupByKey(x => x.DEST_COUNTRY_NAME).mapValues(grpSum2).count().take(5)
```

We can even create new manipulations and define how groups should be reduced:

```
def sum2(left:Flight, right:Flight) = {
  Flight(left.DEST_COUNTRY_NAME, null, left.count + right.count)
}
flights.groupByKey(x => x.DEST_COUNTRY_NAME).reduceGroups((l, r) => sum2(l, r))
  .take(5)
```

It should be straightfoward enough to understand that this is a more expensive process than aggregating immediately after scanning, especially because it ends up in the same end result:

```
flights.groupBy("DEST_COUNTRY_NAME").count().explain

== Physical Plan ==
*HashAggregate(keys=[DEST_COUNTRY_NAME#1308], functions=[count(1)])
+- Exchange hashpartitioning(DEST_COUNTRY_NAME#1308, 200)
   +- *HashAggregate(keys=[DEST_COUNTRY_NAME#1308], functions=[partial_count(1)])
      +- *FileScan parquet [DEST_COUNTRY_NAME#1308] Batched: tru...
```

This should motivate using Datasets only with user-defined encoding surgically and only where it makes sense. This might be at the beginning of a big data pipeline or at the end of one.

Conclusion

In this chapter, we covered the basics of Datasets and provided some motivating examples. Although short, this chapter actually teaches you basically all that you need to know about Datasets and how to use them. It can be helpful to think of them as a blend between the higher-level Structured APIs and the low-level RDD APIs, which is the topic of Chapter 12.

PART III
Low-Level APIs

Resilient Distributed Datasets (RDDs)

The previous part of the book covered Spark's Structured APIs. You should heavily favor these APIs in almost all scenarios. That being said, there are times when higher-level manipulation will not meet the business or engineering problem you are trying to solve. For those cases, you might need to use Spark's lower-level APIs, specifically the Resilient Distributed Dataset (RDD), the SparkContext, and distributed *shared variables* like accumulators and broadcast variables. The chapters that follow in this part cover these APIs and how to use them.

If you are brand new to Spark, this is not the place to start. Start with the Structured APIs, you'll be more productive more quickly!

What Are the Low-Level APIs?

There are two sets of low-level APIs: there is one for manipulating distributed data (RDDs), and another for distributing and manipulating distributed shared variables (broadcast variables and accumulators).

When to Use the Low-Level APIs?

You should generally use the lower-level APIs in three situations:

- You need some functionality that you cannot find in the higher-level APIs; for example, if you need very tight control over physical data placement across the cluster.
- You need to maintain some legacy codebase written using RDDs.

- You need to do some custom shared variable manipulation. We will discuss shared variables more in Chapter 14.

Those are the reasons why you should *use* these lower-level tools, buts it's still helpful to *understand* these tools because all Spark workloads compile down to these fundamental primitives. When you're calling a DataFrame transformation, it actually just becomes a set of RDD transformations. This understanding can make your task easier as you begin debugging more and more complex workloads.

Even if you are an advanced developer hoping to get the most out of Spark, we still recommend focusing on the Structured APIs. However, there are times when you might want to "drop down" to some of the lower-level tools to complete your task. You might need to drop down to these APIs to use some legacy code, implement some custom partitioner, or update and track the value of a variable over the course of a data pipeline's execution. These tools give you more fine-grained control at the expense of safeguarding you from shooting yourself in the foot.

How to Use the Low-Level APIs?

A `SparkContext` is the entry point for low-level API functionality. You access it through the `SparkSession`, which is the tool you use to perform computation across a Spark cluster. We discuss this further in Chapter 15 but for now, you simply need to know that you can access a SparkContext via the following call:

```
spark.sparkContext
```

About RDDs

RDDs were the primary API in the Spark 1.X series and are still available in 2.X, but they are not as commonly used. However, as we've pointed out earlier in this book, virtually all Spark code you run, whether DataFrames or Datasets, compiles down to an RDD. The Spark UI, covered in the next part of the book, also describes job execution in terms of RDDs. Therefore, it will behoove you to have at least a basic understanding of what an RDD is and how to use it.

In short, an RDD represents an immutable, partitioned collection of records that can be operated on in parallel. Unlike DataFrames though, where each record is a structured row containing fields with a known schema, in RDDs the records are just Java, Scala, or Python objects of the programmer's choosing.

RDDs give you complete control because every record in an RDD is a just a Java or Python object. You can store anything you want in these objects, in any format you want. This gives you great power, but not without potential issues. Every manipulation and interaction between values must be defined by hand, meaning that you must "reinvent the wheel" for whatever task you are trying to carry out. Also, optimizations are going to require much more manual work, because Spark does not understand the inner structure of your records as it does with the Structured APIs. For instance, Spark's Structured APIs automatically store data in an optimzied, compressed binary format, so to achieve the same space-efficiency and performance, you'd also need to implement this type of format inside your objects and all the low-level operations to compute over it. Likewise, optimizations like reordering filters and aggregations that occur automatically in Spark SQL need to be implemented by hand. For this reason and others, we highly recommend using the Spark Structured APIs when possible.

The RDD API is similar to the `Dataset`, which we saw in the previous part of the book, except that RDDs are not stored in, or manipulated with, the structured data engine. However, it is trivial to convert back and forth between RDDs and Datasets, so you can use both APIs to take advantage of each API's strengths and weaknesses. We'll show how to do this throughout this part of the book.

Types of RDDs

If you look through Spark's API documentation, you will notice that there are lots of subclasses of RDD. For the most part, these are internal representations that the Data-Frame API uses to create optimized physical execution plans. As a user, however, you will likely only be creating two types of RDDs: the "generic" RDD type or a key-value RDD that provides additional functions, such as aggregating by key. For your purposes, these will be the only two types of RDDs that matter. Both just represent a collection of objects, but key-value RDDs have special operations as well as a concept of custom partitioning by key.

Let's formally define RDDs. Internally, each RDD is characterized by five main properties:

- A list of partitions
- A function for computing each split
- A list of dependencies on other RDDs
- Optionally, a `Partitioner` for key-value RDDs (e.g., to say that the RDD is hash-partitioned)
- Optionally, a list of preferred locations on which to compute each split (e.g., block locations for a Hadoop Distributed File System [HDFS] file)

 The `Partitioner` is probably one of the core reasons why you might want to use RDDs in your code. Specifying your own custom `Partitioner` can give you significant performance and stability improvements if you use it correctly. This is discussed in more depth in Chapter 13 when we introduce Key–Value Pair RDDs.

These properties determine all of Spark's ability to schedule and execute the user program. Different kinds of RDDs implement their own versions of each of the aforementioned properties, allowing you to define new data sources.

RDDs follow the exact same Spark programming paradigms that we saw in earlier chapters. They provide *transformations*, which evaluate lazily, and *actions*, which evaluate eagerly, to manipulate data in a distributed fashion. These work the same way as transformations and actions on DataFrames and Datasets. However, there is no concept of "rows" in RDDs; individual records are just raw Java/Scala/Python objects, and you manipulate those manually instead of tapping into the repository of functions that you have in the structured APIs.

The RDD APIs are available in Python as well as Scala and Java. For Scala and Java, the performance is for the most part the same, the large costs incurred in manipulating the raw objects. Python, however, can lose a substantial amount of performance when using RDDs. Running Python RDDs equates to running Python user-defined functions (UDFs) row by row. Just as we saw in Chapter 6. We serialize the data to the Python process, operate on it in Python, and then serialize it back to the Java Virtual Machine (JVM). This causes a high overhead for Python RDD manipulations. Even though many people ran production code with them in the past, we recommend building on the Structured APIs in Python and only dropping down to RDDs if absolutely necessary.

When to Use RDDs?

In general, you should not manually create RDDs unless you have a very, very specific reason for doing so. They are a much lower-level API that provides a lot of power but also lacks a lot of the optimizations that are available in the Structured APIs. For the vast majority of use cases, DataFrames will be more efficient, more stable, and more expressive than RDDs.

The most likely reason for why you'll want to use RDDs is because you need fine-grained control over the physical distribution of data (custom partitioning of data).

Datasets and RDDs of Case Classes

We noticed this question on the web and found it to be an interesting one: what is the difference between RDDs of Case Classes and Datasets? The difference is that Datasets can still take advantage of the wealth of functions and optimizations that the Structured APIs have to offer. With Datasets, you do not need to choose between only operating on JVM types or on Spark types, you can choose whatever is either easiest to do or most flexible. You get the both of best worlds.

Creating RDDs

Now that we discussed some key RDD properties, let's begin applying them so that you can better understand how to use them.

Interoperating Between DataFrames, Datasets, and RDDs

One of the easiest ways to get RDDs is from an existing DataFrame or Dataset. Converting these to an RDD is simple: just use the rdd method on any of these data types. You'll notice that if you do a conversion from a Dataset[T] to an RDD, you'll get the appropriate native type T back (remember this applies only to Scala and Java):

```
// in Scala: converts a Dataset[Long] to RDD[Long]
spark.range(500).rdd
```

Because Python doesn't have Datasets—it has only DataFrames—you will get an RDD of type Row:

```
# in Python
spark.range(10).rdd
```

To operate on this data, you will need to convert this Row object to the correct data type or extract values out of it, as shown in the example that follows. This is now an RDD of type Row:

```
// in Scala
spark.range(10).toDF().rdd.map(rowObject => rowObject.getLong(0))

# in Python
spark.range(10).toDF("id").rdd.map(lambda row: row[0])
```

You can use the same methodology to create a DataFrame or Dataset from an RDD. All you need to do is call the toDF method on the RDD:

```
// in Scala
spark.range(10).rdd.toDF()

# in Python
spark.range(10).rdd.toDF()
```

This command creates an RDD of type Row. This row is the internal Catalyst format that Spark uses to represent data in the Structured APIs. This functionality makes it possible for you to jump between the Structured and low-level APIs as it suits your use case. (We talk about this in Chapter 13.)

The RDD API will feel quite similar to the Dataset API in Chapter 11 because they are extremely similar to each other (RDDs being a lower-level representation of Datasets) that do not have a lot of the convenient functionality and interfaces that the Structured APIs do.

From a Local Collection

To create an RDD from a collection, you will need to use the `parallelize` method on a `SparkContext` (within a SparkSession). This turns a single node collection into a parallel collection. When creating this parallel collection, you can also explicitly state the number of partitions into which you would like to distribute this array. In this case, we are creating two partitions:

```scala
// in Scala
val myCollection = "Spark The Definitive Guide : Big Data Processing Made Simple"
  .split(" ")
val words = spark.sparkContext.parallelize(myCollection, 2)
```

```python
# in Python
myCollection = "Spark The Definitive Guide : Big Data Processing Made Simple"\
  .split(" ")
words = spark.sparkContext.parallelize(myCollection, 2)
```

An additional feature is that you can then name this RDD to show up in the Spark UI according to a given name:

```scala
// in Scala
words.setName("myWords")
words.name // myWords
```

```python
# in Python
words.setName("myWords")
words.name() # myWords
```

From Data Sources

Although you can create RDDs from data sources or text files, it's often preferable to use the Data Source APIs. RDDs do not have a notion of "Data Source APIs" like DataFrames do; they primarily define their dependency structures and lists of partitions. The Data Source API that we saw in Chapter 9 is almost always a better way to read in data. That being said, you can also read data as RDDs using `sparkContext`. For example, let's read a text file line by line:

```
spark.sparkContext.textFile("/some/path/withTextFiles")
```

This creates an RDD for which each record in the RDD represents a line in that text file or files. Alternatively, you can read in data for which each text file should become a single record. The use case here would be where each file is a file that consists of a large JSON object or some document that you will operate on as an individual:

```
spark.sparkContext.wholeTextFiles("/some/path/withTextFiles")
```

In this RDD, the name of the file is the first object and the value of the text file is the second string object.

Manipulating RDDs

You manipulate RDDs in much the same way that you manipulate DataFrames. As mentioned, the core difference being that you manipulate raw Java or Scala objects instead of Spark types. There is also a dearth of "helper" methods or functions that you can draw upon to simplify calculations. Rather, you must define each filter, map functions, aggregation, and any other manipulation that you want as a function.

To demonstrate some data manipulation, let's use the simple RDD (words) we created previously to define some more details.

Transformations

For the most part, many transformations mirror the functionality that you find in the Structured APIs. Just as you do with DataFrames and Datasets, you specify *transformations* on one RDD to create another. In doing so, we define an RDD as a dependency to another along with some manipulation of the data contained in that RDD.

distinct

A `distinct` method call on an RDD removes duplicates from the RDD:

```
words.distinct().count()
```

This gives a result of 10.

filter

Filtering is equivalent to creating a SQL-like where clause. You can look through our records in the RDD and see which ones match some predicate function. This function just needs to return a Boolean type to be used as a filter function. The input should be whatever your given row is. In this next example, we filter the RDD to keep only the words that begin with the letter "S":

```scala
// in Scala
def startsWithS(individual:String) = {
  individual.startsWith("S")
}
```

```python
# in Python
def startsWithS(individual):
  return individual.startswith("S")
```

Now that we defined the function, let's filter the data. This should feel quite familiar if you read Chapter 11 because we simply use a function that operates record by record in the RDD. The function is defined to work on each record in the RDD individually:

```scala
// in Scala
words.filter(word => startsWithS(word)).collect()
```

```
# in Python
words.filter(lambda word: startsWithS(word)).collect()
```

This gives a result of *Spark* and *Simple*. We can see, like the Dataset API, that this returns native types. That is because we never coerce our data into type Row, nor do we need to convert the data after collecting it.

map

Mapping is again the same operation that you can read about in Chapter 11. You specify a function that returns the value that you want, given the correct input. You then apply that, record by record. Let's perform something similar to what we just did. In this example, we'll map the current word to the word, its starting letter, and whether the word begins with "S."

Notice in this instance that we define our functions completely inline using the relevant lambda syntax:

```
// in Scala
val words2 = words.map(word => (word, word(0), word.startsWith("S")))
```
```
# in Python
words2 = words.map(lambda word: (word, word[0], word.startswith("S")))
```

You can subsequently filter on this by selecting the relevant Boolean value in a new function:

```
// in Scala
words2.filter(record => record._3).take(5)
```
```
# in Python
words2.filter(lambda record: record[2]).take(5)
```

This returns a tuple of "Spark," "S," and "true," as well as "Simple," "S," and "True."

flatMap

flatMap provides a simple extension of the map function we just looked at. Sometimes, each current row should return multiple rows, instead. For example, you might want to take your set of words and flatMap it into a set of characters. Because each word has multiple characters, you should use flatMap to expand it. flatMap requires that the ouput of the map function be an iterable that can be expanded:

```
// in Scala
words.flatMap(word => word.toSeq).take(5)
```
```
# in Python
words.flatMap(lambda word: list(word)).take(5)
```

This yields *S, P, A, R, K*.

sort

To sort an RDD you must use the `sortBy` method, and just like any other RDD operation, you do this by specifying a function to extract a value from the objects in your RDDs and then sort based on that. For instance, the following example sorts by word length from longest to shortest:

```scala
// in Scala
words.sortBy(word => word.length() * -1).take(2)
```

```python
# in Python
words.sortBy(lambda word: len(word) * -1).take(2)
```

Random Splits

We can also randomly split an RDD into an `Array` of RDDs by using the `randomSplit` method, which accepts an `Array` of weights and a random seed:

```scala
// in Scala
val fiftyFiftySplit = words.randomSplit(Array[Double](0.5, 0.5))
```

```python
# in Python
fiftyFiftySplit = words.randomSplit([0.5, 0.5])
```

This returns an array of RDDs that you can manipulate individually.

Actions

Just as we do with DataFrames and Datasets, we specify *actions* to kick off our specified transformations. Actions either collect data to the driver or write to an external data source.

reduce

You can use the `reduce` method to specify a function to "reduce" an RDD of any kind of value to one value. For instance, given a set of numbers, you can reduce this to its sum by specifying a function that takes as input two values and reduces them into one. If you have experience in functional programming, this should not be a new concept:

```scala
// in Scala
spark.sparkContext.parallelize(1 to 20).reduce(_ + _) // 210
```

```python
# in Python
spark.sparkContext.parallelize(range(1, 21)).reduce(lambda x, y: x + y) # 210
```

You can also use this to get something like the longest word in our set of words that we defined a moment ago. The key is just to define the correct function:

```scala
// in Scala
def wordLengthReducer(leftWord:String, rightWord:String): String = {
```

```
  if (leftWord.length > rightWord.length)
    return leftWord
  else
    return rightWord
}

words.reduce(wordLengthReducer)
# in Python
def wordLengthReducer(leftWord, rightWord):
  if len(leftWord) > len(rightWord):
    return leftWord
  else:
    return rightWord

words.reduce(wordLengthReducer)
```

This reducer is a good example because you can get one of two outputs. Because the reduce operation on the partitions is not deterministic, you can have either "definitive" or "processing" (both of length 10) as the "left" word. This means that sometimes you can end up with one, whereas other times you end up with the other.

count

This method is fairly self-explanatory. Using it, you could, for example, count the number of rows in the RDD:

```
words.count()
```

countApprox

Even though the return signature for this type is a bit strange, it's quite sophisticated. This is an approximation of the count method we just looked at, but it must execute within a timeout (and can return incomplete results if it exceeds the timeout).

The confidence is the probability that the error bounds of the result will contain the true value. That is, if countApprox were called repeatedly with confidence 0.9, we would expect 90% of the results to contain the true count. The confidence must be in the range [0,1], or an exception will be thrown:

```
val confidence = 0.95
val timeoutMilliseconds = 400
words.countApprox(timeoutMilliseconds, confidence)
```

countApproxDistinct

There are two implementations of this, both based on streamlib's implementation of "HyperLogLog in Practice: Algorithmic Engineering of a State-of-the-Art Cardinality Estimation Algorithm."

In the first implementation, the argument we pass into the function is the relative accuracy. Smaller values create counters that require more space. The value must be greater than 0.000017:

```
words.countApproxDistinct(0.05)
```

With the other implementation you have a bit more control; you specify the relative accuracy based on two parameters: one for "regular" data and another for a sparse representation.

The two arguments are p and sp where p is precision and sp is sparse precision. The relative accuracy is approximately 1.054 / $sqrt(2^p)$. Setting a nonzero (sp > p) can reduce the memory consumption and increase accuracy when the cardinality is small. Both values are integers:

```
words.countApproxDistinct(4, 10)
```

countByValue

This method counts the number of values in a given RDD. However, it does so by finally loading the result set into the memory of the driver. You should use this method only if the resulting map is expected to be small because the entire thing is loaded into the driver's memory. Thus, this method makes sense only in a scenario in which either the total number of rows is low or the number of distinct items is low:

```
words.countByValue()
```

countByValueApprox

This does the same thing as the previous function, but it does so as an approximation. This must execute within the specified timeout (first parameter) (and can return incomplete results if it exceeds the timeout).

The confidence is the probability that the error bounds of the result will contain the true value. That is, if countApprox were called repeatedly with confidence 0.9, we would expect 90% of the results to contain the true count. The confidence must be in the range [0,1], or an exception will be thrown:

```
words.countByValueApprox(1000, 0.95)
```

first

The first method returns the first value in the dataset:

```
words.first()
```

max and min

max and min return the maximum values and minimum values, respectively:

```
spark.sparkContext.parallelize(1 to 20).max()
spark.sparkContext.parallelize(1 to 20).min()
```

take

take and its derivative methods take a number of values from your RDD. This works by first scanning one partition and then using the results from that partition to estimate the number of additional partitions needed to satisfy the limit.

There are many variations on this function, such as takeOrdered, takeSample, and top. You can use takeSample to specify a fixed-size random sample from your RDD. You can specify whether this should be done by using withReplacement, the number of values, as well as the random seed. top is effectively the opposite of takeOrdered in that it selects the top values according to the implicit ordering:

```
words.take(5)
words.takeOrdered(5)
words.top(5)
val withReplacement = true
val numberToTake = 6
val randomSeed = 100L
words.takeSample(withReplacement, numberToTake, randomSeed)
```

Saving Files

Saving files means writing to plain-text files. With RDDs, you cannot actually "save" to a data source in the conventional sense. You must iterate over the partitions in order to save the contents of each partition to some external database. This is a low-level approach that reveals the underlying operation that is being performed in the higher-level APIs. Spark will take each partition, and write that out to the destination.

saveAsTextFile

To save to a text file, you just specify a path and optionally a compression codec:

```
words.saveAsTextFile("file:/tmp/bookTitle")
```

To set a compression codec, we must import the proper codec from Hadoop. You can find these in the org.apache.hadoop.io.compress library:

```
// in Scala
import org.apache.hadoop.io.compress.BZip2Codec
words.saveAsTextFile("file:/tmp/bookTitleCompressed", classOf[BZip2Codec])
```

SequenceFiles

Spark originally grew out of the Hadoop ecosystem, so it has a fairly tight integration with a variety of Hadoop tools. A `sequenceFile` is a flat file consisting of binary key–value pairs. It is extensively used in MapReduce as input/output formats.

Spark can write to `sequenceFiles` using the `saveAsObjectFile` method or by explicitly writing key–value pairs, as described in Chapter 13:

```
words.saveAsObjectFile("/tmp/my/sequenceFilePath")
```

Hadoop Files

There are a variety of different Hadoop file formats to which you can save. These allow you to specify classes, output formats, Hadoop configurations, and compression schemes. (For information on these formats, read *Hadoop: The Definitive Guide* [O'Reilly, 2015].) These formats are largely irrelevant except if you're working deeply in the Hadoop ecosystem or with some legacy mapReduce jobs.

Caching

The same principles apply for caching RDDs as for DataFrames and Datasets. You can either cache or persist an RDD. By default, cache and persist only handle data in memory. We can name it if we use the `setName` function that we referenced previously in this chapter:

```
words.cache()
```

We can specify a storage level as any of the storage levels in the singleton object: `org.apache.spark.storage.StorageLevel`, which are combinations of memory only; disk only; and separately, off heap.

We can subsequently query for this storage level (we talk about storage levels when we discuss persistence in Chapter 20):

```
// in Scala
words.getStorageLevel

# in Python
words.getStorageLevel()
```

Checkpointing

One feature not available in the DataFrame API is the concept of *checkpointing*. Checkpointing is the act of saving an RDD to disk so that future references to this RDD point to those intermediate partitions on disk rather than recomputing the RDD from its original source. This is similar to caching except that it's not stored in memory, only disk. This can be helpful when performing iterative computation, similar to the use cases for caching:

```
spark.sparkContext.setCheckpointDir("/some/path/for/checkpointing")
words.checkpoint()
```

Now, when we reference this RDD, it will derive from the checkpoint instead of the source data. This can be a helpful optimization.

Pipe RDDs to System Commands

The pipe method is probably one of Spark's more interesting methods. With pipe, you can return an RDD created by piping elements to a forked external process. The resulting RDD is computed by executing the given process once per partition. All elements of each input partition are written to a process's stdin as lines of input separated by a newline. The resulting partition consists of the process's stdout output, with each line of stdout resulting in one element of the output partition. A process is invoked even for empty partitions.

The print behavior can be customized by providing two functions.

We can use a simple example and pipe each partition to the command wc. Each row will be passed in as a new line, so if we perform a line count, we will get the number of lines, one per partition:

```
words.pipe("wc -l").collect()
```

In this case, we got five lines per partition.

mapPartitions

The previous command revealed that Spark operates on a per-partition basis when it comes to actually executing code. You also might have noticed earlier that the return signature of a map function on an RDD is actually MapPartitionsRDD. This is because map is just a row-wise alias for mapPartitions, which makes it possible for you to map an individual partition (represented as an iterator). That's because physically on the cluster we operate on each partition individually (and not a specific row). A simple example creates the value "1" for every partition in our data, and the sum of the following expression will count the number of partitions we have:

```
// in Scala
words.mapPartitions(part => Iterator[Int](1)).sum() // 2

# in Python
words.mapPartitions(lambda part: [1]).sum() # 2
```

Naturally, this means that we operate on a per-partition basis and allows us to perform an operation on that *entire* partition. This is valuable for performing something on an entire subdataset of your RDD. You can gather all values of a partition class or group into one partition and then operate on that entire group using arbitrary functions and controls. An example use case of this would be that you could pipe this through some custom machine learning algorithm and train an individual model for that company's portion of the dataset. A Facebook engineer has an interesting demonstration of their particular implementation of the `pipe` operator with a similar use case demonstrated at Spark Summit East 2017 (*https://spark-summit.org/east-2017/ events/experiences-with-sparks-rdd-apis-for-complex-custom-applications/*).

Other functions similar to `mapPartitions` include `mapPartitionsWithIndex`. With this you specify a function that accepts an index (within the partition) and an iterator that goes through all items within the partition. The partition index is the partition number in your RDD, which identifies where each record in our dataset sits (and potentially allows you to debug). You might use this to test whether your map functions are behaving correctly:

```scala
// in Scala
def indexedFunc(partitionIndex:Int, withinPartIterator: Iterator[String]) = {
  withinPartIterator.toList.map(
    value => s"Partition: $partitionIndex => $value").iterator
}
words.mapPartitionsWithIndex(indexedFunc).collect()
```

```python
# in Python
def indexedFunc(partitionIndex, withinPartIterator):
  return ["partition: {} => {}".format(partitionIndex,
    x) for x in withinPartIterator]
words.mapPartitionsWithIndex(indexedFunc).collect()
```

foreachPartition

Although `mapPartitions` needs a return value to work properly, this next function does not. `foreachPartition` simply iterates over all the partitions of the data. The difference is that the function has no return value. This makes it great for doing something with each partition like writing it out to a database. In fact, this is how many data source connectors are written. You can create our own text file source if you want by specifying outputs to the temp directory with a random ID:

```scala
words.foreachPartition { iter =>
  import java.io._
  import scala.util.Random
  val randomFileName = new Random().nextInt()
  val pw = new PrintWriter(new File(s"/tmp/random-file-${randomFileName}.txt"))
  while (iter.hasNext) {
      pw.write(iter.next())
  }
  pw.close()
}
```

You'll find these two files if you scan your */tmp* directory.

glom

`glom` is an interesting function that takes every partition in your dataset and converts them to arrays. This can be useful if you're going to collect the data to the driver and want to have an array for each partition. However, this can cause serious stability issues because if you have large partitions or a large number of partitions, it's simple to crash the driver.

In the following example, you can see that we get two partitions and each word falls into one partition each:

```scala
// in Scala
spark.sparkContext.parallelize(Seq("Hello", "World"), 2).glom().collect()
// Array(Array(Hello), Array(World))
```

```python
# in Python
spark.sparkContext.parallelize(["Hello", "World"], 2).glom().collect()
# [['Hello'], ['World']]
```

Conclusion

In this chapter, you saw the basics of the RDD APIs, including single RDD manipulation. Chapter 13 touches on more advanced RDD concepts, such as joins and key-value RDDs.

Advanced RDDs

Chapter 12 explored the basics of single RDD manipulation. You learned how to create RDDs and why you might want to use them. In addition, we discussed map, filter, reduce, and how to create functions to transform single RDD data. This chapter covers the advanced RDD operations and focuses on key–value RDDs, a powerful abstraction for manipulating data. We also touch on some more advanced topics like custom partitioning, a reason you might want to use RDDs in the first place. With a custom partitioning function, you can control exactly how data is laid out on the cluster and manipulate that individual partition accordingly. Before we get there, let's summarize the key topics we will cover:

- Aggregations and key–value RDDs
- Custom partitioning
- RDD joins

 This set of APIs has been around since, essentially, the beginning of Spark, and there are a *ton* of examples all across the web on this set of APIs. This makes it trivial to search and find examples that will show you how to use these operations.

Let's use the same dataset we used in the last chapter:

```scala
// in Scala
val myCollection = "Spark The Definitive Guide : Big Data Processing Made Simple"
  .split(" ")
val words = spark.sparkContext.parallelize(myCollection, 2)
```

```python
# in Python
myCollection = "Spark The Definitive Guide : Big Data Processing Made Simple"\
```

```
    .split(" ")
words = spark.sparkContext.parallelize(myCollection, 2)
```

Key-Value Basics (Key-Value RDDs)

There are many methods on RDDs that require you to put your data in a key–value format. A hint that this is required is that the method will include <some-operation>ByKey. Whenever you see ByKey in a method name, it means that you can perform this only on a PairRDD type. The easiest way is to just map over your current RDD to a basic key–value structure. This means having two values in each record of your RDD:

```
// in Scala
words.map(word => (word.toLowerCase, 1))

# in Python
words.map(lambda word: (word.lower(), 1))
```

keyBy

The preceding example demonstrated a simple way to create a key. However, you can also use the keyBy function to achieve the same result by specifying a function that creates the key from your current value. In this case, you are keying by the first letter in the word. Spark then keeps the record as the value for the keyed RDD:

```
// in Scala
val keyword = words.keyBy(word => word.toLowerCase.toSeq(0).toString)

# in Python
keyword = words.keyBy(lambda word: word.lower()[0])
```

Mapping over Values

After you have a set of key–value pairs, you can begin manipulating them as such. If we have a tuple, Spark will assume that the first element is the key, and the second is the value. When in this format, you can explicitly choose to map-over the values (and ignore the individual keys). Of course, you could do this manually, but this can help prevent errors when you know that you are just going to modify the values:

```
// in Scala
keyword.mapValues(word => word.toUpperCase).collect()

# in Python
keyword.mapValues(lambda word: word.upper()).collect()
```

Here's the output in Python:

```
[('s', 'SPARK'),
 ('t', 'THE'),
 ('d', 'DEFINITIVE'),
 ('g', 'GUIDE'),
```

```
(':', ':'),
('b', 'BIG'),
('d', 'DATA'),
('p', 'PROCESSING'),
('m', 'MADE'),
('s', 'SIMPLE')]
```

(The values in Scala are the same but omitted for brevity.)

You can `flatMap` over the rows, as we saw in Chapter 12, to expand the number of rows that you have to make it so that each row represents a character. In the following example, we will omit the output, but it would simply be each character as we converted them into arrays:

```scala
// in Scala
keyword.flatMapValues(word => word.toUpperCase).collect()
```

```python
# in Python
keyword.flatMapValues(lambda word: word.upper()).collect()
```

Extracting Keys and Values

When we are in the key–value pair format, we can also extract the specific keys or values by using the following methods:

```scala
// in Scala
keyword.keys.collect()
keyword.values.collect()
```

```python
# in Python
keyword.keys().collect()
keyword.values().collect()
```

lookup

One interesting task you might want to do with an RDD is look up the result for a particular key. Note that there is *no* enforcement mechanism with respect to there being only one key for each input, so if we `lookup` "s", we are going to get both values associated with that—"Spark" and "Simple":

```
keyword.lookup("s")
```

sampleByKey

There are two ways to sample an RDD by a set of keys. We can do it via an approximation or exactly. Both operations can do so with or without replacement as well as sampling by a fraction by a given key. This is done via simple random sampling with one pass over the RDD, which produces a sample of size that's approximately equal to the sum of `math.ceil(numItems * samplingRate)` over all key values:

```scala
// in Scala
val distinctChars = words.flatMap(word => word.toLowerCase.toSeq).distinct
  .collect()
import scala.util.Random
val sampleMap = distinctChars.map(c => (c, new Random().nextDouble())).toMap
words.map(word => (word.toLowerCase.toSeq(0), word))
  .sampleByKey(true, sampleMap, 6L)
  .collect()
```

```python
# in Python
import random
distinctChars = words.flatMap(lambda word: list(word.lower())).distinct()\
  .collect()
sampleMap = dict(map(lambda c: (c, random.random()), distinctChars))
words.map(lambda word: (word.lower()[0], word))\
  .sampleByKey(True, sampleMap, 6).collect()
```

This method differs from `sampleByKey` in that you make additional passes over the RDD to create a sample size that's exactly equal to the sum of `math.ceil(numItems * samplingRate)` over all key values with a 99.99% confidence. When sampling without replacement, you need one additional pass over the RDD to guarantee sample size; when sampling with replacement, you need two additional passes:

```scala
// in Scala
words.map(word => (word.toLowerCase.toSeq(0), word))
  .sampleByKeyExact(true, sampleMap, 6L).collect()
```

Aggregations

You can perform aggregations on plain RDDs or on PairRDDs, depending on the method that you are using. Let's use some of our datasets to demonstrate this:

```scala
// in Scala
val chars = words.flatMap(word => word.toLowerCase.toSeq)
val KVcharacters = chars.map(letter => (letter, 1))
def maxFunc(left:Int, right:Int) = math.max(left, right)
def addFunc(left:Int, right:Int) = left + right
val nums = sc.parallelize(1 to 30, 5)
```

```python
# in Python
chars = words.flatMap(lambda word: word.lower())
KVcharacters = chars.map(lambda letter: (letter, 1))
def maxFunc(left, right):
  return max(left, right)
def addFunc(left, right):
  return left + right
nums = sc.parallelize(range(1,31), 5)
```

After you have this, you can do something like `countByKey`, which counts the items per each key.

countByKey

You can count the number of elements for each key, collecting the results to a local Map. You can also do this with an approximation, which makes it possible for you to specify a timeout and confidence when using Scala or Java:

```scala
// in Scala
val timeout = 1000L //milliseconds
val confidence = 0.95
KVcharacters.countByKey()
KVcharacters.countByKeyApprox(timeout, confidence)
```

```python
# in Python
KVcharacters.countByKey()
```

Understanding Aggregation Implementations

There are several ways to create your key–value PairRDDs; however, the implementation is actually quite important for job stability. Let's compare the two fundamental choices, groupBy and reduce. We'll do these in the context of a key, but the same basic principles apply to the groupBy and reduce methods.

groupByKey

Looking at the API documentation, you might think groupByKey with a map over each grouping is the best way to sum up the counts for each key:

```scala
// in Scala
KVcharacters.groupByKey().map(row => (row._1, row._2.reduce(addFunc))).collect()
```

```python
# in Python
KVcharacters.groupByKey().map(lambda row: (row[0], reduce(addFunc, row[1])))\
  .collect()
# note this is Python 2, reduce must be imported from functools in Python 3
```

However, this is, for the majority of cases, the wrong way to approach the problem. The fundamental issue here is that each executor must hold *all values* for a given key in memory before applying the function to them. Why is this problematic? If you have massive key skew, some partitions might be completely overloaded with a ton of values for a given key, and you will get OutOfMemoryErrors. This obviously doesn't cause an issue with our current dataset, but it can cause serious problems at scale. This is not guaranteed to happen, but it *can* happen.

There are use cases when groupByKey does make sense. If you have consistent value sizes for each key and know that they will fit in the memory of a given executor, you're going to be just fine. It's just good to know exactly what you're getting yourself into when you do this. There is a preferred approach for additive use cases: reduceBy Key.

reduceByKey

Because we are performing a simple count, a much more stable approach is to perform the same `flatMap` and then just perform a `map` to map each letter instance to the number one, and then perform a `reduceByKey` with a summation function in order to collect back the array. This implementation is much more stable because the reduce happens within each partition and doesn't need to put everything in memory. Additionally, there is no incurred shuffle during this operation; everything happens at each worker individually before performing a final reduce. This greatly enhances the speed at which you can perform the operation as well as the stability of the operation:

```
KVcharacters.reduceByKey(addFunc).collect()
```

Here's the result of the operation:

```
Array((d,4), (p,3), (t,3), (b,1), (h,1), (n,2),
...
(a,4), (i,7), (k,1), (u,1), (o,1), (g,3), (m,2), (c,1))
```

The `reduceByKey` method returns an RDD of a group (the key) and sequence of elements that are not guranteed to have an ordering. Therefore this method is completely appropriate when our workload is associative but inappropriate when the order matters.

Other Aggregation Methods

There exist a number of advanced aggregation methods. For the most part these are largely implementation details depending on your specific workload. We find it very rare that users come across this sort of workload (or need to perform this kind of operation) in modern-day Spark. There just aren't that many reasons for using these extremely low-level tools when you can perform much simpler aggregations using the Structured APIs. These functions largely allow you very specific, very low-level control on exactly how a given aggregation is performed on the cluster of machines.

aggregate

Another function is `aggregate`. This function requires a null and start value and then requires you to specify two different functions. The first aggregates within partitions, the second aggregates across partitions. The start value will be used at both aggregation levels:

```scala
// in Scala
nums.aggregate(0)(maxFunc, addFunc)
```

```python
# in Python
nums.aggregate(0, maxFunc, addFunc)
```

`aggregate` does have some performance implications because it performs the final aggregation on the driver. If the results from the executors are too large, they can take down the driver with an `OutOfMemoryError`. There is another method, `treeAggre gate` that does the same thing as aggregate (at the user level) but does so in a different way. It basically "pushes down" some of the subaggregations (creating a tree from executor to executor) before performing the final aggregation on the driver. Having multiple levels can help you to ensure that the driver does not run out of memory in the process of the aggregation. These tree-based implementations are often to try to improve stability in certain operations:

```scala
// in Scala
val depth = 3
nums.treeAggregate(0)(maxFunc, addFunc, depth)
```

```python
# in Python
depth = 3
nums.treeAggregate(0, maxFunc, addFunc, depth)
```

aggregateByKey

This function does the same as `aggregate` but instead of doing it partition by partition, it does it by key. The start value and functions follow the same properties:

```scala
// in Scala
KVcharacters.aggregateByKey(0)(addFunc, maxFunc).collect()
```

```python
# in Python
KVcharacters.aggregateByKey(0, addFunc, maxFunc).collect()
```

combineByKey

Instead of specifying an aggregation function, you can specify a combiner. This combiner operates on a given key and merges the values according to some function. It then goes to merge the different outputs of the combiners to give us our result. We can specify the number of output partitions as a custom output partitioner as well:

```scala
// in Scala
val valToCombiner = (value:Int) => List(value)
val mergeValuesFunc = (vals:List[Int], valToAppend:Int) => valToAppend :: vals
val mergeCombinerFunc = (vals1:List[Int], vals2:List[Int]) => vals1 ::: vals2
// now we define these as function variables
val outputPartitions = 6
KVcharacters
  .combineByKey(
    valToCombiner,
    mergeValuesFunc,
    mergeCombinerFunc,
    outputPartitions)
  .collect()
```

```python
# in Python
def valToCombiner(value):
  return [value]
def mergeValuesFunc(vals, valToAppend):
```

```
    vals.append(valToAppend)
    return vals
  def mergeCombinerFunc(vals1, vals2):
    return vals1 + vals2
outputPartitions = 6
KVcharacters\
  .combineByKey(
    valToCombiner,
    mergeValuesFunc,
    mergeCombinerFunc,
    outputPartitions)\
  .collect()
```

foldByKey

foldByKey merges the values for each key using an associative function and a neutral "zero value," which can be added to the result an arbitrary number of times, and must not change the result (e.g., 0 for addition, or 1 for multiplication):

```
// in Scala
KVcharacters.foldByKey(0)(addFunc).collect()
```

```
# in Python
KVcharacters.foldByKey(0, addFunc).collect()
```

CoGroups

CoGroups give you the ability to group together up to three key–value RDDs together in Scala and two in Python. This joins the given values by key. This is effectively just a group-based join on an RDD. When doing this, you can also specify a number of output partitions or a custom partitioning function to control exactly how this data is distributed across the cluster (we talk about partitioning functions later on in this chapter):

```
// in Scala
import scala.util.Random
val distinctChars = words.flatMap(word => word.toLowerCase.toSeq).distinct
val charRDD = distinctChars.map(c => (c, new Random().nextDouble()))
val charRDD2 = distinctChars.map(c => (c, new Random().nextDouble()))
val charRDD3 = distinctChars.map(c => (c, new Random().nextDouble()))
charRDD.cogroup(charRDD2, charRDD3).take(5)
```

```
# in Python
import random
distinctChars = words.flatMap(lambda word: word.lower()).distinct()
charRDD = distinctChars.map(lambda c: (c, random.random()))
charRDD2 = distinctChars.map(lambda c: (c, random.random()))
charRDD.cogroup(charRDD2).take(5)
```

The result is a group with our key on one side, and all of the relevant values on the other side.

Joins

RDDs have much the same joins as we saw in the Structured API, although RDDs are much more involved for you. They all follow the same basic format: the two RDDs we would like to join, and, optionally, either the number of output partitions or the customer partition function to which they should output. We'll talk about partitioning functions later on in this chapter.

Inner Join

We'll demonstrate an inner join now. Notice how we are setting the number of output partitions we would like to see:

```scala
// in Scala
val keyedChars = distinctChars.map(c => (c, new Random().nextDouble()))
val outputPartitions = 10
KVcharacters.join(keyedChars).count()
KVcharacters.join(keyedChars, outputPartitions).count()
```

```python
# in Python
keyedChars = distinctChars.map(lambda c: (c, random.random()))
outputPartitions = 10
KVcharacters.join(keyedChars).count()
KVcharacters.join(keyedChars, outputPartitions).count()
```

We won't provide an example for the other joins, but they all follow the same basic format. You can learn about the following join types at the conceptual level in Chapter 8:

- `fullOuterJoin`
- `leftOuterJoin`
- `rightOuterJoin`
- `cartesian` (This, again, is very dangerous! It does not accept a join key and can have a massive output.)

zips

The final type of join isn't really a join at all, but it does combine two RDDs, so it's worth labeling it as a join. `zip` allows you to "zip" together two RDDs, assuming that they have the same length. This creates a `PairRDD`. The two RDDs must have the same number of partitions as well as the same number of elements:

```scala
// in Scala
val numRange = sc.parallelize(0 to 9, 2)
words.zip(numRange).collect()
```

```python
# in Python
numRange = sc.parallelize(range(10), 2)
words.zip(numRange).collect()
```

This gives us the following result, an array of keys zipped to the values:

```
[('Spark', 0),
 ('The', 1),
 ('Definitive', 2),
 ('Guide', 3),
 (':', 4),
 ('Big', 5),
 ('Data', 6),
 ('Processing', 7),
 ('Made', 8),
 ('Simple', 9)]
```

Controlling Partitions

With RDDs, you have control over how data is exactly physically distributed across the cluster. Some of these methods are basically the same from what we have in the Structured APIs but the key addition (that does not exist in the Structured APIs) is the ability to specify a partitioning function (formally a custom `Partitioner`, which we discuss later when we look at basic methods).

coalesce

`coalesce` effectively collapses partitions on the same worker in order to avoid a shuffle of the data when repartitioning. For instance, our `words` RDD is currently two partitions, we can collapse that to one partition by using `coalesce` without bringing about a shuffle of the data:

```scala
// in Scala
words.coalesce(1).getNumPartitions // 1
```

```python
# in Python
words.coalesce(1).getNumPartitions() # 1
```

repartition

The `repartition` operation allows you to repartition your data up or down but performs a shuffle across nodes in the process. Increasing the number of partitions can increase the level of parallelism when operating in map- and filter-type operations:

```
words.repartition(10) // gives us 10 partitions
```

repartitionAndSortWithinPartitions

This operation gives you the ability to repartition as well as specify the ordering of each one of those output partitions. We'll omit the example because the documentation for it is good, but both the partitioning and the key comparisons can be specified by the user.

Custom Partitioning

This ability is one of the primary reasons you'd want to use RDDs. Custom partitioners are not available in the Structured APIs because they don't really have a logical counterpart. They're a low-level, implementation detail that can have a significant effect on whether your jobs run successfully. The canonical example to motivate custom partition for this operation is PageRank whereby we seek to control the layout of the data on the cluster and avoid shuffles. In our shopping dataset, this might mean partitioning by each customer ID (we'll get to this example in a moment).

In short, the sole goal of custom partitioning is to even out the distribution of your data across the cluster so that you can work around problems like data skew.

If you're going to use custom partitioners, you should drop down to RDDs from the Structured APIs, apply your custom partitioner, and then convert it back to a DataFrame or Dataset. This way, you get the best of both worlds, only dropping down to custom partitioning when you need to.

To perform custom partitioning you need to implement your own class that extends `Partitioner`. You need to do this only when you have lots of domain knowledge about your problem space—if you're just looking to partition on a value or even a set of values (columns), it's worth just doing it in the DataFrame API.

Let's dive into an example:

```scala
// in Scala
val df = spark.read.option("header", "true").option("inferSchema", "true")
  .csv("/data/retail-data/all/")
val rdd = df.coalesce(10).rdd
```

```python
# in Python
df = spark.read.option("header", "true").option("inferSchema", "true")\
  .csv("/data/retail-data/all/")
rdd = df.coalesce(10).rdd
```

```
df.printSchema()
```

Spark has two built-in Partitioners that you can leverage off in the RDD API, a `Hash Partitioner` for discrete values and a `RangePartitioner`. These two work for discrete values and continuous values, respectively. Spark's Structured APIs will already use these, although we can use the same thing in RDDs:

```scala
// in Scala
import org.apache.spark.HashPartitioner
rdd.map(r => r(6)).take(5).foreach(println)
val keyedRDD = rdd.keyBy(row => row(6).asInstanceOf[Int].toDouble)

keyedRDD.partitionBy(new HashPartitioner(10)).take(10)
```

Although the hash and range partitioners are useful, they're fairly rudimentary. At times, you will need to perform some very low-level partitioning because you're working with very large data and large *key skew*. Key skew simply means that some keys have many, many more values than other keys. You want to break these keys as much as possible to improve parallelism and prevent `OutOfMemoryErrors` during the course of execution.

One instance might be that you need to partition more keys if and only if the key matches a certain format. For instance, we might know that there are two customers in your dataset that always crash your analysis and we need to break them up further than other customer IDs. In fact, these two are so skewed that they need to be operated on alone, whereas all of the others can be lumped into large groups. This is obviously a bit of a caricatured example, but you might see similar situations in your data, as well:

```scala
// in Scala
import org.apache.spark.Partitioner
class DomainPartitioner extends Partitioner {
  def numPartitions = 3
  def getPartition(key: Any): Int = {
    val customerId = key.asInstanceOf[Double].toInt
    if (customerId == 17850.0 || customerId == 12583.0) {
      return 0
    } else {
      return new java.util.Random().nextInt(2) + 1
    }
  }
}

keyedRDD
  .partitionBy(new DomainPartitioner).map(_._1).glom().map(_.toSet.toSeq.length)
  .take(5)
```

After you run this, you will see the count of results in each partition. The second two numbers will vary, because we're distributing them randomly (as you will see when we do the same in Python) but the same principles apply:

```python
# in Python
def partitionFunc(key):
  import random
  if key == 17850 or key == 12583:
    return 0
  else:
    return random.randint(1,2)
```

```
keyedRDD = rdd.keyBy(lambda row: row[6])
keyedRDD\
  .partitionBy(3, partitionFunc)\
  .map(lambda x: x[0])\
  .glom()\
  .map(lambda x: len(set(x)))\
  .take(5)
```

This custom key distribution logic is available only at the RDD level. Of course, this is a simple example, but it does show the power of using arbitrary logic to distribute the data around the cluster in a physical manner.

Custom Serialization

The last advanced topic that is worth talking about is the issue of *Kryo serialization*. Any object that you hope to parallelize (or function) must be serializable:

```
// in Scala
class SomeClass extends Serializable {
  var someValue = 0
  def setSomeValue(i:Int) = {
    someValue = i
    this
  }
}

sc.parallelize(1 to 10).map(num => new SomeClass().setSomeValue(num))
```

The default serialization can be quite slow. Spark can use the Kryo library (version 2) to serialize objects more quickly. Kryo is significantly faster and more compact than Java serialization (often as much as 10x), but does not support all serializable types and requires you to register the classes you'll use in the program in advance for best performance.

You can use Kryo by initializing your job with a SparkConf and setting the value of "spark.serializer" to "org.apache.spark.serializer.KryoSerializer" (we discuss this in the next part of the book). This setting configures the serializer used for shuffling data between worker nodes and serializing RDDs to disk. The only reason Kryo is not the default is because of the custom registration requirement, but we recommend trying it in any network-intensive application. Since Spark 2.0.0, we internally use Kryo serializer when shuffling RDDs with simple types, arrays of simple types, or string type.

Spark automatically includes Kryo serializers for the many commonly used core Scala classes covered in the AllScalaRegistrar from the Twitter chill library.

To register your own custom classes with Kryo, use the registerKryoClasses method:

```scala
// in Scala
val conf = new SparkConf().setMaster(...).setAppName(...)
conf.registerKryoClasses(Array(classOf[MyClass1], classOf[MyClass2]))
val sc = new SparkContext(conf)
```

Conclusion

In this chapter we discussed many of the more advanced topics regarding RDDs. Of particular note was the section on custom partitioning, which allows you very specific functions to layout your data. In Chapter 14, we discuss another of Spark's low-level tools: distributed variables.

Distributed Shared Variables

In addition to the Resilient Distributed Dataset (RDD) interface, the second kind of low-level API in Spark is two types of "distributed shared variables": broadcast variables and accumulators. These are variables you can use in your user-defined functions (e.g., in a map function on an RDD or a DataFrame) that have special properties when running on a cluster. Specifically, *accumulators* let you add together data from all the tasks into a shared result (e.g., to implement a counter so you can see how many of your job's input records failed to parse), while *broadcast variables* let you save a large value on all the worker nodes and reuse it across many Spark actions without re-sending it to the cluster. This chapter discusses some of the motivation for each of these variable types as well as how to use them.

Broadcast Variables

Broadcast variables are a way you can share an immutable value efficiently around the cluster without encapsulating that variable in a function closure. The normal way to use a variable in your driver node inside your tasks is to simply reference it in your function closures (e.g., in a map operation), but this can be inefficient, especially for large variables such as a lookup table or a machine learning model. The reason for this is that when you use a variable in a closure, it must be deserialized on the worker nodes many times (one per task). Moreover, if you use the same variable in multiple Spark actions and jobs, it will be re-sent to the workers with every job instead of once.

This is where broadcast variables come in. Broadcast variables are shared, immutable variables that are cached on every machine in the cluster instead of serialized with every single task. The canonical use case is to pass around a large lookup table that fits in memory on the executors and use that in a function, as illustrated in Figure 14-1.

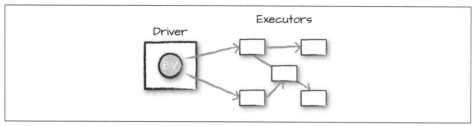

Figure 14-1. Broadcast variables

For example, suppose that you have a list of words or values:

```
// in Scala
val myCollection = "Spark The Definitive Guide : Big Data Processing Made Simple"
  .split(" ")
val words = spark.sparkContext.parallelize(myCollection, 2)
```

```
# in Python
my_collection = "Spark The Definitive Guide : Big Data Processing Made Simple"\
  .split(" ")
words = spark.sparkContext.parallelize(my_collection, 2)
```

You would like to supplement your list of words with other information that you have, which is many kilobytes, megabytes, or potentially even gigabytes in size. This is technically a right join if we thought about it in terms of SQL:

```
// in Scala
val supplementalData = Map("Spark" -> 1000, "Definitive" -> 200,
                           "Big" -> -300, "Simple" -> 100)
```

```
# in Python
supplementalData = {"Spark":1000, "Definitive":200,
                    "Big":-300, "Simple":100}
```

We can broadcast this structure across Spark and reference it by using `suppBroadcast`. This value is immutable and is lazily replicated across all nodes in the cluster when we trigger an action:

```
// in Scala
val suppBroadcast = spark.sparkContext.broadcast(supplementalData)
```

```
# in Python
suppBroadcast = spark.sparkContext.broadcast(supplementalData)
```

We reference this variable via the `value` method, which returns the exact value that we had earlier. This method is accessible within serialized functions without having to serialize the data. This can save you a great deal of serialization and deserialization costs because Spark transfers data more efficiently around the cluster using broadcasts:

```
// in Scala
suppBroadcast.value
```

```python
# in Python
suppBroadcast.value
```

Now we could transform our RDD using this value. In this instance, we will create a key–value pair according to the value we might have in the map. If we lack the value, we will simply replace it with 0:

```scala
// in Scala
words.map(word => (word, suppBroadcast.value.getOrElse(word, 0)))
  .sortBy(wordPair => wordPair._2)
  .collect()
```

```python
# in Python
words.map(lambda word: (word, suppBroadcast.value.get(word, 0)))\
  .sortBy(lambda wordPair: wordPair[1])\
  .collect()
```

This returns the following value in Python and the same values in an array type in Scala:

```
[('Big', -300),
 ('The', 0),
 ...
 ('Definitive', 200),
 ('Spark', 1000)]
```

The only difference between this and passing it into the closure is that we have done this in a much more efficient manner (Naturally, this depends on the amount of data and the number of executors. For very small data (low KBs) on small clusters, it might not be). Although this small dictionary probably is not too large of a cost, if you have a much larger value, the cost of serializing the data for every task can be quite significant.

One thing to note is that we used this in the context of an RDD; we can also use this in a UDF or in a Dataset and achieve the same result.

Accumulators

Accumulators (Figure 14-2), Spark's second type of shared variable, are a way of updating a value inside of a variety of transformations and propagating that value to the driver node in an efficient and fault-tolerant way.

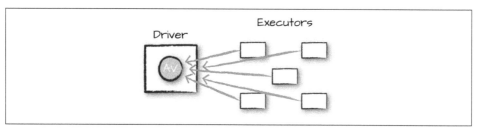

Figure 14-2. Accumulator variable

Accumulators provide a mutable variable that a Spark cluster can safely update on a per-row basis. You can use these for debugging purposes (say to track the values of a certain variable per partition in order to intelligently use it over time) or to create low-level aggregation. Accumulators are variables that are "added" to only through an associative and commutative operation and can therefore be efficiently supported in parallel. You can use them to implement counters (as in MapReduce) or sums. Spark natively supports accumulators of numeric types, and programmers can add support for new types.

For accumulator updates performed inside *actions only*, Spark guarantees that each task's update to the accumulator will be applied only once, meaning that restarted tasks will not update the value. In transformations, you should be aware that each task's update can be applied more than once if tasks or job stages are reexecuted.

Accumulators do not change the lazy evaluation model of Spark. If an accumulator is being updated within an operation on an RDD, its value is updated only once that RDD is actually computed (e.g., when you call an action on that RDD or an RDD that depends on it). Consequently, accumulator updates are not guaranteed to be executed when made within a lazy transformation like map().

Accumulators can be both named and unnamed. Named accumulators will display their running results in the Spark UI, whereas unnamed ones will not.

Basic Example

Let's experiment by performing a custom aggregation on the Flight dataset that we created earlier in the book. In this example, we will use the Dataset API as opposed to the RDD API, but the extension is quite similar:

```scala
// in Scala
case class Flight(DEST_COUNTRY_NAME: String,
                  ORIGIN_COUNTRY_NAME: String, count: BigInt)
val flights = spark.read
  .parquet("/data/flight-data/parquet/2010-summary.parquet")
  .as[Flight]
```

```python
# in Python
flights = spark.read\
  .parquet("/data/flight-data/parquet/2010-summary.parquet")
```

Now let's create an accumulator that will count the number of flights to or from China. Even though we could do this in a fairly straightfoward manner in SQL, many things might not be so straightfoward. Accumulators provide a programmatic way of allowing for us to do these sorts of counts. The following demonstrates creating an unnamed accumulator:

```scala
// in Scala
import org.apache.spark.util.LongAccumulator
val accUnnamed = new LongAccumulator
val acc = spark.sparkContext.register(accUnnamed)
```

```python
# in Python
accChina = spark.sparkContext.accumulator(0)
```

Our use case fits a named accumulator a bit better. There are two ways to do this: a short-hand method and a long-hand one. The simplest is to use the SparkContext. Alternatively, we can instantiate the accumulator and register it with a name:

```scala
// in Scala
val accChina = new LongAccumulator
val accChina2 = spark.sparkContext.longAccumulator("China")
spark.sparkContext.register(accChina, "China")
```

We specify the name of the accumulator in the string value that we pass into the function, or as the second parameter into the `register` function. Named accumulators will display in the Spark UI, whereas unnamed ones will not.

The next step is to define the way we add to our accumulator. This is a fairly straightforward function:

```scala
// in Scala
def accChinaFunc(flight_row: Flight) = {
  val destination = flight_row.DEST_COUNTRY_NAME
  val origin = flight_row.ORIGIN_COUNTRY_NAME
  if (destination == "China") {
    accChina.add(flight_row.count.toLong)
  }
  if (origin == "China") {
    accChina.add(flight_row.count.toLong)
  }
}
```

```python
# in Python
def accChinaFunc(flight_row):
  destination = flight_row["DEST_COUNTRY_NAME"]
  origin = flight_row["ORIGIN_COUNTRY_NAME"]
  if destination == "China":
    accChina.add(flight_row["count"])
```

```
if origin == "China":
    accChina.add(flight_row["count"])
```

Now, let's iterate over every row in our flights dataset via the `foreach` method. The reason for this is because `foreach` is an action, and Spark can provide guarantees that perform only inside of actions.

The `foreach` method will run once for each row in the input DataFrame (assuming that we did not filter it) and will run our function against each row, incrementing the accumulator accordingly:

```scala
// in Scala
flights.foreach(flight_row => accChinaFunc(flight_row))
```

```python
# in Python
flights.foreach(lambda flight_row: accChinaFunc(flight_row))
```

This will complete fairly quickly, but if you navigate to the Spark UI, you can see the relevant value, on a per-Executor level, even before querying it programmatically, as demonstrated in Figure 14-3.

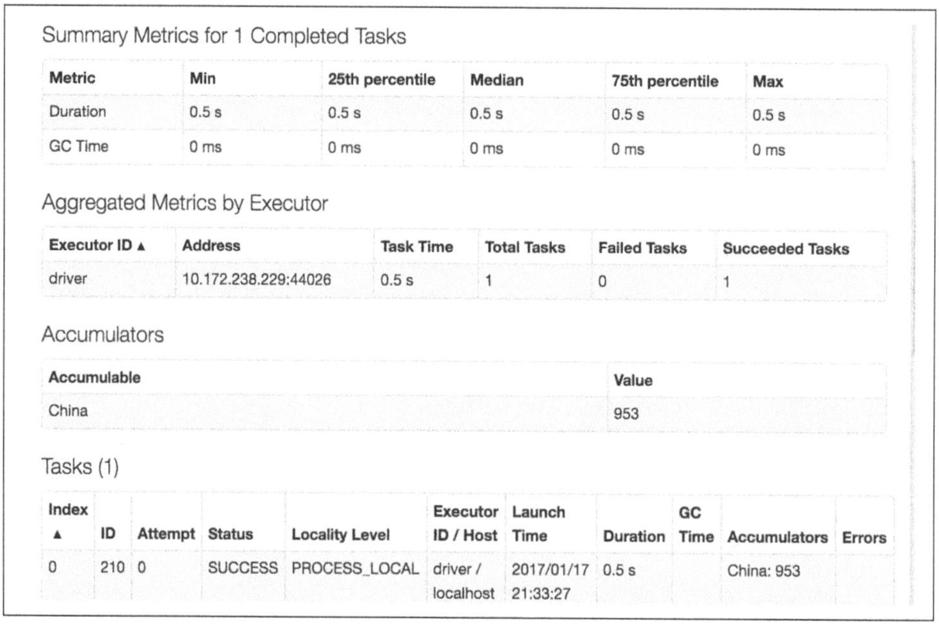

Summary Metrics for 1 Completed Tasks

Metric	Min	25th percentile	Median	75th percentile	Max
Duration	0.5 s	0.5 s	0.5 s	0.5 s	0.5 s
GC Time	0 ms	0 ms	0 ms	0 ms	0 ms

Aggregated Metrics by Executor

Executor ID ▲	Address	Task Time	Total Tasks	Failed Tasks	Succeeded Tasks
driver	10.172.238.229:44026	0.5 s	1	0	1

Accumulators

Accumulable	Value
China	953

Tasks (1)

Index ▲	ID	Attempt	Status	Locality Level	Executor ID / Host	Launch Time	Duration	GC Time	Accumulators	Errors
0	210	0	SUCCESS	PROCESS_LOCAL	driver / localhost	2017/01/17 21:33:27	0.5 s		China: 953	

Figure 14-3. Executor Spark UI

Of course, we can query it programmatically, as well. To do this, we use the `value` property:

```scala
// in Scala
accChina.value // 953
```

```python
# in Python
accChina.value # 953
```

Custom Accumulators

Although Spark does provide some default accumulator types, sometimes you might want to build your own custom accumulator. In order to do this you need to subclass the AccumulatorV2 class. There are several abstract methods that you need to implement, as you can see in the example that follows. In this example, you we will add only values that are even to the accumulator. Although this is again simplistic, it should show you how easy it is to build up your own accumulators:

```scala
// in Scala
import scala.collection.mutable.ArrayBuffer
import org.apache.spark.util.AccumulatorV2

val arr = ArrayBuffer[BigInt]()

class EvenAccumulator extends AccumulatorV2[BigInt, BigInt] {
  private var num:BigInt = 0
  def reset(): Unit = {
    this.num = 0
  }
  def add(intValue: BigInt): Unit = {
    if (intValue % 2 == 0) {
        this.num += intValue
    }
  }
  def merge(other: AccumulatorV2[BigInt,BigInt]): Unit = {
    this.num += other.value
  }
  def value():BigInt = {
    this.num
  }
  def copy(): AccumulatorV2[BigInt,BigInt] = {
    new EvenAccumulator
  }
  def isZero():Boolean = {
    this.num == 0
  }
}
val acc = new EvenAccumulator
val newAcc = sc.register(acc, "evenAcc")
```

```scala
// in Scala
acc.value // 0
flights.foreach(flight_row => acc.add(flight_row.count))
acc.value // 31390
```

If you are predominantly a Python user, you can also create your own custom accumulators by subclassing AccumulatorParam (*https://spark.apache.org/docs/1.1.0/api/*

python/pyspark.accumulators.AccumulatorParam-class.html) and using it as we saw in
the previous example.

Conclusion

In this chapter, we covered distributed variables. These can be helpful tools for optimizations or for debugging. In Chapter 15, we define how Spark runs on a cluster to
better understand when these can be helpful.

## PART IV

Production Applications

How Spark Runs on a Cluster

Thus far in the book, we focused on Spark's properties as a programming interface. We have discussed how the structured APIs take a logical operation, break it up into a logical plan, and convert that to a physical plan that actually consists of Resilient Distributed Dataset (RDD) operations that execute across the cluster of machines. This chapter focuses on what happens when Spark goes about executing that code. We discuss this in an implementation-agnostic way—this depends on neither the cluster manager that you're using nor the code that you're running. At the end of the day, all Spark code runs the same way.

This chapter covers several key topics:

- The architecture and components of a Spark Application
- The life cycle of a Spark Application inside and outside of Spark
- Important low-level execution properties, such as pipelining
- What it takes to run a Spark Application, as a segue into Chapter 16.

Let's begin with the architecture.

The Architecture of a Spark Application

In Chapter 2, we discussed some of the high-level components of a Spark Application. Let's review those again:

The Spark driver
> The driver is the process "in the driver seat" of your Spark Application. It is the controller of the execution of a Spark Application and maintains all of the state of the Spark cluster (the state and tasks of the executors). It must interface with the cluster manager in order to actually get physical resources and launch executors.

At the end of the day, this is just a process on a physical machine that is responsible for maintaining the state of the application running on the cluster.

The Spark executors

Spark executors are the processes that perform the tasks assigned by the Spark driver. Executors have one core responsibility: take the tasks assigned by the driver, run them, and report back their state (success or failure) and results. Each Spark Application has its own separate executor processes.

The cluster manager

The Spark Driver and Executors do not exist in a void, and this is where the cluster manager comes in. The cluster manager is responsible for maintaining a cluster of machines that will run your Spark Application(s). Somewhat confusingly, a cluster manager will have its own "driver" (sometimes called master) and "worker" abstractions. The core difference is that these are tied to physical machines rather than processes (as they are in Spark). Figure 15-1 shows a basic cluster setup. The machine on the left of the illustration is the *Cluster Manager Driver Node*. The circles represent daemon processes running on and managing each of the individual worker nodes. There is no Spark Application running as of yet—these are just the processes from the cluster manager.

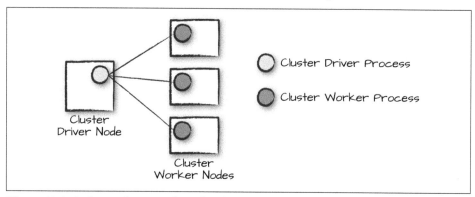

Figure 15-1. A cluster driver and worker (no Spark Application yet)

When it comes time to actually run a Spark Application, we request resources from the cluster manager to run it. Depending on how our application is configured, this can include a place to run the Spark driver or might be just resources for the executors for our Spark Application. Over the course of Spark Application execution, the cluster manager will be responsible for managing the underlying machines that our application is running on.

Spark currently supports three cluster managers: a simple built-in standalone cluster manager, Apache Mesos, and Hadoop YARN. However, this list will continue to grow, so be sure to check the documentation for your favorite cluster manager.

Now that we've covered the basic components of an application, let's walk through one of the first choices you will need to make when running your applications: choosing the execution mode.

Execution Modes

An execution *mode* gives you the power to determine where the aforementioned resources are physically located when you go to run your application. You have three modes to choose from:

- Cluster mode
- Client mode
- Local mode

We will walk through each of these in detail using Figure 15-1 as a template. In the following section, rectangles with solid borders represent Spark *driver process* whereas those with dotted borders represent the *executor processes*.

Cluster mode

Cluster mode is probably the most common way of running Spark Applications. In cluster mode, a user submits a pre-compiled JAR, Python script, or R script to a cluster manager. The cluster manager then launches the driver process on a worker node inside the cluster, in addition to the executor processes. This means that the cluster manager is responsible for maintaining all Spark Application–related processes. Figure 15-2 shows that the cluster manager placed our driver on a worker node and the executors on other worker nodes.

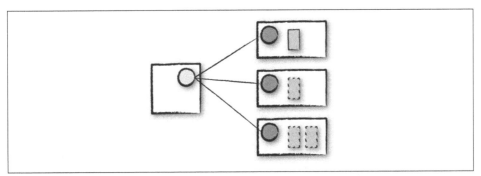

Figure 15-2. Spark's cluster mode

Client mode

Client mode is nearly the same as cluster mode except that the Spark driver remains on the client machine that submitted the application. This means that the client machine is responsible for maintaining the Spark driver process, and the cluster manager maintains the executor processses. In Figure 15-3, we are running the Spark Application from a machine that is not colocated on the cluster. These machines are commonly referred to as *gateway machines* or *edge nodes*. In Figure 15-3, you can see that the driver is running on a machine outside of the cluster but that the workers are located on machines in the cluster.

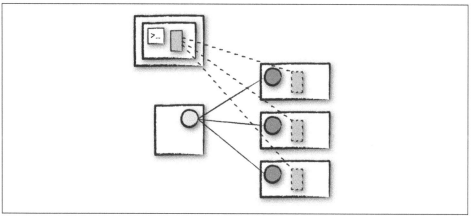

Figure 15-3. Spark's client mode

Local mode

Local mode is a significant departure from the previous two modes: it runs the entire Spark Application on a single machine. It achieves parallelism through threads on that single machine. This is a common way to learn Spark, to test your applications, or experiment iteratively with local development. However, we do not recommend using local mode for running production applications.

The Life Cycle of a Spark Application (Outside Spark)

This chapter has thus far covered the vocabulary necessary for discussing Spark Applications. It's now time to talk about the overall life cycle of Spark Applications from "outside" the actual Spark code. We will do this with an illustrated example of an application run with `spark-submit` (introduced in Chapter 3). We assume that a cluster is already running with four nodes, a driver (not a Spark driver but cluster manager driver) and three worker nodes. The actual cluster manager does not matter at this point: this section uses the vocabulary from the previous section to walk through a step-by-step Spark Application life cycle from initialization to program exit.

This section also makes use of illustrations and follows the same notation that we introduced previously. Additionally, we now introduce lines that represent network communication. Darker arrows represent communication by Spark or Spark-related processes, whereas dashed lines represent more general communication (like cluster management communication).

Client Request

The first step is for you to submit an actual application. This will be a pre-compiled JAR or library. At this point, you are executing code on your local machine and you're going to make a request to the cluster manager driver node (Figure 15-4). Here, we are explicitly asking for resources for the *Spark driver process* only. We assume that the cluster manager accepts this offer and places the driver onto a node in the cluster. The client process that submitted the original job exits and the application is off and running on the cluster.

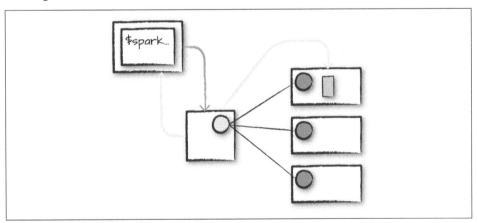

Figure 15-4. Requesting resources for a driver

To do this, you'll run something like the following command in your terminal:

```
./bin/spark-submit \
  --class <main-class> \
  --master <master-url> \
  --deploy-mode cluster \
  --conf <key>=<value> \
  ... # other options
  <application-jar> \
  [application-arguments]
```

Launch

Now that the driver process has been placed on the cluster, it begins running user code (Figure 15-5). This code must include a SparkSession that initializes a Spark cluster (e.g., driver + executors). The SparkSession will subsequently communicate with the cluster manager (the darker line), asking it to launch Spark executor processes across the cluster (the lighter lines). The number of executors and their relevant configurations are set by the user via the command-line arguments in the original spark-submit call.

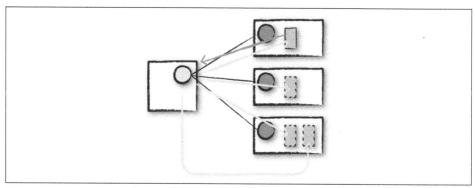

Figure 15-5. Launching the Spark Application

The cluster manager responds by launching the executor processes (assuming all goes well) and sends the relevant information about their locations to the driver process. After everything is hooked up correctly, we have a "Spark Cluster" as you likely think of it today.

Execution

Now that we have a "Spark Cluster," Spark goes about its merry way executing code, as shown in Figure 15-6. The driver and the workers communicate among themselves, executing code and moving data around. The driver schedules tasks onto each worker, and each worker responds with the status of those tasks and success or failure. (We cover these details shortly.)

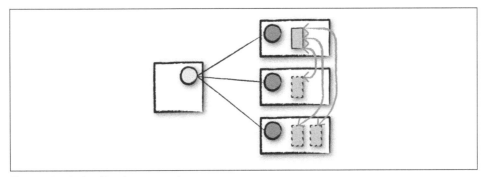

Figure 15-6. Application execution

Completion

After a Spark Application completes, the driver processs exits with either success or failure (Figure 15-7). The cluster manager then shuts down the executors in that Spark cluster for the driver. At this point, you can see the success or failure of the Spark Application by asking the cluster manager for this information.

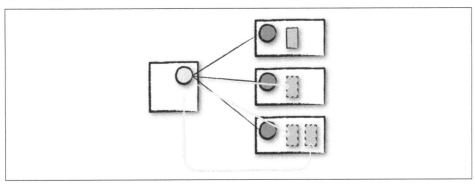

Figure 15-7. Shutting down the application

The Life Cycle of a Spark Application (Inside Spark)

We just examined the life cycle of a Spark Application outside of user code (basically the infrastructure that supports Spark), but it's arguably more important to talk about what happens within Spark when you run an application. This is "user-code" (the actual code that you write that defines your Spark Application). Each application is made up of one or more *Spark jobs*. Spark jobs within an application are executed serially (unless you use threading to launch multiple actions in parallel).

The SparkSession

The first step of any Spark Application is creating a SparkSession. In many interactive modes, this is done for you, but in an application, you must do it manually.

Some of your legacy code might use the new `SparkContext` pattern. This should be avoided in favor of the builder method on the `SparkSession`, which more robustly instantiates the Spark and SQL Contexts and ensures that there is no context conflict, given that there might be multiple libraries trying to create a session in the same Spark Appication:

```scala
// Creating a SparkSession in Scala
import org.apache.spark.sql.SparkSession
val spark = SparkSession.builder().appName("Databricks Spark Example")
  .config("spark.sql.warehouse.dir", "/user/hive/warehouse")
  .getOrCreate()
```

```python
# Creating a SparkSession in Python
from pyspark.sql import SparkSession
spark = SparkSession.builder.master("local").appName("Word Count")\
    .config("spark.some.config.option", "some-value")\
    .getOrCreate()
```

After you have a `SparkSession`, you should be able to run your Spark code. From the `SparkSession`, you can access all of low-level and legacy contexts and configurations accordingly, as well. Note that the `SparkSession` class was only added in Spark 2.X. Older code you might find would instead directly create a `SparkContext` and a `SQLContext` for the structured APIs.

The SparkContext

A `SparkContext` object within the `SparkSession` represents the connection to the Spark cluster. This class is how you communicate with some of Spark's lower-level APIs, such as RDDs. It is commonly stored as the variable `sc` in older examples and documentation. Through a `SparkContext`, you can create RDDs, accumulators, and broadcast variables, and you can run code on the cluster.

For the most part, you should not need to explicitly initialize a `SparkContext`; you should just be able to access it through the `SparkSession`. If you do want to, you should create it in the most general way, through the `getOrCreate` method:

```scala
// in Scala
import org.apache.spark.SparkContext
val sc = SparkContext.getOrCreate()
```

The SparkSession, SQLContext, and HiveContext

In previous versions of Spark, the `SQLContext` and `HiveContext` provided the ability to work with DataFrames and Spark SQL and were commonly stored as the variable `sqlContext` in examples, documentation, and legacy code. As a historical point, Spark 1.X had effectively two contexts. The `SparkContext` and the `SQLContext`. These two each performed different things. The former focused on more fine-grained control of Spark's central abstractions, whereas the latter focused on the higher-level tools like Spark SQL. In Spark 2.X, the communtiy combined the two APIs into the centralized `SparkSession` that we have today. However, both of these APIs still exist and you can access them via the `SparkSession`. It is important to note that you should never need to use the `SQLContext` and rarely need to use the `SparkContext`.

After you initialize your SparkSession, it's time to execute some code. As we know from previous chapters, all Spark code compiles down to RDDs. Therefore, in the next section, we will take some logical instructions (a DataFrame job) and walk through, step by step, what happens over time.

Logical Instructions

As you saw in the beginning of the book, Spark code essentially consists of transformations and actions. How you build these is up to you—whether it's through SQL, low-level RDD manipulation, or machine learning algorithms. Understanding how we take declarative instructions like DataFrames and convert them into physical execution plans is an important step to understanding how Spark runs on a cluster. In this section, be sure to run this in a fresh environment (a new Spark shell) to follow along with the job, stage, and task numbers.

Logical instructions to physical execution

We mentioned this in Part II, but it's worth reiterating so that you can better understand how Spark takes your code and actually runs the commands on the cluster. We will walk through some more code, line by line, explain what's happening behind the scenes so that you can walk away with a better understanding of your Spark Applications. In later chapters, when we discuss monitoring, we will perform a more detailed tracking of a Spark job through the Spark UI. In this current example, we'll take a simpler approach. We are going to do a three-step job: using a simple DataFrame, we'll repartition it, perform a value-by-value manipulation, and then aggregate some values and collect the final result.

This code was written and runs with Spark 2.2 in Python (you'll get the same result in Scala, so we've omitted it). The number of jobs is unlikely to change drastically but there might be improvements to Spark's underlying optimizations that change physical execution strategies.

```python
# in Python
df1 = spark.range(2, 10000000, 2)
df2 = spark.range(2, 10000000, 4)
step1 = df1.repartition(5)
step12 = df2.repartition(6)
step2 = step1.selectExpr("id * 5 as id")
step3 = step2.join(step12, ["id"])
step4 = step3.selectExpr("sum(id)")

step4.collect() # 2500000000000
```

When you run this code, we can see that your action triggers one complete Spark job. Let's take a look at the explain plan to ground our understanding of the physical execution plan. We can access this information on the SQL tab (after we actually run a query) in the Spark UI, as well:

```
step4.explain()

== Physical Plan ==
*HashAggregate(keys=[], functions=[sum(id#15L)])
+- Exchange SinglePartition
   +- *HashAggregate(keys=[], functions=[partial_sum(id#15L)])
      +- *Project [id#15L]
         +- *SortMergeJoin [id#15L], [id#10L], Inner
            :- *Sort [id#15L ASC NULLS FIRST], false, 0
            :  +- Exchange hashpartitioning(id#15L, 200)
            :     +- *Project [(id#7L * 5) AS id#15L]
            :        +- Exchange RoundRobinPartitioning(5)
            :           +- *Range (2, 10000000, step=2, splits=8)
            +- *Sort [id#10L ASC NULLS FIRST], false, 0
               +- Exchange hashpartitioning(id#10L, 200)
                  +- Exchange RoundRobinPartitioning(6)
                     +- *Range (2, 10000000, step=4, splits=8)
```

What you have when you call `collect` (or any action) is the execution of a Spark *job* that individually consist of *stages* and *tasks*. Go to localhost:4040 if you are running this on your local machine to see the Spark UI. We will follow along on the "jobs" tab eventually jumping to stages and tasks as we proceed to further levels of detail.

A Spark Job

In general, there should be one Spark job for one action. Actions always return results. Each job breaks down into a series of *stages*, the number of which depends on how many shuffle operations need to take place.

This job breaks down into the following stages and tasks:

- Stage 1 with 8 Tasks
- Stage 2 with 8 Tasks
- Stage 3 with 6 Tasks
- Stage 4 with 5 Tasks
- Stage 5 with 200 Tasks
- Stage 6 with 1 Task

I hope you're at least somewhat confused about how we got to these numbers so that we can take the time to better understand what is going on!

Stages

Stages in Spark represent groups of tasks that can be executed together to compute the same operation on multiple machines. In general, Spark will try to pack as much work as possible (i.e., as many transformations as possible inside your job) into the same stage, but the engine starts new stages after operations called *shuffles*. A shuffle represents a physical repartitioning of the data—for example, sorting a DataFrame, or grouping data that was loaded from a file by key (which requires sending records with the same key to the same node). This type of repartitioning requires coordinating across executors to move data around. Spark starts a new stage after each shuffle, and keeps track of what order the stages must run in to compute the final result.

In the job we looked at earlier, the first two stages correspond to the range that you perform in order to create your DataFrames. By default when you create a DataFrame with range, it has eight partitions. The next step is the repartitioning. This changes the number of partitions by shuffling the data. These DataFrames are shuffled into six partitions and five partitions, corresponding to the number of tasks in stages 3 and 4.

Stages 3 and 4 perform on each of those DataFrames and the end of the stage represents the join (a shuffle). Suddenly, we have 200 tasks. This is because of a Spark SQL configuration. The `spark.sql.shuffle.partitions` default value is 200, which means that when there is a shuffle performed during execution, it outputs 200 shuffle partitions by default. You can change this value, and the number of output partitions will change.

We cover the number of partitions in a bit more detail in Chapter 19 because it's such an important parameter. This value should be set according to the number of cores in your cluster to ensure efficient execution. Here's how to set it:

```
spark.conf.set("spark.sql.shuffle.partitions", 50)
```

A good rule of thumb is that the number of partitions should be larger than the number of executors on your cluster, potentially by multiple factors depending on the workload. If you are running code on your local machine, it would behoove you to set this value lower because your local machine is unlikely to be able to execute that number of tasks in parallel. This is more of a default for a cluster in which there might be many more executor cores to use. Regardless of the number of partitions, that entire stage is computed in parallel. The final result aggregates those partitions individually, brings them all to a single partition before finally sending the final result to the driver. We'll see this configuration several times over the course of this part of the book.

Tasks

Stages in Spark consist of *tasks*. Each task corresponds to a combination of blocks of data and a set of transformations that will run on a single executor. If there is one big partition in our dataset, we will have one task. If there are 1,000 little partitions, we will have 1,000 tasks that can be executed in parallel. A task is just a unit of computation applied to a unit of data (the partition). Partitioning your data into a greater number of partitions means that more can be executed in parallel. This is not a panacea, but it is a simple place to begin with optimization.

Execution Details

Tasks and stages in Spark have some important properties that are worth reviewing before we close out this chapter. First, Spark automatically *pipelines* stages and tasks that can be done together, such as a map operation followed by another map operation. Second, for all shuffle operations, Spark writes the data to stable storage (e.g., disk), and can reuse it across multiple jobs. We'll discuss these concepts in turn because they will come up when you start inspecting applications through the Spark UI.

Pipelining

An important part of what makes Spark an "in-memory computation tool" is that unlike the tools that came before it (e.g., MapReduce), Spark performs as many steps as it can at one point in time before writing data to memory or disk. One of the key optimizations that Spark performs is *pipelining*, which occurs at and below the RDD level. With pipelining, any sequence of operations that feed data directly into each other, without needing to move it across nodes, is collapsed into a single stage of tasks that do all the operations together. For example, if you write an RDD-based program that does a map, then a filter, then another map, these will result in a *single* stage of tasks that immediately read each input record, pass it through the first map, pass it through the filter, and pass it through the last map function if needed. This pipelined version of the computation is much faster than writing the intermediate results to memory or disk after each step. The same kind of pipelining happens for a Data-Frame or SQL computation that does a `select`, `filter`, and `select`.

From a practical point of view, pipelining will be transparent to you as you write an application—the Spark runtime will automatically do it—but you will see it if you ever inspect your application through the Spark UI or through its log files, where you will see that multiple RDD or DataFrame operations were pipelined into a single stage.

Shuffle Persistence

The second property you'll sometimes see is shuffle persistence. When Spark needs to run an operation that has to move data *across* nodes, such as a reduce-by-key operation (where input data for each key needs to first be brought together from many nodes), the engine can't perform pipelining anymore, and instead it performs a cross-network shuffle. Spark always executes shuffles by first having the "source" tasks (those sending data) write *shuffle files* to their local disks during their execution stage. Then, the stage that does the grouping and reduction launches and runs tasks that fetch their corresponding records from each shuffle file and performs that computation (e.g., fetches and processes the data for a specific range of keys). Saving the shuffle files to disk lets Spark run this stage later in time than the source stage (e.g., if there are not enough executors to run both at the same time), and also lets the engine re-launch reduce tasks on failure without rerunning all the input tasks.

One side effect you'll see for shuffle persistence is that running a new job over data that's already been shuffled does not rerun the "source" side of the shuffle. Because the shuffle files were already written to disk earlier, Spark knows that it can use them to run the later stages of the job, and it need not redo the earlier ones. In the Spark UI and logs, you will see the pre-shuffle stages marked as "skipped". This automatic optimization can save time in a workload that runs multiple jobs over the same data, but of course, for even better performance you can perform your own caching with the DataFrame or RDD `cache` method, which lets you control exactly which data is saved and where. You'll quickly grow accustomed to this behavior after you run some Spark actions on aggregated data and inspect them in the UI.

Conclusion

In this chapter, we discussed what happens to Spark Applications when we go to execute them on a cluster. This means how the cluster will actually go about running that code as well as what happens within Spark Applications during the process. At this point, you should feel quite comfortable understanding what happens within and outside of a Spark Application. This will give you a starting point for debugging your applications. Chapter 16 will discuss writing Spark Applications and the things you should consider when doing so.

Developing Spark Applications

In Chapter 15, you learned about how Spark runs your code on the cluster. We'll now show you how easy it is to develop a standalone Spark application and deploy it on a cluster. We'll do this using a simple template that shares some easy tips for how to structure your applications, including setting up build tools and unit testing. This template is available in the book's code repository (*https://github.com/databricks/ Spark-The-Definitive-Guide*). This template is not really necessary, because writing applications from scratch isn't hard, but it helps. Let's get started with our first application.

Writing Spark Applications

Spark Applications are the combination of two things: a Spark cluster and your code. In this case, the cluster will be local mode and the application will be one that is predefined. Let's walk through an application in each language.

A Simple Scala-Based App

Scala is Spark's "native" language and naturally makes for a great way to write applications. It's really no different than writing a Scala application.

Scala can seem intimidating, depending on your background, but it's worth learning if only to understand Spark just a bit better. Additionally, you do not need to learn all the language's ins and outs; begin with the basics and you'll see that it's easy to be productive in Scala in no time. Using Scala will also open up a lot of doors. With a little practice, it's not to difficult to do code-level tracing through Spark's codebase.

You can build applications using sbt or Apache Maven, two Java Virtual Machine (JVM)–based build tools. As with any build tool, they each have their own quirks, but it's probably easiest to begin with sbt. You can download, install, and learn about sbt on the sbt website (*http://www.scala-sbt.org/index.html*). You can install Maven from its respective website (*https://maven.apache.org/*), as well.

To configure an sbt build for our Scala application, we specify a *build.sbt* file to manage the package information. Inside the *build.sbt* file, there are a few key things to include:

- Project metadata (package name, package versioning information, etc.)
- Where to resolve dependencies
- Dependencies needed for your library

There are many more options that you can specify; however, they are beyond the scope of this book (you can find information about this on the web and in the sbt documentation). There are also some books on the subject (*http://shop.oreilly.com/product/9781783282678.do*) that can serve as a helpful reference as soon as you've gone beyond anything nontrivial. Here's what a sample Scala *built.sbt* file might look like (and the one that we include in the template (*https://github.com/databricks/Spark-The-Definitive-Guide/blob/master/project-templates/scala/build.sbt*)). Notice how we must specify the Scala version as well as the Spark version:

```
name := "example"
organization := "com.databricks"
version := "0.1-SNAPSHOT"
scalaVersion := "2.11.8"

// Spark Information
val sparkVersion = "2.2.0"

// allows us to include spark packages
resolvers += "bintray-spark-packages" at
  "https://dl.bintray.com/spark-packages/maven/"

resolvers += "Typesafe Simple Repository" at
  "http://repo.typesafe.com/typesafe/simple/maven-releases/"

resolvers += "MavenRepository" at
  "https://mvnrepository.com/"

libraryDependencies ++= Seq(
  // spark core
  "org.apache.spark" %% "spark-core" % sparkVersion,
  "org.apache.spark" %% "spark-sql" % sparkVersion,
// the rest of the file is omitted for brevity
  )
```

Now that we've defined the build file, we can actually go about adding code to our project. We'll use the standard Scala project structure, which you can find in the sbt reference manual (*http://www.scala-sbt.org/0.13/docs/Directories.html*) (this is the same directory structure as Maven projects):

```
src/
  main/
    resources/
       <files to include in main jar here>
    scala/
       <main Scala sources>
    java/
       <main Java sources>
  test/
    resources
       <files to include in test jar here>
    scala/
       <test Scala sources>
    java/
       <test Java sources>
```

We put the source code in the Scala and Java directories. In this case, we put something like the following in a file; this initializes the SparkSession, runs the application, and then exits:

```
object DataFrameExample extends Serializable {
  def main(args: Array[String]) = {

    val pathToDataFolder = args(0)

    // start up the SparkSession
    // along with explicitly setting a given config
    val spark = SparkSession.builder().appName("Spark Example")
      .config("spark.sql.warehouse.dir", "/user/hive/warehouse")
      .getOrCreate()

    // udf registration
    spark.udf.register("myUDF", someUDF(_:String):String)
    val df = spark.read.json(pathToDataFolder + "data.json")
    val manipulated = df.groupBy(expr("myUDF(group)")).sum().collect()
      .foreach(x => println(x))

  }
}
```

Notice how we defined a main class that we can run from the command line when we use spark-submit to submit it to our cluster for execution.

Now that we have our project set up and have added some code to it, it's time to build it. We can use sbt assemble to build an "uber-jar" or "fat-jar" that contains all of the dependencies in one JAR. This can be simple for some deployments but cause complications (especially dependency conflicts) for others. A lighter-weight approach is to run sbt package, which will gather all of your dependencies into the target folder but will not package all of them into one big JAR.

Running the application

The target folder contains the JAR that we can use as an argument to spark-submit. After building the Scala package (*https://github.com/databricks/Spark-The-Definitive-Guide/tree/master/project-templates/scala*), you end up with something that you can spark-submit on your local machine by using the following code (this snippet takes advantage of aliasing to create the $SPARK_HOME variable; you could replace $SPARK_HOME with the exact directory that contains your downloaded version of Spark):

```
$SPARK_HOME/bin/spark-submit \
    --class com.databricks.example.DataFrameExample \
    --master local \
    target/scala-2.11/example_2.11-0.1-SNAPSHOT.jar "hello"
```

Writing Python Applications

Writing PySpark Applications is really no different than writing normal Python applications or packages. It's quite similar to writing command-line applications in particular. Spark doesn't have a build concept, just Python scripts, so to run an application, you simply execute the script against the cluster.

To facilitate code reuse, it is common to package multiple Python files into egg or ZIP files of Spark code. To include those files, you can use the --py-files argument of spark-submit to add *.py*, *.zip*, or *.egg* files to be distributed with your application.

When it's time to run your code, you create the equivalent of a "Scala/Java main class" in Python. Specify a certain script as an executable script that builds the SparkSession. This is the one that we will pass as the main argument to spark-submit:

```python
# in Python
from __future__ import print_function
if __name__ == '__main__':
    from pyspark.sql import SparkSession
    spark = SparkSession.builder \
        .master("local") \
        .appName("Word Count") \
        .config("spark.some.config.option", "some-value") \
        .getOrCreate()

    print(spark.range(5000).where("id > 500").selectExpr("sum(id)").collect())
```

When you do this, you're going to get a `SparkSession` that you can pass around your application. It is best practice to pass around this variable at runtime rather than instantiating it within every Python class.

One helpful tip when developing in Python is to use `pip` (*https://pypi.python.org/pypi/pip*) to specify PySpark as a dependency. You can do this by running the command `pip install pyspark`. This allows you to use it in a way that you might use other Python packages. This makes for very helpful code completion in many `editors`, as well. This is brand new in Spark 2.2, so it might take a version or two to be completely production ready, but Python is very popular in the Spark community, and it's sure to be a cornerstone of Spark's future.

Running the application

After you've written your code, it's time to submit it for execution. (We're executing the same code that we have in the project template (*https://github.com/databricks/Spark-The-Definitive-Guide/tree/master/project-templates/python/pyspark_template*).) You just need to call `spark-submit` with that information:

```
$SPARK_HOME/bin/spark-submit --master local pyspark_template/main.py
```

Writing Java Applications

Writing Java Spark Applications is, if you squint, the same as writing Scala applications. The core differences involve how you specify your dependencies.

This example assumes that you are using Maven to specify your dependencies. In this case, you'll use the following format. In Maven, you must add the Spark Packages repository so that you can fetch dependencies from those locations:

```xml
<dependencies>
    <dependency>
        <groupId>org.apache.spark</groupId>
        <artifactId>spark-core_2.11</artifactId>
        <version>2.1.0</version>
    </dependency>
    <dependency>
        <groupId>org.apache.spark</groupId>
        <artifactId>spark-sql_2.11</artifactId>
        <version>2.1.0</version>
    </dependency>
    <dependency>
        <groupId>graphframes</groupId>
        <artifactId>graphframes</artifactId>
        <version>0.4.0-spark2.1-s_2.11</version>
    </dependency>
</dependencies>
<repositories>
    <!-- list of other repositories -->
```

```
    <repository>
        <id>SparkPackagesRepo</id>
        <url>http://dl.bintray.com/spark-packages/maven</url>
    </repository>
</repositories>
```

Naturally, you follow the same directory structure as in the Scala project version (seeing as they both conform to the Maven specification). We then just follow the relevant Java examples to actually build and execute the code. Now we can create a simple example that specifies a `main` class for us to execute against (more on this at the end of the chapter):

```java
import org.apache.spark.sql.SparkSession;
public class SimpleExample {
    public static void main(String[] args) {
        SparkSession spark = SparkSession
                .builder()
                .getOrCreate();
        spark.range(1, 2000).count();
    }
}
```

We then package it by using `mvn package` (you need to have Maven installed to do so).

Running the application

This operation is going to be the exact same as running the Scala application (or the Python application, for that matter). Simply use `spark-submit`:

```
$SPARK_HOME/bin/spark-submit \
    --class com.databricks.example.SimpleExample \
    --master local \
    target/spark-example-0.1-SNAPSHOT.jar "hello"
```

Testing Spark Applications

You now know what it takes to write and run a Spark Application, so let's move on to a less exciting but still very important topic: testing. Testing Spark Applications relies on a couple of key principles and tactics that you should keep in mind as you're writing your applications.

Strategic Principles

Testing your data pipelines and Spark Applications is just as important as actually writing them. This is because you want to ensure that they are resilient to future change, in data, logic, and output. In this section, we'll first discuss *what* you might want to test in a typical Spark Application, then discuss *how* to organize your code for easy testing.

Input data resilience

Being resilient to different kinds of input data is something that is quite fundamental to how you write your data pipelines. The data will change because the business needs will change. Therefore your Spark Applications and pipelines should be resilient to at least some degree of change in the input data or otherwise ensure that these failures are handled in a graceful and resilient way. For the most part this means being smart about writing your tests to handle those edge cases of different inputs and making sure that the pager only goes off when it's something that is truly important.

Business logic resilience and evolution

The business logic in your pipelines will likely change as well as the input data. Even more importantly, you want to be sure that what you're deducing from the raw data is what you actually think that you're deducing. This means that you'll need to do robust logical testing with realistic data to ensure that you're actually getting what you want out of it. One thing to be wary of here is trying to write a bunch of "Spark Unit Tests" that just test Spark's functionality. You don't want to be doing that; instead, you want to be testing your business logic and ensuring that the complex business pipeline that you set up is actually doing what you think it should be doing.

Resilience in output and atomicity

Assuming that you're prepared for departures in the structure of input data and that your business logic is well tested, you now want to ensure that your output structure is what you expect. This means you will need to gracefully handle output schema resolution. It's not often that data is simply dumped in some location, never to be read again—most of your Spark pipelines are probably feeding other Spark pipelines. For this reason you're going to want to make certain that your downstream consumers understand the "state" of the data—this could mean how frequently it's updated as well as whether the data is "complete" (e.g., there is no late data) or that there won't be any last-minute corrections to the data.

All of the aforementioned issues are principles that you should be thinking about as you build your data pipelines (actually, regardless of whether you're using Spark). This strategic thinking is important for laying down the foundation for the system that you would like to build.

Tactical Takeaways

Although strategic thinking is important, let's talk a bit more in detail about some of the tactics that you can actually use to make your application easy to test. The highest value approach is to verify that your business logic is correct by employing proper unit testing and to ensure that you're resilient to changing input data or have structured it so that schema evolution will not become unwielding in the future. The decision for how to do this largely falls on you as the developer because it will vary according to your business domain and domain expertise.

Managing SparkSessions

Testing your Spark code using a unit test framework like JUnit or ScalaTest is relatively easy because of Spark's local mode—just create a local mode SparkSession as part of your test harness to run it. However, to make this work well, you should try to perform dependency injection as much as possible when managing SparkSessions in your code. That is, initialize the SparkSession only once and pass it around to relevant functions and classes at runtime in a way that makes it easy to substitute during testing. This makes it much easier to test each individual function with a dummy SparkSession in unit tests.

Which Spark API to Use?

Spark offers several choices of APIs, ranging from SQL to DataFrames and Datasets, and each of these can have different impacts for maintainability and testability of your application. To be perfectly honest, the right API depends on your team and its needs: some teams and projects will need the less strict SQL and DataFrame APIs for speed of development, while others will want to use type-safe Datasets or RDDs.

In general, we recommend documenting and testing the input and output types of each function regardless of which API you use. The type-safe API automatically enforces a minimal contract for your function that makes it easy for other code to build on it. If your team prefers to use DataFrames or SQL, then spend some time to document *and test* what each function returns and what types of inputs it accepts to avoid surprises later, as in any dynamically typed programming language. While the lower-level RDD API is also statically typed, we recommend going into it only if you need low-level features such as partitioning that are not present in Datasets, which should not be very common; the Dataset API allows more performance optimizations and is likely to provide even more of them in the future.

A similar set of considerations applies to which programming language to use for your application: there certainly is no right answer for every team, but depending on your needs, each language will provide different benefits. We generally recommend using statically typed languages like Scala and Java for larger applications or those where you want to be able to drop into low-level code to fully control performance, but Python and R may be significantly better in other cases—for example, if you need to use some of their other libraries. Spark code should easily be testable in the standard unit testing frameworks in every language.

Connecting to Unit Testing Frameworks

To unit test your code, we recommend using the standard frameworks in your language (e.g., JUnit or ScalaTest), and setting up your test harnesses to create and clean up a SparkSession for each test. Different frameworks offer different mechanisms to do this, such as "before" and "after" methods. We have included some sample unit testing code in the application templates for this chapter.

Connecting to Data Sources

As much as possible, you should make sure your testing code does not connect to production data sources, so that developers can easily run it in isolation if these data sources change. One easy way to make this happen is to have all your business logic functions take DataFrames or Datasets as input instead of directly connecting to various sources; after all, subsequent code will work the same way no matter what the data source was. If you are using the structured APIs in Spark, another way to make this happen is named tables: you can simply register some dummy datasets (e.g., loaded from small text file or from in-memory objects) as various table names and go from there.

The Development Process

The development process with Spark Applications is similar to development workflows that you have probably already used. First, you might maintain a scratch space, such as an interactive notebook or some equivalent thereof, and then as you build key components and algorithms, you move them to a more permanent location like a library or package. The notebook experience is one that we often recommend (and are using to write this book) because of its simplicity in experimentation. There are also some tools, such as Databricks, that allow you to run notebooks as production applications as well.

When running on your local machine, the `spark-shell` and its various language-specific implementations are probably the best way to develop applications. For the most part, the shell is for interactive applications, whereas `spark-submit` is for production applications on your Spark cluster. You can use the shell to interactively run Spark, just as we showed you at the beginning of this book. This is the mode with which you will run PySpark, Spark SQL, and SparkR. In the `bin` folder, when you download Spark, you will find the various ways of starting these shells. Simply run `spark-shell`(for Scala), `spark-sql`, `pyspark`, and `sparkR`.

After you've finished your application and created a package or script to run, `spark-submit` will become your best friend to submit this job to a cluster.

Launching Applications

The most common way for running Spark Applications is through `spark-submit`. Previously in this chapter, we showed you how to run `spark-submit`; you simply specify your options, the application JAR or script, and the relevant arguments:

```
./bin/spark-submit \
  --class <main-class> \
  --master <master-url> \
  --deploy-mode <deploy-mode> \
  --conf <key>=<value> \
  ... # other options
  <application-jar-or-script> \
  [application-arguments]
```

You can always specify whether to run in client or cluster mode when you submit a Spark job with `spark-submit`. However, you should almost always favor running in cluster mode (or in client mode on the cluster itself) to reduce latency between the executors and the driver.

When submitting applciations, pass a *.py* file in the place of a *.jar*, and add Python `.zip`, `.egg`, or `.py` to the search path with `--py-files`.

For reference, Table 16-1 lists all of the available `spark-submit` options, including those that are particular to some cluster managers. To enumerate all these options yourself, run `spark-submit` with `--help`.

Table 16-1. Spark submit help text

Parameter	Description
`--master MASTER_URL`	spark://host:port, mesos://host:port, yarn, or local
`--deploy-mode DEPLOY_MODE`	Whether to launch the driver program locally ("client") or on one of the worker machines inside the cluster ("cluster") (Default: client)
`--class CLASS_NAME`	Your application's main class (for Java / Scala apps).
`--name NAME`	A name of your application.
`--jars JARS`	Comma-separated list of local JARs to include on the driver and executor classpaths.
`--packages`	Comma-separated list of Maven coordinates of JARs to include on the driver and executor classpaths. Will search the local Maven repo, then Maven Central and any additional remote repositories given by `--repositories`. The format for the coordinates should be `groupId:artifactId:version`.
`--exclude-packages`	Comma-separated list of `groupId:artifactId`, to exclude while resolving the dependencies provided in `--packages` to avoid dependency conflicts.
`--repositories`	Comma-separated list of additional remote repositories to search for the Maven coordinates given with `--packages`.
`--py-files PY_FILES`	Comma-separated list of *.zip*, *.egg*, or *.py* files to place on the PYTHONPATH for Python apps.

Parameter	Description
`--files FILES`	Comma-separated list of files to be placed in the working directory of each executor.
`--conf PROP=VALUE`	Arbitrary Spark configuration property.
`--properties-file FILE`	Path to a file from which to load extra properties. If not specified, this will look for `conf/spark-defaults.conf`.
`--driver-memory MEM`	Memory for driver (e.g., 1000M, 2G) (Default: 1024M).
`--driver-java-options`	Extra Java options to pass to the driver.
`--driver-library-path`	Extra library path entries to pass to the driver.
`--driver-class-path`	Extra class path entries to pass to the driver. Note that JARs added with `--jars` are automatically included in the classpath.
`--executor-memory MEM`	Memory per executor (e.g., 1000M, 2G) (Default: 1G).
`--proxy-user NAME`	User to impersonate when submitting the application. This argument does not work with `--principal` / `--keytab`.
`--help, -h`	Show this help message and exit.
`--verbose, -v`	Print additional debug output.
`--version`	Print the version of current Spark.

There are some deployment-specific configurations as well (see Table 16-2).

Table 16-2. Deployment Specific Configurations

Cluster Managers	Modes	Conf	Description
Standalone	Cluster	`--driver-cores NUM`	Cores for driver (Default: 1).
Standalone/ Mesos	Cluster	`--supervise`	If given, restarts the driver on failure.
Standalone/ Mesos	Cluster	`--kill SUBMIS SION_ID`	If given, kills the driver specified.
Standalone/ Mesos	Cluster	`--status SUBMIS SION_ID`	If given, requests the status of the driver specified.
Standalone/ Mesos	Either	`--total-executor-cores NUM`	Total cores for all executors.
Standalone/ YARN	Either	`--executor-cores NUM1`	Number of cores per executor. (Default: 1 in YARN mode or all available cores on the worker in standalone mode)
YARN	Either	`--driver-cores NUM`	Number of cores used by the driver, only in cluster mode (Default: 1).
YARN	Either	`queue QUEUE_NAME`	The YARN queue to submit to (Default: "default").

Cluster Managers	Modes	Conf	Description
YARN	Either	`--num-executors NUM`	Number of executors to launch (Default: 2). If dynamic allocation is enabled, the initial number of executors will be at least NUM.
YARN	Either	`--archives ARCHIVES`	Comma-separated list of archives to be extracted into the working directory of each executor.
YARN	Either	`--principal PRIN CIPAL`	Principal to be used to log in to KDC, while running on secure HDFS.
YARN	Either	`--keytab KEYTAB`	The full path to the file that contains the keytab for the principal specified above. This keytab will be copied to the node running the Application Master via the Secure Distributed Cache, for renewing the login tickets and the delegation tokens periodically.

Application Launch Examples

We already covered some local-mode application examples previously in this chapter, but it's worth looking at how we use some of the aforementioned options, as well. Spark also includes several examples and demonstration applications in the *examples* directory that is included when you download Spark. If you're stuck on how to use certain parameters, simply try them first on your local machine and use the SparkPi class as the main class:

```
./bin/spark-submit \
  --class org.apache.spark.examples.SparkPi \
  --master spark://207.184.161.138:7077 \
  --executor-memory 20G \
  --total-executor-cores 100 \
  replace/with/path/to/examples.jar \
  1000
```

The following snippet does the same for Python. You run it from the Spark directory and this will allow you to submit a Python application (all in one script) to the stand-alone cluster manager. You can also set the same executor limits as in the preceding example:

```
./bin/spark-submit \
  --master spark://207.184.161.138:7077 \
  examples/src/main/python/pi.py \
  1000
```

You can change this to run in local mode as well by setting the master to local or local[*] to run on all the cores on your machine. You will also need to change the /path/to/examples.jar to the relevant Scala and Spark versions you are running.

Configuring Applications

Spark includes a number of different configurations, some of which we covered in Chapter 15. There are many different configurations, depending on what you're hoping to achieve. This section covers those very details. For the most part, this information is included for reference and is probably worth skimming only, unless you're looking for something in particular. The majority of configurations fall into the following categories:

- Application properties
- Runtime environment
- Shuffle behavior
- Spark UI
- Compression and serialization
- Memory management
- Execution behavior
- Networking
- Scheduling
- Dynamic allocation
- Security
- Encryption
- Spark SQL
- Spark streaming
- SparkR

Spark provides three locations to configure the system:

- Spark properties control most application parameters and can be set by using a `SparkConf` object
- Java system properties
- Hardcoded configuration files

There are several templates that you can use, which you can find in the */conf* directory available in the root of the Spark home folder. You can set these properties as hardcoded variables in your applications or by specifying them at runtime. You can use environment variables to set per-machine settings, such as the IP address, through the `conf/spark-env.sh` script on each node. Lastly, you can configure logging through `log4j.properties`.

The SparkConf

The SparkConf manages all of our application configurations. You create one via the import statement, as shown in the example that follows. After you create it, the Spark Conf is immutable for that specific Spark Application:

```scala
// in Scala
import org.apache.spark.SparkConf
val conf = new SparkConf().setMaster("local[2]").setAppName("DefinitiveGuide")
  .set("some.conf", "to.some.value")
```

```python
# in Python
from pyspark import SparkConf
conf = SparkConf().setMaster("local[2]").setAppName("DefinitiveGuide")\
  .set("some.conf", "to.some.value")
```

You use the SparkConf to configure individual Spark Applications with Spark properties. These Spark properties control how the Spark Application runs and how the cluster is configured. The example that follows configures the local cluster to have two threads and specifies the application name that shows up in the Spark UI.

You can configure these at runtime, as you saw previously in this chapter through command-line arguments. This is helpful when starting a Spark Shell that will automatically include a basic Spark Application for you; for instance:

```
./bin/spark-submit --name "DefinitiveGuide" --master local[4] ...
```

Of note is that when setting time duration-based properties, you should use the following format:

- 25ms (milliseconds)
- 5s (seconds)
- 10m or 10min (minutes)
- 3h (hours)
- 5d (days)
- 1y (years)

Application Properties

Application properties are those that you set either from spark-submit or when you create your Spark Application. They define basic application metadata as well as some execution characteristics. Table 16-3 presents a list of current application properties.

Table 16-3. Application properties

Property name	Default	Meaning
`spark.app.name`	(none)	The name of your application. This will appear in the UI and in log data.
`spark.driver.cores`	1	Number of cores to use for the driver process, only in cluster mode.
`spark.driver.maxResult Size`	1g	Limit of total size of serialized results of all partitions for each Spark action (e.g., collect). Should be at least `1M`, or `0` for unlimited. Jobs will be aborted if the total size exceeds this limit. Having a high limit can cause `OutOfMemoryErrors` in the driver (depends on `spark.driver.memory` and memory overhead of objects in JVM). Setting a proper limit can protect the driver from `OutOfMemoryErrors`.
`spark.driver.memory`	1g	Amount of memory to use for the driver process, where `SparkContext` is initialized. (e.g. 1g, 2g). Note: in client mode, this must not be set through the `SparkConf` directly in your application, because the driver JVM has already started at that point. Instead, set this through the `--driver-memory` command-line option or in your default properties file.
`spark.executor.memory`	1g	Amount of memory to use per executor process (e.g., 2g, 8g).
`spark.extraListeners`	(none)	A comma-separated list of classes that implement `SparkListener`; when initializing `SparkContext`, instances of these classes will be created and registered with Spark's listener bus. If a class has a single-argument constructor that accepts a `SparkConf`, that constructor will be called; otherwise, a zero-argument constructor will be called. If no valid constructor can be found, the `SparkContext` creation will fail with an exception.
`spark.logConf`	FALSE	Logs the effective `SparkConf` as INFO when a `SparkContext` is started.
`spark.master`	(none)	The cluster manager to connect to. See the list of allowed master URLs.
`spark.submit.deploy Mode`	(none)	The deploy mode of the Spark driver program, either "client" or "cluster," which means to launch driver program locally ("client") or remotely ("cluster") on one of the nodes inside the cluster.
`spark.log.callerCon text`	(none)	Application information that will be written into Yarn RM log/HDFS audit log when running on Yarn/HDFS. Its length depends on the Hadoop configuration `hadoop.caller.context.max.size`. It should be concise, and typically can have up to 50 characters.
`spark.driver.supervise`	FALSE	If true, restarts the driver automatically if it fails with a non-zero exit status. Only has effect in Spark standalone mode or Mesos cluster deploy mode.

You can ensure that you've correctly set these values by checking the application's web UI on port 4040 of the driver on the "Environment" tab. Only values explicitly specified through *spark-defaults.conf*, `SparkConf`, or the command line will appear. For all other configuration properties, you can assume the default value is used.

Runtime Properties

Although less common, there are times when you might also need to configure the runtime environment of your application. Due to space limitations, we cannot include the entire configuration set here. Refer to the relevant table on the Runtime Environment (*http://bit.ly/2FlsX2i*) in the Spark documentation (*http://bit.ly/*

1qnQ26w). These properties allow you to configure extra classpaths and python paths for both drivers and executors, Python worker configurations, as well as miscellaneous logging properties.

Execution Properties

These configurations are some of the most relevant for you to configure because they give you finer-grained control on actual execution. Due to space limitations, we cannot include the entire configuration set here. Refer to the relevant table on Execution Behavior (*http://bit.ly/2nggXYy*) in the Spark documentation (*http://bit.ly/1qnQ26w*). The most common configurations to change are `spark.executor.cores` (to control the number of available cores) and `spark.files.maxPartitionBytes` (maximum partition size when reading files).

Configuring Memory Management

There are times when you might need to manually manage the memory options to try and optimize your applications. Many of these are not particularly relevant for end users because they involve a lot of legacy concepts or fine-grained controls that were obviated in Spark 2.X because of automatic memory management. Due to space limitations, we cannot include the entire configuration set here. Refer to the relevant table on Memory Management (*http://bit.ly/2DSESrk*) in the Spark documentation (*http://bit.ly/1qnQ26w*).

Configuring Shuffle Behavior

We've emphasized how shuffles can be a bottleneck in Spark jobs because of their high communication overhead. Therefore there are a number of low-level configurations for controlling shuffle behavior. Due to space limitations, we cannot include the entire configuration set here. Refer to the relevant table on Shuffle Behavior (*http://bit.ly/1EZHL46*) in the Spark documentation (*http://bit.ly/1qnQ26w*).

Environmental Variables

You can configure certain Spark settings through environment variables, which are read from the *conf/spark-env.sh* script in the directory where Spark is installed (or *conf/spark-env.cmd* on Windows). In Standalone and Mesos modes, this file can give machine-specific information such as hostnames. It is also sourced when running local Spark Applications or submission scripts.

Note that *conf/spark-env.sh* does not exist by default when Spark is installed. However, you can copy *conf/spark-env.sh.template* to create it. Be sure to make the copy executable.

The following variables can be set in *spark-env.sh*:

JAVA_HOME
  Location where Java is installed (if it's not on your default PATH).

PYSPARK_PYTHON
  Python binary executable to use for PySpark in both driver and workers (default
  is python2.7 if available; otherwise, python). Property spark.pyspark.python
  takes precedence if it is set.

PYSPARK_DRIVER_PYTHON
  Python binary executable to use for PySpark in driver only (default is
  PYSPARK_PYTHON). Property spark.pyspark.driver.python takes precedence if
  it is set.

SPARKR_DRIVER_R
  R binary executable to use for SparkR shell (default is R). Property
  spark.r.shell.command takes precedence if it is set.

SPARK_LOCAL_IP
  IP address of the machine to which to bind.

SPARK_PUBLIC_DNS
  Hostname your Spark program will advertise to other machines.

In addition to the variables ust listed, there are also options for setting up the Spark
standalone cluster scripts, such as number of cores to use on each machine and maximum memory. Because *spark-env.sh* is a shell script, you can set some of these programmatically; for example, you might compute SPARK_LOCAL_IP by looking up the
IP of a specific network interface.

> When running Spark on YARN in cluster mode, you need to set
> environment variables by using the spark.yarn.appMasterEnv.
> [*EnvironmentVariableName*] property in your *conf/spark-
> defaults.conf* file. Environment variables that are set in *spark-env.sh*
> will not be reflected in the YARN Application Master process in
> cluster mode. See the YARN-related Spark Properties for more
> information.

Job Scheduling Within an Application

Within a given Spark Application, multiple parallel jobs can run simultaneously if
they were submitted from separate threads. By job, in this section, we mean a Spark
action and any tasks that need to run to evaluate that action. Spark's scheduler is fully
thread-safe and supports this use case to enable applications that serve multiple
requests (e.g., queries for multiple users).

By default, Spark's scheduler runs jobs in *FIFO* fashion. If the jobs at the head of the queue don't need to use the entire cluster, later jobs can begin to run right away, but if the jobs at the head of the queue are large, later jobs might be delayed significantly.

It is also possible to configure fair sharing between jobs. Under fair sharing, Spark assigns tasks between jobs in a round-robin fashion so that all jobs get a roughly equal share of cluster resources. This means that short jobs submitted while a long job is running can begin receiving resources right away and still achieve good response times without waiting for the long job to finish. This mode is best for multi-user settings.

To enable the fair scheduler, set the `spark.scheduler.mode` property to `FAIR` when configuring a `SparkContext`.

The fair scheduler also supports grouping jobs into pools, and setting different scheduling options, or weights, for each pool. This can be useful to create a high-priority pool for more important jobs or to group the jobs of each user together and give users equal shares regardless of how many concurrent jobs they have instead of giving jobs equal shares. This approach is modeled after the Hadoop Fair Scheduler.

Without any intervention, newly submitted jobs go into a default pool, but jobs pools can be set by adding the `spark.scheduler.pool` local property to the `SparkContext` in the thread that's submitting them. This is done as follows (assuming `sc` is your `SparkContext`:

```
sc.setLocalProperty("spark.scheduler.pool", "pool1")
```

After setting this local property, all jobs submitted within this thread will use this pool name. The setting is per-thread to make it easy to have a thread run multiple jobs on behalf of the same user. If you'd like to clear the pool that a thread is associated with, set it to null.

Conclusion

This chapter covered a lot about Spark Applications; we learned how to write, test, run, and configure them in all of Spark's languages. In Chapter 17, we talk about deploying and the cluster management options you have when it comes to running Spark Applications.

Deploying Spark

This chapter explores the infrastructure you need in place for you and your team to be able to run Spark Applications:

- Cluster deployment choices
- Spark's different cluster managers
- Deployment considerations and configuring deployments

For the most, part Spark should work similarly with all the supported cluster managers; however, customizing the setup means understanding the intricacies of each of the cluster management systems. The hard part is deciding on the cluster manager (or choosing a managed service). Although we would be happy to include all the minute details about how you can configure different cluster with different cluster managers, it's simply impossible for this book to provide hyper-specific details for every situation in every single enviroment. The goal of this chapter, therefore, is not to discuss each of the cluster managers in full detail, but rather to look at their fundamental differences and to provide a reference for a lot of the material already available on the Spark website. Unfortunately, there is no easy answer to "which is the easiest cluster manager to run" because it varies so much by use case, experience, and resources. The Spark documentation site (*http://spark.apache.org/docs/latest/cluster-overview.html*) offers a lot of detail about deploying Spark with actionable examples. We do our best to discuss the most relevant points.

As of this writing, Spark has three officially supported cluster managers:

- Standalone mode
- Hadoop YARN

- Apache Mesos

These cluster managers maintain a set of machines onto which you can deploy Spark Applications. Naturally, each of these cluster managers has an opinionated view toward management, and so there are trade-offs and semantics that you will need to keep in mind. However, they all run Spark applications the same way (as covered in Chapter 16). Let's begin with the first point: where to deploy your cluster.

Where to Deploy Your Cluster to Run Spark Applications

There are two high-level options for where to deploy Spark clusters: deploy in an on-premises cluster or in the public cloud. This choice is consequential and is therefore worth discussing.

On-Premises Cluster Deployments

Deploying Spark to an on-premises cluster is sometimes a reasonable option, especially for organizations that already manage their own datacenters. As with everything else, there are trade-offs to this approach. An on-premises cluster gives you full control over the hardware used, meaning you can optimize performance for your specific workload. However, it also introduces some challenges, especially when it comes to data analytics workloads like Spark. First, with on-premises deployment, your cluster is fixed in size, whereas the resource demands of data analytics workloads are often elastic. If you make your cluster too small, it will be hard to launch the occasional very large analytics query or training job for a new machine learning model, whereas if you make it large, you will have resources sitting idle. Second, for on-premises clusters, you need to select and operate your own storage system, such as a Hadoop file system or scalable key-value store. This includes setting up georeplication and disaster recovery if required.

If you are going to deploy on-premises, the best way to combat the resource utilization problem is to use a cluster manager that allows you to run many Spark applications and dynamically reassign resources between them, or even allows non-Spark applications on the same cluster. All of Spark's supported cluster managers allow multiple concurrent applications, but YARN and Mesos have better support for dynamic sharing and also additionally support non-Spark workloads. Handling resource sharing is likely going to be the biggest difference your users see day to day with Spark on-premise versus in the cloud: in public clouds, it's easy to give each application its own cluster of exactly the required size for just the duration of that job.

For storage, you have several different options, but covering all the trade-offs and operational details in depth would probably require its own book. The most common storage systems used for Spark are distributed file systems such as Hadoop's HDFS and key-value stores such as Apache Cassandra. Streaming message bus systems such as Apache Kafka are also often used for ingesting data. All these systems have varying degrees of support for management, backup, and georeplication, sometimes built into the system and sometimes only through third-party commercial tools. Before choosing a storage option, we recommend evaluating the performance of its Spark connector and evaluating the available management tools.

Spark in the Cloud

While early big data systems were designed for on-premises deployment, the cloud is now an increasingly common platform for deploying Spark. The public cloud has several advantages when it comes to big data workloads. First, resources can be launched and shut down elastically, so you can run that occasional "monster" job that takes hundreds of machines for a few hours without having to pay for them all the time. Even for normal operation, you can choose a different type of machine and cluster size for each application to optimize its cost performance—for example, launch machines with Graphics Processing Units (GPUs) just for your deep learning jobs. Second, public clouds include low-cost, georeplicated storage that makes it easier to manage large amounts of data.

Many companies looking to migrate to the cloud imagine they'll run their applications in the same way that they run their on-premises clusters. All the major cloud providers (Amazon Web Services [AWS], Microsoft Azure, Google Cloud Platform [GCP], and IBM Bluemix) include managed Hadoop clusters for their customers, which provide HDFS for storage as well as Apache Spark. This is actually *not* a great way to run Spark in the cloud, however, because by using a fixed-size cluster and file system, you are not going to be able to take advantage of elasticity. Instead, it is generally a better idea to use global storage systems that are decoupled from a specific cluster, such as Amazon S3, Azure Blob Storage, or Google Cloud Storage and spin up machines dynamically for each Spark workload. With decoupled compute and storage, you will be able to pay for computing resources only when needed, scale them up dynamically, and mix different hardware types. Basically, keep in mind that running Spark in the cloud need not mean migrating an on-premises installation to virtual machines: you can run Spark natively against cloud storage to take full advantage of the cloud's elasticity, cost-saving benefit, and management tools without having to manage an on-premise computing stack within your cloud environment.

Several companies provide "cloud-native" Spark-based services, and all installations of Apache Spark can of course connect to cloud storage. Databricks, the company started by the Spark team from UC Berkeley, is one example of a service provider built specifically for Spark in the cloud. Databricks provides a simple way to run Spark workloads without the heavy baggage of a Hadoop installation. The company provides a number of features for running Spark more efficiently in the cloud, such as auto-scaling, auto-termination of clusters, and optimized connectors to cloud storage, as well as a collaborative environment for working on notebooks and standalone jobs. The company also provides a free Community Edition (*https://databricks.com/ try-databricks*) for learning Spark where you can run notebooks on a small cluster and share them live with others. A fun fact is that this *entire book* was written using the free Community Edition of Databricks, because we found the integrated Spark notebooks, live collaboration, and cluster management the easiest way to produce and test this content.

If you run Spark in the cloud, much of the content in this chapter might not be relevant because you can often create a separate, short-lived Spark cluster for each job you execute. In that case, the standalone cluster manager is likely the easiest to use. However, you may still want to read this content if you'd like to share a longer-lived cluster among many applications, or to install Spark on virtual machines yourself.

Cluster Managers

Unless you are using a high-level managed service, you will have to decide on the cluster manager to use for Spark. Spark supports three aforementioned cluster managers: standalone clusters, Hadoop YARN, and Mesos. Let's review each of these.

Standalone Mode

Spark's standalone cluster manager is a lightweight platform built specifically for Apache Spark workloads. Using it, you can run multiple Spark Applications on the same cluster. It also provides simple interfaces for doing so but can scale to large Spark workloads. The main disadvantage of the standalone mode is that it's more limited than the other cluster managers—in particular, your cluster can *only* run Spark. It's probably the best starting point if you just want to quickly get Spark running on a cluster, however, and you do not have experience using YARN or Mesos.

Starting a standalone cluster

Starting a standalone cluster requires provisioning the machines for doing so. That means starting them up, ensuring that they can talk to one another over the network, and getting the version of Spark you would like to run on those sets of machines. After that, there are two ways to start the cluster: by hand or using built-in launch scripts.

Let's first launch a cluster by hand. The first step is to start the master process on the machine that we want that to run on, using the following command:

```
$SPARK_HOME/sbin/start-master.sh
```

When we run this command, the cluster manager master process will start up on that machine. Once started, the master prints out a `spark://HOST:PORT` URI. You use this when you start each of the worker nodes of the cluster, and you can use it as the master argument to your SparkSession on application initialization. You can also find this

URI on the master's web UI, which is *http://master-ip-address:8080* by default. With that URI, start the worker nodes by logging in to each machine and running the following script using the URI you just received from the master node. The master machine must be available on the network of the worker nodes you are using, and the port must be open on the master node, as well:

```
$SPARK_HOME/sbin/start-slave.sh <master-spark-URI>
```

As soon as you've run that on another machine, you have a Spark cluster running! This process is naturally a bit manual; thankfully there are scripts that can help to automate this process.

Cluster launch scripts

You can configure cluster launch scripts that can automate the launch of standalone clusters. To do this, create a file called *conf/slaves* in your Spark directory that will contain the hostnames of all the machines on which you intend to start Spark workers, one per line. If this file does not exist, everything will launch locally. When you go to actually start the cluster, the master machine will access each of the worker machines via Secure Shell (SSH). By default, SSH is run in parallel and requires that you configure password-less (using a private key) access. If you do not have a password-less setup, you can set the environment variable SPARK_SSH_FOREGROUND and serially provide a password for each worker.

After you set up this file, you can launch or stop your cluster by using the following shell scripts, based on Hadoop's deploy scripts, and available in $SPARK_HOME/sbin:

$SPARK_HOME/sbin/start-master.sh
    Starts a master instance on the machine on which the script is executed.

$SPARK_HOME/sbin/start-slaves.sh
    Starts a slave instance on each machine specified in the *conf/slaves* file.

$SPARK_HOME/sbin/start-slave.sh
    Starts a slave instance on the machine on which the script is executed.

$SPARK_HOME/sbin/start-all.sh
    Starts both a master and a number of slaves as described earlier.

$SPARK_HOME/sbin/stop-master.sh
    Stops the master that was started via the *bin/start-master.sh* script.

$SPARK_HOME/sbin/stop-slaves.sh
    Stops all slave instances on the machines specified in the *conf/slaves* file.

$SPARK_HOME/sbin/stop-all.sh
    Stops both the master and the slaves as described earlier.

Standalone cluster configurations

Standalone clusters have a number of configurations that you can use to tune your application. These control everything from what happens to old files on each worker for terminated applications to the worker's core and memory resources. These are controlled via environment variables or via application properties. Due to space limitations, we cannot include the entire configuration set here. Refer to the relevant table on Standalone Environment Variables (*http://spark.apache.org/docs/latest/spark-standalone.html#cluster-launch-scripts*) in the Spark documentation (*http://spark.apache.org/docs/latest/index.html*).

Submitting applications

After you create the cluster, you can submit applications to it using the `spark://` URI of the master. You can do this either on the master node itself or another machine using `spark-submit`. There are some specific command-line arguments for standalone mode, which we covered in "Launching Applications" on page 272.

Spark on YARN

Hadoop YARN is a framework for job scheduling and cluster resource management. Even though Spark is often (mis)classified as a part of the "Hadoop Ecosystem," in reality, Spark has little to do with Hadoop. Spark does natively support the Hadoop YARN cluster manager but it requires nothing from Hadoop itself.

You can run your Spark jobs on Hadoop YARN by specifying the master as YARN in the `spark-submit` command-line arguments. Just like with standalone mode, there are a number of knobs that you are able to tune according to what you would like the cluster to do. The number of knobs is naturally larger than that of Spark's standalone mode because Hadoop YARN is a generic scheduler for a large number of different execution frameworks.

Setting up a YARN cluster is beyond the scope of this book, but there are some great books (*http://shop.oreilly.com/product/0636920033448.do*) on the topic as well as managed services that can simplify this experience.

Submitting applications

When submitting applications to YARN, the core difference from other deployments is that `--master` will become `yarn` as opposed the master node IP, as it is in standalone mode. Instead, Spark will find the YARN configuration files using the environment variable `HADOOP_CONF_DIR` or `YARN_CONF_DIR`. Once you have set those environment variables to your Hadoop installation's configuration directory, you can just run `spark-submit` like we saw in Chapter 16.

There are two deployment modes that you can use to launch Spark on YARN. As discussed in previous chapters, cluster mode has the spark driver as a process managed by the YARN cluster, and the client can exit after creating the application. In client mode, the driver will run in the client process and therefore YARN will be responsible only for granting executor resources to the application, not maintaining the master node. Also of note is that in cluster mode, Spark doesn't necessarily run on the same machine on which you're executing. Therefore libraries and external jars must be distributed manually or through the --jars command-line argument.

There are a few YARN-specific properties that you can set by using spark-submit. These allow you to control priority queues and things like keytabs for security. We covered these in "Launching Applications" on page 272 in Chapter 16.

Configuring Spark on YARN Applications

Deploying Spark as YARN applications requires you to understand the variety of different configurations and their implications for your Spark applications. This section covers some best practices for basic configurations and includes references to some of the important configuration for running your Spark applications.

Hadoop configurations

If you plan to read and write from HDFS using Spark, you need to include two Hadoop configuration files on Spark's classpath: *hdfs-site.xml*, which provides default behaviors for the HDFS client; and *core-site.xml*, which sets the default file system name. The location of these configuration files varies across Hadoop versions, but a common location is inside of */etc/hadoop/conf*. Some tools create these configurations on the fly, as well, so it's important to understand how your managed service might be deploying these, as well.

To make these files visible to Spark, set HADOOP_CONF_DIR in *$SPARK_HOME/spark-env.sh* to a location containing the configuration files or as an environment variable when you go to spark-submit your application.

Application properties for YARN

There are a number of Hadoop-related configurations and things that come up that largely don't have much to do with Spark, just running or securing YARN in a way that influences how Spark runs. Due to space limitations, we cannot include the configuration set here. Refer to the relevant table on YARN Configurations (*http://spark.apache.org/docs/latest/running-on-yarn.html#configuration*) in the Spark documentation (*http://spark.apache.org/docs/latest/index.html*).

Spark on Mesos

Apache Mesos is another clustering system that Spark can run on. A fun fact about Mesos is that the project was also started by many of the original authors of Spark, including one of the authors of this book. In the Mesos project's own words:

> Apache Mesos abstracts CPU, memory, storage, and other compute resources away from machines (physical or virtual), enabling fault-tolerant and elastic distributed systems to easily be built and run effectively.

For the most part, Mesos intends to be a datacenter scale-cluster manager that manages not just short-lived applications like Spark, but long-running applications like web applications or other resource interfaces. Mesos is the heaviest-weight cluster manager, simply because you might choose this cluster manager only if your organization already has a large-scale deployment of Mesos, but it makes for a good cluster manager nonetheless.

Mesos is a large piece of infrastructure, and unfortunately there's simply too much information for us to cover how to deploy and maintain Mesos clusters. There are many great books on the subject for that, including Dipa Dubhashi and Akhil Das's *Mastering Mesos* (O'Reilly, 2016). The goal here is to bring up some of the considerations that you'll need to think about when running Spark Applications on Mesos.

For instance, one common thing you will hear about Spark on Mesos is fine-grained versus coarse-grained mode. Historically Mesos supported a variety of different modes (fine-grained and coarse-grained), but at this point, it supports only coarse-grained scheduling (fine-grained has been deprecated). Coarse-grained mode means that each Spark executor runs as a single Mesos task. Spark executors are sized according to the following application properties:

- `spark.executor.memory`
- `spark.executor.cores`
- `spark.cores.max/spark.executor.cores`

Submitting applications

Submitting applications to a Mesos cluster is similar to doing so for Spark's other cluster managers. For the most part you should favor cluster mode when using Mesos. Client mode requires some extra configuration on your part, especially with regard to distributing resources around the cluster.

For instance, in client mode, the driver needs extra configuration information in *spark-env.sh* to work with Mesos.

In *spark-env.sh* set some environment variables:

```
export MESOS_NATIVE_JAVA_LIBRARY=<path to libmesos.so>
```

This path is typically *<prefix>/lib/libmesos.so* where the prefix is */usr/local* by default. On Mac OS X, the library is called *libmesos.dylib* instead of *libmesos.so*:

```
export SPARK_EXECUTOR_URI=<URL of spark-2.2.0.tar.gz uploaded above>
```

Finally, set the Spark Application property `spark.executor.uri` to `<URL of spark-2.2.0.tar.gz>`. Now, when starting a Spark application against the cluster, pass a `mesos://` URL as the master when creating a `SparkContex`, and set that property as a parameter in your `SparkConf` variable or the initialization of a `SparkSession`:

```scala
// in Scala
import org.apache.spark.sql.SparkSession
val spark = SparkSession.builder
  .master("mesos://HOST:5050")
  .appName("my app")
  .config("spark.executor.uri", "<path to spark-2.2.0.tar.gz uploaded above>")
  .getOrCreate()
```

Submitting cluster mode applications is fairly straightforward and follows the same `spark-submit` structure you read about before. We covered these in "Launching Applications" on page 272.

Configuring Mesos

Just like any other cluster manager, there are a number of ways that we can configure our Spark Applications when they're running on Mesos. Due to space limitations, we cannot include the entire configuration set here. Refer to the relevant table on Mesos Configurations (*http://bit.ly/2DPmLTf*) in the Spark documentation (*http://bit.ly/1qnQ26w*).

Secure Deployment Configurations

Spark also provides some low-level ability to make your applications run more securely, especially in untrusted environments. Note that the majority of this setup will happen outside of Spark. These configurations are primarily network-based to help Spark run in a more secure manner. This means authentication, network encryption, and setting TLS and SSL configurations. Due to space limitations, we cannot include the entire configuration set here. Refer to the relevant table on Security Configurations (*http://bit.ly/2DJ0BTp*) in the Spark documentation (*http://bit.ly/1qnQ26w*).

Cluster Networking Configurations

Just as shuffles are important, there can be some things worth tuning on the network. This can also be helpful when performing custom deployment configurations for your Spark clusters when you need to use proxies in between certain nodes. If you're looking to increase Spark's performance, these should not be the first configurations you go to tune, but may come up in custom deployment scenarios. Due to space limitations, we cannot include the entire configuration set here. Refer to the relevant table on Networking Configurations (*http://bit.ly/2DGfT7v*) in the Spark documentation (*http://bit.ly/1qnQ26w*).

Application Scheduling

Spark has several facilities for scheduling resources between computations. First, recall that, as described earlier in the book, each Spark Application runs an independent set of executor processes. Cluster managers provide the facilities for scheduling across Spark applications. Second, within each Spark application, multiple jobs (i.e., Spark actions) may be running concurrently if they were submitted by different threads. This is common if your application is serving requests over the network. Spark includes a *fair scheduler* to schedule resources within each application. We introduced this topic in the previous chapter.

If multiple users need to share your cluster and run different Spark Applications, there are different options to manage allocation, depending on the cluster manager. The simplest option, available on all cluster managers, is static partitioning of resources. With this approach, each application is given a maximum amount of resources that it can use, and holds onto those resources for the entire duration. In `spark-submit` there are a number of properties that you can set to control the resource allocation of a particular application. Refer to Chapter 16 for more information. In addition, *dynamic allocation* (described next) can be turned on to let applications scale up and down dynamically based on their current number of pending tasks. If, instead, you want users to be able to share memory and executor resources in a fine-grained manner, you can launch a single Spark Application and use thread scheduling within it to serve multiple requests in parallel.

Dynamic allocation

If you would like to run multiple Spark Applications on the same cluster, Spark provides a mechanism to dynamically adjust the resources your application occupies based on the workload. This means that your application can give resources back to the cluster if they are no longer used, and request them again later when there is demand. This feature is particularly useful if multiple applications share resources in your Spark cluster.

This feature is disabled by default and available on all coarse-grained cluster managers; that is, standalone mode, YARN mode, and Mesos coarse-grained mode. There are two requirements for using this feature. First, your application must set `spark.dynamicAllocation.enabled` to `true`. Second, you must set up an external shuffle service on each worker node in the same cluster and set `spark.shuffle.ser` `vice.enabled` to `true` in your application. The purpose of the external shuffle service is to allow executors to be removed without deleting shuffle files written by them. This is set up differently for each cluster manager and is described in the job scheduling configuration (*http://bit.ly/2DQ3ocB*). Due to space limitations, we cannot include the configuration set for dynamic allocation. Refer to the relevant table on Dynamic Allocation Configurations (*http://bit.ly/2ne8jL3*).

Miscellaneous Considerations

There several other topics to consider when deploying Spark applications that may affect your choice of cluster manager and its setup. These are just things that you should think about when comparing different deployment options.

One of the more important considerations is the number and type of applications you intend to be running. For instance, YARN is great for HDFS-based applications but is not commonly used for much else. Additionally, it's not well designed to support the cloud, because it expects information to be available on HDFS. Also, compute and storage is largely coupled together, meaning that scaling your cluster involves scaling both storage and compute instead of just one or the other. Mesos does improve on this a bit conceptually, and it supports a wide range of application types, but it still requires pre-provisioning machines and, in some sense, requires buy-in at a much larger scale. For instance, it doesn't really make sense to have a Mesos cluster for only running Spark Applications. Spark standalone mode is the lightest-weight cluster manager and is relatively simple to understand and take advantage of, but then you're going to be building more application management infrastructure that you could get much more easily by using YARN or Mesos.

Another challenge is managing different Spark versions. Your hands are largely tied if you want to try to run a variety of different applications running different Spark versions, and unless you use a well-managed service, you're going to need to spend a fair amount of time either managing different setup scripts for different Spark services or removing the ability for your users to use a variety of different Spark applications.

Regardless of the cluster manager that you choose, you're going to want to consider how you're going to set up logging, store logs for future reference, and allow end users to debug their applications. These are more "out of the box" for YARN or Mesos and might need some tweaking if you're using standalone.

One thing you might want to consider—or that might influence your decision making—is maintaining a metastore in order to maintain metadata about your stored datasets, such as a table catalog. We saw how this comes up in Spark SQL when we are creating and maintaining tables. Maintaining an Apache Hive metastore, a topic beyond the scope of this book, might be something that's worth doing to facilitate more productive, cross-application referencing to the same datasets.

Depending on your workload, it might be worth considering using Spark's external shuffle service. Typically Spark stores shuffle blocks (shuffle output) on a local disk on that particular node. An external shuffle service allows for storing those shuffle blocks so that they are available to all executors, meaning that you can arbitrarily kill executors and still have their shuffle outputs available to other applications.

Finally, you're going to need to configure at least some basic monitoring solution and help users debug their Spark jobs running on their clusters. This is going to vary across cluster management options and we touch on some of the things that you might want to set up in Chapter 18.

Conclusion

This chapter looked at the world of configuration options that you have when choosing how to deploy Spark. Although most of the information is irrelevant to the majority of users, it is worth mentioning if you're performing more advanced use cases. It might seem fallacious, but there are other configurations that we have omitted that control even lower-level behavior. You can find these in the Spark documentation or in the Spark source code. Chapter 18 talks about some of the options that we have when monitoring Spark Applications.

Monitoring and Debugging

This chapter covers the key details you need to monitor and debug your Spark Applications. To do this, we will walk through the Spark UI with an example query designed to help you understand how to trace your own jobs through the execution life cycle. The example we'll look at will also help you understand how to debug your jobs and where errors are likely to occur.

The Monitoring Landscape

At some point, you'll need to monitor your Spark jobs to understand where issues are occuring in them. It's worth reviewing the different things that we can actually monitor and outlining some of the options for doing so. Let's review the components we can monitor (see Figure 18-1).

Spark Applications and Jobs

The first thing you'll want to begin monitoring when either debugging or just understanding better how your application executes against the cluster is the Spark UI and the Spark logs. These report information about the applications currently running at the level of concepts in Spark, such as RDDs and query plans. We talk in detail about how to use these Spark monitoring tools throughout this chapter.

JVM

Spark runs the executors in individual Java Virtual Machines (JVMs). Therefore, the next level of detail would be to monitor the individual virtual machines (VMs) to better understand how your code is running. JVM utilities such as *jstack* for providing stack traces, *jmap* for creating heap-dumps, *jstat* for reporting time–series statistics, and *jconsole* for visually exploring various JVM properties are useful for those comfortable with JVM internals. You can also use a tool like *jvisualvm* to help profile Spark jobs. Some of this information is provided in the Spark UI, but for very low-level debugging, the aforementioned tools can come in handy.

OS/Machine

The JVMs run on a host operating system (OS) and it's important to monitor the state of those machines to ensure that they are healthy. This includes monitoring things like CPU, network, and I/O. These are often reported in cluster-level monitoring solutions; however, there are more specific tools that you can use, including *dstat*, *iostat*, and *iotop*.

Cluster

Naturally, you can monitor the cluster on which your Spark Application(s) will run. This might be a YARN, Mesos, or standalone cluster. Usually it's important to have some sort of monitoring solution here because, somewhat obviously, if your cluster is not working, you should probably know pretty quickly. Some popular cluster-level monitoring tools include *Ganglia* and *Prometheus*.

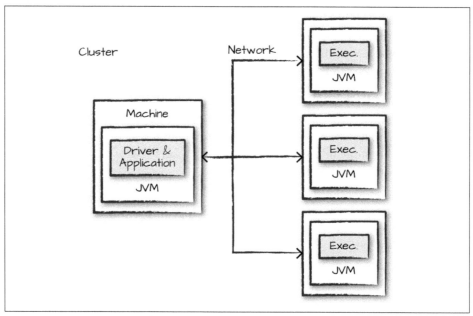

Figure 18-1. Components of a Spark application that you can monitor

What to Monitor

After that brief tour of the monitoring landscape, let's discuss how we can go about monitoring and debugging our Spark Applications. There are two main things you will want to monitor: the *processes* running your application (at the level of CPU usage, memory usage, etc.), and the *query execution* inside it (e.g., jobs and tasks).

Driver and Executor Processes

When you're monitoring a Spark application, you're definitely going to want to keep an eye on the driver. This is where all of the state of your application lives, and you'll need to be sure it's running in a stable manner. If you could monitor only one machine or a single JVM, it would definitely be the driver. With that being said, understanding the state of the executors is also extremely important for monitoring individual Spark jobs. To help with this challenge, Spark has a configurable metrics system based on the Dropwizard Metrics Library (*http://metrics.dropwizard.io*). The metrics system is configured via a configuration file that Spark expects to be present at *$SPARK_HOME/conf/metrics.properties*. A custom file location can be specified by changing the `spark.metrics.conf` configuration property. These metrics can be output to a variety of different sinks, including cluster monitoring solutions like Ganglia.

Queries, Jobs, Stages, and Tasks

Although the driver and executor processes are important to monitor, sometimes you need to debug what's going on at the level of a specific query. Spark provides the ability to dive into *queries*, *jobs*, *stages*, and *tasks*. (We learned about these in Chapter 15.) This information allows you to know exactly what's running on the cluster at a given time. When looking for performance tuning or debugging, this is where you are most likely to start.

Now that we know what we want to monitor, let's look at the two most common ways of doing so: the Spark logs and the Spark UI.

Spark Logs

One of the most detailed ways to monitor Spark is through its log files. Naturally, strange events in Spark's logs, or in the logging that you added to your Spark Application, can help you take note of exactly where jobs are failing or what is causing that failure. If you use the application template provided with the book (*https://github.com/databricks/Spark-The-Definitive-Guide*), the logging framework we set up in the template will allow your application logs to show up along Spark's own logs, making them very easy to correlate. One challenge, however, is that Python won't be able to integrate directly with Spark's Java-based logging library. Using Python's `log ging` module or even simple print statements will still print the results to standard error, however, and make them easy to find.

To change Spark's log level, simply run the following command:

```
spark.sparkContext.setLogLevel("INFO")
```

This will allow you to read the logs, and if you use our application template, you can log your own relevant information along with these logs, allowing you to inspect both your own application and Spark. The logs themselves will be printed to standard error when running a local mode application, or saved to files by your cluster manager when running Spark on a cluster. Refer to each cluster manager's documentation about how to find them—typically, they are available through the cluster manager's web UI.

You won't always find the answer you need simply by searching logs, but it can help you pinpoint the given problem that you're encountering and possibly add new log statements in your application to better understand it. It's also convenient to collect logs over time in order to reference them in the future. For instance, if your application crashes, you'll want to debug why, without access to the now-crashed application. You may also want to ship logs off the machine they were written on to hold onto them if a machine crashes or gets shut down (e.g., if running in the cloud).

The Spark UI

The Spark UI provides a visual way to monitor applications while they are running as well as metrics about your Spark workload, at the Spark and JVM level. Every Spark Context running launches a web UI, by default on port 4040, that displays useful information about the application. When you run Spark in local mode, for example, just navigate to *http://localhost:4040* to see the UI when running a Spark Application on your local machine. If you're running multiple applications, they will launch web UIs on increasing port numbers (4041, 4042, …). Cluster managers will also link to each application's web UI from their own UI.

Figure 18-2 shows all of the tabs available in the Spark UI.

Figure 18-2. Spark UI tabs

These tabs are accessible for each of the things that we'd like to monitor. For the most part, each of these should be self-explanatory:

- The Jobs tab refers to Spark jobs.
- The Stages tab pertains to individual stages (and their relevant tasks).
- The Storage tab includes information and the data that is currently cached in our Spark Application.

- The Environment tab contains relevant information about the configurations and current settings of the Spark application.

- The SQL tab refers to our Structured API queries (including SQL and DataFrames).

- The Executors tab provides detailed information about each executor running our application.

Let's walk through an example of how you can drill down into a given query. Open a new Spark shell, run the following code, and we will trace its execution through the Spark UI:

```python
# in Python
spark.read\
  .option("header", "true")\
  .csv("/data/retail-data/all/online-retail-dataset.csv")\
  .repartition(2)\
  .selectExpr("instr(Description, 'GLASS') >= 1 as is_glass")\
  .groupBy("is_glass")\
  .count()\
  .collect()
```

This results in three rows of various values. The code kicks off a SQL query, so let's navigate to the SQL tab, where you should see something similar to Figure 18-3.

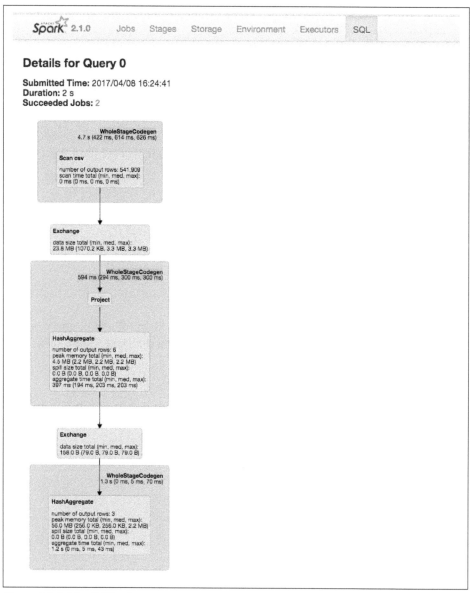

Figure 18-3. The SQL tab

The first thing you see is aggregate statistics about this query:

```
Submitted Time: 2017/04/08 16:24:41
Duration: 2 s
Succeeded Jobs: 2
```

These will become important in a minute, but first let's take a look at the Directed Acyclic Graph (DAG) of Spark stages. Each blue box in these tabs represent a stage of Spark tasks. The entire group of these stages represent our Spark job. Let's take a look at each stage in detail so that we can better understand what is going on at each level, starting with Figure 18-4.

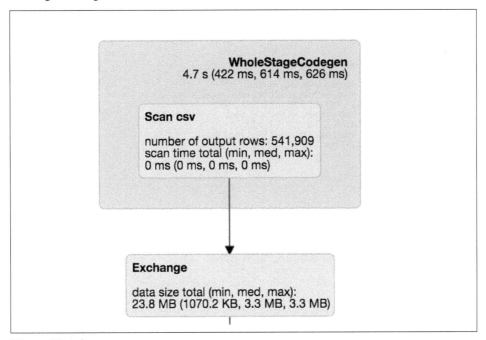

Figure 18-4. Stage one

The box on top, labeled WholeStateCodegen, represents a full scan of the CSV file. The box below that represents a shuffle that we forced when we called repartition. This turned our original dataset (of a yet to be specified number of partitions) into two partitions.

The next step is our projection (selecting/adding/filtering columns) and the aggregation. Notice that in Figure 18-5 the number of output rows is six. This convienently lines up with the number of output rows multiplied by the number of partitions at aggregation time. This is because Spark performs an aggregation for each partition (in this case a hash-based aggregation) before shuffling the data around in preparation for the final stage.

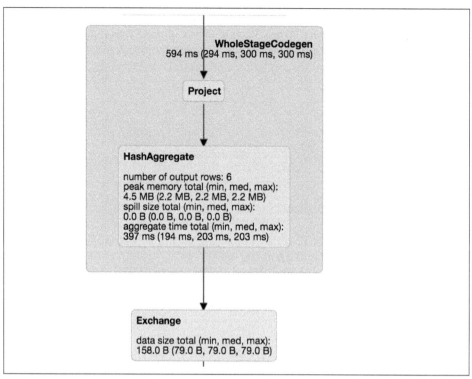

Figure 18-5. Stage two

The last stage is the aggregation of the subaggregations that we saw happen on a per-partition basis in the previous stage. We combine those two partitions in the final three rows that are the output of our total query (Figure 18-6).

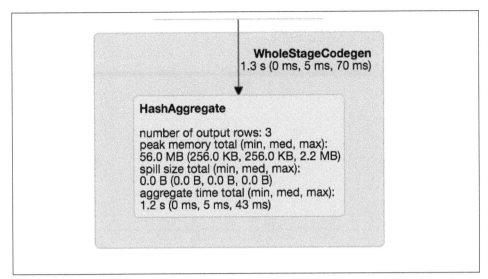

WholeStageCodegen
1.3 s (0 ms, 5 ms, 70 ms)

HashAggregate

number of output rows: 3
peak memory total (min, med, max):
56.0 MB (256.0 KB, 256.0 KB, 2.2 MB)
spill size total (min, med, max):
0.0 B (0.0 B, 0.0 B, 0.0 B)
aggregate time total (min, med, max):
1.2 s (0 ms, 5 ms, 43 ms)

Figure 18-6. Stage three

Let's look further into the job's execution. On the Jobs tab, next to Succeeded Jobs, click 2. As Figure 18-7 demonstrates, our job breaks down into three stages (which corresponds to what we saw on the SQL tab).

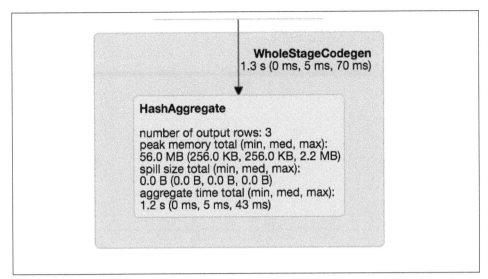

Figure 18-7. The Jobs tab

These stages have more or less the same information as what's shown in Figure 18-6, but clicking the label for one of them will show the details for a given stage. In this example, three stages ran, with eight, two, and then two hundred tasks each. Before diving into the stage detail, let's review why this is the case.

The first stage has eight tasks. CSV files are splittable, and Spark broke up the work to be distributed relatively evenly between the different cores on the machine. This happens at the cluster level and points to an important optimization: how you store your files. The following stage has two tasks because we explicitly called a repartition to move the data into two partitions. The last stage has 200 tasks because the default shuffle partitions value is 200.

Now that we reviewed how we got here, click the stage with eight tasks to see the next level of detail, as shown in Figure 18-8.

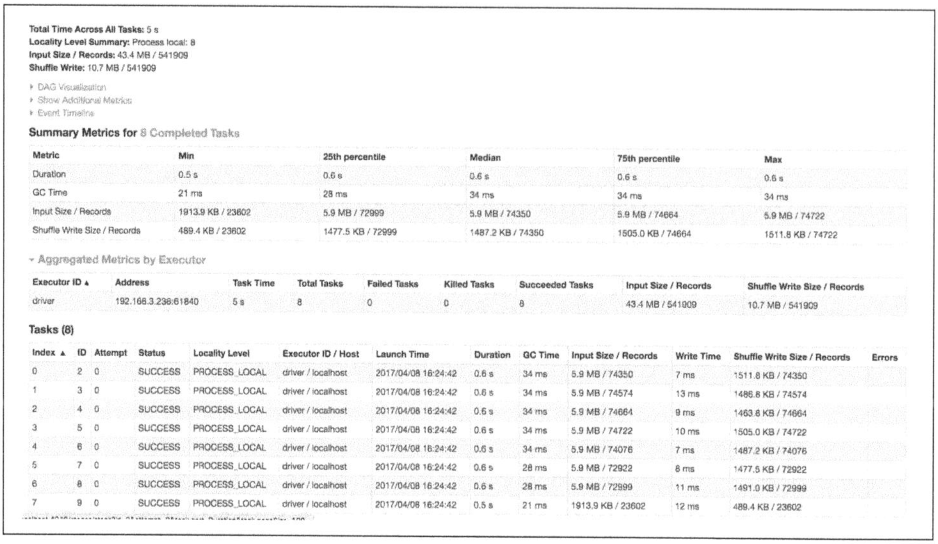
Total Time Across All Tasks: 5 s
Locality Level Summary: Process local: 8
Input Size / Records: 43.4 MB / 541909
Shuffle Write: 10.7 MB / 541909

- DAG Visualization
- Show Additional Metrics
- Event Timeline

Summary Metrics for 8 Completed Tasks

Metric	Min	25th percentile	Median	75th percentile	Max
Duration	0.5 s	0.6 s	0.6 s	0.6 s	0.6 s
GC Time	21 ms	28 ms	34 ms	34 ms	34 ms
Input Size / Records	1913.9 KB / 23602	5.9 MB / 72999	5.9 MB / 74350	5.9 MB / 74664	5.9 MB / 74722
Shuffle Write Size / Records	489.4 KB / 23602	1477.5 KB / 72999	1487.2 KB / 74350	1505.0 KB / 74664	1511.8 KB / 74722

- Aggregated Metrics by Executor

Executor ID ▲	Address	Task Time	Total Tasks	Failed Tasks	Killed Tasks	Succeeded Tasks	Input Size / Records	Shuffle Write Size / Records
driver	192.168.3.238:61840	5 s	8	0	0	8	43.4 MB / 541909	10.7 MB / 541909

Tasks (8)

Index ▲	ID	Attempt	Status	Locality Level	Executor ID / Host	Launch Time	Duration	GC Time	Input Size / Records	Write Time	Shuffle Write Size / Records	Errors
0	2	0	SUCCESS	PROCESS_LOCAL	driver / localhost	2017/04/08 16:24:42	0.6 s	34 ms	5.9 MB / 74350	7 ms	1511.8 KB / 74350	
1	3	0	SUCCESS	PROCESS_LOCAL	driver / localhost	2017/04/08 16:24:42	0.6 s	34 ms	5.9 MB / 74574	13 ms	1486.8 KB / 74574	
2	4	0	SUCCESS	PROCESS_LOCAL	driver / localhost	2017/04/08 16:24:42	0.6 s	34 ms	5.9 MB / 74664	9 ms	1463.8 KB / 74664	
3	5	0	SUCCESS	PROCESS_LOCAL	driver / localhost	2017/04/08 16:24:42	0.6 s	34 ms	5.9 MB / 74722	10 ms	1505.0 KB / 74722	
4	6	0	SUCCESS	PROCESS_LOCAL	driver / localhost	2017/04/08 16:24:42	0.6 s	34 ms	5.9 MB / 74076	7 ms	1487.2 KB / 74076	
5	7	0	SUCCESS	PROCESS_LOCAL	driver / localhost	2017/04/08 16:24:42	0.6 s	28 ms	5.9 MB / 72922	8 ms	1477.5 KB / 72922	
6	8	0	SUCCESS	PROCESS_LOCAL	driver / localhost	2017/04/08 16:24:42	0.6 s	28 ms	5.9 MB / 72999	11 ms	1491.0 KB / 72999	
7	9	0	SUCCESS	PROCESS_LOCAL	driver / localhost	2017/04/08 16:24:42	0.5 s	21 ms	1913.9 KB / 23602	12 ms	489.4 KB / 23602	

Figure 18-8. Spark tasks

Spark provides a lot of detail about what this job did when it ran. Toward the top, notice the Summary Metrics section. This provides a synopsis of statistics regarding various metrics. What you want to be on the lookout for is uneven distributions of the values (we touch on this in Chapter 19). In this case, everything looks very consistent; there are no wide swings in the distribution of values. In the table at the bottom, we can also examine on a per-executor basis (one for every core on this particular machine, in this case). This can help identify whether a particular executor is struggling with its workload.

Spark also makes available a set of more detailed metrics, as shown in Figure 18-8, which are probably not relevant to the large majority of users. To view those, click Show Additional Metrics, and then either choose (De)select All or select individual metrics, depending on what you want to see.

You can repeat this basic analysis for each stage that you want to analyze. We leave that as an exercise for the reader.

Other Spark UI tabs

The remaining Spark tabs, Storage, Environment, and Executors, are fairly self-explanatory. The Storage tab shows information about the cached RDDs/DataFrames on the cluster. This can help you see if certain data has been evicted from the cache over time. The Environment tab shows you information about the Runtime Environment, including information about Scala and Java as well as the various Spark Properties that you configured on your cluster.

Configuring the Spark user interface

There are a number of configurations that you can set regarding the Spark UI. Many of them are networking configurations such as enabling access control. Others let you configure how the Spark UI will behave (e.g., how many jobs, stages, and tasks are stored). Due to space limitations, we cannot include the entire configuration set here. Consult the relevant table on Spark UI Configurations (*http://spark.apache.org/docs/latest/monitoring.html#spark-configuration-options*) in the Spark documentation.

Spark REST API

In addition to the Spark UI, you can also access Spark's status and metrics via a REST API. This is is available at *http://localhost:4040/api/v1* and is a way of building visualizations and monitoring tools on top of Spark itself. For the most part this API exposes the same information presented in the web UI, except that it doesn't include any of the SQL-related information. This can be a useful tool if you would like to build your own reporting solution based on the information available in the Spark UI. Due to space limitations, we cannot include the list of API endpoints here. Consult the relevant table on REST API Endpoints (*http://spark.apache.org/docs/latest/monitoring.html#rest-api*) in the Spark documentation.

Spark UI History Server

Normally, the Spark UI is only available while a SparkContext is running, so how can you get to it after your application crashes or ends? To do this, Spark includes a tool called the Spark History Server that allows you to reconstruct the Spark UI and REST API, provided that the application was configured to save an *event log*. You can find up-to-date information about how to use this tool in the Spark documentation (*https://spark.apache.org/docs/latest/monitoring.html*).

To use the history server, you first need to configure your application to store event logs to a certain location. You can do this by by enabling `spark.eventLog.enabled` and the event log location with the configuration `spark.eventLog.dir`. Then, once you have stored the events, you can run the history server as a standalone application, and it will automatically reconstruct the web UI based on these logs. Some cluster managers and cloud services also configure logging automatically and run a history server by default.

There are a number of other configurations for the history server. Due to space limitations, we cannot include the entire configuration set here. Refer to the relevant table on Spark History Server Configurations (*http://spark.apache.org/docs/latest/monitoring.html#spark-configuration-options*) in the Spark documentation.

Debugging and Spark First Aid

The previous sections defined some core "vital signs"—that is, things that we can monitor to check the health of a Spark Application. For the remainder of the chapter we're going to take a "first aid" approach to Spark debugging: We'll review some signs and symptoms of problems in your Spark jobs, including signs that you might observe (e.g., slow tasks) as well as symptoms from Spark itself (e.g., `OutOfMemoryEr ror`). There are many issues that may affect Spark jobs, so it's impossible to cover everything. But we will discuss some of the more common Spark issues you may encounter. In addition to the signs and symptoms, we'll also look at some potential treatments for these issues.

Most of the recommendations about fixing issues refer to the configuration tools discussed in Chapter 16.

Spark Jobs Not Starting

This issue can arise frequently, especially when you're just getting started with a fresh deployment or environment.

Signs and symptoms

- Spark jobs don't start.
- The Spark UI doesn't show any nodes on the cluster except the driver.
- The Spark UI seems to be reporting incorrect information.

Potential treatments

This mostly occurs when your cluster or your application's resource demands are not configured properly. Spark, in a distributed setting, does make some assumptions about networks, file systems, and other resources. During the process of setting up the cluster, you likely configured something incorrectly, and now the node that runs the driver cannot talk to the executors. This might be because you didn't specify what IP and port is open or didn't open the correct one. This is most likely a cluster level, machine, or configuration issue. Another option is that your application requested more resources per executor than your cluster manager currently has free, in which case the driver will be waiting forever for executors to be launched.

- Ensure that machines can communicate with one another on the ports that you expect. Ideally, you should open up all ports between the worker nodes unless you have more stringent security constraints.
- Ensure that your Spark resource configurations are correct and that your cluster manager is properly set up for Spark. Try running a simple application first to see

if that works. One common issue may be that you requested more memory per executor than the cluster manager has free to allocate, so check how much it is reporting free (in its UI) and your `spark-submit` memory configuration.

Errors Before Execution

This can happen when you're developing a new application and have previously run code on this cluster, but now some new code won't work.

Signs and symptoms

- Commands don't run at all and output large error messages.
- You check the Spark UI and no jobs, stages, or tasks seem to run.

Potential treatments

After checking and confirming that the Spark UI environment tab shows the correct information for your application, it's worth double-checking your code. Many times, there might be a simple typo or incorrect column name that is preventing the Spark job from compiling into its underlying Spark plan (when using the DataFrame API).

- You should take a look at the error returned by Spark to confirm that there isn't an issue in your code, such as providing the wrong input file path or field name.
- Double-check to verify that the cluster has the network connectivity that you expect between your driver, your workers, and the storage system you are using.
- There might be issues with libraries or classpaths that are causing the wrong version of a library to be loaded for accessing storage. Try simplifying your application until you get a smaller version that reproduces the issue (e.g., just reading one dataset).

Errors During Execution

This kind of issue occurs when you already are working on a cluster or parts of your Spark Application run before you encounter an error. This can be a part of a scheduled job that runs at some interval or a part of some interactive exploration that seems to fail after some time.

Signs and symptoms

- One Spark job runs successfully on the entire cluster but the next one fails.
- A step in a multistep query fails.

- A scheduled job that ran yesterday is failing today.
- Difficult to parse error message.

Potential treatments

- Check to see if your data exists or is in the format that you expect. This can change over time or some upstream change may have had unintended consequences on your application.
- If an error quickly pops up when you run a query (i.e., before tasks are launched), it is most likely an *analysis error* while planning the query. This means that you likely misspelled a column name referenced in the query or that a column, view, or table you referenced does not exist.
- Read through the stack trace to try to find clues about what components are involved (e.g., what operator and stage it was running in).
- Try to isolate the issue by progressively double-checking input data and ensuring the data conforms to your expectations. Also try removing logic until you can isolate the problem in a smaller version of your application.
- If a job runs tasks for some time and then fails, it could be due to a problem with the input data itself, wherein the schema might be specified incorrectly or a particular row does not conform to the expected schema. For instance, sometimes your schema might specify that the data contains no nulls but your data does actually contain nulls, which can cause certain transformations to fail.
- It's also possible that your own code for processing the data is crashing, in which case Spark will show you the exception thrown by your code. In this case, you will see a task marked as "failed" on the Spark UI, and you can also view the logs on that machine to understand what it was doing when it failed. Try adding more logs inside your code to figure out which data record was being processed.

Slow Tasks or Stragglers

This issue is quite common when optimizing applications, and can occur either due to work not being evenly distributed across your machines ("skew"), or due to one of your machines being slower than the others (e.g., due to a hardware problem).

Signs and symptoms

Any of the following are appropriate symptoms of the issue:

- Spark stages seem to execute until there are only a handful of tasks left. Those tasks then take a long time.

- These slow tasks show up in the Spark UI and occur consistently on the same dataset(s).
- These occur in stages, one after the other.
- Scaling up the number of machines given to the Spark Application doesn't really help—some tasks still take much longer than others.
- In the Spark metrics, certain executors are reading and writing much more data than others.

Potential treatments

Slow tasks are often called "stragglers." There are many reasons they may occur, but most often the source of this issue is that your data is partitioned unevenly into Data-Frame or RDD partitions. When this happens, some executors might need to work on much larger amounts of work than others. One particularly common case is that you use a group-by-key operation and one of the keys just has more data than others. In this case, when you look at the Spark UI, you might see that the shuffle data for some nodes is much larger than for others.

- Try increasing the number of partitions to have less data per partition.
- Try repartitioning by another combination of columns. For example, stragglers can come up when you partition by a skewed ID column, or a column where many values are null. In the latter case, it might make sense to first filter out the null values.
- Try increasing the memory allocated to your executors if possible.
- Monitor the executor that is having trouble and see if it is the same machine across jobs; you might also have an unhealthy executor or machine in your cluster—for example, one whose disk is nearly full.
- If this issue is associated with a join or an aggregation, see "Slow Joins" on page 309 or "Slow Aggregations" on page 308.
- Check whether your user-defined functions (UDFs) are wasteful in their object allocation or business logic. Try to convert them to DataFrame code if possible.
- Ensure that your UDFs or User-Defined Aggregate Functions (UDAFs) are running on a small enough batch of data. Oftentimes an aggregation can pull a lot of data into memory for a common key, leading to that executor having to do a lot more work than others.
- Turning on *speculation*, which we discuss in "Slow Reads and Writes" on page 310, will have Spark run a second copy of tasks that are extremely slow. This can be helpful if the issue is due to a faulty node because the task will get to run on a faster one. Speculation does come at a cost, however, because it consumes addi-

tional resources. In addition, for some storage systems that use eventual consistency, you could end up with duplicate output data if your writes are not idempotent. (We discussed speculation configurations in Chapter 17.)

- Another common issue can arise when you're working with Datasets. Because Datasets perform a lot of object instantiation to convert records to Java objects for UDFs, they can cause a lot of garbage collection. If you're using Datasets, look at the garbage collection metrics in the Spark UI to see if they're consistent with the slow tasks.

Stragglers can be one of the most difficult issues to debug, simply because there are so many possible causes. However, in all likelihood, the cause will be some kind of data skew, so definitely begin by checking the Spark UI for imbalanced amounts of data across tasks.

Slow Aggregations

If you have a slow aggregation, start by reviewing the issues in the "Slow Tasks" section before proceeding. Having tried those, you might continue to see the same problem.

Signs and symptoms

- Slow tasks during a `groupBy` call.
- Jobs after the aggregation are slow, as well.

Potential treatments

Unfortunately, this issue can't always be solved. Sometimes, the data in your job just has some skewed keys, and the operation you want to run on them needs to be slow.

- Increasing the number of partitions, prior to an aggregation, might help by reducing the number of different keys processed in each task.

- Increasing executor memory can help alleviate this issue, as well. If a single key has lots of data, this will allow its executor to spill to disk less often and finish faster, although it may still be much slower than executors processing other keys.

- If you find that tasks after the aggregation are also slow, this means that your dataset might have remained unbalanced after the aggregation. Try inserting a `repartition` call to partition it randomly.

- Ensuring that all filters and `SELECT` statements that can be are above the aggregation can help to ensure that you're working only on the data that you need to be working on and nothing else. Spark's query optimizer will automatically do this for the structured APIs.

- Ensure null values are represented correctly (using Spark's concept of `null`) and not as some default value like " " or `"EMPTY"`. Spark often optimizes for skipping nulls early in the job when possible, but it can't do so for your own placeholder values.

- Some aggregation functions are also just inherently slower than others. For instance, `collect_list` and `collect_set` are very slow aggregation functions because they *must* return all the matching objects to the driver, and should be avoided in performance-critical code.

Slow Joins

Joins and aggregations are both shuffles, so they share some of the same general symptoms as well as treatments.

Signs and symptoms

- A join stage seems to be taking a long time. This can be one task or many tasks.
- Stages before and after the join seem to be operating normally.

Potential treatments

- Many joins can be optimized (manually or automatically) to other types of joins. We covered how to select different join types in Chapter 8.

- Experimenting with different join orderings can really help speed up jobs, especially if some of those joins filter out a large amount of data; do those first.

- Partitioning a dataset prior to joining can be very helpful for reducing data movement across the cluster, especially if the same dataset will be used in multiple join operations. It's worth experimenting with different prejoin partitioning. Keep in mind, again, that this isn't "free" and does come at the cost of a shuffle.

- Slow joins can also be caused by data skew. There's not always a lot you can do here, but sizing up the Spark application and/or increasing the size of executors can help, as described in earlier sections.

- Ensuring that all filters and select statements that can be are above the join can help to ensure that you're working only on the data that you need for the join.

- Ensure that null values are handled correctly (that you're using `null`) and not some default value like " " or `"EMPTY"`, as with aggregations.

- Sometimes Spark can't properly plan for a broadcast join if it doesn't know any statistics about the input DataFrame or table. If you know that one of the tables that you are joining is small, you can try to force a broadcast (as discussed in

Chapter 8), or use Spark's statistics collection commands to let it analyze the table.

Slow Reads and Writes

Slow I/O can be difficult to diagnose, especially with networked file systems.

Signs and symptoms

- Slow reading of data from a distributed file system or external system.
- Slow writes from network file systems or blob storage.

Potential treatments

- Turning on speculation (set `spark.speculation` to `true`) can help with slow reads and writes. This will launch additional tasks with the same operation in an attempt to see whether it's just some transient issue in the first task. Speculation is a powerful tool and works well with consistent file systems. However, it can cause duplicate data writes with some eventually consistent cloud services, such as Amazon S3, so check whether it is supported by the storage system connector you are using.
- Ensuring sufficient network connectivity can be important—your Spark cluster may simply not have enough total network bandwidth to get to your storage system.
- For distributed file systems such as HDFS running on the same nodes as Spark, make sure Spark sees the same hostnames for nodes as the file system. This will enable Spark to do locality-aware scheduling, which you will be able to see in the "locality" column in the Spark UI. We'll talk about locality a bit more in the next chapter.

Driver OutOfMemoryError or Driver Unresponsive

This is usually a pretty serious issue because it will crash your Spark Application. It often happens due to collecting too much data back to the driver, making it run out of memory.

Signs and symptoms

- Spark Application is unresponsive or crashed.
- `OutOfMemoryErrors` or garbage collection messages in the driver logs.

- Commands take a very long time to run or don't run at all.
- Interactivity is very low or non-existent.
- Memory usage is high for the driver JVM.

Potential treatments

There are a variety of potential reasons for this happening, and diagnosis is not always straightforward.

- Your code might have tried to collect an overly large dataset to the driver node using operations such as `collect`.
- You might be using a broadcast join where the data to be broadcast is too big. Use Spark's maximum broadcast join configuration to better control the size it will broadcast.
- A long-running application generated a large number of objects on the driver and is unable to release them. Java's *jmap* tool can be useful to see what objects are filling most of the memory of your driver JVM by printing a histogram of the heap. However, take note that *jmap* will pause that JVM while running.
- Increase the driver's memory allocation if possible to let it work with more data.
- Issues with JVMs running out of memory can happen if you are using another language binding, such as Python, due to data conversion between the two requiring too much memory in the JVM. Try to see whether your issue is specific to your chosen language and bring back less data to the driver node, or write it to a file instead of bringing it back as in-memory objects.
- If you are sharing a SparkContext with other users (e.g., through the SQL JDBC server and some notebook environments), ensure that people aren't trying to do something that might be causing large amounts of memory allocation in the driver (like working overly large arrays in their code or collecting large datasets).

Executor OutOfMemoryError or Executor Unresponsive

Spark applications can sometimes recover from this automatically, depending on the true underlying issue.

Signs and symptoms

- `OutOfMemoryErrors` or garbage collection messages in the executor logs. You can find these in the Spark UI.
- Executors that crash or become unresponsive.

- Slow tasks on certain nodes that never seem to recover.

Potential treatments

- Try increasing the memory available to executors and the number of executors.
- Try increasing PySpark worker size via the relevant Python configurations.
- Look for garbage collection error messages in the executor logs. Some of the tasks that are running, especially if you're using UDFs, can be creating lots of objects that need to be garbage collected. Repartition your data to increase parallelism, reduce the amount of records per task, and ensure that all executors are getting the same amount of work.
- Ensure that null values are handled correctly (that you're using `null`) and not some default value like " " or "EMPTY", as we discussed earlier.
- This is more likely to happen with RDDs or with Datasets because of object instantiations. Try using fewer UDFs and more of Spark's structured operations when possible.
- Use Java monitoring tools such as *jmap* to get a histogram of heap memory usage on your executors, and see which classes are taking up the most space.
- If executors are being placed on nodes that also have other workloads running on them, such as a key-value store, try to isolate your Spark jobs from other jobs.

Unexpected Nulls in Results

Signs and symptoms

- Unexpected `null` values after transformations.
- Scheduled production jobs that used to work no longer work, or no longer produce the right results.

Potential treatments

- It's possible that your data format has changed without adjusting your business logic. This means that code that worked before is no longer valid.
- Use an accumulator to try to count records or certain types, as well as parsing or processing errors where you skip a record. This can be helpful because you might think that you're parsing data of a certain format, but some of the data doesn't. Most often, users will place the accumulator in a UDF when they are parsing their raw data into a more controlled format and perform the counts there. This

allows you to count valid and invalid records and then operate accordingly after the fact.

- Ensure that your transformations actually result in valid query plans. Spark SQL sometimes does implicit type coercions that can cause confusing results. For instance, the SQL expression `SELECT 5*"23"` results in 115 because the string "25" converts to an the value 25 as an integer, but the expression `SELECT 5 * " "` results in `null` because casting the empty string to an integer gives `null`. Make sure that your intermediate datasets have the schema you expect them to (try using `printSchema` on them), and look for any `CAST` operations in the final query plan.

No Space Left on Disk Errors

Signs and symptoms

- You see "no space left on disk" errors and your jobs fail.

Potential treatments

- The easiest way to alleviate this, of course, is to add more disk space. You can do this by sizing up the nodes that you're working on or attaching external storage in a cloud environment.

- If you have a cluster with limited storage space, some nodes may run out first due to skew. Repartitioning the data as described earlier may help here.

- There are also a number of storage configurations with which you can experiment. Some of these determine how long logs should be kept on the machine before being removed. For more information, see the Spark executor logs rolling configurations in Chapter 16.

- Try manually removing some old log files or old shuffle files from the machine(s) in question. This can help alleviate some of the issue although obviously it's not a permanent fix.

Serialization Errors

Signs and symptoms

- You see serialization errors and your jobs fail.

Potential treatments

- This is very uncommon when working with the Structured APIs, but you might be trying to perform some custom logic on executors with UDFs or RDDs and either the task that you're trying to serialize to these executors or the data you are trying to share cannot be serialized. This often happens when you're working with either some code or data that cannot be serialized into a UDF or function, or if you're working with strange data types that cannot be serialized. If you are using (or intend to be using Kryo serialization), verify that you're actually registering your classes so that they are indeed serialized.

- Try not to refer to any fields of the enclosing object in your UDFs when creating UDFs inside a Java or Scala class. This can cause Spark to try to serialize the whole enclosing object, which may not be possible. Instead, copy the relevant fields to local variables in the same scope as closure and use those.

Conclusion

This chapter covered some of the main tools that you can use to monitor and debug your Spark jobs and applications, as well as the most common issues we see and their resolutions. As with debugging any complex software, we recommend taking a principled, step-by-step approach to debug issues. Add logging statements to figure out where your job is crashing and what type of data arrives at each stage, try to isolate the problem to the smallest piece of code possible, and work up from there. For data skew issues, which are unique to parallel computing, use Spark's UI to get a quick overview of how much work each task is doing. In Chapter 19, we discuss performance tuning in particular and various tools you can use for that.

Performance Tuning

Chapter 18 covered the Spark user interface (UI) and basic first-aid for your Spark Application. Using the tools outlined in that chapter, you should be able to ensure that your jobs run reliably. However, sometimes you'll also need them to run faster or more efficiently for a variety of reasons. That's what this chapter is about. Here, we present a discussion of some of the performance choices that are available to make your jobs run faster.

Just as with monitoring, there are a number of different levels that you can try to tune at. For instance, if you had an extremely fast network, that would make many of your Spark jobs faster because shuffles are so often one of the costlier steps in a Spark job. Most likely, you won't have much ability to control such things; therefore, we're going to discuss the things you can control through code choices or configuration.

There are a variety of different parts of Spark jobs that you might want to optimize, and it's valuable to be specific. Following are some of the areas:

- Code-level design choices (e.g., RDDs versus DataFrames)
- Data at rest
- Joins
- Aggregations
- Data in flight
- Individual application properties
- Inside of the Java Virtual Machine (JVM) of an executor
- Worker nodes
- Cluster and deployment properties

This list is by no means exhaustive, but it does at least ground the conversation and the topics that we cover in this chapter. Additionally, there are two ways of trying to achieve the execution characteristics that we would like out of Spark jobs. We can either do so *indirectly* by setting configuration values or changing the runtime environment. These should improve things across Spark Applications or across Spark jobs. Alternatively, we can try to *directly* change execution characteristic or design choices at the individual Spark job, stage, or task level. These kinds of fixes are very specific to that one area of our application and therefore have limited overall impact. There are numerous things that lie on both sides of the *indirect* versus *direct* divide, and we will draw lines in the sand accordingly.

One of the best things you can do to figure out how to improve performance is to implement good monitoring and job history tracking. Without this information, it can be difficult to know whether you're really improving job performance.

Indirect Performance Enhancements

As discussed, there are a number of indirect enhancements that you can perform to help your Spark jobs run faster. We'll skip the obvious ones like "improve your hardware" and focus more on the things within your control.

Design Choices

Although good design choices seem like a somewhat obvious way to optimize performance, we often don't prioritize this step in the process. When designing your applications, making good design choices is very important because it not only helps you to write better Spark applications but also to get them to run in a more stable and consistent manner over time and in the face of external changes or variations. We've already discussed some of these topics earlier in the book, but we'll summarize some of the fundamental ones again here.

Scala versus Java versus Python versus R

This question is nearly impossible to answer in the general sense because a lot will depend on your use case. For instance, if you want to perform some single-node machine learning after performing a large ETL job, we might recommend running your Extract, Transform, and Load (ETL) code as SparkR code and then using R's massive machine learning ecosystem to run your single-node machine learning algorithms. This gives you the best of both worlds and takes advantage of the strength of R as well as the strength of Spark without sacrifices. As we mentioned numerous times, Spark's Structured APIs are consistent across languages in terms of speed and stability. That means that you should code with whatever language you are most comfortable using or is best suited for your use case.

Things do get a bit more complicated when you need to include custom transformations that cannot be created in the Structured APIs. These might manifest themselves as RDD transformations or user-defined functions (UDFs). If you're going to do this, R and Python are not necessarily the best choice simply because of how this is actually executed. It's also more difficult to provide stricter guarantees of types and manipulations when you're defining functions that jump across languages. We find that using Python for the majority of the application, and porting some of it to Scala or writing specific UDFs in Scala as your application evolves, is a powerful technique —it allows for a nice balance between overall usability, maintainability, and performance.

DataFrames versus SQL versus Datasets versus RDDs

This question also comes up frequently. The answer is simple. Across all languages, DataFrames, Datasets, and SQL are equivalent in speed. This means that if you're using DataFrames in any of these languages, performance is equal. However, if you're going to be defining UDFs, you'll take a performance hit writing those in Python or R, and to some extent a lesser performance hit in Java and Scala. If you want to optimize for pure performance, it would behoove you to try and get back to DataFrames and SQL as quickly as possible. Although all DataFrame, SQL, and Dataset code compiles down to RDDs, Spark's optimization engine will write "better" RDD code than you can manually and certainly do it with orders of magnitude less effort. Additionally, you will lose out on new optimizations that are added to Spark's SQL engine every release.

Lastly, if you want to use RDDs, we definitely recommend using Scala or Java. If that's not possible, we recommend that you restrict the "surface area" of RDDs in your application to the bare minimum. That's because when Python runs RDD code, it's serializes a lot of data to and from the Python process. This is very expensive to run over very big data and can also decrease stability.

Although it isn't exactly relevant to performance tuning, it's important to note that there are also some gaps in what functionality is supported in each of Spark's languages. We discussed this in Chapter 16.

Object Serialization in RDDs

In Part III, we briefly discussed the serialization libraries that can be used within RDD transformations. When you're working with custom data types, you're going to want to serialize them using Kryo (*https://github.com/EsotericSoftware/kryo*) because it's both more compact and much more efficient than Java serialization. However, this does come at the inconvenience of registering the classes that you will be using in your application.

You can use Kryo serialization by setting `spark.serializer` to `org.apache.spark.serializer.KryoSerializer`. You will also need to explicitly register the classes that you would like to register with the Kryo serializer via the `spark.kryo.classesToRegister` configuration. There are also a number of advanced parameters for controlling this in greater detail that are described in the Kryo documentation (*https://github.com/EsotericSoftware/kryo*).

To register your classes, use the `SparkConf` that you just created and pass in the names of your classes:

```
conf.registerKryoClasses(Array(classOf[MyClass1], classOf[MyClass2]))
```

Cluster Configurations

This area has huge potential benefits but is probably one of the more difficult to prescribe because of the variation across hardware and use cases. In general, monitoring how the machines themselves are performing will be the most valuable approach toward optimizing your cluster configurations, especially when it comes to running multiple applications (whether they are Spark or not) on a single cluster.

Cluster/application sizing and sharing

This somewhat comes down to a resource sharing and scheduling problem; however, there are a lot of options for how you want to share resources at the cluster level or at the application level. Take a look at the configurations listed at the end of Chapter 16 as well as some configurations in Chapter 17.

Dynamic allocation

Spark provides a mechanism to dynamically adjust the resources your application occupies based on the workload. This means that your application can give resources back to the cluster if they are no longer used, and request them again later when there is demand. This feature is particularly useful if multiple applications share resources in your Spark cluster. This feature is disabled by default and available on all coarse-grained cluster managers; that is, standalone mode, YARN mode, and Mesos coarse-grained mode. If you'd like to enable this feature, you should set `spark.dynamicAllocation.enabled` to `true`. The Spark documentation (*https://spark.apache.org/docs/latest/job-scheduling.html#configuration-and-setup*) presents a number of individual parameters that you can tune.

Scheduling

Over the course of the previous chapters, we discussed a number of different potential optimizations that you can take advantage of to either help Spark jobs run in parallel with scheduler pools or help Spark applications run in parallel with something like dynamic allocation or setting `max-executor-cores`. Scheduling optimizations do involve some research and experimentation, and unfortunately there are not super-quick fixes beyond setting `spark.scheduler.mode` to `FAIR` to allow better sharing of resources across multiple users, or setting `--max-executor-cores`, which specifies the maximum number of executor cores that your application will need. Specifying this value can ensure that your application does not take up all the resources on the cluster. You can also change the default, depending on your cluster manager, by setting the configuration `spark.cores.max` to a default of your choice. Cluster managers also provide some scheduling primitives that can be helpful when optimizing multiple Spark Applications, as discussed in Chapters 16 and 17.

Data at Rest

More often that not, when you're saving data it will be read many times as other folks in your organization access the same datasets in order to run different analyses. Making sure that you're storing your data for effective reads later on is absolutely essential to successful big data projects. This involves choosing your storage system, choosing your data format, and taking advantage of features such as data partitioning in some storage formats.

File-based long-term data storage

There are a number of different file formats available, from simple comma-separated values (CSV) files and binary blobs, to more sophisticated formats like Apache Parquet. One of the easiest ways to optimize your Spark jobs is to follow best practices when storing data and choose the most efficient storage format possible.

Generally you should always favor structured, binary types to store your data, especially when you'll be accessing it frequently. Although files like "CSV" seem well-structured, they're very slow to parse, and often also full of edge cases and pain points. For instance, improperly escaped new-line characters can often cause a lot of trouble when reading a large number of files. The most efficient file format you can generally choose is Apache Parquet. Parquet stores data in binary files with column-oriented storage, and also tracks some statistics about each file that make it possible to quickly skip data not needed for a query. It is well integrated with Spark through the built-in Parquet data source.

Splittable file types and compression

Whatever file format you choose, you should make sure it is "splittable", which means that different tasks can read different parts of the file in parallel. We saw why this is important in Chapter 18. When we read in the file, all cores were able to do part of the work. That's because the file was splittable. If we didn't use a splittable file type—

say something like a malformed JSON file—we're going to need to read in the entire file on a single machine, greatly reducing parallelism.

The main place splittability comes in is compression formats. A ZIP file or TAR archive cannot be split, which means that even if we have 10 files in a ZIP file and 10 cores, only one core can read in that data because we cannot parallelize access to the ZIP file. This is a poor use of resources. In contrast, files compressed using gzip, bzip2, or lz4 are generally splittable if they were written by a parallel processing framework like Hadoop or Spark. For your own input data, the simplest way to make it splittable is to upload it as separate files, ideally each no larger than a few hundred megabytes.

Table partitioning

We discussed table partitioning in Chapter 9, and will only use this section as a reminder. Table partitioning refers to storing files in separate directories based on a key, such as the date field in the data. Storage managers like Apache Hive support this concept, as do many of Spark's built-in data sources. Partitioning your data correctly allows Spark to skip many irrelevant files when it only requires data with a specific range of keys. For instance, if users frequently filter by "date" or "customerId" in their queries, partition your data by those columns. This will greatly reduce the amount of data that end users must read by most queries, and therefore dramatically increase speed.

The one downside of partitioning, however, is that if you partition at too fine a granularity, it can result in many small files, and a great deal of overhead trying to list all the files in the storage system.

Bucketing

We also discussed bucketing in Chapter 9, but to recap, the essense is that bucketing your data allows Spark to "pre-partition" data according to how joins or aggregations are likely to be performed by readers. This can improve performance and stability because data can be consistently distributed across partitions as opposed to skewed into just one or two. For instance, if joins are frequently performed on a column immediately after a read, you can use bucketing to ensure that the data is well partitioned according to those values. This can help prevent a shuffle before a join and therefore help speed up data access. Bucketing generally works hand-in-hand with partitioning as a second way of physically splitting up data.

The number of files

In addition to organizing your data into buckets and partitions, you'll also want to consider the number of files and the size of files that you're storing. If there are lots of small files, you're going to pay a price listing and fetching each of those individual files. For instance, if you're reading a data from Hadoop Distributed File System (HDFS), this data is managed in blocks that are up to 128 MB in size (by default). This means if you have 30 files, of 5 MB each, you're going to have to potentially request 30 blocks, even though the same data could have fit into 2 blocks (150 MB total).

Although there is not necessarily a panacea for how you want to store your data, the trade-off can be summarized as such. Having lots of small files is going to make the scheduler work much harder to locate the data and launch all of the read tasks. This can increase the network and scheduling overhead of the job. Having fewer large files eases the pain off the scheduler but it will also make tasks run longer. In this case, though, you can always launch more tasks than there are input files if you want more parallelism—Spark will split each file across multiple tasks assuming you are using a splittable format. In general, we recommend sizing your files so that they each con-tain at least a few tens of megabytes of data.

One way of controlling data partitioning when you write your data is through a write option introduced in Spark 2.2. To control how many records go into each file, you can specify the `maxRecordsPerFile` option to the write operation.

Data locality

Another aspect that can be important in shared cluster environments is data locality. Data locality basically specifies a preference for certain nodes that hold certain data, rather than having to exchange these blocks of data over the network. If you run your storage system on the same nodes as Spark, and the system supports locality hints, Spark will try to schedule tasks close to each input block of data. For example HDFS storage provides this option. There are several configurations that affect locality, but it will generally be used by default if Spark detects that it is using a local storage sys-tem. You will also see data-reading tasks marked as "local" in the Spark web UI.

Statistics collection

Spark includes a cost-based query optimizer that plans queries based on the proper-ties of the input data when using the structured APIs. However, to allow the cost-based optimizer to make these sorts of decisions, you need to collect (and maintain) *statistics* about your tables that it can use. There are two kinds of statistics: table-level and column-level statistics. Statistics collection is available only on named tables, not on arbitrary DataFrames or RDDs.

To collect table-level statistics, you can run the following command:

```
ANALYZE TABLE table_name COMPUTE STATISTICS
```

To collect column-level statistics, you can name the specific columns:

```
ANALYZE TABLE table_name COMPUTE STATISTICS FOR
COLUMNS column_name1, column_name2, ...
```

Column-level statistics are slower to collect, but provide more information for the cost-based optimizer to use about those data columns. Both types of statistics can help with joins, aggregations, filters, and a number of other potential things (e.g., automatically choosing when to do a broadcast join). This is a fast-growing part of Spark, so different optimizations based on statistics will likely be added in the future.

> You can follow the progress of cost-based optimization on its JIRA issue (*https://issues.apache.org/jira/browse/SPARK-16026*). You can also read through the design document on SPARK-16026 (*https://issues.apache.org/jira/browse/SPARK-16026*) to learn more about this feature. This is an active area of development in Spark at the time of writing.

Shuffle Configurations

Configuring Spark's external shuffle service (discussed in Chapters 16 and 17) can often increase performance because it allows nodes to read shuffle data from remote machines even when the executors on those machines are busy (e.g., with garbage collection). This does come at the cost of complexity and maintenance, however, so it might not be worth it in your deployment. Beyond configuring this external service, there are also a number of configurations for shuffles, such as the number of concurrent connections per executor, although these usually have good defaults.

In addition, for RDD-based jobs, the serialization format has a large impact on shuffle performance—always prefer Kryo over Java serialization, as described in "Object Serialization in RDDs" on page 317. Furthermore, for all jobs, the number of partitions of a shuffle matters. If you have too few partitions, then too few nodes will be doing work and there may be skew, but if you have too many partitions, there is an overhead to launching each one that may start to dominate. Try to aim for at least a few tens of megabytes of data per output partition in your shuffle.

Memory Pressure and Garbage Collection

During the course of running Spark jobs, the executor or driver machines may struggle to complete their tasks because of a lack of sufficient memory or "memory pressure." This may occur when an application takes up too much memory during execution or when garbage collection runs too frequently or is slow to run as large numbers of objects are created in the JVM and subsequently garbage collected as they are no longer used. One strategy for easing this issue is to ensure that you're using the Structured APIs as much as possible. These will not only increase the efficiency with which your Spark jobs will execute, but it will also greatly reduce memory pressure because JVM objects are never realized and Spark SQL simply performs the computation on its internal format.

The Spark documentation includes some great pointers on tuning garbage collection for RDD and UDF based applications, and we paraphrase the following sections from that information.

Measuring the impact of garbage collection

The first step in garbage collection tuning is to gather statistics on how frequently garbage collection occurs and the amount of time it takes. You can do this by adding `-verbose:gc -XX:+PrintGCDetails -XX:+PrintGCTimeStamps` to Spark's JVM options using the `spark.executor.extraJavaOptions` configuration parameter. The next time you run your Spark job, you will see messages printed in the worker's logs each time a garbage collection occurs. These logs will be on your cluster's worker nodes (in the stdout files in their work directories), not in the driver.

Garbage collection tuning

To further tune garbage collection, you first need to understand some basic information about memory management in the JVM:

- Java heap space is divided into two regions: Young and Old. The Young generation is meant to hold short-lived objects whereas the Old generation is intended for objects with longer lifetimes.
- The Young generation is further divided into three regions: Eden, Survivor1, and Survivor2.

Here's a simplified description of the garbage collection procedure:

1. When Eden is full, a minor garbage collection is run on Eden and objects that are alive from Eden and Survivor1 are copied to Survivor2.
2. The Survivor regions are swapped.
3. If an object is old enough or if Survivor2 is full, that object is moved to Old.
4. Finally, when Old is close to full, a full garbage collection is invoked. This involves tracing through all the objects on the heap, deleting the unreferenced ones, and moving the others to fill up unused space, so it is generally the slowest garbage collection operation.

The goal of garbage collection tuning in Spark is to ensure that only long-lived cached datasets are stored in the Old generation and that the Young generation is sufficiently sized to store all short-lived objects. This will help avoid full garbage collections to collect temporary objects created during task execution. Here are some steps that might be useful.

Gather garbage collection statistics to determine whether it is being run too often. If a full garbage collection is invoked multiple times before a task completes, it means that there isn't enough memory available for executing tasks, so you should decrease the amount of memory Spark uses for caching (`spark.memory.fraction`).

If there are too many minor collections but not many major garbage collections, allocating more memory for Eden would help. You can set the size of the Eden to be an over-estimate of how much memory each task will need. If the size of Eden is determined to be E, you can set the size of the Young generation using the option `-Xmn=4/3*E`. (The scaling up by 4/3 is to account for space used by survivor regions, as well.)

As an example, if your task is reading data from HDFS, the amount of memory used by the task can be estimated by using the size of the data block read from HDFS. Note that the size of a decompressed block is often two or three times the size of the block. So if you want to have three or four tasks' worth of working space, and the HDFS block size is 128 MB, we can estimate size of Eden to be 43,128 MB.

Try the G1GC garbage collector with `-XX:+UseG1GC`. It can improve performance in some situations in which garbage collection is a bottleneck and you don't have a way to reduce it further by sizing the generations. Note that with large executor heap sizes, it can be important to increase the G1 region size with `-XX:G1HeapRegionSize`.

Monitor how the frequency and time taken by garbage collection changes with the new settings.

Our experience suggests that the effect of garbage collection tuning depends on your application and the amount of memory available. There are many more tuning options described online, but at a high level, managing how frequently full garbage collection takes place can help in reducing the overhead. You can specify garbage collection tuning flags for executors by setting `spark.executor.extraJavaOptions` in a job's configuration.

Direct Performance Enhancements

In the previous section, we touched on some general performance enhancements that apply to all jobs. Be sure to skim the previous couple of pages before jumping to this section and the solutions here. These solutions here are intended as "band-aids" of sorts for issues with specific stages or jobs, but they require inspecting and optimizing each stage or job separately.

Parallelism

The first thing you should do whenever trying to speed up a specific stage is to increase the degree of parallelism. In general, we recommend having at least two or three tasks per CPU core in your cluster if the stage processes a large amount of data. You can set this via the `spark.default.parallelism` property as well as tuning the `spark.sql.shuffle.partitions` according to the number of cores in your cluster.

Improved Filtering

Another frequent source of performance enhancements is moving filters to the earliest part of your Spark job that you can. Sometimes, these filters can be pushed into the data sources themselves and this means that you can avoid reading and working with data that is irrelevant to your end result. Enabling partitioning and bucketing also helps achieve this. Always look to be filtering as much data as you can early on, and you'll find that your Spark jobs will almost always run faster.

Repartitioning and Coalescing

Repartition calls can incur a shuffle. However, doing some can optimize the overall execution of a job by balancing data across the cluster, so they can be worth it. In general, you should try to shuffle the least amount of data possible. For this reason, if you're reducing the number of overall partitions in a DataFrame or RDD, first try `coalesce` method, which will not perform a shuffle but rather merge partitions on the same node into one partition. The slower `repartition` method will also shuffle data across the network to achieve even load balancing. Repartitions can be particularly helpful when performing joins or prior to a `cache` call. Remember that repartitioning is not free, but it can improve overall application performance and parallelism of your jobs.

Custom partitioning

If your jobs are still slow or unstable, you might want to explore performing custom partitioning at the RDD level. This allows you to define a custom partition function that will organize the data across the cluster to a finer level of precision than is available at the DataFrame level. This is very rarely necessary, but it is an option. For more information, see Part III.

User-Defined Functions (UDFs)

In general, avoiding UDFs is a good optimization opportunity. UDFs are expensive because they force representing data as objects in the JVM and sometimes do this multiple times per record in a query. You should try to use the Structured APIs as much as possible to perform your manipulations simply because they are going to perform the transformations in a much more efficient manner than you can do in a high-level language. There is also ongoing work to make data available to UDFs in batches, such as the Vectorized UDF (*https://issues.apache.org/jira/browse/*

SPARK-21190) extension for Python that gives your code multiple records at once using a Pandas data frame. We discussed UDFs and their costs in Chapter 18.

Temporary Data Storage (Caching)

In applications that reuse the same datasets over and over, one of the most useful optimizations is caching. Caching will place a DataFrame, table, or RDD into temporary storage (either memory or disk) across the executors in your cluster, and make subsequent reads faster. Although caching might sound like something we should do all the time, it's not always a good thing to do. That's because caching data incurs a serialization, deserialization, and storage cost. For example, if you are only going to process a dataset *once* (in a later transformation), caching it will only slow you down.

The use case for caching is simple: as you work with data in Spark, either within an interactive session or a standalone application, you will often want to reuse a certain dataset (e.g., a DataFrame or RDD). For example, in an interactive data science session, you might load and clean your data and then reuse it to try multiple statistical models. Or in a standalone application, you might run an iterative algorithm that reuses the same dataset. You can tell Spark to cache a dataset using the `cache` method on DataFrames or RDDs.

Caching is a lazy operation, meaning that things will be cached only as they are accessed. The RDD API and the Structured API differ in how they actually perform caching, so let's review the gory details before going over the storage levels. When we cache an RDD, we cache the actual, physical data (i.e., the bits). The bits. When this data is accessed again, Spark returns the proper data. This is done through the RDD reference. However, in the Structured API, caching is done based on the *physical plan*. This means that we effectively store the physical plan as our key (as opposed to the object reference) and perform a lookup prior to the execution of a Structured job. This can cause confusion because sometimes you might be expecting to access raw data but because someone else already cached the data, you're actually accessing their cached version. Keep that in mind when using this feature.

There are different *storage levels* that you can use to cache your data, specifying what type of storage to use. Table 19-1 lists the levels.

Table 19-1. Data cache storage levels

Storage level	Meaning
MEMORY_ONLY	Store RDD as deserialized Java objects in the JVM. If the RDD does not fit in memory, some partitions will not be cached and will be recomputed on the fly each time they're needed. This is the default level.
MEMORY_AND_DISK	Store RDD as deserialized Java objects in the JVM. If the RDD does not fit in memory, store the partitions that don't fit on disk, and read them from there when they're needed.

Storage level	Meaning
MEMORY_ONLY_SER (Java and Scala)	Store RDD as serialized Java objects (one byte array per partition). This is generally more space-efficient than deserialized objects, especially when using a fast serializer, but more CPU-intensive to read.
MEMORY_AND_DISK_SER (Java and Scala)	Similar to MEMORY_ONLY_SER, but spill partitions that don't fit in memory to disk instead of recomputing them on the fly each time they're needed.
DISK_ONLY	Store the RDD partitions only on disk.
MEMORY_ONLY_2, MEMORY_AND_DISK_2, etc.	Same as the previous levels, but replicate each partition on two cluster nodes.
OFF_HEAP (experimental)	Similar to MEMORY_ONLY_SER, but store the data in off-heap memory. This requires off-heap memory to be enabled.

For more information on these options, take a look at "Configuring Memory Management" on page 278.

Figure 19-1 presents a simple illustrations of the process. We load an initial DataFrame from a CSV file and then derive some new DataFrames from it using transformations. We can avoid having to recompute the original DataFrame (i.e., load and parse the CSV file) many times by adding a line to cache it along the way.

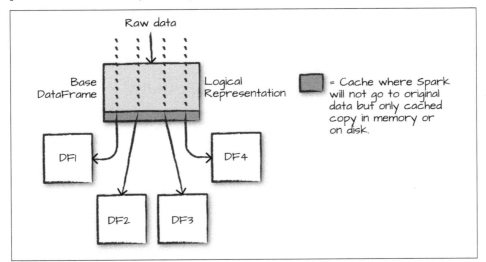

Figure 19-1. A cached DataFrame

Now let's walk through the code:

```
# in Python
# Original loading code that does *not* cache DataFrame
DF1 = spark.read.format("csv")\
  .option("inferSchema", "true")\
  .option("header", "true")\
  .load("/data/flight-data/csv/2015-summary.csv")
```

```
DF2 = DF1.groupBy("DEST_COUNTRY_NAME").count().collect()
DF3 = DF1.groupBy("ORIGIN_COUNTRY_NAME").count().collect()
DF4 = DF1.groupBy("count").count().collect()
```

You'll see here that we have our "lazily" created DataFrame (DF1), along with three other DataFrames that access data in DF1. All of our downstream DataFrames share that common parent (DF1) and will repeat the same work when we perform the preceding code. In this case, it's just reading and parsing the raw CSV data, but that can be a fairly intensive process, especially for large datasets.

On my machine, those commands take a second or two to run. Luckily caching can help speed things up. When we ask for a DataFrame to be cached, Spark will save the data in memory or on disk the first time it computes it. Then, when any other queries come along, they'll just refer to the one stored in memory as opposed to the original file. You do this using the DataFrame's `cache` method:

```
DF1.cache()
DF1.count()
```

We used the count above to eagerly cache the data (basically perform an action to force Spark to store it in memory), because caching itself is lazy—the data is cached only on the first time you run an action on the DataFrame. Now that the data is cached, the previous commands will be faster, as we can see by running the following code:

```
# in Python
DF2 = DF1.groupBy("DEST_COUNTRY_NAME").count().collect()
DF3 = DF1.groupBy("ORIGIN_COUNTRY_NAME").count().collect()
DF4 = DF1.groupBy("count").count().collect()
```

When we ran this code, it cut the time by more than half! This might not seem that wild, but picture a large dataset or one that requires a lot of computation to create (not just reading in a file). The savings can be immense. It's also great for iterative machine learning workloads because they'll often need to access the same data a number of times, which we'll see shortly.

The `cache` command in Spark always places data in memory by default, caching only part of the dataset if the cluster's total memory is full. For more control, there is also a `persist` method that takes a `StorageLevel` object to specify where to cache the data: in memory, on disk, or both.

Joins

Joins are a common area for optimization. The biggest weapon you have when it comes to optimizing joins is simply educating yourself about what each join does and how it's performed. This will help you the most. Additionally, equi-joins are the easiest for Spark to optimize at this point and therefore should be preferred wherever possible. Beyond that, simple things like trying to use the filtering ability of inner joins by changing join ordering can yield large speedups. Additionally, using broadcast join hints can help Spark make intelligent planning decisions when it comes to creating query plans, as described in Chapter 8. Avoiding Cartesian joins or even full outer joins is often low-hanging fruit for stability and optimizations because these can often be optimized into different filtering style joins when you look at the entire data flow instead of just that one particular job area. Lastly, following some of the other sections in this chapter can have a significant effect on joins. For example, collecting statistics on tables prior to a join will help Spark make intelligent join decisions. Additionally, bucketing your data appropriately can also help Spark avoid large shuffles when joins are performed.

Aggregations

For the most part, there are not too many ways that you can optimize specific aggregations beyond filtering data before the aggregation having a sufficiently high number of partitions. However, if you're using RDDs, controlling exactly how these aggregations are performed (e.g., using reduceByKey when possible over groupByKey) can be very helpful and improve the speed and stability of your code.

Broadcast Variables

We touched on broadcast joins and variables in previous chapters, and these are a good option for optimization. The basic premise is that if some large piece of data will be used across multiple UDF calls in your program, you can broadcast it to save just a single read-only copy on each node and avoid re-sending this data with each job. For example, broadcast variables may be useful to save a lookup table or a machine learning model. You can also broadcast arbitrary objects by creating broadcast variables using your SparkContext, and then simply refer to those variables in your tasks, as we discussed in Chapter 14.

Conclusion

There are many different ways to optimize the performance of your Spark Applications and make them run faster and at a lower cost. In general, the main things you'll want to prioritize are (1) reading as little data as possible through partitioning and efficient binary formats, (2) making sure there is sufficient parallellism and no data skew on the cluster using partitioning, and (3) using high-level APIs such as the Structured APIs as much as possible to take already optimized code. As with any other software optimization work, you should also make sure you are optimizing the *right* operations for your job: the Spark monitoring tools described in Chapter 18 will let you see which stages are taking the longest time and focus your efforts on those. Once you have identified the work that you believe can be optimized, the tools in this chapter will cover the most important performance optimization opportunities for the majority of users.

PART V
Streaming

## CHAPTER 20

Stream Processing Fundamentals

Stream processing is a key requirement in many big data applications. As soon as an application computes something of value—say, a report about customer activity, or a new machine learning model—an organization will want to compute this result continuously in a production setting. As a result, organizations of all sizes are starting to incorporate stream processing, often even in the first version of a new application.

Luckily, Apache Spark has a long history of high-level support for streaming. In 2012, the project incorporated Spark Streaming and its DStreams API, one of the first APIs to enable stream processing using high-level functional operators like map and reduce. Hundreds of organizations now use DStreams in production for large real-time applications, often processing terabytes of data per hour. Much like the Resilient Distributed Dataset (RDD) API, however, the DStreams API is based on relatively low-level operations on Java/Python objects that limit opportunities for higher-level optimization. Thus, in 2016, the Spark project added Structured Streaming, a new streaming API built directly on DataFrames that supports both rich optimizations and significantly simpler integration with other DataFrame and Dataset code. The Structured Streaming API was marked as stable in Apache Spark 2.2, and has also seen swift adoption throughout the Spark community.

In this book, we will focus only on the Structured Streaming API, which integrates directly with the DataFrame and Dataset APIs we discussed earlier in the book and is the framework of choice for writing new streaming applications. If you are interested in DStreams, many other books cover that API, including several dedicated books on Spark Streaming only, such as *Learning Spark Streaming* by Francois Garillot and Gerard Maas (O'Reilly, 2017). Much as with RDDs versus DataFrames, however, Structured Streaming offers a superset of the majority of the functionality of DStreams, and will often perform better due to code generation and the Catalyst optimizer.

Before we discuss the streaming APIs in Spark, let's more formally define streaming and batch processing. This chapter will discuss some of the core concepts in this area that we will need throughout this part of the book. It won't be a dissertation on this topic, but will cover enough of the concepts to let you make sense of systems in this space.

What Is Stream Processing?

Stream processing is the act of continuously incorporating new data to compute a result. In stream processing, the input data is unbounded and has no predetermined beginning or end. It simply forms a series of events that arrive at the stream processing system (e.g., credit card transactions, clicks on a website, or sensor readings from Internet of Things [IoT] devices). User applications can then compute various queries over this stream of events (e.g., tracking a running count of each type of event or aggregating them into hourly windows). The application will output multiple versions of the result as it runs, or perhaps keep it up to date in an external "sink" system such as a key-value store.

Naturally, we can compare streaming to *batch processing*, in which the computation runs on a fixed-input dataset. Oftentimes, this might be a large-scale dataset in a data warehouse that contains all the historical events from an application (e.g., all website visits or sensor readings for the past month). Batch processing also takes a query to compute, similar to stream processing, but only computes the result once.

Although streaming and batch processing sound different, in practice, they often need to work together. For example, streaming applications often need to *join* input data against a dataset written periodically by a batch job, and the *output* of streaming jobs is often files or tables that are queried in batch jobs. Moreover, any business logic in your applications needs to work consistently across streaming and batch execution: for example, if you have a custom code to compute a user's billing amount, it would be harmful to get a different result when running it in a streaming versus batch fashion! To handle these needs, Structured Streaming was designed from the beginning to *interoperate easily* with the rest of Spark, including batch applications. Indeed, the Structured Streaming developers coined the term *continuous applications* to capture end-to-end applications (*http://bit.ly/2bvecOm*) that consist of streaming, batch, and interactive jobs all working on the same data to deliver an end product. Structured Streaming is focused on making it simple to build such applications in an end-to-end fashion instead of only handling stream-level per-record processing.

Stream Processing Use Cases

We defined stream processing as the incremental processing of unbounded datasets, but that's a strange way to motivate a use case. Before we get into advantages and disadvantages of streaming, let's explain why you might want to use streaming. We'll describe six common use cases with varying requirements from the underlying stream processing system.

Notifications and alerting

Probably the most obvious streaming use case involves notifications and alerting. Given some series of events, a notification or alert should be triggered if some sort of event or series of events occurs. This doesn't necessarily imply autonomous or pre-programmed decision making; alerting can also be used to notify a human counterpart of some action that needs to be taken. An example might be driving an alert to an employee at a fulfillment center that they need to get a certain item from a location in the warehouse and ship it to a customer. In either case, the notification needs to happen quickly.

Real-time reporting

Many organizations use streaming systems to run real-time dashboards that any employee can look at. For example, this book's authors leverage Structured Streaming every day to run real-time reporting dashboards throughout Databricks (where both authors of this book work). We use these dashboards to monitor total platform usage, system load, uptime, and even usage of new features as they are rolled out, among other applications.

Incremental ETL

One of the most common streaming applications is to reduce the latency companies must endure while retreiving information into a data warehouse—in short, "my batch job, but streaming." Spark batch jobs are often used for Extract, Transform, and Load (ETL) workloads that turn raw data into a structured format like Parquet to enable efficient queries. Using Structured Streaming, these jobs can incorporate new data within seconds, enabling users to query it faster downstream. In this use case, it is critical that data is processed exactly once and in a fault-tolerant manner: we don't want to *lose* any input data before it makes it to the warehouse, and we don't want to load the same data twice. Moreover, the streaming system needs to make updates to the data warehouse transactionally so as not to confuse the queries running on it with partially written data.

Update data to serve in real time

Streaming systems are frequently used to compute data that gets served interactively by another application. For example, a web analytics product such as Google Analytics might continuously track the number of visits to each page, and use a streaming system to keep these counts up to date. When users interact with the product's UI, this web application queries the latest counts. Supporting this use case requires that the streaming system can perform *incremental* updates to a key–value store (or other serving system) as a sync, and often also that these updates are *transactional*, as in the ETL case, to avoid corrupting the data in the application.

Real-time decision making

Real-time decision making on a streaming system involves analyzing new inputs and responding to them automatically using business logic. An example use case would be a bank that wants to automatically verify whether a new transaction on a customer's credit card represents fraud based on their recent history, and deny the transaction if the charge is determined fradulent. This decision needs to be made in real-time while processing each transaction, so developers could implement this business logic in a streaming system and run it against the stream of transactions. This type of application will likely need to maintain a significant amount of *state* about each user to track their current spending patterns, and automatically compare this state against each new transaction.

Online machine learning

A close derivative of the real-time decision-making use case is online machine learning. In this scenario, you might want to train a model on a combination of streaming and historical data from multiple users. An example might be more sophisticated than the aforementioned credit card transaction use case: rather than reacting with hardcoded rules based on *one* customer's behavior, the company may want to continuously update a model from *all* customers' behavior and test each transaction against it. This is the most challenging use case of the bunch for stream processing systems because it requires aggregation across multiple customers, joins against static datasets, integration with machine learning libraries, and low-latency response times.

Advantages of Stream Processing

Now that we've seen some use cases for streaming, let's crystallize some of the advantages of stream processing. For the most part, batch is much simpler to understand, troubleshoot, and write applications in for the majority of use cases. Additionally, the ability to process data in batch allows for vastly higher data processing throughput than many streaming systems. However, stream processing is essential in two cases. First, stream processing enables *lower latency*: when your application needs to respond quickly (on a timescale of minutes, seconds, or milliseconds), you will need a streaming system that can keep state in memory to get acceptable performance. Many of the decision making and alerting use cases we described fall into this camp. Second, stream processing can also be more *efficient* in updating a result than repeated batch jobs, because it automatically incrementalizes the computation. For example, if we want to compute web traffic statistics over the past 24 hours, a naively implemented batch job might scan all the data each time it runs, always processing 24 hours' worth of data. In contrast, a streaming system can remember state from the previous computation and only count the new data. If you tell the streaming system to update your report every hour, for example, it would only need to process 1 hour's worth of data each time (the new data since the last report). In a batch system, you would have to implement this kind of incremental computation by hand to get the same performance, resulting in a lot of extra work that the streaming system will automatically give you out of the box.

Challenges of Stream Processing

We discussed motivations and advantages of stream processing, but as you likely know, there's never a free lunch. Let's discuss some of the challenges of operating on streams.

To ground this example, let's imagine that our application receives input messages from a sensor (e.g., inside a car) that report its value at different times. We then want to search within this stream for certain values, or certain patterns of values. One specific challenge is that the input records might arrive to our application out-of-order: due to delays and retransmissions, for example, we might receive the following sequence of updates in order, where the time field shows the time when the value was actually measured:

```
{value: 1, time: "2017-04-07T00:00:00"}
{value: 2, time: "2017-04-07T01:00:00"}
{value: 5, time: "2017-04-07T02:00:00"}
{value: 10, time: "2017-04-07T01:30:00"}
{value: 7, time: "2017-04-07T03:00:00"}
```

In any data processing system, we can construct logic to perform some action based on receiving the single value of "5." In a streaming system, we can also respond to this individual event quickly. However, things become more complicated if you want only to trigger some action based on a specific *sequence* of values received, say, 2 then 10 then 5. In the case of batch processing, this is not particularly difficult because we can simply sort all the events we have by time field to see that 10 did come between 2 and 5. However, this is harder for stream processing systems. The reason is that the streaming system is going to receive each event individually, and will need to track some *state* across events to remember the 2 and 5 events and realize that the 10 event was between them. The need to remember such state over the stream creates more challenges. For instance, what if you have a massive data volume (e.g., millions of sensor streams) and the state itself is massive? What if a machine in the sytem fails, losing some state? What if the load is imbalanced and one machine is slow? And how can your application signal downstream consumers when analysis for some event is "done" (e.g., the pattern 2-10-5 did *not* occur)? Should it wait a fixed amount of time or remember some state indefinitely? All of these challenges and others—such as making the input and the output of the system transactional—can come up when you want to deploy a streaming application.

To summarize, the challenges we described in the previous paragraph and a couple of others, are as follows:

- Processing out-of-order data based on application timestamps (also called *event time*)
- Maintaining large amounts of state
- Supporting high-data throughput
- Processing each event exactly once despite machine failures
- Handling load imbalance and stragglers
- Responding to events at low latency
- Joining with external data in other storage systems
- Determining how to update output sinks as new events arrive
- Writing data transactionally to output systems
- Updating your application's business logic at runtime

Each of these topics are an active area of research and development in large-scale streaming systems. To understand how different streaming systems have tackled these challenges, we describe a few of the most common design concepts you will see across them.

Stream Processing Design Points

To support the stream processing challenges we described, including high through-put, low latency, and out-of-order data, there are multiple ways to design a streaming system. We describe the most common design options here, before describing Spark's choices in the next section.

Record-at-a-Time Versus Declarative APIs

The simplest way to design a streaming API would be to just pass each event to the application and let it react using custom code. This is the approach that many early streaming systems, such as Apache Storm, implemented, and it has an important place when applications need full control over the processing of data. Streaming that provide this kind of *record-at-a-time* API just give the user a collection of "plumbing" to connect together into an application. However, the downside of these systems is that most of the complicating factors we described earlier, such as maintaining state, are solely governed by the application. For example, with a record-at-a-time API, you are responsible for tracking state over longer time periods, dropping it after some time to clear up space, and responding differently to duplicate events after a failure.

Programming these systems correctly can be quite challenging. At its core, low-level APIs require deep expertise to be develop and maintain.

As a result, many newer streaming systems provide *declarative* APIs, where your application specifies *what* to compute but not *how* to compute it in response to each new event and how to recover from failure. Spark's original DStreams API, for example, offered functional API based on operations like *map*, *reduce* and *filter* on streams. Internally, the DStream API automatically tracked how much data each operator had processed, saved any relevant state reliably, and recovered the computation from failure when needed. Systems such as Google Dataflow and Apache Kafka Streams provide similar, functional APIs. Spark's Structured Streaming actually takes this concept even further, switching from *functional* operations to *relational* (SQL-like) ones that enable even richer automatic optimization of the execution without programming effort.

Event Time Versus Processing Time

For the systems with declarative APIs, a second concern is whether the system natively supports *event time*. Event time is the idea of processing data based on timestamps inserted into each record at the source, as opposed to the time when the record is received at the streaming application (which is called *processing time*). In particular, when using event time, records may arrive to the system *out of order* (e.g., if they traveled back on different network paths), and different sources may also be out of sync with each other (some records may arrive later than other records for the same event time). If your application collects data from remote sources that may be delayed, such as mobile phones or IoT devices, event-time processing is crucial: without it, you will miss important patterns when some data is late. In contrast, if your application only processes local events (e.g., ones generated in the same datacenter), you may not need sophisticated event-time processing.

When using event-time, several issues become common concerns across applications, including tracking state in a manner that allows the system to incorporate late events, and determining when it is safe to output a result for a given time window in event time (i.e., when the system is likely to have received all the input up to that point). Because of this, many declarative systems, including Structured Streaming, have "native" support for event time integrated into all their APIs, so that these concerns can be handled automatically across your whole program.

Continuous Versus Micro-Batch Execution

The final design decision you will often see come up is about continuous versus micro-batch execution. In *continuous processing*-based systems, each node in the system is continually listening to messages from other nodes and outputting new updates to its child nodes. For example, suppose that your application implements a map-reduce computation over several input streams. In a continuous processing system, each of the nodes implementing map would read records one by one from an input source, compute its function on them, and send them to the appropriate reducer. The reducer would then update its state whenever it gets a new record. The key idea is that this happens on each individual record, as illustrated in Figure 20-1.

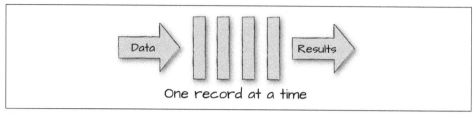

Figure 20-1. Continuous processing

Continuous processing has the advantage of offering the lowest possible *latency* when the total input rate is relatively low, because each node responds immediately to a new message. However, continuous processing systems generally have lower maximum *throughput*, because they incur a significant amount of overhead per-record (e.g., calling the operating system to send a packet to a downstream node). In addition, continous systems generally have a fixed topology of operators that cannot be moved at runtime without stopping the whole system, which can introduce load balancing issues.

In contrast, *micro-batch* systems wait to accumulate small batches of input data (say, 500 ms' worth), then process each batch in parallel using a distributed collection of tasks, similar to the execution of a batch job in Spark. Micro-batch systems can often achieve high throughput per node because they leverage the same optimizations as batch systems (e.g., vectorized processing), and do not incur any extra per-record overhead, as illustrated in Figure 20-2.

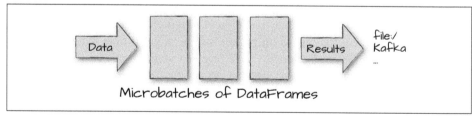

Figure 20-2. Micro-batch

Thus, they need fewer nodes to process the same rate of data. Micro-batch systems can also use dynamic load balancing techniques to handle changing workloads (e.g., increasing or decreasing the number of tasks). The downside, however, is a higher base latency due to waiting to accumulate a micro-batch. In practice, the streaming applications that are large-scale enough to need to *distribute* their computation tend to prioritize throughput, so Spark has traditionally implemented micro-batch processing. In Structured Streaming, however, there is an active development effort to *also* support a continuous processing mode beneath the same API.

When choosing between these two execution modes, the main factors you should keep in mind are your desired latency and total cost of operation (TCO). Micro-batch systems can comfortably deliver latencies from 100 ms to a second, depending on the application. Within this regime, they will generally require fewer nodes to achieve the same throughput, and hence lower operational cost (including lower maintenance cost due to less frequent node failures). For much lower latencies, you should consider a continuous processing system, or using a micro-batch system in conjunction with a fast serving layer to provide low-latency *queries* (e.g., outputting data into MySQL or Apache Cassandra, where it can be served to clients in milliseconds).

Spark's Streaming APIs

We covered some high-level design approaches to stream processing, but thus far we have not discussed Spark's APIs in detail. Spark includes two streaming APIs, as we discussed at the beginning of this chapter. The earlier DStream API in Spark Streaming is purely micro-batch oriented. It has a declarative (functional-based) API but no support for event time. The newer Structured Streaming API adds higher-level optimizations, event time, and support for continuous processing.

The DStream API

Spark's original DStream API has been used broadly for stream processing since its first release in 2012. For example, DStreams was the most widely used processing engine in Datanami's 2016 survey (*https://www.datanami.com/2016/07/07/ investments-fast-data-analytics-surge/*). Many companies use and operate Spark Streaming at scale in production today due to its high-level API interface and simple exactly-once semantics. Interactions with RDD code, such as joins with static data, are also natively supported in Spark Streaming. Operating Spark Streaming isn't much more difficult than operating a normal Spark cluster. However, the DStreams API has several limitations. First, it is based purely on Java/Python objects and functions, as opposed to the richer concept of structured tables in DataFrames and Datasets. This limits the engine's opportunity to perform optimizations. Second, the API is purely based on processing time—to handle event-time operations, applications need to implement them on their own. Finally, DStreams can only operate in a micro-batch fashion, and exposes the duration of micro-batches in some parts of its API, making it difficult to support alternative execution modes.

Structured Streaming

Structured Streaming is a higher-level streaming API built from the ground up on Spark's Structured APIs. It is available in all the environments where structured processing runs, including Scala, Java, Python, R, and SQL. Like DStreams, it is a declarative API based on high-level operations, but by building on the structured data model introduced in the previous part of the book, Structured Streaming can perform more types of optimizations automatically. However, unlike DStreams, Structured Streaming has native support for event time data (all of its the windowing operators automatically support it). As of Apache Spark 2.2, the system only runs in a micro-batch model, but the Spark team at Databricks has announced an effort called Continuous Processing (*https://issues.apache.org/jira/browse/SPARK-20928*) to add a continuous execution mode. This should become an option for users in Spark 2.3.

More fundamentally, beyond simplifying stream processing, Structured Streaming is also designed to make it easy to build *end-to-end* continuous applications using Apache Spark that combine streaming, batch, and interactive queries. For example, Structured Streaming does not use a separate API from DataFrames: you simply write a normal DataFrame (or SQL) computation and launch it on a stream. Structured Streaming will automatically update the result of this computation in an incremental fashion as data arrives. This is a major help when writing end-to-end data applications: developers do not need to maintain a separate streaming version of their batch code, possibly for a different execution system, and risk having these two versions of the code fall out of sync. As another example, Structured Streaming can output data to standard sinks usable by Spark SQL, such as Parquet tables, making it easy to query your stream state from another Spark applications. In future versions of Apache Spark, we expect more and more components of the project to integrate with Structured Streaming, including online learning algorithms in MLlib.

In general, Structured Streaming is meant to be an easier-to-use and higher-performance evolution of Spark Streaming's DStream API, so we will focus solely on this new API in this book. Many of the concepts, such as building a computation out of a graph of transformations, also apply to DStreams, but we leave the exposition of that to other books.

Conclusion

This chapter covered the basic concepts and ideas that you're going to need to understand stream processing. The design approaches introduced in this chapter should clarify how you can evaluate streaming systems for a given application. You should also feel comfortable understanding what trade-offs the authors of DStreams and Structured Streaming have made, and why the direct support for DataFrame programs is a big help when using Structured Streaming: there is no need to duplicate your application logic. In the upcoming chapters, we'll dive right into Structured Streaming to understand how to use it.

## CHAPTER 21

Structured Streaming Basics

Now that we have covered a brief overview of stream processing, let's dive right into Structured Streaming. In this chapter, we will, again, state some of the key concepts behind Structured Streaming and then apply them with some code examples that show how easy the system is to use.

Structured Streaming Basics

Structured Streaming, as we discussed at the end of Chapter 20, is a stream processing framework built on the Spark SQL engine. Rather than introducing a separate API, Structured Streaming uses the existing structured APIs in Spark (DataFrames, Datasets, and SQL), meaning that all the operations you are familiar with there are supported. Users express a streaming computation in the same way they'd write a batch computation on static data. Upon specifying this, and specifying a streaming destination, the Structured Streaming engine will take care of running your query incrementally and continuously as new data arrives into the system. These logical instructions for the computation are then executed using the same Catalyst engine discussed in Part II of this book, including query optimization, code generation, etc. Beyond the core structured processing engine, Structured Streaming includes a number of features specifically for streaming. For instance, Structured Streaming ensures end-to-end, exactly-once processing as well as fault-tolerance through checkpointing and write-ahead logs.

The main idea behind Structured Streaming is to treat a *stream* of data as a *table* to which data is continuously appended. The job then periodically checks for new input data, process it, updates some internal state located in a state store if needed, and updates its result. A cornerstone of the API is that you should not have to change your query's code when doing batch or stream processing—you should have to specify only whether to run that query in a batch or streaming fashion. Internally, Structured Streaming will automatically figure out how to "incrementalize" your query, i.e., update its result efficiently whenever new data arrives, and will run it in a fault-tolerant fashion.

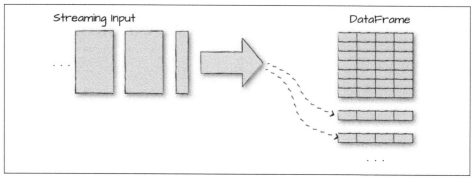

Figure 21-1. Structured streaming input

In simplest terms, Structured Streaming is "your DataFrame, but streaming." This makes it very easy to get started using streaming applications. You probably already have the code for them! There are some limits to the types of queries Structured Streaming will be able to run, however, as well as some new concepts you have to think about that are specific to streaming, such as event-time and out-of-order data. We will discuss these in this and the following chapters.

Finally, by integrating with the rest of Spark, Structured Streaming enables users to build what we call continuous applications (*https://databricks.com/blog/2016/07/28/continuous-applications-evolving-streaming-in-apache-spark-2-0.html*). A continous application is an *end-to-end* application that reacts to data in real time by combining a variety of tools: streaming jobs, batch jobs, joins between streaming and offline data, and interactive ad-hoc queries. Because most streaming jobs today *are* deployed within the context of a larger continuous application, the Spark developers sought to make it easy to specify the whole application in one framework and get consistent results across these different portions of it. For example, you can use Structured Streaming to continuously update a table that users query interactively with Spark SQL, serve a machine learning model trained by MLlib, or join streams with offline data in any of Spark's data sources—applications that would be much more complex to build using a mix of different tools.

Core Concepts

Now that we introduced the high-level idea, let's cover some of the important concepts in a Structured Streaming job. One thing you will hopefully find is that there aren't many. That's because Structured Streaming is designed to be *simple*. Read some other big data streaming books and you'll notice that they begin by introducing terminology like *distributed stream processing topologies for skewed data reducers* (a caricature, but accurate) and other complex verbiage. Spark's goal is to handle these concerns automatically and give users a simple way to run any Spark computation on a stream.

Transformations and Actions

Structured Streaming maintains the same concept of transformations and actions that we have seen throughout this book. The transformations available in Structured Streaming are, with a few restrictions, the exact same transformations that we saw in Part II. The restrictions usually involve some types of queries that the engine cannot incrementalize yet, although some of the limitations are being lifted in new versions of Spark. There is generally only one action available in Structured Streaming: that of starting a stream, which will then run continuously and output results.

Input Sources

Structured Streaming supports several *input sources* for reading in a streaming fashion. As of Spark 2.2, the supported input sources are as follows:

- Apache Kafka 0.10
- Files on a distributed file system like HDFS or S3 (Spark will continuously read new files in a directory)
- A socket source for testing

We discuss these in depth later in this chapter, but it's worth mentioning that the authors of Spark are working on a stable source API so that you can build your own streaming connectors.

Sinks

Just as sources allow you to get data into Structured Streaming, *sinks* specify the destination for the result set of that stream. Sinks and the execution engine are also responsible for reliably tracking the exact progress of data processing. Here are the supported output sinks as of Spark 2.2:

- Apache Kafka 0.10
- Almost any file format
- A foreach sink for running arbitary computation on the output records
- A console sink for testing
- A memory sink for debugging

We discuss these in more detail later in the chapter when we discuss sources.

Output Modes

Defining a sink for our Structured Streaming job is only half of the story. We also need to define how we want Spark to write data to that sink. For instance, do we only want to append new information? Do we want to update rows as we receive more information about them over time (e.g., updating the click count for a given web page)? Do we want to completely overwrite the result set every single time (i.e. always write a file with the complete click counts for all pages)? To do this, we define an *output mode*, similar to how we define output modes in the static Structured APIs.

The supported output modes are as follows:

- Append (only add new records to the output sink)
- Update (update changed records in place)
- Complete (rewrite the full output)

One important detail is that certain queries, and certain sinks, only support certain output modes, as we will discuss later in the book. For example, suppose that your job is just performing a map on a stream. The output data will grow indefinitely as new records arrive, so it would not make sense to use Complete mode, which requires writing *all* the data to a new file at once. In contrast, if you are doing an aggregation into a limited number of keys, Complete and Update modes would make sense, but Append would not, because the values of some keys' need to be updated over time.

Triggers

Whereas output modes define *how* data is output, triggers define *when* data is output —that is, when Structured Streaming should check for new input data and update its result. By default, Structured Streaming will look for new input records as soon as it has finished processing the last group of input data, giving the lowest latency possible for new results. However, this behavior can lead to writing many small output files when the sink is a set of files. Thus, Spark also supports triggers based on processing time (only look for new data at a fixed interval). In the future, other types of triggers may also be supported.

Event-Time Processing

Structured Streaming also has support for event-time processing (i.e., processing data based on timestamps included in the record that may arrive out of order). There are two key ideas that you will need to understand here for the moment; we will talk about both of these in much more depth in the next chapter, so don't worry if you're not perfectly clear on them at this point.

Event-time data

Event-time means time fields that are embedded in your data. This means that rather than processing data according to the time it reaches your system, you process it according to the time that it was generated, even if records arrive out of order at the streaming application due to slow uploads or network delays. Expressing event-time processing is simple in Structured Streaming. Because the system views the input data as a table, the event time is just another field in that table, and your application can do grouping, aggregation, and windowing using standard SQL operators. However, under the hood, Structured Streaming can take some special actions when it knows that one of your columns is an event-time field, including optimizing query execution or determining when it is safe to forget state about a time window. Many of these actions can be controlled using *watermarks*.

Watermarks

Watermarks are a feature of streaming systems that allow you to specify how late they expect to see data in event time. For example, in an application that processes logs from mobile devices, one might expect logs to be up to 30 minutes late due to upload delays. Systems that support event time, including Structured Streaming, usually allow setting watermarks to limit how long they need to remember old data. Watermarks can also be used to control when to output a result for a particular event time window (e.g., waiting until the watermark for it has passed).

Structured Streaming in Action

Let's get to an applied example of how you might use Structured Streaming. For our examples, we're going to be working with the Heterogeneity Human Activity Recognition Dataset. The data consists of smartphone and smartwatch sensor readings from a variety of devices—specifically, the accelerometer and gyroscope, sampled at the highest possible frequency supported by the devices. Readings from these sensors were recorded while users performed activities like biking, sitting, standing, walking, and so on. There are several different smartphones and smartwatches used, and nine total users. You can download the data here (*https://github.com/databricks/Spark-The-Definitive-Guide/tree/master/data*), in the activity data folder.

This Dataset is fairly large. If it's too large for your machine, you can remove some of the files and it will work just fine.

Let's read in the static version of the dataset as a DataFrame:

```scala
// in Scala
val static = spark.read.json("/data/activity-data/")
val dataSchema = static.schema
```

```python
# in Python
static = spark.read.json("/data/activity-data/")
dataSchema = static.schema
```

Here's the schema:

```
root
 |-- Arrival_Time: long (nullable = true)
 |-- Creation_Time: long (nullable = true)
 |-- Device: string (nullable = true)
 |-- Index: long (nullable = true)
 |-- Model: string (nullable = true)
 |-- User: string (nullable = true)
 |-- _corrupt_record: string (nullable = true)
 |-- gt: string (nullable = true)
 |-- x: double (nullable = true)
 |-- y: double (nullable = true)
 |-- z: double (nullable = true)
```

Here's a sample of the DataFrame:

```
+-------------+------------------+--------+-----+------+----+--------+-----+-----
| Arrival_Time|     Creation_Time| Device|Index| Model|User|_c...ord|.  gt|    x
|1424696634224|142469663222623685|nexus4_1|   62|nexus4|   a|    null|stand|-0...
...
|1424696660715|142469665872381726|nexus4_1| 2342|nexus4|   a|    null|stand|-0...
+-------------+------------------+--------+-----+------+----+--------+-----+-----
```

You can see in the preceding example, which includes a number of timestamp columns, models, user, and device information. The gt field specifies what activity the user was doing at that time.

Next, let's create a streaming version of the same Dataset, which will read each input file in the dataset one by one as if it was a stream.

Streaming DataFrames are largely the same as static DataFrames. We create them within Spark applications and then perform transformations on them to get our data into the correct format. Basically, all of the transformations that are available in the static Structured APIs apply to Streaming DataFrames. However, one small difference is that Structured Streaming does not let you perform schema inference without explicitly enabling it. You can enable schema inference for this by setting the configuration spark.sql.streaming.schemaInference to true. Given that fact, we will read the schema from one file (that we know has a valid schema) and pass the dataSchema object from our static DataFrame to our streaming DataFrame. As mentioned, you should avoid doing this in a production scenario where your data may (accidentally) change out from under you:

```scala
// in Scala
val streaming = spark.readStream.schema(dataSchema)
  .option("maxFilesPerTrigger", 1).json("/data/activity-data")
```

```python
# in Python
streaming = spark.readStream.schema(dataSchema).option("maxFilesPerTrigger", 1)\
  .json("/data/activity-data")
```

 We discuss `maxFilesPerTrigger` a little later on in this chapter but essentially it allows you to control how quickly Spark will read all of the files in the folder. By specifying this value lower, we're artificially limiting the flow of the stream to one file per trigger. This helps us demonstrate how Structured Streaming runs incrementally in our example, but probably isn't something you'd use in production.

Just like with other Spark APIs, streaming DataFrame creation and execution is lazy. In particular, we can now specify *transformations* on our streaming DataFrame before finally calling an action to start the stream. In this case, we'll show one simple transformation—we will group and count data by the `gt` column, which is the activity being performed by the user at that point in time:

```scala
// in Scala
val activityCounts = streaming.groupBy("gt").count()
```

```python
# in Python
activityCounts = streaming.groupBy("gt").count()
```

Because this code is being written in local mode on a small machine, we are going to set the shuffle partitions to a small value to avoid creating too many shuffle partitions:

```
spark.conf.set("spark.sql.shuffle.partitions", 5)
```

Now that we set up our transformation, we need only to specify our action to start the query. As mentioned previously in the chapter, we will specify an output destination, or output sink for our result of this query. For this basic example, we are going to write to a *memory sink* which keeps an in-memory table of the results.

In the process of specifying this sink, we're going to need to define *how* Spark will output that data. In this example, we use the *complete* output mode. This mode rewrites all of the keys along with their counts after every trigger:

```scala
// in Scala
val activityQuery = activityCounts.writeStream.queryName("activity_counts")
  .format("memory").outputMode("complete")
  .start()
```

```python
# in Python
activityQuery = activityCounts.writeStream.queryName("activity_counts")\
  .format("memory").outputMode("complete")\
  .start()
```

We are now writing out our stream! You'll notice that we set a *unique* query name to represent this stream, in this case `activity_counts`. We specified our format as an in-memory table and we set the output mode.

When we run the preceding code, we also want to include the following line:

```
activityQuery.awaitTermination()
```

After this code is executed, the streaming computation will have started in the background. The query object is a handle to that active streaming query, and we must specify that we would like to wait for the termination of the query using `activity Query.awaitTermination()` to prevent the driver process from exiting while the query is active. We will omit this from our future parts of the book for readability, but it must be included in your production applications; otherwise, your stream won't be able to run.

Spark lists this stream, and other active ones, under the active streams in our `Spark Session`. We can see a list of those streams by running the following:

```
spark.streams.active
```

Spark also assigns each stream a UUID, so if need be you could iterate through the list of running streams and select the above one. In this case, we assigned it to a variable, so that's not necessary.

Now that this stream is running, we can experiment with the results by querying the in-memory table it is maintaining of the current output of our streaming aggregation. This table will be called `activity_counts`, the same as the stream. To see the current data in this output table, we simply need to query it! We'll do this in a simple loop that will print the results of the streaming query every second:

```scala
// in Scala
for( i <- 1 to 5 ) {
    spark.sql("SELECT * FROM activity_counts").show()
    Thread.sleep(1000)
}
```

```python
# in Python
from time import sleep
for x in range(5):
    spark.sql("SELECT * FROM activity_counts").show()
    sleep(1)
```

As the preceding queries run, you should see the counts for each activity change over time. For instance, the first show call displays the following result (because we queried it while the stream was reading the first file):

```
+---+-----+
| gt|count|
+---+-----+
+---+-----+
```

The previous show call shows the following result—note that the result will probably vary when you're running this code personally because you will likely start it at a different time:

```
+----------+-----+
|        gt|count|
+----------+-----+
|       sit| 8207|
...
|      null| 6966|
|      bike| 7199|
+----------+-----+
```

With this simple example, the power of Structured Streaming should become clear. You can take the same operations that you use in batch and run them on a stream of data with very few code changes (essentially just specifying that it's a stream). The rest of this chapter touches on some of the details about the various manipulations, sources, and sinks that you can use with Structured Streaming.

Transformations on Streams

Streaming transformations, as we mentioned, include almost all static DataFrame transformations that you already saw in Part II. All select, filter, and simple transformations are supported, as are all DataFrame functions and individual column manipulations. The limitations arise on transformations that do not make sense in context of streaming data. For example, as of Apache Spark 2.2, users cannot sort streams that are not aggregated, and cannot perform multiple levels of aggregation without using Stateful Processing (covered in the next chater). These limitations may be lifted as Structured Streaming continues to develop, so we encourage you to check the documentation (*http://spark.apache.org/docs/latest/structured-streaming-programming-guide.html*) of your version of Spark for updates.

Selections and Filtering

All select and filter transformations are supported in Structured Streaming, as are all DataFrame functions and individual column manipulations. We show a simple example using selections and filtering below. In this case, because we are not updating any keys over time, we will use the Append output mode, so that new results are appended to the output table:

```scala
// in Scala
import org.apache.spark.sql.functions.expr
val simpleTransform = streaming.withColumn("stairs", expr("gt like '%stairs%'"))
  .where("stairs")
  .where("gt is not null")
  .select("gt", "model", "arrival_time", "creation_time")
  .writeStream
```

```
  .queryName("simple_transform")
  .format("memory")
  .outputMode("append")
  .start()

# in Python
from pyspark.sql.functions import expr
simpleTransform = streaming.withColumn("stairs", expr("gt like '%stairs%'"))\
  .where("stairs")\
  .where("gt is not null")\
  .select("gt", "model", "arrival_time", "creation_time")\
  .writeStream\
  .queryName("simple_transform")\
  .format("memory")\
  .outputMode("append")\
  .start()
```

Aggregations

Structured Streaming has excellent support for aggregations. You can specify arbitrary aggregations, as you saw in the Structured APIs. For example, you can use a more exotic aggregation, like a cube, on the phone model and activity and the average x, y, z accelerations of our sensor (jump back to Chapter 7 in order to see potential aggregations that you can run on your stream):

```
// in Scala
val deviceModelStats = streaming.cube("gt", "model").avg()
  .drop("avg(Arrival_time)")
  .drop("avg(Creation_Time)")
  .drop("avg(Index)")
  .writeStream.queryName("device_counts").format("memory").outputMode("complete")
  .start()

# in Python
deviceModelStats = streaming.cube("gt", "model").avg()\
  .drop("avg(Arrival_time)")\
  .drop("avg(Creation_Time)")\
  .drop("avg(Index)")\
  .writeStream.queryName("device_counts").format("memory")\
  .outputMode("complete")\
  .start()
```

Querying that table allows us to see the results:

```
SELECT * FROM device_counts

+----------+------+-------------------+-------------------+-------------------+
|        gt| model|             avg(x)|             avg(y)|             avg(z)|
+----------+------+-------------------+-------------------+-------------------+
|       sit|  null|-3.682775300344...|1.242033094787975...|-4.22021191297611...|
|     stand|  null|-4.415368069618...|-5.30657295890281...|2.264837548081631...|
...
|      walk|nexus4|-0.007342235359...|0.004341030525168...|-6.01620400184307...|
```

```
|stairsdown|nexus4|0.0309175199508...|-0.02869185568293...| 0.11661923308518365|
...
+----------+------+-----------------+--------------------+--------------------+
```

In addition to these aggregations on raw columns in the dataset, Structured Streaming has special support for columns that represent event time, including watermark support and windowing. We will discuss these in more detail in Chapter 22.

 As of Spark 2.2, the one limitation of aggregations is that multiple "chained" aggregations (aggregations on streaming aggregations) are not supported at this time. However, you can achieve this by writing out to an intermediate sink of data, like Kafka or a file sink. This will change in the future as the Structured Streaming community adds this functionality.

Joins

As of Apache Spark 2.2, Structured Streaming supports joining streaming DataFrames to static DataFrames. Spark 2.3 will add the ability to join multiple streams together. You can do multiple column joins and supplement streaming data with that from static data sources:

```scala
// in Scala
val historicalAgg = static.groupBy("gt", "model").avg()
val deviceModelStats = streaming.drop("Arrival_Time", "Creation_Time", "Index")
  .cube("gt", "model").avg()
  .join(historicalAgg, Seq("gt", "model"))
  .writeStream.queryName("device_counts").format("memory").outputMode("complete")
  .start()
```

```python
# in Python
historicalAgg = static.groupBy("gt", "model").avg()
deviceModelStats = streaming.drop("Arrival_Time", "Creation_Time", "Index")\
  .cube("gt", "model").avg()\
  .join(historicalAgg, ["gt", "model"])\
  .writeStream.queryName("device_counts").format("memory")\
  .outputMode("complete")\
  .start()
```

In Spark 2.2, full outer joins, left joins with the stream on the right side, and right joins with the stream on the left are not supported. Structured Streaming also does not yet support stream-to-stream joins, but this is also a feature under active development.

Input and Output

This section dives deeper into the details of how sources, sinks, and output modes work in Structured Streaming. Specifically, we discuss how, when, and where data flows into and out of the system. As of this writing, Structured Streaming supports several sources and sinks, including Apache Kafka, files, and several sources and sinks for testing and debugging. More sources may be added over time, so be sure to check the documentation (*http://spark.apache.org/docs/latest/structured-streaming-programming-guide.html*) for the most up-to-date information. We discuss the *source* and *sink* for a particular storage system together in this chapter, but in reality you can mix and match them (e.g., use a Kafka input source with a file sink).

Where Data Is Read and Written (Sources and Sinks)

Structured Streaming supports several production sources and sinks (files and Apache Kafka), as well as some debugging tools like the memory table sink. We mentioned these at the beginning of the chapter, but now let's cover the details of each one.

File source and sink

Probably the simplest source you can think of is the simple file source. It's easy to reason about and understand. While essentially any file source should work, the ones that we see in practice are Parquet, text, JSON, and CSV.

The only difference between using the file source/sink and Spark's static file source is that with streaming, we can control the number of files that we read in during each trigger via the `maxFilesPerTrigger` option that we saw earlier.

Keep in mind that any files you *add* into an input directory for a streaming job need to appear in it atomically. Otherwise, Spark will process partially written files before you have finished. On file systems that show partial writes, such as local files or HDFS, this is best done by writing the file in an external directory and moving it into the input directory when finished. On Amazon S3, objects normally only appear once fully written.

Kafka source and sink

Apache Kafka is a distributed publish-and-subscribe system for streams of data. Kafka lets you publish and subscribe to streams of records like you might do with a message queue—these are stored as streams of records in a fault-tolerant way. Think of Kafka like a distributed buffer. Kafka lets you store streams of records in categories that are referred to as *topics*. Each *record* in Kafka consists of a key, a value, and a timestamp. Topics consist of immutable sequences of records for which the position of a record in a sequence is called an *offset*. Reading data is called *subscribing* to a topic and writing data is as simple as *publishing* to a topic.

Spark allows you to read from Kafka with both batch and streaming DataFrames.

As of Spark 2.2, Structured Streaming supports Kafka version 0.10. This too is likely to expand in the future, so be sure to check the documentation (*http://spark.apache.org/docs/latest/structured-streaming-programming-guide.html*) for more information about the Kafka versions available. There are only a few options that you need to specify when you read from Kafka.

Reading from the Kafka Source

To read, you first need to choose one of the following options: `assign`, `subscribe`, or `subscribePattern`. Only one of these can be present as an option when you go to read from Kafka. Assign is a fine-grained way of specifying not just the topic but also the topic partitions from which you would like to read. This is specified as a JSON string `{"topicA":[0,1],"topicB":[2,4]}`. `subscribe` and `subscribePattern` are ways of subscribing to one or more topics either by specifying a list of topics (in the former) or via a pattern (via the latter).

Second, you will need to specify the `kafka.bootstrap.servers` that Kafka provides to connect to the service.

After you have specified your options, you have several other options to specify:

`startingOffsets` *and* `endingOffsets`
   The start point when a query is started, either `earliest`, which is from the earliest offsets; `latest`, which is just from the latest offsets; or a JSON string specifying a starting offset for each `TopicPartition`. In the JSON, `-2` as an offset can be used to refer to earliest, `-1` to latest. For example, the JSON specification could be `{"topicA":{"0":23,"1":-1},"topicB":{"0":-2}}`. This applies only when a new Streaming query is started, and that resuming will always pick up from where the query left off. Newly discovered partitions during a query will start at earliest. The ending offsets for a given query.

`failOnDataLoss`
   Whether to fail the query when it's possible that data is lost (e.g., topics are deleted, or offsets are out of range). This might be a false alarm. You can disable it when it doesn't work as you expected. The default is `true`.

`maxOffsetsPerTrigger`
   The total number of offsets to read in a given trigger.

There are also options for setting Kafka consumer timeouts, fetch retries, and intervals.

To read from Kafka, do the following in Structured Streaming:

```scala
// in Scala
// Subscribe to 1 topic
val ds1 = spark.readStream.format("kafka")
```

```scala
  .option("kafka.bootstrap.servers", "host1:port1,host2:port2")
  .option("subscribe", "topic1")
  .load()
// Subscribe to multiple topics
val ds2 = spark.readStream.format("kafka")
  .option("kafka.bootstrap.servers", "host1:port1,host2:port2")
  .option("subscribe", "topic1,topic2")
  .load()
// Subscribe to a pattern of topics
val ds3 = spark.readStream.format("kafka")
  .option("kafka.bootstrap.servers", "host1:port1,host2:port2")
  .option("subscribePattern", "topic.*")
  .load()
```

Python is quite similar:

```python
# in Python
# Subscribe to 1 topic
df1 = spark.readStream.format("kafka")\
  .option("kafka.bootstrap.servers", "host1:port1,host2:port2")\
  .option("subscribe", "topic1")\
  .load()
# Subscribe to multiple topics
df2 = spark.readStream.format("kafka")\
  .option("kafka.bootstrap.servers", "host1:port1,host2:port2")\
  .option("subscribe", "topic1,topic2")\
  .load()
# Subscribe to a pattern
df3 = spark.readStream.format("kafka")\
  .option("kafka.bootstrap.servers", "host1:port1,host2:port2")\
  .option("subscribePattern", "topic.*")\
  .load()
```

Each row in the source will have the following schema:

- key: binary
- value: binary
- topic: string
- partition: int
- offset: long
- timestamp: long

Each message in Kafka is likely to be serialized in some way. Using native Spark functions in the Structured APIs, or a User-Defined Function (UDF), you can parse the message into a more structured format analysis. A common pattern is to use JSON or Avro to read and write to Kafka.

Writing to the Kafka Sink

Writing to Kafka queries is largely the same as reading from them except for fewer parameters. You'll still need to specify the Kafka bootstrap servers, but the only other option you will need to supply is either a column with the topic specification or supply that as an option. For example, the following writes are equivalent:

```scala
// in Scala
ds1.selectExpr("topic", "CAST(key AS STRING)", "CAST(value AS STRING)")
  .writeStream.format("kafka")
  .option("checkpointLocation", "/to/HDFS-compatible/dir")
  .option("kafka.bootstrap.servers", "host1:port1,host2:port2")
  .start()
ds1.selectExpr("CAST(key AS STRING)", "CAST(value AS STRING)")
  .writeStream.format("kafka")
  .option("kafka.bootstrap.servers", "host1:port1,host2:port2")
  .option("checkpointLocation", "/to/HDFS-compatible/dir")\
  .option("topic", "topic1")
  .start()
```

```python
# in Python
df1.selectExpr("topic", "CAST(key AS STRING)", "CAST(value AS STRING)")\
  .writeStream\
  .format("kafka")\
  .option("kafka.bootstrap.servers", "host1:port1,host2:port2")\
  .option("checkpointLocation", "/to/HDFS-compatible/dir")\
  .start()
df1.selectExpr("CAST(key AS STRING)", "CAST(value AS STRING)")\
  .writeStream\
  .format("kafka")\
  .option("kafka.bootstrap.servers", "host1:port1,host2:port2")\
  .option("checkpointLocation", "/to/HDFS-compatible/dir")\
  .option("topic", "topic1")\
  .start()
```

Foreach sink

The `foreach` sink is akin to `foreachPartitions` in the Dataset API. This operation allows arbitrary operations to be computed on a per-partition basis, in parallel. This is available in Scala and Java initially, but it will likely be ported to other languages in the future. To use the `foreach` sink, you must implement the `ForeachWriter` interface, which is available in the Scala/Java documents, which contains three methods: open, process, and close. The relevant methods will be called whenever there is a sequence of rows generated as output after a trigger.

Here are some important details:

- The writer must be Serializable, as it were a UDF or a Dataset map function.
- The three methods (open, process, close) will be called on each executor.

- The writer must do all its initialization, like opening connections or starting transactions only in the open method. A common source of errors is that if initialization occurs outside of the open method (say in the class that you're using), that happens on the driver instead of the executor.

Because the Foreach sink runs arbitrary user code, one key issue you must consider when using it is fault tolerance. If Structured Streaming asked your sink to write some data, but then crashed, it cannot know whether your original write succeeded. Therefore, the API provides some additional parameters to help you achieve exactly-once processing.

First, the open call on your ForeachWriter receives two parameters that uniquely identify the set of rows that need to be acted on. The version parameter is a monotonically increasing ID that increases on a per-trigger basis, and partitionId is the ID of the partition of the output in your task. Your open method should return whether to process this set of rows. If you track your sink's output externally and see that this set of rows was already output (e.g., you wrote the last version and partitionId written in your storage system), you can return false from open to skip processing this set of rows. Otherwise, return true. Your ForeachWriter will be opened again for each trigger's worth of data to write.

Next, the process method will be called for each record in the data, assuming your open method returned true. This is fairly straightforward—just process or write your data.

Finally, whenever open is called, the close method is also called (unless the node crashed before that), regardless of whether open returned true. If Spark witnessed an error during processing, the close method receives that error. It is your responsibility to clean up any open resources during close.

Together, the ForeachWriter interface effectively lets you implement your own sink, including your own logic for tracking which triggers' data has been written or safely overwriting it on failures. We show an example of passing a ForeachWriter below:

```scala
//in Scala
datasetOfString.write.foreach(new ForeachWriter[String] {
  def open(partitionId: Long, version: Long): Boolean = {
    // open a database connection
  }
  def process(record: String) = {
    // write string to connection
  }
  def close(errorOrNull: Throwable): Unit = {
    // close the connection
  }
})
```

Sources and sinks for testing

Spark also includes several test sources and sinks that you can use for prototyping or debugging your streaming queries (these should be used only during development and not in production scenarios, because they do not provide end-to-end fault tolerance for your application):

Socket source

The socket source allows you to send data to your Streams via TCP sockets. To start one, specify a host and port to read data from. Spark will open a new TCP connection to read from that address. The socket source should *not* be used in production because the socket sits on the driver and does not provide end-to-end fault-tolerance guarantees.

Here is a short example of setting up this source to read from `localhost:9999`:

```scala
// in Scala
val socketDF = spark.readStream.format("socket")
  .option("host", "localhost").option("port", 9999).load()
```

```python
# in Python
socketDF = spark.readStream.format("socket")\
  .option("host", "localhost").option("port", 9999).load()
```

If you'd like to actually write data to this application, you will need to run a server that listens on port 9999. On Unix-like systems, you can do this using the NetCat utility, which will let you type text into the first connection that is opened to port 9999. Run the command below before starting your Spark application, then write into it:

```
nc -lk 9999
```

The socket source will return a table of text strings, one per line in the input data.

Console sink

The console sink allows you to write out some of your streaming query to the console. This is useful for debugging but is not fault-tolerant. Writing out to the console is simple and only prints some rows of your streaming query to the console. This supports both append and complete output modes:

```
activityCounts.format("console").write()
```

Memory sink

The memory sink is a simple source for testing your streaming system. It's similar to the console sink except that rather than printing to the console, it collects the data to the driver and then makes the data available as an in-memory table that is available for interactive querying. This sink is not fault tolerant, and you shouldn't use it in production, but is great for testing and querying your stream during development. This supports both append and complete output modes:

```scala
// in Scala
activityCounts.writeStream.format("memory").queryName("my_device_table")
```

If you do want to output data to a table for interactive SQL queries in production, the authors recommend using the Parquet file sink on a distributed file system (e.g., S3). You can then query the data from any Spark application.

How Data Is Output (Output Modes)

Now that you know where your data can go, let's discuss how the result Dataset will look when it gets there. This is what we call the *output mode*. As we mentioned, they're the same concept as save modes on static DataFrames. There are three modes supported by Structured Streaming. Let's look at each of them.

Append mode

Append mode is the default behavior and the simplest to understand. When new rows are added to the result table, they will be output to the sink based on the trigger (explained next) that you specify. This mode ensures that each row is output once (and only once), assuming that you have a fault-tolerant sink. When you use append mode with event-time and watermarks (covered in Chapter 22), only the final result will output to the sink.

Complete mode

Complete mode will output the entire state of the result table to your output sink. This is useful when you're working with some stateful data for which all rows are expected to change over time or the sink you are writing does not support row-level updates. Think of it like the state of a stream at the time the previous batch had run.

Update mode

Update mode is similar to complete mode except that only the rows that are different from the previous write are written out to the sink. Naturally, your sink must support row-level updates to support this mode. If the query doesn't contain aggregations, this is equivalent to append mode.

When can you use each mode?

Structured Streaming limits your use of each mode to queries where it makes sense. For example, if your query just does a map operation, Structured Streaming will not allow complete mode, because this would require it to remember all input records since the start of the job and rewrite the whole output table. This requirement is bound to get prohibitively expensive as the job runs. We will discuss when each mode is supported in more detail in the next chapter, once we also cover event-time processing and watermarks. If your chosen mode is not available, Spark Streaming will throw an exception when you start your stream.

Here's a handy table from the documentation that lays all of this out. Keep in mind that this will change in the future, so you'll want to check the documentation for the most up-to-date version.

Table 21-1 shows when you can use each output mode.

Table 21-1. Structured streaming output modes as of Spark 2.2

Query Type	Query type (continued)	Supported Output Modes	Notes
Queries with aggregation	Aggregation on event-time with watermark	Append, Update, Complete	Append mode uses watermark to drop old aggregation state. This means that as new rows are brought into the table, Spark will only keep around rows that are below the "watermark". Update mode also uses the watermark to remove old aggregation state. By definition, complete mode does not drop old aggregation state since this mode preserves all data in the Result Table.
	Other aggregations	Complete, Update	Since no watermark is defined (only defined in other category), old aggregation state is not dropped. Append mode is not supported as aggregates can update thus violating the semantics of this mode.
Queries with mapGroupsWithState		Update	
Queries with flatMapGroupsWithState	Append operation mode	Append	Aggregations are allowed after flatMapGroupsWithState.
	Update operation mode	Update	Aggregations not allowed after flatMapGroupsWithState.
Other queries		Append, Update	Complete mode not supported as it is infeasible to keep all unaggregated data in the Result Table.

When Data Is Output (Triggers)

To control when data is output to our sink, we set a *trigger*. By default, Structured Streaming will start data as soon as the previous trigger completes processing. You can use triggers to ensure that you do not overwhelm your output sink with too many updates or to try and control file sizes in the output. Currently, there is one periodic trigger type, based on processing time, as well as a "once" trigger to manually run a processing step once. More triggers will likely be added in the future.

Processing time trigger

For the processing time trigger, we simply specify a duration as a string (you may also use a `Duration` in Scala or `TimeUnit` in Java). We'll show the string format below.

```scala
// in Scala
import org.apache.spark.sql.streaming.Trigger

activityCounts.writeStream.trigger(Trigger.ProcessingTime("100 seconds"))
  .format("console").outputMode("complete").start()
```

```python
# in Python
activityCounts.writeStream.trigger(processingTime='5 seconds')\
  .format("console").outputMode("complete").start()
```

The `ProcessingTime` trigger will wait for multiples of the given duration in order to output data. For example, with a trigger duration of one minute, the trigger will fire at 12:00, 12:01, 12:02, and so on. If a trigger time is missed because the previous processing has not yet completed, then Spark will wait until the next trigger point (i.e., the next minute), rather than firing immediately after the previous processing completes.

Once trigger

You can also just run a streaming job once by setting that as the trigger. This might seem like a weird case, but it's actually extremely useful in both development and production. During development, you can test your application on just one trigger's worth of data at a time. During production, the Once trigger can be used to run your job manually at a low rate (e.g., import new data into a summary table just occasionally). Because Structured Streaming still fully tracks all the input files processed and the state of the computation, this is easier than writing your own custom logic to track this in a batch job, and saves a lot of resources over running a continuous job 24/7 (*http://bit.ly/2BuQUSR*):

```scala
// in Scala
import org.apache.spark.sql.streaming.Trigger

activityCounts.writeStream.trigger(Trigger.Once())
  .format("console").outputMode("complete").start()
```

```python
# in Python
activityCounts.writeStream.trigger(once=True)\
  .format("console").outputMode("complete").start()
```

Streaming Dataset API

One final thing to note about Structured Streaming is that you are not limited to just the DataFrame API for streaming. You can also use Datasets to perform the same computation but in type-safe manner. You can turn a streaming DataFrame into a Dataset the same way you did with a static one. As before, the Dataset's elements need to be Scala case classes or Java bean classes. Other than that, the DataFrame and Dataset operators work as they did in a static setting, and will also turn into a streaming execution plan when run on a stream.

Here's an example using the same dataset that we used in Chapter 11:

```scala
// in Scala
case class Flight(DEST_COUNTRY_NAME: String, ORIGIN_COUNTRY_NAME: String,
  count: BigInt)
val dataSchema = spark.read
  .parquet("/data/flight-data/parquet/2010-summary.parquet/")
  .schema
val flightsDF = spark.readStream.schema(dataSchema)
  .parquet("/data/flight-data/parquet/2010-summary.parquet/")
val flights = flightsDF.as[Flight]
def originIsDestination(flight_row: Flight): Boolean = {
  return flight_row.ORIGIN_COUNTRY_NAME == flight_row.DEST_COUNTRY_NAME
}
flights.filter(flight_row => originIsDestination(flight_row))
  .groupByKey(x => x.DEST_COUNTRY_NAME).count()
  .writeStream.queryName("device_counts").format("memory").outputMode("complete")
  .start()
```

Conclusion

It should be clear that Structured Streaming presents a powerful way to write streaming applications. Taking a batch job you already run and turning it into a streaming job with almost no code changes is both simple and extremely helpful from an engineering standpoint if you need to have this job interact closely with the rest of your data processing application. Chapter 22 dives into two advanced streaming-related concepts: event-time processing and stateful processing. Then, after that, Chapter 23 addresses what you need to do to run Structured Streaming in production.

Event-Time and Stateful Processing

Chapter 21 covered the core concepts and basic APIs; this chapter dives into event-time and stateful processing. Event-time processing is a hot topic because we analyze information with respect to the time that it was created, not processed. The key idea between this style of processing is that over the lifetime of the job, Spark will maintain relevant state that it can update over the course of the job before outputting it to the sink.

Let's cover these concepts in greater detail before we begin working with code to show they work.

Event Time

Event time is an important topic to cover discretely because Spark's DStream API does not support processing information with respect to event-time. At a higher level, in stream-processing systems there are effectively two relevant times for each event: the time at which it actually occurred (event time), and the time that it was processed or reached the stream-processing system (processing time).

Event time

Event time is the time that is embedded in the data itself. It is most often, though not required to be, the time that an event actually occurs. This is important to use because it provides a more robust way of comparing events against one another. The challenge here is that event data can be late or out of order. This means that the stream processing system must be able to handle out-of-order or late data.

Processing time

Processing time is the time at which the stream-processing system actually receives data. This is usually less important than event time because when it's processed is largely an implementation detail. This can't ever be out of order because it's a property of the streaming system at a certain time (not an external system like event time).

Those explanations are nice and abstract, so let's use a more tangible example. Suppose that we have a datacenter located in San Francisco. An event occurs in two places at the same time: one in Ecuador, the other in Virginia (see Figure 22-1).

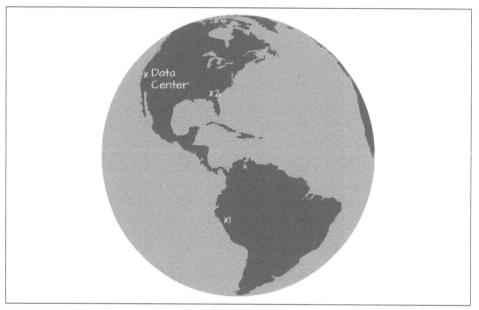

Figure 22-1. Event Time Across the World

Due to the location of the datacenter, the event in Virginia is likely to show up in our datacenter before the event in Ecuador. If we were to analyze this data based on processing time, it would appear that the event in Virginia occurred before the event in Ecuador: something that we know to be wrong. However, if we were to analyze the data based on event time (largely ignoring the time at which it's processed), we would see that these events occurred at the same time.

As we mentioned, the fundamental idea is that the order of the series of events in the processing system does *not* guarantee an ordering in event time. This can be somewhat unintuitive, but is worth reinforcing. Computer networks are unreliable. That means that events can be dropped, slowed down, repeated, or be sent without issue. Because individual events are not guaranteed to suffer one fate or the other, we must acknowledge that any number of things can happen to these events on the way from the source of the information to our stream processing system. For this reason, we need to operate on event time and look at the overall stream with reference to this information contained in the data rather than on when it arrives in the system. This means that we hope to compare events based on the time at which those events occurred.

Stateful Processing

The other topic we need to cover in this chapter is stateful processing. Actually, we already demonstrated this many times in Chapter 21. Stateful processing is only necessary when you need to use or update intermediate information (state) over longer periods of time (in either a microbatch or a record-at-a-time approach). This can happen when you are using event time or when you are performing an aggregation on a key, whether that involves event time or not.

For the most part, when you're performing stateful operations. Spark handles all of this complexity for you. For example, when you specify a grouping, Structured Streaming maintains and updates the information for you. You simply specify the logic. When performing a stateful operation, Spark stores the intermediate information in a *state store*. Spark's current state store implementation is an in-memory state store that is made fault tolerant by storing intermediate state to the checkpoint directory.

Arbitrary Stateful Processing

The stateful processing capabilities described above are sufficient to solve many streaming problems. However, there are times when you need fine-grained control over what state should be stored, how it is updated, and when it should be removed, either explicitly or via a time-out. This is called arbitrary (or custom) stateful processing and Spark allows you to essentially store whatever information you like over the course of the processing of a stream. This provides immense flexibility and power and allows for some complex business logic to be handled quite easily. Just as we did before, let's ground this with some examples:

- You'd like to record information about user sessions on an ecommerce site. For instance, you might want to track what pages users visit over the course of this session in order to provide recommendations in real time during their next session. Naturally, these sessions have completely arbitrary start and stop times that are unique to that user.

- Your company would like to report on errors in the web application but only if five events occur during a user's session. You could do this with count-based windows that only emit a result if five events of some type occur.

- You'd like to deduplicate records over time. To do so, you're going to need to keep track of every record that you see before deduplicating it.

Now that we've explained the core concepts that we're going to need in this chapter, let's cover all of this with some examples that you can follow along with and explain some of the important caveats that you need to consider when processing in this manner.

Event-Time Basics

Let's begin with the same dataset from the previous chapter. When working with event time, it's just another column in our dataset, and that's really all we need to concern ourselves with; we simply use that column, as demonstrated here:

```
// in Scala
spark.conf.set("spark.sql.shuffle.partitions", 5)
val static = spark.read.json("/data/activity-data")
val streaming = spark
  .readStream
  .schema(static.schema)
  .option("maxFilesPerTrigger", 10)
  .json("/data/activity-data")
```

```
# in Python
spark.conf.set("spark.sql.shuffle.partitions", 5)
static = spark.read.json("/data/activity-data")
streaming = spark\
  .readStream\
  .schema(static.schema)\
  .option("maxFilesPerTrigger", 10)\
  .json("/data/activity-data")
```

```
streaming.printSchema()

root
 |-- Arrival_Time: long (nullable = true)
 |-- Creation_Time: long (nullable = true)
 |-- Device: string (nullable = true)
 |-- Index: long (nullable = true)
 |-- Model: string (nullable = true)
 |-- User: string (nullable = true)
 |-- gt: string (nullable = true)
 |-- x: double (nullable = true)
 |-- y: double (nullable = true)
 |-- z: double (nullable = true)
```

In this dataset, there are two time-based columns. The `Creation_Time` column defines when an event was created, whereas the `Arrival_Time` defines when an event hit our servers somewhere upstream. We will use `Creation_Time` in this chapter. This example reads from a file but, as we saw in the previous chapter, it would be simple to change it to Kafka if you already have a cluster up and running.

Windows on Event Time

The first step in event-time analysis is to convert the timestamp column into the proper Spark SQL timestamp type. Our current column is unixtime nanoseconds (represented as a long), therefore we're going to have to do a little manipulation to get it into the proper format:

```scala
// in Scala
val withEventTime = streaming.selectExpr(
  "*",
  "cast(cast(Creation_Time as double)/1000000000 as timestamp) as event_time")
```

```python
# in Python
withEventTime = streaming\.selectExpr(
  "*",
  "cast(cast(Creation_Time as double)/1000000000 as timestamp) as event_time")
```

We're now prepared to do arbitrary operations on event time! Note how this experience is just like we'd do in batch operations—there's no special API or DSL. We simply use columns, just like we might in batch, the aggregation, and we're working with event time.

Tumbling Windows

The simplest operation is simply to count the number of occurrences of an event in a given window. Figure 22-2 depicts the process when performing a simple summation based on the input data and a key.

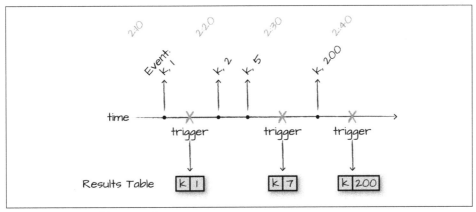

Figure 22-2. Tumbling Windows

We're performing an aggregation of keys over a window of time. We update the result table (depending on the output mode) when every trigger runs, which will operate on the data received since the last trigger. In the case of our actual dataset (and Figure 22-2), we'll do so in 10-minute windows without any overlap between them (each, and only one event can fall into one window). This will update in real time, as well, meaning that if new events were being added upstream to our system, Structured Streaming would update those counts accordingly. This is the complete output mode, Spark will output the entire result table regardless of whether we've seen the entire dataset:

```scala
// in Scala
import org.apache.spark.sql.functions.{window, col}
withEventTime.groupBy(window(col("event_time"), "10 minutes")).count()
  .writeStream
  .queryName("events_per_window")
  .format("memory")
  .outputMode("complete")
  .start()
```

```python
# in Python
from pyspark.sql.functions import window, col
withEventTime.groupBy(window(col("event_time"), "10 minutes")).count()\
  .writeStream\
  .queryName("pyevents_per_window")\
  .format("memory")\
  .outputMode("complete")\
  .start()
```

Now we're writing out to the in-memory sink for debugging, so we can query it with SQL after we have the stream running:

```
spark.sql("SELECT * FROM events_per_window").printSchema()

SELECT * FROM events_per_window
```

This shows us something like the following result, depending on the amount of data processed when you had run the query:

```
+---------------------------------------------+-----+
|window                                       |count|
+---------------------------------------------+-----+
|[2015-02-23 10:40:00.0,2015-02-23 10:50:00.0]|11035|
|[2015-02-24 11:50:00.0,2015-02-24 12:00:00.0]|18854|
...
|[2015-02-23 13:40:00.0,2015-02-23 13:50:00.0]|20870|
|[2015-02-23 11:20:00.0,2015-02-23 11:30:00.0]|9392 |
+---------------------------------------------+-----+
```

For reference, here's the schema we get from the previous query:

```
root
 |-- window: struct (nullable = false)
 |    |-- start: timestamp (nullable = true)
 |    |-- end: timestamp (nullable = true)
 |-- count: long (nullable = false)
```

Notice how window is actually a struct (a complex type). Using this we can query this struct for the start and end times of a particular window.

Of importance is the fact that we can also perform an aggregation on multiple columns, including the event time column. Just like we saw in the previous chapter, we can even perform these aggregations using methods like cube. While we won't repeat the fact that we can perform the multi-key aggregation below, this does apply to any window-style aggregation (or stateful computation) we would like:

```scala
// in Scala
import org.apache.spark.sql.functions.{window, col}
withEventTime.groupBy(window(col("event_time"), "10 minutes"), "User").count()
  .writeStream
  .queryName("events_per_window")
  .format("memory")
  .outputMode("complete")
  .start()
```

```python
# in Python
from pyspark.sql.functions import window, col
withEventTime.groupBy(window(col("event_time"), "10 minutes"), "User").count()\
  .writeStream\
  .queryName("pyevents_per_window")\
  .format("memory")\
  .outputMode("complete")\
  .start()
```

Sliding windows

The previous example was simple counts in a given window. Another approach is that we can decouple the window from the starting time of the window. Figure 22-3 illustrates what we mean.

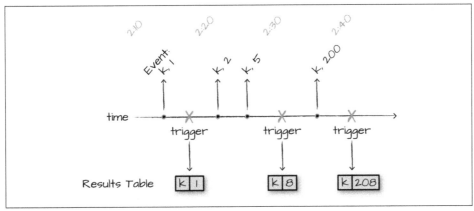

Figure 22-3. Sliding Windows

In the figure, we are running a sliding window through which we look at an hour increment, but we'd like to get the state every 10 minutes. This means that we will update the values over time and will include the last hours of data. In this example, we have 10-minute windows, starting every five minutes. Therefore each event will fall into two different windows. You can tweak this further according to your needs:

```scala
// in Scala
import org.apache.spark.sql.functions.{window, col}
withEventTime.groupBy(window(col("event_time"), "10 minutes", "5 minutes"))
  .count()
  .writeStream
  .queryName("events_per_window")
  .format("memory")
  .outputMode("complete")
  .start()
```

```python
# in Python
from pyspark.sql.functions import window, col
withEventTime.groupBy(window(col("event_time"), "10 minutes", "5 minutes"))\
  .count()\
  .writeStream\
  .queryName("pyevents_per_window")\
  .format("memory")\
  .outputMode("complete")\
  .start()
```

Naturally, we can query the in-memory table:

```
SELECT * FROM events_per_window
```

This query gives us the following result. Note that the starting times for each window are now in 5-minute intervals instead of 10, like we saw in the previous query:

```
+---------------------------------------------+-----+
|window                                       |count|
+---------------------------------------------+-----+
|[2015-02-23 14:15:00.0,2015-02-23 14:25:00.0]|40375|
|[2015-02-24 11:50:00.0,2015-02-24 12:00:00.0]|56549|
...
|[2015-02-24 11:45:00.0,2015-02-24 11:55:00.0]|51898|
|[2015-02-23 10:40:00.0,2015-02-23 10:50:00.0]|33200|
+---------------------------------------------+-----+
```

Handling Late Data with Watermarks

The preceding examples are great, but they have a flaw. We never specified *how late* we expect to see data. This means that Spark is going to need to store that intermediate data forever because we never specified a watermark, or a time at which we don't expect to see any more data. This applies to all stateful processing that operates on event time. We must specify this watermark in order to age-out data in the stream (and, therefore, state) so that we don't overwhelm the system over a long period of time.

Concretely, a watermark is an amount of time following a given event or set of events after which we do not expect to see any more data from that time. We know this can happen due to delays on the network, devices that lose a connection, or any number of other issues. In the DStreams API, there was no robust way to handle late data in this way—if an event occurred at a certain time but did not make it to the processing system by the time the batch for a given window started, it would show up in other processing batches. Structured Streaming remedies this. In event time and stateful processing, a given window's state or set of data is decoupled from a processing window. That means that as more events come in, Structured Streaming will continue to update a window with more information.

Let's return back to our event time example from the beginning of the chapter, shown now in Figure 22-4.

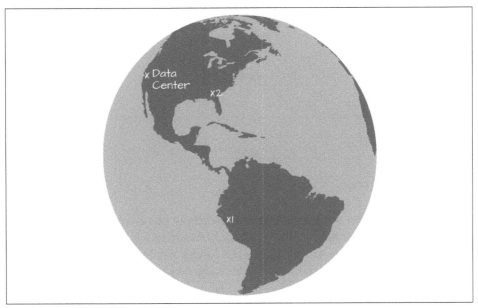

Figure 22-4. Event Time Watermarking

In this example, let's imagine that we frequently see some amount of delay from our customers in Latin America. Therefore, we specify a watermark of 10 minutes. When doing this, we instruct Spark that any event that occurs more than 10 "event-time" minutes past a previous event should be ignored. Conversely, this also states that we expect to see every event within 10 minutes. After that, Spark should remove intermediate state and, depending on the output mode, do something with the result. As mentioned at the beginning of the chapter, we need to specify watermarks because if we did not, we'd need to keep all of our windows around forever, expecting them to be updated forever. This brings us to the core question when working with event-time: "how late do I expect to see data?" The answer to this question will be the watermark that you'll configure for your data.

Returning to our dataset, if we know that we typically see data as produced downstream in minutes but we have seen delays in events up to five hours after they occur (perhaps the user lost cell phone connectivity), we'd specify the watermark in the following way:

```scala
// in Scala
import org.apache.spark.sql.functions.{window, col}
withEventTime
  .withWatermark("event_time", "5 hours")
  .groupBy(window(col("event_time"), "10 minutes", "5 minutes"))
  .count()
  .writeStream
  .queryName("events_per_window")
  .format("memory")
  .outputMode("complete")
  .start()
```

```python
# in Python
from pyspark.sql.functions import window, col
withEventTime\
  .withWatermark("event_time", "30 minutes")\
  .groupBy(window(col("event_time"), "10 minutes", "5 minutes"))\
  .count()\
  .writeStream\
  .queryName("pyevents_per_window")\
  .format("memory")\
  .outputMode("complete")\
  .start()
```

It's pretty amazing, but almost nothing changed about our query. We essentially just added another configuration. Now, Structured Streaming will wait until 30 minutes after the final timestamp of this 10-minute rolling window before it finalizes the result of that window. We can query our table and see the intermediate results because we're using complete mode—they'll be updated over time. In append mode, this information won't be output until the window closes.

```
SELECT * FROM events_per_window

+---------------------------------------------+-----+
|window                                       |count|
+---------------------------------------------+-----+
|[2015-02-23 14:15:00.0,2015-02-23 14:25:00.0]|9505 |
|[2015-02-24 11:50:00.0,2015-02-24 12:00:00.0]|13159|
...
|[2015-02-24 11:45:00.0,2015-02-24 11:55:00.0]|12021|
|[2015-02-23 10:40:00.0,2015-02-23 10:50:00.0]|7685 |
+---------------------------------------------+-----+
```

At this point, you really know all that you need to know about handling late data. Spark does all of the heavy lifting for you. Just to reinforce the point, if you do not specify how late you think you will see data, then Spark will maintain that data in memory forever. Specifying a watermark allows it to free those objects from memory, allowing your stream to continue running for a long time.

Dropping Duplicates in a Stream

One of the more difficult operations in record-at-a-time systems is removing duplicates from the stream. Almost by definition, you must operate on a batch of records at a time in order to find duplicates—there's a high coordination overhead in the processing system. Deduplication is an important tool in many applications, especially when messages might be delivered multiple times by upstream systems. A perfect example of this are Internet of Things (IoT) applications that have upstream producers generating messages in nonstable network environments, and the same message might end up being sent multiple times. Your downstream applications and aggregations should be able to assume that there is only one of each message.

Essentially, Structured Streaming makes it easy to take message systems that provide at-least-once semantics, and convert them into exactly-once by dropping duplicate messages as they come in, based on arbitrary keys. To de-duplicate data, Spark will maintain a number of user specified keys and ensure that duplicates are ignored.

 Just like other stateful processing applications, you need to specify a watermark to ensure that the maintained state does not grow infinitely over the course of your stream.

Let's begin the de-duplication process. The goal here will be to de-duplicate the number of events per user by removing duplicate events. Notice how you need to specify the event time column as a duplicate column along with the column you should de-duplicate. The core assumption is that duplicate events will have the same timestamp as well as identifier. In this model, rows with two different timestamps are two different records:

```scala
// in Scala
import org.apache.spark.sql.functions.expr

withEventTime
  .withWatermark("event_time", "5 seconds")
  .dropDuplicates("User", "event_time")
  .groupBy("User")
  .count()
  .writeStream
  .queryName("deduplicated")
  .format("memory")
  .outputMode("complete")
  .start()
```

```python
# in Python
from pyspark.sql.functions import expr

withEventTime\
  .withWatermark("event_time", "5 seconds")\
  .dropDuplicates(["User", "event_time"])\
  .groupBy("User")\
  .count()\
  .writeStream\
  .queryName("pydeduplicated")\
  .format("memory")\
  .outputMode("complete")\
  .start()
```

The result will be similar to the following and will continue to update over time as more data is read by your stream:

```
+----+-----+
|User|count|
+----+-----+
|   a| 8085|
|   b| 9123|
|   c| 7715|
|   g| 9167|
|   h| 7733|
|   e| 9891|
|   f| 9206|
|   d| 8124|
|   i| 9255|
+----+-----+
```

Arbitrary Stateful Processing

The first section if this chapter demonstrates how Spark maintains information and updates windows based on our specifications. But things differ when you have more complex concepts of windows; this is, where arbitrary stateful processing comes in. This section includes several examples of different use cases along with examples that show you how you might go about setting up your business logic. Stateful processing is available only in Scala in Spark 2.2. This will likely change in the future.

When performing stateful processing, you might want to do the following:

- Create window based on counts of a given key
- Emit an alert if there is a number of events within a certain time frame
- Maintain user sessions of an undetermined amount of time and save those sessions to perform some analysis on later.

At the end of the day, there are two things you will want to do when performing this style of processing:

- Map over groups in your data, operate on each group of data, and generate at most a single row for each group. The relevant API for this use case is `mapGroups WithState`.

- Map over groups in your data, operate on each group of data, and generate one or more rows for each group. The relevant API for this use case is `flatMapGroups WithState`.

When we say "operate" on each group of data, that means that you can arbitrarily update each group independent of any other group of data. This means that you can define arbitrary window types that don't conform to tumbling or sliding windows like we saw previously in the chapter. One important benefit that we get when we perform this style of processing is control over configuring time-outs on state. With windows and watermarks, it's very simple: you simply time-out a window when the watermark passes the window start. This doesn't apply to arbitrary stateful processing, because you manage the state based on user-defined concepts. Therefore, you need to properly time-out your state. Let's discuss this a bit more.

Time-Outs

As mentioned in Chapter 21, a time-out specifies how long you should wait before timing-out some intermediate state. A time-out is a global parameter across all groups that is configured on a per-group basis. Time-outs can be either based on processing time (`GroupStateTimeout.ProcessingTimeTimeout`) or event time (`GroupSta teTimeout.EventTimeTimeout`). When using time-outs, check for time-out first before processing the values. You can get this information by checking the `state.has TimedOut` flag or checking whether the values iterator is empty. You need to set some state (i.e., state must be defined, not removed) for time-outs to be set.

With a time-out based on processing time, you can set the time-out duration by calling `GroupState.setTimeoutDuration` (we'll see code examples of this later in this section of the chapter). The time-out will occur when the clock has advanced by the set duration. Guarantees provided by this time-out with a duration of D ms are as follows:

- Time-out will never occur before the clock time has advanced by D ms

- Time-out will occur eventually when there is a trigger in the query (i.e., after D ms). So there is a no strict upper bound on when the time-out would occur. For example, the trigger interval of the query will affect when the time-out actually occurs. If there is no data in the stream (for any group) for a while, there won't be any trigger and the time-out function call will not occur until there is data.

Because the processing time time-out is based on the clock time, it is affected by the variations in the system clock. This means that time zone changes and clock skew are important variables to consider.

With a time-out based on event time, the user also must specify the event-time watermark in the query using watermarks. When set, data older than the watermark is filtered out. As the developer, you can set the timestamp that the watermark should reference by setting a time-out timestamp using the `GroupState.setTimeoutTimestamp(...)` API. The time-out would occur when the watermark advances beyond the set timestamp. Naturally, you can control the time-out delay by either specifying longer watermarks or simply updating the time-out as you process your stream. Because you can do this in arbitrary code, you can do it on a per-group basis. The guarantee provided by this time-out is that it will never occur before the watermark has exceeded the set time-out.

Similar to processing-time time-outs, there is a no strict upper bound on the delay when the time-out actually occurs. The watermark can advance only when there is data in the stream, and the event time of the data has actually advanced.

 We mentioned this a few moments ago, but it's worth reinforcing. Although time-outs are important, they might not always function as you expect. For instance, as of this writing, Structured Streaming does not have asynchronous job execution, which means that Spark will not output data (or time-out data) between the time that a epoch finishes and the next one starts, because it is not processing any data at that time. Also, if a processing batch of data has no records (keep in mind this is a batch, not a group), there are no updates and there cannot be an event-time time-out. This might change in future versions.

Output Modes

One last "gotcha" when working with this sort of arbitrary stateful processing is the fact that not all output modes discussed in Chapter 21 are supported. This is sure to change as Spark continues to change, but, as of this writing, `mapGroupsWithState` supports only the `update` output mode, whereas `flatMapGroupsWithState` supports `append` and `update`. `append` mode means that only after the time-out (meaning the watermark has passed) will data show up in the result set. This does not happen automatically, it is your responsibility to output the proper row or rows.

Please see Table 21-1 to see which output modes can be used when.

mapGroupsWithState

Our first example of stateful processing uses a feature called mapGroupsWithState. This is similar to a user-defined aggregation function that takes as input an update set of data and then resolves it down to a specific key with a set of values. There are several things you're going to need to define along the way:

- Three class definitions: an input definition, a state definition, and optionally an output definition.
- A function to update the state based on a key, an iterator of events, and a previous state.
- A time-out parameter (as described in the time-outs section).

With these objects and definitions, you can control arbitrary state by creating it, updating it over time, and removing it. Let's begin with a example of simply updating the key based on a certain amount of state, and then move onto more complex things like sessionization.

Because we're working with sensor data, let's find the first and last timestamp that a given user performed one of the activities in the dataset. This means that the key we will be grouping on (and mapping on) is a user and activity combination.

 When you use mapGroupsWithState, the output of the dream will contain only one row per key (or group) at all times. If you would like each group to have multiple outputs, you should use flatMap GroupsWithState (covered shortly).

Let's establish the input, state, and output definitions:

```
case class InputRow(user:String, timestamp:java.sql.Timestamp, activity:String)
case class UserState(user:String,
  var activity:String,
  var start:java.sql.Timestamp,
  var end:java.sql.Timestamp)
```

For readability, set up the function that defines how you will update your state based on a given row:

```
def updateUserStateWithEvent(state:UserState, input:InputRow):UserState = {
  if (Option(input.timestamp).isEmpty) {
    return state
  }
  if (state.activity == input.activity) {

    if (input.timestamp.after(state.end)) {
      state.end = input.timestamp
    }
```

```
    if (input.timestamp.before(state.start)) {
      state.start = input.timestamp
    }
  } else {
    if (input.timestamp.after(state.end)) {
      state.start = input.timestamp
      state.end = input.timestamp
      state.activity = input.activity
    }
  }

  state
}
```

Now, write the function that defines the way state is updated based on an epoch of rows:

```
import org.apache.spark.sql.streaming.{GroupStateTimeout, OutputMode, GroupState}
def updateAcrossEvents(user:String,
  inputs: Iterator[InputRow],
  oldState: GroupState[UserState]):UserState = {
  var state:UserState = if (oldState.exists) oldState.get else UserState(user,
        "",
        new java.sql.Timestamp(6284160000000L),
        new java.sql.Timestamp(6284160L)
    )
  // we simply specify an old date that we can compare against and
  // immediately update based on the values in our data

  for (input <- inputs) {
    state = updateUserStateWithEvent(state, input)
    oldState.update(state)
  }
  state
}
```

When we have that, it's time to start your query by passing in the relevant information. The one thing that you're going to have to add when you specify `mapGroupsWith State` is whether you need to time-out a given group's state. This just gives you a mechanism to control what should be done with state that receives no update after a certain amount of time. In this case, you want to maintain state indefinitely, so specify that Spark should not time-out.

Use the `update` output mode so that you get updates on the user activity:

```
import org.apache.spark.sql.streaming.GroupStateTimeout
withEventTime
  .selectExpr("User as user",
    "cast(Creation_Time/1000000000 as timestamp) as timestamp", "gt as activity")
  .as[InputRow]
  .groupByKey(_.user)
  .mapGroupsWithState(GroupStateTimeout.NoTimeout)(updateAcrossEvents)
```

```
  .writeStream
  .queryName("events_per_window")
  .format("memory")
  .outputMode("update")
  .start()

SELECT * FROM events_per_window order by user, start
```

Here's a sample of our result set:

```
+----+--------+--------------------+-------------------+
|user|activity|               start|                end|
+----+--------+--------------------+-------------------+
|   a|    bike|2015-02-23 13:30:...|2015-02-23 14:06:...|
|   a|    bike|2015-02-23 13:30:...|2015-02-23 14:06:...|
...
|   d|    bike|2015-02-24 13:07:...|2015-02-24 13:42:...|
+----+--------+--------------------+-------------------+
```

An interesting aspect of our data is that the last activity performed at any given time is "bike." This is related to how the experiment was likely run, in which they had each participant perform the same activities in order.

Example: Count-Based Windows

Typical window operations are built from start and end times for which all events that fall in between those two points contribute to the counting or summation that you're performing. However, there are times when instead of creating windows based on time, you'd rather create them based on a number of events regardless of state and event times, and perform some aggregation on that window of data. For example, we may want to compute a value for every 500 events received, regardless of when they are received.

The next example analyzes the activity dataset from this chapter and outputs the average reading of each device periodically, creating a window based on the *count* of events and outputting it each time it has accumulated 500 events for that device. You define two case classes for this task: the input row format (which is simply a device and a timestamp); and the state and output rows (which contain the current count of records collected, device ID, and an array of readings for the events in the window).

Here are our various, self-describing case class definitions:

```
case class InputRow(device: String, timestamp: java.sql.Timestamp, x: Double)
case class DeviceState(device: String, var values: Array[Double],
  var count: Int)
case class OutputRow(device: String, previousAverage: Double)
```

Now, you can define the function to update the individual state based on a single input row. You could write this inline or in a number of other ways, but this example makes it easy to see exactly how you update based on a given row:

```scala
def updateWithEvent(state:DeviceState, input:InputRow):DeviceState = {
  state.count += 1
  // maintain an array of the x-axis values
  state.values = state.values ++ Array(input.x)
  state
}
```

Now it's time to define the function that updates across a series of input rows. Notice in the example that follows that we have a specific key, the iterator of inputs, and the old state, and we update that old state over time as we receive new events. This, in turn, will return our output rows with the updates on a per-device level based on the number of counts it sees. This case is quite straightforward, after a given number of events, you update the state and reset it. You then create an output row. You can see this row in the output table:

```scala
import org.apache.spark.sql.streaming.{GroupStateTimeout, OutputMode,
  GroupState}

def updateAcrossEvents(device:String, inputs: Iterator[InputRow],
  oldState: GroupState[DeviceState]):Iterator[OutputRow] = {
  inputs.toSeq.sortBy(_.timestamp.getTime).toIterator.flatMap { input =>
    val state = if (oldState.exists) oldState.get
      else DeviceState(device, Array(), 0)

    val newState = updateWithEvent(state, input)
    if (newState.count >= 500) {
      // One of our windows is complete; replace our state with an empty
      // DeviceState and output the average for the past 500 items from
      // the old state
      oldState.update(DeviceState(device, Array(), 0))
      Iterator(OutputRow(device,
        newState.values.sum / newState.values.length.toDouble))
    }
    else {
      // Update the current DeviceState object in place and output no
      // records
      oldState.update(newState)
      Iterator()
    }
  }
}
```

Now you can run your stream. You will notice that you need to explicitly state the output mode, which is append. You also need to set a GroupStateTimeout. This time-out specifies the amount of time you want to wait before a window should be output as complete (even if it did not reach the required count). In that case, set an infinite time-out, meaning if a device never gets to that required 500 count threshold, it will maintain that state forever as "incomplete" and not output it to the result table.

By specifying both of those parameters you can pass in the updateAcrossEvents function and start the stream:

```
import org.apache.spark.sql.streaming.GroupStateTimeout

withEventTime
  .selectExpr("Device as device",
    "cast(Creation_Time/1000000000 as timestamp) as timestamp", "x")
  .as[InputRow]
  .groupByKey(_.device)
  .flatMapGroupsWithState(OutputMode.Append,
    GroupStateTimeout.NoTimeout)(updateAcrossEvents)
  .writeStream
  .queryName("count_based_device")
  .format("memory")
  .outputMode("append")
  .start()
```

After you start the stream, it's time to query it. Here are the results:

```
SELECT * FROM count_based_device

+--------+--------------------+
| device|     previousAverage|
+--------+--------------------+
|nexus4_1|       4.660034012E-4|
|nexus4_1|0.001436279298199...|
...
|nexus4_1|1.049804683999999...|
|nexus4_1|-0.01837188737960...|
+--------+--------------------+
```

You can see the values change over each of those windows as you append new data to the result set.

flatMapGroupsWithState

Our second example of stateful processing will use a feature called `flatMapGroups WithState`. This is quite similar to `mapGroupsWithState` except that rather than just having a single key with at most one output, a single key can have many outputs. This can provide us a bit more flexibility and the same fundamental structure as `map GroupsWithState` applies. Here's what we'll need to define.

- Three class definitions: an input definition, a state definition, and optionally an output definition.
- A function to update the state based on a key, an iterator of events, and a previous state.
- A time-out parameter (as described in the time-outs section).

With these objects and definitions, we can control arbitrary state by creating it, updating it over time, and removing it. Let's start with an example of sessionization.

Example: Sessionization

Sessions are simply unspecified time windows with a series of events that occur. Typically, you want to record these different events in an array in order to compare these sessions to other sessions in the future. In a session, you will likely have arbitrary logic to maintain and update your state over time as well as certain actions to define when state ends (like a count) or a simple time-out. Let's build on the previous example and define it a bit more strictly as a session.

At times, you might have an explicit session ID that you can use in your function. This obviously makes it much easier because you can just perform a simple aggregation and might not even need your own stateful logic. In this case, you're creating sessions on the fly from a user ID and some time information and if you see no new event from that user in five seconds, the session terminates. You'll also notice that this code uses time-outs differently than we have in other examples.

You can follow the same process of creating your classes, defining our single event update function and then the multievent update function:

```
case class InputRow(uid:String, timestamp:java.sql.Timestamp, x:Double,
  activity:String)
case class UserSession(val uid:String, var timestamp:java.sql.Timestamp,
  var activities: Array[String], var values: Array[Double])
case class UserSessionOutput(val uid:String, var activities: Array[String],
  var xAvg:Double)

def updateWithEvent(state:UserSession, input:InputRow):UserSession = {
  // handle malformed dates
  if (Option(input.timestamp).isEmpty) {
    return state
  }

  state.timestamp = input.timestamp
  state.values = state.values ++ Array(input.x)
  if (!state.activities.contains(input.activity)) {
    state.activities = state.activities ++ Array(input.activity)
  }
  state
}

import org.apache.spark.sql.streaming.{GroupStateTimeout, OutputMode,
  GroupState}

def updateAcrossEvents(uid:String,
  inputs: Iterator[InputRow],
  oldState: GroupState[UserSession]):Iterator[UserSessionOutput] = {

  inputs.toSeq.sortBy(_.timestamp.getTime).toIterator.flatMap { input =>
    val state = if (oldState.exists) oldState.get else UserSession(
    uid,
```

```scala
    new java.sql.Timestamp(6284160000000L),
    Array(),
    Array())
  val newState = updateWithEvent(state, input)

  if (oldState.hasTimedOut) {
    val state = oldState.get
    oldState.remove()
    Iterator(UserSessionOutput(uid,
    state.activities,
    newState.values.sum / newState.values.length.toDouble))
  } else if (state.values.length > 1000) {
    val state = oldState.get
    oldState.remove()
    Iterator(UserSessionOutput(uid,
    state.activities,
    newState.values.sum / newState.values.length.toDouble))
  } else {
    oldState.update(newState)
    oldState.setTimeoutTimestamp(newState.timestamp.getTime(), "5 seconds")
    Iterator()
  }

  }
}
```

You'll see in this one that we only expect to see an event at most five seconds late. Anything other than that and we will ignore it. We will use an `EventTimeTimeout` to set that we want to time-out based on the event time in this stateful operation:

```scala
import org.apache.spark.sql.streaming.GroupStateTimeout

withEventTime.where("x is not null")
  .selectExpr("user as uid",
    "cast(Creation_Time/1000000000 as timestamp) as timestamp",
    "x", "gt as activity")
  .as[InputRow]
  .withWatermark("timestamp", "5 seconds")
  .groupByKey(_.uid)
  .flatMapGroupsWithState(OutputMode.Append,
    GroupStateTimeout.EventTimeTimeout)(updateAcrossEvents)
  .writeStream
  .queryName("count_based_device")
  .format("memory")
  .start()
```

Querying this table will show you the output rows for each user over this time period:

```
SELECT * FROM count_based_device

+---+--------------------+--------------------+
|uid|          activities|                xAvg|
+---+--------------------+--------------------+
|  a|  [stand, null, sit]|-9.10908533566433...|
```

```
|  a|   [sit, null, walk]|-0.00654280428601...|
...
|  c|[null, stairsdown...|-0.03286657789999995|
+---+--------------------+--------------------+
```

As you might expect, sessions that have a number of activities in them have a higher x-axis gyroscope value than ones that have fewer activities. It should be trivial to extend this example to problem sets more relevant to your own domain, as well.

Conclusion

This chapter covered some of the more advanced topics in Structured Streaming, including event time and stateful processing. This is effectively the user guide to help you actually build out your application logic and turn it into something that provides value. Next, we will discuss what we'll need to do in order to take this application to production and maintain and update it over time.

## CHAPTER 23

Structured Streaming in Production

The previous chapters of this part of the book have covered Structured Streaming from a user's perspective. Naturally this is the core of your application. This chapter covers some of the operational tools needed to run Structured Streaming robustly in production after you've developed an application.

Structured Streaming was marked as production-ready in Apache Spark 2.2.0, meaning that this release has all the features required for production use and stabilizes the API. Many organizations are already using the system in production because, frankly, it's not much different from running other production Spark applications. Indeed, through features such as transactional sources/sinks and exactly-once processing, the Structured Streaming designers sought to make it as easy to operate as possible. This chapter will walk you through some of the key operational tasks specific to Structured Streaming. This should supplement everything we saw and learned about Spark operations in Part II.

Fault Tolerance and Checkpointing

The most important operational concern for a streaming application is failure recovery. Faults are inevitable: you're going to lose a machine in the cluster, a schema will change by accident without a proper migration, or you may even intentionally restart the cluster or application. In any of these cases, Structured Streaming allows you to recover an application by just restarting it. To do this, you must configure the application to use checkpointing and write-ahead logs, both of which are handled automatically by the engine. Specifically, you must configure a query to write to a *checkpoint location* on a reliable file system (e.g., HDFS, S3, or any compatible filesystem). Structured Streaming will then periodically save all relevant progress information (for instance, the range of offsets processed in a given trigger) as well as the current intermediate state values to the checkpoint location. In a failure scenario, you simply need to restart your application, making sure to point to the same checkpoint location, and it will automatically recover its state and start processing data where it left off. You do not have to manually manage this state on behalf of the application—Structured Streaming does it for you.

To use checkpointing, specify your checkpoint location *before* starting your application through the `checkpointLocation` option on `writeStream`. You can do this as follows:

```scala
// in Scala
val static = spark.read.json("/data/activity-data")
val streaming = spark
  .readStream
  .schema(static.schema)
  .option("maxFilesPerTrigger", 10)
  .json("/data/activity-data")
  .groupBy("gt")
  .count()
val query = streaming
  .writeStream
  .outputMode("complete")
  .option("checkpointLocation", "/some/location/")
  .queryName("test_stream")
  .format("memory")
  .start()
```

```python
# in Python
static = spark.read.json("/data/activity-data")
streaming = spark\
  .readStream\
  .schema(static.schema)\
  .option("maxFilesPerTrigger", 10)\
  .json("/data/activity-data")\
  .groupBy("gt")\
  .count()
query = streaming\
  .writeStream\
  .outputMode("complete")\
  .option("checkpointLocation", "/some/python/location/")\
  .queryName("test_python_stream")\
  .format("memory")\
  .start()
```

If you lose your checkpoint directory or the information inside of it, your application will not be able to recover from failures and you will have to restart your stream from scratch.

Updating Your Application

Checkpointing is probably the most important thing to enable in order to run your applications in production. This is because the checkpoint will store all of the information about what your stream has processed thus far and what the intermediate state it may be storing is. However, checkpointing does come with a small catch— you're going to have to reason about your old checkpoint data when you update your streaming application. When you update your application, you're going to have to ensure that your update is not a breaking change. Let's cover these in detail when we review the two types of updates: either an update to your application code or running a new Spark version.

Updating Your Streaming Application Code

Structured Streaming is designed to allow certain types of changes to the application code between application restarts. Most importantly, you are allowed to change user-defined functions (UDFs) as long as they have the same type signature. This feature can be very useful for bug fixes. For example, imagine that your application starts receiving a new type of data, and one of the data parsing functions in your current logic crashes. With Structured Streaming, you can recompile the application with a new version of that function and pick up at the same point in the stream where it crashed earlier.

While small adjustments like adding a new column or changing a UDF are not breaking changes and do not require a new checkpoint directory, there are larger changes that do require an entirely new checkpoint directory. For example, if you update your streaming application to add a new aggregation key or fundamentally change the query itself, Spark cannot construct the required state for the new query from an old checkpoint directory. In these cases, Structured Streaming will throw an exception saying it cannot begin from a checkpoint directory, and you must start from scratch with a new (empty) directory as your checkpoint location.

Updating Your Spark Version

Structured Streaming applications should be able to restart from an old checkpoint directory across patch version updates to Spark (e.g., moving from Spark 2.2.0 to 2.2.1 to 2.2.2). The checkpoint format is designed to be forward-compatible, so the only way it may be broken is due to critical bug fixes. If a Spark release cannot recover from old checkpoints, this will be clearly documented in its release notes. The Structured Streaming developers also aim to keep the format compatible across *minor* version updates (e.g., Spark 2.2.x to 2.3.x), but you should check the release notes to see whether this is supported for each upgrade. In either case, if you cannot start from a checkpoint, you will need to start your application again using a new checkpoint directory.

Sizing and Rescaling Your Application

In general, the size of your cluster should be able to comfortably handle bursts above your data rate. The key metrics you should be monitoring in your application and cluster are discussed as follows. In general, if you see that your input rate is much higher than your processing rate (elaborated upon momentarily), it's time to scale up your cluster or application. Depending on your resource manager and deployment, you may just be able to dynamically add executors to your application. When it comes time, you can scale-down your application in the same way—remove executors (potentially through your cloud provider) or restart your application with lower resource counts. These changes will likely incur some processing delay (as data is recomputed or partitions are shuffled around when executors are removed). In the end, it's a business decision as to whether it's worthwhile to create a system with more sophisticated resource management capabilities.

While making underlying infrastructure changes to the cluster or application are sometimes necessary, other times a change may only require a restart of the application or stream with a new configuration. For instance, changing `spark.sql.shuffle.partitions` is not supported while a stream is currently running (it won't actually change the number of shuffle partitions). This requires restarting the actual stream, not necessarily the entire application. Heavier weight changes, like changing arbitrary Spark application configurations, will likely require an application restart.

Metrics and Monitoring

Metrics and monitoring in streaming applications is largely the same as for general Spark applications using the tools described in Chapter 18. However, Structured Streaming does add several more specifics in order to help you better understand the state of your application. There are two key APIs you can leverage to query the status of a streaming query and see its recent execution progress. With these two APIs, you can get a sense of whether or not your stream is behaving as expected.

Query Status

The query status is the most basic monitoring API, so it's a good starting point. It aims to answer the question, "What processing is my stream performing right now?" This information is reported in the `status` field of the query object returned by `startStream`. For example, you might have a simple counts stream that provides counts of IOT devices defined by the following query (here we're just using the same query from the previous chapter without the initialization code):

```
query.status
```

To get the status of a given query, simply running the command `query.status` will return the current status of the stream. This gives us details about what is happening at that point in time in the stream. Here's a sample of what you'll get back when querying this status:

```
{
  "message" : "Getting offsets from ...",
  "isDataAvailable" : true,
  "isTriggerActive" : true
}
```

The above snippet describes getting the offsets from a Structured Streaming data source (hence the message describing getting offsets). There are a variety of messages to describe the stream's status.

We have shown the status command inline here the way you would call it in a Spark shell. However, for a standalone application, you may not have a shell attached to run arbitrary code inside your process. In that case, you can expose its status by implementing a monitoring server, such as a small HTTP server that listens on a port and returns `query.status` when it gets a request. Alternatively, you can use the richer `StreamingQueryListener` API described later to listen to more events.

Recent Progress

While the query's current status is useful to see, equally important is an ability to view the query's progress. The progress API allows us to answer questions like "At what rate am I processing tuples?" or "How fast are tuples arriving from the source?" By running `query.recentProgress`, you'll get access to more time-based information like the processing rate and batch durations. The streaming query progress also includes information about the input sources and output sinks behind your stream.

```
query.recentProgress
```

Here's the result of the Scala version after we ran the code from before; the Python one will be similar:

```
Array({
  "id" : "d9b5eac5-2b27-4655-8dd3-4be626b1b59b",
  "runId" : "f8da8bc7-5d0a-4554-880d-d21fe43b983d",
  "name" : "test_stream",
  "timestamp" : "2017-08-06T21:11:21.141Z",
  "numInputRows" : 780119,
  "processedRowsPerSecond" : 19779.89350912779,
  "durationMs" : {
    "addBatch" : 38179,
    "getBatch" : 235,
    "getOffset" : 518,
    "queryPlanning" : 138,
    "triggerExecution" : 39440,
```

```
    "walCommit" : 312
  },
  "stateOperators" : [ {
    "numRowsTotal" : 7,
    "numRowsUpdated" : 7
  } ],
  "sources" : [ {
    "description" : "FileStreamSource[/some/stream/source/]",
    "startOffset" : null,
    "endOffset" : {
      "logOffset" : 0
    },
    "numInputRows" : 780119,
    "processedRowsPerSecond" : 19779.89350912779
  } ],
  "sink" : {
    "description" : "MemorySink"
  }
})
```

As you can see from the output just shown, this includes a number of details about the state of the stream. It is important to note that this is a snapshot in time (according to when we asked for the query progress). In order to consistently get output about the state of the stream, you'll need to query this API for the updated state repeatedly. The majority of the fields in the previous output should be self-explanatory. However, let's review some of the more consequential fields in detail.

Input rate and processing rate

The input rate specifies how much data is flowing into Structured Streaming from our input source. The processing rate is how quickly the application is able to analyze that data. In the ideal case, the input and processing rates should vary together. Another case might be when the input rate is much greater than the processing rate. When this happens, the stream is falling behind and you will need to scale the cluster up to handle the larger load.

Batch duration

Nearly all streaming systems utilize batching to operate at any reasonable throughput (some have an option of high latency in exchange for lower throughput). Structured Streaming achieves both. As it operates on the data, you will likely see batch duration oscillate as Structured Streaming processes varying numbers of events over time. Naturally, this metric will have little to no relevance when the continuous processing engine is made an execution option.

Generally it's a best practice to visualize the changes in batch duration and input and processing rates. It's much more helpful than simply reporting changes over time.

Spark UI

The Spark web UI, covered in detail in Chapter 18, also shows tasks, jobs, and data processing metrics for Structured Streaming applications. On the Spark UI, each streaming application will appear as a sequence of short jobs, one for each trigger. However, you can use the same UI to see metrics, query plans, task durations, and logs from your application. One departure of note from the DStream API is that the Streaming Tab is not used by Structured Streaming.

Alerting

Understanding and looking at the metrics for your Structured Streaming queries is an important first step. However, this involves constantly watching a dashboard or the metrics in order to discover potential issues. You're going to need robust *automatic* alerting to notify you when your jobs are failing or not keeping up with the input data rate without monitoring them manually. There are several ways to integrate existing alerting tools with Spark, generally building on the recent progress API we covered before. For example, you may directly feed the metrics to a monitoring system such as the open source Coda Hale Metrics library or Prometheus, or you may simply log them and use a log aggregation system like Splunk. In addition to monitoring and alerting on queries, you're also going to want to monitor and alert on the state of the cluster and the overall application (if you're running multiple queries together).

Advanced Monitoring with the Streaming Listener

We already touched on some of the high-level monitoring tools in Structured Streaming. With a bit of glue logic, you can use the status and queryProgress APIs to output monitoring events into your organization's monitoring platform of choice (e.g., a log aggregation system or Prometheus dashboard). Beyond these approaches, there is also a lower-level but more powerful way to observe an application's execution: the StreamingQueryListener class.

The StreamingQueryListener class will allow you to receive asynchronous updates from the streaming query in order to automatically output this information to other systems and implement robust monitoring and alerting mechanisms. You start by developing your own object to extend StreamingQueryListener, then attach it to a running SparkSession. Once you attach your custom listener with sparkSes sion.streams.addListener(), your class will receive notifications when a query is started or stopped, or progress is made on an active query. Here's a simple example of a listener from the Structured Streaming documentation:

```
val spark: SparkSession = ...

spark.streams.addListener(new StreamingQueryListener() {
    override def onQueryStarted(queryStarted: QueryStartedEvent): Unit = {
        println("Query started: " + queryStarted.id)
    }
    override def onQueryTerminated(
      queryTerminated: QueryTerminatedEvent): Unit = {
        println("Query terminated: " + queryTerminated.id)
    }
    override def onQueryProgress(queryProgress: QueryProgressEvent): Unit = {
        println("Query made progress: " + queryProgress.progress)
    }
})
```

Streaming listeners allow you to process each progress update or status change using custom code and pass it to external systems. For example, the following code for a `StreamingQueryListener` that will forward all query progress information to Kafka. You'll have to parse this JSON string once you read data from Kafka in order to access the actual metrics:

```
class KafkaMetrics(servers: String) extends StreamingQueryListener {
  val kafkaProperties = new Properties()
  kafkaProperties.put(
    "bootstrap.servers",
    servers)
  kafkaProperties.put(
    "key.serializer",
    "kafkashaded.org.apache.kafka.common.serialization.StringSerializer")
  kafkaProperties.put(
    "value.serializer",
    "kafkashaded.org.apache.kafka.common.serialization.StringSerializer")

  val producer = new KafkaProducer[String, String](kafkaProperties)

  import org.apache.spark.sql.streaming.StreamingQueryListener
  import org.apache.kafka.clients.producer.KafkaProducer

  override def onQueryProgress(event:
    StreamingQueryListener.QueryProgressEvent): Unit = {
    producer.send(new ProducerRecord("streaming-metrics",
      event.progress.json))
  }
  override def onQueryStarted(event:
    StreamingQueryListener.QueryStartedEvent): Unit = {}
  override def onQueryTerminated(event:
    StreamingQueryListener.QueryTerminatedEvent): Unit = {}
}
```

Using the `StreamingQueryListener` interface, you can even monitor Structured Streaming applications on one cluster by running a Structured Streaming application on that same (or another) cluster. You could also manage multiple streams in this way.

Conclusion

In this chapter, we covered the main tools needed to run Structured Streaming in production: checkpoints for fault tolerance and various monitoring APIs that let you observe how your application is running. Lucky for you, if you're running Spark in production already, many of the concepts and tools are similar, so you should be able to reuse a lot of your existing knowledge. Be sure to check Part IV to see some other helpful tools for monitoring Spark Applications.

PART VI
Advanced Analytics and Machine Learning

## CHAPTER 24

Advanced Analytics and Machine Learning Overview

Thus far, we have covered fairly general data flow APIs. This part of the book will dive deeper into some of the more specific advanced analytics APIs available in Spark. Beyond large-scale SQL analysis and streaming, Spark also provides support for statistics, machine learning, and graph analytics. These encompass a set of workloads that we will refer to as advanced analytics. This part of the book will cover advanced analytics tools in Spark, including:

- Preprocessing your data (cleaning data and feature engineering)
- Supervised learning
- Recommendation learning
- Unsupervised engines
- Graph analytics
- Deep learning

This chapter offers a basic overview of advanced analytics, some example use cases, and a basic advanced analytics workflow. Then we'll cover the analytics tools just listed and teach you how to apply them.

This book is not intended to teach you everything you need to know about machine learning from scratch. We won't go into strict mathematical definitions and formulations—not for lack of importance but simply because it's too much information to include. This part of the book is *not* an algorithm guide that will teach you the mathematical underpinnings of every available algorithm nor the in-depth implementation strategies used. The chapters included here serve as a guide for *users*, with the purpose of outlining what you need to know to use Spark's advanced analytics APIs.

A Short Primer on Advanced Analytics

Advanced analytics refers to a variety of techniques aimed at solving the core problem of deriving insights and making predictions or recommendations based on data. The best ontology for machine learning is structured based on the task that you'd like to perform. The most common tasks include:

- Supervised learning, including classification and regression, where the goal is to predict a label for each data point based on various features.

- Recommendation engines to suggest products to users based on behavior.

- Unsupervised learning, including clustering, anomaly detection, and topic modeling, where the goal is to discover structure in the data.

- Graph analytics tasks such as searching for patterns in a social network.

Before discussing Spark's APIs in detail, let's review each of these tasks along with some common machine learning and advanced analytics use cases. While we have certainly tried to make this introduction as accessible as possible, at times you may need to consult other resources in order to fully understand the material. O'Reilly should we link to or mention any specific ones? Additionally, we will cite the following books throughout the next few chapters because they are great resources for learning more about the individual analytics (and, as a bonus, they are freely available on the web):

- *An Introduction to Statistical Learning* (*http://www-bcf.usc.edu/~gareth/ISL/*) by Gareth James, Daniela Witten, Trevor Hastie, and Robert Tibshirani. We refer to this book as "ISL."

- *Elements of Statistical Learning* (*https://web.stanford.edu/~hastie/ElemStatLearn/*) by Trevor Hastie, Robert Tibshirani, and Jerome Friedman. We refer to this book as "ESL."

- *Deep Learning* (*http://www.deeplearningbook.org/*) by Ian Goodfellow, Yoshua Bengio, and Aaron Courville. We refer to this book as "DLB."

Supervised Learning

Supervised learning is probably the most common type of machine learning. The goal is simple: using historical data that already has labels (often called the dependent variables), train a model to predict the values of those labels based on various features of the data points. One example would be to predict a person's income (the dependent variable) based on age (a feature). This training process usually proceeds through an iterative optimization algorithm such as gradient descent. The training algorithm starts with a basic model and gradually improves it by adjusting various internal parameters (coefficients) during each training iteration. The result of this process is a trained model that you can use to make predictions on new data. There are a number of different tasks we'll need to complete as part of the process of training and making predictions, such as measuring the success of trained models before using them in the field, but the fundamental principle is simple: train on historical data, ensure that it generalizes to data we didn't train on, and then make predictions on new data.

We can further organize supervised learning based on the type of variable we're looking to predict. We'll get to that next.

Classification

One common type of supervised learning is classification. Classification is the act of training an algorithm to predict a dependent variable that is *categorical* (belonging to a discrete, finite set of values). The most common case is *binary classification*, where our resulting model will make a prediction that a given item belongs to one of two groups. The canonical example is classifying email spam. Using a set of historical emails that are organized into groups of spam emails and not spam emails, we train an algorithm to analyze the words in, and any number of properties of, the historical emails and make predictions about them. Once we are satisfied with the algorithm's performance, we use that model to make predictions about future emails the model has never seen before.

When we classify items into more than just two categories, we call this *multiclass classification*. For example, we may have four different categories of email (as opposed to the two categories in the previous paragraph): spam, personal, work related, and other. There are many use cases for classification, including:

Predicting disease
   A doctor or hospital might have a historical dataset of behavioral and physiological attributes of a set of patients. They could use this dataset to train a model on this historical data (and evaluate its success and ethical implications before applying it) and then leverage it to predict whether or not a patient has heart disease or not. This is an example of binary classification (healthy heart, unhealthy heart) or multiclass classification (healthly heart, or one of several different diseases).

Classifying images
There are a number of applications from companies like Apple, Google, or Facebook that can predict who is in a given photo by running a classification model that has been trained on historical images of people in your past photos. Another common use case is to classify images or label the objects in images.

Predicting customer churn
A more business-oriented use case might be predicting customer churn—that is, which customers are likely to stop using a service. You can do this by training a binary classifier on past customers that have churned (and not churned) and using it to try and predict whether or not current customers will churn.

Buy or won't buy
Companies often want to predict whether visitors of their website will purchase a given product. They might use information about users' browsing pattern or attributes such as location in order to drive this prediction.

There are many more use cases for classification beyond these examples. We will introduce more use cases, as well as Spark's classification APIs, in Chapter 26.

Regression

In classification, our dependent variable is a set of discrete values. In regression, we instead try to predict a continuous variable (a real number). In simplest terms, rather than predicting a category, we want to predict a value on a number line. The rest of the process is largely the same, which is why they're both forms of supervised learning. We will train on historical data to make predictions about data we have never seen. Here are some typical examples:

Predicting sales
A store may want to predict total product sales on given data using historical sales data. There are a number of potential input variables, but a simple example might be using last week's sales data to predict the next day's data.

Predicting height
Based on the heights of two individuals, we might want to predict the heights of their potential children.

Predicting the number of viewers of a show
A media company like Netflix might try to predict how many of their subscribers will watch a particular show.

We will introduce more use cases, as well as Spark's methods for regression, in Chapter 27.

Recommendation

Recommendation is one of the most intuitive applications of advanced analytics. By studying people's explicit preferences (through ratings) or implicit ones (through observed behavior) for various products or items, an algorithm can make recommendations on what a user may like by drawing similarities between the users or items. By looking at these similarities, the algorithm makes recommendations to users based on what similar users liked, or what other products resemble the ones the user already purchased. Recommendation is a common use case for Spark and well suited to big data. Here are some example use cases:

Movie recommendations

Netflix uses Spark (*http://bit.ly/2Fkx4Mm*), although not necessarily its built-in libraries, to make large-scale movie recommendations to its users. It does this by studying what movies users watch and do not watch in the Netflix application. In addition, Netflix likely takes into consideration how similar a given user's ratings are to other users'.

Product recommendations

Amazon uses product recommendations as one of its main tools to increase sales. For instance, based on the items in our shopping cart, Amazon may recommend other items that were added to similar shopping carts in the past. Likewise, on every product page, Amazon shows similar products purchased by other users.

We will introduce more recommendation use cases, as well as Spark's methods for generating recommendations, in Chapter 28.

Unsupervised Learning

Unsupervised learning is the act of trying to find patterns or discover the underlying structure in a given set of data. This differs from supervised learning because there is no dependent variable (label) to predict.

Some example use cases for unsupervised learning include:

Anomaly detection

Given some standard event type often occuring over time, we might want to report when a nonstandard type of event occurs. For example, a security officer might want to receive notifications when a strange object (think vehicle, skater, or bicyclist) is observed on a pathway.

User segmentation

Given a set of user behaviors, we might want to better understand what attributes certain users share with other users. For instance, a gaming company might cluster users based on properties like the number of hours played in a given game. The algorithm might reveal that casual players have very different behavior than hardcore gamers, for example, and allow the company to offer different recommendations or rewards to each player.

Topic modeling

Given a set of documents, we might analyze the different words contained therein to see if there is some underlying relation between them. For example, given a number of web pages on data analytics, a topic modeling algorithm can cluster them into pages about machine learning, SQL, streaming, and so on based on groups of words that are more common in one topic than in others.

Intuitively, it is easy to see how segmenting customers could help a platform cater better to each set of users. However, it may be hard to discover whether or not this set of user segments is "correct". For this reason, it can be difficult to determine whether a particular model is good or not. We will discuss unsupervised learning in detail in Chapter 29.

Graph Analytics

While less common than classification and regression, graph analytics is a powerful tool. Fundamentally, graph analytics is the study of structures in which we specify *vertices* (which are objects) and *edges* (which represent the relationships between those objects). For example, the vertices might represent people and products, and edges might represent a purchase. By looking at the properties of vertices and edges, we can better understand the connections between them and the overall structure of the graph. Since graphs are all about relationships, anything that specifies a relationship is a great use case for graph analytics. Some examples include:

Fraud prediction

Capital One uses Spark's graph analytics capabilities (*https://youtu.be/ q5HFMVoN_rc*) to better understand fraud networks. By using historical fraudulent information (like phone numbers, addresses, or names) they discover fraudulent credit requests or transactions. For instance, any user accounts within two hops of a fraudulent phone number might be considered suspicious.

Anomaly detection

By looking at how networks of individuals connect with one another, outliers and anomalies can be flagged for manual analysis. For instance, if typically in our data each vertex has ten edges associated with it and a given vertex only has one edge, that might be worth investigating as something strange.

Classification

Given some facts about certain vertices in a network, you can classify other vertices according to their connection to the original node. For instance, if a certain individual is labeled as an influencer in a social network, we could classify other individuals with similar network structures as influencers.

Recommendation

Google's original web recommendation algorithm, PageRank, is a graph algorithm that analyzes website relationships in order to rank the importance of web pages. For example, a web page that has a lot of links to it is ranked as more important than one with no links to it.

We'll discuss more examples of graph analytics in Chapter 30.

The Advanced Analytics Process

You should have a firm grasp of some fundamental use cases for machine learning and advanced analytics. However, finding a use case is only a small part of the actual advanced analytics process. There is a lot of work in preparing your data for analysis, testing different ways of modeling it, and evaluating these models. This section will provide structure to the overall anaytics process and the steps we have to take to not just perform one of the tasks just outlined, but actually evaluate success objectively in order to understand whether or not we should apply our model to the real world (Figure 24-1).

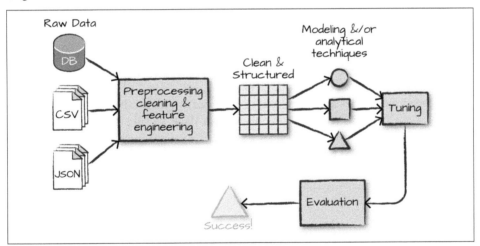

Figure 24-1. The machine learning workflow

The overall process involves, the following steps (with some variation):

1. Gathering and collecting the relevant data for your task.

2. Cleaning and inspecting the data to better understand it.

3. Performing feature engineering to allow the algorithm to leverage the data in a suitable form (e.g., converting the data to numerical vectors).

4. Using a portion of this data as a training set to train one or more algorithms to generate some candidate models.

5. Evaluating and comparing models against your success criteria by objectively measuring results on a subset of the same data that was not used for training. This allows you to better understand how your model may perform in the wild.

6. Leveraging the insights from the above process and/or using the model to make predictions, detect anomalies, or solve more general business challenges.

These steps won't be the same for every advanced analytics task. However, this workflow does serve as a general framework for what you're going to need to be successful with advanced analytics. Just as we did with the various advanced analytics tasks earlier in the chapter, let's break down the process to better understand the overall objective of each step.

Data collection

Naturally it's hard to create a training set without first collecting data. Typically this means at least gathering the datasets you'll want to leverage to train your algorithm. Spark is an excellent tool for this because of its ability to speak to a variety of data sources and work with data big and small.

Data cleaning

After you've gathered the proper data, you're going to need to clean and inspect it. This is typically done as part of a process called exploratory data analysis (*https://en.wikipedia.org/wiki/Exploratory_data_analysis*), or EDA. EDA generally means using interactive queries and visualization methods in order to better understand distributions, correlations, and other details in your data. During this process you may notice you need to remove some values that may have been misrecorded upstream or that other values may be missing. Whatever the case, it's always good to know what is in your data to avoid mistakes down the road. The multitude of Spark functions in the structured APIs will provide a simple way to clean and report on your data.

Feature engineering

Now that you collected and cleaned your dataset, it's time to convert it to a form suitable for machine learning algorithms, which generally means numerical features. Proper feature engineering can often make or break a machine learning application, so this is one task you'll want to do carefully. The process of feature engineering includes a variety of tasks, such as normalizing data, adding variables to represent the interactions of other variables, manipulating categorical variables, and converting them to the proper format to be input into our machine learning model. In MLlib, Spark's machine learning library, all variables will usually have to be input as vectors of doubles (regardless of what they actually represent). We cover the process of feature engineering in great depth in Chapter 25. As you will see in that chapter, Spark provides the essentials you'll need to manipulate your data using a variety of machine learning statistical techniques.

 The following few steps (training models, model tuning, and evaluation) are not relevant to all use cases. This is a general workflow that may vary significantly based on the end objective you would like to achieve.

Training models

At this point in the process we have a dataset of historical information (e.g., spam or not spam emails) and a task we would like to complete (e.g., classifying spam emails). Next, we will want to train a model to predict the correct output, given some input. During the training process, the parameters inside of the model will change according to how well the model performed on the input data. For instance, to classify spam emails, our algorithm will likely find that certain words are better predictors of spam than others and therefore weight the parameters associated with those words higher. In the end, the trained model will find that certain words should have more influence (because of their consistent association with spam emails) than others. The output of the training process is what we call a model. Models can then be used to gain insights or to make future predictions. To make predictions, you will give the model an input and it will produce an output based on a mathematical manipulation of these inputs. Using the classification example, given the properties of an email, it will predict whether that email is spam or not by comparing to the historical spam and not spam emails that it was trained on.

However, just training a model isn't the objective—we want to leverage our model to produce insights. Thus, we must answer the question: how do we know our model is any good at what it's supposed to do? That's where model tuning and evaluation come in.

Model tuning and evaluation

You likely noticed earlier that we mentioned that you should split your data into multiple portions and use only one for training. This is an essential step in the machine learning process because when you build an advanced analytics model you want that model to generalize to data it has not seen before. Splitting our dataset into multiple portions allows us to objectively test the effectiveness of the trained model against a set of data that it has never seen before. The objective is to see if your model understands something fundamental about this data process or whether or not it just noticed the things particular to only the training set (sometimes called *overfitting*). That's why it is called a *test set*. In the process of training models, we also might take another, separate subset of data and treat that as another type of test set, called a *validation set*, in order to try out different *hyperparameters* (parameters that affect the training process) and compare different variations of the same model without overfitting to the test set.

 Following proper training, validation, and test set best practices is essential to successfully using machine learning. It's easy to end up overfitting (training a model that does not generalize well to new data) if we do not properly isolate these sets of data. We cannot cover this problem in depth in this book, but almost any machine learning book will cover this topic.

To continue with the classification example we referenced previously, we have three sets of data: a training set for training models, a validation set for testing different variations of the models that we're training, and lastly, a test set we will use for the final evaluation of our different model variations to see which one performed the best.

Leveraging the model and/or insights

After running the model through the training process and ending up with a well-performing model, you are now ready to use it! Taking your model to production can be a significant challenge in and of itself. We will discuss some tactics later on in this chapter.

Spark's Advanced Analytics Toolkit

The previous overview is just an example workflow and doesn't encompass all use cases or potential workflows. In addition, you probably noticed that we did not discuss Spark almost at all. This section will discuss Spark's advanced analytics capabilities. Spark includes several core packages and many external packages for performing advanced analytics. The primary package is MLlib, which provides an interface for building machine learning pipelines.

What Is MLlib?

MLlib is a package, built on and included in Spark, that provides interfaces for gathering and cleaning data, feature engineering and feature selection, training and tuning large-scale supervised and unsupervised machine learning models, and using those models in production.

MLlib actually consists of two packages that leverage different core data structures. The package `org.apache.spark.ml` includes an interface for use with DataFrames. This package also offers a high-level interface for building machine learning pipelines that help standardize the way in which you perform the preceding steps. The lower-level package, `org.apache.spark.mllib`, includes interfaces for Spark's low-level RDD APIs. This book will focus exclusively on the DataFrame API. The RDD API is the lower-level interface, which is in maintenance mode (meaning it will only receive bug fixes, not new features) at this time. It has also been covered fairly extensively in older books on Spark and is therefore omitted here.

When and why should you use MLlib (versus scikit-learn, TensorFlow, or foo package)

At a high level, MLlib might sound like a lot of other machine learning packages you've probably heard of, such as scikit-learn for Python or the variety of R packages for performing similar tasks. So why should you bother with MLlib at all? There are numerous tools for performing machine learning on a single machine, and while there are several great options to choose from, these single machine tools do have their limits either in terms of the size of data you can train on or the processing time. This means single-machine tools are usually *complementary* to MLlib. When you hit those scalability issues, take advantage of Spark's abilities.

There are two key use cases where you want to leverage Spark's ability to scale. First, you want to leverage Spark for preprocessing and feature generation to reduce the amount of time it might take to produce training and test sets from a large amount of data. Then you might leverage single-machine learning libraries to train on those given data sets. Second, when your input data or model size become too difficult or inconvenient to put on one machine, use Spark to do the heavy lifting. Spark makes distributed machine learning very simple.

An important caveat to all of this is that while training and data preparation are made simple, there are still some complexities you will need to keep in mind, especially when it comes to deploying a trained model. For example, Spark does not provide a built-in way to serve low-latency predictions from a model, so you may want to export the model to another serving system or a custom application to do that. MLlib is generally designed to allow inspecting and exporting models to other tools where possible.

High-Level MLlib Concepts

In MLlib there are several fundamental "structural" types: transformers, estimators, evaluators, and pipelines. By structural, we mean you will think in terms of these types when you define an end-to-end machine learning pipeline. They'll provide the common language for defining what belongs in what part of the pipeline. Figure 24-2 illustrates the overall workflow that you will follow when developing machine learning models in Spark.

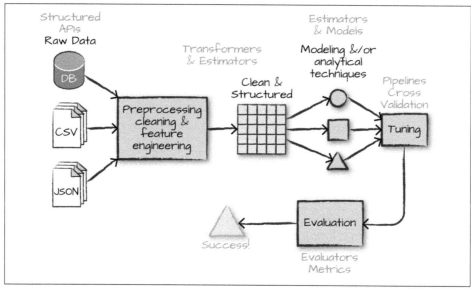

Figure 24-2. The machine learning workflow, in Spark

Transformers are functions that convert raw data in some way. This might be to create a new interaction variable (from two other variables), normalize a column, or simply change an `Integer` into a `Double` type to be input into a model. An example of a transformer is one that converts string categorical variables into numerical values that can be used in MLlib. Transformers are primarily used in preprocessing and feature engineering. Transformers take a DataFrame as input and produce a new DataFrame as output, as illustrated in Figure 24-3.

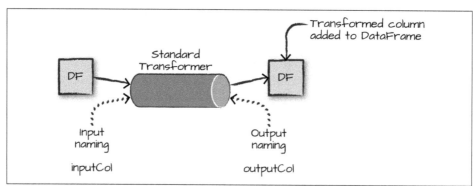

Figure 24-3. A standard transformer

Estimators are one of two kinds of things. First, estimators can be a kind of transformer that is initialized with data. For instance, to normalize numerical data we'll need to initialize our transformation with some information about the current values in the column we would like to normalize. This requires two passes over our data—the initial pass generates the initialization values and the second actually applies the generated function over the data. In the Spark's nomenclature, algorithms that allow users to train a model from data are also referred to as estimators.

An *evaluator* allows us to see how a given model performs according to criteria we specify like a receiver operating characteristic (ROC) curve. After we use an evaluator to select the best model from the ones we tested, we can then use that model to make predictions.

From a high level we can specify each of the transformations, estimations, and evaluations one by one, but it is often easier to specify our steps as *stages* in a *pipeline*. This pipeline is similar to scikit-learn's pipeline concept.

Low-level data types

In addition to the structural types for building pipelines, there are also several lower-level data types you may need to work with in MLlib (Vector being the most common). Whenever we pass a set of features into a machine learning model, we must do it as a vector that consists of Doubles. This vector can be either sparse (where most of the elements are zero) or dense (where there are many unique values). Vectors are created in different ways. To create a dense vector, we can specify an array of all the values. To create a sparse vector, we can specify the total size and the indices and values of the non-zero elements. Sparse is the best format, as you might have guessed, when the majority of values are zero as this is a more compressed representation. Here is an example of how to manually create a Vector:

```scala
// in Scala
import org.apache.spark.ml.linalg.Vectors
val denseVec = Vectors.dense(1.0, 2.0, 3.0)
val size = 3
val idx = Array(1,2) // locations of non-zero elements in vector
val values = Array(2.0,3.0)
val sparseVec = Vectors.sparse(size, idx, values)
sparseVec.toDense
denseVec.toSparse
```

```python
# in Python
from pyspark.ml.linalg import Vectors
denseVec = Vectors.dense(1.0, 2.0, 3.0)
size = 3
idx = [1, 2] # locations of non-zero elements in vector
values = [2.0, 3.0]
sparseVec = Vectors.sparse(size, idx, values)
```

Confusingly, there are similar datatypes that refer to ones that can be used in DataFrames and others that can only be used in RDDs. The RDD implementations fall under the mllib package while the DataFrame implementations fall under ml.

MLlib in Action

Now that we have described some of the core pieces you can expect to come across, let's create a simple pipeline to demonstrate each of the components. We'll use a small synthetic dataset that will help illustrate our point. Let's read the data in and see a sample before talking about it further:

```scala
// in Scala
var df = spark.read.json("/data/simple-ml")
df.orderBy("value2").show()
```

```python
# in Python
df = spark.read.json("/data/simple-ml")
df.orderBy("value2").show()
```

Here's a sample of the data:

```
+-----+----+------+------------------+
|color| lab|value1|            value2|
+-----+----+------+------------------+
|green|good|     1|14.386294994851129|
...
|  red| bad|    16|14.386294994851129|
|green|good|    12|14.386294994851129|
+-----+----+------+------------------+
```

This dataset consists of a categorical label with two values (good or bad), a categorical variable (color), and two numerical variables. While the data is synthetic, let's imagine that this dataset represents a company's customer health. The "color" column represents some categorical health rating made by a customer service representative. The "lab" column represents the true customer health. The other two values are some numerical measures of activity within an application (e.g., minutes spent on site and purchases). Suppose that we want to train a classification model where we hope to predict a binary variable—the label—from the other values.

Apart from JSON, there are some specific data formats commonly used for supervised learning, including LIBSVM. These formats have real valued labels and sparse input data. Spark can read and write for these formats using its data source API. Here's an example of how to read in data from a libsvm file using that Data Source API.

```
spark.read.format("libsvm").load(
    "/data/sample_libsvm_data.txt")
```

For more information on LIBSVM, see the documentation (*http://www.csie.ntu.edu.tw/~cjlin/libsvm/*).

Feature Engineering with Transformers

As already mentioned, transformers help us manipulate our current columns in one way or another. Manipulating these columns is often in pursuit of building features (that we will input into our model). Transformers exist to either cut down the number of features, add more features, manipulate current ones, or simply to help us format our data correctly. Transformers add new columns to DataFrames.

When we use MLlib, all inputs to machine learning algorithms (with several exceptions discussed in later chapters) in Spark must consist of type `Double` (for labels) and `Vector[Double]` (for features). The current dataset does *not* meet that requirement and therefore we need to transform it to the proper format.

To achieve this in our example, we are going to specify an `RFormula`. This is a declarative language for specifying machine learning transformations and is simple to use once you understand the syntax. `RFormula` supports a limited subset of the R operators that in practice work quite well for simple models and manipulations (we demonstrate the manual approach to this problem in Chapter 25). The basic RFormula operators are:

~

Separate target and terms

+

Concat terms; "+ 0" means removing the intercept (this means that the *y*-intercept of the line that we will fit will be 0)

-

Remove a term; "- 1" means removing the intercept (this means that the *y*-intercept of the line that we will fit will be 0—yes, this does the same thing as "+ 0"

:

Interaction (multiplication for numeric values, or binarized categorical values)

- All columns except the target/dependent variable

In order to specify transformations with this syntax, we need to import the relevant class. Then we go through the process of defining our formula. In this case we want to use all available variables (the .) and also add in the interactions between value1 and color and value2 and color, treating those as new features:

```scala
// in Scala
import org.apache.spark.ml.feature.RFormula
val supervised = new RFormula()
  .setFormula("lab ~ . + color:value1 + color:value2")
```

```python
# in Python
from pyspark.ml.feature import RFormula
supervised = RFormula(formula="lab ~ . + color:value1 + color:value2")
```

At this point, we have declaratively specified how we would like to change our data into what we will train our model on. The next step is to *fit* the RFormula transformer to the data to let it discover the possible values of each column. Not all transformers have this requirement but because RFormula will automatically handle categorical variables for us, it needs to determine which columns are categorical and which are not, as well as what the distinct values of the categorical columns are. For this reason, we have to call the fit method. Once we call fit, it returns a "trained" version of our transformer we can then use to actually transform our data.

We're using the RFormula transformer because it makes performing several transformations extremely easy to do. In Chapter 25, we'll show other ways to specify a similar set of transformations and outline the component parts of the RFormula when we cover the specific transformers in MLlib.

Now that we covered those details, let's continue on and prepare our DataFrame:

```scala
// in Scala
val fittedRF = supervised.fit(df)
val preparedDF = fittedRF.transform(df)
preparedDF.show()
```

```python
# in Python
fittedRF = supervised.fit(df)
preparedDF = fittedRF.transform(df)
preparedDF.show()
```

Here's the output from the training and transformation process:

```
+-----+----+------+-------------------+--------------------+-----+
|color| lab|value1|             value2|            features|label|
+-----+----+------+-------------------+--------------------+-----+
|green|good|     1|14.386294994851129|(10,[1,2,3,5,8],[...|  1.0|
```

```
...
|  red| bad|     2|14.386294994851129|(10,[0,2,3,4,7],[...|  0.0|
+-----+----+------+------------------+--------------------+-----+
```

In the output we can see the result of our transformation—a column called features that has our previously raw data. What's happening behind the scenes is actually pretty simple. RFormula inspects our data during the fit call and outputs an object that will transform our data according to the specified formula, which is called an RFormulaModel. This "trained" transformer always has the word Model in the type signature. When we use this transformer, Spark automatically converts our categorical variable to Doubles so that we can input it into a (yet to be specified) machine learning model. In particular, it assigns a numerical value to each possible color category, creates additional features for the interaction variables between colors and value1/value2, and puts them all into a single vector. We then call transform on that object in order to transform our input data into the expected output data.

Thus far you (pre)processed the data and added some features along the way. Now it is time to actually train a model (or a set of models) on this dataset. In order to do this, you first need to prepare a test set for evaluation.

Having a good test set is probably the most important thing you can do to ensure you train a model you can actually use in the real world (in a dependable way). Not creating a representative test set or using your test set for hyperparameter tuning are surefire ways to create a model that does not perform well in real-world scenarios. Don't skip creating a test set—it's a requirement to know how well your model actually does!

Let's create a simple test set based off a random split of the data now (we'll be using this test set throughout the remainder of the chapter):

```scala
// in Scala
val Array(train, test) = preparedDF.randomSplit(Array(0.7, 0.3))
```

```python
# in Python
train, test = preparedDF.randomSplit([0.7, 0.3])
```

Estimators

Now that we have transformed our data into the correct format and created some valuable features, it's time to actually fit our model. In this case we will use a classification algorithm called logistic regression. To create our classifier we instantiate an instance of LogisticRegression, using the default configuration or hyperparameters. We then set the label columns and the feature columns; the column names we are setting—label and features—are actually the default labels for all estimators in Spark MLlib, and in later chapters we omit them:

```scala
// in Scala
import org.apache.spark.ml.classification.LogisticRegression
val lr = new LogisticRegression().setLabelCol("label").setFeaturesCol("features")
```

```python
# in Python
from pyspark.ml.classification import LogisticRegression
lr = LogisticRegression(labelCol="label",featuresCol="features")
```

Before we actually go about training this model, let's inspect the parameters. This is also a great way to remind yourself of the options available for each particular model:

```scala
// in Scala
println(lr.explainParams())
```

```python
# in Python
print lr.explainParams()
```

While the output is too large to reproduce here, it shows an explanation of all of the parameters for Spark's implementation of logistic regression. The explainParams method exists on all algorithms available in MLlib.

Upon instantiating an untrained algorithm, it becomes time to fit it to data. In this case, this returns a LogisticRegressionModel:

```scala
// in Scala
val fittedLR = lr.fit(train)
```

```python
# in Python
fittedLR = lr.fit(train)
```

This code will kick off a Spark job to train the model. As opposed to the transformations that you saw throughout the book, the fitting of a machine learning model is eager and performed immediately.

Once complete, you can use the model to make predictions. Logically this means tranforming features into labels. We make predictions with the transform method. For example, we can transform our training dataset to see what labels our model assigned to the training data and how those compare to the true outputs. This, again, is just another DataFrame we can manipulate. Let's perform that prediction with the following code snippet:

```
fittedLR.transform(train).select("label", "prediction").show()
```

This results in:

```
+-----+----------+
|label|prediction|
+-----+----------+
|  0.0|       0.0|
 ...
|  0.0|       0.0|
+-----+----------+
```

Our next step would be to manually evaluate this model and calculate performance metrics like the true positive rate, false negative rate, and so on. We might then turn around and try a different set of parameters to see if those perform better. However, while this is a useful process, it can also be quite tedious. Spark helps you avoid manually trying different models and evaluation criteria by allowing you to specify your workload as a declarative pipeline of work that includes all your transformations as well as tuning your hyperparameters.

A Review of Hyperparameters

Although we mentioned them previously, let's more formally define hyperparameters. Hyperparameters are configuration parameters that affect the training process, such as model architecture and regularization. They are set prior to starting training. For instance, logistic regression has a hyperparameter that determines how much regularization should be performed on our data through the training phase (regularization is a technique that pushes models against overfitting data). You'll see in the next couple of pages that we can set up our pipeline to try different hyperparameter values (e.g., different regularization values) in order to compare different variations of the same model against one another.

Pipelining Our Workflow

As you probably noticed, if you are performing a lot of transformations, writing all the steps and keeping track of DataFrames ends up being quite tedious. That's why Spark includes the `Pipeline` concept. A pipeline allows you to set up a dataflow of the relevant transformations that ends with an estimator that is automatically tuned according to your specifications, resulting in a tuned model ready for use. Figure 24-4 illustrates this process.

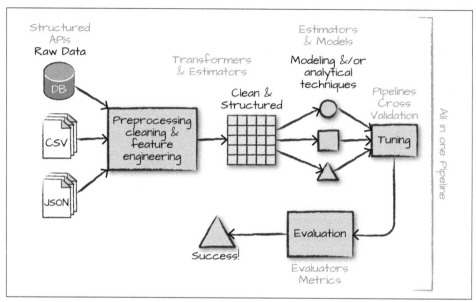

Figure 24-4. Pipelining the ML workflow

Note that it is essential that instances of transformers or models are *not* reused across different pipelines. Always create a new instance of a model before creating another pipeline.

In order to make sure we don't overfit, we are going to create a holdout test set and tune our hyperparameters based on a validation set (note that we create this validation set based on the original dataset, not the `preparedDF` used in the previous pages):

```
// in Scala
val Array(train, test) = df.randomSplit(Array(0.7, 0.3))
```

```
# in Python
train, test = df.randomSplit([0.7, 0.3])
```

Now that you have a holdout set, let's create the base stages in our pipeline. A stage simply represents a transformer or an estimator. In our case, we will have two estimators. The RFomula will first analyze our data to understand the types of input features and then transform them to create new features. Subsequently, the LogisticRegression object is the algorithm that we will train to produce a model:

```
// in Scala
val rForm = new RFormula()
val lr = new LogisticRegression().setLabelCol("label").setFeaturesCol("features")
```

```
# in Python
rForm = RFormula()
lr = LogisticRegression().setLabelCol("label").setFeaturesCol("features")
```

We will set the potential values for the RFormula in the next section. Now instead of manually using our transformations and then tuning our model we just make them stages in the overall pipeline, as in the following code snippet:

```scala
// in Scala
import org.apache.spark.ml.Pipeline
val stages = Array(rForm, lr)
val pipeline = new Pipeline().setStages(stages)
```

```python
# in Python
from pyspark.ml import Pipeline
stages = [rForm, lr]
pipeline = Pipeline().setStages(stages)
```

Training and Evaluation

Now that you arranged the logical pipeline, the next step is training. In our case, we won't train just one model (like we did previously); we will train several variations of the model by specifying different combinations of hyperparameters that we would like Spark to test. We will then select the best model using an Evaluator that compares their predictions on our validation data. We can test different hyperparameters in the entire pipeline, even in the RFormula that we use to manipulate the raw data. This code shows how we go about doing that:

```scala
// in Scala
import org.apache.spark.ml.tuning.ParamGridBuilder
val params = new ParamGridBuilder()
  .addGrid(rForm.formula, Array(
    "lab ~ . + color:value1",
    "lab ~ . + color:value1 + color:value2"))
  .addGrid(lr.elasticNetParam, Array(0.0, 0.5, 1.0))
  .addGrid(lr.regParam, Array(0.1, 2.0))
  .build()
```

```python
# in Python
from pyspark.ml.tuning import ParamGridBuilder
params = ParamGridBuilder()\
  .addGrid(rForm.formula, [
    "lab ~ . + color:value1",
    "lab ~ . + color:value1 + color:value2"])\
  .addGrid(lr.elasticNetParam, [0.0, 0.5, 1.0])\
  .addGrid(lr.regParam, [0.1, 2.0])\
  .build()
```

In our current paramter grid, there are three hyperparameters that will diverge from the defaults:

- Two different versions of the RFormula

- Three different options for the ElasticNet parameter

- Two different options for the regularization parameter

This gives us a total of 12 different combinations of these parameters, which means we will be training 12 different versions of logistic regression. We explain the `Elastic Net` parameter as well as the regularization options in Chapter 26.

Now that the grid is built, it's time to specify our evaluation process. The *evaluator* allows us to automatically and objectively compare multiple models to the same evaluation metric. There are evaluators for classification and regression, covered in later chapters, but in this case we will use the `BinaryClassificationEvaluator`, which has a number of potential evaluation metrics, as we'll discuss in Chapter 26. In this case we will use `areaUnderROC`, which is the total area under the receiver operating characteristic, a common measure of classification performance:

```Scala
// in Scala
import org.apache.spark.ml.evaluation.BinaryClassificationEvaluator
val evaluator = new BinaryClassificationEvaluator()
  .setMetricName("areaUnderROC")
  .setRawPredictionCol("prediction")
  .setLabelCol("label")
```

```Python
# in Python
from pyspark.ml.evaluation import BinaryClassificationEvaluator
evaluator = BinaryClassificationEvaluator()\
  .setMetricName("areaUnderROC")\
  .setRawPredictionCol("prediction")\
  .setLabelCol("label")
```

Now that we have a pipeline that specifies how our data should be transformed, we will perform model selection to try out different hyperparameters in our logistic regression model and measure success by comparing their performance using the `areaUnderROC` metric.

As we discussed, it is a best practice in machine learning to fit hyperparameters on a validation set (instead of your test set) to prevent overfitting. For this reason, we cannot use our holdout test set (that we created before) to tune these parameters. Luckily, Spark provides two options for performing hyperparameter tuning automatically. We can use `TrainValidationSplit`, which will simply perform an arbitrary random split of our data into two different groups, or `CrossValidator`, which performs K-fold cross-validation by splitting the dataset into k non-overlapping, randomly partitioned folds:

```Scala
// in Scala
import org.apache.spark.ml.tuning.TrainValidationSplit
val tvs = new TrainValidationSplit()
  .setTrainRatio(0.75) // also the default.
  .setEstimatorParamMaps(params)
  .setEstimator(pipeline)
  .setEvaluator(evaluator)
```

```python
# in Python
from pyspark.ml.tuning import TrainValidationSplit
tvs = TrainValidationSplit()\
  .setTrainRatio(0.75)\
  .setEstimatorParamMaps(params)\
  .setEstimator(pipeline)\
  .setEvaluator(evaluator)
```

Let's run the entire pipeline we constructed. To review, running this pipeline will test out every version of the model against the validation set. Note the type of `tvsFitted` is `TrainValidationSplitModel`. Any time we fit a given model, it outputs a "model" type:

```scala
// in Scala
val tvsFitted = tvs.fit(train)
```

```python
# in Python
tvsFitted = tvs.fit(train)
```

And of course evaluate how it performs on the test set!

```scala
evaluator.evaluate(tvsFitted.transform(test)) // 0.9166666666666667
```

We can also see a training summary for some models. To do this we extract it from the pipeline, cast it to the proper type, and print our results. The metrics available on each model are discussed throughout the next several chapters. Here's how we can see the results:

```scala
// in Scala
import org.apache.spark.ml.PipelineModel
import org.apache.spark.ml.classification.LogisticRegressionModel
val trainedPipeline = tvsFitted.bestModel.asInstanceOf[PipelineModel]
val TrainedLR = trainedPipeline.stages(1).asInstanceOf[LogisticRegressionModel]
val summaryLR = TrainedLR.summary
summaryLR.objectiveHistory // 0.6751425885789243, 0.5543659647777687, 0.473776...
```

The objective history shown here provides details related to how our algorithm performed over each training iteration. This can be helpful because we can note the progress our algorithm is making toward the best model. Large jumps are typically expected at the beginning, but over time the values should become smaller and smaller, with only small amounts of variation between the values.

Persisting and Applying Models

Now that we trained this model, we can persist it to disk to use it for prediction purposes later on:

```scala
tvsFitted.write.overwrite().save("/tmp/modelLocation")
```

After writing out the model, we can load it into another Spark program to make predictions. To do this, we need to use a "model" version of our particular algorithm to load our persisted model from disk. If we were to use `CrossValidator`, we'd have to read in the persisted version as the `CrossValidatorModel`, and if we were to use `LogisticRegression` manually we would have to use `LogisticRegressionModel`. In this case, we use `TrainValidationSplit`, which outputs `TrainValidationSplitModel`:

```scala
// in Scala
import org.apache.spark.ml.tuning.TrainValidationSplitModel
val model = TrainValidationSplitModel.load("/tmp/modelLocation")
model.transform(test)
```

Deployment Patterns

In Spark there are several different deployment patterns for putting machine learning models into production. Figure 24-5 illustrates common workflows.

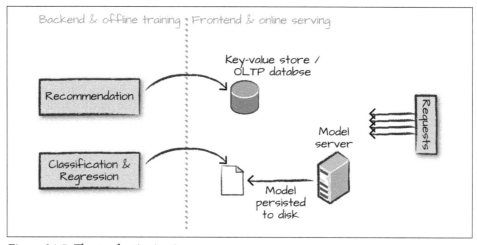

Figure 24-5. The productionization process

Here are the various options for how you might go about deploying a Spark model. These are the general options you should be able to link to the process illustrated in Figure 24-5.

- Train your machine learning (ML) model offline and then supply it with offline data. In this context, we mean offline data to be data that is stored for analysis, and not data that you need to get an answer from quickly. Spark is well suited to this sort of deployment.

- Train your model offline and then put the results into a database (usually a key-value store). This works well for something like recommendation but poorly for something like classification or regression where you cannot just look up a value for a given user but must calculate one based on the input.

- Train your ML algorithm offline, persist the model to disk, and then use that for serving. This is not a low-latency solution if you use Spark for the serving part, as the overhead of starting up a Spark job can be high, even if you're not running on a cluster. Additionally this does not parallelize well, so you'll likely have to put a load balancer in front of multiple model replicas and build out some REST API integration yourself. There are some interesting potential solutions to this problem, but no standards currently exist for this sort of model serving.

- Manually (or via some other software) convert your distributed model to one that can run much more quickly on a single machine. This works well when there is not too much manipulation of the raw data in Spark but can be hard to maintain over time. Again, there are several solutions in progress. For example, MLlib can export some models to PMML, a common model interchange format.

- Train your ML algorithm online and use it online. This is possible when used in conjunction with Structured Streaming, but can be complex for some models.

While these are some of the options, there are many other ways of performing model deployment and management. This is an area under heavy development and many potential innovations are currently being worked on.

Conclusion

In this chapter we covered the core concepts behind advanced analytics and MLlib. We also showed you how to use them. The next chapter will discuss preprocessing in depth, including Spark's tools for feature engineering and data cleaning. Then we'll move into detailed descriptions of each algorithm available in MLlib along with some tools for graph analytics and deep learning.

## CHAPTER 25

Preprocessing and Feature Engineering

Any data scientist worth her salt knows that one of the biggest challenges (and time sinks) in advanced analytics is preprocessing. It's not that it's particularly complicated programming, but rather that it requires deep knowledge of the data you are working with and an understanding of what your model needs in order to successfully leverage this data. This chapter covers the details of how you can use Spark to perform preprocessing and feature engineering. We'll walk through the core requirements you'll need to meet in order to train an MLlib model in terms of how your data is structured. We will then discuss the different tools Spark makes available for performing this kind of work.

Formatting Models According to Your Use Case

To preprocess data for Spark's different advanced analytics tools, you must consider your end objective. The following list walks through the requirements for input data structure for each advanced analytics task in MLlib:

- In the case of most classification and regression algorithms, you want to get your data into a column of type `Double` to represent the label and a column of type `Vector` (either dense or sparse) to represent the features.

- In the case of recommendation, you want to get your data into a column of users, a column of items (say movies or books), and a column of ratings.

- In the case of unsupervised learning, a column of type `Vector` (either dense or sparse) is needed to represent the features.

- In the case of graph analytics, you will want a DataFrame of vertices and a DataFrame of edges.

The best way to get your data in these formats is through transformers. Transformers are functions that accept a DataFrame as an argument and return a new DataFrame as a response. This chapter will focus on what transformers are relevant for particular use cases rather than attempting to enumerate every possible transformer.

 Spark provides a number of transformers as part of the `org.apache.spark.ml.feature` package. The corresponding package in Python is `pyspark.ml.feature`. New transformers are constantly popping up in Spark MLlib and therefore it is impossible to include a definitive list in this book. The most up-to-date information can be found on the Spark documentation site (*http://spark.apache.org/docs/latest/ml-features.html*).

Before we proceed, we're going to read in several different sample datasets, each of which has different properties we will manipulate in this chapter:

```scala
// in Scala
val sales = spark.read.format("csv")
  .option("header", "true")
  .option("inferSchema", "true")
  .load("/data/retail-data/by-day/*.csv")
  .coalesce(5)
  .where("Description IS NOT NULL")
val fakeIntDF = spark.read.parquet("/data/simple-ml-integers")
var simpleDF = spark.read.json("/data/simple-ml")
val scaleDF = spark.read.parquet("/data/simple-ml-scaling")
```

```python
# in Python
sales = spark.read.format("csv")\
  .option("header", "true")\
  .option("inferSchema", "true")\
  .load("/data/retail-data/by-day/*.csv")\
  .coalesce(5)\
  .where("Description IS NOT NULL")
fakeIntDF = spark.read.parquet("/data/simple-ml-integers")
simpleDF = spark.read.json("/data/simple-ml")
scaleDF = spark.read.parquet("/data/simple-ml-scaling")
```

In addition to this realistic sales data, we're going to use several simple synthetic datasets as well. `FakeIntDF`, `simpleDF`, and `scaleDF` all have very few rows. This will give you the ability to focus on the exact data manipulation we are performing instead of the various inconsistencies of any particular dataset. Because we're going to be accessing the sales data a number of times, we're going to cache it so we can read it efficiently from memory as opposed to reading it from disk every time we need it. Let's also check out the first several rows of data in order to better understand what's in the dataset:

```
sales.cache()
sales.show()
```

```
+---------+---------+--------------------+--------+-------------------+--------
|InvoiceNo|StockCode|         Description|Quantity|        InvoiceDate|UnitPr...
+---------+---------+--------------------+--------+-------------------+--------
|   580538|    23084|  RABBIT NIGHT LIGHT|      48|2011-12-05 08:38:00|      1...
...
|   580539|    22375|AIRLINE BAG VINTA...|       4|2011-12-05 08:39:00|      4...
+---------+---------+--------------------+--------+-------------------+--------
```

It is important to note that we filtered out null values here. MLlib does not always play nicely with null values at this point in time. This is a frequent cause for problems and errors and a great first step when you are debugging. Improvements are also made with every Spark release to improve algorithm handling of null values.

Transformers

We discussed transformers in the previous chapter, but it's worth reviewing them again here. Transformers are functions that convert raw data in some way. This might be to create a new interaction variable (from two other variables), to normalize a column, or to simply turn it into a `Double` to be input into a model. Transformers are primarily used in preprocessing or feature generation.

Spark's transformer only includes a transform method. This is because it will not change based on the input data. Figure 25-1 is a simple illustration. On the left is an input DataFrame with the column to be manipulated. On the right is the input Data-Frame with a new column representing the output transformation.

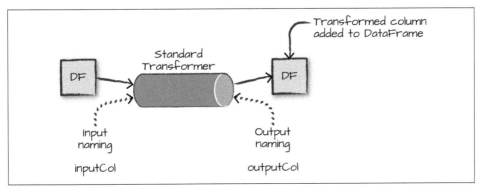

Figure 25-1. A Spark transformer

The `Tokenizer` is an example of a transformer. It tokenizes a string, splitting on a given character, and has nothing to learn from our data; it simply applies a function. We'll discuss the tokenizer in more depth later in this chapter, but here's a small code snippet showing how a tokenizer is built to accept the input column, how it transforms the data, and then the output from that transformation:

```scala
// in Scala
import org.apache.spark.ml.feature.Tokenizer
val tkn = new Tokenizer().setInputCol("Description")
tkn.transform(sales.select("Description")).show(false)
```

```
+-------------------------------------+-------------------------------------------+
|Description                          |tok_7de4dfc81ab7__output                   |
+-------------------------------------+-------------------------------------------+
|RABBIT NIGHT LIGHT                   |[rabbit, night, light]                     |
|DOUGHNUT LIP GLOSS                   |[doughnut, lip, gloss]                     |
...
|AIRLINE BAG VINTAGE WORLD CHAMPION   |[airline, bag, vintage, world, champion]   |
|AIRLINE BAG VINTAGE JET SET BROWN    |[airline, bag, vintage, jet, set, brown]   |
+-------------------------------------+-------------------------------------------+
```

Estimators for Preprocessing

Another tool for preprocessing are estimators. An *estimator* is necessary when a transformation you would like to perform must be initialized with data or information about the input column (often derived by doing a pass over the input column itself). For example, if you wanted to scale the values in our column to have mean zero and unit variance, you would need to perform a pass over the entire data in order to calculate the values you would use to normalize the data to mean zero and unit variance. In effect, an estimator can be a transformer configured according to your particular input data. In simplest terms, you can either blindly apply a transformation (a "regular" transformer type) or perform a transformation based on your data (an estimator type). Figure 25-2 is a simple illustration of an estimator fitting to a particular input dataset, generating a transformer that is then applied to the input dataset to append a new column (of the transformed data).

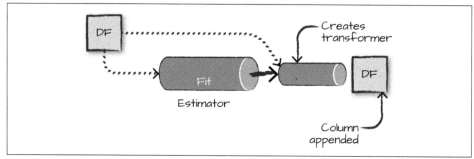

Figure 25-2. A Spark estimator

An example of this type of estimator is the StandardScaler, which scales your input column according to the range of values in that column to have a zero mean and a variance of 1 in each dimension. For that reason it must first perform a pass over the data to create the transformer. Here's a sample code snippet showing the entire process, as well as the output:

```
// in Scala
import org.apache.spark.ml.feature.StandardScaler
val ss = new StandardScaler().setInputCol("features")
ss.fit(scaleDF).transform(scaleDF).show(false)

+---+--------------+-----------------------------------------------------------+
|id |features      |stdScal_d66fbeac10ea__output                               |
+---+--------------+-----------------------------------------------------------+
|0  |[1.0,0.1,-1.0]|[1.1952286093343936,0.02337622911060922,-0.5976143046671968]|
...
|1  |[3.0,10.1,3.0]|[3.5856858280031805,2.3609991401715313,1.7928429140015902] |
+---+--------------+-----------------------------------------------------------+
```

We will use both estimators and transformers throughout and cover more about these particular estimators (and add examples in Python) later on in this chapter.

Transformer Properties

All transformers require you to specify, at a minimum, the `inputCol` and the `output Col`, which represent the column name of the input and output, respectively. You set these with `setInputCol` and `setOutputCol`. There are some defaults (you can find these in the documentation), but it is a best practice to manually specify them yourself for clarity. In addition to input and output columns, all transformers have different parameters that you can tune (whenever we mention a parameter in this chapter you must set it with a `set()` method). In Python, we also have another method to set these values with keyword arguments to the object's constructor. We exclude these from the examples in the next chapter for consistency. Estimators require you to `fit` the transformer to your particular dataset and then call `transform` on the resulting object.

 Spark MLlib stores metadata about the columns it uses in each DataFrame as an attribute on the column itself. This allows it to properly store (and annotate) that a column of `Doubles` may actually represent a series of categorical variables instead of continuous values. However, metadata won't show up when you print the schema or the DataFrame.

High-Level Transformers

High-level transformers, such as the `RFormula` we saw in the previous chapter, allow you to concisely specify a number of transformations in one. These operate at a "high level", and allow you to avoid doing data manipulations or transformations one by one. In general, you should try to use the highest level transformers you can, in order to minimize the risk of error and help you focus on the business problem instead of the smaller details of implementation. While this is not always possible, it's a good objective.

RFormula

The RFormula is the easiest transfomer to use when you have "conventionally" formatted data. Spark borrows this transformer from the R language to make it simple to declaratively specify a set of transformations for your data. With this transformer, values can be either numerical or categorical and you do not need to extract values from strings or manipulate them in any way. The RFormula will automatically handle categorical inputs (specified as strings) by performing something called *one-hot encoding*. In brief, one-hot encoding converts a set of values into a set of binary columns specifying whether or not the data point has each particular value (we'll discuss one-hot encoding in more depth later in the chapter). With the RFormula, numeric columns will be cast to Double but will *not* be one-hot encoded. If the label column is of type String, it will be first transformed to Double with StringIndexer.

> Automatic casting of numeric columns to Double without one-hot encoding has some important implications. If you have numerically valued categorical variables, they will *only* be cast to Double, implicitly specifying an order. It is important to ensure the input types correspond to the expected conversion. If you have categorical variables that really have no order relation, they should be cast to String. You can also manually index columns (see "Working with Categorical Features" on page 441).

The RFormula allows you to specify your transformations in declarative syntax. It is simple to use once you understand the syntax. Currently, RFormula supports a limited subset of the R operators that in practice work quite well for simple transformations. The basic operators are:

~

Separate target and terms

+

Concatenate terms; "+ 0" means removing the intercept (this means the y-intercept of the line that we will fit will be 0)

-

Remove a term; "- 1" means removing intercept (this means the y-intercept of the line that we will fit will be 0)

:

Interaction (multiplication for numeric values, or binarized categorical values)

.

All columns except the target/dependent variable

RFormula also uses default columns of label and features to label, you guessed it, the label and the set of features that it outputs (for supervised machine learning). The models covered later on in this chapter by default require those column names, making it easy to pass the resulting transformed DataFrame into a model for training. If this doesn't make sense yet, don't worry—it'll become clear once we actually start using models in later chapters.

Let's use RFormula in an example. In this case, we want to use all available variables (the .) and then specify an interaction between value1 and color and value2 and color as additional features to generate:

```scala
// in Scala
import org.apache.spark.ml.feature.RFormula
val supervised = new RFormula()
  .setFormula("lab ~ . + color:value1 + color:value2")
supervised.fit(simpleDF).transform(simpleDF).show()
```

```python
# in Python
from pyspark.ml.feature import RFormula

supervised = RFormula(formula="lab ~ . + color:value1 + color:value2")
supervised.fit(simpleDF).transform(simpleDF).show()
```

```
+-----+----+------+------------------+--------------------+-----+
|color| lab|value1|            value2|            features|label|
+-----+----+------+------------------+--------------------+-----+
|green|good|     1|14.386294994851129|(10,[1,2,3,5,8],[...|  1.0|
| blue| bad|     8|14.386294994851129|(10,[2,3,6,9],[8....|  0.0|
...
|  red| bad|     1| 38.97187133755819|(10,[0,2,3,4,7],[...|  0.0|
|  red| bad|     2|14.386294994851129|(10,[0,2,3,4,7],[...|  0.0|
+-----+----+------+------------------+--------------------+-----+
```

SQL Transformers

A SQLTransformer allows you to leverage Spark's vast library of SQL-related manipulations just as you would a MLlib transformation. Any SELECT statement you can use in SQL is a valid transformation. The only thing you need to change is that instead of using the table name, you should just use the keyword *THIS*. You might want to use SQLTransformer if you want to formally codify some DataFrame manipulation as a preprocessing step, or try different SQL expressions for features during hyperparameter tuning. Also note that the output of this transformation will be appended as a column to the output DataFrame.

You might want to use an SQLTransformer in order to represent all of your manipulations on the very rawest form of your data so you can version different variations of manipulations as transformers. This gives you the benefit of building and testing varying pipelines, all by simply swapping out transformers. The following is a basic example of using `SQLTransformer`:

```scala
// in Scala
import org.apache.spark.ml.feature.SQLTransformer

val basicTransformation = new SQLTransformer()
  .setStatement("""
    SELECT sum(Quantity), count(*), CustomerID
    FROM __THIS__
    GROUP BY CustomerID
    """)

basicTransformation.transform(sales).show()
```

```python
# in Python
from pyspark.ml.feature import SQLTransformer

basicTransformation = SQLTransformer()\
  .setStatement("""
    SELECT sum(Quantity), count(*), CustomerID
    FROM __THIS__
    GROUP BY CustomerID
    """)

basicTransformation.transform(sales).show()
```

Here's a sample of the output:

```
-------------+--------+----------+
|sum(Quantity)|count(1)|CustomerID|
+-------------+--------+----------+
|          119|      62|   14452.0|
...
|          138|      18|   15776.0|
+-------------+--------+----------+
```

For extensive samples of these transformations, refer back to Part II.

VectorAssembler

The VectorAssembler is a tool you'll use in nearly every single pipeline you generate. It helps concatenate all your features into one big vector you can then pass into an estimator. It's used typically in the last step of a machine learning pipeline and takes as input a number of columns of `Boolean`, `Double`, or `Vector`. This is particularly helpful if you're going to perform a number of manipulations using a variety of transformers and need to gather all of those results together.

The output from the following code snippet will make it clear how this works:

```scala
// in Scala
import org.apache.spark.ml.feature.VectorAssembler
```

```
val va = new VectorAssembler().setInputCols(Array("int1", "int2", "int3"))
va.transform(fakeIntDF).show()

# in Python
from pyspark.ml.feature import VectorAssembler
va = VectorAssembler().setInputCols(["int1", "int2", "int3"])
va.transform(fakeIntDF).show()

+----+----+----+-------------------------------------------+
|int1|int2|int3|VectorAssembler_403ab93eacd5585ddd2d__output|
+----+----+----+-------------------------------------------+
|   1|   2|   3|                              [1.0,2.0,3.0]|
|   4|   5|   6|                              [4.0,5.0,6.0]|
|   7|   8|   9|                              [7.0,8.0,9.0]|
+----+----+----+-------------------------------------------+
```

Working with Continuous Features

Continuous features are just values on the number line, from positive infinity to negative infinity. There are two common transformers for continuous features. First, you can convert continuous features into categorical features via a process called bucketing, or you can scale and normalize your features according to several different requirements. These transformers will *only* work on Double types, so make sure you've turned any other numerical values to Double:

```
// in Scala
val contDF = spark.range(20).selectExpr("cast(id as double)")

# in Python
contDF = spark.range(20).selectExpr("cast(id as double)")
```

Bucketing

The most straightforward approach to bucketing or binning is using the Bucketizer. This will split a given continuous feature into the buckets of your designation. You specify how buckets should be created via an array or list of Double values. This is useful because you may want to simplify the features in your dataset or simplify their representations for interpretation later on. For example, imagine you have a column that represents a person's weight and you would like to predict some value based on this information. In some cases, it might be simpler to create three buckets of "overweight," "average," and "underweight."

To specify the bucket, set its borders. For example, setting splits to 5.0, 10.0, 250.0 on our contDF will actually fail because we don't cover all possible input ranges. When specifying your bucket points, the values you pass into splits must satisfy three requirements:

- The minimum value in your splits array must be less than the minimum value in your DataFrame.

- The maximum value in your splits array must be greater than the maximum value in your DataFrame.

- You need to specify at a minimum three values in the splits array, which creates two buckets.

 The Bucketizer can be confusing because we specify bucket borders via the splits method, but these are not actually splits.

To cover all possible ranges, scala.Double.NegativeInfinity might be another split option, with scala.Double.PositiveInfinity to cover all possible ranges outside of the inner splits. In Python we specify this in the following way: float("inf"), float("-inf").

In order to handle null or NaN values, we must specify the handleInvalid parameter as a certain value. We can either keep those values (keep), error or null, or skip those rows. Here's an example of using bucketing:

```scala
// in Scala
import org.apache.spark.ml.feature.Bucketizer
val bucketBorders = Array(-1.0, 5.0, 10.0, 250.0, 600.0)
val bucketer = new Bucketizer().setSplits(bucketBorders).setInputCol("id")
bucketer.transform(contDF).show()
```

```python
# in Python
from pyspark.ml.feature import Bucketizer
bucketBorders = [-1.0, 5.0, 10.0, 250.0, 600.0]
bucketer = Bucketizer().setSplits(bucketBorders).setInputCol("id")
bucketer.transform(contDF).show()
```

```
+----+---------------------------------------+
|  id|Bucketizer_4cb1be19f4179cc2545d__output|
+----+---------------------------------------+
| 0.0|                                    0.0|
...
|10.0|                                    2.0|
|11.0|                                    2.0|
...
+----+---------------------------------------+
```

In addition to splitting based on hardcoded values, another option is to split based on percentiles in our data. This is done with QuantileDiscretizer, which will bucket the values into user-specified buckets with the splits being determined by approximate quantiles values. For instance, the 90th quantile is the point in your data at which 90% of the data is below that value. You can control how finely the buckets should be split by setting the relative error for the approximate quantiles calculation using `setRelativeError`. Spark does this is by allowing you to specify the number of buckets you would like out of the data and it will split up your data accordingly. The following is an example:

```scala
// in Scala
import org.apache.spark.ml.feature.QuantileDiscretizer
val bucketer = new QuantileDiscretizer().setNumBuckets(5).setInputCol("id")
val fittedBucketer = bucketer.fit(contDF)
fittedBucketer.transform(contDF).show()
```

```python
# in Python
from pyspark.ml.feature import QuantileDiscretizer
bucketer = QuantileDiscretizer().setNumBuckets(5).setInputCol("id")
fittedBucketer = bucketer.fit(contDF)
fittedBucketer.transform(contDF).show()
```

```
+----+----------------------------------------+
|  id|quantileDiscretizer_cd87d1a1fb8e__output|
+----+----------------------------------------+
| 0.0|                                     0.0|
...
| 6.0|                                     1.0|
| 7.0|                                     2.0|
...
|14.0|                                     3.0|
|15.0|                                     4.0|
...
+----+----------------------------------------+
```

Advanced bucketing techniques

The techniques descriubed here are the most common ways of bucketing data, but there are a number of other ways that exist in Spark today. All of these processes are the same from a data flow perspective: start with continuous data and place them in buckets so that they become categorical. Differences arise depending on the algorithm used to compute these buckets. The simple examples we just looked at are easy to intepret and work with, but more advanced techniques such as locality sensitivity hashing (LSH) are also available in MLlib.

Scaling and Normalization

We saw how we can use bucketing to create groups out of continuous variables. Another common task is to scale and normalize continuous data. While not always necessary, doing so is usually a best practice. You might want to do this when your data contains a number of columns based on different scales. For instance, say we have a DataFrame with two columns: weight (in ounces) and height (in feet). If you don't scale or normalize, the algorithm will be less sensitive to variations in height because height values in feet are much lower than weight values in ounces. That's an example where you should scale your data.

An example of normalization might involve transforming the data so that each point's value is a representation of its distance from the mean of that column. Using the same example from before, we might want to know how far a given individual's height is from the mean height. Many algorithms assume that their input data is normalized.

As you might imagine, there are a multitude of algorithms we can apply to our data to scale or normalize it. Enumerating them all is unnecessary here because they are covered in many other texts and machine learning libraries. If you're unfamiliar with the concept in detail, check out any of the books referenced in the previous chapter. Just keep in mind the fundamental goal—we want our data on the same scale so that values can easily be compared to one another in a sensible way. In MLlib, this is always done on columns of type `Vector`. MLlib will look across all the rows in a given column (of type `Vector`) and then treat every dimension in those vectors as its own particular column. It will then apply the scaling or normalization function on each dimension separately.

A simple example might be the following vectors in a column:

```
1,2
3,4
```

When we apply our scaling (but not normalization) function, the "3" and the "1" will be adjusted according to those two values while the "2" and the "4" will be adjusted according to one another. This is commonly referred to as component-wise comparisons.

StandardScaler

The `StandardScaler` standardizes a set of features to have zero mean and a standard deviation of 1. The flag `withStd` will scale the data to unit standard deviation while the flag `withMean` (false by default) will center the data prior to scaling it.

> Centering can be very expensive on sparse vectors because it generally turns them into dense vectors, so be careful before centering your data.

Here's an example of using a `StandardScaler`:

```scala
// in Scala
import org.apache.spark.ml.feature.StandardScaler
```

```scala
val sScaler = new StandardScaler().setInputCol("features")
sScaler.fit(scaleDF).transform(scaleDF).show()
```

```python
# in Python
from pyspark.ml.feature import StandardScaler
sScaler = StandardScaler().setInputCol("features")
sScaler.fit(scaleDF).transform(scaleDF).show()
```

The output is shown below:

```
+---+-------------+-------------------------------------------------------------+
|id |features     |StandardScaler_41aaa6044e7c3467adc3__output                  |
+---+-------------+-------------------------------------------------------------+
|0  |[1.0,0.1,-1.0]|[1.1952286093343936,0.02337622911060922,-0.5976143046671968]|
...
|1  |[3.0,10.1,3.0]|[3.5856858280031805,2.3609991401715313,1.7928429140015902]  |
+---+-------------+-------------------------------------------------------------+
```

MinMaxScaler

The `MinMaxScaler` will scale the values in a vector (component wise) to the proportional values on a scale from a given min value to a max value. If you specify the minimum value to be 0 and the maximum value to be 1, then all the values will fall in between 0 and 1:

```scala
// in Scala
import org.apache.spark.ml.feature.MinMaxScaler
val minMax = new MinMaxScaler().setMin(5).setMax(10).setInputCol("features")
val fittedminMax = minMax.fit(scaleDF)
fittedminMax.transform(scaleDF).show()
```

```python
# in Python
from pyspark.ml.feature import MinMaxScaler
minMax = MinMaxScaler().setMin(5).setMax(10).setInputCol("features")
fittedminMax = minMax.fit(scaleDF)
fittedminMax.transform(scaleDF).show()
```

```
+---+-------------+------------------------------------------+
| id|     features|MinMaxScaler_460cbafafbe6b9ab7c62__output|
+---+-------------+------------------------------------------+
|  0|[1.0,0.1,-1.0]|                           [5.0,5.0,5.0]|
...
|  1|[3.0,10.1,3.0]|                        [10.0,10.0,10.0]|
+---+-------------+------------------------------------------+
```

MaxAbsScaler

The max absolute scaler (`MaxAbsScaler`) scales the data by dividing each value by the maximum absolute value in this feature. All values therefore end up between −1 and 1. This transformer does not shift or center the data at all in the process:

```scala
// in Scala
import org.apache.spark.ml.feature.MaxAbsScaler
```

```scala
val maScaler = new MaxAbsScaler().setInputCol("features")
val fittedmaScaler = maScaler.fit(scaleDF)
fittedmaScaler.transform(scaleDF).show()
```

```python
# in Python
from pyspark.ml.feature import MaxAbsScaler
maScaler = MaxAbsScaler().setInputCol("features")
fittedmaScaler = maScaler.fit(scaleDF)
fittedmaScaler.transform(scaleDF).show()
```

```
+---+-------------+-----------------------------------------------------------+
|id |features     |MaxAbsScaler_402587e1d9b6f268b927__output                  |
+---+-------------+-----------------------------------------------------------+
|0  |[1.0,0.1,-1.0]|[0.3333333333333333,0.009900990099009901,-0.3333333333333]|
...
|1  |[3.0,10.1,3.0]|[1.0,1.0,1.0]                                             |
+---+-------------+-----------------------------------------------------------+
```

ElementwiseProduct

The `ElementwiseProduct` allows us to scale each value in a vector by an arbitrary value. For example, given the vector below and the row "1, 0.1, -1" the output will be "10, 1.5, -20." Naturally the dimensions of the scaling vector must match the dimensions of the vector inside the relevant column:

```scala
// in Scala
import org.apache.spark.ml.feature.ElementwiseProduct
import org.apache.spark.ml.linalg.Vectors
val scaleUpVec = Vectors.dense(10.0, 15.0, 20.0)
val scalingUp = new ElementwiseProduct()
  .setScalingVec(scaleUpVec)
  .setInputCol("features")
scalingUp.transform(scaleDF).show()
```

```python
# in Python
from pyspark.ml.feature import ElementwiseProduct
from pyspark.ml.linalg import Vectors
scaleUpVec = Vectors.dense(10.0, 15.0, 20.0)
scalingUp = ElementwiseProduct()\
  .setScalingVec(scaleUpVec)\
  .setInputCol("features")
scalingUp.transform(scaleDF).show()
```

```
+---+-------------+-------------------------------------------------+
| id|      features|ElementwiseProduct_42b29ea5a55903e9fea6__output|
+---+-------------+-------------------------------------------------+
|  0|[1.0,0.1,-1.0]|                              [10.0,1.5,-20.0]|
...
|  1|[3.0,10.1,3.0]|                              [30.0,151.5,60.0]|
+---+-------------+-------------------------------------------------+
```

Normalizer

The normalizer allows us to scale multidimensional vectors using one of several power norms, set through the parameter "p". For example, we can use the Manhattan norm (or Manhattan distance) with p = 1, Euclidean norm with p = 2, and so on. The Manhattan distance is a measure of distance where you can only travel from point to point along the straight lines of an axis (like the streets in Manhattan).

Here's an example of using the `Normalizer`:

```scala
// in Scala
import org.apache.spark.ml.feature.Normalizer
val manhattanDistance = new Normalizer().setP(1).setInputCol("features")
manhattanDistance.transform(scaleDF).show()
```

```python
# in Python
from pyspark.ml.feature import Normalizer
manhattanDistance = Normalizer().setP(1).setInputCol("features")
manhattanDistance.transform(scaleDF).show()
```

```
+---+--------------+-----------------------------+
| id|      features|normalizer_1bf2cd17ed33__output|
+---+--------------+-----------------------------+
|  0|[1.0,0.1,-1.0]|         [0.47619047619047...|
|  1| [2.0,1.1,1.0]|         [0.48780487804878...|
|  0|[1.0,0.1,-1.0]|         [0.47619047619047...|
|  1| [2.0,1.1,1.0]|         [0.48780487804878...|
|  1|[3.0,10.1,3.0]|         [0.18633540372670...|
+---+--------------+-----------------------------+
```

Working with Categorical Features

The most common task for categorical features is indexing. Indexing converts a categorical variable in a column to a numerical one that you can plug into machine learning algorithms. While this is conceptually simple, there are some catches that are important to keep in mind so that Spark can do this in a stable and repeatable manner.

In general, we recommend re-indexing every categorical variable when preprocessing just for consistency's sake. This can be helpful in maintaining your models over the long run as your encoding practices may change over time.

StringIndexer

The simplest way to index is via the `StringIndexer`, which maps strings to different numerical IDs. Spark's `StringIndexer` also creates metadata attached to the DataFrame that specify what inputs correspond to what outputs. This allows us later to get inputs back from their respective index values:

```scala
// in Scala
import org.apache.spark.ml.feature.StringIndexer
val lblIndxr = new StringIndexer().setInputCol("lab").setOutputCol("labelInd")
val idxRes = lblIndxr.fit(simpleDF).transform(simpleDF)
idxRes.show()
```

```python
# in Python
from pyspark.ml.feature import StringIndexer
lblIndxr = StringIndexer().setInputCol("lab").setOutputCol("labelInd")
idxRes = lblIndxr.fit(simpleDF).transform(simpleDF)
idxRes.show()
```

```
+-----+----+------+------------------+--------+
|color| lab|value1|            value2|labelInd|
+-----+----+------+------------------+--------+
|green|good|     1|14.386294994851129|     1.0|
...
|  red| bad|     2|14.386294994851129|     0.0|
+-----+----+------+------------------+--------+
```

We can also apply `StringIndexer` to columns that are not strings, in which case, they will be converted to strings before being indexed:

```scala
// in Scala
val valIndexer = new StringIndexer()
  .setInputCol("value1")
  .setOutputCol("valueInd")

valIndexer.fit(simpleDF).transform(simpleDF).show()
```

```python
# in Python
valIndexer = StringIndexer().setInputCol("value1").setOutputCol("valueInd")
valIndexer.fit(simpleDF).transform(simpleDF).show()
```

```
+-----+----+------+------------------+--------+
|color| lab|value1|            value2|valueInd|
+-----+----+------+------------------+--------+
|green|good|     1|14.386294994851129|     1.0|
...
|  red| bad|     2|14.386294994851129|     0.0|
+-----+----+------+------------------+--------+
```

Keep in mind that the `StringIndexer` is an estimator that must be fit on the input data. This means it must see all inputs to select a mapping of inputs to IDs. If you train a `StringIndexer` on inputs "a," "b," and "c" and then go to use it against input "d," it will throw an error by default. Another option is to skip the entire row if the input value was not a value seen during training. Going along with the previous example, an input value of "d" would cause that row to be skipped entirely. We can set this option before or after training the indexer or pipeline. More options may be added to this feature in the future but as of Spark 2.2, you can only skip or throw an error on invalid inputs.

```
valIndexer.setHandleInvalid("skip")
valIndexer.fit(simpleDF).setHandleInvalid("skip")
```

Converting Indexed Values Back to Text

When inspecting your machine learning results, you're likely going to want to map back to the original values. Since MLlib classification models make predictions using the indexed values, this conversion is useful for converting model predictions (indices) back to the original categories. We can do this with `IndexToString`. You'll notice that we do not have to input our value to the `String` key; Spark's MLlib maintains this metadata for you. You can optionally specify the outputs.

```scala
// in Scala
import org.apache.spark.ml.feature.IndexToString
val labelReverse = new IndexToString().setInputCol("labelInd")
labelReverse.transform(idxRes).show()
```

```python
# in Python
from pyspark.ml.feature import IndexToString
labelReverse = IndexToString().setInputCol("labelInd")
labelReverse.transform(idxRes).show()
```

```
+-----+----+------+------------------+--------+--------------------------------+
|color| lab|value1|            value2|labelInd|IndexToString_415...2a0d__output|
+-----+----+------+------------------+--------+--------------------------------+
|green|good|     1|14.386294994851129|     1.0|                            good|
...
|  red| bad|     2|14.386294994851129|     0.0|                             bad|
+-----+----+------+------------------+--------+--------------------------------+
```

Indexing in Vectors

`VectorIndexer` is a helpful tool for working with categorical variables that are already found inside of vectors in your dataset. This tool will automatically find categorical features inside of your input vectors and convert them to categorical features with zero-based category indices. For example, in the following DataFrame, the first column in our `Vector` is a categorical variable with two different categories while the rest of the variables are continuous. By setting `maxCategories` to 2 in our `VectorIndexer`, we are instructing Spark to take any column in our vector with two or less distinct values and convert it to a categorical variable. This can be helpful when you know how many unique values there are in your largest category because you can specify this and it will automatically index the values accordingly. Conversely, Spark changes the data based on this parameter, so if you have continuous variables that don't appear particularly continuous (lots of repeated values) these can be unintentionally converted to categorical variables if there are too few unique values.

```scala
// in Scala
import org.apache.spark.ml.feature.VectorIndexer
import org.apache.spark.ml.linalg.Vectors
```

```scala
val idxIn = spark.createDataFrame(Seq(
  (Vectors.dense(1, 2, 3),1),
  (Vectors.dense(2, 5, 6),2),
  (Vectors.dense(1, 8, 9),3)
)).toDF("features", "label")
val indxr = new VectorIndexer()
  .setInputCol("features")
  .setOutputCol("idxed")
  .setMaxCategories(2)
indxr.fit(idxIn).transform(idxIn).show
```

```python
# in Python
from pyspark.ml.feature import VectorIndexer
from pyspark.ml.linalg import Vectors
idxIn = spark.createDataFrame([
  (Vectors.dense(1, 2, 3),1),
  (Vectors.dense(2, 5, 6),2),
  (Vectors.dense(1, 8, 9),3)
]).toDF("features", "label")
indxr = VectorIndexer()\
  .setInputCol("features")\
  .setOutputCol("idxed")\
  .setMaxCategories(2)
indxr.fit(idxIn).transform(idxIn).show()
```

```
+-------------+-----+-------------+
|     features|label|        idxed|
+-------------+-----+-------------+
|[1.0,2.0,3.0]|    1|[0.0,2.0,3.0]|
|[2.0,5.0,6.0]|    2|[1.0,5.0,6.0]|
|[1.0,8.0,9.0]|    3|[0.0,8.0,9.0]|
+-------------+-----+-------------+
```

One-Hot Encoding

Indexing categorical variables is only half of the story. One-hot encoding is an extremely common data transformation performed after indexing categorical variables. This is because indexing does not always represent our categorical variables in the correct way for downstream models to process. For instance, when we index our "color" column, you will notice that some colors have a higher value (or index number) than others (in our case, blue is 1 and green is 2).

This is incorrect because it gives the mathematical appearance that the input to the machine learning algorithm seems to specify that green > blue, which makes no sense in the case of the current categories. To avoid this, we use OneHotEncoder, which will convert each distinct value to a Boolean flag (1 or 0) as a component in a vector. When we encode the color value, then we can see these are no longer ordered, making them easier for downstream models (e.g., a linear model) to process:

```scala
// in Scala
import org.apache.spark.ml.feature.{StringIndexer, OneHotEncoder}
```

```scala
val lblIndxr = new StringIndexer().setInputCol("color").setOutputCol("colorInd")
val colorLab = lblIndxr.fit(simpleDF).transform(simpleDF.select("color"))
val ohe = new OneHotEncoder().setInputCol("colorInd")
ohe.transform(colorLab).show()
```

```python
# in Python
from pyspark.ml.feature import OneHotEncoder, StringIndexer
lblIndxr = StringIndexer().setInputCol("color").setOutputCol("colorInd")
colorLab = lblIndxr.fit(simpleDF).transform(simpleDF.select("color"))
ohe = OneHotEncoder().setInputCol("colorInd")
ohe.transform(colorLab).show()
```

```
+-----+--------+--------------------------------------------+
|color|colorInd|OneHotEncoder_46b5ad1ef147bb355612__output|
+-----+--------+--------------------------------------------+
|green|     1.0|                             (2,[1],[1.0])|
| blue|     2.0|                                (2,[],[])|
...
|  red|     0.0|                             (2,[0],[1.0])|
|  red|     0.0|                             (2,[0],[1.0])|
+-----+--------+--------------------------------------------+
```

Text Data Transformers

Text is always tricky input because it often requires lots of manipulation to map to a format that a machine learning model will be able to use effectively. There are generally two kinds of texts you'll see: free-form text and string categorical variables. This section primarily focuses on free-form text because we already discussed categorical variables.

Tokenizing Text

Tokenization is the process of converting free-form text into a list of "tokens" or individual words. The easiest way to do this is by using the `Tokenizer` class. This transformer will take a string of words, separated by whitespace, and convert them into an array of words. For example, in our dataset we might want to convert the Description field into a list of tokens.

```scala
// in Scala
import org.apache.spark.ml.feature.Tokenizer
val tkn = new Tokenizer().setInputCol("Description").setOutputCol("DescOut")
val tokenized = tkn.transform(sales.select("Description"))
tokenized.show(false)
```

```python
# in Python
from pyspark.ml.feature import Tokenizer
tkn = Tokenizer().setInputCol("Description").setOutputCol("DescOut")
tokenized = tkn.transform(sales.select("Description"))
tokenized.show(20, False)
```

```
+--------------------------------+-----------------------------------------------+
|Description                     | DescOut                                       |
+--------------------------------+-----------------------------------------------+
|RABBIT NIGHT LIGHT              |[rabbit, night, light]                         |
|DOUGHNUT LIP GLOSS              |[doughnut, lip, gloss]                         |
...
|AIRLINE BAG VINTAGE WORLD CHAMPION |[airline, bag, vintage, world, champion]    |
|AIRLINE BAG VINTAGE JET SET BROWN  |[airline, bag, vintage, jet, set, brown]    |
+--------------------------------+-----------------------------------------------+
```

We can also create a `Tokenizer` that is not just based white space but a regular expression with the `RegexTokenizer`. The format of the regular expression should conform to the Java Regular Expression (RegEx) syntax:

```scala
// in Scala
import org.apache.spark.ml.feature.RegexTokenizer
val rt = new RegexTokenizer()
  .setInputCol("Description")
  .setOutputCol("DescOut")
  .setPattern(" ") // simplest expression
  .setToLowercase(true)
rt.transform(sales.select("Description")).show(false)
```

```python
# in Python
from pyspark.ml.feature import RegexTokenizer
rt = RegexTokenizer()\
  .setInputCol("Description")\
  .setOutputCol("DescOut")\
  .setPattern(" ")\
  .setToLowercase(True)
rt.transform(sales.select("Description")).show(20, False)
```

```
+--------------------------------+-----------------------------------------------+
|Description                     | DescOut                                       |
+--------------------------------+-----------------------------------------------+
|RABBIT NIGHT LIGHT              |[rabbit, night, light]                         |
|DOUGHNUT LIP GLOSS              |[doughnut, lip, gloss]                         |
...
|AIRLINE BAG VINTAGE WORLD CHAMPION |[airline, bag, vintage, world, champion]    |
|AIRLINE BAG VINTAGE JET SET BROWN  |[airline, bag, vintage, jet, set, brown]    |
+--------------------------------+-----------------------------------------------+
```

Another way of using the `RegexTokenizer` is to use it to output values matching the provided pattern instead of using it as a gap. We do this by setting the `gaps` parameter to false. Doing this with a space as a pattern returns all the spaces, which is not too useful, but if we made our pattern capture individual words, we could return those:

```scala
// in Scala
import org.apache.spark.ml.feature.RegexTokenizer
val rt = new RegexTokenizer()
  .setInputCol("Description")
  .setOutputCol("DescOut")
  .setPattern(" ")
```

```
  .setGaps(false)
  .setToLowercase(true)
rt.transform(sales.select("Description")).show(false)

# in Python
from pyspark.ml.feature import RegexTokenizer
rt = RegexTokenizer()\
  .setInputCol("Description")\
  .setOutputCol("DescOut")\
  .setPattern(" ")\
  .setGaps(False)\
  .setToLowercase(True)
rt.transform(sales.select("Description")).show(20, False)

+-----------------------------------+------------------+
|Description                        |DescOut           |
+-----------------------------------+------------------+
|RABBIT NIGHT LIGHT                 |[ , ]             |
|DOUGHNUT LIP GLOSS                 |[ , , ]           |
...
|AIRLINE BAG VINTAGE WORLD CHAMPION |[ , , , , ]       |
|AIRLINE BAG VINTAGE JET SET BROWN  |[ , , , , ]       |
+-----------------------------------+------------------+
```

Removing Common Words

A common task after tokenization is to filter *stop words*, common words that are not relevant in many kinds of analysis and should thus be removed. Frequently occurring stop words in English include "the," "and," and "but." Spark contains a list of default stop words you can see by calling the following method, which can be made case insensitive if necessary (as of Spark 2.2, supported languages for stopwords are "danish," "dutch," "english," "finnish," "french," "german," "hungarian," "italian," "norwegian," "portuguese," "russian," "spanish," "swedish," and "turkish"):

```
// in Scala
import org.apache.spark.ml.feature.StopWordsRemover
val englishStopWords = StopWordsRemover.loadDefaultStopWords("english")
val stops = new StopWordsRemover()
  .setStopWords(englishStopWords)
  .setInputCol("DescOut")
stops.transform(tokenized).show()

# in Python
from pyspark.ml.feature import StopWordsRemover
englishStopWords = StopWordsRemover.loadDefaultStopWords("english")
stops = StopWordsRemover()\
  .setStopWords(englishStopWords)\
  .setInputCol("DescOut")
stops.transform(tokenized).show()
```

The following output shows how this works:

```
+--------------------+--------------------+------------------------------------+
|         Description|             DescOut|StopWordsRemover_4ab18...6ed__output|
+--------------------+--------------------+------------------------------------+
...
|SET OF 4 KNICK KN...|[set, of, 4, knic...|                  [set, 4, knick, k...|
...
+--------------------+--------------------+------------------------------------+
```

Notice how the word of is removed in the output column. That's because it's such a common word that it isn't relevant to any downstream manipulation and simply adds noise to our dataset.

Creating Word Combinations

Tokenizing our strings and filtering stop words leaves us with a clean set of words to use as features. It is often of interest to look at combinations of words, usually by looking at colocated words. Word combinations are technically referred to as *n-grams* —that is, sequences of words of length n. An n-gram of length 1 is called a *unigrams*; those of length 2 are called *bigrams*, and those of length 3 are called *trigrams* (anything above those are just four-gram, five-gram, etc.), Order matters with n-gram creation, so converting a sentence with three words into bigram representation would result in two bigrams. The goal when creating n-grams is to better capture sentence structure and more information than can be gleaned by simply looking at all words individually. Let's create some n-grams to illustrate this concept.

The bigrams of "Big Data Processing Made Simple" are:

- "Big Data"
- "Data Processing"
- "Processing Made"
- "Made Simple"

While the trigrams are:

- "Big Data Processing"
- "Data Processing Made"
- "Procesing Made Simple"

With n-grams, we can look at sequences of words that commonly co-occur and use them as inputs to a machine learning algorithm. These can create better features than simply looking at all of the words individually (say, tokenized on a space character):

```scala
// in Scala
import org.apache.spark.ml.feature.NGram
val unigram = new NGram().setInputCol("DescOut").setN(1)
val bigram = new NGram().setInputCol("DescOut").setN(2)
```

```
unigram.transform(tokenized.select("DescOut")).show(false)
bigram.transform(tokenized.select("DescOut")).show(false)

# in Python
from pyspark.ml.feature import NGram
unigram = NGram().setInputCol("DescOut").setN(1)
bigram = NGram().setInputCol("DescOut").setN(2)
unigram.transform(tokenized.select("DescOut")).show(False)
bigram.transform(tokenized.select("DescOut")).show(False)


+------------------------------------------+------------------------------------
DescOut                                    |ngram_104c4da6a01b__output      ...
+------------------------------------------+------------------------------------
|[rabbit, night, light]                    |[rabbit, night, light]          ...
|[doughnut, lip, gloss]                    |[doughnut, lip, gloss]          ...
...
|[airline, bag, vintage, world, champion]  |[airline, bag, vintage, world, cha...
|[airline, bag, vintage, jet, set, brown]  |[airline, bag, vintage, jet, set, ...
+------------------------------------------+------------------------------------
```

And the result for bigrams:

```
+------------------------------------------+------------------------------------
DescOut                                    |ngram_6e68fb3a642a__output      ...
+------------------------------------------+------------------------------------
|[rabbit, night, light]                    |[rabbit night, night light]     ...
|[doughnut, lip, gloss]                    |[doughnut lip, lip gloss]       ...
...
|[airline, bag, vintage, world, champion]  |[airline bag, bag vintage, vintag...
|[airline, bag, vintage, jet, set, brown]  |[airline bag, bag vintage, vintag...
+------------------------------------------+------------------------------------
```

Converting Words into Numerical Representations

Once you have word features, it's time to start counting instances of words and word combinations for use in our models. The simplest way is just to include binary counts of a word in a given document (in our case, a row). Essentially, we're measuring whether or not each row contains a given word. This is a simple way to normalize for document sizes and occurrence counts and get numerical features that allow us to classify documents based on content. In addition, we can count words using a Count Vectorizer, or reweigh them according to the prevalence of a given word in all the documents using a TF–IDF transformation (discussed next).

A CountVectorizer operates on our tokenized data and does two things:

1. During the fit process, it finds the set of words in all the documents and then counts the occurrences of those words in those documents.

2. It then counts the occurrences of a given word in each row of the DataFrame column during the transformation process and outputs a vector with the terms that occur in that row.

Conceptually this tranformer treats every row as a *document* and every word as a *term* and the total collection of all terms as the *vocabulary*. These are all tunable parameters, meaning we can set the minimum term frequency (minTF) for the term to be included in the vocabulary (effectively removing rare words from the vocabulary); minimum number of documents a term must appear in (minDF) before being included in the vocabulary (another way to remove rare words from the vocabulary); and finally, the total maximum vocabulary size (vocabSize). Lastly, by default the CountVectorizer will output the counts of a term in a document. To just return whether or not a word exists in a document, we can use setBinary(true). Here's an example of using CountVectorizer:

```scala
// in Scala
import org.apache.spark.ml.feature.CountVectorizer
val cv = new CountVectorizer()
  .setInputCol("DescOut")
  .setOutputCol("countVec")
  .setVocabSize(500)
  .setMinTF(1)
  .setMinDF(2)
val fittedCV = cv.fit(tokenized)
fittedCV.transform(tokenized).show(false)
```

```python
# in Python
from pyspark.ml.feature import CountVectorizer
cv = CountVectorizer()\
  .setInputCol("DescOut")\
  .setOutputCol("countVec")\
  .setVocabSize(500)\
  .setMinTF(1)\
  .setMinDF(2)
fittedCV = cv.fit(tokenized)
fittedCV.transform(tokenized).show(False)
```

While the output looks a little complicated, it's actually just a sparse vector that contains the total vocabulary size, the index of the word in the vocabulary, and then the counts of that particular word:

```
+---------------------------------+------------------------------------------------+
DescOut                           |countVec                                        |
+---------------------------------+------------------------------------------------+
|[rabbit, night, light]           |(500,[150,185,212],[1.0,1.0,1.0])               |
|[doughnut, lip, gloss]           |(500,[462,463,492],[1.0,1.0,1.0])               |
...
|[airline, bag, vintage, world,...|(500,[2,6,328],[1.0,1.0,1.0])                   |
|[airline, bag, vintage, jet, s...|(500,[0,2,6,328,405],[1.0,1.0,1.0,1.0,1.0])     |
+---------------------------------+------------------------------------------------+
```

Term frequency–inverse document frequency

Another way to approach the problem of converting text into a numerical representation is to use term frequency–inverse document frequency (TF–IDF). In simplest terms, *TF–IDF* measures how often a word occurs in each document, weighted according to how many documents that word occurs in. The result is that words that occur in a few documents are given more weight than words that occur in many documents. In practice, a word like "the" would be weighted very low because of its prevalence while a more specialized word like "streaming" would occur in fewer documents and thus would be weighted higher. In a way, TF–IDF helps find documents that share similar topics. Let's take a look at an example—first, we'll inspect some of the documents in our data containing the word "red":

```scala
// in Scala
val tfIdfIn = tokenized
  .where("array_contains(DescOut, 'red')")
  .select("DescOut")
  .limit(10)
tfIdfIn.show(false)
```

```python
# in Python
tfIdfIn = tokenized\
  .where("array_contains(DescOut, 'red')")\
  .select("DescOut")\
  .limit(10)
tfIdfIn.show(10, False)
```

```
+----------------------------------------+
DescOut                                  |
+----------------------------------------+
|[gingham, heart, , doorstop, red]       |
...
|[red, retrospot, oven, glove]           |
|[red, retrospot, plate]                 |
+----------------------------------------+
```

We can see some overlapping words in these documents, but these words provide at least a rough topic-like representation. Now let's input that into TF–IDF. To do this, we're going to hash each word and convert it to a numerical representation, and then weigh each word in the voculary according to the inverse document frequency. Hashing is a similar process as CountVectorizer, but is irreversible—that is, from our output index for a word, we cannot get our input word (multiple words might map to the same output index):

```scala
// in Scala
import org.apache.spark.ml.feature.{HashingTF, IDF}
val tf = new HashingTF()
  .setInputCol("DescOut")
  .setOutputCol("TFOut")
  .setNumFeatures(10000)
val idf = new IDF()
```

```
  .setInputCol("TFOut")
  .setOutputCol("IDFOut")
  .setMinDocFreq(2)

# in Python
from pyspark.ml.feature import HashingTF, IDF
tf = HashingTF()\
  .setInputCol("DescOut")\
  .setOutputCol("TFOut")\
  .setNumFeatures(10000)
idf = IDF()\
  .setInputCol("TFOut")\
  .setOutputCol("IDFOut")\
  .setMinDocFreq(2)

// in Scala
idf.fit(tf.transform(tfIdfIn)).transform(tf.transform(tfIdfIn)).show(false)

# in Python
idf.fit(tf.transform(tfIdfIn)).transform(tf.transform(tfIdfIn)).show(10, False)
```

While the output is too large to include here, notice that a certain value is assigned to "red" and that this value appears in every document. Also note that this term is weighted extremely low because it appears in every document. The output format is a sparse Vector we can subsequently input into a machine learning model in a form like this:

```
(10000,[2591,4291,4456],[1.0116009116784799,0.0,0.0])
```

This vector is represented using three different values: the total vocabulary size, the hash of every word appearing in the document, and the weighting of each of those terms. This is similar to the CountVectorizer output.

Word2Vec

Word2Vec is a deep learning–based tool for computing a vector representation of a set of words. The goal is to have similar words close to one another in this vector space, so we can then make generalizations about the words themselves. This model is easy to train and use, and has been shown to be useful in a number of natural language processing applications, including entity recognition, disambiguation, parsing, tagging, and machine translation.

Word2Vec is notable for capturing relationships between words based on their semantics. For example, if v~king, v~queen, v~man, and v~women represent the vectors for those four words, then we will often get a representation where v~king − v~man + v~woman ~= v~queen. To do this, Word2Vec uses a technique called "skip-grams" to convert a sentence of words into a vector representation (optionally of a specific size). It does this by building a vocabulary, and then for every sentence, it removes a token and trains the model to predict the missing token in the "n-gram" representation. Word2Vec works best with continuous, free-form text in the form of tokens.

Here's a simple example from the documentation:

```scala
// in Scala
import org.apache.spark.ml.feature.Word2Vec
import org.apache.spark.ml.linalg.Vector
import org.apache.spark.sql.Row
// Input data: Each row is a bag of words from a sentence or document.
val documentDF = spark.createDataFrame(Seq(
  "Hi I heard about Spark".split(" "),
  "I wish Java could use case classes".split(" "),
  "Logistic regression models are neat".split(" ")
).map(Tuple1.apply)).toDF("text")
// Learn a mapping from words to Vectors.
val word2Vec = new Word2Vec()
  .setInputCol("text")
  .setOutputCol("result")
  .setVectorSize(3)
  .setMinCount(0)
val model = word2Vec.fit(documentDF)
val result = model.transform(documentDF)
result.collect().foreach { case Row(text: Seq[_], features: Vector) =>
  println(s"Text: [${text.mkString(", ")}] => \nVector: $features\n") }
}
```

```python
# in Python
from pyspark.ml.feature import Word2Vec
# Input data: Each row is a bag of words from a sentence or document.
documentDF = spark.createDataFrame([
    ("Hi I heard about Spark".split(" "), ),
    ("I wish Java could use case classes".split(" "), ),
    ("Logistic regression models are neat".split(" "), )
], ["text"])
# Learn a mapping from words to Vectors.
word2Vec = Word2Vec(vectorSize=3, minCount=0, inputCol="text",
  outputCol="result")
model = word2Vec.fit(documentDF)
result = model.transform(documentDF)
for row in result.collect():
    text, vector = row
    print("Text: [%s] => \nVector: %s\n" % (", ".join(text), str(vector)))
```

```
Text: [Hi, I, heard, about, Spark] =>
Vector: [-0.008142343163490296,0.02051363289356232,0.03255096450448036]

Text: [I, wish, Java, could, use, case, classes] =>
Vector: [0.043090314205203734,0.035048123182994974,0.023512658663094044]

Text: [Logistic, regression, models, are, neat] =>
Vector: [0.038572299480438235,-0.03250147425569594,-0.01552378609776497]
```

Spark's Word2Vec implementation includes a variety of tuning parameters that can be found in the documentation (*http://bit.ly/2DRnljk*).

Feature Manipulation

While nearly every transformer in ML manipulates the feature space in some way, the following algorithms and tools are automated means of either expanding the input feature vectors or reducing them to a lower number of dimensions.

PCA

Principal Components Analysis (PCA) is a mathematical technique for finding the most important aspects of our data (the principal components). It changes the feature representation of our data by creating a new set of features ("aspects"). Each new feature is a combination of the original features. The power of PCA is that it can create a smaller set of more meaningful features to be input into your model, at the potential cost of interpretability.

You'd want to use PCA if you have a large input dataset and want to reduce the total number of features you have. This frequently comes up in text analysis where the entire feature space is massive and many of the features are largely irrelevant. Using PCA, we can find the most important combinations of features and only include those in our machine learning model. PCA takes a parameter k, specifying the number of output features to create. Generally, this should be much smaller than your input vectors' dimension.

 Picking the right k is nontrivial and there's no prescription we can give. Check out the relevant chapters in ESL (*http://statweb.stan ford.edu/~tibs/ElemStatLearn/*) and ISL (*http://www-bcf.usc.edu/ ~gareth/ISL/*) for more information.

Let's train PCA with a k of 2:

```scala
// in Scala
import org.apache.spark.ml.feature.PCA
val pca = new PCA().setInputCol("features").setK(2)
pca.fit(scaleDF).transform(scaleDF).show(false)
```

```python
# in Python
from pyspark.ml.feature import PCA
pca = PCA().setInputCol("features").setK(2)
pca.fit(scaleDF).transform(scaleDF).show(20, False)
```

```
+---+--------------+----------------------------------------+
|id |features      |pca_7c5c4aa7674e__output                |
+---+--------------+----------------------------------------+
|0  |[1.0,0.1,-1.0]|[0.0713719499248418,-0.4526654888147822]|
```

```
...
|1  |[3.0,10.1,3.0]|[-10.872398139848944,0.030962697060150646]|
+---+-------------+-----------------------------------------+
```

Interaction

In some cases, you might have domain knowledge about specific variables in your dataset. For example, you might know that a certain interaction between the two variables is an important variable to include in a downstream estimator. The feature transformer Interaction allows you to create an interaction between two variables manually. It just multiplies the two features together—something that a typical linear model would not do for every possible pair of features in your data. This transformer is currently only available directly in Scala but can be called from any language using the RFormula. We recommend users just use RFormula instead of manually creating interactions.

Polynomial Expansion

Polynomial expansion is used to generate interaction variables of all the input columns. With polynomial expansion, we specify to what degree we would like to see various interactions. For example, for a degree-2 polynomial, Spark takes every value in our feature vector, multiplies it by every other value in the feature vector, and then stores the results as features. For instance, if we have two input features, we'll get four output features if we use a second degree polynomial (2x2). If we have three input features, we'll get nine output features (3x3). If we use a third-degree polynomial, we'll get 27 output features (3x3x3) and so on. This transformation is useful when you want to see interactions between particular features but aren't necessarily sure about which interactions to consider.

 Polynomial expansion can greatly increase your feature space, leading to both high computational costs and overfitting. Use it with caution, especially for higher degrees.

Here's an example of a second degree polynomial:

```scala
// in Scala
import org.apache.spark.ml.feature.PolynomialExpansion
val pe = new PolynomialExpansion().setInputCol("features").setDegree(2)
pe.transform(scaleDF).show(false)
```

```python
# in Python
from pyspark.ml.feature import PolynomialExpansion
pe = PolynomialExpansion().setInputCol("features").setDegree(2)
pe.transform(scaleDF).show()
```

```
+---+-------------+----------------------------------------------------------+
|id |features     |poly_9b2e603812cb__output                                 |
+---+-------------+----------------------------------------------------------+
|0  |[1.0,0.1,-1.0]|[1.0,1.0,0.1,0.1,0.010000000000000002,-1.0,-1.0,-0.1,1.0] |
...
|1  |[3.0,10.1,3.0]|[3.0,9.0,10.1,30.299999999999997,102.00999999999999,3.0... |
+---+-------------+----------------------------------------------------------+
```

Feature Selection

Often, you will have a large range of possible features and want to select a smaller subset to use for training. For example, many features might be correlated, or using too many features might lead to overfitting. This process is called feature selection. There are a number of ways to evaluate feature importance once you've trained a model but another option is to do some rough filtering beforehand. Spark has some simple options for doing that, such as ChiSqSelector.

ChiSqSelector

ChiSqSelector leverages a statistical test to identify features that are not independent from the label we are trying to predict, and drop the uncorrelated features. It's often used with categorical data in order to reduce the number of features you will input into your model, as well as to reduce the dimensionality of text data (in the form of frequencies or counts). Since this method is based on the Chi-Square test, there are several different ways we can pick the "best" features. The methods are numTopFeatures, which is ordered by p-value; percentile, which takes a proportion of the input features (instead of just the top N features); and fpr, which sets a cut off p-value.

We will demonstrate this with the output of the CountVectorizer created earlier in this chapter:

```scala
// in Scala
import org.apache.spark.ml.feature.{ChiSqSelector, Tokenizer}
val tkn = new Tokenizer().setInputCol("Description").setOutputCol("DescOut")
val tokenized = tkn
  .transform(sales.select("Description", "CustomerId"))
  .where("CustomerId IS NOT NULL")
val prechi = fittedCV.transform(tokenized)
val chisq = new ChiSqSelector()
  .setFeaturesCol("countVec")
  .setLabelCol("CustomerId")
  .setNumTopFeatures(2)
chisq.fit(prechi).transform(prechi)
  .drop("customerId", "Description", "DescOut").show()
```

```python
# in Python
from pyspark.ml.feature import ChiSqSelector, Tokenizer
```

```
tkn = Tokenizer().setInputCol("Description").setOutputCol("DescOut")
tokenized = tkn\
  .transform(sales.select("Description", "CustomerId"))\
  .where("CustomerId IS NOT NULL")
prechi = fittedCV.transform(tokenized)\
  .where("CustomerId IS NOT NULL")
chisq = ChiSqSelector()\
  .setFeaturesCol("countVec")\
  .setLabelCol("CustomerId")\
  .setNumTopFeatures(2)
chisq.fit(prechi).transform(prechi)\
  .drop("customerId", "Description", "DescOut").show()
```

Advanced Topics

There are several advanced topics surrounding transformers and estimators. Here we touch on the two most common, persisting transformers as well as writing custom ones.

Persisting Transformers

Once you've used an estimator to configure a transformer, it can be helpful to write it to disk and simply load it when necessary (e.g., for use in another Spark session). We saw this in the previous chapter when we persisted an entire pipeline. To persist a transformer individually, we use the `write` method on the fitted transformer (or the standard transformer) and specify the location:

```scala
// in Scala
val fittedPCA = pca.fit(scaleDF)
fittedPCA.write.overwrite().save("/tmp/fittedPCA")
```

```python
# in Python
fittedPCA = pca.fit(scaleDF)
fittedPCA.write().overwrite().save("/tmp/fittedPCA")
```

We can then load it back in:

```scala
// in Scala
import org.apache.spark.ml.feature.PCAModel
val loadedPCA = PCAModel.load("/tmp/fittedPCA")
loadedPCA.transform(scaleDF).show()
```

```python
# in Python
from pyspark.ml.feature import PCAModel
loadedPCA = PCAModel.load("/tmp/fittedPCA")
loadedPCA.transform(scaleDF).show()
```

Writing a Custom Transformer

Writing a custom transformer can be valuable when you want to encode some of your own business logic in a form that you can fit into an ML Pipeline, pass on to hyper-parameter search, and so on. In general you should try to use the built-in modules (e.g., SQLTransformer) as much as possible because they are optimized to run efficiently. But sometimes we do not have that luxury. Let's create a simple tokenizer to demonstrate:

```
import org.apache.spark.ml.UnaryTransformer
import org.apache.spark.ml.util.{DefaultParamsReadable, DefaultParamsWritable,
  Identifiable}
import org.apache.spark.sql.types.{ArrayType, StringType, DataType}
import org.apache.spark.ml.param.{IntParam, ParamValidators}

class MyTokenizer(override val uid: String)
  extends UnaryTransformer[String, Seq[String],
    MyTokenizer] with DefaultParamsWritable {

  def this() = this(Identifiable.randomUID("myTokenizer"))

  val maxWords: IntParam = new IntParam(this, "maxWords",
    "The max number of words to return.",
  ParamValidators.gtEq(0))

  def setMaxWords(value: Int): this.type = set(maxWords, value)

  def getMaxWords: Integer = $(maxWords)

  override protected def createTransformFunc: String => Seq[String] = (
    inputString: String) => {
      inputString.split("\\s").take($(maxWords))
  }

  override protected def validateInputType(inputType: DataType): Unit = {
    require(
      inputType == StringType, s"Bad input type: $inputType. Requires String.")
  }

  override protected def outputDataType: DataType = new ArrayType(StringType,
    true)
}

// this will allow you to read it back in by using this object.
object MyTokenizer extends DefaultParamsReadable[MyTokenizer]

val myT = new MyTokenizer().setInputCol("someCol").setMaxWords(2)
myT.transform(Seq("hello world. This text won't show.").toDF("someCol")).show()
```

It is also possible to write a custom estimator where you must customize the transformation based on the actual input data. However, this isn't as common as writing a standalone transformer and is therefore not included in this book. A good way to do this is to look at one of the simple estimators we saw before and modify the code to suit your use case. A good place to start might be the StandardScaler (*http://bit.ly/2FkPIn4*).

Conclusion

This chapter gave a whirlwind tour of many of the most common preprocessing transformations Spark has available. There are several domain-specific ones we did not have enough room to cover (e.g., Discrete Cosine Transform), but you can find more information in the documentation (*http://bit.ly/2pE51jZ*). This area of Spark is also constantly growing as the community develops new ones.

Another important aspect of this feature engineering toolkit is consistency. In the previous chapter we covered the pipeline concept, an essential tool to package and train end-to-end ML workflows. In the next chapter we will start going through the variety of machine learning tasks you may have and what algorithms are available for each one.

## CHAPTER 26

Classification

Classification is the task of predicting a label, category, class, or discrete variable given some input features. The key difference from other ML tasks, such as regression, is that the output label has a finite set of possible values (e.g., three classes).

Use Cases

Classification has many use cases, as we discussed in Chapter 24. Here are a few more to consider as a reinforcement of the multitude of ways classification can be used in the real world.

Predicting credit risk
  A financing company might look at a number of variables before offering a loan to a company or individual. Whether or not to offer the loan is a binary classification problem.

News classification
  An algorithm might be trained to predict the topic of a news article (sports, politics, business, etc.).

Classifying human activity
  By collecting data from sensors such as a phone accelerometer or smart watch, you can predict the person's activity. The output will be one of a finite set of classes (e.g., walking, sleeping, standing, or running).

Types of Classification

Before we continue, let's review several different types of classification.

Binary Classification

The simplest example of classification is *binary classification*, where there are only two labels you can predict. One example is fraud analytics, where a given transaction can be classified as fraudulent or not; or email spam, where a given email can be classified as spam or not spam.

Multiclass Classification

Beyond binary classification lies *multiclass classification*, where one label is chosen from more than two distinct possible labels. A typical example is Facebook predicting the people in a given photo or a meterologist predicting the weather (rainy, sunny, cloudy, etc.). Note how there is always a finite set of classes to predict; it's never unbounded. This is also called multinomial classification.

Multilabel Classification

Finally, there is *multilabel classification*, where a given input can produce multiple labels. For example, you might want to predict a book's genre based on the text of the book itself. While this could be multiclass, it's probably better suited for multilabel because a book may fall into multiple genres. Another example of multilabel classification is identifying the number of objects that appear in an image. Note that in this example, the number of output predictions is not necessarily fixed, and could vary from image to image.

Classification Models in MLlib

Spark has several models available for performing binary and multiclass classification out of the box. The following models are available for classification in Spark:

- Logistic regression
- Decision trees
- Random forests
- Gradient-boosted trees

Spark does not support making multilabel predictions natively. In order to train a multilabel model, you must train one model per label and combine them manually.

Once manually constructed, there are built-in tools that support measuring these kinds of models (discussed at the end of the chapter).

This chapter will cover the basics of each of these models by providing:

- A simple explanation of the model and the intuition behind it
- Model hyperparameters (the different ways we can initialize the model)
- Training parameters (parameters that affect how the model is trained)
- Prediction parameters (parameters that affect how predictions are made)

You can set the hyperparameters and training parameters in a `ParamGrid` as we saw in Chapter 24.

Model Scalability

Model scalability is an important consideration when choosing your model. In general, Spark has great support for training large-scale machine learning models (note, these are *large scale*; on single-node workloads there are a number of other tools that also perform well). Table 26-1 is a simple model scalability scorecard to use to find the best model for your particular task (if scalability is your core consideration). The actual scalability will depend on your configuration, machine size, and other specifics but should make for a good heuristic.

Table 26-1. Model scalability reference

Model	Features count	Training examples	Output classes
Logistic regression	1 to 10 million	No limit	Features x Classes < 10 million
Decision trees	1,000s	No limit	Features x Classes < 10,000s
Random forest	10,000s	No limit	Features x Classes < 100,000s
Gradient-boosted trees	1,000s	No limit	Features x Classes < 10,000s

We can see that nearly all these models scale to large collections of input data and there is ongoing work to scale them even further. The reason *no limit* is in place for the number of training examples is because these are trained using methods like stochastic gradient descent and L-BFGS. These methods are optimized specifically for working with massive datasets and to remove any constraints that might exist on the number of training examples you would hope to learn on.

Let's start looking at the classification models by loading in some data:

```scala
// in Scala
val bInput = spark.read.format("parquet").load("/data/binary-classification")
  .selectExpr("features", "cast(label as double) as label")
```

```python
# in Python
bInput = spark.read.format("parquet").load("/data/binary-classification")\
  .selectExpr("features", "cast(label as double) as label")
```

Like our other advanced analytics chapters, this one cannot teach you the mathematical underpinnings of every model. See Chapter 4 in ISL (*http://www-bcf.usc.edu/~gareth/ISL/*) and ESL (*http://stat web.stanford.edu/~tibs/ElemStatLearn/*) for a review of classification.

Logistic Regression

Logistic regression is one of the most popular methods of classification. It is a linear method that combines each of the individual inputs (or features) with specific weights (these weights are generated during the training process) that are then combined to get a probability of belonging to a particular class. These weights are helpful because they are good representations of feature importance; if you have a large weight, you can assume that variations in that feature have a significant effect on the outcome (assuming you performed normalization). A smaller weight means the feature is less likely to be important.

See ISL 4.3 (*http://www-bcf.usc.edu/~gareth/ISL/*) and ESL 4.4 (*http://statweb.stan ford.edu/~tibs/ElemStatLearn/*) for more information.

Model Hyperparameters

Model hyperparameters are configurations that determine the basic structure of the model itself. The following hyperparameters are available for logistic regression:

family

  Can be multinomial (two or more distinct labels; multiclass classification) or binary (only two distinct labels; binary classification).

elasticNetParam

  A floating-point value from 0 to 1. This parameter specifies the mix of L1 and L2 regularization according to elastic net regularization (which is a linear combination of the two). Your choice of L1 or L2 depends a lot on your particular use case but the intuition is as follows: L1 regularization (a value of 1) will create sparsity in the model because certain feature weights will become zero (that are of little consequence to the output). For this reason, it can be used as a simple feature-selection method. On the other hand, L2 regularization (a value of 0) does not create sparsity because the corresponding weights for particular features will only be driven toward zero, but will never completely reach zero. ElasticNet gives us the best of both worlds—we can choose a value between 0 and 1 to specify a mix of L1 and L2 regularization. For the most part, you should be tuning this by testing different values.

fitIntercept
Can be true or false. This hyperparameter determines whether or not to fit the intercept or the arbitrary number that is added to the linear combination of inputs and weights of the model. Typically you will want to fit the intercept if we haven't normalized our training data.

regParam
A value ≥ 0. that determines how much weight to give to the regularization term in the objective function. Choosing a value here is again going to be a function of noise and dimensionality in our dataset. In a pipeline, try a wide range of values (e.g., 0, 0.01, 0.1, 1).

standardization
Can be true or false, whether or not to standardize the inputs before passing them into the model. See Chapter 25 for more information.

Training Parameters

Training parameters are used to specify how we perform our training. Here are the training parameters for logistic regression.

maxIter
Total number of iterations over the data before stopping. Changing this parameter probably won't change your results a ton, so it shouldn't be the first parameter you look to adjust. The default is 100.

tol
This value specifies a threshold by which changes in parameters show that we optimized our weights enough, and can stop iterating. It lets the algorithm stop before maxIter iterations. The default value is 1.0E-6. This also shouldn't be the first parameter you look to tune.

weightCol
The name of a weight column used to weigh certain rows more than others. This can be a useful tool if you have some other measure of how important a particular training example is and have a weight associated with it. For example, you might have 10,000 examples where you know that some labels are more accurate than others. You can weigh the labels you know are correct more than the ones you don't.

Prediction Parameters

These parameters help determine how the model should actually be making predictions at prediction time, but do not affect training. Here are the prediction parameters for logistic regression:

threshold
> A Double in the range of 0 to 1. This parameter is the probability threshold for when a given class should be predicted. You can tune this parameter according to your requirements to balance between false positives and false negatives. For instance, if a mistaken prediction would be costly—you might want to make its prediction threshold very high.

thresholds
> This parameter lets you specify an array of threshold values for each class when using multiclass classification. It works similarly to the single threshold parameter described previously.

Example

Here's a simple example using the LogisticRegression model. Notice how we didn't specify any parameters because we'll leverage the defaults and our data conforms to the proper column naming. In practice, you probably won't need to change many of the parameters:

```scala
// in Scala
import org.apache.spark.ml.classification.LogisticRegression
val lr = new LogisticRegression()
println(lr.explainParams()) // see all parameters
val lrModel = lr.fit(bInput)
```

```python
# in Python
from pyspark.ml.classification import LogisticRegression
lr = LogisticRegression()
print lr.explainParams() # see all parameters
lrModel = lr.fit(bInput)
```

Once the model is trained you can get information about the model by taking a look at the coefficients and the intercept. The coefficients correspond to the individual feature weights (each feature weight is multiplied by each respective feature to compute the prediction) while the intercept is the value of the italics-intercept (if we chose to fit one when specifying the model). Seeing the coefficients can be helpful for inspecting the model that you built and comparing how features affect the prediction:

```scala
// in Scala
println(lrModel.coefficients)
println(lrModel.intercept)
```

```python
# in Python
print lrModel.coefficients
print lrModel.intercept
```

For a multinomial model (the current one is binary), `lrModel.coefficientMatrix` and `lrModel.interceptVector` can be used to get the coefficients and intercept. These will return `Matrix` and `Vector` types representing the values or each of the given classes.

Model Summary

Logistic regression provides a model summary that gives you information about the final, trained model. This is analogous to the same types of summaries we see in many R language machine learning packages. The model summary is currently only available for binary logistic regression problems, but multiclass summaries will likely be added in the future. Using the binary summary, we can get all sorts of information about the model itself including the area under the ROC curve, the f measure by threshold, the precision, the recall, the recall by thresholds, and the ROC curve. Note that for the area under the curve, instance weighting is not taken into account, so if you wanted to see how you performed on the values you weighed more highly, you'd have to do that manually. This will probably change in future Spark versions. You can see the summary using the following APIs:

```scala
// in Scala
import org.apache.spark.ml.classification.BinaryLogisticRegressionSummary
val summary = lrModel.summary
val bSummary = summary.asInstanceOf[BinaryLogisticRegressionSummary]
println(bSummary.areaUnderROC)
bSummary.roc.show()
bSummary.pr.show()
```

```python
# in Python
summary = lrModel.summary
print summary.areaUnderROC
summary.roc.show()
summary.pr.show()
```

The speed at which the model descends to the final result is shown in the objective history. We can access this through the objective history on the model summary:

```
summary.objectiveHistory
```

This is an array of doubles that specify how, over each training iteration, we are performing with respect to our objective function. This information is helpful to see if we have sufficient iterations or need to be tuning other parameters.

Decision Trees

Decision trees are one of the more friendly and interpretable models for performing classification because they're similar to simple decision models that humans use quite often. For example, if you have to predict whether or not someone will eat ice cream when offered, a good feature might be whether or not that individual likes ice cream. In pseudocode, if person.likes("ice_cream"), they will eat ice cream; otherwise, they won't eat ice cream. A decision tree creates this type of structure with all the inputs and follows a set of branches when it comes time to make a prediction. This makes it a great starting point model because it's easy to reason about, easy to inspect, and makes very few assumptions about the structure of the data. In short, rather than trying to train coeffiecients in order to model a function, it simply creates a big tree of decisions to follow at prediction time. This model also supports multiclass classification and provides outputs as predictions and probabilities in two different columns.

While this model is usually a great start, it does come at a cost. It can overfit data *extremely* quickly. By that we mean that, unrestrained, the decision tree will create a pathway from the start based on every single training example. That means it encodes all of the information in the training set in the model. This is bad because then the model won't generalize to new data (you will see poor test set prediction performance). However, there are a number of ways to try and rein in the model by limiting its branching structure (e.g., limiting its height) to get good predictive power.

See ISL 8.1 (*http://www-bcf.usc.edu/~gareth/ISL/*) and ESL 9.2 (*http://statweb.stan ford.edu/~tibs/ElemStatLearn/*) for more information.

Model Hyperparameters

There are many different ways to configure and train decision trees. Here are the hyperparameters that Spark's implementation supports:

maxDepth
    Since we're training a tree, it can be helpful to specify a max depth in order to avoid overfitting to the dataset (in the extreme, every row ends up as its own leaf node). The default is 5.

maxBins
    In decision trees, continuous features are converted into categorical features and maxBins determines how many bins should be created from continous features. More bins gives a higher level of granularity. The value must be greater than or equal to 2 and greater than or equal to the number of categories in any categorical feature in your dataset. The default is 32.

`impurity`

To build up a "tree" you need to configure when the model should branch. Impurity represents the metric (information gain) to determine whether or not the model should split at a particular leaf node. This parameter can be set to either be "entropy" or "gini" (default), two commonly used impurity metrics.

`minInfoGain`

This parameter determines the minimum information gain that can be used for a split. A higher value can prevent overfitting. This is largely something that needs to be determined from testing out different variations of the decision tree model. The default is zero.

`minInstancePerNode`

This parameter determines the minimum number of training instances that need to end in a particular node. Think of this as another manner of controlling max depth. We can prevent overfitting by limiting depth or we can prevent it by specifying that at minimum a certain number of training values need to end up in a particular leaf node. If it's not met we would "prune" the tree until that requirement is met. A higher value can prevent overfitting. The default is 1, but this can be any value greater than 1.

Training Parameters

These are configurations we specify in order to manipulate how we perform our training. Here is the training parameter for decision trees:

`checkpointInterval`

Checkpointing is a way to save the model's work over the course of training so that if nodes in the cluster crash for some reason, you don't lose your work. A value of 10 means the model will get checkpointed every 10 iterations. Set this to -1 to turn off checkpointing. This parameter needs to be set together with a `checkpointDir` (a directory to checkpoint to) and with `useNodeIdCache=true`. Consult the Spark documentation for more information on checkpointing.

Prediction Parameters

There is only one prediction parameter for decision trees: `thresholds`. Refer to the explanation for thresholds under "Logistic Regression" on page 464.

Here's a minimal but complete example of using a decision tree classifier:

```scala
// in Scala
import org.apache.spark.ml.classification.DecisionTreeClassifier
val dt = new DecisionTreeClassifier()
println(dt.explainParams())
val dtModel = dt.fit(bInput)
```

```python
# in Python
from pyspark.ml.classification import DecisionTreeClassifier
dt = DecisionTreeClassifier()
print dt.explainParams()
dtModel = dt.fit(bInput)
```

Random Forest and Gradient-Boosted Trees

These methods are extensions of the decision tree. Rather than training one tree on all of the data, you train multiple trees on varying subsets of the data. The intuition behind doing this is that various decision trees will become "experts" in that particular domain while others become experts in others. By combining these various experts, you then get a "wisdom of the crowds" effect, where the group's performance exceeds any individual. In addition, these methods can help prevent overfitting.

Random forests and gradient-boosted trees are two distinct methods for combining decision trees. In random forests, we simply train a lot of trees and then average their response to make a prediction. With gradient-boosted trees, each tree makes a weighted prediction (such that some trees have more predictive power for some classes than others). They have largely the same parameters, which we note below. One current limitation is that gradient-boosted trees currently only support binary labels.

 There are several popular tools for learning tree-based models. For example, the XGBoost (*https://xgboost.readthedocs.io/en/latest/*) library provides an integration package for Spark that can be used to run it on Spark.

See ISL (*http://www-bcf.usc.edu/~gareth/ISL/*) 8.2 and ESL (*http://statweb.stanford.edu/~tibs/ElemStatLearn/*) 10.1 for more information on these tree ensemble models.

Model Hyperparameters

Random forests and gradient-boosted trees provide all of the same model hyperparameters supported by decision trees. In addition, they add several of their own.

Random forest only

numTrees
    The total number of trees to train.

featureSubsetStrategy
    This parameter determines how many features should be considered for splits. This can be a variety of different values including "auto", "all", "sqrt", "log2", or a number "n." When your input is "n" the model will use n * number of features

during training. When n is in the range (1, number of features), the model will use n features during training. There's no one-size-fits-all solution here, so it's worth experimenting with different values in your pipeline.

Gradient-boosted trees (GBT) only

lossType

This is the loss function for gradient-boosted trees to minimize during training. Currently, only logistic loss is supported.

maxIter

Total number of iterations over the data before stopping. Changing this probably won't change your results a ton, so it shouldn't be the first parameter you look to adjust. The default is 100.

stepSize

This is the learning rate for the algorithm. A larger step size means that larger jumps are made between training iterations. This can help in the optimization process and is something that should be tested in training. The default is 0.1 and this can be any value from 0 to 1.

Training Parameters

There is only one training parameter for these models, checkpointInterval. Refer back to the explanation under "Decision Trees" on page 468 for details on checkpointing.

Prediction Parameters

These models have the same prediction parameters as decision trees. Consult the prediction parameters under that model for more information.

Here's a short code example of using each of these classifiers:

```scala
// in Scala
import org.apache.spark.ml.classification.RandomForestClassifier
val rfClassifier = new RandomForestClassifier()
println(rfClassifier.explainParams())
val trainedModel = rfClassifier.fit(bInput)

// in Scala
import org.apache.spark.ml.classification.GBTClassifier
val gbtClassifier = new GBTClassifier()
println(gbtClassifier.explainParams())
val trainedModel = gbtClassifier.fit(bInput)

# in Python
from pyspark.ml.classification import RandomForestClassifier
rfClassifier = RandomForestClassifier()
```

```python
print rfClassifier.explainParams()
trainedModel = rfClassifier.fit(bInput)

# in Python
from pyspark.ml.classification import GBTClassifier
gbtClassifier = GBTClassifier()
print gbtClassifier.explainParams()
trainedModel = gbtClassifier.fit(bInput)
```

Naive Bayes

Naive Bayes classifiers are a collection of classifiers based on Bayes' theorem. The core assumption behind the models is that all features in your data are independent of one another. Naturally, strict independence is a bit naive, but even if this is violated, useful models can still be produced. Naive Bayes classifiers are commonly used in text or document classification, although it can be used as a more general-purpose classifier as well. There are two different model types: either a *multivariate Bernoulli model*, where indicator variables represent the existence of a term in a document; or the *multinomial model*, where the total counts of terms are used.

One important note when it comes to Naive Bayes is that all input features must be non-negative.

See ISL 4.4 (*http://www-bcf.usc.edu/~gareth/ISL/*) and ESL 6.6 (*http://statweb.stanford.edu/~tibs/ElemStatLearn/*) for more background on these models.

Model Hyperparameters

These are configurations we specify to determine the basic structure of the models:

modelType
   Either "bernoulli" or "multinomial." See the previous section for more information on this choice.

weightCol
   Allows weighing different data points differently. Refer back to "Training Parameters" on page 465 for the explanation of this hyperparameter.

Training Parameters

These are configurations that specify how we perform our training:

smoothing
   This determines the amount of regularization that should take place using additive smoothing (*https://en.wikipedia.org/wiki/Additive_smoothing*). This helps smooth out categorical data and avoid overfitting on the training data by changing the expected probability for certain classes. The default value is 1.

Prediction Parameters

Naive Bayes shares the same prediction parameter, thresholds, as all of our other models. Refer back to the previous explanation for threshold to see how to use this.

Here's an example of using a Naive Bayes classifier.

```scala
// in Scala
import org.apache.spark.ml.classification.NaiveBayes
val nb = new NaiveBayes()
println(nb.explainParams())
val trainedModel = nb.fit(bInput.where("label != 0"))
```

```python
# in Python
from pyspark.ml.classification import NaiveBayes
nb = NaiveBayes()
print nb.explainParams()
trainedModel = nb.fit(bInput.where("label != 0"))
```

Note that in this example dataset, we have features that have negative values. In this case, the rows with negative features correspond to rows with label "0". Therefore we're just going to filter them out (via the label) instead of processing them further to demonstrate the naive bayes API.

Evaluators for Classification and Automating Model Tuning

As we saw in Chapter 24, evaluators allow us to specify the metric of success for our model. An evaluator doesn't help too much when it stands alone; however, when we use it in a pipeline, we can automate a grid search of our various parameters of the models and transformers—trying all combinations of the parameters to see which ones perform the best. Evaluators are most useful in this pipeline and parameter grid context. For classification, there are two evaluators, and they expect two columns: a predicted label from the model and a true label. For binary classification we use the BinaryClassificationEvaluator. This supports optimizing for two different metrics "areaUnderROC" and areaUnderPR." For multiclass classification, we need to use the MulticlassClassificationEvaluator, which supports optimizing for "f1", "weightedPrecision", "weightedRecall", and "accuracy".

To use evaluators, we build up our pipeline, specify the parameters we would like to test, and then run it and see the results. See Chapter 24 for a code example.

Detailed Evaluation Metrics

MLlib also contains tools that let you evaluate multiple classification metrics at once. Unfortunately, these metrics classes have not been ported over to Spark's DataFrame-based ML package from the underlying RDD framework. So, at the time of this writing, you still have to create an RDD to use these. In the future, this functionality will likely be ported to DataFrames and the following may no longer be the best way to see metrics (although you will still be able to use these APIs).

There are three different classification metrics we can use:

- Binary classification metrics
- Multiclass classification metrics
- Multilabel classification metrics

All of these measures follow the same approximate style. We'll compare generated outputs with true values and the model calculates all of the relevant metrics for us. Then we can query the object for the values for each of the metrics:

```scala
// in Scala
import org.apache.spark.mllib.evaluation.BinaryClassificationMetrics
val out = model.transform(bInput)
  .select("prediction", "label")
  .rdd.map(x => (x(0).asInstanceOf[Double], x(1).asInstanceOf[Double]))
val metrics = new BinaryClassificationMetrics(out)
```

```python
# in Python
from pyspark.mllib.evaluation import BinaryClassificationMetrics
out = model.transform(bInput)\
  .select("prediction", "label")\
  .rdd.map(lambda x: (float(x[0]), float(x[1])))
metrics = BinaryClassificationMetrics(out)
```

Once we've done that, we can see typical classification success metrics on this metric's object using a similar API to the one we saw with logistic regression:

```scala
// in Scala
metrics.areaUnderPR
metrics.areaUnderROC
println("Receiver Operating Characteristic")
metrics.roc.toDF().show()
```

```python
# in Python
print metrics.areaUnderPR
print metrics.areaUnderROC
print "Receiver Operating Characteristic"
metrics.roc.toDF().show()
```

One-vs-Rest Classifier

There are some MLlib models that don't support multiclass classification. In these cases, users can leverage a one-vs-rest classifier in order to perform multiclass classification given only a binary classifier. The intuition behind this is that for every class you hope to predict, the one-vs-rest classifier will turn the problem into a binary classification problem by isolating one class as the target class and grouping all of the other classes into one. Thus the prediction of the class becomes binary (is it this class or *not* this class?).

One-vs-rest is implemented as an estimator. For the base classifier it takes instances of the classifier and creates a binary classification problem for each of the k classes. The classifier for class i is trained to predict whether the label is i or not, distinguishing class i from all other classes.

Predictions are done by evaluating each binary classifier and the index of the most confident classifier is output as the label.

See the Spark documentation for a nice example of the use of one-vs-rest (*http://bit.ly/2BxBwVI*).

Multilayer Perceptron

The multilayer perceptron is a classifier based on neural networks with a configurable number of layers (and layer sizes). We will discuss it in Chapter 31.

Conclusion

In this chapter we covered the majority of tools Spark provides for classification: predicting one of a finite set of labels for each data point based on its features. In the next chapter, we'll look at regression, where the required output is continuous instead of categorical.

## CHAPTER 27

Regression

Regression is a logical extension of classification. Rather than just predicting a single value from a set of values, *regression* is the act of predicting a real number (or continuous variable) from a set of features (represented as numbers).

Regression can be harder than classification because, from a mathematical perspective, there are an infinite number of possible output values. Furthermore, we aim to optimize some metric of error between the predicted and true value, as opposed to an accuracy rate. Aside from that, regression and classification are fairly similar. For this reason, we will see a lot of the same underlying concepts applied to regression as we did with classification.

Use Cases

The following is a small set of regression use cases that can get you thinking about potential regression problems in your own domain:

Predicting movie viewership
Given information about a movie and the movie-going public, such as how many people have watched the trailer or shared it on social media, you might want to predict how many people are likely to watch the movie when it comes out.

Predicting company revenue
Given a current growth trajectory, the market, and seasonality, you might want to predict how much revenue a company will gain in the future.

Predicting crop yield
Given information about the particular area in which a crop is grown, as well as the current weather throughout the year, you might want to predict the total crop yield for a particular plot of land.

Regression Models in MLlib

There are several fundamental regression models in MLlib. Some of these models are carryovers from Chapter 26. Others are only relevant to the regression problem domain. This list is current as of Spark 2.2 but will grow:

- Linear regression
- Generalized linear regression
- Isotonic regression
- Decision trees
- Random forest
- Gradient-boosted trees
- Survival regression

This chapter will cover the basics of each of these particular models by providing:

- A simple explanation of the model and the intuition behind the algorithm
- Model hyperparameters (the different ways that we can initialize the model)
- Training parameters (parameters that affect how the model is trained)
- Prediction parameters (parameters that affect how predictions are made)

You can search over the hyperparameters and training parameters using a `ParamGrid`, as we saw in Chapter 24.

Model Scalability

The regression models in MLlib all scale to large datasets. Table 27-1 is a simple model scalability scorecard that will help you in choosing the best model for your particular task (if scalability is your core consideration). These will depend on your configuration, machine size, and other factors.

Table 27-1. Regression scalability reference

Model	Number features	Training examples
Linear regression	1 to 10 million	No limit
Generalized linear regression	4,096	No limit
Isotonic regression	N/A	Millions
Decision trees	1,000s	No limit
Random forest	10,000s	No limit
Gradient-boosted trees	1,000s	No limit
Survival regression	1 to 10 million	No limit

Like our other advanced analytics chapters, this one cannot teach you the mathematical underpinnings of every model. See Chapter 3 in ISL (*http://www-bcf.usc.edu/~gareth/ISL/*) and ESL (*http://stat web.stanford.edu/~tibs/ElemStatLearn/*) for a review of regression.

Let's read in some sample data that we will use throughout the chapter:

```scala
// in Scala
val df = spark.read.load("/data/regression")
```

```python
# in Python
df = spark.read.load("/data/regression")
```

Linear Regression

Linear regression assumes that a linear combination of your input features (the sum of each feature multiplied by a weight) results along with an amount of Gaussian error in the output. This linear assumption (along with Gaussian error) does not always hold true, but it does make for a simple, interpretable model that's hard to overfit. Like logistic regression, Spark implements ElasticNet regularization for this, allowing you to mix L1 and L2 regularization.

See ISL (*http://www-bcf.usc.edu/~gareth/ISL/*) 3.2 and ESL (*http://statweb.stan ford.edu/~tibs/ElemStatLearn/*) 3.2 for more information.

Model Hyperparameters

Linear regression has the same model hyperparameters as logistic regression. See Chapter 26 for more information.

Training Parameters

Linear regression also shares all of the same training parameters from logistic regression. Refer back to Chapter 26 for more on this topic.

Example

Here's a short example of using linear regression on our sample dataset:

```scala
// in Scala
import org.apache.spark.ml.regression.LinearRegression
val lr = new LinearRegression().setMaxIter(10).setRegParam(0.3)\
  .setElasticNetParam(0.8)
println(lr.explainParams())
val lrModel = lr.fit(df)
```

```python
# in Python
from pyspark.ml.regression import LinearRegression
```

```
lr = LinearRegression().setMaxIter(10).setRegParam(0.3).setElasticNetParam(0.8)
print lr.explainParams()
lrModel = lr.fit(df)
```

Training Summary

Just as in logistic regression, we get detailed training information back from our model. The code font method is a simple shorthand for accessing these metrics. It reports several conventional metrics for measuring the success of a regression model, allowing you to see how well your model is actually fitting the line.

The summary method returns a summary object with several fields. Let's go through these in turn. The residuals are simply the weights for each of the features that we input into the model. The objective history shows how our training is going at every iteration. The root mean squared error is a measure of how well our line is fitting the data, determined by looking at the distance between each predicted value and the actual value in the data. The R-squared variable is a measure of the proportion of the variance of the predicted variable that is captured by the model.

There are a number of metrics and summary information that may be relevant to your use case. This section demonstrates the API, but does not comprehensively cover every metric (consult the API documentation for more information).

Here are some of the attributes of the model summary for linear regression:

```
// in Scala
val summary = lrModel.summary
summary.residuals.show()
println(summary.objectiveHistory.toSeq.toDF.show())
println(summary.rootMeanSquaredError)
println(summary.r2)
```

```
# in Python
summary = lrModel.summary
summary.residuals.show()
print summary.totalIterations
print summary.objectiveHistory
print summary.rootMeanSquaredError
print summary.r2
```

Generalized Linear Regression

The standard linear regression that we saw in this chapter is actually a part of a family of algorithms called *generalized linear regression*. Spark has two implementations of this algorithm. One is optimized for working with very large sets of features (the simple linear regression covered previously in this chapter), while the other is more general, includes support for more algorithms, and doesn't currently scale to large numbers of features.

The generalized form of linear regression gives you more fine-grained control over what kind of regression model you use. For instance, these allow you to select the expected noise distribution from a variety of families, including Gaussian (linear regression), binomial (logistic regression), poisson (poisson regression), and gamma (gamma regression). The generalized models also support setting a link function that specifies the relationship between the linear predictor and the mean of the distribution function. Table 27-2 shows the available link functions for each family.

Table 27-2. Regression families, response types, and link functions

Family	Response type	Supported links
Gaussian	Continuous	Identity*, Log, Inverse
Binomial	Binary	Logit*, Probit, CLogLog
Poisson	Count	Log*, Identity, Sqrt
Gamma	Continuous	Inverse*, Idenity, Log
Tweedie	Zero-inflated continuous	Power link function

The asterisk signifies the canonical link function for each family.

See ISL 3.2 (*http://www-bcf.usc.edu/~gareth/ISL/*) and ESL 3.2 (*http://statweb.stan ford.edu/~tibs/ElemStatLearn/*) for more information on generalized linear models.

> A fundamental limitation as of Spark 2.2 is that generalized linear regression only accepts a maximum of 4,096 features for inputs. This will likely change for later versions of Spark, so be sure to refer to the documentation.

Model Hyperparameters

These are configurations that we specify to determine the basic structure of the model itself. In addition to `fitIntercept` and `regParam` (mentioned in "Regression" on page 404), generalized linear regression includes several other hyperparameters:

`family`
  A description of the error distribution to be used in the model. Supported options are Poisson, binomial, gamma, Gaussian, and tweedie.

`link`
  The name of link function which provides the relationship between the linear predictor and the mean of the distribution function. Supported options are cloglog, probit, logit, inverse, sqrt, identity, and log (default: identity).

solver
The solver algorithm to be used for optimization. The only currently supported solver is `irls` (iteratively reweighted least squares).

variancePower
The power in the variance function of the Tweedie distribution, which characterizes the relationship between the variance and mean of the distribution. Only applicable to the Tweedie family. Supported values are 0 and [1, Infinity). The default is 0.

linkPower
The index in the power link function for the Tweedie family.

Training Parameters

The training parameters are the same that you will find for logistic regression. Consult Chapter 26 for more information.

Prediction Parameters

This model adds one prediction parameter:

linkPredictionCol
A column name that will hold the output of our link function for each prediction.

Example

Here's an example of using `GeneralizedLinearRegression`:

```scala
// in Scala
import org.apache.spark.ml.regression.GeneralizedLinearRegression
val glr = new GeneralizedLinearRegression()
  .setFamily("gaussian")
  .setLink("identity")
  .setMaxIter(10)
  .setRegParam(0.3)
  .setLinkPredictionCol("linkOut")
println(glr.explainParams())
val glrModel = glr.fit(df)
```

```python
# in Python
from pyspark.ml.regression import GeneralizedLinearRegression
glr = GeneralizedLinearRegression()\
  .setFamily("gaussian")\
  .setLink("identity")\
  .setMaxIter(10)\
  .setRegParam(0.3)\
  .setLinkPredictionCol("linkOut")
```

```
print glr.explainParams()
glrModel = glr.fit(df)
```

Training Summary

As for the simple linear model in the previous section, the training summary provided by Spark for the generalized linear model can help you ensure that your model is a good fit for the data that you used as the training set. It is important to note that this does not replace running your algorithm against a proper test set, but it can provide more information. This information includes a number of different potential metrics for analyzing the fit of your algorithm, including some of the most common success metrics:

R squared
  The coefficient of determination; a measure of fit.

The residuals
  The difference between the label and the predicted value.

Be sure to inspect the summary object on the model to see all the available methods.

Decision Trees

Decision trees as applied to regression work fairly similarly to decision trees applied to classification. The main difference is that decision trees for regression output a single number per leaf node instead of a label (as we saw with classification). The same interpretability properties and model structure still apply. In short, rather than trying to train coefficients to model a function, decision tree regression simply creates a tree to predict the numerical outputs. This is of significant consequence because unlike generalized linear regression, we can predict nonlinear functions in the input data. This also creates a significant risk of overfitting the data, so we need to be careful when tuning and evaluating these models.

We also covered decision trees in Chapter 26 (refer to "Decision Trees" on page 468). For more information on this topic, consult ISL 8.1 (*http://www-bcf.usc.edu/~gareth/ISL*) and ESL 9.2 (*http://statweb.stanford.edu/~tibs/ElemStatLearn/*).

Model Hyperparameters

The model hyperparameters that apply decision trees for regression are the same as those for classification except for a slight change to the impurity parameter. See Chapter 26 for more information on the other hyperparameters:

impurity

The impurity parameter represents the metric (information gain) for whether or not the model should split at a particular leaf node with a particular value or keep it as is. The only metric currently supported for regression trees is "variance."

Training Parameters

In addition to hyperparameters, classification and regression trees also share the same training parameters. See "Training Parameters" on page 465 for these parameters.

Example

Here's a short example of using a decision tree regressor:

```scala
// in Scala
import org.apache.spark.ml.regression.DecisionTreeRegressor
val dtr = new DecisionTreeRegressor()
println(dtr.explainParams())
val dtrModel = dtr.fit(df)
```

```python
# in Python
from pyspark.ml.regression import DecisionTreeRegressor
dtr = DecisionTreeRegressor()
print dtr.explainParams()
dtrModel = dtr.fit(df)
```

Random Forests and Gradient-Boosted Trees

The random forest and gradient-boosted tree models can be applied to both classification and regression. As a review, these both follow the same basic concept as the decision tree, except rather than training one tree, many trees are trained to perform a regression. In the random forest model, many de-correlated trees are trained and then averaged. With gradient-boosted trees, each tree makes a weighted prediction (such that some trees have more predictive power for some classes over others). Random forest and gradient-boosted tree regression have the same model hyperparameters and training parameters as the corresponding classification models, except for the purity measure (as is the case with DecisionTreeRegressor).

See ISL 8.2 (*http://www-bcf.usc.edu/~gareth/ISL/*) and ESL 10.1 (*http://statweb.stanford.edu/~tibs/ElemStatLearn/*) for more information on tree ensembles.

Model Hyperparameters

These models share many of the same parameters as we saw in the previous chapter as well as for regression decision trees. Refer back to "Model Hyperparameters" on page 464 for a thorough explanation of these parameters. As for a single regression tree, however, the only `impurity` metric currently supported is `variance`.

Training Parameters

These models support the same `checkpointInterval` parameter as classification trees, as described in Chapter 26.

Example

Here's a small example of how to use these two models to perform a regression:

```scala
// in Scala
import org.apache.spark.ml.regression.RandomForestRegressor
import org.apache.spark.ml.regression.GBTRegressor
val rf = new RandomForestRegressor()
println(rf.explainParams())
val rfModel = rf.fit(df)
val gbt = new GBTRegressor()
println(gbt.explainParams())
val gbtModel = gbt.fit(df)
```

```python
# in Python
from pyspark.ml.regression import RandomForestRegressor
from pyspark.ml.regression import GBTRegressor
rf =  RandomForestRegressor()
print rf.explainParams()
rfModel = rf.fit(df)
gbt = GBTRegressor()
print gbt.explainParams()
gbtModel = gbt.fit(df)
```

Advanced Methods

The preceding methods are highly general methods for performing a regression. The models are by no means exhaustive, but do provide the essential regression types that many folks use. This next section will cover some of the more specialized regression models that Spark includes. We omit code examples simply because they follow the same patterns as the other algorithms.

Survival Regression (Accelerated Failure Time)

Statisticians use survival analysis to understand the survival rate of individuals, typically in controlled experiments. Spark implements the accelerated failure time model, which, rather than describing the actual survival time, models the log of the survival time. This variation of survival regression is implemented in Spark because the more well-known Cox Proportional Hazard's model is semi-parametric and does not scale well to large datasets. By contrast, accelerated failure time does because each instance (row) contributes to the resulting model independently. Accelerated failure time does have different assumptions than the Cox survival model and therefore one is not necessarily a drop-in replacement for the other. Covering these differing assumptions is outside of the scope of this book. See L. J. Wei's paper (*http://bit.ly/2rKxqcW*) on accelerated failure time for more information.

The requirement for input is quite similar to that of other regressions. We will tune coefficients according to feature values. However, there is one departure, and that is the introduction of a censor variable column. A test subject *censors* during a scientific study when that individual drops out of a study, since their state at the end of the experiment may be unknown. This is important because we cannot assume an outcome for an individual that censors (doesn't report that state to the researchers) at some intermediate point in a study.

See more about survival regression with AFT in the documentation (*http://bit.ly/2nht2wD*).

Isotonic Regression

Isotonic regression is another specialized regression model, with some unique requirements. Essentially, *isotonic regression* specifies a piecewise linear function that is always monotonically increasing. It cannot decrease. This means that if your data is going up and to the right in a given plot, this is an appropriate model. If it varies over the course of input values, then this is not appropriate.

The illustration of isotonic regression's behavior in Figure 27-1 makes it much easier to understand.

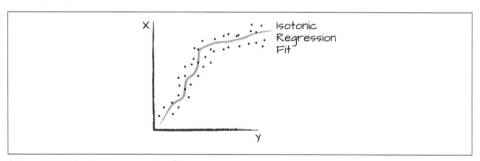

Figure 27-1. Isotonic regression line

Notice how this gets a better fit than the simple linear regression. See more about how to use this model in the Spark documentation (*http://spark.apache.org/docs/latest/ml-classification-regression.html#isotonic-regression*).

Evaluators and Automating Model Tuning

Regression has the same core model tuning functionality that we saw with classification. We can specify an evaluator, pick a metric to optimize for, and then train our pipeline to perform that parameter tuning on our part. The evaluator for regression, unsurprisingly, is called the RegressionEvaluator and allows us to optimize for a number of common regression success metrics. Just like the classification evaluator, RegressionEvaluator expects two columns, a column representing the prediction and another representing the true label. The supported metrics to optimize for are the root mean squared error ("rmse"), the mean squared error ("mse"), the r^2 metric ("r2"), and the mean absolute error ("mae").

To use RegressionEvaluator, we build up our pipeline, specify the parameters we would like to test, and then run it. Spark will automatically select the model that performs best and return this to us:

```scala
// in Scala
import org.apache.spark.ml.evaluation.RegressionEvaluator
import org.apache.spark.ml.regression.GeneralizedLinearRegression
import org.apache.spark.ml.Pipeline
import org.apache.spark.ml.tuning.{CrossValidator, ParamGridBuilder}
val glr = new GeneralizedLinearRegression()
  .setFamily("gaussian")
  .setLink("identity")
val pipeline = new Pipeline().setStages(Array(glr))
val params = new ParamGridBuilder().addGrid(glr.regParam, Array(0, 0.5, 1))
  .build()
val evaluator = new RegressionEvaluator()
  .setMetricName("rmse")
  .setPredictionCol("prediction")
  .setLabelCol("label")
val cv = new CrossValidator()
  .setEstimator(pipeline)
  .setEvaluator(evaluator)
  .setEstimatorParamMaps(params)
  .setNumFolds(2) // should always be 3 or more but this dataset is small
val model = cv.fit(df)
```

```python
# in Python
from pyspark.ml.evaluation import RegressionEvaluator
from pyspark.ml.regression import GeneralizedLinearRegression
from pyspark.ml import Pipeline
from pyspark.ml.tuning import CrossValidator, ParamGridBuilder
glr = GeneralizedLinearRegression().setFamily("gaussian").setLink("identity")
pipeline = Pipeline().setStages([glr])
params = ParamGridBuilder().addGrid(glr.regParam, [0, 0.5, 1]).build()
evaluator = RegressionEvaluator()\
  .setMetricName("rmse")\
  .setPredictionCol("prediction")\
  .setLabelCol("label")
```

```
cv = CrossValidator()\
  .setEstimator(pipeline)\
  .setEvaluator(evaluator)\
  .setEstimatorParamMaps(params)\
  .setNumFolds(2) # should always be 3 or more but this dataset is small
model = cv.fit(df)
```

Metrics

Evaluators allow us to evaluate and fit a model according to one specific metric, but we can also access a number of regression metrics via the `RegressionMetrics` object. As for the classification metrics in the previous chapter, `RegressionMetrics` operates on RDDs of (prediction, label) pairs. For instance, let's see how we can inspect the results of the previously trained model.

```scala
// in Scala
import org.apache.spark.mllib.evaluation.RegressionMetrics
val out = model.transform(df)
  .select("prediction", "label")
  .rdd.map(x => (x(0).asInstanceOf[Double], x(1).asInstanceOf[Double]))
val metrics = new RegressionMetrics(out)
println(s"MSE = ${metrics.meanSquaredError}")
println(s"RMSE = ${metrics.rootMeanSquaredError}")
println(s"R-squared = ${metrics.r2}")
println(s"MAE = ${metrics.meanAbsoluteError}")
println(s"Explained variance = ${metrics.explainedVariance}")
```

```python
# in Python
from pyspark.mllib.evaluation import RegressionMetrics
out = model.transform(df)\
  .select("prediction", "label").rdd.map(lambda x: (float(x[0]), float(x[1])))
metrics = RegressionMetrics(out)
print "MSE: " + str(metrics.meanSquaredError)
print "RMSE: " + str(metrics.rootMeanSquaredError)
print "R-squared: " + str(metrics.r2)
print "MAE: " + str(metrics.meanAbsoluteError)
print "Explained variance: " + str(metrics.explainedVariance)
```

Consult the Spark documentation (*http://bit.ly/2rFTbef*) for the latest methods.

Conclusion

In this chapter, we covered the basics of regression in Spark, including how we train models and how we measure success. In the next chapter, we'll take a look at recommendation engines, one of the more popular applications of MLlib.

## CHAPTER 28

Recommendation

The task of recommendation is one of the most intuitive. By studying people's explicit preferences (through ratings) or implicit preferences (through observed behavior), you can make recommendations on what one user may like by drawing similarities between the user and other users, or between the products they liked and other products. Using the underlying similarities, recommendation engines can make new recommendations to other users.

Use Cases

Recommendation engines are one of the best use cases for big data. It's fairly easy to collect training data about users' past preferences at scale, and this data can be used in many domains to connect users with new content. Spark is an open source tool of choice used across a variety of companies for large-scale recommendations:

Movie recommendations
> Amazon, Netflix, and HBO all want to provide relevant film and TV content to their users. Netflix utilizes Spark (*https://youtu.be/II8GlmbDg9M*), to make large scale movie recommendations to their users.

Course recommendations
> A school might want to recommend courses to students by studying what courses similar students have liked or taken. Past enrollment data makes for a very easy to collect training dataset for this task.

In Spark, there is one workhorse recommendation algorithm, Alternating Least Squares (ALS). This algorithm leverages a technique called *collaborative filtering*, which makes recommendations based only on which items users interacted with in the past. That is, it does not require or use any additional features about the users or the items. It supports several ALS variants (e.g., explicit or implicit feedback). Apart from ALS, Spark provides Frequent Pattern Mining for finding association rules in market basket analysis. Finally, Spark's RDD API (*http://spark.apache.org/docs/latest/mllib-collaborative-filtering.html*) also includes a lower-level matrix factorization method that will not be covered in this book.

Collaborative Filtering with Alternating Least Squares

ALS finds a k-dimensional feature vector for each user and item such that the dot product of each user's feature vector with each item's feature vector approximates the user's rating for that item. Therefore this only requires an input dataset of existing ratings between user-item pairs, with three columns: a user ID column, an item ID column (e.g., a movie), and a rating column. The ratings can either be *explicit*—a numerical rating that we aim to predict directly—or *implicit*—in which case each rating represents the strength of interactions observed between a user and item (e.g., number of visits to a particular page), which measures our level of confidence in the user's preference for that item. Given this input DataFrame, the model will produce feature vectors that you can use to predict users' ratings for items they have not yet rated.

One issue to note in practice is that this algorithm does have a preference for serving things that are very common or that it has a lot of information on. If you're introducing a new product that no users have expressed a preference for, the algorithm isn't going to recommend it to many people. Additionally, if new users are onboarding onto the platform, they may not have any ratings in the training set. Therefore, the algorithm won't know what to recommend them. These are examples of what we call the *cold start problem*, which we discuss later on in the chapter.

In terms of scalability, one reason for Spark's popularity for this task is that the algorithm and implementation in MLlib can scale to millions of users, millions of items, and billions of ratings.

Model Hyperparameters

These are configurations that we can specify to determine the structure of the model as well as the specific collaborative filtering problem we wish to solve:

rank
> The rank term determines the dimension of the feature vectors learned for users and items. This should normally be tuned through experimentation. The core trade-off is that by specifying too high a rank, the algorithm may overfit the training data; but by specifying a low rank, then it may not make the best possible predictions. The default value is 10.

`alpha`

When training on implicit feedback (behavioral observations), the alpha sets a baseline confidence for preference. This has a default of 1.0 and should be driven through experimentation.

`regParam`

Controls regularization to prevent overfitting. You should test out different values for the regularization parameter to find the optimal value for your problem. The default is 0.1.

`implicitPrefs`

This Boolean value specifies whether you are training on implicit (`true`) or explicit (`false`) (refer back to the preceding discussion for an explanation of the difference between explicit and implicit). This value should be set based on the data that you're using as input to the model. If the data is based off passive endorsement of a product (say, via a click or page visit), then you should use implicit preferences. In contrast, if the data is an explicit rating (e.g., the user gave this restaurant 4/5 stars), you should use explicit preferences. Explicit preferences are the default.

`nonnegative`

If set to true, this parameter configures the model to place non-negative constraints on the least-squares problem it solves and only return non-negative feature vectors. This can improve performance in some applications. The default value is `false`.

Training Parameters

The training parameters for alternating least squares are a bit different from those that we have seen in other models. That's because we're going to get more low-level control over how the data is distributed across the cluster. The groups of data that are distributed around the cluster are called *blocks*. Determining how much data to place in each block can have a significant impact on the time it takes to train the algorithm (but not the final result). A good rule of thumb is to aim for approximately one to five million ratings per block. If you have less data than that in each block, more blocks will not improve the algorithm's performance.

`numUserBlocks`

This determines how many blocks to split the users into. The default is 10.

`numItemBlocks`

This determines how many blocks to split the items into. The default is 10.

`maxIter`
Total number of iterations over the data before stopping. Changing this probably won't change your results a ton, so this shouldn't be the first parameter you adjust. The default is `10`. An example of when you might want to increase this is that after inspecting your objective history and noticing that it doesn't flatline after a certain number of training iterations.

`checkpointInterval`
Checkpointing allows you to save model state during training to more quickly recover from node failures. You can set a checkpoint directory using `SparkCon text.setCheckpointDir`.

`seed`
Specifying a random seed can help you replicate your results.

Prediction Parameters

Prediction parameters determine how a trained model should actually make predictions. In our case, there's one parameter: the cold start strategy (set through `cold StartStrategy`). This setting determines what the model should predict for users or items that did not appear in the training set.

The cold start challenge commonly arises when you're serving a model in production, and new users and/or items have no ratings history, and therefore the model has no recommendation to make. It can also occur when using simple random splits as in Spark's `CrossValidator` or `TrainValidationSplit`, where it is very common to encounter users and/or items in the evaluation set that are not in the training set.

By default, Spark will assign `NaN` prediction values when it encounters a user and/or item that is not present in the actual model. This can be useful because you design your overall system to fall back to some default recommendation when a new user or item is in the system. However, this is undesirable during training because it will ruin the ability for your evaluator to properly measure the success of your model. This makes model selection impossible. Spark allows users to set the `coldStartStrategy` parameter to `drop` in order to drop any rows in the DataFrame of predictions that contain `NaN` values. The evaluation metric will then be computed over the non-`NaN` data and will be valid. `drop` and `nan` (the default) are the only currently supported cold-start strategies.

Example

This example will make use of a dataset that we have not used thus far in the book, the MovieLens movie rating dataset. This dataset, naturally, has information relevant for making movie recommendations. We will first use this dataset to train a model:

```scala
// in Scala
import org.apache.spark.ml.recommendation.ALS
val ratings = spark.read.textFile("/data/sample_movielens_ratings.txt")
  .selectExpr("split(value , '::') as col")
  .selectExpr(
    "cast(col[0] as int) as userId",
    "cast(col[1] as int) as movieId",
    "cast(col[2] as float) as rating",
    "cast(col[3] as long) as timestamp")
val Array(training, test) = ratings.randomSplit(Array(0.8, 0.2))
val als = new ALS()
  .setMaxIter(5)
  .setRegParam(0.01)
  .setUserCol("userId")
  .setItemCol("movieId")
  .setRatingCol("rating")
println(als.explainParams())
val alsModel = als.fit(training)
val predictions = alsModel.transform(test)
```

```python
# in Python
from pyspark.ml.recommendation import ALS
from pyspark.sql import Row
ratings = spark.read.text("/data/sample_movielens_ratings.txt")\
  .rdd.toDF()\
  .selectExpr("split(value , '::') as col")\
  .selectExpr(
    "cast(col[0] as int) as userId",
    "cast(col[1] as int) as movieId",
    "cast(col[2] as float) as rating",
    "cast(col[3] as long) as timestamp")
training, test = ratings.randomSplit([0.8, 0.2])
als = ALS()\
  .setMaxIter(5)\
  .setRegParam(0.01)\
  .setUserCol("userId")\
  .setItemCol("movieId")\
  .setRatingCol("rating")
print als.explainParams()
alsModel = als.fit(training)
predictions = alsModel.transform(test)
```

We can now output the top k recommendations for each user or movie. The model's
recommendForAllUsers method returns a DataFrame of a userId, an array of recommendations, as well as a rating for each of those movies. recommendForAllItems
returns a DataFrame of a movieId, as well as the top users for that movie:

```scala
// in Scala
alsModel.recommendForAllUsers(10)
  .selectExpr("userId", "explode(recommendations)").show()
alsModel.recommendForAllItems(10)
  .selectExpr("movieId", "explode(recommendations)").show()
```

```python
# in Python
alsModel.recommendForAllUsers(10)\
  .selectExpr("userId", "explode(recommendations)").show()
alsModel.recommendForAllItems(10)\
  .selectExpr("movieId", "explode(recommendations)").show()
```

Evaluators for Recommendation

When covering the cold-start strategy, we can set up an automatic model evaluator when working with ALS. One thing that may not be immediately obvious is that this recommendation problem is really just a kind of regression problem. Since we're predicting values (ratings) for given users, we want to optimize for reducing the total difference between our users' ratings and the true values. We can do this using the same `RegressionEvaluator` that we saw in Chapter 27. You can place this in a pipeline to automate the training process. When doing this, you should also set the cold-start strategy to be `drop` instead of `NaN` and then switch it back to `NaN` when it comes time to actually make predictions in your production system:

```scala
// in Scala
import org.apache.spark.ml.evaluation.RegressionEvaluator
val evaluator = new RegressionEvaluator()
  .setMetricName("rmse")
  .setLabelCol("rating")
  .setPredictionCol("prediction")
val rmse = evaluator.evaluate(predictions)
println(s"Root-mean-square error = $rmse")
```

```python
# in Python
from pyspark.ml.evaluation import RegressionEvaluator
evaluator = RegressionEvaluator()\
  .setMetricName("rmse")\
  .setLabelCol("rating")\
  .setPredictionCol("prediction")
rmse = evaluator.evaluate(predictions)
print("Root-mean-square error = %f" % rmse)
```

Metrics

Recommendation results can be measured using both the standard regression metrics and some recommendation-specific metrics. It should come as no surprise that there are more sophisticated ways of measuring recommendation success than simply evaluating based on regression. These metrics are particularly useful for evaluating your final model.

Regression Metrics

We can recycle the regression metrics for recommendation. This is because we can simply see how close each prediction is to the actual rating for that user and item:

```scala
// in Scala
import org.apache.spark.mllib.evaluation.{
  RankingMetrics,
  RegressionMetrics}
val regComparison = predictions.select("rating", "prediction")
  .rdd.map(x => (x.getFloat(0).toDouble,x.getFloat(1).toDouble))
val metrics = new RegressionMetrics(regComparison)
```

```python
# in Python
from pyspark.mllib.evaluation import RegressionMetrics
regComparison = predictions.select("rating", "prediction")\
  .rdd.map(lambda x: (x(0), x(1)))
metrics = RegressionMetrics(regComparison)
```

Ranking Metrics

More interestingly, we also have another tool: ranking metrics. A RankingMetric allows us to compare our recommendations with an actual set of ratings (or preferences) expressed by a given user. RankingMetric does not focus on the value of the rank but rather whether or not our algorithm recommends an already ranked item again to a user. This does require some data preparation on our part. You may want to refer to Part II for a refresher on some of the methods. First, we need to collect a set of highly ranked movies for a given user. In our case, we're going to use a rather low threshold: movies ranked above 2.5. Tuning this value will largely be a business decision:

```scala
// in Scala
import org.apache.spark.mllib.evaluation.{RankingMetrics, RegressionMetrics}
import org.apache.spark.sql.functions.{col, expr}
val perUserActual = predictions
  .where("rating > 2.5")
  .groupBy("userId")
  .agg(expr("collect_set(movieId) as movies"))
```

```python
# in Python
from pyspark.mllib.evaluation import RankingMetrics, RegressionMetrics
from pyspark.sql.functions import col, expr
perUserActual = predictions\
  .where("rating > 2.5")\
  .groupBy("userId")\
  .agg(expr("collect_set(movieId) as movies"))
```

At this point, we have a collection of users, along with a truth set of previously ranked movies for each user. Now we will get our top 10 recommendations from our algorithm on a per-user basis. We will then see if the top 10 recommendations show up in our truth set. If we have a well-trained model, it will correctly recommend the movies a user already liked. If it doesn't, it may not have learned enough about each particular user to successfully reflect their preferences:

```scala
// in Scala
val perUserPredictions = predictions
```

```
  .orderBy(col("userId"), col("prediction").desc)
  .groupBy("userId")
  .agg(expr("collect_list(movieId) as movies"))

# in Python
perUserPredictions = predictions\
  .orderBy(col("userId"), expr("prediction DESC"))\
  .groupBy("userId")\
  .agg(expr("collect_list(movieId) as movies"))
```

Now we have two DataFrames, one of predictions and another the top-ranked items for a particular user. We can pass them into the RankingMetrics object. This object accepts an RDD of these combinations, as you can see in the following join and RDD conversion:

```
// in Scala
val perUserActualvPred = perUserActual.join(perUserPredictions, Seq("userId"))
  .map(row => (
    row(1).asInstanceOf[Seq[Integer]].toArray,
    row(2).asInstanceOf[Seq[Integer]].toArray.take(15)
  ))
val ranks = new RankingMetrics(perUserActualvPred.rdd)

# in Python
perUserActualvPred = perUserActual.join(perUserPredictions, ["userId"]).rdd\
  .map(lambda row: (row[1], row[2][:15]))
ranks = RankingMetrics(perUserActualvPred)
```

Now we can see the metrics from that ranking. For instance, we can see how precise our algorithm is with the mean average precision. We can also get the precision at certain ranking points, for instance, to see where the majority of the positive recommendations fall:

```
// in Scala
ranks.meanAveragePrecision
ranks.precisionAt(5)

# in Python
ranks.meanAveragePrecision
ranks.precisionAt(5)
```

Frequent Pattern Mining

In addition to ALS, another tool that MLlib provides for creating recommendations is frequent pattern mining. *Frequent pattern mining*, sometimes referred to as *market basket analysis*, looks at raw data and finds association rules. For instance, given a large number of transactions it might identify that users who buy hot dogs almost always purchase hot dog buns. This technique can be applied in the recommendation context, especially when people are filling shopping carts (either on or offline). Spark implements the FP-growth algorithm for frequent pattern mining. See the Spark documentation (*https://spark.apache.org/docs/latest/ml-frequent-pattern-mining.html#fp-growth*) and ESL 14.2 for more information about this algorithm.

Conclusion

In this chapter, we discussed one of Spark's most popular machine learning algorithms in practice—alternating least squares for recommendation. We saw how we can train, tune, and evaluate this model. In the next chapter, we'll move to unsupervised learning and discuss clustering.

## CHAPTER 29

Unsupervised Learning

This chapter will cover the details of Spark's available tools for unsupervised learning, focusing specifically on clustering. Unsupervised learning is, generally speaking, used less often than supervised learning because it's usually harder to apply and measure success (from an end-result perspective). These challenges can become exacerbated at scale. For instance, clustering in high-dimensional space can create odd clusters simply because of the properties of high-dimensional spaces, something referred to as *the curse of dimensionality*. The curse of dimensionality describes the fact that as a feature space expands in dimensionality, it becomes increasingly sparse. This means that the data needed to fill this space for statistically meaningful results increases rapidly with any increase in dimensionality. Additionally, with high dimensions comes more noise in the data. This, in turn, may cause your model to hone in on noise instead of the true factors causing a particular result or grouping. Therefore in the model scalability table, we include computational limits, as well as a set of statistical recommendations. These are heuristics and should be helpful guides, not requirements.

At its core, *unsupervised learning* is trying to discover patterns or derive a concise representation of the underlying structure of a given dataset.

Use Cases

Here are some potential use cases. At its core, these patterns might reveal topics, anomalies, or groupings in our data that may not have been obvious beforehand:

Finding anomalies in data
   If the majority of values in a dataset cluster into a larger group with several small groups on the outside, those groups might warrant further investigation.

Topic modeling
By looking at large bodies of text, it is possible to find topics that exist across those different documents.

Model Scalability

Just like with our other models, it's important to mention the basic model scalability requirements along with statistical recommendations.

Table 29-1. Clustering model scalability reference

Model	Statistical recommendation	Computation limits	Training examples
k-means	50 to 100 maximum	Features x clusters < 10 million	No limit
Bisecting k-means	50 to 100 maximum	Features x clusters < 10 million	No limit
GMM	50 to 100 maximum	Features x clusters < 10 million	No limit
LDA	An interpretable number	1,000s of topics	No limit

Let's get started by loading some example numerical data:

```Scala
// in Scala
import org.apache.spark.ml.feature.VectorAssembler

val va = new VectorAssembler()
  .setInputCols(Array("Quantity", "UnitPrice"))
  .setOutputCol("features")

val sales = va.transform(spark.read.format("csv")
  .option("header", "true")
  .option("inferSchema", "true")
  .load("/data/retail-data/by-day/*.csv")
  .limit(50)
  .coalesce(1)
  .where("Description IS NOT NULL"))

sales.cache()
```

```Python
# in Python
from pyspark.ml.feature import VectorAssembler
va = VectorAssembler()\
  .setInputCols(["Quantity", "UnitPrice"])\
  .setOutputCol("features")

sales = va.transform(spark.read.format("csv")
  .option("header", "true")
  .option("inferSchema", "true")
  .load("/data/retail-data/by-day/*.csv")
  .limit(50)
  .coalesce(1)
  .where("Description IS NOT NULL"))
```

```
sales.cache()
```

k-means

k-means is one of the most popular clustering algorithms. In this algorithm, a user-specified number of clusters (k) are randomly assigned to different points in the dataset. The unassigned points are then "assigned" to a cluster based on their proximity (measured in Euclidean distance) to the previously assigned point. Once this assignment happens, the center of this cluster (called the *centroid*) is computed, and the process repeats. All points are assigned to a particular centroid, and a new centroid is computed. We repeat this process for a finite number of iterations or until convergence (i.e., when our centroid locations stop changing). This does not, however, mean that our clusters are always sensical. For instance, a given "logical" cluster of data might be split right down the middle simply because of the starting points of two distinct clusters. Thus, it is often a good idea to perform multiple runs of k-means starting with different initializations.

Choosing the right value for k is an extremely important aspect of using this algorithm successfully, as well as a hard task. There's no real prescription for the number of clusters you need, so you'll likely have to experiment with different values and consider what you would like the end result to be.

For more information on k-means, see ISL 10.3 (*http://www-bcf.usc.edu/~gareth/ISL/*) and ESL 14.3 (*http://statweb.stanford.edu/~tibs/ElemStatLearn/*).

Model Hyperparameters

These are configurations that we specify to determine the basic structure of the model:

k
   This is the number of clusters that you would like to end up with.

Training Parameters

`initMode`
   The initialization mode is the algorithm that determines the starting locations of the centroids. The supported options are `random` and `k-means||` (the default). The latter is a parallelized variant of the `k-means||` (*http://theory.stanford.edu/~sergei/papers/kMeansPP-soda.pdf*) method. While the details are not within the scope of this book, the thinking behind the latter method is that rather than simply choosing random initialization locations, the algorithm chooses cluster centers that are already well spread out to generate a better clustering.

initSteps

The number of steps for k-means|| initialization mode. Must be greater than 0. (The default value is 2.)

maxIter

Total number of iterations over the data before stopping. Changing this probably won't change your results a ton, so don't make this the first parameter you look to adjust. The default is 20.

tol

Specifies a threshold by which changes in centroids show that we optimized our model enough, and can stop iterating early, before maxIter iterations. The default value is 0.0001.

This algorithm is generally robust to these parameters, and the main trade-off is that running more initialization steps and iterations may lead to a better clustering at the expense of longer training time:

Example

```scala
// in Scala
import org.apache.spark.ml.clustering.KMeans
val km = new KMeans().setK(5)
println(km.explainParams())
val kmModel = km.fit(sales)
```

```python
# in Python
from pyspark.ml.clustering import KMeans
km = KMeans().setK(5)
print km.explainParams()
kmModel = km.fit(sales)
```

k-means Metrics Summary

k-means includes a summary class that we can use to evaluate our model. This class provides some common measures for k-means success (whether these apply to your problem set is another question). The k-means summary includes information about the clusters created, as well as their relative sizes (number of examples).

We can also compute the *within set sum of squared errors*, which can help measure how close our values are from each cluster centroid, using computeCost. The implicit goal in k-means is that we want to minimize the within set sum of squared error, subject to the given number k of clusters:

```scala
// in Scala
val summary = kmModel.summary
summary.clusterSizes // number of points
kmModel.computeCost(sales)
```

```
println("Cluster Centers: ")
kmModel.clusterCenters.foreach(println)

# in Python
summary = kmModel.summary
print summary.clusterSizes # number of points
kmModel.computeCost(sales)
centers = kmModel.clusterCenters()
print("Cluster Centers: ")
for center in centers:
    print(center)
```

Bisecting k-means

Bisecting k-means is a variant of k-means. The core difference is that instead of clustering points by starting "bottom-up" and assigning a bunch of different groups in the data, this is a top-down clustering method. This means that it will start by creating a single group and then splitting that group into smaller groups in order to end up with the k number of clusters specified by the user. This is usually a faster method than k-means and will yield different results.

Model Hyperparameters

These are configurations that we specify to determine the basic structure of the model:

k

This is the number of clusters that you would like to end up with.

Training Parameters

minDivisibleClusterSize

The minimum number of points (if greater than or equal to 1.0) or the minimum proportion of points (if less than 1.0) of a divisible cluster. The default is 1.0, meaning that there must be at least one point in each cluster.

maxIter

Total number of iterations over the data before stopping. Changing this probably won't change your results a ton, so don't make this the first parameter you look to adjust. The default is 20.

Most of the parameters in this model should be tuned in order to find the best result. There's no rule that applies to all datasets.

Example

```
// in Scala
import org.apache.spark.ml.clustering.BisectingKMeans
```

```scala
val bkm = new BisectingKMeans().setK(5).setMaxIter(5)
println(bkm.explainParams())
val bkmModel = bkm.fit(sales)
```

```python
# in Python
from pyspark.ml.clustering import BisectingKMeans
bkm = BisectingKMeans().setK(5).setMaxIter(5)
bkmModel = bkm.fit(sales)
```

Bisecting k-means Summary

Bisecting k-means includes a summary class that we can use to evaluate our model, that is largely the same as the k-means summary. This includes information about the clusters created, as well as their relative sizes (number of examples):

```scala
// in Scala
val summary = bkmModel.summary
summary.clusterSizes // number of points
kmModel.computeCost(sales)
println("Cluster Centers: ")
kmModel.clusterCenters.foreach(println)
```

```python
# in Python
summary = bkmModel.summary
print summary.clusterSizes # number of points
kmModel.computeCost(sales)
centers = kmModel.clusterCenters()
print("Cluster Centers: ")
for center in centers:
    print(center)
```

Gaussian Mixture Models

Gaussian mixture models (GMM) are another popular clustering algorithm that makes different assumptions than bisecting k-means or k-means do. Those algorithms try to group data by reducing the sum of squared distances from the center of the cluster. Gaussian mixture models, on the other hand, assume that each cluster produces data based upon random draws from a Gaussian distribution. This means that clusters of data should be less likely to have data at the edge of the cluster (reflected in the Guassian distribution) and much higher probability of having data in the center. Each Gaussian cluster can be of arbitrary size with its own mean and standard deviation (and hence a possibly different, ellipsoid shape). There are still k user-specified clusters that will be created during training.

A simplified way of thinking about Gaussian mixture models is that they're like a soft version of k-means. k-means creates very rigid clusters—each point is only within one cluster. GMMs allow for a more nuanced cluster associated with probabilities, instead of rigid boundaries.

For more information, see ESL (*http://statweb.stanford.edu/~tibs/ElemStatLearn/*) 14.3.

Model Hyperparameters

These are configurations that we specify to determine the basic structure of the model:

k

This is the number of clusters that you would like to end up with.

Training Parameters

maxIter

Total number of iterations over the data before stopping. Changing this probably won't change your results a ton, so don't make this the first parameter you look to adjust. The default is 100.

tol

This value simply helps us specify a threshold by which changes in parameters show that we optimized our weights enough. A smaller value can lead to higher accuracy at the cost of performing more iterations (although never more than maxIter). The default value is 0.01.

As with our *k*-means model, these training parameters are less likely to have an impact than the number of clusters, *k*.

Example

```scala
// in Scala
import org.apache.spark.ml.clustering.GaussianMixture
val gmm = new GaussianMixture().setK(5)
println(gmm.explainParams())
val model = gmm.fit(sales)
```

```python
# in Python
from pyspark.ml.clustering import GaussianMixture
gmm = GaussianMixture().setK(5)
print gmm.explainParams()
model = gmm.fit(sales)
```

Gaussian Mixture Model Summary

Like our other clustering algorithms, Gaussian mixture models include a summary class to help with model evaluation. This includes information about the clusters created, like the weights, the means, and the covariance of the Gaussian mixture, which can help us learn more about the underlying structure inside of our data:

```scala
// in Scala
val summary = model.summary
model.weights
model.gaussiansDF.show()
summary.cluster.show()
summary.clusterSizes
summary.probability.show()
```

```python
# in Python
summary = model.summary
print model.weights
model.gaussiansDF.show()
summary.cluster.show()
summary.clusterSizes
summary.probability.show()
```

Latent Dirichlet Allocation

Latent Dirichlet Allocation (LDA) is a hierarchical clustering model typically used to perform topic modelling on text documents. LDA tries to extract high-level topics from a series of documents and keywords associated with those topics. It then interprets each document as having a variable number of contributions from multiple input topics. There are two implementations that you can use: online LDA and expectation maximization. In general, online LDA will work better when there are more examples, and the expectation maximization optimizer will work better when there is a larger input vocabulary. This method is also capable of scaling to hundreds or thousands of topics.

To input our text data into LDA, we're going to have to convert it into a numeric format. You can use the `CountVectorizer` to achieve this.

Model Hyperparameters

These are configurations that we specify to determine the basic structure of the model:

k

> The total number of topics to infer from the data. The default is 10 and must be a positive number.

docConcentration

> Concentration parameter (commonly named "alpha") for the prior placed on documents' distributions over topics ("theta"). This is the parameter to a Dirichlet distribution, where larger values mean more smoothing (more regularization).

If not set by the user, then docConcentration is set automatically. If set to single-ton vector [alpha], then alpha is replicated to a vector of length k in fitting. Otherwise, the docConcentration vector must be length k.

topicConcentration

The concentration parameter (commonly named "beta" or "eta") for the prior placed on a topic's distributions over terms. This is the parameter to a symmetric Dirichlet distribution. If not set by the user, then topicConcentration is set automatically.

Training Parameters

These are configurations that specify how we perform training:

maxIter

Total number of iterations over the data before stopping. Changing this probably won't change your results a ton, so don't make this the first parameter you look to adjust. The default is 20.

optimizer

This determines whether to use EM or online training optimization to determine the LDA model. The default is online.

learningDecay

Learning rate, set as an exponential decay rate. This should be between (0.5, 1.0] to guarantee asymptotic convergence. The default is 0.51 and only applies to the online optimizer.

learningOffset

A (positive) learning parameter that downweights early iterations. Larger values make early iterations count less. The default is 1,024.0 and only applies to the online optimizer.

optimizeDocConcentration

Indicates whether the docConcentration (Dirichlet parameter for document-topic distribution) will be optimized during training. The default is true but only applies to the online optimizer.

subsamplingRate

The fraction of the corpus to be sampled and used in each iteration of mini-batch gradient descent, in range (0, 1]. The default is 0.5 and only applies to the online optimizer.

seed

This model also supports specifying a random seed for reproducibility.

checkpointInterval

This is the same checkpoint feature that we saw in Chapter 26.

Prediction Parameters

topicDistributionCol

The column that will hold the output of the topic mixture distribution for each document.

Example

```scala
// in Scala
import org.apache.spark.ml.feature.{Tokenizer, CountVectorizer}
val tkn = new Tokenizer().setInputCol("Description").setOutputCol("DescOut")
val tokenized = tkn.transform(sales.drop("features"))
val cv = new CountVectorizer()
  .setInputCol("DescOut")
  .setOutputCol("features")
  .setVocabSize(500)
  .setMinTF(0)
  .setMinDF(0)
  .setBinary(true)
val cvFitted = cv.fit(tokenized)
val prepped = cvFitted.transform(tokenized)
```

```python
# in Python
from pyspark.ml.feature import Tokenizer, CountVectorizer
tkn = Tokenizer().setInputCol("Description").setOutputCol("DescOut")
tokenized = tkn.transform(sales.drop("features"))
cv = CountVectorizer()\
  .setInputCol("DescOut")\
  .setOutputCol("features")\
  .setVocabSize(500)\
  .setMinTF(0)\
  .setMinDF(0)\
  .setBinary(True)
cvFitted = cv.fit(tokenized)
prepped = cvFitted.transform(tokenized)
```

```scala
// in Scala
import org.apache.spark.ml.clustering.LDA
val lda = new LDA().setK(10).setMaxIter(5)
println(lda.explainParams())
val model = lda.fit(prepped)
```

```python
# in Python
from pyspark.ml.clustering import LDA
lda = LDA().setK(10).setMaxIter(5)
print lda.explainParams()
model = lda.fit(prepped)
```

After we train the model, you will see some of the top topics. This will return the term indices, and we'll have to look these up using the `CountVectorizerModel` that we trained in order to find out the true words. For instance, when we trained on the data our top 3 topics were hot, home, and brown after looking them up in our vocabulary:

```scala
// in Scala
model.describeTopics(3).show()
cvFitted.vocabulary
```

```python
# in Python
model.describeTopics(3).show()
cvFitted.vocabulary
```

These methods result in detailed information about the vocabulary used as well as the emphasis on particular terms. These can be helpful for better understanding the underlying topics. Due to space constraints, we can't show this output. Using similar APIs, we can get some more technical measures like the log likelihood and perplexity. The goal of these tools is to help you optimize the number of topics, based on your data. When using perplexity in your success criteria, you should apply these metrics to a holdout set to reduce the overall perplexity of the model. Another option is to optimize to increase the log likelihood value on the holdout set. We can calculate each of these by passing a dataset into the following functions: `model.logLikelihood` and `model.logPerplexity`.

Conclusion

This chapter covered the most popular algorithms that Spark includes for unsupervised learning. The next chapter will bring us out of MLlib and talk about some of the advanced analytics ecosystem that has grown outside of Spark.

## CHAPTER 30

Graph Analytics

The previous chapter covered some conventional unsupervised techniques. This chapter is going to dive into a more specialized toolset: graph processing. Graphs are data structures composed of *nodes*, or *vertices*, which are arbitrary objects, and *edges* that define relationships between these nodes. *Graph analytics* is the process of analyzing these relationships. An example graph might be your friend group. In the context of graph analytics, each vertex or node would represent a person, and each edge would represent a relationship. Figure 30-1 shows a sample graph.

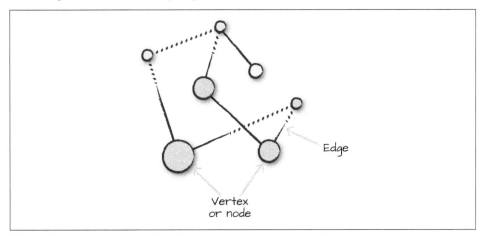

Figure 30-1. A sample graph with seven nodes and seven edges

This particular graph is *undirected*, in that the edges do not have a specified "start" and "end" vertex. There are also *directed* graphs that specify a start and end. Figure 30-2 shows a *directed* graph where the edges are directional.

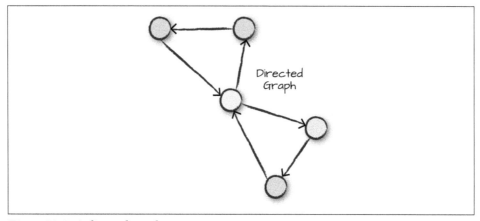

Figure 30-2. A directed graph

Edges and vertices in graphs can also have data associated with them. In our friend example, the weight of the edge might represent the intimacy between different friends; acquaintances would have low-weight edges between them, while married individuals would have edges with large weights. We could set this value by looking at communication frequency between nodes and weighting the edges accordingly. Each vertex (person) might also have data such as a name.

Graphs are a natural way of describing relationships and many different problem sets, and Spark provides several ways of working in this analytics paradigm. Some business use cases could be detecting credit card fraud, motif finding, determining importance of papers in bibliographic networks (i.e., which papers are most referenced), and ranking web pages, as Google famously used the PageRank algorithm to do.

Spark has long contained an RDD-based library for performing graph processing: GraphX. This provided a very low-level interface that was extremely powerful, but just like RDDs, wasn't easy to use or optimize. GraphX remains a core part of Spark. Companies continue to build production applications on top of it, and it still sees some minor feature development. The GraphX API is well documented simply because it hasn't changed much since its creation. However, some of the developers of Spark (including some of the original authors of GraphX) have recently created a next-generation graph analytics library on Spark: GraphFrames. GraphFrames extends GraphX to provide a DataFrame API and support for Spark's different language bindings so that users of Python can take advantage of the scalability of the tool. In this book, we will focus on GraphFrames.

GraphFrames (*http://graphframes.github.io/index.html*) is currently available as a Spark package (*http://spark-packages.org/package/graphframes/graphframes*), an external package that you need to load when you start up your Spark application, but may be merged into the core of Spark in the future. For the most part, there should be little difference in performance between the two (except for a huge user experience improvement in GraphFrames). There is some small overhead when using Graph-Frames, but for the most part it tries to call down to GraphX where appropriate; and for most, the user experience gains greatly outweigh this minor overhead.

How Does GraphFrames Compare to Graph Databases?

Spark is not a database. Spark is a distributed computation engine, but it does not store data long-term or perform transactions. You can build a graph computation on top of Spark, but that's fundamentally different from a database. GraphFrames can scale to much larger workloads than many graph databases and performs well for analytics but does not support transactional processing and serving.

The goal of this chapter is to show you how to use GraphFrames to perform graph analytics on Spark. We are going to be doing this with publicly available bike data from the Bay Area Bike Share portal (*http://www.bayareabikeshare.com/open-data*).

During the course of writing this book, this map and data have changed dramatically (even the naming!). We include a copy of the dataset inside the *data* folder (*https://github.com/databricks/Spark-The-Definitive-Guide/tree/master/data*) of this book's repository. Be sure to use that dataset to replicate the following results; and when you're feeling adventurous, expand to the whole dataset!

To get set up, you're going to need to point to the proper package. To do this from the command line, you'll run:

```
./bin/spark-shell --packages graphframes:graphframes:0.5.0-spark2.2-s_2.11
```

```
// in Scala
val bikeStations = spark.read.option("header","true")
  .csv("/data/bike-data/201508_station_data.csv")
val tripData = spark.read.option("header","true")
  .csv("/data/bike-data/201508_trip_data.csv")
```

```
# in Python
bikeStations = spark.read.option("header","true")\
  .csv("/data/bike-data/201508_station_data.csv")
tripData = spark.read.option("header","true")\
  .csv("/data/bike-data/201508_trip_data.csv")
```

Building a Graph

The first step is to build the graph. To do this we need to define the vertices and edges, which are DataFrames with some specifically named columns. In our case, we're creating a *directed graph*. This graph will point from the source to the location.

In the context of this bike trip data, this will point from a trip's starting location to a trip's ending location. To define the graph, we use the naming conventions for columns presented in the GraphFrames library. In the vertices table we define our identifier as `id` (in our case this is of string type), and in the edges table we label each edge's source vertex ID as `src` and the destination ID as `dst`:

```scala
// in Scala
val stationVertices = bikeStations.withColumnRenamed("name", "id").distinct()
val tripEdges = tripData
  .withColumnRenamed("Start Station", "src")
  .withColumnRenamed("End Station", "dst")
```

```python
# in Python
stationVertices = bikeStations.withColumnRenamed("name", "id").distinct()
tripEdges = tripData\
  .withColumnRenamed("Start Station", "src")\
  .withColumnRenamed("End Station", "dst")
```

We can now build a GraphFrame object, which represents our graph, from the vertex and edge DataFrames we have so far. We will also leverage caching because we'll be accessing this data frequently in later queries:

```scala
// in Scala
import org.graphframes.GraphFrame
val stationGraph = GraphFrame(stationVertices, tripEdges)
stationGraph.cache()
```

```python
# in Python
from graphframes import GraphFrame
stationGraph = GraphFrame(stationVertices, tripEdges)
stationGraph.cache()
```

Now we can see the basic statistics about graph (and query our original DataFrame to ensure that we see the expected results):

```scala
// in Scala
println(s"Total Number of Stations: ${stationGraph.vertices.count()}")
println(s"Total Number of Trips in Graph: ${stationGraph.edges.count()}")
println(s"Total Number of Trips in Original Data: ${tripData.count()}")
```

```python
# in Python
print "Total Number of Stations: " + str(stationGraph.vertices.count())
print "Total Number of Trips in Graph: " + str(stationGraph.edges.count())
print "Total Number of Trips in Original Data: " + str(tripData.count())
```

This returns the following results:

```
Total Number of Stations: 70
Total Number of Trips in Graph: 354152
Total Number of Trips in Original Data: 354152
```

Querying the Graph

The most basic way of interacting with the graph is simply querying it, performing things like counting trips and filtering by given destinations. GraphFrames provides simple access to both vertices and edges as DataFrames. Note that our graph retained all the additional columns in the data in addition to IDs, sources, and destinations, so we can also query those if needed:

```scala
// in Scala
import org.apache.spark.sql.functions.desc
stationGraph.edges.groupBy("src", "dst").count().orderBy(desc("count")).show(10)
```

```python
# in Python
from pyspark.sql.functions import desc
stationGraph.edges.groupBy("src", "dst").count().orderBy(desc("count")).show(10)
```

```
+-------------------+-------------------+-----+
|                src|                dst|count|
+-------------------+-------------------+-----+
|San Francisco Cal...|     Townsend at 7th| 3748|
|Harry Bridges Pla...|Embarcadero at Sa...| 3145|
...
|      Townsend at 7th|San Francisco Cal...| 2192|
|Temporary Transba...|San Francisco Cal...| 2184|
+-------------------+-------------------+-----+
```

We can also filter by any valid DataFrame expression. In this instance, I want to look at one specific station and the count of trips in and out of that station:

```scala
// in Scala
stationGraph.edges
  .where("src = 'Townsend at 7th' OR dst = 'Townsend at 7th'")
  .groupBy("src", "dst").count()
  .orderBy(desc("count"))
  .show(10)
```

```python
# in Python
stationGraph.edges\
  .where("src = 'Townsend at 7th' OR dst = 'Townsend at 7th'")\
  .groupBy("src", "dst").count()\
  .orderBy(desc("count"))\
  .show(10)
```

```
+-------------------+-------------------+-----+
|                src|                dst|count|
+-------------------+-------------------+-----+
|San Francisco Cal...|     Townsend at 7th| 3748|
|      Townsend at 7th|San Francisco Cal...| 2734|
...
|    Steuart at Market|     Townsend at 7th|  746|
|      Townsend at 7th|Temporary Transba...|  740|
+-------------------+-------------------+-----+
```

Subgraphs

Subgraphs are just smaller graphs within the larger one. We saw in the last section how we can query a given set of edges and vertices. We can use this query ability to create subgraphs:

```scala
// in Scala
val townAnd7thEdges = stationGraph.edges
  .where("src = 'Townsend at 7th' OR dst = 'Townsend at 7th'")
val subgraph = GraphFrame(stationGraph.vertices, townAnd7thEdges)
```

```python
# in Python
townAnd7thEdges = stationGraph.edges\
  .where("src = 'Townsend at 7th' OR dst = 'Townsend at 7th'")
subgraph = GraphFrame(stationGraph.vertices, townAnd7thEdges)
```

We can then apply the following algorithms to either the original graph or the subgraph.

Motif Finding

Motifs are a way of expresssing structural patterns in a graph. When we specify a motif, we are querying for patterns in the data instead of actual data. In GraphFrames, we specify our query in a domain-specific language similar to Neo4J's Cypher language. This language lets us specify combinations of vertices and edges and assign then names. For example, if we want to specify that a given vertex a connects to another vertex b through an edge ab, we would specify (a)-[ab]->(b). The names inside parentheses or brackets do not signify values but instead what the columns for matching vertices and edges should be named in the resulting DataFrame. We can omit the names (e.g., (a)-[]->()) if we do not intend to query the resulting values.

Let's perform a query on our bike data. In plain English, let's find all the rides that form a "triangle" pattern between three stations. We express this with the following motif, using the find method to query our GraphFrame for that pattern. (a) signifies the starting station, and [ab] represents an edge from (a) to our next station (b). We repeat this for stations (b) to (c) and then from (c) to (a):

```scala
// in Scala
val motifs = stationGraph.find("(a)-[ab]->(b); (b)-[bc]->(c); (c)-[ca]->(a)")
```

```python
# in Python
motifs = stationGraph.find("(a)-[ab]->(b); (b)-[bc]->(c); (c)-[ca]->(a)")
```

Figure 30-3 presents a visual representation of this query.

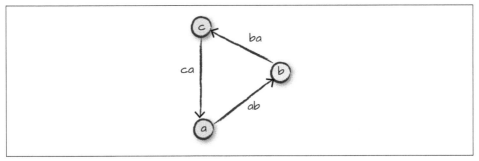

Figure 30-3. Triangle motif in our triangle query

The DataFrame we get from running this query contains nested fields for vertices a, b, and c, as well as the respective edges. We can now query this as we would a DataFrame. For example, given a certain bike, what is the shortest trip the bike has taken from station a, to station b, to station c, and back to station a? The following logic will parse our timestamps, into Spark timestamps and then we'll do comparisons to make sure that it's the same bike, traveling from station to station, and that the start times for each trip are correct:

```scala
// in Scala
import org.apache.spark.sql.functions.expr
motifs.selectExpr("*",
    "to_timestamp(ab.`Start Date`, 'MM/dd/yyyy HH:mm') as abStart",
    "to_timestamp(bc.`Start Date`, 'MM/dd/yyyy HH:mm') as bcStart",
    "to_timestamp(ca.`Start Date`, 'MM/dd/yyyy HH:mm') as caStart")
  .where("ca.`Bike #` = bc.`Bike #`").where("ab.`Bike #` = bc.`Bike #`")
  .where("a.id != b.id").where("b.id != c.id")
  .where("abStart < bcStart").where("bcStart < caStart")
  .orderBy(expr("cast(caStart as long) - cast(abStart as long)"))
  .selectExpr("a.id", "b.id", "c.id", "ab.`Start Date`", "ca.`End Date`")
  .limit(1).show(false)
```

```python
# in Python
from pyspark.sql.functions import expr
motifs.selectExpr("*",
    "to_timestamp(ab.`Start Date`, 'MM/dd/yyyy HH:mm') as abStart",
    "to_timestamp(bc.`Start Date`, 'MM/dd/yyyy HH:mm') as bcStart",
    "to_timestamp(ca.`Start Date`, 'MM/dd/yyyy HH:mm') as caStart")\
  .where("ca.`Bike #` = bc.`Bike #`").where("ab.`Bike #` = bc.`Bike #`")\
  .where("a.id != b.id").where("b.id != c.id")\
  .where("abStart < bcStart").where("bcStart < caStart")\
  .orderBy(expr("cast(caStart as long) - cast(abStart as long)"))\
  .selectExpr("a.id", "b.id", "c.id", "ab.`Start Date`", "ca.`End Date`")
  .limit(1).show(1, False)
```

We see the fastest trip is approximately 20 minutes. Pretty fast for three different people (we assume) using the same bike!

Note also that we had to filter the triangles returned by our motif query in this example. In general, different vertex IDs used in the query will not be forced to match distinct vertices, so you should perform this type of filtering if you want distinct vertices. One of the most powerful features of GraphFrames is that you can combine motif finding with DataFarme queries over the resulting tables to further narrow down, sort, or aggregate the patterns found.

Graph Algorithms

A graph is just a logical representation of data. Graph theory provides numerous algorithms for analyzing data in this format, and GraphFrames allows us to leverage many algorithms out of the box. Development continues as new algorithms are added to GraphFrames, so this list will most likely continue to grow.

PageRank

One of the most prolific graph algorithms is PageRank (*https://en.wikipedia.org/wiki/ PageRank*). Larry Page, cofounder of Google, created PageRank as a research project for how to rank web pages. Unfortunately, a complete explanation of how PageRank works is outside the scope of this book. However, to quote Wikipedia, the high-level explanation is as follows:

> PageRank works by counting the number and quality of links to a page to determine a rough estimate of how important the website is. The underlying assumption is that more important websites are likely to receive more links from other websites.

PageRank generalizes quite well outside of the web domain. We can apply this right to our own data and get a sense for important bike stations (specifically, those that receive a lot of bike traffic). In this example, important bike stations will be assigned large PageRank values:

```scala
// in Scala
import org.apache.spark.sql.functions.desc
val ranks = stationGraph.pageRank.resetProbability(0.15).maxIter(10).run()
ranks.vertices.orderBy(desc("pagerank")).select("id", "pagerank").show(10)
```

```python
# in Python
from pyspark.sql.functions import desc
ranks = stationGraph.pageRank(resetProbability=0.15, maxIter=10)
ranks.vertices.orderBy(desc("pagerank")).select("id", "pagerank").show(10)
```

```
+--------------------+------------------+
|                  id|          pagerank|
+--------------------+------------------+
|San Jose Diridon ...|  4.051504835989922|
|San Francisco Cal...| 3.3511832964279518|
...
|     Townsend at 7th|  1.568456580534273|
```

```
|Embarcadero at Sa...|1.5414242087749768|
+--------------------+------------------+
```

Graph Algorithm APIs: Parameters and Return Values

Most algorithms in GraphFrames are accessed as methods which take parameters (e.g., `resetProbability` in this PageRank example). Most algorithms return either a new GraphFrame or a single DataFrame. The results of the algorithm are stored as one or more columns in the GraphFrame's vertices and/or edges or the DataFrame. For PageRank, the algorithm returns a GraphFrame, and we can extract the estimated PageRank values for each vertex from the new `pagerank` column.

 Depending on the resources available on your machine, this may take some time. You can always try a smaller set of data before running this to see the results. On Databricks Community Edition, this takes about 20 seconds to run, although some reviewers found it to take much longer on their machines.

Interestingly, we see that Caltrain stations rank quite highly. This makes sense because these are natural connection points where a lot of bike trips might end up. Either as commuters move from home to the Caltrain station for their commute or from the Caltrain station to home.

In-Degree and Out-Degree Metrics

Our graph is a directed graph. This is due to the bike trips being directional, starting in one location and ending in another. One common task is to count the number of trips into or out of a given station. To measure trips in and out of stations, we will use a metric called in-degree and out-degree, respectively, as seen in Figure 30-4.

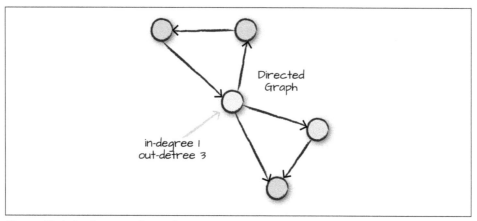

Figure 30-4. In-degree and out-degree

This is particularly applicable in the context of social networking because certain users may have many more inbound connections (i.e., followers) than outbound connections (i.e., people they follow). Using the following query, you can find interesting people in the social network who might have more influence than others. GraphFrames provides a simple way to query our graph for this information:

```scala
// in Scala
val inDeg = stationGraph.inDegrees
inDeg.orderBy(desc("inDegree")).show(5, false)
```

```python
# in Python
inDeg = stationGraph.inDegrees
inDeg.orderBy(desc("inDegree")).show(5, False)
```

The result of querying for the stations sorted by the highest in-degree:

```
+----------------------------------------+--------+
|id                                      |inDegree|
+----------------------------------------+--------+
|San Francisco Caltrain (Townsend at 4th)|34810   |
|San Francisco Caltrain 2 (330 Townsend) |22523   |
|Harry Bridges Plaza (Ferry Building)    |17810   |
|2nd at Townsend                         |15463   |
|Townsend at 7th                         |15422   |
+----------------------------------------+--------+
```

We can query the out degrees in the same fashion:

```scala
// in Scala
val outDeg = stationGraph.outDegrees
outDeg.orderBy(desc("outDegree")).show(5, false)
```

```python
# in Python
outDeg = stationGraph.outDegrees
outDeg.orderBy(desc("outDegree")).show(5, False)
```

```
+-----------------------------------------------+---------+
|id                                             |outDegree|
+-----------------------------------------------+---------+
|San Francisco Caltrain (Townsend at 4th)       |26304    |
|San Francisco Caltrain 2 (330 Townsend)        |21758    |
|Harry Bridges Plaza (Ferry Building)           |17255    |
|Temporary Transbay Terminal (Howard at Beale)  |14436    |
|Embarcadero at Sansome                         |14158    |
+-----------------------------------------------+---------+
```

The ratio of these two values is an interesting metric to look at. A higher ratio value will tell us where a large number of trips end (but rarely begin), while a lower value tells us where trips often begin (but infrequently end):

```scala
// in Scala
val degreeRatio = inDeg.join(outDeg, Seq("id"))
  .selectExpr("id", "double(inDegree)/double(outDegree) as degreeRatio")
degreeRatio.orderBy(desc("degreeRatio")).show(10, false)
degreeRatio.orderBy("degreeRatio").show(10, false)
```

```python
# in Python
degreeRatio = inDeg.join(outDeg, "id")\
  .selectExpr("id", "double(inDegree)/double(outDegree) as degreeRatio")
degreeRatio.orderBy(desc("degreeRatio")).show(10, False)
degreeRatio.orderBy("degreeRatio").show(10, False)
```

Those queries result in the following data:

```
+-----------------------------------------+------------------+
|id                                       |degreeRatio       |
+-----------------------------------------+------------------+
|Redwood City Medical Center              |1.5333333333333334|
|San Mateo County Center                  |1.4724409448818898|
...
|Embarcadero at Vallejo                   |1.2201707365495336|
|Market at Sansome                        |1.2173913043478262|
+-----------------------------------------+------------------+


+-----------------------------------+------------------+
|id                                 |degreeRatio       |
+-----------------------------------+------------------+
|Grant Avenue at Columbus Avenue    |0.5180520570948782|
|2nd at Folsom                      |0.5909488686085761|
...
|San Francisco City Hall            |0.7928849902534113|
|Palo Alto Caltrain Station         |0.8064516129032258|
+-----------------------------------+------------------+
```

Breadth-First Search

Breadth-first search will search our graph for how to connect two sets of nodes, based on the edges in the graph. In our context, we might want to do this to find the shortest paths to different stations, but the algorithm also works for *sets* of nodes specified through a SQL expression. We can specify the maximum of edges to follow with the `maxPathLength`, and we can also specify an `edgeFilter` to filter out edges that do not meet a requirement, like trips during nonbusiness hours.

We'll choose two fairly close stations so that this does not run too long. However, you can do interesting graph traversals when you have sparse graphs that have distant connections. Feel free to play around with the stations (especially those in other cities) to see if you can get distant stations to connect:

```scala
// in Scala
stationGraph.bfs.fromExpr("id = 'Townsend at 7th'")
  .toExpr("id = 'Spear at Folsom'").maxPathLength(2).run().show(10)
```

```python
# in Python
stationGraph.bfs(fromExpr="id = 'Townsend at 7th'",
  toExpr="id = 'Spear at Folsom'", maxPathLength=2).show(10)
```

```
+--------------------+--------------------+--------------------+
|                from|                  e0|                  to|
+--------------------+--------------------+--------------------+
|[65,Townsend at 7...|[913371,663,8/31/...|[49,Spear at Fols...|
|[65,Townsend at 7...|[913265,658,8/31/...|[49,Spear at Fols...|
...
|[65,Townsend at 7...|[903375,850,8/24/...|[49,Spear at Fols...|
|[65,Townsend at 7...|[899944,910,8/21/...|[49,Spear at Fols...|
+--------------------+--------------------+--------------------+
```

Connected Components

A *connected component* defines an (undirected) subgraph that has connections to itself but does not connect to the greater graph, as illustrated in Figure 30-5.

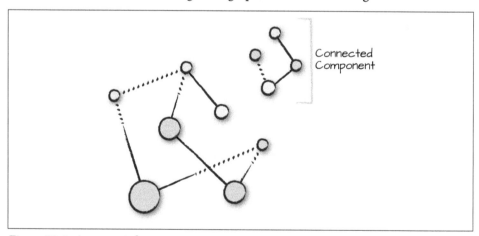

Figure 30-5. A connected component

The connected components algorithm does not directly relate to our current problem because they assume an undirected graph. However, we can still run the algorithm, which just assumes that there are is no directionality associated with our edges. In fact, if we look at the bike share map, we assume that we would get two distinct connected components (Figure 30-6).

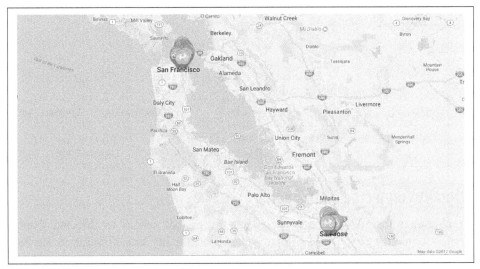

Figure 30-6. A map of Bay Area bike share locations

To run this algorithm, you will need to set a checkpoint directory which will store the state of the job at every iteration. This allows you to continue where you left off if the job crashes. This is probably one of the most expensive algorithms currently in Graph-Frames, so expect delays.

One thing you will likely have to do to run this algorithm on your local machine is take a sample of the data, just as we do in the following code example (taking a sample can help you get to a result without crashing the Spark application with garbage collection issues):

```scala
// in Scala
spark.sparkContext.setCheckpointDir("/tmp/checkpoints")
```

```python
# in Python
spark.sparkContext.setCheckpointDir("/tmp/checkpoints")
```

```scala
// in Scala
val minGraph = GraphFrame(stationVertices, tripEdges.sample(false, 0.1))
val cc = minGraph.connectedComponents.run()
```

```python
# in Python
minGraph = GraphFrame(stationVertices, tripEdges.sample(False, 0.1))
cc = minGraph.connectedComponents()
```

From this query we get two connected components but not necessarily the ones we might expect. Our sample may not have all of the correct data or information so we'd probably need more compute resources to investigate further:

```scala
// in Scala
cc.where("component != 0").show()
```

```python
# in Python
cc.where("component != 0").show()
```

```
+----------+------------------+---------+-----------+---------+-----------+-----
|station_id|                id|      lat|       long|dockcount|   landmark|in...
+----------+------------------+---------+-----------+---------+-----------+-----
|          |                47|  Post at Kearney|37.788975|-122.403452|       19|San Franc...|  ...
|          |                46|Washington at K...|37.795425|-122.404767|       15|San Franc...|  ...
+----------+------------------+---------+-----------+---------+-----------+-----
```

Strongly Connected Components

GraphFrames includes another related algorithm that relates to directed graphs: *strongly connected components*, which takes directionality into account. A strongly connected component is a subgraph that has paths between all pairs of vertices inside it.

```scala
// in Scala
val scc = minGraph.stronglyConnectedComponents.maxIter(3).run()
```

```python
# in Python
scc = minGraph.stronglyConnectedComponents(maxIter=3)

scc.groupBy("component").count().show()
```

Advanced Tasks

This is just a short selection of some of the features of GraphFrames. The Graph-Frames library also includes features such as writing your own algorithms via a message-passing interface, triangle counting, and converting to and from GraphX. You can find more information in the GraphFrames documentation.

Conclusion

In this chapter, we took a tour of GraphFrames, a library for performing graph analysis on Apache Spark. We took a more tutorial-based approach, since this processing technique is not necessarily the first tool that people use when performing advanced analytics. It is nonetheless a powerful tool for analyzing relationships between different objects, and critical in many domains. The next chapter will talk about more cutting-edge functionality—specifically, deep learning.

## CHAPTER 31

Deep Learning

Deep learning is one of the most exciting areas of development around Spark due to its ability to solve several previously difficult machine learning problems, especially those involving unstructured data such as images, audio, and text. This chapter will cover how Spark works in tandem with deep learning, and some of the different approaches you can use to work with Spark and deep learning together.

Because deep learning is still a new field, many of the newest tools are implemented in external libraries. This chapter will not focus on packages that are necessarily core to Spark but rather on the massive amount of innovation in libraries built on top of Spark. We will start with several high-level ways to use deep learning on Spark, discuss when to use each one, and then go over the libraries available for them. As usual, we will include end-to-end examples.

 To make the most of this chapter you should know at least the basics of deep learning as well as the basics of Spark. With that being said, we point to an excellent resource at the beginning of this part of the book called the Deep Learning Book (*http://www.deeplearningbook.org/*), by some of the top researchers in this area.

What Is Deep Learning?

To define deep learning, we must first define neural networks. A neural network is a graph of nodes with weights and activation functions. These nodes are organized into *layers* that are stacked on top of one another. Each layer is connected, either partially or completely, to the previous layer in the network. By stacking layers one after the other, these simple functions can learn to recognize more and more complex signals in the input: simple lines with one layer, circles and squares with the next layer, complex textures in another, and finally the full object or output you hope to identify. The goal is to train the network to associate certain inputs with certain outputs by tuning the weights associated with each connection and the values of each node in the network. Figure 31-1 shows the simple neural network.

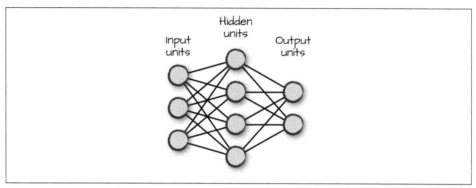

Figure 31-1. A neural network

Deep learning, or *deep neural networks*, stack many of these layers together into various different architectures. Neural networks themselves have existed for decades, and have waxed and waned in terms of popularity for various machine learning problems. Recently, however, a combination of much larger datasets (e.g., the ImageNet corpus for object recognition), powerful hardware (clusters and GPUs), and new training algorithms have enabled training much larger neural networks that outperform previous approaches in many machine learning tasks. Typical machine learning techniques typically cannot continue to perform well as more data is added; their performance hits a ceiling. Deep learning can benefit from enormous amounts of data and information and it is not uncommon for deep learning datasets to be orders of magnitude larger than other machine learning datasets. Deep neural networks have now become the standard in computer vision, speech processing, and some natural language tasks, where they often "learn" better features than previous hand-tuned models. They are also actively being applied in other areas of machine learning. Apache Spark's strength as a big data and parallel computing system makes it a natural framework to use with deep learning.

Researchers and engineers have put a lot of effort into speeding up these neural network-like calculations. Nowadays, the most popular way to use neural networks or deep learning is to use a framework, implemented by a research institute or corporation. The most popular as of the time of this writing are TensorFlow, MXNet, Keras, and PyTorch. This area is rapidly evolving so it's always worth searching around for others.

Ways of Using Deep Learning in Spark

For the most part, regardless of which application you are targeting, there are three major ways to use deep learning in Spark:

Inference

The simplest way to use deep learning is to take a pretrained model and apply it to large datasets in parallel using Spark. For example, you could use an image classification model, trained using a standard dataset like ImageNet, and apply it to your own image collection to identify pandas, flowers, or cars. Many organizations publish large, pretrained models on common datasets (e.g., Faster R-CNN and YOLO for object detection), so you can often take a model from your favorite deep learning framework and apply it in parallel using a Spark function. Using PySpark, you could simply call a framework such as TensorFlow or PyTorch in a map function to get distributed inference, though some of the libraries we discuss for it make further optimizations beyond simply calling these libraries in a map function.

Featurization and transfer learning

The next level of complexity is to use an existing model as a *featurizer* instead of taking its final output. Many deep learning models learn useful feature representations in their lower layers as they get trained for an end-to-end task. For example, a classifier trained on the ImageNet dataset will also learn low-level features present in all natural images, such as edges and textures. We can then use these features to learn models for a new problem not covered by the original dataset. This method is called *transfer learning*, and generally involves the last few layers of a pretrained model and retraining them with the data of interest. Transfer learning is also especially useful if you do not have a large amount of training data: training a full-blown network from scratch requires a dataset of hundreds of thousands of images, like ImageNet, to avoid overfitting, which will not be available in many business contexts. In contrast, transfer learning can work even with a few thousand images because it updates fewer parameters.

Model training

Spark can also be used to train a new deep learning model from scratch. There are two common methods here. First, you can use a Spark cluster to parallelize the training of a *single* model over multiple servers, communicating updates between them. Alternatively, some libraries let the user train *multiple* instances of similar models in parallel to try various model architectures and hyperparameters, accelerating the model search and tuning process. In both cases, Spark's deep learning libraries make it simple to pass data from RDDs and DataFrames to deep learning algorithms. Finally, even if you do not wish to train your model in parallel, these libraries can be used to extract data from a cluster and export it to a single-machine training script using the native data format of frameworks like TensorFlow.

In all three cases, the deep learning code typically runs as part of a larger application that includes Extract, Transform, and Load (ETL) steps to parse the input data, I/O from various sources, and potentially batch or streaming inference. For these other parts of the application, you can simply use the DataFrame, RDD, and MLlib APIs described earlier in this book. One of Spark's strengths is the ease of combining these steps into a single parallel workflow.

Deep Learning Libraries

In this section, we'll survey a few of the most popular libraries available for deep learning in Spark. We will describe the main use cases of the library and link them to references or examples when possible. This list is not meant to be exhaustive, because the field is rapidly evolving. We encourage you to check each library's website and the Spark documentation for the latest updates.

MLlib Neural Network Support

Spark's MLlib currently has native support for a single deep learning algorithm: the `ml.classification.MultilayerPerceptronClassifier` class's multilayer perceptron classifier. This class is limited to training relatively shallow networks containing fully connected layers with the sigmoid activation function and an output layer with a softmax activation function. This class is most useful for training the last few layers of a classification model when using transfer learning on top of an existing deep learning–based featurizer. For example, it can be added on top of the Deep Learning Pipelines library we describe later in this chapter to quickly perform transfer learning over Keras and TensorFlow models.

TensorFrames

TensorFrames (*https://github.com/databricks/tensorframes*) is an inference and transfer learning-oriented library that makes it easy to pass data between Spark DataFrames and TensorFlow. It supports Python and Scala interfaces and focuses on providing a simple but optimized interface to pass data from TensorFlow to Spark and back. In particular, using TensorFrames to apply a model over Spark DataFrames is generally more efficient than calling a Python `map` function that directly invokes the TensorFlow model, due to faster data transfer and amortization of the startup cost. TensorFrames is most useful for inference, in both streaming and batch settings, and for transfer learning, where you can apply an existing model over raw data to featurize it, then learn the last layers using a `MultilayerPerceptronClassifier` or even a simpler logistic regression or random forest classifier over the data.

BigDL

BigDL (*https://github.com/intel-analytics/BigDL*) is a distributed deep learning framework for Apache Spark primarily developed by Intel. It aims to support distributed training of large models as well as fast applications of these models using inference. One key advantage of BigDL over the other libraries described here is that it is primarily optimized to use CPUs instead of GPUs, making it efficient to run on an existing, CPU-based cluster (e.g., an Apache Hadoop deployment). BigDL provides high-level APIs to build neural networks from scratch and automatically distributes all operations by default. It can also train models described with the Keras DL library.

TensorFlowOnSpark

TensorFlowOnSpark (*https://github.com/yahoo/TensorFlowOnSpark*) is a widely used library that can train TensorFlow models in a parallel fashion on Spark clusters. TensorFlow includes some foundations to do distributed training, but it still needs to rely on a cluster manager for managing the hardware and data communications. It does not come with a cluster manager or a distributed I/O layer out of the box. TensorFlowOnSpark launches TensorFlow's existing distributed mode inside a Spark job, and automatically feeds data from Spark RDDs or DataFrames into the TensorFlow job. If you already know how to use TensorFlow's distributed mode, TensorFlowOnSpark makes it easy to launch your job inside a Spark cluster and pass it data processed with other Spark libraries (e.g., DataFrame transformations) from any input source Spark supports. TensorFlowOnSpark was originally developed at Yahoo! and is also used in production at other large organizations. The project also integrates with Spark's ML Pipelines API.

DeepLearning4J

DeepLearning4j (*https://deeplearning4j.org/spark*) is an open-source, distributed deep learning project in Java and Scala that provides both single-node and distributed training options. One of its advantages over Python-based deep learning frameworks is that it was primarily designed for the JVM, making it more convenient for groups that do not wish to add Python to their development process. It includes a wide variety of training algorithms and support for CPUs as well as GPUs.

Deep Learning Pipelines

Deep Learning Pipelines (*https://github.com/databricks/spark-deep-learning*) is an open source package from Databricks that integrates deep learning functionality into Spark's ML Pipelines API. The package existing deep learning frameworks (TensorFlow and Keras at the time of writing), but focuses on two goals:

- Incorporating these frameworks into standard Spark APIs (such as ML Pipelines and Spark SQL) to make them very easy to use
- Distributing all computation by default

For example, Deep Learning Pipelines provides a `DeepImageFeaturizer` class that acts as a transformer in the Spark ML Pipeline API, allowing you to build a transfer learning pipeline in just a few lines of code (e.g., by adding a perceptron or logistic regression classifier on top). Likewise, the library supports parallel grid search over multiple model parameters using MLlib's grid search and cross-validation API. Finally, users can export an ML model as a Spark SQL user-defined function and make it available to analysts using SQL or streaming applications. At the time of writing (summer 2017), Deep Learning Pipelines is under heavy development, so we encourage you to check its website for the latest updates.

Table 31-1 summarizes the various deep learning libraries and the main use cases they support:

Table 31-1. Deep learning libraries

Library	Underlying DL framework	Use cases
BigDL	BigDL	Distributed training, inference, ML Pipeline integration
DeepLearning4J	DeepLearning4J	Inference, transfer learning, distributed training
Deep Learning Pipelines	TensorFlow, Keras	Inference, transfer learning, multi-model training, ML Pipeline and Spark SQL integration
MLlib Perceptron	Spark	Distributed training, ML Pipeline integration
TensorFlowOnSpark	TensorFlow	Distributed training, ML Pipeline integration
TensorFrames	TensorFlow	Inference, transfer learning, DataFrame integration

While there are several approaches different companies have taken to integrating Spark and deep learning libraries, the one currently aiming for the closest integration with MLlib and DataFrames is Deep Learning Pipelines. This library aims to improve Spark's support for image and tensor data (which will be integrated into the core Spark codebase in Spark 2.3), and to make all deep learning functionality available in the ML Pipeline API. Its friendly API makes it the simplest way to run deep learning on Spark today and will be the focus of the remaining sections in this chapter.

A Simple Example with Deep Learning Pipelines

As we described, Deep Learning Pipelines provides high-level APIs for scalable deep learning by integrating popular deep learning frameworks with ML Pipelines and Spark SQL.

Deep Learning Pipelines builds on Spark's ML Pipelines for training and on Spark DataFrames and SQL for deploying models. It includes high-level APIs for common aspects of deep learning so they can be done efficiently in a few lines of code:

- Working with images in Spark DataFrames;
- Applying deep learning models at scale, whether they are your own or standard popular models, to image and tensor data;
- Transfer learning using common pretrained deep learning models;
- Exporting models as Spark SQL functions to make it simple for all kinds of users to take advantage of deep learning; and
- Distributed deep learning hyperparameter tuning via ML Pipelines.

Deep Learning Pipelines currently only offers an API in Python, which is designed to work closely with existing Python deep learning packages such as TensorFlow and Keras.

Setup

Deep Learning Pipelines (*https://github.com/databricks/spark-deep-learning*) is a Spark Package, so we'll load it just like we loaded GraphFrames. Deep Learning Pipelines works on Spark 2.x and the package can be found here (*https://spark-packages.org/package/databricks/spark-deep-learning*). You're going to need to install a few Python dependencies, including TensorFrames (*https://spark-packages.org/package/databricks/tensorframes*), TensorFlow (*https://www.tensorflow.org/*), Keras (*https://keras.io/*), and h5py (*http://www.h5py.org/*). Make sure these are installed across both your driver and worker machines.

We'll use the flowers dataset from the TensorFlow retraining tutorial (*https://www.tensorflow.org/tutorials/image_retraining*). Now if you're running this on a cluster of machines, you're going to need a way to put these files on a distributed file system once you download them. We include a sample of these images in the book's GitHub Repository (*https://github.com/databricks/Spark-The-Definitive-Guide*).

Images and DataFrames

One of the historical challenges when working with images in Spark is that getting them into a DataFrame was difficult and tedious. Deep Learning Pipelines includes utility functions that make loading and decoding images in a distributed fashion easy. This is an area that's changing rapidly. Currently, this is a part of Deep Learning Pipelines. Basic image loading and representation will be included in Spark 2.3. While it is not released yet, all of the examples in this chapter should be compatible with this upcoming version of Spark:

```python
from sparkdl import readImages
img_dir = '/data/deep-learning-images/'
image_df = readImages(img_dir)
```

The resulting DataFrame contains the path and then the image along with some associated metadata:

```
image_df.printSchema()

root
 |-- filePath: string (nullable = false)
 |-- image: struct (nullable = true)
 |    |-- mode: string (nullable = false)
 |    |-- height: integer (nullable = false)
 |    |-- width: integer (nullable = false)
 |    |-- nChannels: integer (nullable = false)
 |    |-- data: binary (nullable = false)
```

Transfer Learning

Now that we have some data, we can get started with some simple transfer learning. Remember, this means leveraging a model that someone else created and modifying it to better suit our own purposes. First, we will load the data for each type of flower and create a training and test set:

```python
from sparkdl import readImages
from pyspark.sql.functions import lit
tulips_df = readImages(img_dir + "/tulips").withColumn("label", lit(1))
daisy_df = readImages(img_dir + "/daisy").withColumn("label", lit(0))
tulips_train, tulips_test = tulips_df.randomSplit([0.6, 0.4])
daisy_train, daisy_test = daisy_df.randomSplit([0.6, 0.4])
train_df = tulips_train.unionAll(daisy_train)
test_df = tulips_test.unionAll(daisy_test)
```

In the next step we will leverage a transformer called the DeepImageFeaturizer. This will allow us to leverage a pretrained model called Inception, a powerful neural network successfully used to identify patterns in images. The version we are using is pretrained to work well with images of various common objects and animals. This is one of the standard pretrained models that ship with the Keras library. However, this particular neural network is not trained to recognize daisies and roses. So we're going to use transfer learning in order to make it into something useful for our own purposes: distinguishing different flower types.

Note that we can use the same ML Pipeline concepts we learned about throughout this part of the book and leverage them with Deep Learning Pipelines: DeepImageFea turizer is just an ML transformer. Additionally, all that we've done to extend this model is add on a logistic regression model in order to facilitate the training of our end model. We could use another classifier in its place. The following code snippet demonstrates adding this model (note this may take time to complete as it's a fairly resource intensive process):

```
from pyspark.ml.classification import LogisticRegression
from pyspark.ml import Pipeline
from sparkdl import DeepImageFeaturizer
featurizer = DeepImageFeaturizer(inputCol="image", outputCol="features",
  modelName="InceptionV3")
lr = LogisticRegression(maxIter=1, regParam=0.05, elasticNetParam=0.3,
  labelCol="label")
p = Pipeline(stages=[featurizer, lr])
p_model = p.fit(train_df)
```

Once we've trained the model, we can use the same classification evaluator we used in Chapter 25. We can specify the metric we'd like to test and then evaluate it:

```
from pyspark.ml.evaluation import MulticlassClassificationEvaluator
tested_df = p_model.transform(test_df)
evaluator = MulticlassClassificationEvaluator(metricName="accuracy")
print("Test set accuracy = " + str(evaluator.evaluate(tested_df.select(
  "prediction", "label"))))
```

With our DataFrame of examples, we can inspect the rows and images in which we made mistakes in the previous training:

```
from pyspark.sql.types import DoubleType
from pyspark.sql.functions import expr
# a simple UDF to convert the value to a double
def _p1(v):
  return float(v.array[1])
p1 = udf(_p1, DoubleType())
df = tested_df.withColumn("p_1", p1(tested_df.probability))
wrong_df = df.orderBy(expr("abs(p_1 - label)"), ascending=False)
wrong_df.select("filePath", "p_1", "label").limit(10).show()
```

Applying deep learning models at scale

Spark DataFrames are a natural construct for applying deep learning models to a large-scale dataset. Deep Learning Pipelines provides a set of Transformers for applying TensorFlow graphs and TensorFlow-backed Keras models at scale. In addition, popular image models can be applied out of the box, without requiring any TensorFlow or Keras code. The transformers, backed by the Tensorframes library, efficiently handle the distribution of models and data to Spark tasks.

Applying Popular Models

There are many standard deep learning models for images. If the task at hand is very similar to what the models provide (e.g., object recognition with ImageNet classes), or merely for exploration, you can use the transformer DeepImagePredictor by simply specifying the model name. Deep Learning Pipelines supports a variety of standard models included in Keras, which are listed on its website. The following is an example of using DeepImagePredictor:

```
from sparkdl import readImages, DeepImagePredictor
image_df = readImages(img_dir)
predictor = DeepImagePredictor(
  inputCol="image",
  outputCol="predicted_labels",
  modelName="InceptionV3",
  decodePredictions=True,
  topK=10)
predictions_df = predictor.transform(image_df)
```

Notice that the `predicted_labels` column shows "daisy" as a high probability class for all sample flowers using this base model. However, as can be seen from the differences in the probability values, the neural network has the information to discern the two flower types. As we can see, our transfer learning example was able to properly learn the differences between daisies and tulips starting from the base model:

```
df = p_model.transform(image_df)
```

Applying custom Keras models

Deep Learning Pipelines also allows us to apply a Keras model in a distributed manner using Spark. To do this, check the user guide (*http://bit.ly/2Edb6eQ*) on the `KerasImageFileTransformer`. This loads a Keras model and applies it to a DataFrame column.

Applying TensorFlow models

Deep Learning Pipelines, through its integration with TensorFlow, can be used to create custom transformers that manipulate images using TensorFlow. For instance, you could create a transformer to change the size of an image or modify the color spectrum. To do this, use the `TFImageTransformer` class.

Deploying models as SQL functions

Another option is to deploy a model as a SQL function allowing any user who knows SQL to be able to use a deep learning model. Once this function is used, the resulting UDF function takes a column and produces the output of the particular model. For instance, you could apply Inception v3 to a variety of images by using the `register KeraImageUDF` class:

```
from keras.applications import InceptionV3
from sparkdl.udf.keras_image_model import registerKerasImageUDF
from keras.applications import InceptionV3
registerKerasImageUDF("my_keras_inception_udf", InceptionV3(weights="imagenet"))
```

This way, the power of deep learning is available to any Spark user, not just the specialist who built the model.

Conclusion

This chapter discussed several common approaches to using deep learning in Spark. We covered a variety of available libraries and then worked through some basic examples of common tasks. This area of Spark is under very active development and will continue to advance as time moves on so it's worth checking in on the libraries to learn more as time goes on! Over time, the authors of this book hope to keep this chapter up to date with current developments.

PART VII
Ecosystem

## CHAPTER 32

Language Specifics: Python (PySpark) and R (SparkR and sparklyr)

This chapter will cover some of the more nuanced language specifics of Apache Spark. We've seen a huge number of PySpark examples throughout the book. In Chapter 1, we discussed at a high level how Spark runs code from other languages. Let's talk through some of the more specific integrations:

- PySpark
- SparkR
- sparklyr

As a reminder, Figure 32-1 shows the fundamental architecture for these specific languages.

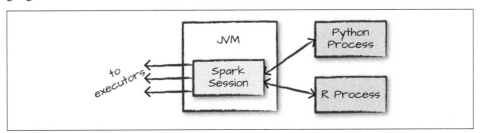

Figure 32-1. The Spark Driver

Now let's cover each of these in depth.

PySpark

We covered a ton of PySpark throughout this book. In fact, PySpark is included alongside Scala and SQL in nearly every chapter in this book. Therefore, this section will be short and sweet, covering only the details that are relevant to Spark itself. As we discussed in Chapter 1, Spark 2.2 included a way to install PySpark with `pip`. Simply, `pip install pyspark` will make it available as a package on your local machine. This is new, so there may be some bugs to fix, but it is something that you can leverage in your projects today.

Fundamental PySpark Differences

If you're using the structured APIs, your code should run just about as fast as if you had written it in Scala, except if you're not using UDFs in Python. If you're using a UDF, you may have a performance impact. Refer back to Chapter 6 for more information on why this is the case.

If you're using the unstructured APIs, specifically RDDs, then your performance is going to suffer (at the cost of a bit more flexibility). We touch on this reasoning in Chapter 12, but the fundamental idea is that Spark is going to have to work a lot harder converting information from something that Spark and the JVM can understand to Python and back again. This includes both functions as well as data and is a process known as *serialization*. We're not saying it never makes sense to use them; it's just something to be aware of when doing so.

Pandas Integration

One of the powers of PySpark is its ability to work across programming models. For instance, a common pattern is to perform very large-scale ETL work with Spark and then collect the (single-machine-sized) result to the driver and then leverage Pandas to manipulate it further. This allows you to use a best-in-class tool for the best task at hand—Spark for big data and Pandas for small data:

```
import pandas as pd
df = pd.DataFrame({"first":range(200), "second":range(50,250)})

sparkDF = spark.createDataFrame(df)

newPDF = sparkDF.toPandas()
newPDF.head()
```

These niceties make working with data big and small easy with Spark. Spark's community continues to focus on improving this interoperability with various other projects, so the integration between Spark and Python will continue to improve. For example, at the time of writing, the community is actively working on Vectorized UDFs (SPARK-21190 (*https://issues.apache.org/jira/browse/SPARK-21190*)), which add a `mapBatches` API to let you process a Spark DataFrame as a series of Pandas data frames in Python instead of converting each individual row to a Python object. This feature is targeted to appear in Spark 2.3.

R on Spark

The rest of this chapter will cover R, Spark's newest officially supported language. R is a language and environment for statistical computing and graphics. It is similar to the S language and environment developed at Bell Laboratories by John Chambers (of no relation to one of the authors of this book) and colleagues. The R language has been around for decades and is consistently popular among statisticians and those doing research in numerical computing. R is steadily becoming a first-class citizen in Spark and provides the simplest open source interface for distributed computation to the R language.

The popularity of R for performing single-machine data analysis and advanced analytics makes it an excellent complement to Spark. There are two core initiatives to making this partnership a reality: SparkR and `sparklyr`. These packages take slightly different approaches to provide similar functionality. SparkR provides a DataFrame API similar to R's `data.frame`, while `sparklyr` is based on the popular `dplyr` package for accessing structured data. You can use whichever you prefer in your code, but over time we expect that the community might converge toward a single integrated package.

We will cover both packages here to let you choose which API you prefer. For the most part, both of these projects are mature and well supported, albeit by slightly different communities. They both support Spark's structured APIs and allow for machine learning. We will elaborate on their differences in the next sections.

SparkR

SparkR is an R package (originating as a collaborative research project between UC Berkeley, Databricks, and MIT CSAIL) that provides a frontend to Apache Spark based on familiar R APIs. SparkR is *conceptually* similar to R's built-in `data.frame` API, except for some departures from the API semantics, such as lazy evaluation. SparkR is a part of the official Spark project and is supported as such. See the documentation for SparkR for more information (*http://spark.apache.org/docs/latest/sparkr.html*).

Pros and cons of using SparkR instead of other languages

The reasons we would recommend that you use SparkR as opposed to PySpark are the following.

- You are familiar with R and want to take the smallest step to leverage the capabilities of Spark:

- You want to leverage R-specific functionality or libraries (say the excellent ggplot2 library) and would like to work with big data in the process.

R is a powerful programming language that provides a lot of advantages over other languages when it comes to certain tasks. However, it has its share of shortcomings like natively working with distributed data. SparkR aims to fill this gap and does a great job enabling users to be successful on both small and large data, in a conceptual way similar to PySpark and Pandas.

Setup

Let's take a look at how to use SparkR. Naturally, you will need to have R installed on your system to follow along in this chapter. To start up the shell, in your Spark home folder, run **./bin/sparkR** to start SparkR. This will automatically create a SparkSession for you. If you were to run SparkR from RStudio, you would have to do something like the following:

```
library(SparkR)
spark <- sparkR.session()
```

Once we've started the shell, we can run Spark commands. For instance, we can read in a CSV file like we saw in Chapter 9:

```
retail.data <- read.df(
  "/data/retail-data/all/",
  "csv",
  header="true",
  inferSchema="true")
print(str(retail.data))
```

We can take some rows from this SparkDataFrame and convert them to a standard R data.frame type:

```
local.retail.data <- take(retail.data, 5)
print(str(local.retail.data))
```

Key Concepts

Now that we saw some very basic code, let's reiterate key concepts. First, SparkR is still Spark. Basically, all the tools that you have seen across the entire book apply directly to SparkR. It runs according to the same principles as PySpark and has almost all of the same functionality available as PySpark.

As shown in Figure 32-1, there is a gateway that connects the R process to the JVM that contains a SparkSession, and SparkR converts user code into structured Spark manipulations across the cluster. This makes its efficiency on par with Python and

Scala when using the structured APIs. SparkR has *no support* for RDDs or other low-level APIs.

While SparkR is used less than PySpark or Scala, it's still popular and continues to grow. For those that want to know enough Spark to leverage SparkR effectively, we recommend reading the following section, along with Parts I and II of this book. When working through those other chapters, feel free to try and use SparkR in place of Python or Scala. You'll see that once you get the hang of it, it's easy to translate between the various languages.

The rest of this chapter will explain the most important differences between SparkR and "standard" R to make it easier to be productive with SparkR faster.

The first thing we should cover is the different between local types and Spark types. A data.frame type's core difference with the Spark version is that it is available in memory and is usually directly available in that particular process. A SparkDataFrame is just a logical representation of a series of manipulations. Therefore when we manipulate a data.frame, we'll see our results right away. On a SparkDataFrame, we are going to logically manipulate the data using the same *transformation* and *action* concepts that we saw throughout the book.

Once we have a SparkDataFrame, we can collect it to a data.frame similar to how we can read in data using Spark. We can also collect it into a local data.frame with the following code (using the SparkDataFrame we created in "Setup" on page 544):

```
# collect brings it from Spark to your local environment
collect(count(groupBy(retail.data, "country")))
# createDataFrame comverts a data.frame
# from your local environment to Spark
```

This difference is of consequence for end users. Certain functions or assumptions that apply to local data.frames do not apply in Spark. For instance, we cannot index a SparkDataFrame according to a particular row. Additionally, we cannot change point values in a SparkDataFrame but can do that in a local data.frame.

Function masking

One frequent "gotcha" when users come to SparkR is that certain functions are masked by SparkR. When I imported SparkR, I received the following message:

```
The following objects are masked from 'package:stats':

    cov, filter, lag, na.omit, predict, sd, var, window

The following objects are masked from 'package:base':

    as.data.frame, colnames, ...
```

This means that if we wish to call these masked functions, we need to be explicit about the package that we're calling them from or at least understand which function masks another. The ? can be helpful in determining these conflicts:

```
?na.omit # refers to SparkR due to package loading order
?stats::na.omit # refers explicitly to stats
?SparkR::na.omit # refers explicitly to sparkR's null value filtering
```

SparkR functions only apply to SparkDataFrames

One implication of function masking is that functions that worked on objects previously may no longer work on them after you bring in the SparkR package. This is because SparkR functions only apply on Spark objects. For instance, we cannot use the `sample` function on a standard `data.frame` because Spark takes that function name:

```
sample(mtcars) # fails
```

What you have to do instead is explicitly use the base sample function. Additionally the function signatures differ between the two functions, which means that even if you are familiar with the syntax and argument order for one particular library, it does not necessarily mean it's the same order for SparkR:

```
base::sample(some.r.data.frame) # some.r.data.frame = R data.frame type
```

Data manipulation

Data manipulation in SparkR is conceptually the same as Spark's DataFrame API in other languages. The core difference is in the syntax, largely due to us running R code and not another language. Aggregations, filtering, and many of the functions that you can find in the other chapters throughout this book are also available in R. For the most part, you can look at the names of functions or manipulations that you find throughout this book and find out if they are available in SparkR by running `?<function-name>`. This should work the vast majority of the time, as there is good coverage of structured SQL functions:

```
?to_date # to Data DataFrame column manipulation
```

SQL is largely the same. We can specify SQL commands that we can then manipulate as DataFrames. For instance, we can find all tables that contain the word "production" in them:

```
tbls <- sql("SHOW TABLES")

collect(
  select(
    filter(tbls, like(tbls$tableName, "%production%")),
    "tableName",
    "isTemporary"))
```

We can also use the popular `magrittr` package to make this code more readable, leveraging the piping operator to chain our transformations in a more functional and readable syntax:

```
library(magrittr)

tbls %>%
  filter(like(tbls$tableName, "%production%")) %>%
  select("tableName", "isTemporary") %>%
  collect()
```

Data sources

SparkR supports all of the data sources that Spark supports, including third-party packages. We can see in the following snippet that we simply specify the options using a slightly different syntax:

```
retail.data <- read.df(
  "/data/retail-data/all/",
  "csv",
  header="true",
  inferSchema="true")
flight.data <- read.df(
  "/data/flight-data/parquet/2010-summary.parquet",
  "parquet")
```

Refer back to Chapter 9 for more information.

Machine learning

Machine learning is a fundamental part of the R language, as well as of Spark. From SparkR there is a decent availability of Spark MLlib algorithms. Typically they arrive in R one or two versions after they are introduced in Scala or Python. As of Spark 2.1, the following algorithms are supported in SparkR:

- `spark.glm` or `glm`: Generalized linear model
- `spark.survreg`: Accelerated failure time (AFT) survival regression model
- `spark.naiveBayes`: Naive Bayes model
- `spark.kmeans`: k-means model
- `spark.logit`: Logistic regression model
- `spark.isoreg`: Isotonic regression model
- `spark.gaussianMixture`: Gaussian mixture model
- `spark.lda`: Latent Dirichlet allocation (LDA) model
- `spark.mlp`: Multilayer perceptron classification model
- `spark.gbt`: Gradient boosted tree model for regression and classification

- `spark.randomForest`: Random forest model for regression and classification
- `spark.als`: Alternating least squares (ALS) matrix factorization model
- `spark.kstest`: Kolmogorov-Smirnov test

Under the hood, SparkR uses MLlib to train the model, which means that most everything covered in Part VI is relevant for SparkR users. Users can call `summary` to print a summary of the fitted model, `predict` to make predictions on new data, and `write.ml`/`read.ml` to save/load fitted models. SparkR supports a subset of the available R formula operators for model fitting, including ~, ., :, +, and -. Here's an example of running a simple regression on the retail dataset:

```
model <- spark.glm(retail.data, Quantity ~ UnitPrice + Country,
  family='gaussian')
summary(model)
predict(model, retail.data)

write.ml(model, "/tmp/myModelOutput", overwrite=T)
newModel <- read.ml("/tmp/myModelOutput")
```

The API is consistent across models, although not all models support detailed summary outputs like we saw with glm. For more information about specific models or preprocessing techniques, see the corresponding chapters in Part VI.

While this pales in comparison to R's extensive collection of statistical algorithms and analysis libraries, many users do not require the scale that Spark provides for the actual training and usage of their machine learning algorithms. Users have the opportunity to build training sets on large data using Spark and then collect that dataset to their local environment for training on a local `data.frame`.

User-defined functions

In SparkR, there are several ways of running user-defined functions. A *user-defined function* is one that is created in the native language and run on the server in that same native language. These run, for the most part, in the same way that a Python UDF runs, by performing serialization into and out of the JVM of the function.

The different kinds of UDFs you can define are as follows:

First, `spark.lapply` lets you run multiple instances of a function in Spark on different parameter values provided in an R collection. This is a great way of performing grid search and comparing the results:

```
families <- c("gaussian", "poisson")
train <- function(family) {
  model <- glm(Sepal.Length ~ Sepal.Width + Species, iris, family = family)
  summary(model)
}
# Return a list of model's summaries
```

```r
model.summaries <- spark.lapply(families, train)

# Print the summary of each model
print(model.summaries)
```

Second, `dapply` and `dapplyCollect` let you process SparkDataFrame data using custom code. In particular, these functions will take each partition of the SparkDataFrame, convert it to an R `data.frame` inside of an executor, and then call your R code over that partition (represented as an R `data.frame`). They will then return the results: a SparkDataFrame for `dapply` or a local `data.frame` for `dapplyCollect`.

To use `dapply`, which returns a SparkDataFrame, you must specify the output schema that will result from the transformation so that Spark understands what kind of data you will return. For example, the following code will allow you to train a local R model per partition in your SparkDataFrame, assuming you partition your data according to the correct keys:

```r
df <- withColumnRenamed(createDataFrame(as.data.frame(1:100)), "1:100", "col")
outputSchema <- structType(
  structField("col", "integer"),
  structField("newColumn", "double"))

udfFunc <- function (remote.data.frame) {
  remote.data.frame['newColumn'] = remote.data.frame$col * 2
  remote.data.frame
}
# outputs SparkDataFrame, so it requires a schema
take(dapply(df, udfFunc, outputSchema), 5)
# collects all results to a, so no schema required.
# however this will fail if the result is large
dapplyCollect(df, udfFunc)
```

Finally, the `gapply` and `gapplyCollect` functions apply a UDF to a group of data in a fashion similar to `dapply`. In fact, these two methods are largely the same, except that one operates on a generic SparkDataFrame, and the other applies to a grouped DataFrame. The `gapply` function will apply this function on a per-group basis and by passing in the key as the first parameter to the function that you define. In this way, you can be sure to have a function customized according to each particular group:

```r
local <- as.data.frame(1:100)
local['groups'] <- c("a", "b")

df <- withColumnRenamed(createDataFrame(local), "1:100", "col")

outputSchema <- structType(
  structField("col", "integer"),
  structField("groups", "string"),
  structField("newColumn", "double"))

udfFunc <- function (key, remote.data.frame) {
```

```r
  if (key == "a") {
    remote.data.frame['newColumn'] = remote.data.frame$col * 2
  } else if (key == "b") {
    remote.data.frame['newColumn'] = remote.data.frame$col * 3
  } else if (key == "c") {
    remote.data.frame['newColumn'] = remote.data.frame$col * 4
  }

  remote.data.frame
}
# outputs SparkDataFrame, so it requires a schema
take(gapply(df,
            "groups",
            udfFunc,
            outputSchema), 50)

gapplyCollect(df,
              "groups",
              udfFunc)
```

SparkR will continue to grow as a part of Spark; and if you're familiar with R and a little bit of Spark, this can be a very powerful tool.

sparklyr

sparklyr is a newer package from the RStudio team based on the popular dplyr package for structured data. This package is fundamentally different from SparkR and its authors take a more opinionated stance toward what the integration between Spark and R should do. This means that sparklyr sheds some of the Spark concepts that are available throughout this book, like the SparkSession, and uses its own ideas instead. For some, this means that sparklyr takes a R-first approach instead of SparkR's approach of closely matching Python and Scala APIs. That approach speaks to its origins as a framework; sparklyr was created within the R community by the folks at RStudio (the popular R IDE), rather than being created by the Spark community. Whether sparklyr's or SparkR's approach is better or worse completely depends on the end user's preference.

In short, sparklyr provides an improved experience for R users familiar with dplyr, with slightly less overall functionality than SparkR (which may change over time). Specifically, sparklyr provides a complete dplyr backend to Spark, making it easy to take the dplyr code that you run today on your local machine and make it distributed. The implication of the dplyr backend architecture is that the same functions you use on local data.frame objects apply in a distributed manner to distributed Spark DataFrames. In essence, scaling up requires no code changes. Since functions apply to both single node and distributed DataFrames, this architecture addresses one of the core challenges with SparkR today, where function masking can lead to strange debugging scenarios. In addition, this architectural choice makes spar klyr an easier transition than simply using SparkR. Like SparkR, sparklyr is an evolving project; and when this book is published, the sparklyr project will have evolved further. For the most up-to-date reference, you should see the sparklyr website (*http://spark.rstudio.com/index.html*). The following sections provide a lightweight comparison and won't go into depth on this particular project. Let's get started with some hands-on examples of sparklyr. The first thing we need to do is install the package:

```
install.packages("sparklyr")
library(sparklyr)
```

Key concepts

sparklyr ignores some of the fundamental concepts that Spark has and that we discussed throughout this book. We posit that this is because these concepts are unfamiliar (and potentially irrelevant) to the typical R user. For instance, rather than a SparkSession, there's simply spark_connect, which allows you to connect to a Spark cluster:

```
sc <- spark_connect(master = "local")
```

The returned variable is a remote dplyr data source. This connection, even though it resembles a SparkContext, is *not* the same SparkContext we mentioned in this book. This is a purely sparklyr concept that represents a Spark cluster connect. This function is largely the entire interface for how you will define configurations that you would like to use in your spark environment. Through this interface, you can specify initialization configurations for the spark cluster as a whole:

```
spark_connect(master = "local", config = spark_config())
```

This works by using the config package in R to specify the configurations you would like to set on your Spark cluster. These details are covered in the sparklyr deployment documentation (*http://spark.rstudio.com/deployment.html*).

Using this variable, we can manipulate remote Spark data from a local R process, thus the result of spark_connect performs roughly the same administrative role for end users as a SparkContext.

No DataFrames

sparklyr ignores the concept of a unique SparkDataFrame type. Instead it leverages tables (which are still mapped to DataFrames inside Spark) similar to other dplyr data sources and allows you to manipulate those. This aligns more with the typical R workflow, which is to use dplyr and magrittr to functionally define transformations from a source table. However, it means that some of Spark's built-in functions and APIs may not be accessible unless dplyr also supports them.

Data manipulation

Once we connect to our cluster, we can run all the available `dplyr` functions and manipulations as if they were a local `dplyr data.frame`. This architectural choice gives those familiar with R the ability to do the same transformations using the same code, at scale. This means there's no new syntax or concepts for R users to learn.

While `sparklyr` does improve the R end-user experience, it comes at a cost of reducing the overall power available to `sparklyr` users, since the concepts are R concepts, not necessarily Spark concepts. For instance, `sparklyr` does not support user-defined functions that you can create and apply in SparkR using `dapply`, `gapply`, and `lapply`. As `sparklyr` continues to mature, it may add this sort of functionality, but at the time of this writing this capability does not exist. `sparklyr` is under very active development and more functionality is being added so refer to the sparklyr homepage (*https://spark.rstudio.com/index.html*) for more information.

Executing SQL

While there is less direct Spark integration, users can execute arbitrary SQL code against the cluster using the `DBI` library corresponding to almost the same SQL interface we have seen in previous chapters:

```
library(DBI)
allTables <- dbGetQuery(sc, "SHOW TABLES")
```

This SQL interface provides a convenient lower-level interface to the `SparkSession`. For instance, users can use DBI's interface to set Spark SQL specific properties on the Spark cluster:

```
setShufflePartitions <- dbGetQuery(sc, "SET spark.sql.shuffle.partitions=10")
```

Unfortunately, neither DBI nor `spark_connect` does not give you an interface for setting Spark-specific properties, which you are going to have to specify when you connect to your cluster.

Data sources

Users can leverage many of the same data sources available in Spark using `sparklyr`. For example, you should be able to create table statements using arbitrary data sources. However, only CSV, JSON, and Parquet formats are supported as first-class citizens using the following function definitions:

```
spark_write_csv(tbl_name, location)
spark_write_json(tbl_name, location)
spark_write_parquet(tbl_name, location)
```

Machine learning

`sparklyr` also has support for some of the core machine learning algorithms that we saw in previous chapters. A list of the supported algorithms (at the time of this writing) includes:

- `ml_kmeans`: *k*-means clustering
- `ml_linear_regression`: Linear regression
- `ml_logistic_regression`: Logistic regression
- `ml_survival_regression`: Survival regression
- `ml_generalized_linear_regression`: Generalized linear regression
- `ml_decision_tree`: Decision trees
- `ml_random_forest`: Random forests
- `ml_gradient_boosted_trees`: Gradient-boosted trees
- `ml_pca`: Principal components analysis
- `ml_naive_bayes`: Naive-Bayes
- `ml_multilayer_perceptron`: Multilayer perceptron
- `ml_lda`: Latent Dirichlet allocation
- `ml_one_vs_rest`: One versus rest (allowing you to make a binary classifier into a multiclass classifier)

However, development does continue, so check MLlib (*http://spark.rstudio.com/mllib.html*) for more information.

Conclusion

SparkR and `sparklyr` are areas of rapid growth in the Spark project, so visit their websites to find out the latest updates about each one. Moreover, the entire Spark project continues to grow as new members, tools, integrations, and packages join the community. The next chapter will discuss the Spark community and some of the other resources available to you.

## CHAPTER 33

Ecosystem and Community

One of Spark's biggest selling points is the sheer volume of resources, tools, and con‐ tributors. At the time of this writing, there are over 1,000 contributors to the Spark codebase. This is orders of magnitude more than most other projects dream of ach‐ ieving and a testament to Spark's amazing community—both in terms of contributors and stewards. The Spark project shows no sign of slowing down, as companies large and small seek to join the community. This environment has stimulated a large num‐ ber of projects that complement and extend Spark's features, including formal Spark packages and informal extensions that users can use in Spark.

Spark Packages

Spark has a package repository for packages specific to Spark: Spark Packages (*https://spark-packages.org/*). These packages were discussed in Chapters 9 and 24. Spark packages are libraries for Spark applications that can easily be shared with the community. GraphFrames (*http://graphframes.github.io/*) is a perfect example; it makes graph analysis available on Spark's structured APIs in ways much easier to use than the lower-level (GraphX) API built into Spark. There are numerous other pack‐ ages, including many machine learning and deep learning ones, that leverage Spark as the core and extend its functionality.

Beyond these advanced analytics packages, others exist to solve problems in particu‐ lar verticals. Healthcare and genomics have seen a surge in opportunity for big data applications. For example, the ADAM Project (*http://bdgenomics.org/*) leverages unique, internal optimizations to Spark's Catalyst engine to provide a scalable API & CLI for genome processing. Another package, Hail (*https://hail.is/*), is an open source, scalable framework for exploring and analyzing genomic data. Starting from sequencing or microarray data in VCF and other formats, Hail provides scalable algorithms to enable statistical analysis of gigabyte-scale data on a laptop or terabyte-scale data on cluster.

At the time of this writing, there are nearly 400 different packages to choose. As a user, you can specify Spark packages as dependencies in your build files (as seen in this book's book GitHub repository (*https://github.com/databricks/Spark-The-Definitive-Guide/*)). You can also download the pre-built jars and include them in your class path without explicitly adding them to your build file. Spark packages can also be included at runtime by passing a parameter to the spark-shell or spark-submit command-line tools.

An Abridged List of Popular Packages

As mentioned, there are nearly 400 Spark packages. Including all of these is not relevant to you as a user because you can search for specific packages on the Spark package website. However, it is worth mentioning some of the more popular packages:

Spark Cassandra Connector (https://github.com/datastax/spark-cassandra-connector/)
    This connector helps you get data in and out of the Cassandra database.

Spark Redshift Connector (https://github.com/databricks/spark-redshift)
    This connector helps you get data in and out of the Redshift database.

Spark bigquery (https://github.com/spotify/spark-bigquery)
    This connector helps you get data in and out of Google's BigQuery.

Spark Avro (https://github.com/databricks/spark-avro)
    This package allows you to read and write Avro files.

Elasticsearch (https://github.com/elastic/elasticsearch-hadoop)
    This package allows you to get data into and out of Elasticsearch.

Magellan (https://github.com/harsha2010/magellan)
    Allows you to perform geo-spatial data analytics on top of Spark.

GraphFrames (http://graphframes.github.io/)
    Allows you to perform graph analysis with DataFrames.

Spark Deep Learning (https://github.com/databricks/spark-deep-learning)
    Allows you to leverage Deep Learning and Spark together.

Using Spark Packages

There are two core ways you can include Spark Packages in your projects. In Scala or Java, you can include it as a build dependency, or you can also specify your packages at runtime (for Python or R). Let's review the ways in which you can include this information.

In Scala

Including the following resolver in your *build.sbt* file will allow you to include Spark packages as dependencies. For example, we can add this resolver:

```
// allows us to include spark packages
resolvers += "bintray-spark-packages" at
  "https://dl.bintray.com/spark-packages/maven/"
```

Now that we added this line, we can include a library dependency for our Spark package:

```
libraryDependencies ++= Seq(
...
  // spark packages
  "graphframes" % "graphframes" % "0.4.0-spark2.1-s_2.11",

)
```

This is to include the GraphFrames library. There are slight versioning differences between packages, but you can always find this information on the Spark packages website.

In Python

At the time of this writing , there is no explicit way to include a Spark package as a dependency in a Python package. These sorts of dependencies must be set at runtime.

At runtime

We saw how we can specify Spark packages in Scala packages, but we can also include these packages at runtime. This is as simple as including a new argument to the spark-shell and spark-submit that you would use to run your code.

For example, to include the magellan library:

```
$SPARK_HOME/bin/spark-shell --packages harsha2010:magellan:1.0.4-s_2.11
```

External Packages

In addition to the formal Spark Packages, there are a number of informal packages that are built on or leverage Spark's capabilities. A prime example is the popular gradient-boosted, decision-tree framework XGBoost (*https://github.com/dmlc/xgboost*), which makes use of Spark for scheduling distributed training on individual partitions. A number of these are liberally licensed, public projects available on GitHub. Using your favorite search engine is a great way to discover projects that may already exist, rather than having to write your own.

Community

Spark has a large, robust community. It is so much larger than the packages and direct contributions. The ecosystem of end users who build Spark into their products and write tutorials is an ever-growing group. As of this writing, there are over 1,000 contributors to the repository on Github.

The official Spark website (*http://spark.apache.org/community.html*) maintains the most up-to-date community information, including mailing lists, improvement proposals, and project committers. This website also includes many resources about new Spark versions, documentation, and release notes for the community.

Spark Summit

Spark Summits are events that occur across the globe at various times a year. This is the canonical event for Spark-related talks, where thousands of end users and developers attend these summits to learn about the cutting edge in Spark and hear about use cases. There are hundreds of tracks and training courses over the course of several days. In 2016, there were three events: New York (Spark Summit East), San Francisco (Spark Summit West), and Amsterdam (Spark Summit Europe). In 2017, there were Spark Summits in Boston, San Francisco, and Dublin. Coming in 2018—and beyond—there will be even more events. Find out more at at the Spark Summit website (*https://spark-summit.org/*).

There are hundreds of freely available Spark Summit videos (*https://www.youtube.com/user/TheApacheSpark*) for learning about use cases, Spark's development, and strategies and tactics that you can use to get the most out of Spark. You can browse historical Spark Summit talks and videos on the website (*https://spark-summit.org/*).

Local Meetups

There are many Spark-related meetup groups on meetup.com (*https://www.meetup.com*). Figure 33-1 shows a map of Spark-related meetups on Meetup.com.

Figure 33-1. Spark meetup map

Spark's "official meetup group" in the Bay Area (founded by one of the authors of this book), can be found here (*https://www.meetup.com/spark-users/*). However, there are over 600 Spark-related meetups around the world, totaling nearly 350,000 members. These meetups continue to spring up and grow, so be sure to find one in your area.

Conclusion

This whirlwind chapter discussed nontechnical resources that Spark makes available. One important fact is that one of Spark's greatest assets is the Spark community. We are extremely proud of the community's involvement in the development of Spark and love to hear about what companies, academic institutions, and individuals build with Spark.

We sincerely hope that you've enjoyed this book and we look forward to seeing you at a Spark Summit!

Index

About the Authors

Bill Chambers is a product manager at Databricks focused on helping customers succeed with their large scale data science and analytics initiatives using Spark and Databricks.

Bill also regularly blogs about data science and big data and presents at conferences and meetups. He has a Master's degree in Information Systems from the UC Berkeley School of Information, where he focused on data science.

Matei Zaharia is an assistant professor of computer science at Stanford University and chief technologist at Databricks. He started the Spark project at UC Berkeley in 2009, where he was a PhD student, and he continues to serve as its vice president at Apache. Matei also co-started the Apache Mesos project and is a committer on Apache Hadoop. Matei's research work was recognized through the 2014 ACM Doctoral Dissertation Award and the VMware Systems Research Award.

Colophon

The animal on the cover of *Spark: The Definitive Guide* is the swallow-tailed kite (*Elanoides forficatus*). Found in woodland and wetland locations ranging from southern Brazil to the southeastern United States, these raptors subsist on small reptiles, ambhibians, and mammals, as well as large insects. They build their nests near water.

Swallow-tailed kites tend to be 20–27 inches in length, and coast through the air on wings spanning around 4 feet, using their sharply forked tails to steer. Their plumage grows in a strikingly contrasting black and white, and they spend most of their time in the air, even grazing the surface of bodies of water to drink rather than staying put on the ground.

Among the raptor species, *Elanoides forficatus* are social animals, and often nest in close proximity or roost for the night in large communal groups. During migration, they may travel in groups numbering in the hundreds or thousands.

Many of the animals on O'Reilly covers are endangered; all of them are important to the world. To learn more about how you can help, go to *animals.oreilly.com*.

The cover image is from Lydekker's *The Royal Natural History*. The cover fonts are URW Typewriter and Guardian Sans. The text font is Adobe Minion Pro; the heading font is Adobe Myriad Condensed; and the code font is Dalton Maag's Ubuntu Mono.